Microsoft® SharePoint
Technologies

Related Titles from Digital Press

Kieran McCorry, *Microsoft Exchange 2003 Deployment and Migration,*
ISBN 1-55558-316, 400pp, 2004

Pierre Bijaoui, *Scaling Microsoft Exchange Server,* ISBN 1-55558-239-7, 552pp, 2002

Sue Mosher, *Microsoft Outlook Programming: Jumpstart for Administrators, Developers,
and Power Users,* ISBN 1-55558-286-9, 620pp, 2002

Jerry Cochran, *Mission-Critical Microsoft® Exchange 2003: Designing and Building Reliable
Exchange Servers,* ISBN 1-55558-294-X, 480pp, 2003

Micky Balladelli and Jan DeClercq, *Mission-Critical Active Directory: Architecting a
Secure and Scalable Infrastructure,* ISBN 1-55558-240-0, 512pp, 2001

Mike Daugherty, *Monitoring and Managing Microsoft Exchange 2000 Server,*
ISBN 1-55558-232-X, 432pp, 2001

Mike Daugherty, *Monitoring and Managing Microsoft Exchange 2003 Server,*
ISBN 1-55558-302-4, 512pp, 2004

Kevin Laahs, Emer McKenna, and Don Vickers, *Microsoft SharePoint Portal Server:
Building Knowledge Sharing Applications,* ISBN 1-55558-244-3, 544pp, 2002

Tony Redmond, *Tony Redmond's Microsoft® Exchange Server 2003 with SP1,*
ISBN 1-55558-330-X, 1008pp, 2005.

Jan DeClercq, *Windows 2003 Server Security Infrastructures,* ISBN 1-55558-283-4, 800pp, 2004

Alain Lissoir, *Understanding WMI: Exploiting Microsoft's Windows Management Instrumentation
in Mission-Critical Computing Infrastructures,* ISBN 1-55558-266-4, 580pp, 2003

Alain Lissoir, *Leveraging WMI: Using Windows Management Instrumentation to Solve
Windows Management Problems,* ISBN 1-55558-299-0, 924pp, 2003

**For more information or to order these and other Digital Press titles,
please visit our Web site at www.books.elsevier.com/digitalpress**

At www.books.elsevier.com/digitalpress you can:

- Join the Digital Press Email Service and have news about
our books delivered right to your desktop
- Read the latest news on titles
- Sample chapters on featured titles for free
- Question our expert authors and editors
- Download free software to accompany select texts

Microsoft® SharePoint Technologies

Technologies

Planning, Design, and Implementation

Kevin Laahs
Emer McKenna
Veli-Matti Vanamo

ELSEVIER
DIGITAL
PRESS

Amsterdam • Boston • Heidelberg • London • New York • Oxford
Paris • San Diego • San Francisco • Singapore • Sydney • Tokyo

Elsevier Digital Press
30 Corporate Drive, Suite 400, Burlington, MA 01803, USA
Linacre House, Jordan Hill, Oxford OX2 8DP, UK

 Recognizing the importance of preserving what has been written, Elsevier prints its books on acid-free paper whenever possible.

Library of Congress Cataloging-in-Publication Data

Application submitted.

ISBN-13: 978-1-55558-301-9
ISBN-10: 1-55558-301-6

British Library Cataloguing-in-Publication Data

A catalogue record for this book is available from the British Library.

For information on all Elsevier Digital Press publications, visit our Web site at www.books.elsevier.com.

05 06 07 08 09 10 9 8 7 6 5 4 3

Printed in the United States of America

Contents

Foreword

I love software that runs and delivers value out of the box. SharePoint Portal Server (SPS) 2001 certainly delivered great value to customers, because it was easy to deploy and use. SPS 2001 also affected the economics of the portal market, because its pricing made it viable for companies to dip their toes into portal deployment without incurring huge cost. All software evolves over time, and we now have a new version of SPS, plus the addition of Windows SharePoint Services as part of the base Windows operating system. So, now is a good time to take the opportunity to consider the value that companies can extract from SharePoint.

While SharePoint delivers value out of the box, you'll only get limited value if you accept everything as is. For the software to be truly valuable, I believe that you have to consider the needs of the business and then look at how SharePoint can help you address those needs. Bending SharePoint to meet what you think the business wants is probably pointless. Sometimes you'll succeed, but most of the time you'll end up with frustrated and unhappy users. Experience is tremendously important, too, because without experience, you'll never quite know where the limits exist and where you can apply tweaks to satisfy business needs.

This book is late. I have moaned at the authors on this point for a long time, but they quote my own arguments back to me, citing the need to capture their experience of meeting real business needs within HP as we deploy and use SPS and Windows SharePoint Services to help our people be more productive. Experience takes time to accumulate, so I guess I shouldn't be surprised that the book is late. Now that it has appeared, the content in the book shows real experience of technology in action in many places, and that's its real value. Many people can sit down, learn a technology, and describe it in a book. Few can tell the story from the perspective of experience and make their hard-earned knowledge available in an accessible form. Although it took time, I think this book hits the target, and I'm sure it will be valuable to you, especially if you face the challenge of migrating from the original SharePoint architecture as implemented in the 2001 release to the new technology platform exploited by SPS 2003. Migrating data is easy enough; the challenge exists in understanding how to best exploit the new architectural capabilities and what you need to do with the customized Web Parts and other tweaks that administrators and programmers deploy to meet business requirements.

As with any book, you have to take the information presented here and put it into context with your own experience, requirements, and pressures (time and other). Dip into the book, find its delights, and use them to your advantage.

Enjoy!

Tony Redmond
Vice President and Chief Technology Officer
HP Services

Preface

Mergers, mergers, mergers . . .

SharePoint Products and Technologies are the second generation of the SharePoint family, whose roots are to be found in the Version 1 products called SharePoint Team Services and SharePoint Portal Server (SPS) 2001. Since our first book on SPS 2001, we have lived through many forms of mergers (both personal and business, including the largest IT merger in history between HP and Compaq) and have learned that great things can come from successful mergers. Successful mergers tend to leverage the individual strengths of all involved into a single, stronger force that benefits all concerned.

And this is also the case with SharePoint. The very loosely coupled Version 1 products have come together to produce a more tightly integrated and richer platform, upon which successful collaboration and information sharing can occur. As well as finally delivering on the SharePoint brand, the overall offering merges nicely with other major Microsoft directions, such as Windows 2003, the .NET Framework, and Visual Studio .NET. The delivery of the SharePoint platform also offers benefits to others that play in the collaboration space, as seen with the likes of Office, Project, and Info-Path as they consume underlying SharePoint services.

We, the authors of this book, all work for HP Services and are involved with SharePoint at many different levels—through consulting directly with customers, presenting at industry conferences on SharePoint technologies, contributing to industry publications, and architecting and building HP Service's internal knowledge network based upon SharePoint. We hope that the range of our experience helps you achieve success in your encounters with SharePoint.

Book structure

This book does not cover every single aspect of SharePoint, and if we have missed your favorite topic, then we apologize. We do feel, however, that we have tackled the most important areas, as well as those subjects in which our experience complements the standard product documentation and other books that are out there. We urge you to use your favorite search engine if the answer you seek is not contained here!

We understand that your interest in SharePoint may derive from many different sources, and therefore, we have structured the book into three distinct parts. Part I is for those of you who want to find out about what SharePoint can actually do for you in end-user terms. If you are new to SharePoint and want to see if it can do a job for you, then we recommend you read Part I.

Part II is for system architects who want to know how to plan, design, implement, and manage a SharePoint environment. If you are tasked with rolling out SharePoint to support your business, then we recommend that you read Part II.

Part III is for those who want to extend base functionality to meet specific business needs. If you are a developer who is tasked with enhancing a SharePoint environment, then we recommend that you read Part III.

Note that there will be some slight repetition among the three parts in places. We are aware of this, and it was a deliberate choice in order that you could read each part in isolation from the others. The repetition is merely to ensure that you have the prerequisite information to follow along with the current topic.

Where there's a merger, there's a divestiture . . .

Almost as common as mergers are divestitures, and again, we have experienced many over the past years. We're glad to say that none of us has experienced divorce, albeit writing a book could be cited as a justifiable reason in any such action. We just wanted to say that Don Vickers, who coauthored the first book, could not join us for this second journey and we wish him continued success in all that he does. We did manage to find an excellent replacement in Veli-Matti Vanamo, who, aside from being an alphabetically handy replacement, has also matured sufficiently to appreciate (and spell correctly) Laphroaig.

Kevin, Emer, Veli

Acknowledgments

It is with great relief that we find ourselves writing this section of the book; there were times during this process that we didn't think we'd make it, but here we are! While writing a book provides many benefits, including an opportunity for personal growth, it requires an enormous commitment—not only from the authors but from many other sources. The acknowledgments section gives us each a chance to express our thanks to the people who helped to get us here by providing their ongoing advice, encouragement, and support.

We'd like to thank the publishing team—namely Alan Rose, Lauralee Reinke, and Theron Shreve—for their incredible patience, dedication, flexibility, commitment, and support throughout. You truly are a wonderful team and it was a pleasure working with you. Special thanks go to Tony Redmond for his support and providing the Foreword; Mike Topalovich, Gary Adams, and Adam Rosenblatt for taking the time to provide their reviews; and Eric Tipton for his contribution to the review process.

We are fortunate to work inside a company that has a wealth of experience and a sharing culture that allows us to draw on this experience in many ways. So thanks to all our colleagues at HP. We are also fortunate to have a very close working relationship with Microsoft, and we'd like to thank all our friends there for their willingness to help us and answer our many questions—we promise to continue bombarding you guys with e-mails!

Before we move on to our individual acknowledgements, collectively we'd like to thank those of you who ordered this book many months ago and didn't cancel your order—thank you so much for your patience; we hope you find it worth the wait!

Personal Acknowledgments

To Emer and Veli, my family and friends, and to my wife, Wendy, and children, Jenny and Euan—thanks for putting up with me.

—Kevin Laahs

I'd like to thank Kevin and Veli for their knowledge, expertise, and dedication—as always, it was great working with you guys.

Most of all, I would like to thank my wonderful husband, Michael, and my beautiful little girl, Caoimhe, for supporting my contribution to this book, which required countless nights and weekends away from both. I am so relieved that we can spend time as a family once more. I love you both dearly. XOXO

—Emer McKenna

First of all, I would like to thank Kevin and Emer for the opportunity to co-author the book, and for the countless hours you folks spent pulling me through it. I'd like to thank my wife, Audrey, for her enormous support and even agreeing to go through with the wedding during the lengthy writing process. Finally, many thanks to my family for all the advice and support throughout the years.

—Veli-Matti Vanamo

Part I

Introduction to SharePoint Products and Technologies

How Did We Get Here?

1.1   From whence we came

This is our second book with the word "SharePoint" in its title. Our first, entitled *Microsoft SharePoint Portal Server: Building Knowledge-Sharing Applications* (2001), dealt primarily with Microsoft SharePoint Portal Server 2001 (SPS 2001). I guess it would be natural to assume that this offering is merely an update covering the next release of this product—Microsoft Office SharePoint Portal Server 2003 (SPS 2003)—but this is a false assumption. This book actually covers Microsoft SharePoint Products and Technologies, an umbrella name for those offerings from Microsoft that facilitate collaboration. Now, while SPS is still a major player in this area, it is only part of a strategy designed to connect people to information across all levels of an organization.

This strategy is significantly different from the one that was around when we wrote our first book. It is therefore important to understand how Microsoft has arrived at such a strategy, as this will help you appreciate the thinking behind the current product offerings. Hopefully, this will then assist you in making informed decisions about how to deploy a SharePoint environment for your specific collaborative needs.

1.1.1   Wasn't Exchange meant to be the collaboration platform?

If you cast your mind back to 2000, you will recall the launch of Exchange Server 2000. A significantly different architecture from that of Exchange 5.5, it was hailed as not just a messaging server, but also as a collaboration server. Additionally, it brought new technologies to the table that would be used by other Microsoft product offerings. Witness here the Web Storage System, which is at the core of SPS 2001.

As a collaboration server Microsoft was clearly trying to offer something that could compete with Lotus Notes. Few would argue that Exchange provided the best messaging platform, while Notes provided the best collaborative application platform, and both products were trying to make ground in their "weaker" areas. Thus, a major focus of Exchange 2000 was providing a platform upon which developers could build collaborative applications in addition to delivering the best-in-class messaging server. As it turned out, Exchange's strength as a messaging server alone was enough to keep the threat of Notes at bay, and this is one reason why Microsoft has subsequently de-emphasized Exchange as a collaboration platform and focused it firmly as a pure messaging server. Indeed, you only have to look at Exchange Server 2003 and note that real-time collaboration options such as Instant Messaging, which were part of Exchange Server 2000, are no longer part of the Exchange offering.

However, the consideration that the messaging battle had been "won" was not the only reason for the de-emphasis. The failure of Exchange Server 2000 to become a ubiquitous collaboration platform was another. True, some applications were built on top of Exchange, but it basically failed to capture the interest of the majority of application developers out there. It also met with resistance from administrators, whose primary purpose in life was to ensure a highly performing messaging server. E-mail is mission critical for most organizations these days, and anything that might jeopardize its availability or service-level agreements is met with scorn!

Understanding the reasons for the failure has helped shape the current strategy. At the time, Microsoft had three major goals for Exchange as a collaborative application development platform:

1.   Make Exchange-based data widely available through many protocols and APIs. If the Web Storage System were to be the place to store all sorts of information, then it would have to be ubiquitously available.

2.   Provide an extensible platform. In order to meet a wide variety of needs, new services would need to integrate easily into the platform.

3.   Deliver a compelling environment for the development of rich, collaborative applications. Encourage developers to use the Web Storage System as their platform of choice.

Let's take a look at each goal and see how it fared. First, Microsoft certainly did provide ubiquitous access to Exchange data. The primary APIs were ActiveX Data Objects (ADO), Collaboration Data Objects for

Exchange (CDOEX), and Web-based Distributed Authoring and Versioning (WebDAV). The support of ADO meant that developers who were used to coding against, say, SQL or Oracle, could code against the Web Storage System in much the same way. This met with Microsoft's goal of making the Web Storage System appeal to the masses. CDOEX provided a rich API that made it easy to handle typical Exchange items such as messages, calendars, contacts, and tasks. WebDAV support made building Web-based clients using the HTTP protocol a reality—Outlook Web Access (OWA) being a prime example here. Indeed, using any mixture of these three APIs, you could quite easily access and manipulate items in user mailboxes and public folders.

Sounds like a pretty good picture for data access, so why wasn't it successful? Well, while ADO and CDOEX were robust and powerful APIs, they could only run on the Exchange Server. This meant that applications themselves would have to be installed and run on the Exchange Server. "Not on MY Messaging Server!" would be the response of most Exchange administrators. You see, administrators tend to be passionate about their messaging service and do not want to risk compromising the service it provides to end users. Therefore, it was very difficult to put forward a good case for installing such applications onto the Exchange Server. The only other alternative would be to supply Exchange Servers that were separate from the core messaging service specifically for these applications—clearly a prohibitive expense!

WebDAV is different from ADO and CDOEX in that it can run remotely. In other words, you can run your custom application on one server and have it access Exchange-based data on another server. Now, while this approach appeased Exchange administrators, writing raw WebDAV applications was rather complex. Thus, developers did not embrace this as a viable solution.

Finally, with the provision of these multiple APIs, there were multiple ways to achieve the same aim. For example, there are eight different ways to create a folder in the Web Storage System, so which is the right one to use? This plethora of options merely confused rather than assisted the developer.

Providing an extensible platform was achieved mainly through the support of events at three different levels—SMTP Protocol, SMTP Transport, and Store. Events allowed you to write your own custom code that could react appropriately as messages traversed your environment and as items were manipulated in the Web Storage System. A couple of examples will help clarify the power of events. First, SPS 2001 actually relied heavily on a Store event in order to ensure the integrity of documents as they were checked in and published (remember SPS 2001 uses the Web Storage System that was initially provided by the Exchange group). As documents are created in an SPS 2001 document library, the Store event ensures that valid profiles are filled in, version numbers are maintained, and so forth.

The second example is that of third-party antivirus vendors, who typically harness the SMTP Transport events in order to scan messages before they are actually delivered to a user's mailbox. This is a great example of how new services could be layered easily on top of the platform.

Now, much like the problems with ADO and CDOEX, any application utilizing events would ultimately have to be installed directly onto the Exchange Server. While it is true that SMTP events could run on boundary servers not hosting user mailboxes, Store events would typically have to be on mailbox and public folder servers if they were to add any significant value. Yet, again, Exchange administrators hollered, "Not on MY Exchange Server!" A secondary issue that relates particularly to SMTP events was that you really needed to be able to code in a language such as C++ in order to exploit their capabilities fully. This alienated a lot of those people who would not consider themselves to be hard-core developers and meant that the feature was not overly utilized, as it did not appeal to the masses.

The third goal of delivering a compelling platform for the development of collaborative applications had its challenges as well. Microsoft wanted to lure developers into using the Web Storage System as their primary platform, not just for the data associated with an application but for all its collateral, including source code, forms, and the like. As such Microsoft envisaged all application code and data to be stored within public folders. To this end it provided supporting technologies and showcase applications such as Web Storage System Forms, FrontPage Extensions for Web Storage System Forms, sample public folder–based applications, a workflow engine/designer, and regular updates to the Exchange Software Developer Kit. Interestingly, the workflow engine actually leveraged Store events and was a great example of how the overall platform could be extended.

Did these features attract the application developer? Unfortunately, the answer was no, due mainly to the fact that the whole paradigm was confusing and inconsistent when compared with other Microsoft initiatives. For example, writing a Web application with Visual Studio 6.0 was fairly straightforward for a developer, but there was no direct support for utilizing the Web Storage System as the storage mechanism for such an application. Furthermore, the whole approach seemed detached from the main development story emanating from Microsoft—that being the .NET Framework, Visual Studio .NET, and the whole Web Services world.

So the bottom line here was that the strategy was confusing, inconsistent, and impractical, and there was a big message from administrators saying, "Don't mess with my messaging server!" So, clearly, another approach had to be taken to find a suitable platform for building applications that would enhance the lives of information workers in the collaboration area.

Note that the effort made to make Exchange a collaboration platform was not all in vain. I say this because there are pieces of the strategy that align with the future and have made Exchange a good citizen in a .NET world—that being the support of WebDAV such that Exchange services can be consumed by remote applications as and when required. As we will see later, this capability is actually harnessed by Windows SharePoint Services in order to allow documents to be e-mailed into a document library.

1.1.2 What else was going on?

Ever heard of a product called SharePoint Team Services (STS)? I'll bet you probably have, but at the time of its release, SPS 2001 was getting all the airplay. In fact, in our first book we dedicated a whole paragraph to STS (on page 19 if you are really interested), which just goes to show that we did not really understand its true purpose in life (hey, at least we are honest!).

In our defense, Microsoft did not actually give STS the exposure it deserved at that time, and its relation to SPS was purely nominal. Part of the Office XP family, STS came free with a FrontPage 2002 license and, from a technical point of view, had its technology roots firmly planted in FrontPage Server Extensions. It was designed to allow the easy creation of Web sites that users could use as a mechanism for sharing information and collaborating.

It is fair to say that Microsoft did not market the capabilities of STS as well as it could have and put more effort into the technically unrelated SPS product that had shipped a few months previously. The confusion over these two products initially caused STS to lose momentum and not attain its potential in terms of customer uptake. In fact, a common misunderstanding was that an STS team site could only handle groups of up to 50 users. Only after Microsoft publicized its internal usage did STS gain credibility as concerns over scalability were alleviated. With additions such as Self Service Creation, STS proved to be a very popular platform for empowering users with the ability to create team sites instantly and start collaborating without involving IT groups for site creation.

SPS and STS both had their strengths, but were architecturally different and used different development metaphors. For example, to build on SPS required knowledge of the Digital DashBoard Architecture and Web Parts, whereas building on STS required skills with FrontPage Remote Procedure Protocol (RPC) and Collaborative Markup Language (CAML).

However, STS filled a crucial role that couldn't be fulfilled by SPS 2001—it provided an environment in which ad hoc teams could come together, work on some collateral, and then disband. For example, a sales team could get together to work on a new proposal for a customer, or three people could cooperate on the creation of a book. SPS 2001 was designed more to support the publishing and discovery of information than the creation of such information and, therefore, did not lend itself well to the needs of team-based collaboration. The lesson learned is that an effective knowledge-sharing environment must support both the dynamic creation and publishing of information.

Collaboration means working together, especially in a joint intellectual effort. It's fair to say that although the three main offerings from Microsoft in the collaboration space each had its individual merits (Exchange Server 2000, SPS 2001, and STS), they did not exactly benefit from collaborative engineering. Clearly, a more cohesive, consistent, and all-encompassing message was required, and, indeed, this is where the much more compelling story of SharePoint Products and Technologies enters the fray. Which brings us to 2003.

1.2   2003—A vintage year for collaboration

Microsoft released a bundle of products in 2003. This is not really surprising, as it releases many products each year, but "working together" and "joint intellectual effort" are clearly emerging product trends.

The Microsoft Office family of products has been significantly extended, with members sharing much more than just the name. The full list of Office 2003 products is as follows:

- Access
- Excel
- FrontPage
- InfoPath
- Live Communications Server
- Live Meeting
- OneNote

- PowerPoint

- Project

- Publisher

- SharePoint Portal Server

- Visio

- Word

The interesting point here is that formerly "stand-alone" server products have now been brought into the family—in particular SPS and Live Communications Server. This indicates a desire to extend the functionality of personal productivity applications through server-based services.

Completing the major 2003 product set is Windows Server 2003, Windows SharePoint Services, and Microsoft Exchange Server 2003. Note that, as discussed earlier, Exchange 2003 has dropped the "Collaboration" tag and is now firmly positioned as a messaging server. Based on the lessons learned with Exchange 2000, SPS 2001, and STS, the collaboration strategy now focuses on an extensible infrastructure supporting services that citizens of multiple collaborative environments can consume, rather than on one that assumes people only need to collaborate from within their messaging system.

The basis of the collaboration story is now rooted inside Windows itself, through Windows SharePoint Services, and through individual product offerings that can easily leverage these services.

1.2.1　The collaboration ecosystem

As people go about their day-to-day jobs, they encounter many opportunities for collaboration. Indeed, the need to work together with one or more people (or with collateral created by other people) can arise at any moment and is seldom restricted solely to when you are working within a specific application. For example, as I author this part of our book, I think of questions that can be answered by my colleagues, I search for other collateral in the same topic area, and I think of tasks that need to be completed before this book can be published. People collaborate on many different levels and from within many environments. Looking at a pre-2003 Microsoft-centric environment, we see that one-to-one communication is performed via Outlook and Instant Messaging; teamwork on ad hoc projects is performed through a mixture of file shares, public folders, and SharePoint Team Services v1.0; conferencing is performed through either NetMeeting or Exchange Conferencing Server, and publishing is performed through SPS 2001.

Microsoft's collaboration strategy is to provide services that can be consumed "naturally" as information workers go about their day-to-day jobs. By this, I mean that the information workers should not have to divert from their current focus when they need to collaborate. If I am authoring a document in Word and something in the document triggers the need to allocate a task to a colleague, I should be able to do so directly from Word itself and not have to go searching for another application. Collaborative services should be baked into the operating environment and called upon as and when it makes sense.

Another part of the strategy builds upon the realization that in order to collaborate effectively on a piece of work, users need to access multiple information sources—and not just document sources. Connecting people and information is very important. For example, if I am researching a topic and come across an interesting piece of work by a particular person, I may want to see other items that have been authored by that same person or may want to converse immediately with that person through an Instant Messaging conversation. Alternatively, I may want to identify people that have a particular skill set and target them for specific questions. Connecting people and information is therefore something addressed by the strategy.

The strategy therefore is to deliver rich collaboration services built into the infrastructure that go far beyond that of traditional file-sharing services, but are just as easy to use. Endusers are empowered to use these services through the tools they most commonly use—Office, Windows Explorer, and Internet Explorer—and other applications can avail themselves of and build on top of these infrastructure services.

1.3 Delivering the strategy

Four server products form the backbone of the collaboration strategy (Figure 1.1).

1.3.1 Exchange Server 2003

Focusing on Exchange Server 2003's strength as a messaging server, we see that previous collaboration services have been removed from the product. Exchange no longer delivers Instant Messaging and the Exchange Conferencing Service. Exchange also provides the best platform for personal information management in terms of calendars, contacts, and tasks and enables

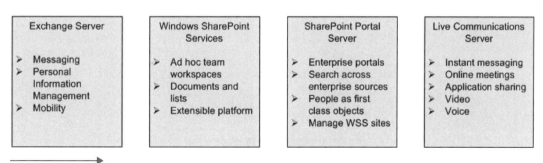

Figure 1.1 *Major products in the collaboration space.*

you to access your mailbox through multiple mobile clients, including Outlook Web Access and Outlook Mobile Access.

1.3.2 Windows SharePoint Services and SPS

Although these products could be seen as upgrades to SharePoint Team Services v1.0 and SPS 2001, it is better to think of them as new products, delivering the core part of Microsoft's collaboration strategy. Together they are known as SharePoint Products and Technologies, and Microsoft had several goals when designing the SharePoint suite.

First, it wanted to provide a scalable base service for collaboration that could be leveraged by many applications. Second, it wanted to ensure that information sharing could happen at all levels of an organization—groups of people, teams of people, departments, and organizations. Third, it wanted to ensure that this environment exploited the .NET Framework and was easily consumed and extended by third-party applications. Finally, it wanted to deliver on the SharePoint brand by ensuring that any Share-Point product utilized the underlying SharePoint services.

Windows SharePoint Services (WSS) is so called because it is part of Windows (available as a free download from Microsoft's Web site), and it provides the base collaborative infrastructure, as we will see in Chapter 2. It is an extensible Web-based environment that lets users quickly provision dynamic Web sites for specific purposes. For example, users can provision a Web site in order to host the collateral of a project or to collaborate on the creation of a particular document. The services offered by WSS are consumable via an object model and Web Services and can therefore be used in any application. Refer to Chapter 3 for details of how Office 2003 consumes the services provided by WSS. WSS provides a scale-out and scale-up three-tier architecture utilizing ASP.NET to deliver Web pages and SQL Server to host data.

SPS 2003 is a product that builds upon the base infrastructure provided by WSS. It utilizes the Web site framework provided by WSS and extends it to provide navigation, aggregated search, application integration services such as single sign-on, audience targeting, and personalized Web sites. As with WSS, these services are accessible via an object model and Web Services for use by third-party applications.

1.3.3   Live Communications Server

Live Communications Server delivers an extensible real-time communication platform and a standards-based, enterprise-ready Instant Messaging solution. It provides presence information that integrates into Microsoft Office and SPS, allowing users to see immediately who is available to collaborate and communicate with. The enterprise IM is delivered to the end user using Windows Messenger v5.0 and includes logging, archiving, file transfer, audio and video conferencing, and application sharing.

Although Live Communications Server effectively only supports one-to-one video conferencing, you can expect to see third-party applications in the future that leverage the platform to provide multiparty conferencing.

Windows SharePoint Services

2.1 Providing the foundation for collaboration

If you only had a base pre-2003 Windows Server (say Windows 2000) at your disposal with no layered applications, then your only means of sharing information between clients would be via network shares. Network shares permit the sharing of files between networked users by providing a common area for storage of such files and the ability to limit access to this area. Thus, the collaborative services provided by Windows 2000 are limited, to say the least.

WSS is at the heart of Microsoft SharePoint Products and Technologies and provides the base platform for collaboration in a Windows Server 2003 environment that goes far beyond traditional file sharing. It provides a consistent experience for users, developers, and IT professionals and is aligned with other Microsoft directions such as the .NET Framework, integrated storage strategy, and the Trustworthy Computing Initiative.

Built upon the .NET Framework, ASP.NET, and SQL Server, it is designed to be extensible and essentially provides a framework that allows "fit-for-purpose" sites (a.k.a., team site or Web site) to be provisioned as and when required. Information is stored inside a site in the form of lists and libraries, and associated ASP.NET pages render the content appropriately. A special type of ASP.NET page called a Web Part Page is used to aggregate information from multiple sources into one Web page. There are many other ways to work with site information, as we will see later.

Lists and their associated views provide a flexible way for storing any kind of information, be it maintaining the top goal scorers in a soccer league or items on an agenda for a business meeting. Libraries, which are just a special form of list, are typically used to store documents and associated metadata. Documents can actually mean anything, including Office documents such as Word and Excel files, images, text files, and the like. Indeed, any file that you can store on disk can also be stored in a WSS library; thus, data from third-party applications can also be stored within a site.

Given that there are no "rules" as to what kind of content is stored within sites, they provide a flexible mechanism for users to avail themselves of as they see fit. For example, in Chapter 3 we see how a WSS site is used for the purpose of supporting multiauthor document collaboration.

Out of the box you can access site content via a browser, such as Internet Explorer, the Windows Explorer, and Office applications. Currently supported browsers include IE5.01 SP2, IE5.5 SP2, IE6 and above, and Netscape Navigator 6.2 or later. Of course, given that WSS is extensible and provides a rich object model in addition to many Web Services, it can be integrated into third-party applications as well.

Self-service site creation can be enabled to empower users to create their own sites for their own collaborative needs. Site templates, which define the initial content and layout of the site, are used to assist the user in creating suitable and consistent sites. IT folks may be concerned at the thought of users being able to create such sites at their leisure, because it is likely that the number of sites will grow into the hundreds of thousands. This is a valid concern, but the good news is that the architecture enables a highly scalable, available, secure, manageable, and well-performing platform with flexible deployment options.

Let's now take a brief look at the architecture of WSS in order to understand how it meets the following goals:

- Performance

- Scalability and availability

- Flexibility in deployments

- Consistency of experience for all concerned

- Integration of storage

- Security

- Showcasing of the .NET application

2.2   Main architectural ingredients

WSS only runs on Windows Server 2003 and, as such, embraces many of its technologies—the .NET Framework and Internet Information Services (IIS)

6.0 being prime examples. WSS uses ASP.NET and SQL Server to deliver a site framework upon which Web-based team sites can be created. The browser is the primary vehicle for interacting with the site, and ASP.NET is used as the Web page rendering technology. Basic Web pages (ASP.NET) are supported, but the primary type of page is a Web Part Page, which consists of one or more Web Parts. Typical Web Parts contain data from libraries and lists, but custom Web Parts can be created to retrieve data from almost anywhere. The use of ASP.NET is essential in order to deliver a high-performing, secure, and stable platform for delivering Web Part Pages.

Aligning with the goal of integrated storage and consistency, all configuration information, site details, documents, lists, views, and Web Part definitions are stored in SQL Server. Indeed, the only major structures that are not stored inside SQL Server are the indexes for full-text search, which are stored in NTFS on the search and index servers, various files for site definitions, help files, default Web pages, binaries, and so forth. The vast majority of these files are stored on the server where WSS was installed at `\Program Files\Common Files\Microsoft Shared\web server extensions\ 60`. SQL Server is Microsoft's strategic database and is likely to become the primary storage for many other applications in the future (such as Exchange).

A scalable platform is delivered by allowing rendering and data storage and retrieval to be separated onto multiple physical servers. This was not possible in STS and SPS v1.0, because their hybrid storage of Web server, file system, SQL, and windows registry dictated that all content be tied to the same server doing the Web page rendering, thus limiting deployment scenarios and scalability.

Multiple stateless front-end servers provide the rendering service, while clustered back-end SQL Servers deal with data storage and retrieval. The fact that they are stateless means they have no persistent local data and, as such, can be load-balanced to meet the needs of the largest enterprises. Meanwhile, the SQL Servers at the back end can be clustered and combined with the multiple front ends, which ensures a highly flexible, scalable, and available platform.

A multiserver deployment is known as a farm, but note that you do have the flexibility to deploy on a single server, which may be sufficient for smaller organizations. In such cases you do not even need to deploy SQL Server because a special instance of (Windows) Microsoft SQL Server 2000 Desktop Engine (WMSDE) can be used for storage. I say "special" instance, because some of the standard restrictions of MSDE have been removed from this version, such as the 2-GB maximum and the limit on concurrent user connections. However, other restrictions still apply, and you cannot augment the database tables with your own—in other words, the WMSDE is solely for use with WSS!

Support for Web Services, a managed object library, and Visual Studio .NET means that .NET developers can extend and build solutions on WSS in a consistent way. For example, anyone familiar with building ASP.NET controls will be able to build and publish Web Parts for use within Web Part Pages.

Finally, like all new Microsoft products, WSS adheres to the Trustworthy Computing principles, ensuring that during development all software components are subjected to rigorous security audits. This, in conjunction with the security that is built into Windows Server 2003, ensures a very secure platform.

2.3   A WSS site—major components and structures

The major components we should concern ourselves with when looking at a WSS site are a physical Web Server running IIS 6.0, a SQL configuration database, one or more IIS virtual servers with one or more SQL content databases per virtual server, and, finally, site collections and subsites. The virtual servers host the Web sites.

To create WSS sites you must first install WSS and then extend one or more IIS virtual servers using the SharePoint Central Administration utility or the command-line utility called `stsadm` (see the WSS Administrator Guide and the WSS Software Development Kit for full details of this utility). SharePoint Central Administration is installed into its own IIS virtual server, which is created for you during the installation of WSS and is used to administer everything from the physical Web server settings to virtual server settings and to individual Web site settings. Also, when you install WSS the default Web site (an IIS virtual server) is extended for you automatically, so you only need to extend any subsequent virtual servers that you might create. You would typically use more than one IIS virtual server if you wanted to support different namespaces or enable different characteristics on a group of Web sites. For example you may want to support separate Web sites for `http://sales.CompanyA.com` and `http://sales.CompanyB.com`, or you may want to access the same Web sites via multiple URLs (say an internal URL and an external URL). Alternatively, you may want to enable automatic deletion of "dead" Web sites for one group of sites, but not for another.

Extending a virtual server results in an ISAPI filter called `stsfltr.dll` being registered, which processes all URL requests directed at the virtual server. If you need to support non-WSS sites on the same virtual server (such as a completely separate Web application), you must configure these as excluded paths using SharePoint Central Administration.

Installing WSS creates the SQL configuration database, which stores details of all IIS virtual servers that have been extended. Additionally, each virtual server has one or more SQL content databases associated with it, and these details are also held in the configuration database. The content databases store data from the Web sites, including management data such as usernames and permissions, as well as content, such as Web Part Pages, list data, and documents from document libraries. It is possible for more than one virtual server to point to the same content databases. This would be typical in a server farm situation, where you want multiple load-balanced front-end servers, but this technique could also be used, for example, to have different URLs point to the same content (perhaps for extranet users). In the latter case you would want to force SSL and basic authentication on the externally facing virtual server, whereas NTLM would suffice on the internally facing virtual server.

Administrators can define paths used to group WSS sites into a common URL namespace. For example, by default a path called "sites" is automatically created during installation. In this case all top-level WSS sites would be of the form `http://<vserver>/sites/<sitename>`. More than one path can be defined, in which case users can choose where they want their sites created. A common practice would be to create multiple paths to indicate the purpose of the site (e.g., `/projects`, `/teams`, `/social`, etc.). Furthermore, subsites can be created to any depth you like, resulting in URLs of the form `http://<vserver>/<site path>/<sitename>/<subsite1>/<subsite2>`, and so forth.

The term *site collection* is used to refer to a top-level site and all its associated subsites. There are management settings that apply to a site collection and some that apply to individual sites (be it a top-level site or a subsite). For example, automatic site-deletion settings apply to site collections, but usernames and permissions apply to each individual top-level or subsite. So, I may have a site collection named `http://whisky.islay.com/sites/laphroaig`, which consists of a physical top-level Web site of the same name, and a couple of subsites called `http://whisky.islay.com/sites/laphroaig/10 year old` and `http://whisky.islay.com/sites/laphroaig/15 year old`. It is important to understand these naming conventions, particularly when you need to use the WSS object model from within your own applications.

Figure 2.1 shows the logical relationship between physical Web servers, virtual servers, site collections, top-level Web sites, and subsites.

By default, the URLs for individual sites will begin with the virtual server name and the path as in our examples above. Many people want to have unique URLs or "vanity" names, which are shorter and easier to remember. While there are many ways to achieve this, such as creating an IIS virtual server for each namespace, WSS can be configured to run in what is known as host header mode. When this is enabled, each team site can be referenced by a simple and unique URL. For example, using our two URLs above, we could have had `http://ten.year.old` and `http://fifteen.year.old`. This setup would typically be used by ISP who are hosting Web sites for multiple people or companies. Host header mode is documented in the WSS Administrators Guide and has some restrictions.

Figure 2.1
Server and site logical structure.

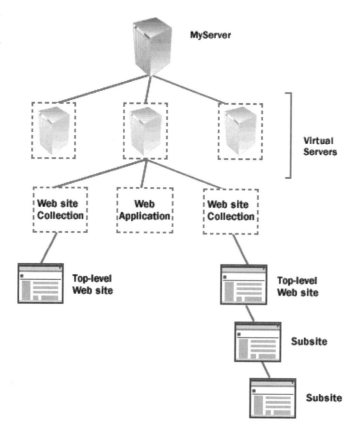

The major restriction is that you can only use the `stsadm` administration utility to create sites—it is not possible to empower users to create their own sites if host header mode is enabled.

2.4 Introducing Web Part Pages and Web Parts

The primary vehicle for end-user access is the browser. A technology called Web Part Pages is employed to deliver the majority of Web pages. Web Part Pages are actually ASP.NET pages that consist of one or more Web Parts contained within Web Part zones. Web Part Pages allow for Web Part personalization, ensuring that each user sees only the most relevant information.

A Web Part is therefore the basic building block of a page. Web Parts are used to consolidate data from multiple sources, be it WSS-based data such as lists or external data such as images and content from other non-WSS-based Web sites. Web Part Pages support personalization, which means that each user can devise his or her own unique view of a Web Part Page by determining which Web Parts are on the page and their individual characteristics. For example, one user may choose to minimize certain Web Parts if the user is not especially interested in their content.

Chapter 14 provides full details on how to build Web Parts and Pages; for the present, suffice it to say, Web Parts are essentially ASP.NET custom server controls, which means they are compiled and digitally signed libraries that result in the best performance and security. Ultimately, a Web Part delivers content that is displayed on the page, and it is up to the developer to ensure the right content is displayed. For example, a Web Part may deliver news content from an external source or sales data from an internal database. The creator of a Web Part can also allow it to be customized directly by the end user in order to let users drive its content and appearance.

Depending upon a user's security role, he or she will be able to create and add new Web Parts to a WSS site and publish these Web Parts into online galleries, where other users can download them. Additionally, users can also add new Web Part Pages to their sites and use them for whatever purpose they see fit (actually, users can also add basic Web pages, which allow for simple content to be authored directly through the browser using a rich-text editor). Multiple Web Parts can be "connected," which allows, for example, the display of a list of items in one part of your Web page and an associated image to be displayed in another part as you select a list item.

2.5 Introducing site definitions, configurations, and custom templates

A WSS site mainly comprises lists, libraries, Web Parts, Web Part Pages, and Basic Web Pages. A *site definition* (which is physically represented as a set of .xml files) is used to define the basics of a site. Among other things, the navigation and quick launch areas of a site are defined, as are the available lists and libraries and the schema definitions for items within these lists and libraries.

Multiple *site configurations* can be derived from a site definition. A configuration determines which actual lists, libraries, and other files are created and configured when an individual site is instantiated. As users create their WSS sites, they must choose a site configuration upon which the new site is based. In the user interface the configurations are displayed during the template selection part of the creation process shown in Figure 2.2.

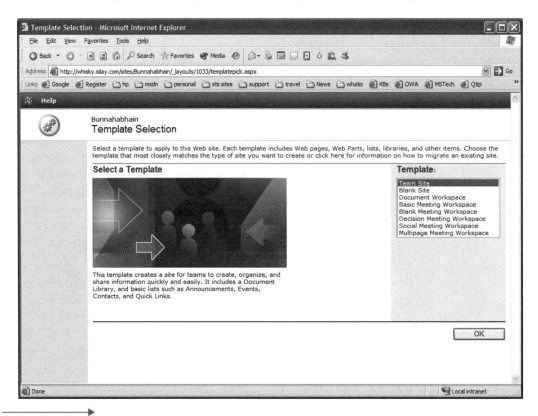

Figure 2.2   *Template selection.*

It is possible to create your own site definitions and site configurations in addition to controlling which site configurations are visible to users on the template selection page. This can be useful because some site configurations may be for internal use only. We cover this in more detail in Chapter 17.

Out-of-the-box WSS ships two site definitions called STS and MPS; as we will see later, SPS extends the available site definitions. The first definition has three configurations defined, called "Team Site," "Blank Site," and "Document Workspace." The second definition relates to sites that are used for meeting purposes and has configurations called "Basic Meeting Workspace," "Blank Meeting Workspace," "Decision Meeting Workspace," "Social Meeting Workspace," and "Multipage Meeting Workspace."

Once a site has been created, it is, of course, extensible and customizable. Users with suitable permissions can add Web Parts and Web Part Pages, modify the definition of lists and libraries, create new lists, change color schemes, and so forth. In order to support the ability to design your own site configurations easily, WSS supports saving customized sites as a *custom template*. There are two types of custom templates—site and list. A custom site template defines a site configuration and a custom list template defines a list configuration. This gives great flexibility and allows you to instantiate other sites from your custom sites, ensuring consistency across sites designed for similar purposes. You don't even need to be a developer to do this, as all of your customizations are performed through the browser, and the custom templates are saved directly from the browser. Custom templates effectively enable a "what you see is what you get" site-design facility.

Custom templates contain the differences between the original site definition from which the site was derived and the state of the site when it was saved. Thus, the usage of a custom template requires that the original site definition be available. As users provision sites they can choose their templates (which in essence define the site definition from which the new site is derived) from the serverwide site configurations, from the central custom template gallery, or from a site collection template gallery. Templates in a site collection gallery can only be applied to sites within that site collection, whereas templates in the central gallery can be applied to any site. Indeed, the central gallery can only be manipulated by server administrators using the stsadm utility, whereas the site collection galleries can be manipulated by any user who has the Add Items right to the site collection gallery (which, by default, applies to the Administrator and Web Designer roles). The stsadm utility is a command-line utility that can be used to manage many aspects of a WSS installation and its associated sites. It is found on a

WSS-enabled server at `\Program Files\Common Files\Microsoft Shared\web server extensions\60\bin\stsadm.exe`, and its operation is documented in the WSS Administrators Help file.

2.6   Lists

I have mentioned lists and list items a few times, and these are a core part of WSS. You can think of a list as being similar to a table in a database or a folder in your mailbox. Each list has its own schema, which defines the data associated with items that are stored in the list. Think of the schema as defining the columns that are associated with each record in your database table. There are many inbuilt lists that ship with WSS—Announcements, Links, Events, Tasks, Contacts, Issues, Surveys, and Discussion Board are a few associated with a default team Web site—but the real power comes from the ability to extend these lists or to define your own custom lists with their own custom schema. You can create lists for any purpose you see fit, be it keeping the list of top scorers in a football league or keeping tabs on the status of current bids. Attachments to list items are supported and list-level permissions are possible. Also, item-level permissions allow you to indicate which items users can read and edit—be it only items they have created, all items, or none. You can also use calculated columns (such as Totals) and lookup columns, which expose values from other lists from within a view. Furthermore, if you are running Office 2003, you can manipulate the contents of lists through a data grid that is rendered into your browser. This gives you an Excel-like experience in dealing with the list. Lists can also be exported and processed offline with Excel or Access and then synchronized back with the server-based content.

Lists can be stored as custom list templates. This allows you to make your custom lists available as a starting point for inclusion in multiple team sites. You can optionally store the actual items associated with a list in the template as well, which is again very handy if you want to ensure that consistent information is delivered across all team sites. Custom list templates are stored in a site collection template gallery and can only be applied to sites within that collection. Custom list templates can be created by users with the Manage Lists right and added to the site collection template gallery by users who have the Add Lists right. See later in this chapter for a discussion on user rights. You save a list as a template by choosing the *Modify Settings and Columns/Save list as template* option.

As mentioned earlier, every WSS site is derived from a base site definition, which can subsequently influence the custom list templates that are

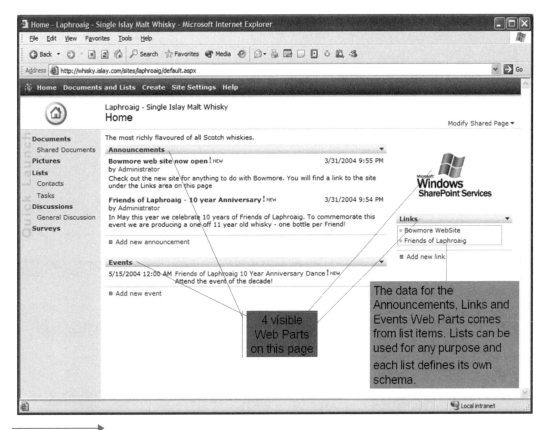

Figure 2.3   *A default WSS site.*

available to that site. Custom list templates can only be applied to WSS sites derived from the same site definition as that where the original custom list was created. Therefore, I cannot, for example, create a custom list template from a list created in a site derived from the STS site definition and subsequently apply this template to a site derived from the MPS site definition.

Figure 2.3 shows a default WSS site with Web Parts exposing list data.

You create lists from the *Create* option on the top menu bar of a site. The site definition controls which options appear on this page, and a default STS site allows you to create a custom list or base your list on an existing list template. Once you give your list a title and description, you can then go ahead and define the columns that make up an item in the list. Each column is given a name, as well as an indication of the type of information it will hold and the characteristics of the data. The type of information can be one of the following:

- Single line of text

- Multiple lines of text

- Choice from a menu of options

- Number

- Currency

- Date and time

- Lookup of information in other lists in the site

- Yes/no check box

- Hyperlink or picture

- Calculation based on other columns

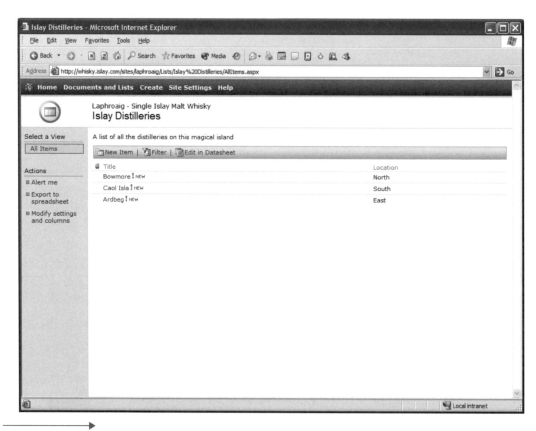

Figure 2.4   *The default view of a list within a site.*

You can also indicate whether a column's value is required and set a default value for each column. As an example of the characteristics that you can apply, you can control whether users are allowed to enter a value into a choice column this is not one of the predefined value.

Each list can be manipulated directly by merely navigating to its URL (also referred to as its Web address). The default view of a list's items is via the `AllItems.aspx` Web page. Figure 2.4 shows the custom list called "Islay Distilleries" on the Laphroaig site.

Furthermore, the contents of a list can be exposed through a Web Part and included on other pages. As we can see in Figure 2.5, a new List View Web Part is made available to us that exposes the newly created list content, allowing us to aggregate this information with other pertinent information. Figure 2.6 shows the new list included in the Home page of the site.

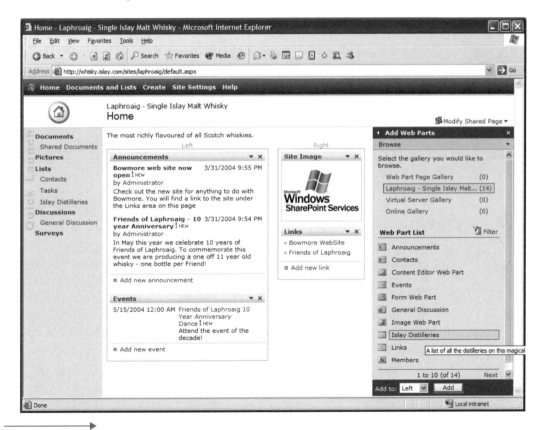

Figure 2.5   *Exposing list content through a Web Part.*

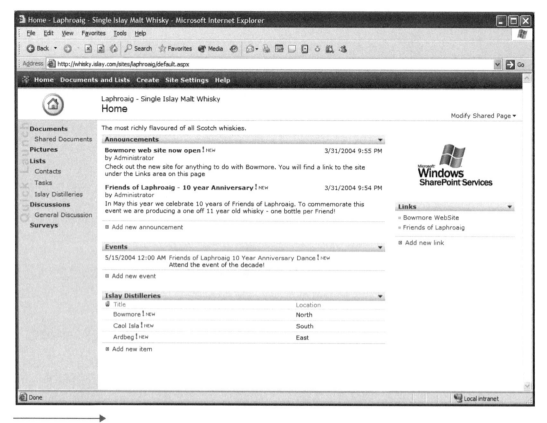

Figure 2.6   *List contents added via Web Part to Home page.*

2.7   Views

Although the concept of lists and views is fairly straightforward, they are very powerful and can be used for many purposes. Readers will more than likely be familiar with the way you can apply different views to items within a folder in Outlook—for example, Unread Messages, By Author, and so forth. Well, as in Outlook, you can define multiple views for your WSS lists and take advantage of the ability to filter, sort, and group items within a view.

For example, WSS allows you to indicate that approvals are required before an item in a list is visible to all users (do this through the *Modify Settings and Columns/Change General Settings* option.) This functionality is achieved through filters on normal views and special views for those users with a security role that enables them to approve items (the Manage Lists right is required for this). For example, enabling approval on my "Islay Distilleries" list results in some new views being available. You can see this by comparing the views available in the left navigation bar in Figures 2.4 and 2.7. The "Approve/reject Items" view utilizes grouping based on item status, the "All Items" view utilizes filtering based on item status to ensure only approved items are shown, and the "My submissions" view utilizes filtering based on the current user.

A view is created using the *Modify settings and columns/create a new view* option, and you can indicate whether the view is a private or public view. Private views are for your own use, whereas public views can be used by anyone who has read access to the site that contains the list. You define a view in terms of the columns that are displayed and their order within the row, how the items are sorted, how items are filtered and grouped, totals, display style, and number of items to display.

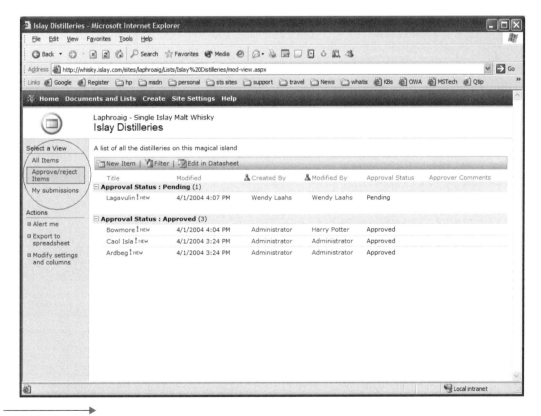

Figure 2.7   *Approval enabled on a list.*

2.8   Libraries

You can create three types of libraries within a WSS site—document, picture, and form. Libraries are merely special types of lists comprising items that have a separate file associated with them. You can think of the file as being the data associated with a special column within the list schema. Just as with standard lists, you can add any number of columns to your library in order to augment the information about the items. This is essential if you are going to exploit your collateral fully, because generally there is much more to a document than merely its contents; for example, you may want to associate a status with an item in a library or a grouping defining the type of item.

Content can be added to a library through the browser by using either the *New Item* or *Upload Item* option as well as by dragging and dropping content through the Explorer view. As with standard lists, any number of views can be associated with a library. Picture libraries, for example, are provisioned with thumbnail and filmstrip views. Another view associated with the three types of libraries is the Explorer view, which allows you to navigate the content of a library using the familiar Windows Explorer interface—in other words, in the same way you would navigate the content of a folder on your C: drive! We discuss accessing library content via the Windows Explorer later in this chapter.

Per-library permissions are supported, but note that, unlike standard lists, per-item permissions are not supported. Thus, if a user has write access to a library, he or she will have write access to all of the items within that library.

2.8.1   Document templates

The definition of a library can include a document template. The document template defines the list of files that can be used as the basis for all new files created in the library via the *New item* option in the browser. Only one file can be associated with the document library at any time, and, during the provisioning of a document library, the user is allowed to choose from the defined list.

The list of available document templates is defined in the site definition from which the site is derived (document templates are actually defined in a file called ONET.XML.) The physical files associated with the individual files defined in the document template originate in the file system on the front-end Web server and, as document libraries are provisioned, the chosen file is copied into the SQL database as part of the site's content.

As an example, we can see, by looking at the `ONET.XML` file from which a "Team Site" is derived, that the file located at `\program files\common files\microsoft shared\web server extensions\60\doctemp\xl\ xltmpl.xls` is copied to `Forms\template.xls` for any document library created using "Microsoft Office Excel spreadsheet" as its document template. This is actually just a blank Excel spreadsheet, but if I wanted to start with some preformatted spreadsheet, I basically have a few options. I could either modify the `xltmpl.xls` file, modify the `ONET.XML` file and point it to an alternate file, add a new document template to `ONET.XML` by inserting an additional `<DocumentTemplate>` node, or create my own site definition and derive my new sites from it. You can also augment the list of available document templates by adding suitably named files to the XML folder of each site configuration. The XML definition from any file whose name begins with `doctemp` is included.

The out-of-the-box STS site definition permits Word, Excel, Power-Point, FrontPage, Basic Web Page, and Web Part Page document templates to be used with document libraries and an InfoPath document template to be used with form libraries. Although I have used the application names here, behind the scenes the extension associated with the physical file is mapped to an application via the `DOCICONS.XML` file, which is part of the site definition.

Note that the default template associated with a document library only affects what happens when a user chooses the *New Item* option and does not restrict in any way the types of items that can be stored within a document library. As we will see, any type of item can be stored in any document library using many different techniques! Consider the creation of a Web Part Page. Web Part Pages can be added to your site and are ultimately stored within a document library. You can do this via the *New Item* option on a document library that has a Web Part Page document template associated with it or by choosing the *Create/Web Part Page* option. The latter will ask you which document library you want to store the Web Part Pages in. The interesting point about creating your own Web Part Pages is that you can select one of eight predefined layouts in terms of zones, and with some customization you can add to the list of predefined layouts.

2.8.2   Managing library items

It is important to know that SharePoint is not intended to be a full-blown document-management system in, say, a Documentum sense. Rather, it provides some management capability to control the publishing of information and is not wholly concerned with the contents or creation of the original content. The ability to require approval before a list or library item becomes public is one example of this.

When it comes to managing items within libraries, WSS supports versioning and the checking in and out of items. Before I explain how these work, you may be wondering how this fits with the capabilities that were in STS v1.0 and SPS 2001. STS allowed you to store items in libraries, but did not give you any control over how these items were published. On the other hand, SPS 2001 allowed you to have two types of document library folders—standard and enhanced. Items placed in a standard folder were automatically published, whereas items in enhanced folders could be checked in and out and multiple versions kept. Additionally, enhanced folders supported a basic routing-and-approval mechanism that could ensure that certain people had authorized the publishing of the document. E-mail was used to notify approvers that items were awaiting their approval or rejection. Finally, profiles could be applied and enforced on document library folders to ensure that the correct metadata was gathered for any document that was to be published.

All told, the document-management capabilities supported out of the box with WSS are not as functional as those in SPS 2001. The ability to define columns on a document library replaced the idea of profiles, but unlike with SPS 2001, you cannot have more than one set of columns on a document library. Thus, emulating the multiprofile capability of an SPS 2001 document folder requires having multiple WSS document libraries instead. WSS does not support the routing-and-approval process that was present in SPS 2001; however, libraries could be extended to support this (and other workflow-type applications) by using events. Finally, note that SPS 2003 can be used with the legacy (SPS 2001) document library store, ensuring full backward compatibility, but this is not the future direction of the SharePoint platform and no enhancements are planned for the legacy store.

So the base functionality in a WSS document library supports check in and out and versioning. Check in and out is available by default on all library types, but versioning has to be enabled on individual libraries that support it (through *Modify settings and columns/Change general settings*). By default only document and picture libraries support versioning. Versioning allows you to keep multiple versions of an item in case a change needs to be reversed. In such a case you can restore a previous version by choosing the *Version History* option on the context-sensitive drop-down menu that appears when you click the down arrow next to an item, as shown in Figure 2.8. (This drop-down menu is customizable such that you can add your own options; details on how to do this are included in Chapter 17.)

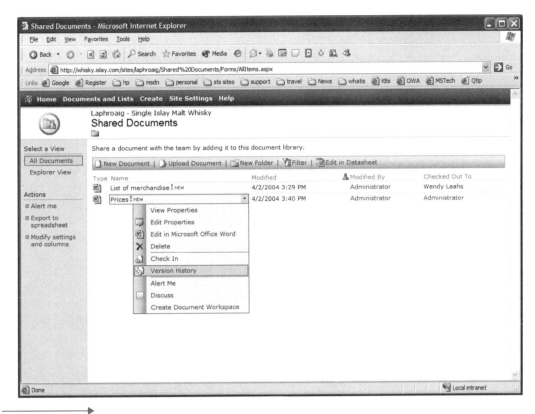

Figure 2.8   *Managing version history.*

Check in and out allows a user to gain exclusive write access to an item. Only the user who has an item checked out can make changes to the document; other users can only read the latest checked-in item. Users who have the Cancel Checkout right can override the checked-out status of an item.

Items in a document library (or indeed any page within the Web site) can also be "discussed." This uses the Web Discussions feature that is available through the Online Collaboration toolbar in Office and the "discuss" button in Internet Explorer. WSS is used as the Web discussion server with individual postings being stored in the Commd table in each content database. Administrators of a site can maintain the contents of Web discussions.

2.9   **Accessing WSS content**

So far, we have basically discussed how to interact with the contents of a WSS site through a browser. Using a browser you can create and populate lists and libraries and define views and Web Part Pages that consume these lists and libraries. Ultimately, you can view the items in a list and library using an HTTP URL; thus, you can hyperlink to content from almost anywhere, be it from within a mail message, a document, or Web application. For example, you can see in Figure 2.9 that I have retrieved the XML representation of the list shown in Figure 2.4 by embedding a request within the URL. A rich object model and Web Services also allow you to access WSS content from within your own applications (see Part III).

WSS also supports the WebDAV protocol, enabling you to interact with the content of sites (in particular libraries) from Office applications and the Windows Explorer. Let's focus on accessing content from Office applications first. The key to understanding this is knowing that every library is accessible via an HTTP URL; therefore, you can directly access a library using this URL from applications that support WebDAV. In situations where you can specify a local folder or a folder on a network share to open or save a file, you can just as easily use the HTTP URL instead to open the

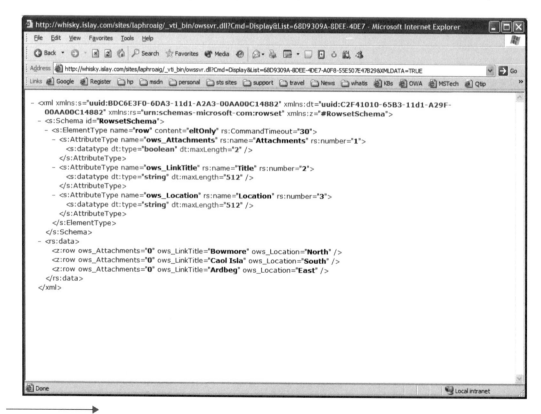

Figure 2.9   *Requesting an XML representation of a list.*

Figure 2.10
Specifying a URL to a site in the Open dialog.

file in or save it to a WSS library. This may seem strange at first, because most users are not accustomed to typing in HTTP URLs when presented with an Open or Save As dialog. But if you look at Figures 2.10 to 2.12, you will see that I can actually browse and open a document stored in a WSS library directly from the File/Open dialog by specifying the relevant HTTP URL in the filename field. Indeed, I needn't even browse the library to open a file because I can just type in the full URL to the file itself. Office applications support the WebDAV protocol natively, which is why you can interact directly with WSS libraries.

Figure 2.11
Navigating the libraries.

Figure 2.12
*Opening an item
from a library.*

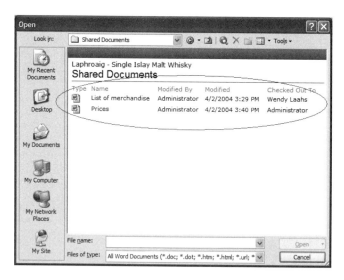

Now, Windows Explorer also allows you to map to WSS sites using something called Web Folders. You can think of Web Folders as being just like the folders on a network share except that the physical folder is accessed over the WebDAV protocol via a Web server, rather than via the traditional Server Message Block (SMB) protocol used for network shares. Using Web Folders you can map a network share and then browse its contents just as you would using Windows Explorer. This functionality means that you can treat WSS libraries in much the same way as you would treat local folders or folders on a network share. Thus, you can cut and paste or drag and drop any file of any type from any folder directly to a WSS library! Clearly, this is a very powerful way to interact with the contents of a WSS library. In Windows XP you create Web Folders by adding a Network Place and pointing it at the relevant HTTP URL. You can choose to point it to the top level of a WSS site, in which case you will be able to browse the site, subsites, and libraries, or you can target it at a specific WSS library. As Figure 2.13 shows, I have created a network place that points to my top-level WSS site.

If you are navigating a WSS library from the browser, you can choose the Explorer view. This basically renders the Windows Explorer into your browser using a Web Folder to display the contents of the library!

Now, one last, but very important, detail about accessing WSS content: If your desktop is running on the Windows XP platform, then you can avail yourself of something called the DAV redirector. This allows you to Open and Save As from any application directly to a WSS library irrespective of whether that application natively supports WebDAV or Web Folders! This

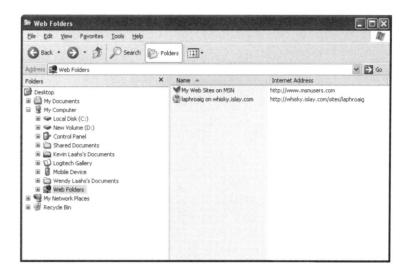

Figure 2.13   *Mapping a Web Folder to a WSS site.*

avoids users having to go through a two-step process (i.e., saving content locally, then opening it up with its native application) to manage non-Office content in a library. To do this you merely map a network share to your WSS library in the same way you would map a traditional share using

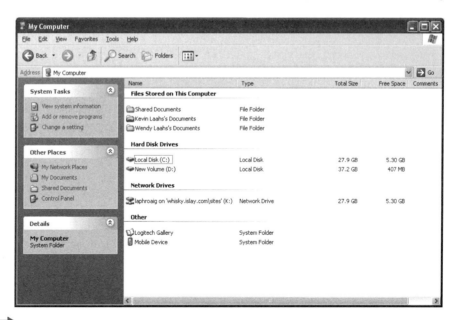

Figure 2.14   *WSS site mapped as a network drive.*

the standard Universal Naming Convention, then use the share's drive letter to open and save items directly. Behind the scenes the DAV redirector converts the standard SMB protocol into WebDAV in order to communicate with the WSS site. We can see this in Figure 2.14, where I have mapped a network share to my WSS site. I can now navigate here from any application via the K: drive as I would with any other network share and open and save files directly to my WSS library.

2.10   Actions

Actions are associated with lists and libraries and certain actions will only apply to certain types of lists and libraries. Some common default actions are "Alert Me" (discussed later), "Export to spreadsheet" (self-explanatory!), and "Modify settings and columns." The latter allows you to manipulate many settings associated with the list or library, such as adding new views or customizing the contents of a list.

As an example of specific actions for specific content types, you will find a View as Slide Show action when you navigate to a picture library.

2.11   Alerts

Alerts, previously called subscriptions in STS, have been enhanced to include more relevant information about the item. You can create alerts for all list types and items and choose to receive e-mail notifications either immediately, once per day, or once per week. Users can manage alerts themselves in the My Alerts page under Site Settings. Note that this only shows the alerts for the current site and that there is no way out of the box to aggregate WSS alerts for all sites and subsites that the user has access to.

2.12   A brief look at site management

Let's take a very brief look at some of the new management options that are available to make the overall management of WSS sites easier than it was in STS v1.0.

As a major downside of STS self-service site creation, users could easily create hundreds of team sites, but had no means of deleting them without contacting an administrator. Thus, it was very common to see hundreds of stale sites lying around with their content just wasting space. With STS it was hard for system administrators to identify which sites were not being used, a task that would have required custom coding to mine the IIS logs.

Administrators are glad to hear that with WSS, site administrators (typically, the people who create the sites) are able to delete the sites as easily as they can create them. WSS also has an out-of-the-box feature for site deletion that mines the IIS logs and identifies unused sites. The site collection owners are sent reminder e-mails to determine whether the site is still active or not. By default the Site Deletion feature sends the first warning after 30 days and a final warning after 60 days, then deletes the site 90 days after the last visit. Because the mail is sent to the site collection owner, it is a good idea to require users to enter a secondary owner when creating a site collection, in case the primary administrator leaves the company or is not around for any reason to deal with the e-mail.

Using the SharePoint Central Administration utility, administrators can also define quotas for a site collection and the maximum size of a file that can be uploaded in a library. Additionally, administrators can control whether self-service site creation is enabled. Also, site usage reports can be enabled allowing the owners of sites to see who is accessing their site, how much quota has been used, and so on.

2.13 Security

WSS allows granular user access control to your Web sites. The security model for WSS is different from that of its predecessor STS v1.0 and, in fact, introduces some rather unexpected anomalies that were not present in STS. The details in this section relate to what happens when running WSS in Domain Account Mode (specifically in an Active Directory [AD] environment) as opposed to Active Directory Account Creation Mode. Also, remember that we are describing here the security within WSS; as it turns out, even though SPS is based on WSS, the security model has some differences, so remember to check the chapter on SPS!

2.13.1 Site creation and user management

The whole idea behind WSS is to empower users to create and manage their own team Web sites without requiring help or intervention from IT support. The inclusion of self-service site creation in WSS bears this fact out, and once it is enabled, you can expect to see your site usage explode. Self-service site creation is enabled at the virtual server level and executed via the `scsignup.aspx` site-creation page. When you enable self-service site creation, an announcement with a link to the sign-up page is added to the Announcements list on the home page of the top-level Web site. You can, of course, advertise a link to the site-creation page in any way you see fit.

Now that you are no longer in control of who creates sites, you have to be confident that users can control appropriate access to their sites without requiring help. This is where user management comes into play. Ultimately, users are identified by their domain logons (`domain\username`) and allocated various rights that grant them the ability to perform specific operations on a Web site. To make the manipulation and allocation of the various rights simple across multiple sites, WSS employs the concept of site groups and cross-site groups. Additionally, there is support for anonymous access, per-list permissions, and subsite permissions inheritance.

2.13.2   User rights

Rights are granted to users to allow them to perform specific actions or tasks, such as creating a subsite, adding or customizing a page to a site, or even using self-service site creation. Certain rights are dependent upon other rights, such as the Add Items right, which requires that the user also have the View Items and View Pages rights.

There is a finite set of rights associated with WSS (21 to be precise!), and these are detailed in the WSS Administrators Help file. The rights are categorized into those that deal with list access, those that deal with site access, and those that deal with personal rights. As an administrator, you can limit the rights that can be granted within a particular virtual server. For example, you could ensure that no pages were added to a Web site merely by removing the Add and Customize Pages right from the virtual server. You do this through the SharePoint Central Administration utility. If a right is not enabled on the virtual server, then it cannot subsequently be added to a site group, which ultimately means it cannot be granted to a user. Additionally, if a right had previously been granted to a site group, removing it from the virtual server would also effectively take it away it from the site group.

2.13.3   Site groups

Site groups are used to allocate rights to users and enable sitewide security. Before users can perform tasks on a site, they have to be associated with one or more site groups. Each site group has a set of rights associated with it. There are five inbuilt site groups (Guest, Reader, Contributor, Web Designer, Administrator), and you can also create your own custom site groups. You can manipulate the rights associated with any of the site groups, except for the inbuilt Guest and Administrator groups. Additionally, note that (1) you cannot assign a user to the Guest site group and (2) that Use Self-Service Site Creation is only applicable to site groups at the top-level Web site of a virtual server. The WSS Administrators Help file lists the rights associated with the default site groups.

Site groups are defined at the site level, which means you can have completely different site groups for different sites. Upon site creation the five default site groups are available (although the Guest group is not visible because it is only used in conjunction with setting per-list permissions), and anyone with the Manage Site Groups right can modify or add site groups to the site. This right is, by default, associated with the Administrator site group, and the creator of a site is automatically assigned to this group.

If a user is a member of multiple site groups, then he or she is granted all the rights that are enabled in all the site groups. Note that there is no way out of the box for normal users to see the accumulated list of rights that they currently have; you need to have the right to view site groups to evaluate the active rights for a particular user.

2.13.4 Cross-site groups

Three types of objects can be associated with a site group—traditional domain user and security group objects, plus a WSS specific object called a cross-site group.

A cross-site group can only contain domain users, and its purpose is to simplify the allocation of the same rights to a group of users across a site collection. In effect it gives WSS users the ability to create their own groups dynamically without having to impose upon IT to create domain security groups that could serve the same purpose.

Consider the following example. I have a site collection containing 10 sites with unique permissions, and I have five users whom I want to add as Readers of all the sites. Therefore, without a cross-site group, my only option is to go through 50 operations to add each individual domain user to each site in the collection. By creating a cross-site group and adding all the domain users as members, I can considerably reduce and simplify the management task. Now I just need to perform 10 operations, adding the cross-site group as a member of the Reader site group for each site in the collection.

Cross-site groups can be defined from any site within a site collection and added as a member to any site group associated with any site in the collection. A user requires the Create Cross-Site Groups right in order to perform these actions. Also note that you can control who can maintain the membership in a cross-site group, even allowing all members to control membership.

2.13.5   Becoming a member of a site

We now need to understand how WSS determines whether you are allowed access to a site, which level of access you are granted, and which details about you are associated with the site.

Users must be associated with one or more site groups before they are allowed any access to a site. The Manage Site Groups right is required in order to use the *Manage Users* option to assign domain users, domain security groups, and cross-site groups to site groups (note that domain distribution groups are not supported, as they are not a security principle). A user could, therefore, be associated with a site group either explicitly via his or her domain user object or implicitly through membership in a domain security group or cross-site group. While the *Manage Users* option allows you to see who has been granted access to a site, the *Site Settings/View information about site users* option lets you see those users who have actually visited the site, including those who have done so implicitly through group membership.

This should all sound straightforward, but it is interesting how WSS retrieves necessary information about a user who is being added to a site and where such information is stored. In addition to a user's domain ID (`<domain>\<userid>`), WSS also stores a display name, e-mail address, notes, and the user's security ID (SID). Now, if you look at the two screen shots in Figure 2.15, you will see an anomaly. Even though I am adding the same user to two different sites, I am presented with different display names and e-mail addresses. Why should this be?

The answer lies in the fact that WSS maintains user details *per-site collection* (recall that a site collection refers to a top-level Web site and all its subsites, so `http://whisky.islay.com/sites/laphroaig` and `http://whisky.islay.com/sites/laphroaig/10 year old` belong to the same site collection, but `http://whisky.islay.com/sites/bowmore` belongs to a different site collection).

A single SQL table called UserInfo contains details for all domain users, domain security groups, and cross-site groups for each site collection. The users' details within this table will be populated the first time they are associated with any cross-site group or any site group within the site collection. Once the details are in this table, they will subsequently be used when

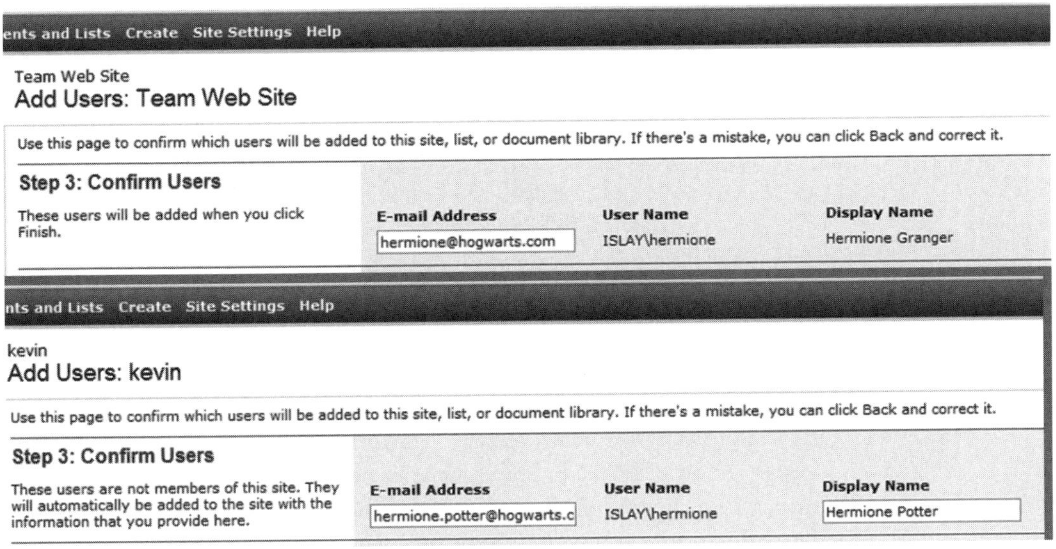

Figure 2.15 *Adding the same user to different sites.*

required for any site within the site collection. Thus, in Figure 2.15 the details in the top panel are from the site collection table, because ISLAY\ hermione had previously been added to a different site within the same site collection. In the bottom panel the details are from an LightWeight Directory Access Protocol (LDAP) call to the Active Directory user object for ISLAY\hermione, because the site belongs to a different site collection, and the user does not yet exist in its site collection user table.

This may seem a moot point, but it can result in a management issue because there is no automatic update of a user's details in site collection tables should his or her corresponding Active Directory user object details change (such as e-mail address, which is certainly not uncommon). And a user will more than likely exist in many site collection tables, so doing this manually will not be a trivial task.

Assuming you have sufficient rights, you can view and modify the details in the site collection table by going to *Site Settings/Go To Site Administration/View site collection user information* from the top-level site within the site collection or *Site Settings/Go To Site Administration/Go To Top-level Site Administration/View site collection user information*. Deleting a user from the site collection table removes that user's access to all sites within the site collection, so you should do this with caution, especially because there is no way to learn in retrospect which site groups the user belonged to within each site.

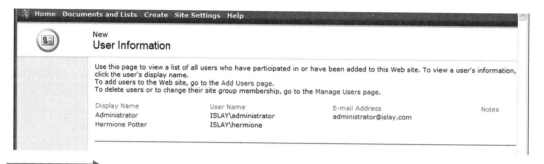

Figure 2.16   *User accesses site via group membership.*

A user can also be added to the site collection table implicitly by accessing a site through domain security group membership. In this case we see even more anomalies, because there is no Active Directory lookup performed to gather the initial details about the user. The details available from the authenticated browser session are used to populate the site collection table; thus, the user's e-mail address is not stored. You can see this in Figure 2.16, where we are looking at the site collection user information. In this example, ISLAY\Hermione's initial access to a site within the site collection was authorized via her membership in a domain security group; thus, the e-mail address has no value.

2.13.6 Requesting access

If a user attempts an operation for which he or she does not have rights, WSS can optionally send a message to the owner of the Web site to request access. This is one reason why all options are shown to users, even though they may not be able to execute them successfully! Users will know if they do not have the right when they are challenged to provide credentials. Any failure to provide suitable credentials (i.e., those of an account that has the appropriate rights) will result in the Request Access Web page being displayed. One good thing about the Request Access page is that it is probably the only place in WSS that shows you your current logon name, which can sometimes be helpful in troubleshooting situations!

Note that the ability to request access can be controlled at the site level, assuming you have the necessary right to do so. You require the Manage Web Site right to enable or disable requests. If they are disabled, then users just get an access denied error when they choose an option for which they do not have the right.

Access requests can also be enabled on a per-list or per-library level.

2.13.7 Subsite permissions

When you create a subsite (assuming that you have the Create Subsites right), you can choose to use the same permissions as its parent site or to use unique permissions. If you use the same permissions as its parent, then all user and site group management options are removed from the subsite, ensuring that these can only be managed from its parent.

If you change the permission inheritance on a subsite to unique permissions, then any existing site groups and their membership to the parent site are recreated on the subsite. If you subsequently revert back to using inherited permissions, any subsite-specific site groups are removed. Therefore, do this with caution, as you will remove access to the subsite for any user who does not also have access to its parent site.

2.13.8 Per-list permissions

You can choose to set per-list permissions on any list within any site. Permissions are applied using normal site groups, and you can enable the majority of the list rights, plus the Manage Personal View right. The current set of rights associated with each site group can be manipulated at the list level in order to apply unique permissions for the list in question. If you choose to apply unique permissions, a new option appears that allows you to revert easily back to the settings that apply to all lists within the site.

2.13.9 Authentication

So far we have discussed authorization, not authentication. In other words, we have described the process of allowing people to do things, but not the process of finding out who people are. We obviously have to be able to identify people before we can grant them authorization to do things.

IIS performs user authentication, and WSS works with anonymous, basic, and integrated Windows Authentication. Additionally, SSL is also supported. You control the authentication method(s) using IIS Manager at the virtual server level. Aside from anonymous access (see next section), nothing further has to be configured within WSS to support authentication.

As a user tries to access a Web site, IIS authenticates him or her to confirm who the user is, but WSS then has to determine whether this user has any access to the Web site he or she is trying to reach. From our previous discussions we know that WSS will need to check for the site groups that the user is associated with, either through his or her domain ID or membership in a domain security group or a cross-site group.

When checking, the user's primary SID is used as a key—not, as you might expect, the actual login ID in the form of `domain\username`. Furthermore, only the primary SID in the user's security token is used and not any that might be present due to the use of `sidHistory`, which is an attribute on a user's AD object that is generally used to store old SIDs. These old SIDs become part of the user's security access token, thus enabling resources that were secured with the legacy SID to be accessible.

Not honoring `sidHistory` is a major issue in the design of WSS, because if a user's SID should change, that user immediately loses access to the Web sites that were authorized through the old SID. In fact, any resource associated with the old SID becomes unavailable, including things such as alerts and personal views.

These issues are most apparent in domain restructuring situations, such as a migration from NT4 to Windows 2000/2003 or the flattening of a multidomain forest. In a typical migration scenario, the new AD account (with its new SID) is usually cloned from the old NT4 account, resulting in `sidHistory` containing the old NT4 SID. As this is clearly something Microsoft wants to encourage, it is disheartening to see such a gaping hole in the manageability of WSS, especially when you consider that STS does not suffer from this issue! STS actually determines a user's rights by membership in a local security group. Thus, if a new account were used, Windows would still recognize a user as part of the local security group due to the use of `sidHistory`.

We can only hope Microsoft will address this issue in the very near future, as its impact is likely to be fairly severe for many customer situations.

2.13.10 Anonymous access

Anonymous access is disabled by default, but you can enable it on a per–Web site basis if anonymous authentication has previously been set on the IIS virtual server. Use *Site Settings/Go To Site Administration/Manage anonymous access* to enable and choose whether it can be used to access the entire Web site or only individual lists and libraries. The default for list access will either be read or nothing, depending upon whether you enable anonymous access to the whole Web site or just lists and libraries. In either case, you can then set more granular access on a per-list basis and allow create and edit access as well.

If anonymous access is allowed to the entire Web site, then the initial access will always be done anonymously. However, in order for authorized users to perform other operations on the Web site (such as removing anonymous access!), a Sign In button is made available on the home page. This allows users to authenticate as an authorized user and avail themselves of their authorized rights.

If anonymous access is only enabled for individual lists and libraries, then users can only have direct access to the list and library Web pages and won't be able to navigate to them through the home page (unless, of course, they can authenticate to the home page, which defeats the purpose of anonymous access!).

2.13.11 Other considerations

There are other ways in which a user can manage WSS and control individual sites. First, accounts in the local administrators' group on the WSS server have full administrative rights and can perform any administrative task, including accessing the contents of all Web sites on the server.

WSS also provides the ability to specify a separate domain group for SharePoint Administrators (note that it has to be a domain group; local groups are not supported). This is useful because adding users to the local administrators' group gives them unnecessary privileges on the server if they only have to administrate WSS. As with the local administrators' group, members of this group can perform all WSS administrative tasks, except those that require updating the IIS metabase.

Finally, any user who has been granted access to a site within a collection has the potential to act as a site collection administrator. This role can be enabled by viewing and editing the list of site users from the top-level Web site. A site collection administrator has the ability to manage the entire site collection without needing to be part of the administrators' site group for individual sites. For example, a site collection administrator can manage users for any site within the collection or even delete the entire site collection by deleting the top-level Web site.

2.14 SQL tables and WSS sites

Let's now take a look behind the scenes at what happens within the SQL database tables when you create, manage, and access WSS sites. Awareness of this can help with troubleshooting, but you should not manipulate the tables directly! This is a very dangerous thing to do, and Microsoft will not support you should you shoot yourself in the foot!

2.14.1   SQL databases

Databases serve two purposes in WSS—hosting configuration information and hosting content. Each WSS installation—be it a single server or a farm—has one configuration database associated with it to host details of the various IIS virtual servers that have been configured for use with WSS. Content databases are associated with each virtual server and host the content of all sites on that virtual server. Content here refers to site, user, library, and list information, as well as to the actual items within lists and libraries. Details about the content databases are stored in the configuration database.

This section focuses mainly on the content database tables used when you create, manage, and access a site. You can view the details about both types of databases using the SharePoint Central Administration utility. The configuration database can be set using the *Set configuration database server* option. To manage the content databases, you must first select the virtual server from the *Configure Virtual Server Settings* option, then choose the *Manage content databases* option.

2.14.2   Configuration database

Before looking at the content database, let's take a quick look at the configuration database tables affected when you extend an IIS virtual server for use with WSS and configure a couple of content databases for the virtual server. In this example, I have created an IIS Web site (a.k.a., virtual server) with a descriptive name of "Islay" and associated a host header called `whisky.islay.com` with it. As we can see in Figure 2.17, the VirtualServers table in the configuration database is updated and a unique ID (Virtu-

VirtualServerId	Name	SmtpServiceId	MailCodePage	FromAddress	ReplyToAddress	LastModified	LastModifiedUser	LastModifieds
{1D3D5E83-8FC6-4966-8B85-5857D6DD9AEF}	Default Web Site	<NULL>	<NULL>	<NULL>	<NULL>	11/03/2004 12:37	Administrator	MS7
3D622286A-CB1B-47D6-B6AA-88EADC41D2A2}	islay	<NULL>	<NULL>	<NULL>	<NULL>	13/03/2004 16:45	Administrator	MS7
{A30362D3-FEC1-468B-ABA1-FF30A7777989}	KAL	<NULL>	<NULL>	<NULL>	<NULL>	03/03/2004 15:27	Administrator	MS7

Figure 2.17   *Virtual server being created.*

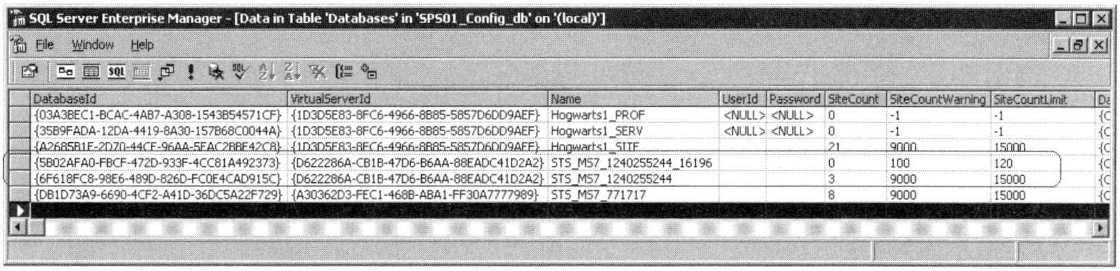

Figure 2.18   *Databases table showing the two content databases.*

alServerId) is allocated to the server. In this case, the ID is {D622286A-CB1B-47D6-B6AA-88EADC41D2A2}.

The initial WSS extension of an IIS Web site will create the first content database, and I have subsequently used the SharePoint Central Administrator to create a second content database. You can create as many content databases as you like and associate a maximum number of sites per database. This allows you some control over the size of each database. You control which SQL server hosts the database, which allows you to partition your content across multiple database servers. New sites are created in the content database that is least full relative to the total number of sites it can hold. Figure 2.18 shows the two content databases created in the Databases table. Note the VirtualServerId column in this table used to tie the databases to the IIS Web site and the SiteCount, SiteCountWarning, and SiteCountLimit columns. In this case, I have already created a few sites that can be seen in the SiteCount column. They were all created in the same database, as it was the least empty.

Let's now look at what happens with the content database as sites are created.

2.14.3   Initial site creation

A site collection refers to a top-level Web site and all of its subsites. Thus, when you create a new site from the site-creation page, you are, in effect, creating a new site collection and its associated top-level Web site. Therefore, details about the site collection and the Web sites within it need to be stored, and the Sites and Webs tables in the content database house these details. You can think of the Sites table as a directory and the Webs table as the starting point for details about items within that directory. Additionally, details about the creator of the site have to be stored, and the UserInfo table comes into play here.

But wait—haven't we forgotten something? How do we know which content database will contain the details? As it turns out, there is also a Sites table in the configuration database that holds an entry for every site collection created in the WSS farm, regardless of which IIS virtual server the site is associated with. To see this in action, let's create a new site using the site-creation page and see which tables get updated. In this example, I have authenticated as the user `islay\kevin` and created a new site called "laphroaig" on the IIS virtual server, referenced by the fully qualified domain name (FQDN) `whisky.islay.com`. I have given some users access to this site using the Manage Users page, as shown in Figure 2.19.

Figure 2.20 shows the Sites table from the configuration database, and we can see that our new site collection has been associated with the second content database (we can also see the three other sites associated with the first content database). I had previously reconfigured the site limit on the first content database to force the creation of the new site collection in the second content database, as Figure 2.21 confirms.

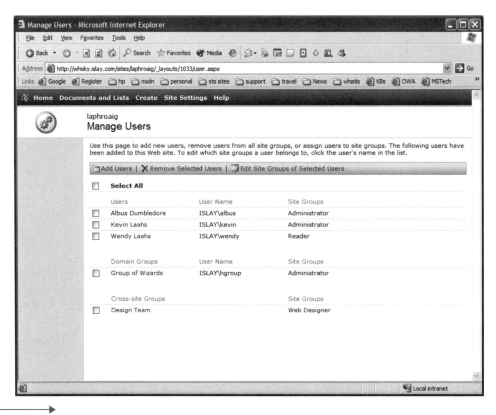

Figure 2.19   *Users added to Web site.*

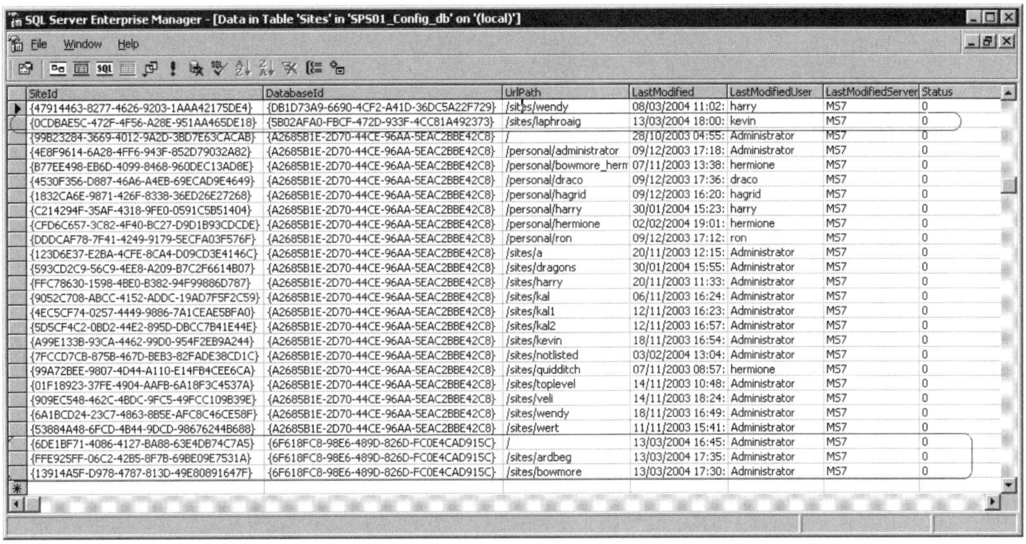

SiteId	DatabaseId	UrlPath	LastModified	LastModifiedUser	LastModifiedServer	Status
{47914463-8277-4626-9203-1AAA42175DE4}	{DB1D73A9-6690-4CF2-A41D-36DC5A22F729}	/sites/wendy	08/03/2004 11:02:	harry	MS7	0
{0CDBAE5C-472F-4F56-A28E-951AA465DE18}	{5B02AFA0-FBCF-472D-933F-4CC81A492373}	/sites/laphroaig	13/03/2004 18:00:	kevin	MS7	0
{99B23284-3669-4012-9A2D-3BD7E63CACAB}	{A2685B1E-2D70-44CE-96AA-5EAC2BBE42C8}	/	28/10/2003 04:55:	Administrator	MS7	0
{4E8F9614-6A28-4FF6-943F-852D79032A82}	{A2685B1E-2D70-44CE-96AA-5EAC2BBE42C8}	/personal/administrator	09/12/2003 17:18:	Administrator	MS7	0
{B77EE498-EB6D-4099-8468-960DEC13AD8E}	{A2685B1E-2D70-44CE-96AA-5EAC2BBE42C8}	/personal/bowmore_herm	07/11/2003 13:38:	hermione	MS7	0
{4530F356-D887-46A6-A4EB-69ECAD9E4649}	{A2685B1E-2D70-44CE-96AA-5EAC2BBE42C8}	/personal/draco	09/12/2003 17:36:	draco	MS7	0
{1832CA6E-9871-426F-8338-36ED26E27268}	{A2685B1E-2D70-44CE-96AA-5EAC2BBE42C8}	/personal/hagrid	09/12/2003 16:20:	hagrid	MS7	0
{C214294F-35AF-4318-9FE0-0591C5B51404}	{A2685B1E-2D70-44CE-96AA-5EAC2BBE42C8}	/personal/harry	30/01/2004 15:23:	harry	MS7	0
{CFD6C657-3C82-4F40-BC27-D9D1B93CDCDE}	{A2685B1E-2D70-44CE-96AA-5EAC2BBE42C8}	/personal/hermione	02/02/2004 19:01:	hermione	MS7	0
{DDDCAF78-7F41-4249-9179-5ECFA03F576F}	{A2685B1E-2D70-44CE-96AA-5EAC2BBE42C8}	/personal/ron	09/12/2003 17:12:	ron	MS7	0
{123D6E37-E2BA-4CFE-8CA4-D09CD3E4146C}	{A2685B1E-2D70-44CE-96AA-5EAC2BBE42C8}	/sites/a	20/11/2003 12:15:	Administrator	MS7	0
{593CD2C9-56C9-4EE8-A209-B7C2F6614B07}	{A2685B1E-2D70-44CE-96AA-5EAC2BBE42C8}	/sites/dragons	30/01/2004 15:55:	Administrator	MS7	0
{FFC78630-1598-4BE0-B382-94F99886D787}	{A2685B1E-2D70-44CE-96AA-5EAC2BBE42C8}	/sites/harry	20/11/2003 11:33:	Administrator	MS7	0
{9052C708-ABCC-4152-ADDC-19AD7F5F2C59}	{A2685B1E-2D70-44CE-96AA-5EAC2BBE42C8}	/sites/kal	06/11/2003 16:24:	Administrator	MS7	0
{4EC5CF74-0257-4449-9886-7A1CEAE5BFA0}	{A2685B1E-2D70-44CE-96AA-5EAC2BBE42C8}	/sites/kal1	12/11/2003 16:23:	Administrator	MS7	0
{5D5CF4C2-0BD2-44E2-895D-DBCC7B41E44E}	{A2685B1E-2D70-44CE-96AA-5EAC2BBE42C8}	/sites/kal2	12/11/2003 16:57:	Administrator	MS7	0
{A99E133B-93CA-4462-99D0-954F2EB9A244}	{A2685B1E-2D70-44CE-96AA-5EAC2BBE42C8}	/sites/kevin	18/11/2003 16:54:	Administrator	MS7	0
{7FCCD7CB-875B-467D-BEB3-82FADE38CD1C}	{A2685B1E-2D70-44CE-96AA-5EAC2BBE42C8}	/sites/notlisted	03/02/2004 13:04:	Administrator	MS7	0
{99A72BEE-9807-4D44-A110-E14FB4CEE6CA}	{A2685B1E-2D70-44CE-96AA-5EAC2BBE42C8}	/sites/quidditch	07/11/2003 08:57:	hermione	MS7	0
{01F18923-37FE-4904-AAFB-6A18F3C4537A}	{A2685B1E-2D70-44CE-96AA-5EAC2BBE42C8}	/sites/toplevel	14/11/2003 10:48:	Administrator	MS7	0
{909EC548-462C-4BDC-9FC5-49FCC109B39E}	{A2685B1E-2D70-44CE-96AA-5EAC2BBE42C8}	/sites/veli	14/11/2003 18:24:	Administrator	MS7	0
{6A1BCD24-23C7-4863-8B5E-AFC8C46CE58F}	{A2685B1E-2D70-44CE-96AA-5EAC2BBE42C8}	/sites/wendy	18/11/2003 16:49:	Administrator	MS7	0
{53884A48-6FCD-4B44-9DCD-98676244B688}	{A2685B1E-2D70-44CE-96AA-5EAC2BBE42C8}	/sites/wert	11/11/2003 15:41:	Administrator	MS7	0
{6DE1BF71-4086-4127-BA88-63E4DB74C7A5}	{6F618FC8-98E6-489D-826D-FC0E4CAD915C}	/	13/03/2004 16:45:	Administrator	MS7	0
{FFE925FF-06C2-42B5-8F7B-69BE09E7531A}	{6F618FC8-98E6-489D-826D-FC0E4CAD915C}	/sites/ardbeg	13/03/2004 17:35:	Administrator	MS7	0
{13914A5F-D978-4787-813D-49E80891647F}	{6F618FC8-98E6-489D-826D-FC0E4CAD915C}	/sites/bowmore	13/03/2004 17:30:	Administrator	MS7	0

Figure 2.20 *Sites being associated with a content database.*

Given that we now know which content database to look at, we can open it up and take a look at the Sites table, as shown in Figure 2.22. Notice how the ID column matches the SiteID column from the configuration database Sites table, as shown in Figure 2.20. As users access a site collection, they are given a unique ID, which serves as a key to their details in the UserInfo table. The Sites table maintains the next key to use in the column NextUserOrGroupId, and it also maintains the key number of the owner in the OwnerID column.

As well as creating a new site collection, WSS creates the top-level Web site for the collection. Details of the Web sites within a site collection are stored in the Webs table, as Figure 2.23 shows. In this example, I have created two subsites called "10 year old" and "15 year old," and you can see

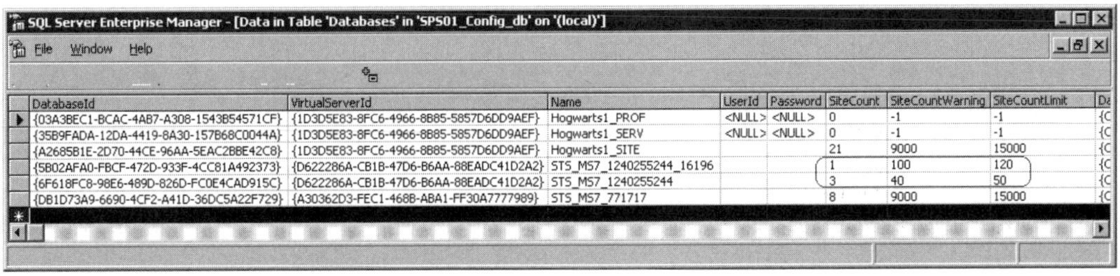

DatabaseId	VirtualServerId	Name	UserId	Password	SiteCount	SiteCountWarning	SiteCountLimit	Da
{03A3BEC1-BCAC-4AB7-A308-1543B54571CF}	{1D3D5E83-8FC6-4966-8B85-5857D6DD9AEF}	Hogwarts1_PROF	<NULL>	<NULL>	0	-1	-1	{C
{35B9FADA-12DA-4419-8A30-157B68C0044A}	{1D3D5E83-8FC6-4966-8B85-5857D6DD9AEF}	Hogwarts1_SERV	<NULL>	<NULL>	0	-1	-1	{C
{A2685B1E-2D70-44CE-96AA-5EAC2BBE42C8}	{1D3D5E83-8FC6-4966-8B85-5857D6DD9AEF}	Hogwarts1_SITE			21	9000	15000	{C
{5B02AFA0-FBCF-472D-933F-4CC81A492373}	{D622286A-CB1B-47D6-B6AA-88EADC41D2A2}	STS_MS7_1240255244_16196			1	100	120	{C
{6F618FC8-98E6-489D-826D-FC0E4CAD915C}	{D622286A-CB1B-47D6-B6AA-88EADC41D2A2}	STS_MS7_1240255244			3	40	50	{C
{DB1D73A9-6690-4CF2-A41D-36DC5A22F729}	{A30362D3-FEC1-468B-ABA1-FF30A7777989}	STS_MS7_771717			8	9000	15000	{C

Figure 2.21 *Databases table showing new site count.*

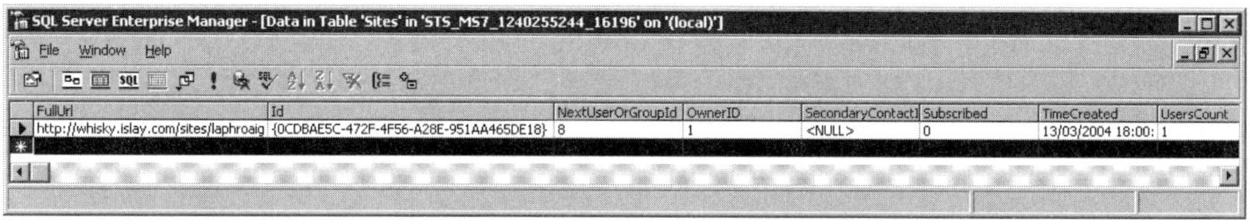

Figure 2.22   *Sites table in the content database.*

each Web site's ID and the associated site collection in the SiteId column. Other interesting columns to note here are FirstUniqueAncestorWebId, which tells you whether this Web site is using unique or inherited permissions, and Author, which is a pointer to the user that created the Web site. The value here is a key into the UserInfo table for the site collection. Many other details are held in this table, such as disk-usage figures, what anonymous users are entitled to do, locales, time zones, and the like.

2.14.4   User information

As discussed previously, a user has to be associated with a site group in order to access a Web site. Association can be explicit or implicit either via membership in a security group or via membership in a cross-site group that has been granted access to the Web site. User details are stored once per-site collection in the UserInfo table, and details are written into this table as users are explicitly added to a Web site or cross-site group. Additionally, user details can be written when users access a Web site via security group membership.

We can see this in Figure 2.24. Notice how islay\kevin and islay\ harry have two entries in this table. This is expected, because user details are stored once per-site collection, and two site collections have been created in this content database. Also, note how the two records for islay\ harry differ in the tp_Title and tp_Email columns. This is because if a user accesses a site collection for the first time via membership in a security

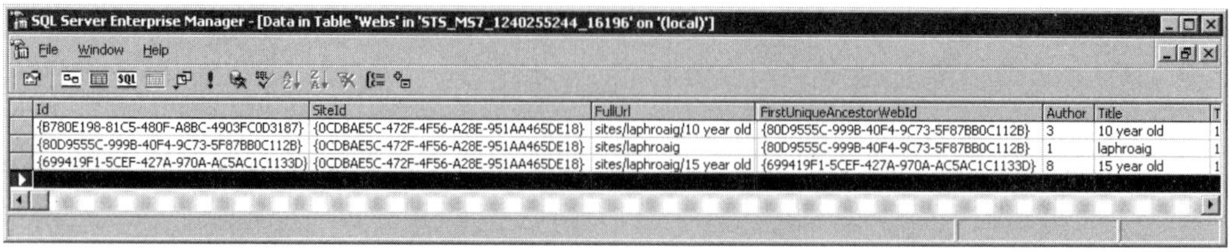

Figure 2.23   *The Webs table.*

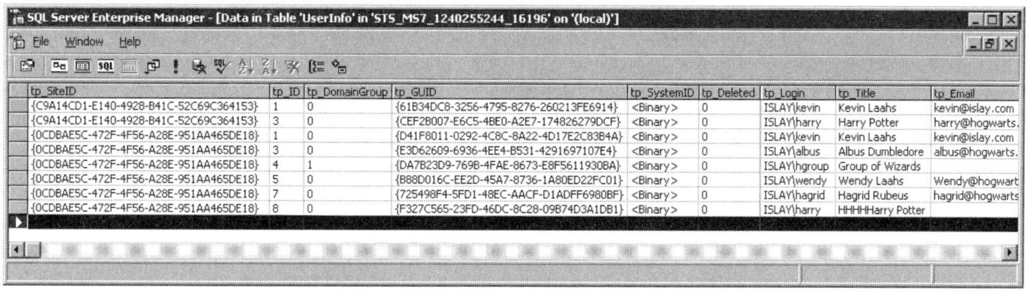

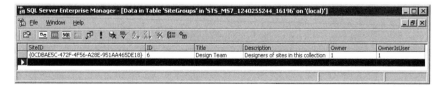

Figure 2.24   *UserInfo table: user details shown once per-site collection.*

group, only the user's title is read from the Active Directory, and there is no way to intervene at creation time either to change this title or to supply an e-mail address. This has to be done after the event by managing the site collection users.

The tp_ID column is the user's or security group's unique number within a site collection (the tp_DomainGroup column identifies groups). You will note that number 2 is missing from both site collections, and number 6 is missing from the second site collection. In the case of the number 6, this was allocated to a cross-site group that was created, as can be seen in Figure 2.25. I can't explain why number 2 is missing, but it would appear that the first user to be added to a Web site aside from the creator always starts at number 3! At a guess, number 2 might be reserved for a secondary owner of the site collection.

The tp_SystemID is the user or security group's SID. Note also that if you delete a user from a site collection, that user is not actually removed from the UserInfo table. The tp_Deleted flag is set, and if you ever readd the user, he or she will pick up his or her former unique number and details. The details that are in the UserInfo table are revealed through the user interface when you look at the site collection users from the top-level Web site via *Site Settings/Go to Site Administration/View site collection user information.*

Figure 2.25   *SiteGroups table: SiteID links to Sites table.*

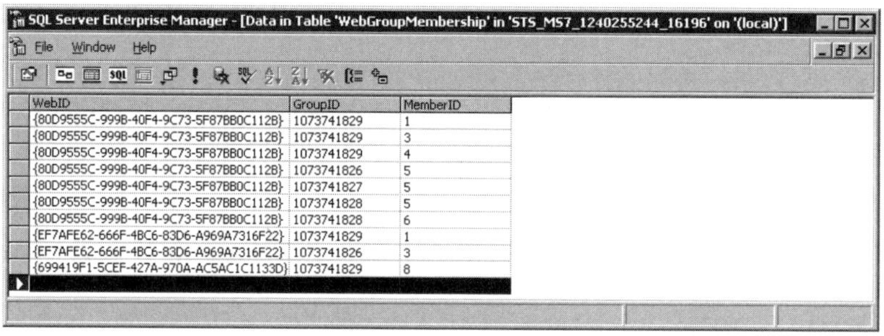

WebID	GroupID	MemberID
{80D9555C-999B-40F4-9C73-5F87BB0C112B}	1073741829	1
{80D9555C-999B-40F4-9C73-5F87BB0C112B}	1073741829	3
{80D9555C-999B-40F4-9C73-5F87BB0C112B}	1073741829	4
{80D9555C-999B-40F4-9C73-5F87BB0C112B}	1073741826	5
{80D9555C-999B-40F4-9C73-5F87BB0C112B}	1073741827	5
{80D9555C-999B-40F4-9C73-5F87BB0C112B}	1073741828	5
{80D9555C-999B-40F4-9C73-5F87BB0C112B}	1073741828	6
{EF7AFE62-666F-4BC6-83D6-A969A7316F22}	1073741829	1
{EF7AFE62-666F-4BC6-83D6-A969A7316F22}	1073741826	3
{699419F1-5CEF-427A-970A-AC5AC1C1133D}	1073741829	8

Figure 2.26 *WebGroupMembership: list of site groups a user is a member of.*

So far, we have only described how users are added to the UserInfo table for the site collection. Each Web site also needs to know which users have been granted access to it and which users have indeed visited the site. The latter information is stored in the WebMembers table and is revealed through the user interface through the *Site Settings/View information about site users.* This option shows you details of all users and whether they have been granted explicit access or implicit access through membership in a security or cross-site group.

The WebGroupMembership table actually stores details of the users, security groups, and cross-site groups that have been granted access to the site via the *Site Settings/Manage Users* option. This table stores one record for each site group that a user is associated with; the GroupID column is the link to the site groups defined in the WebGroups table. These tables can be seen in Figures 2.26 and 2.27.

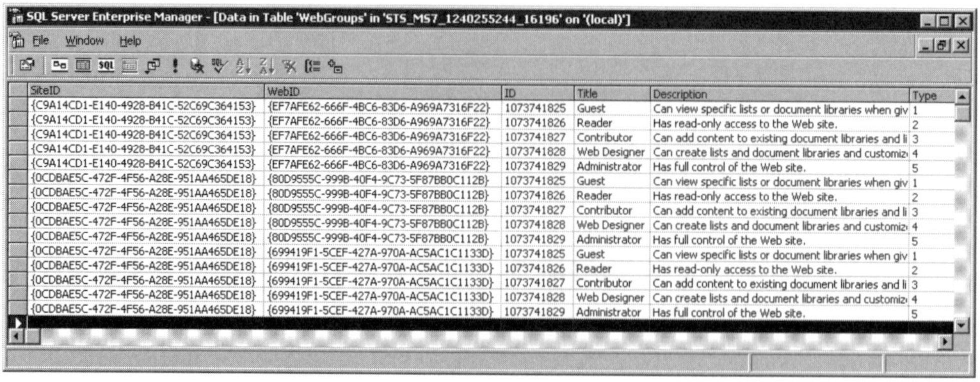

SiteID	WebID	ID	Title	Description	Type
{C9A14CD1-E140-4928-B41C-52C69C364153}	{EF7AFE62-666F-4BC6-83D6-A969A7316F22}	1073741825	Guest	Can view specific lists or document libraries when giv	1
{C9A14CD1-E140-4928-B41C-52C69C364153}	{EF7AFE62-666F-4BC6-83D6-A969A7316F22}	1073741826	Reader	Has read-only access to the Web site.	2
{C9A14CD1-E140-4928-B41C-52C69C364153}	{EF7AFE62-666F-4BC6-83D6-A969A7316F22}	1073741827	Contributor	Can add content to existing document libraries and li	3
{C9A14CD1-E140-4928-B41C-52C69C364153}	{EF7AFE62-666F-4BC6-83D6-A969A7316F22}	1073741828	Web Designer	Can create lists and document libraries and customiz	4
{C9A14CD1-E140-4928-B41C-52C69C364153}	{EF7AFE62-666F-4BC6-83D6-A969A7316F22}	1073741829	Administrator	Has full control of the Web site.	5
{0CDBAE5C-472F-4F56-A28E-951AA465DE18}	{80D9555C-999B-40F4-9C73-5F87BB0C112B}	1073741825	Guest	Can view specific lists or document libraries when giv	1
{0CDBAE5C-472F-4F56-A28E-951AA465DE18}	{80D9555C-999B-40F4-9C73-5F87BB0C112B}	1073741826	Reader	Has read-only access to the Web site.	2
{0CDBAE5C-472F-4F56-A28E-951AA465DE18}	{80D9555C-999B-40F4-9C73-5F87BB0C112B}	1073741827	Contributor	Can add content to existing document libraries and li	3
{0CDBAE5C-472F-4F56-A28E-951AA465DE18}	{80D9555C-999B-40F4-9C73-5F87BB0C112B}	1073741828	Web Designer	Can create lists and document libraries and customiz	4
{0CDBAE5C-472F-4F56-A28E-951AA465DE18}	{80D9555C-999B-40F4-9C73-5F87BB0C112B}	1073741829	Administrator	Has full control of the Web site.	5
{0CDBAE5C-472F-4F56-A28E-951AA465DE18}	{699419F1-5CEF-427A-970A-AC5AC1C1133D}	1073741825	Guest	Can view specific lists or document libraries when giv	1
{0CDBAE5C-472F-4F56-A28E-951AA465DE18}	{699419F1-5CEF-427A-970A-AC5AC1C1133D}	1073741826	Reader	Has read-only access to the Web site.	2
{0CDBAE5C-472F-4F56-A28E-951AA465DE18}	{699419F1-5CEF-427A-970A-AC5AC1C1133D}	1073741827	Contributor	Can add content to existing document libraries and li	3
{0CDBAE5C-472F-4F56-A28E-951AA465DE18}	{699419F1-5CEF-427A-970A-AC5AC1C1133D}	1073741828	Web Designer	Can create lists and document libraries and customiz	4
{0CDBAE5C-472F-4F56-A28E-951AA465DE18}	{699419F1-5CEF-427A-970A-AC5AC1C1133D}	1073741829	Administrator	Has full control of the Web site.	5

Figure 2.27 *WebGroups details.*

3

"Office" Integration

3.1   Building on the framework

In Chapter 2, we discussed how WSS provides the foundation for building sites that can be used by citizens of multiple collaborative ecosystems. In other words, the WSS framework is there to be used for whatever purpose you deem necessary. Of course, you need to build the usage of WSS into your own applications and business processes. In this chapter, we look at how the WSS framework and many of its access vehicles (APIs, Web Services, etc.) are used within the "Office" space. I have deliberately put the word Office in quotes here because, although the main focus is on the Microsoft Office product family, we are talking about an overall environment that includes other products, such as Exchange Server 2003.

The integrations we talk about here provide great examples of what you can do in your own applications to leverage the WSS framework. In particular, we are going to focus on the following areas:

- General WSS enhancements with Office
- Saving Office documents to WSS libraries and property promotion
- Working with WSS lists and Excel/Access
- The Shared Workspace task pane
- Document workspaces
- Meeting workspaces
- Linking lists to Outlook
- InfoPath and form libraries
- Alerts and Outlook
- Exchange Public Folders and WSS libraries
- Outlook Web Access Web Parts

3.2   General WSS enhancements with Office

The Microsoft Office System is not a prerequisite for WSS. In fact, you can create, manage, and work with a WSS site entirely through a browser. However, working directly with the contents of WSS sites is possible to varying degrees from within certain Office applications. This supports the notion of not having to launch many different applications when the need to collaborate arises! The actual functionality available to you is dependent upon the version of Office that you are using. The deepest integration is supported with Office 2003, although Office 2000 and Office 2002 (a.k.a., Office XP) do support certain functions in the area of opening and saving documents directly into a WSS library.

Before we look at specifics, some general integration areas are worthy of note, most of which actually surface through the browser.

3.2.1   Uploading multiple items into a library

As shown in Figure 3.1, there is an option to upload multiple items into a library through your browser session. This option only appears on the upload page under certain conditions (in fact, the option is actually rendered into the page and removed by client-side script if the conditions are not met).

For document and form libraries, a particular ActiveX control needs to be installed on the device where the browser is running. This ActiveX control is called STSUpld.UploadCtl (physically stored in STSUPLD.DLL) and is shipped with Office 2003. It may not, however, be installed with your particular installation—if you experience problems, you need to ensure that WSS Support has been installed. You will find this under Office Tools when doing an advanced customization of applications at install time. If this control is available, then the user is presented with a hierarchical view of his or her computer and can navigate to an individual folder and select any number of items within that single folder for upload. This can be seen in action in Figure 3.2.

For picture libraries the method is slightly different. A check is first made to see if Microsoft Office Picture Manager is installed; if it is, the manager is launched to allow the user to select multiple pictures. If this application is not available, the option falls back to the ActiveX control used with document and form libraries. The benefit of using the Microsoft Office Picture Manager (shown in Figure 3.3) is that it allows the user to manipulate the pictures before uploading. For example, the user can choose

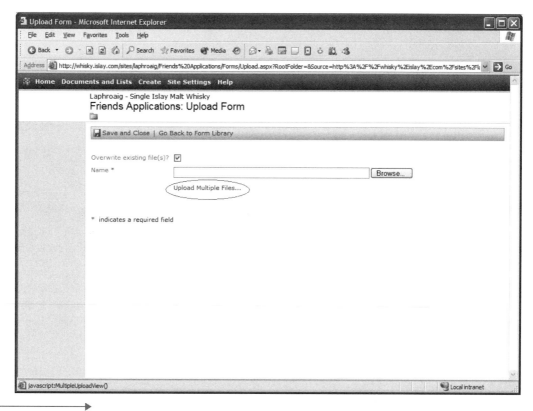

Figure 3.1   *Option to upload multiple files.*

to optimize the pictures for Web viewing, thus reducing the size of the actual data that gets uploaded.

As with the ActiveX control, Picture Manager (actually, the executable is `\Program Files\Microsoft Office\Office 11\OIS.EXE`) is installed by default with Office 2003. During an installation you can control these by indicating that you want advanced customization of applications and navigating to the Office Tools section. Here you will find options for Picture Manager and WSS Support. WSS Support includes the Datasheet control (discussed later) and the Web Capture Client. The latter is the client application used in conjunction with the Web Capture Web Part. The client is used to configure this Web Part, which effectively allows you to screen scrape parts of any HTML page into a Web Part hosted on a WSS site. This Web Part and other useful utilities are part of the "Office 2003 Add-in: Web Parts and Components," which is downloadable from the Microsoft Web site and is also included on the Office 2003 installation CD.

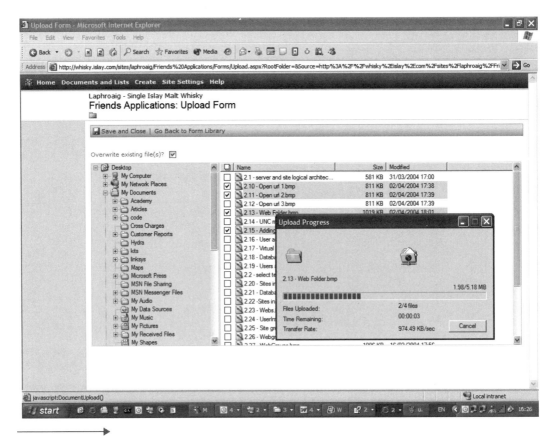

Figure 3.2   *Uploading multiple files in progress.*

Of course, you can also use something like the Custom Installation Wizard from the Office Resource Kit to transform a default installation, thus controlling whether or not the Office Tools are available as part of your installation.

3.2.2   Creating new items in a library

There are many ways to populate a WSS library, including saving directly from an application, using the Web Folders view to drag and drop, or uploading files through the browser. The *New* option on the standard toolbar allows you to create an item from the template associated with the library (as discussed in Chapter 2). Whether this option works depends on the template and the applications that are installed on the device your browser is running on. The template affects the actual code generated to handle the request. For example, if the template is a Web Part Page, then

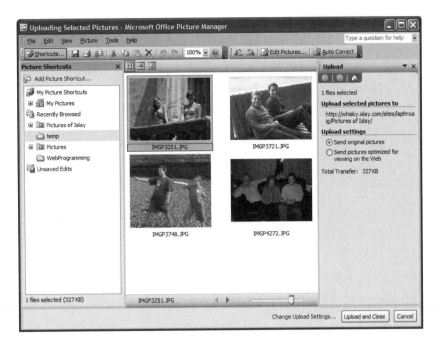

Figure 3.3   *Uploading pictures.*

the *New* option will actually just redirect the browser to another Web page called `spcf.aspx`. If, on the other hand, the template is an Office document, then an attempt is made to launch the associated application.

For a document library you would most typically expect an associated template with a file extension of .doc. This, in theory, should launch Microsoft Word to allow you to edit the contents of the new document. This will happen if Word 2002 or 2003 is installed; otherwise, you will receive an error informing you that you should use the upload document to populate the library. The existence of an ActiveX control called `Share-Point.OpenDocuments.2` (Office 2003) or `SharePoint.OpenDocuments.1` (Office 2002) is required for Word to launch correctly. Similarly, for a form library the existence of `SharePoint.OpenXMLDocuments` is required; this object is installed with InfoPath 2003.

The behavior of the New button can be changed by modifying the `schema.xml` and `docicon.xml` files associated with the site definition. If you want a non-Office application to be used to create, edit, or view an item, then you must provide an ActiveX control (referring to it in the `docicon.xml` file) that supports the same methods as documented in the SharePoint SDK.

3.2.3 Using the Outlook Address Book

WSS allows you to pull information from the Outlook Address Book when managing users (i.e., granting users access to a site) and when importing into a contacts list. Both of these options require that Outlook 2002 or 2003 be installed on the device you are using with a valid MAPI profile. Outlook supplies the `MsSvAbw.AddrBookWrapper` object that supports the `AddressBook` method, which displays the standard Outlook Address Book dialog. For this control to be present, you need to ensure that the Address Book control was included as part of your Outlook installation. From here the user can select multiple entries from any available Address Book source, as shown in Figure 3.4.

Using the Address Book to manage users allows you to discover users' e-mail addresses easily. WSS will then attempt to resolve these e-mail addresses to domain accounts in the normal way (which, incidentally,

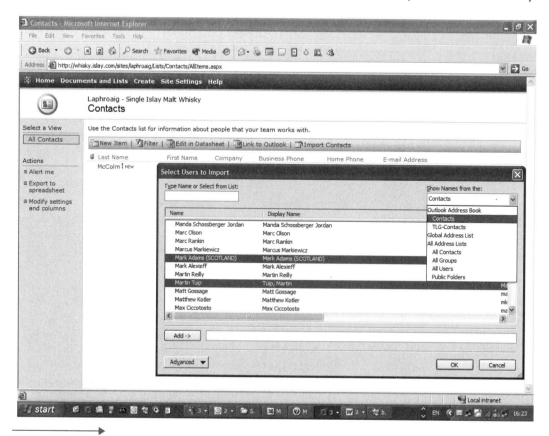

Figure 3.4   *Adding contacts to a list.*

requires WSS to be running in an AD environment, because NT4 accounts have no association with an e-mail address). If you select an Outlook distribution list, then the e-mail address of each member of the list (and any nested lists) is retrieved. Note that this is a point-in-time operation and that there is no ongoing link between the distribution list and the members of your WSS site! This, in fact, is a great way to gather the members of a distribution list for use in another application! You can have WSS expand the list for you, then cut and paste the result into something like Excel for processing.

When you use Address Book to import into a WSS contacts list, a batch Collaborative Application Markup Language (CAML) `Save` method (see Chapter 15 for details on CAML) is used to import each selected entry. Again, any distribution lists are broken down into individual user entries. The properties in the WSS list are stored under the `urn:schemas-microsoft-com:office:office` namespace, and Table 3.1 shows how the details from Address Book entries and WSS contact items are mapped. Be careful if you modify the columns of a contacts list, because if you remove any of the expected columns, the import operation will break. The fields from the Address Book item come from the Outlook 2002 `ContactItem` object. So, for example, the `SMTPAddress` field from the Address Book entry is mapped to the property Uniform Resource Identifier (URI) `urn:schemas-microsoft-com:office:office#Email`. Understanding which property uris are in use is important from an SPS search point of view (see Chapter 6).

Could you include other fields than the Address Book entries in the resulting WSS contact items during an import? The answer is yes, but you would have to modify the schema file for the contact list definition in the site template that was initially used to create the site. Indeed, you could even override the import such that it retrieved its contacts from a location other than the Outlook Address Book; the Active Directory is a good candidate here as an alternative!

The schema file (`schema.xml`, located at `Local_Drive\Program Files\Common Files\Microsoft Shared\Web Server Extensions\ 60\TEMPLATE\LCID\Site_Definition_Name\LISTS\List_Definition_ Name`) defines, among other things, the views and toolbars that are associated with a list. The Import Contacts button is on the toolbar rendered along with the body of a view of a list. This toolbar definition can be found in a `<toolbar>` node inside `schema.xml`, and all the supporting client-side script that controls the import is also defined here. Therefore, you could merely modify the CAML that defines the toolbar such that suitable client-

Table 3.1   *Property Mapping for Address Book Entries*

ContactItem Field	Property URI
FirstName	FirstName
LastName	Title
SMTPAddress	Email
CompanyName	Company
JobTitle	JobTitle
HomeTelephoneNumber	HomePhone
BusinessTelephoneNumber	WorkPhone
MobileTelephoneNumber	CellPhone
BusinessFaxNumber	WorkFax
BusinessAddressStreet	WorkAddress
BusinessAddressCity	WorkCity
BusinessAddressState	WorkState
BusinessAddressPostalCode	WorkZip
BusinessAddressCountry	WorkCountry
WebPage	WebPage
Body	Comments

side script is rendered in order to achieve your goals. Obviously, you need to follow best practice here, and rather than modifying a built-in site template, you should create either your own list or site template and make your modifications to it instead.

To round off this topic, I'd like to point out that the client-side script that calls the Address Book (the main function is called OpenABW) uses a modified form of the Collaboration Data Objects (CDO) AddressBook method. This method only returns a subset of properties from the selected entries; indeed, the only properties of this subset that are not actually imported by default are FullName, MiddleName, and OfficeLocation. Therefore, if you want to import some other properties, you will need to use an alternate method. For example, you could open up each individual contact item returned in the collection via CDO such that you could pull out any property you wished.

3.3   Saving Office documents to WSS libraries

As discussed in Chapter 2, there are many ways to populate the contents of document libraries, such as uploading through the browser, directly from an application, or through Windows Explorer. You can also extend the metadata about items in your libraries by adding new columns and including them in WSS views.

3.3.1   Property promotion

Office documents (Word, Excel, etc.) have their own properties, sometimes referred to as Object Linking and Embedding (OLE) properties. The standard OLE properties are those you see when you call up the File/Properties dialog, such as Subject, Author, Company, and the like. Additionally, you can add your own custom OLE properties to describe the contents of the document further. A typical example here would include adding a property to hold a custom numbering system. Now, these OLE properties are very valuable in terms of identifying the content of a document and should thus be harnessed in views and searches if the document is physically stored inside a WSS library. The term *property promotion* refers to the process that takes OLE properties and replicates them into columns in a library; the term *property demotion* refers to the reverse. The latter ensures that if someone changes the metadata in the library, then these changes will be reflected back into the document. Thus, if the document is taken out of the WSS library and edited elsewhere (perhaps offline on a laptop), then at least the OLE properties will be in sync with the document that resides in the library.

In the SharePoint v1 world, document libraries were in use in two places—STS v1.0 and SPS 2001. With v2 the main focus is on WSS document libraries, although, as mentioned previously, the SPS document library can be used in a legacy mode. Unfortunately, there are some shortcomings with the way WSS libraries handle OLE properties, which results in a deprecated experience from the overall SPS 2001 point of view. I'll first explain each shortcoming and then give an example of how it will affect existing publishing practices. Hopefully Microsoft will address these shortcomings at its earliest convenience!

The first area of concern is with the promotion and demotion of standard OLE properties. By "standard" I refer to the built-in properties, such as Title, Subject, Author, Manager, and so forth. SPS 2001 did this successfully for all standard OLE properties. On the other hand, WSS libraries only promote and demote the Title OLE property, and there is no way to keep any of the other standard OLE properties in sync between the underlying document and the WSS library, even if you create a custom column in your library with the same name as a standard OLE property! In the latter case a new custom OLE property is created with a number after the name to make it unique. So, for example, if I create a column called "Author," when it is demoted it goes into a custom property called "Author0."

Now, why is this a problem? Well, good citizens normally fill in some standard OLE properties when they create content in the first place. Something like the Author field would be filled in automatically, but I try to maintain the discipline of adding a Subject and some Comments so that if someone else publishes the material, that person will at least have some metadata defined by the author. So, for example, if I had given a presentation at an industry conference and you wanted to publish my presentation on your portal, then my name and my description of the content would be used. If the standard OLE properties are not promoted, then you, dear publisher, will have to create your own custom properties and cut and paste the details from the standard properties. This is not ideal—especially if you want to mass publish all material from an industry conference in one go!

The second area of concern relates to when SPS 2003 is in the picture. When it indexes Office content, it does include the standard document properties and actually shows some of these, such as Comments, in search results. Thus, end users cannot see or manipulate standard document properties when browsing the contents of a document library, but they can see them in search results from the same document library! This is clearly a confusing situation.

The third area of concern is with the way that custom OLE properties are handled. In SPS 2001 you only needed to add a same-named property to an SPS document profile, and any subsequent promotion or demotion of that property would occur, regardless of how the document found its way into the SPS 2001 document library or where it was physically stored within the library. Any document that used the profile would happily promote and demote the custom property.

Now, with WSS libraries your first step is to create a same-named column in the WSS document library where you want to store the Office document. Then, property promotion will occur as documents are populated into the library under all circumstances bar one—if you use the *Upload Document* option through your browser to store the document initially! (Note that uploading multiple documents through the browser does not cause this problem.) In this case, the WSS column has a null value, instead of the underlying OLE property value.

Property demotion, on the other hand, works fine, and that is a problem! Why? Because when you next edit a document from the library that was initially uploaded through the browser, the null values are demoted back down and overwrite the original values of the custom OLE properties! The lesson here is that if the source documents that you want to publish into a WSS document library have custom OLE properties, then never use the *Upload Document* option to put them into the library initially. Always either save directly from the application or use the *Multiple Upload* option, Web Folders, or a mapped network drive.

Another problem with custom properties is that you have to define them for every document library in which you want to publish the content. Of course, with careful planning you can skirt this issue by creating site templates with the custom property predefined.

There are a couple of other anomalies with promotion/demotion, which I'll summarize now, but note that most of these existed in the v1 products as well:

- All demoted properties are stored as OLE Text properties, regardless of their type in WSS. Thus, for example, a number column in WSS is represented as Text inside the Office document. This may be an issue if you have applications that expect the data types to match between WSS and the OLE property.

- In STS v1.0 promotion will not occur if the OLE property has an invalid value for the defined type of the column in the library. For example, if the defined type is Number, and you have "abc" in the underlying document, then promotion will not occur. With SPS 2001 and WSS you are presented with a dialog upon saving, which allows you to correct the problem.

- STS v1.0 and WSS promote a value as null if the underlying OLE property is not of type Text. In the same case, SPS 2001 does not promote the value (but demotion still works, so the original value is rewritten to the OLE property on next demotion!).

- In STS v1.0 promotion occurs even if the value of the property does not meet the defined validity checks for the library property. So, for example, a Number property that is outside the accepted value range can be stored in the library. This does not happen with WSS or SPS 2001, which both present the user with a dialog to correct the problem upon save.

3.3.2   Opening and saving documents through Office applications

It is important to ensure that the columns you associate with your document libraries have valid and useful data in them to aid document discovery through browsing and searching. To aid this process, WSS, in conjunction with Office 2002/2003, will display a property view dialog that allows the setting of custom column properties as documents are saved directly into WSS libraries (indeed, you also see this dialog when you choose File/Properties, if the document resides in a WSS library). Of course, this only happens when you save from inside an Office application and does not happen when you drag and drop from Windows Explorer or save from a "non-WSS-aware" application (such as NotePad) that has mapped the site as a network share. Actually, you can also fill in properties through the browser during a single document upload, but not if you choose the multiple document upload option.

Additionally, you can navigate the libraries associated with a WSS site from within an Open or Save dialog, as shown in Figure 3.5. As you traverse a library, you are presented with a Web view of the contents with some common columns. By default the view shows the Type, Name (filename), Modified By, Modified Date, and Checked Out To columns.

The Content view consists of "normal" WSS views defined in the list template that the WSS library was derived from. It is therefore customizable. As usual, care must be taken when you customize any site or list tem-

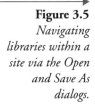

Figure 3.5
Navigating libraries within a site via the Open and Save As dialogs.

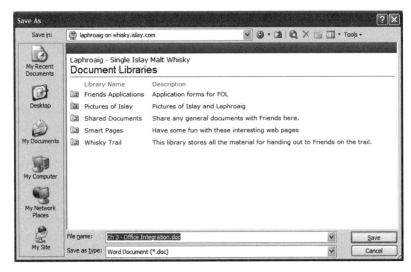

plate. In the case of modifying the Content view, you must ensure that the columns you choose to display do actually exist in all libraries that are instantiated from the template, because a SQL query is actually performed behind the scenes to gather the content. This would fail if a particular column were not in the underlying SQL tables. (Note that neither the library view nor the property view appears to be customizable in the same way as the Content view.)

The Content view could be customized to add extra columns or change the display order. This can be seen in Figure 3.6, where we have replaced the Name (filename) column with the more descriptive Title column and added a Product Type column. The Content view is called "FileDialog" and is defined in the `schema.xml` that is associated with the library definition—usually found at `Program Files\Common Files\Microsoft Shared\web server extensions\60\TEMPLATE\<lcid>\<site configuration>\lists\<list name>\schema.xml`. Inside this file you will find several `<View>` nodes that define the default views created when a library is instantiated; one of them has a Name attribute of "FileDialog." The `<View>` node defines the page to use to render the view (e.g., `allitems.aspx`, `filedlg.htm`), and child nodes of the `<View>` node define the header, body, and footer of the view, the fields in the view and their sort order, and also what to display if the contents of the view are empty.

As you will be aware, WSS libraries support version history and check-in and check-out capabilities. With Office 2003 these options are available

Figure 3.6
A modified Content view.

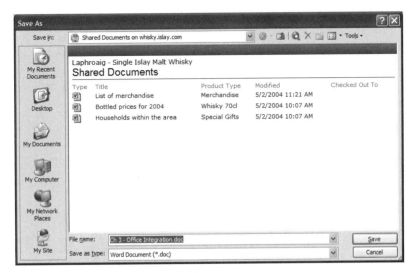

through the File menu, allowing you to retrieve older versions of the document, view historical comments, and so forth without having to leave the Office application. This functionality uses the `versions.asmx` Web Service provided by WSS.

3.4 Working with WSS lists and Excel/Access

If you think about it, the base functionality of a WSS list could easily be emulated using Excel or Access. After all, they both use a tabular row–column paradigm for data. Therefore, it should come as no surprise that there are various ways in which Excel and Access can be used to augment the functionality available with WSS lists.

3.4.1 Importing or saving from Excel to a list

An Excel spreadsheet can be used as the initial source for a WSS list via either an import or saving a list directly from Excel 2003.

To import into a new list you use the *Create/Import Spreadsheet* option to indicate the name of the WSS list you are creating and the spreadsheet that contains the initial content. Again, the presence of an ActiveX control on the device on which the browser is running is required for the option to be fully functional. This control is called `SharePoint.Spreadsheet-Launcher.2` and is installed in the same way as the Upload control except that it is stored within `OWSSUPP.DLL`.

If the control is present (and the browser allows ActiveX controls to run!), then your Excel spreadsheet is launched when you press the Import button, and you are presented with the dialog shown in Figure 3.7. From here you can choose to import your list from a Range of Cells, List Range, or Named Range.

Figure 3.7
Importing from Excel.

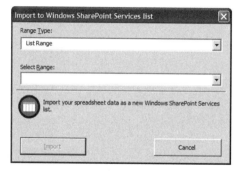

Saving directly to a new list requires Excel 2003, which introduces a new List toolbar for making it easier to manipulate your spreadsheet data as a list (e.g., sorting, filtering). After you have identified a range of cells, you can create an Excel list using the *Data/List* option. The *Publish List* option then allows you to use the list as the initial contents of a new WSS list within a site. Note that it is also possible to link the Excel list and WSS list, thus enabling synchronization between the two, as we will see shortly.

3.4.2   The Datasheet view

Lists are clearly good candidates for editing in an Excel-like fashion as well, and this is indeed doable via the Datasheet view. This view displays a list in a tabular grid within your browser, allowing you to manipulate the contents in a much easier fashion. You can add and edit rows and columns, apply multiple changes in one operation (such as deletions), apply filters and sort orders, display calculated values and totals, and so forth. The Microsoft Office List Datasheet component supports this view. It is installed by default with Office 2003 and requires that the browser allow ActiveX controls to run—the required control being `ListNet.ListNet.11`.

Manipulation of the contents is pretty much an Excel-like experience; for example, you can drag handles to populate a series of cells, insert rows and columns, and use any formula within a cell that you could use in Excel. Unlike interacting with a list through the browser, which effectively only allows you to work with a single list item at a time, you can make changes to multiple items in one operation. Thus, as you make changes to the list on your client, the changes are saved automatically in the background to the server. There is, in fact, a status bar at the bottom right corner of the datasheet that informs you whether any changes you have made are pending.

Obviously, this asynchronous updating could lead to conflicts if another user were to make changes to a list item in the interim. If you are editing an item through the browser, you get a clear message upon trying to save the item that it has been updated; you then need to reapply your changes to the updated version of the item. The datasheet alerts you of conflicts and also gives you the opportunity to resolve certain types of conflicts, such as data being changed in the same item (note that conflicts are identified at the item level and not the individual cell level). Some types of conflicts, such as structural changes to the list, cannot be resolved, and you need to refresh your list data from the server. Resolution allows you to discard or retry your changes such that all other edits are overwritten (Figure 3.8).

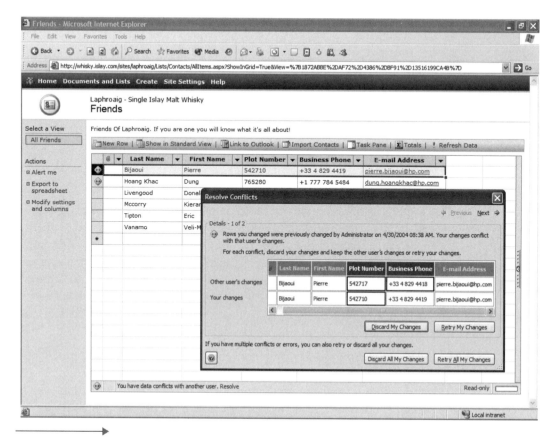

Figure 3.8   *Datasheet and resolution dialog.*

The Datasheet view also supports a task pane, which gives you easy access to frequent operations and allows you to analyze your list data with Excel or Access (see Figure 3.9). You can also link the list with Excel or Access, which enables you to work on the list within those applications.

Access uses its ability to link tables to achieve this. From Access you can create a linked table and specify a WSS list as the source. You can also export a table to a WSS list. A wizard helps you perform both these options; you only have to select Windows SharePoint Services() as the type of file in the File Open or File Save dialog. Behind the scenes Access is using the List Web Service (`lists.asmx`) that WSS provides to read and write to the WSS list. This is also true of the Datasheet view; therefore, the server must be available for you to manipulate the list contents.

Excel uses a different process, which enables you to process list contents while you are offline (e.g., when you are traveling with your laptop) and

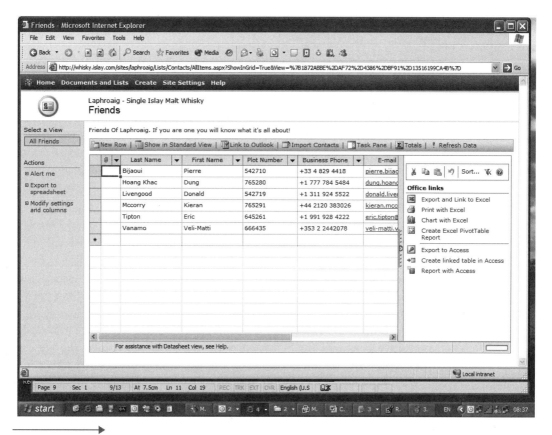

Figure 3.9   *Datasheet and task pane.*

synchronize the contents when you next have a connection to the server. Information workers require seamless offline working due to their peripatetic ways, so this is a welcome addition. Of course, it doesn't give you full offline access to your whole WSS site, but at least it's a start!

3.4.3   Synchronizing with Excel

Excel 2003 introduces the List toolbar and allows you to treat areas of your spreadsheet as a list, making it easy to sort, filter, total, and so forth. An Excel list can be linked with a WSS list in a number of ways. From Excel you can use the *Publish List* option from the List toolbar; during a WSS browser session you can use the *Export to Spreadsheet* or the *Export and Link* option from the Datasheet view. The former uses the WSS List Web Service in order to create the WSS list. The latter creates a Web query file (.iqy), which, when opened in Excel, causes the WSS List Web Service to be called to pull the WSS data into Excel.

Once the Excel list is populated, it remembers the WSS list it is linked to, and we effectively have two separate copies of the list data—one in Excel and one in the WSS site. The presence of this link allows the two copies to be synchronized, and you can choose to break the link at any time using the *Unlink list* option from the List toolbar. Synchronization of local changes and server changes is a manual process via the *Synchronize list* option on the List toolbar. The same conflict-resolution process as described previously for the datasheet also occurs during this process.

Thus, you can work on your Excel copy of the list and synchronize at your leisure. One little nuance that might be confusing occurs when you make a change to an Excel list, but do not synchronize before you close down Excel (which will obviously occur if you are offline and do not have a connection to your server). When you next open the Excel spreadsheet, you receive a message indicating that you have some changes that have not yet been synchronized. If you press the Yes button at this point, the changes you made previously are loaded into the pending-changes queue to be processed when you hit the Synchronize button. If you don't press the Yes button, your only option is to discard these pending changes and refresh the data from the server. However, if the server is not available, then you cannot do anything with the list data! So, best practice is always to click the Yes button to load pending changes if you want to synchronize at any point in the future.

3.5   The Shared Workspace task pane

So, we now know that there are many ways to find yourself inside an Office 2003 application with a document stored in a WSS library that is currently open. Of course, this library is part of a WSS site, and if you are exploiting WSS to its fullest, there will doubtless be other collateral within the site that in some way relates to the document. For example, the members of the site are useful collateral if, while processing the document, you feel the need to contact them for any reason. Additionally, lists such as Tasks and Events could be useful because, often as not, reading a document alerts you to some other activities that need to take place.

Going along with the idea of being able to collaborate directly whenever you feel the urge to do so, Office 2003 introduces the Shared Workspace task pane, designed to allow you to connect quickly with other important collateral contained within the WSS site where the document belongs without having to leave the current application. Now, not all operations that you can perform from the WSS site itself are available from the task pane, but the most likely ones you will need are there. Six separate "pages" within the pane can be used to deal with status information (see section 3.6 about document workspaces), members, tasks, documents, links, and document information. Examples of possible operations include adding a member to the WSS site, updating custom column properties of the currently open document, adding new folders and documents to the library, adding tasks and links to the WSS site, and setting up alerts for WSS site information. Figure 3.10 shows direct updating of the custom properties associated with a document.

Several server components are involved in delivering the document and the site information to the calling application. For example a POST to the ISAPI extension `author.dll` is used to retrieve the document contents, and the Web Service `dws.asmx` is instrumental in gathering the majority of data for the task pane.

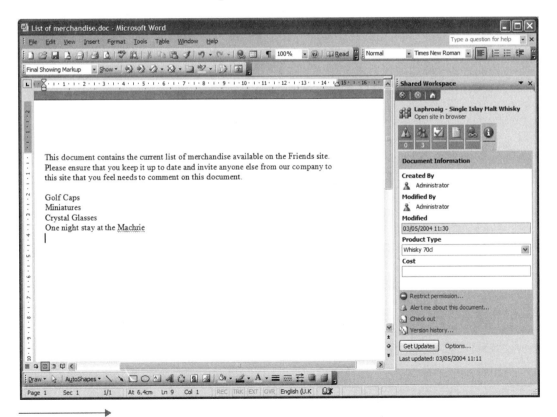

Figure 3.10   *Shared workspace task pane.*

3.6   **Document workspaces**

We talked previously about how WSS sites are designed for multiple purposes and how you can create site templates to tailor sites to your precise
needs. The Office team decided that there was a need to support situations
that involved multiple people creating the actual contents of a document,
be they editors or reviewers.

To this end the team designed a special type of WSS site that supports
typical multiauthor creation activities. The site can be provisioned from
multiple locations and uses its own template to define the Web Parts created within the site. It's most distinguishing feature, however, is that it supports the ability to work on local copies of documents stored within the site
and to update changes periodically to the master copy held in the site. This
is the main feature that allows multiauthor creation of content in that it
allows multiple authors to work on the same document at the same time
without the usual "last writer wins" scenarios and other risks associated with
a "normal" WSS library. Of course the check-in/out capability on any WSS
library can be used for multi-authoring purposes ensuring that at any point
in time a single author has exclusive write access. The big difference with a
library inside a document workspace is that multiple *concurrent* editing is
possible. Automatic updating of changes made by others requires Office
2003 (or later) and works with Word, Excel, PowerPoint, and Visio.

The term *document workspace* defines such a special-purpose WSS site.
As stated, document workspaces are generally used to support the creation
of content, and once the content is complete, it will likely be moved to
another WSS site or an SPS portal area for wider publication. Thus, document workspaces are transient WSS sites, which are quickly provisioned
from multiple locations, used for a specific purpose, and then generally left
to die gracefully through the standard life-cycle management of WSS sites
(although you can choose to be a good citizen and delete the site yourself
once you are finished with it!).

The default configuration of a document workspace is defined in the
ONET.XML file and, out of the box, contains announcements; tasks and
links lists; a document library for storing the document to be worked on;
and a Members Web Part, which reveals the online status of the workspace
members.

There are three places where you can provision a document workspace.
The first is from a document held in a document library within a "normal"
site. In this case the *Create Document Workspace* option appears in the Edit

menu for the document. Why might you want to do this? Well, the most likely case is that the contents of the document need reviewing, and you want multiple people to collaborate on the new contents before republishing. Thus, you can create a new WSS site and invite only those people who need to discuss the new contents to this site as members. Document workspaces created in this way allow you to use the *Publish to Source Location* option to have the document republished to its original location once you are happy with its new content. This feature, used in conjunction with the Shared Workspace task pane, enables a nice environment for jointly working on a document.

You can also manually choose a document workspace as the template during site or subsite creation and manually populate it with documents you want to collaborate on. However, Outlook 2003 provides perhaps the best illustration of document workspaces' intended use.

How many times have you attached a document to an e-mail message and sent it to a group of people along with the instruction: Please update

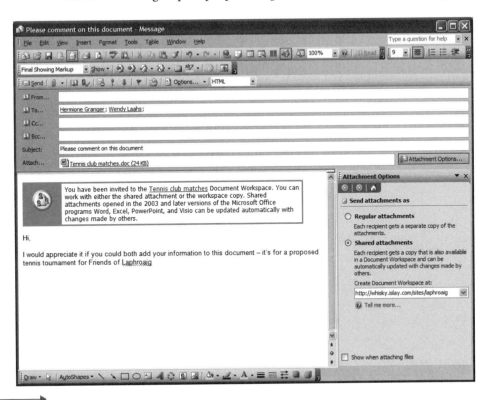

Figure 3.11   *Creating a shared attachment.*

the document and send it back to me—I will then collate all the updates and send the completed document back out to everyone? Well, document workspaces are ideal for making this task much easier! With Outlook 2003 you have the option of marking an attachment as "shared," which results in the dynamic creation of a document workspace; the addition of the message's addressees as members of the workspace; the storing of a master copy of the attachment in a library within the workspace; and the creation of announcement, links, and tasks Web Parts. Finally, some descriptive text is added to the body of the mail message indicating that the attachment is also stored in a document workspace. Note that I say "also stored." As far as Outlook and, more importantly, Exchange are concerned, the attachment is still just like any other attachment. Exchange has no knowledge of the master copy and does not treat the attachment any differently than it does any other attachment. Figures 3.11 and 3.12 show a shared attachment being created and the subsequent document workspace that is generated.

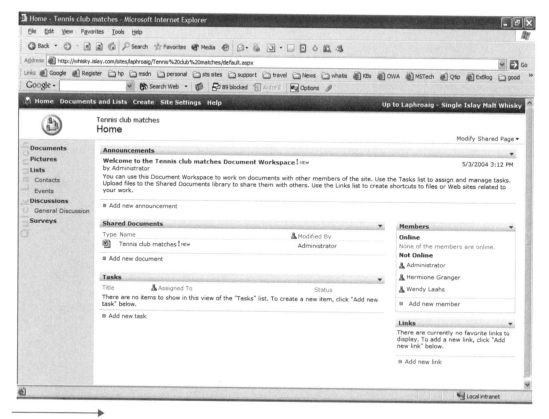

Figure 3.12   *Document workspace created from a shared attachment.*

In the case of a shared attachment, the message originator has to specify where to create the document workspace. It is created as a subsite; therefore, the Create Subsite role is required on the parent site. The Web Service dws.asmx and the ISAPI extension author.dll are used to create the document workspace and to copy the document into its document library.

Only if an attachment is one of the supported Office applications does anything actually happen to it. In this case an attribute is written into the header of the underlying file containing a link to the master copy held in the document workspace. This is done to any Office items that find their way into a document workspace in order that subsequent updates can occur if the document is edited outside of the workspace. Any Office file that has such a link enables the Document Update task pane from within the Office application once the file is opened. This pane allows you to retrieve changes made by others to the master copy of the document and to control when any updates you make are synchronized. There are also options for resolv-

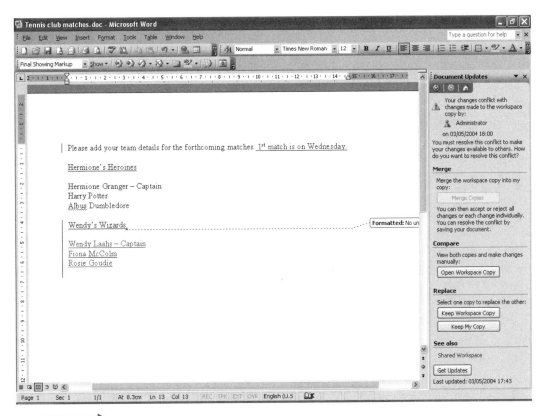

Figure 3.13 *Merging multiple updates.*

ing any conflicts should two users change the same part of a document. In this case you can choose to merge the changes, which utilizes the ability to track changes to show the multiple edits to the user. Figure 3.13 shows the task pane and a sample of multiple edits.

The link inside the Office document can be broken at any time, in which case no automatic updates to the master copy are subsequently possible from this local copy. Obviously, this is required in cases where the document cannot connect back to the document workspace—for example, if a shared attachment e-mail includes an external recipient who cannot physically access the internal network.

One interesting option is made available in the case of a shared e-mail attachment. The recipient can, upon reading the e-mail, choose to open the shared document directly or the local copy attached to the message. Opening the local copy allows the user to see the document as it was at the time when it was attached to the mail message. However, opening the shared document allows the recipient to see it in its current form, which may include changes made in the interim by other recipients of the mail message. In a scenario where all recipients are being invited to add their comments to a document, this allows you to get the most up-to-date information very quickly.

3.7   Meeting workspaces

Meeting workspaces are again just special-purpose WSS sites designed to assist with the typical activities surrounding a meeting. Hosting a successful meeting often requires a lot of collateral, such as agendas, objectives, and outcomes, beyond merely getting the meeting correctly registered in people's diaries.

Meeting workspaces can be provisioned during site or subsite creation and, as you might expect, from Outlook 2003. In the latter case the attendees of the meeting are added as members of the workspace, and a link to the workspace is included in the body of the invitation. Users can choose from multiple meeting workspace templates, depending upon the purpose of their meeting—the template influences the Web Parts that are provisioned into the workspace. As users create a meeting request in Outlook, the Meeting Workspace button brings up a special task pane. From here the user can decide where the meeting workspace should be created and what template to use. Out of the box the available templates are Basic, Blank, Decision, Social, and MultiPage.

Unlike the *Shared Attachments* option, the existence of the Meeting Workspace button can be controlled via a registry key. There are also registry keys that control the possible locations where meeting workspaces can be created. The best way to find out about these keys is to download the Office Resource Kit (ORK) from the Microsoft Web site and play around with the Custom Installation Wizard. The ORK ships a file called `Outlook11.adm`, which can be used to find out about the vast majority of registry keys that affect the way Outlook functions (and can be used as a group policy to enforce these settings). As an example, the key to disable the Meetings Workspace button is defined as follows in the `Outlook11.adm` file:

```
CATEGORY "Meeting Workspace"
POLICY "Disable Meeting Workspace button"
KEYNAME Software\Policies\Microsoft\Office\11.0\
Meetings\Profile
PART "Check to disable Meeting Workspace button" CHECKBOX
      VALUENAME EntryUI
      VALUEON NUMERIC 1
      VALUEOFF NUMERIC 0
   END PART
   END POLICY
```

The Web Service `meetings.asmx` is used to create the meeting workspace and to ensure that any subsequent updates to the Outlook meeting item are kept in sync with the meeting workspace. For example, changing the meeting time or adding or removing attendees will cause the Web Service to be called as the *Send Update* option is chosen on the Outlook item.

3.8   Linking lists to Outlook

Contacts and events are commonly used lists in many WSS sites. Similarly, contacts and calendars are commonly stored in user mailboxes and shared public folders. The option therefore exists to link a WSS contact or event list to Outlook 2003 in order that both sets of contacts and events can be viewed from a single location. I say "viewed" here, because the contents of the WSS list are created inside special read-only folders in a personal storage file (PST) specifically created for this purpose. The items in these folders are not writeable through the Outlook 2003 user interface, and only the background synchronization process can update items in these folders. You can, however, drag and drop items (or indeed the whole folder) from these folders into your own personal folders, but there is no ongoing link or synchronization between your personal copy and the copy in the special folder. This is not ideal, but at least it is a step in the right direction, and we can expect to see Microsoft extending this functionality such that linked items are read/write in the future.

When a user is viewing a WSS events or contacts list in the browser, a *Link to Outlook* option is available on the menu bar. This option will only appear if an ActiveX object called `SharePoint.StssyncHandler` can be created within the current browser session. This object is installed with Office 2003, so clearly Office 2003 has to have been installed on the device you are running your browser on. The very first time a user chooses this option, a check is made to see whether Outlook 2003 is enabled for Share-Point integration; if it is, a special kind of PST is created. By default it is enabled, but this can be controlled via the following registry key:

```
HKCU \ Software \ Policies \ Microsoft \ Office \ 11.0 \
Outlook \ Preferences \
Name: DisallowSTS
Type: DWORD
Value: 1 = disable which means users receive a warning
dialog if they take the "Link to Outlook" option from WSS
```

The PST file is created in the user's Windows profile. Note that the PST is created per MAPI profile, so if you have more than one MAPI profile, and you choose to link WSS folders to them, you will end up with multiple PST files (named `SharePoint Folders.pst`, `SharePoint Folders(2).pst`, etc.). Once the PST file is in place, a new folder is created inside it, and the URL of the WSS list is associated with it. Even though the PST appears like other PSTs, it is effectively read-only, and there is no way through the Outlook user interface to create other folders within it. Only the *Link to Outlook* option is capable of populating new folders into the PST. The Outlook object model introduces some new attributes for the `MAPIfolder` object that allows SharePoint folders to be distinguished. In particular, the Boolean attribute `IsSharePointFolder` indicates whether a folder is a Share-Point-based folder. Other attributes are the date and time the folder was last updated and the list ID from the WSS site.

Now that the folder is in the user's Outlook session, it can be displayed in the same way as other folders of the same type. For example, as shown in Figure 3.14, a folder containing a WSS events list can be displayed side by side with calendar folders from any mailbox the user has access to, plus those contained in public folders. This allows you to create your own personal copy of WSS event list–based items into other Outlook calendar folders through a simple drag and drop. While we are looking at calendar folders, it is worthwhile pointing out a slight issue with time zones. Outlook will always take the current time zone that is set on the client's operating system

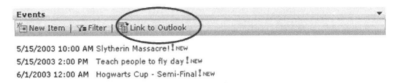

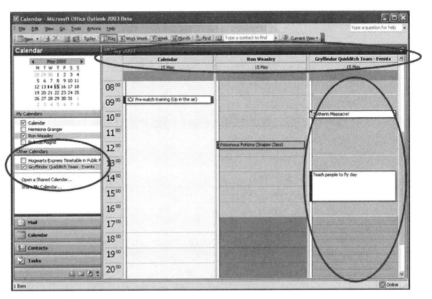

Figure 3.14   *Linking a list to Outlook.*

and use it to display times according to that time zone. On the other hand, each WSS site has a regional time zone setting on the server, which is honored when the site is viewed through a browser. Thus, if your client time zone differs from the WSS site's time zone, then you will see different times for items when viewing them through the synchronized Outlook folder, as opposed to the Browser view of the list. A lesson here is that anyone who creates a WSS event should set its time to be in accordance with the time zone of the WSS space rather than the time zone that the user is currently in. This should ensure that no one misses a meeting!

One-way synchronization occurs both when the user clicks on the folder in Outlook and at timed intervals. Note, however, that even though you can move the WSS folders out of the PST, synchronization only occurs if they are kept inside the SharePoint PST (moving a folder results in the `IsSharePointFolder` property being set to false). This means that you cannot store a SharePoint list in a public folder, a capability that would have been useful for global sharing of WSS lists. The default synchronization frequency is every 20 minutes, but this can be controlled via the following registry key:

```
HKCU \ Software \ Policies \ Microsoft \ Office \ 11.0 \
Outlook \ Preferences \
Name: STSSyncInterval
Type: DWORD
Value: <= 0 do not do auto-synch at timed intervals
       >0 = Number of minutes
```

Synchronization uses the Web Service lists.asmx to pull any updates from the WSS list into the Outlook folder.

3.9   InfoPath and form libraries

InfoPath is a new member of the Office family and allows you to design and process forms in an easy-to-use fashion. The key to its ease of use and interoperability with other systems is the use of XML to represent the data and XSL to render the form.

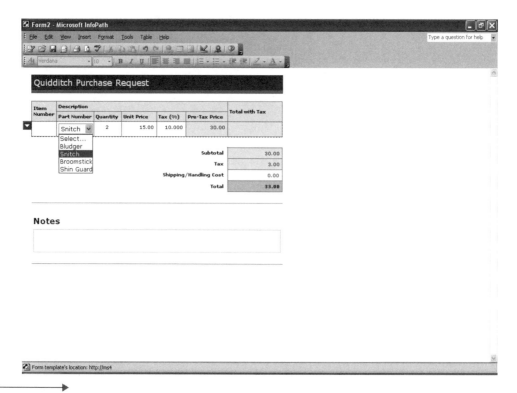

Figure 3.15   *InfoPath form.*

You design InfoPath forms using an Office-like editing environment, allowing you to work in a familiar way with structured documents without needing to know anything about XML. Once you have completed the design, you need to make the form available for use by others by publishing it to a shared location. One publishing location is a WSS site. In this case, a new form library is created in that site, and the InfoPath form is set as the default template for the library. Additionally, fields from the InfoPath form can be promoted into read-only custom columns within the form library, thus allowing form data to be viewable without actually having to invoke InfoPath to render the form. Publishing the InfoPath form to a WSS form library results in InfoPath being launched and the form loaded when users choose the *Fill in this form* option from the library. Of course, InfoPath needs to be installed on the device the user is currently on!

Figures 3.15 and 3.16 show the result of filling in an InfoPath form that is stored as the default template for a WSS form library. Note how certain fields from the form are promoted and displayed as custom columns within the form library listing.

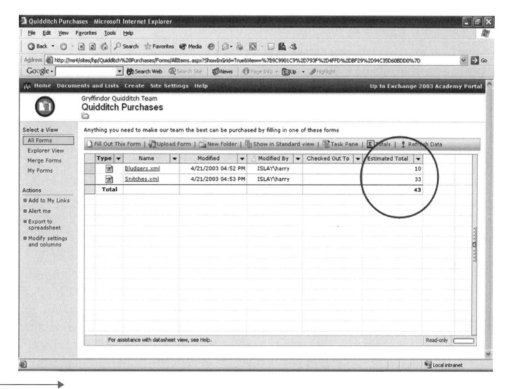

Figure 3.16   *InfoPath and properties being promoted to columns.*

Various ISAPI extensions such as `owssvr.dll` and `author.dll` are used in integrating InfoPath and WSS form libraries.

3.10 Alerts and Outlook

WSS allows you to set up alerts—notifications that something somewhere has changed. (SPS 2003 also has its own way of dealing with alerts, which we will discuss later.) These alerts can be used to monitor lists and libraries, informing you when items are added and deleted or even when individual items are modified. E-mail is the medium used to alert you that something has changed, and you can see which alerts you have set up on a per–WSS site basis using the *Site Settings/My alerts on this site* option.

Given that you may be a member of many WSS sites, it could become cumbersome to manage all the alerts you may have set up. Indeed, it is highly likely that you will forget which particular sites you have alerts set up on. Therefore, to assist you in dealing with this situation, Outlook enables details of all the sources that are sending you alerts to be collated together into one dialog—through the *Rules and Alerts* menu option. From here, you can also delete and create new alerts on any WSS site.

As you choose this option, Outlook 2003 uses the Web Services capabilities of WSS to retrieve your alerts. A POST is made to the `alerts.asmx` and a request to execute the method `GetAlerts` is contained in the XML data sent as part of the body. The returned XML is then rendered and displayed in the Manage Alerts tab of the Rules and Alerts dialog.

How does Outlook 2003 know which WSS servers and sites to ask for details of the alerts you have set up? Well, when you create an alert in the first place, a cookie is written to your machine, and an e-mail message is sent to you to confirm that the alert has been set up successfully. Outlook extracts from this cookie the URL to the server and site that manages the alert and writes these into a hidden folder in your mailbox. This list of alert servers is then used when you choose the *Manage Alerts* option.

There is a slight problem here in that the cookies are not removed from your machine and in that Outlook will parse the cookies once for each MAPI profile used on that machine irrespective of the mailbox the profile is connecting to. Therefore, if you pick up cookies from another person's machine (by creating a profile for your mailbox on his or her machine), you will add his or her alert servers to your list. Now, you won't actually be able to see which alerts have been set up on those servers, because you won't be able to authenticate to WSS as the other user, but Outlook will, nevertheless, still try. Outlook will let you delete the alert servers from your list if it cannot contact them for any reason (server unavailable, invalid authentication, etc.). It makes sense to make this a manual effort, because the alert server may not be available to you for a valid reason; therefore, automatically removing servers from the list would be dangerous.

3.11 Exchange public folders and WSS libraries

A lot of customers use e-mail-enabled public folders to allow internal and external people to contribute documents for sharing. A common request from STS v1.0 and SPS 2001 customers was the ability to e-mail documents directly into document libraries.

This feature is available in WSS and leverages the ability to use WebDAV against the Exchange Store. In theory, mailboxes could be used here, but in practice it is more likely that you will e-mail-enable a public folder and then configure individual WSS document libraries to retrieve attachments from the URL of the public folder. Note that only attachments to mail messages are copied into the WSS document library and not the body of e-mail messages. This is a pity, because taking all items would provide an ideal migration of legacy content from public folders to WSS document libraries. The current feature is designed specifically for e-mailing documents into WSS libraries, but this functionality may well be extended in the future for migration purposes.

A WebDAV SEARCH is issued against the URL for the public folder and asks for any new items in there that have attachments. Because the WebDAV protocol is used, only Exchange 2000 and 2003 servers can be the source for the content, as Exchange 5.5 servers do not support WebDAV. In theory, this enables the pulling of attachments from any folder as long as the SharePoint Services account has permission to access the actual folder. SharePoint administrators set the correct URL on the library (consisting of the root that is applied to the overall virtual server and the part that is associated with the document library in question).

This functionality does not work out of the box due to the fact that the SharePoint Timer Service cannot authenticate to the Exchange virtual directory (the IIS public one). To fix this you need to ensure that the timer service runs under a domain account such that NTLM authentication can work or enable anonymous access to the IIS virtual directory. If you change the timer service account, then you also need to change the IIS 6 SharePoint Admin Application Pool, because the timer service needs to keep in sync with it to read from the SQL database as well.

The SEARCH is performed as follows (using a public folder called "Pilot" as an example and a last run of 2004-04-03 @ 16:06):

```
Select "DAV:href",
"urn:schemas:httpmail:normalizedsubject",
"urn:schemas:httpmail:fromname",
"urn:schemas:httpmail:fromemail",
"urn:schemas:httpmail:datereceived", "http://
schemas.microsoft.com/mapi/proptag/x67090040" FROM
Scope('SHALLOW TRAVERSAL OF "Pilot"') WHERE
"urn:schemas:httpmail:hasattachment" = True AND "http://
schemas.microsoft.com/mapi/proptag/x67090040" &gt '2004-
04-03 16:06:12.357' ORDER BY "http://
schemas.microsoft.com/mapi/proptag/x67090040"
```

If this gets any hits, then a WebDAV X-MS-ENUMATTS is issued to enumerate the list of attachments on each new post, followed by an individual GET performed on each returned attachment.

There is a two-step process to set up this capability. First, you need to enable the feature on a virtual server–basis using the SharePoint Central Administration utility. At this juncture you specify a URL to the top-level Exchange store (or folder) where the root of the search will start and the frequency with which the SharePoint Timer Service will check for any updates to folders associated with WSS libraries. Second, you need to configure each library that you want to be part of the process, indicating which actual Exchange folder under the root is to be searched for content. This is done using the *Modify settings and columns/Change advanced settings* option and is only available for document and form libraries.

3.12 Outlook Web Access Web Parts

WSS offers great potential in the area of personalization, as we will discover in Chapter 5. Users can personalize their views of shared WSS sites and, with SPS in the picture, have their own individual sites. Furthermore, they can provide public and private views of their own sites.

Aggregating information from multiple sources into a site is a requirement, and it is not unusual for users to request to view their own inboxes or calendars inside their own personal sites (as well as, perhaps, shared calendars in public folders). To make this easy to do, the Exchange 2003 team has provided support for simplified Outlook Web Access (OWA) rendering of items within a folder. This is a very welcome addition when you consider all of the extraneous information, such as toolbars and folder hierarchies, rendered when you render a folder URL in Exchange 2000.

These views are generated by passing special query strings to the URL for the folder in question. Integrating these in a WSS site is as simple as providing the correct URL in a Web Part like the Page Viewer Web Part. The "`part=1`" query string indicates that you want a simplified view of the folder in question; it works in conjunction with "`cmd=contents`" or "`cmd=loadmodule`." In a simplified view of the Inbox, the following takes place:

- The toolbar is not rendered.

- The folder name is not displayed.

- If no view is explicitly specified, the two-line view is the default when viewing a mail folder as a Web part.

- The item count is read-only and left aligned; navigation buttons are right aligned.

- The preview pane is disabled.

- The context menu is not available in the view.

- Standard view functions—clickable/sortable column headings, flagging, type-down search, keyboard actions (reply, forward, delete)— are available from the Inbox part.

- The Inbox part should detect the presence of the appropriate version of the S/MIME control and use the correct forms to display S/MIME content.

- Other supported query strings when viewing the Inbox are "`view`" and "`rowsperpage`."

The simplified Calendar part is based on the down-level OWA weekly view, where items are listed and organized daily for a specific week. It is an HTML document—rather than the heavy, rich OWA Calendar control— with two modes: a Quick Agenda view and a Weekly Agenda view. The Quick Agenda view is presented when a date is not explicitly specified; the Calendar part will render appointments beginning the current day, based on the user's time zone settings, and finish at the end of the user-defined week. The Weekly Agenda view is presented when an explicit date is supplied.

When the calendar is displayed as a part, the following occurs:

- The toolbar is not rendered.

- The folder name is not displayed.

- User preference for the start of the week is observed.

- Icons, including recurrence, private, and the invitee heads, are not displayed.

- Days that contain no data display "No appointments scheduled" as their content.

- When in the Quick Agenda view, if the current day and the rest of the week do not contain appointments, the part will only display "No appointments for the rest of the week."

- No navigation from the displayed date span is available in this part.

- An arrow will point to the appointment or appointment(s) that are in progress.

- Hovering over an appointment shows an underline.

- A single-click is used to open an appointment.

Figure 3.17 shows a simplified view of a user's Inbox rendered as a Web Part within a Web Part Page.

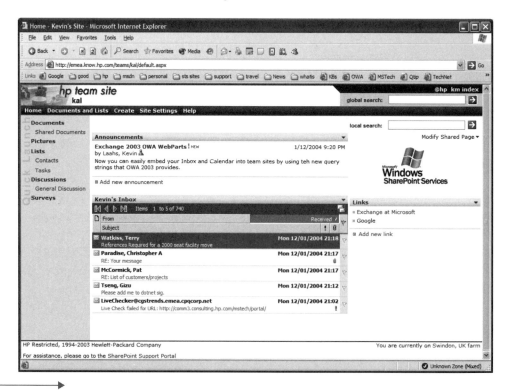

Figure 3.17   *OWA in a Web Part.*

4

SharePoint Portal Server

As discussed in Chapter 2, WSS provides the technological foundation upon which other collaborative services and applications are built. Microsoft Office SPS 2003 is one such product. Not only does it require WSS, but it augments the functionality provided by the WSS site framework. In this chapter, we take a look at the architecture of SPS and the key features that it brings to the collaboration landscape.

4.1   Differentiating WSS and SPS

WSS and SPS both facilitate collaboration and fall under the umbrella name of "Microsoft SharePoint Products and Technologies," which in general conversation is normally shortened to "SharePoint." In discussions of SharePoint, the first issue that usually occurs is that of confusion: confusion about what each product does and which one is right for a particular task. This is understandable given that the functionality provided by SPS is actually a superset of WSS—SPS requires WSS to run!

A simple way of differentiating the two products is to consider that the main focus of WSS is enabling large numbers of small teams to create and collaborate on team-specific information. SPS, on the other hand, focuses on connecting people and information across departments and organizations. Therefore, while WSS is used to collaborate on the creation of team-specific information, SPS enables the publishing of relevant information and its discovery by a wider audience. And we use information in its widest sense here—be it a piece of news, the contents of a document, the phone number of the person who authored a similar document, or the online status of a user who logged a particular transaction in an application-specific database.

As an example of how SPS enables the discovery of information, consider the following. WSS allows sites to be created where teams can generate and collaborate on information. However, this information is effectively in a silo. There is no way, out of the box, for one team to discover any other relevant information possibly being generated by another team. Implementing SPS allows this information to be discovered using a variety of methods—be it linking WSS sites together through navigation, providing a browsable directory of all WSS sites, enabling search across all WSS-based content, or providing publishing areas where topic-based subject matter can be stored and navigated to via a structured hierarchy.

A good example of the latter is two product development teams. Each team has its own WSS site to collaborate on the development of its product specification. Once the teams' individual products are complete, they publish their product specifications to a portal site area for all company products, enabling a wider audience to discover the product specifications by browsing the navigational hierarchy or through searching.

Although I used WSS in the previous example, we are not restricted solely to WSS content. Information from almost anywhere can be aggregated and presented in a relevant way to suit the particular needs of different end users. Indeed, even though WSS is a prerequisite for SPS, you could choose not to allow users to create their own sites for team collaboration and require that they only use SPS to aggregate information from other sources.

4.2   Major SPS components

So SPS has its main focus on making relevant information readily available and discoverable to a wide audience, and it delivers many features that can be used to achieve this goal. Some of these features deal with topics so important that we have dedicated separate chapters to them.

People are considered "first-class objects" in SPS, meaning that discovering information about people is just as important as discovering information contained in documents and lists. Additionally, providing an environment in which people can work with their own personal information in the same way as they would work with shared information is important. Therefore, in Chapter 5, we take a look at how people and personalization are supported in SPS.

Providing an up-to-date and comprehensive index of aggregated content that can be searched with relevant results returned is key for users to find easily the right information regardless of where it is physically stored. Enterprise Search is therefore covered in Chapter 6.

The rest of this chapter looks at the main SPS architecture and the following remaining features:

- Portal areas

- Portal URLs

- Portal content navigation

- Portal listings and news

- Security

- Site directory

- Connecting WSS sites

- Enterprise application integration

4.3   What does SPS require of WSS?

SPS leverages two major technologies provided by WSS—the site framework and Web Part Pages. End users typically view the portal through a Web browser. The content of the Web pages that they view consists of one or more Web Parts, with each gathering its content from a relevant data source. Furthermore, Web Part Pages can be personalized in terms of which Web Parts appear and their characteristics. Thus, the Web Part Pages technology provided by WSS ensures that relevant information can be aggregated and easily accessed by end users.

Before we go any further, let's briefly describe the major architecture in order to get some terminology on the table that will allow us to differentiate between the different types of sites that we will encounter. As with WSS, SPS relies on IIS virtual servers and supports the same types of deployments as WSS. Thus, you can have single-server and farm deployments. The main extra ingredients on top of WSS when SPS is in the mix are search and indexing, both of which can be deployed on separate servers with a farm deployment. Thus, in an SPS environment different roles need to be played, and these roles can be deployed on anything from a single server to multiple, large server farms. The roles in question are front-end Web rendering, indexing, search, job, and SQL database servers. You can control the topology of your environment using the *Configure Server Topology* option from the SPS Central Administration Web page, as shown in Figure 4.1. Any issues with your configuration will be highlighted on this page. As you

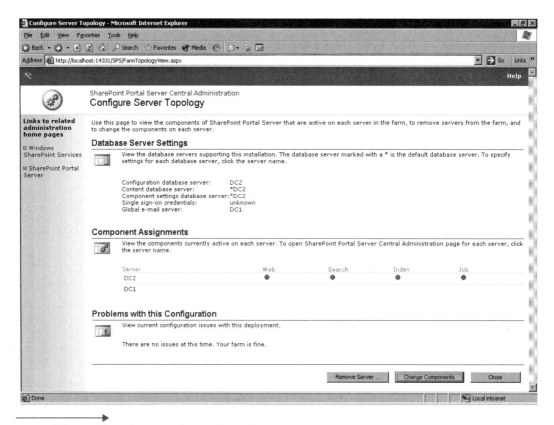

Figure 4.1   *Server topology configuration.*

can see, this screen shot is from a simple and straightforward single-server installation. More detailed configurations are covered later in this book!

After installing SPS you then extend an IIS virtual server to create a portal site. Any SPS deployment (single or farm) can support 15 portal sites, unless you implement Shared Services, in which case you can support up to 100 portal sites (by default IIS only supports 64 virtual servers, so some registry changes, documented in the SPS Administrators Guide, are required if you need to exceed this number). The major reason for only supporting 15 portal sites is the resources required to support the indexing and search catalogs. Each portal site would require its own catalogs, and the single Microsoft SharePoint Search Service running on the indexing and search servers would have to service each individual portal site. Shared Services is a deployment option whereby multiple portal sites share the same index (as well as other services such as the SPS profile); thus, there is only one set of catalogs to deal with and only one indexing server role. Shared Services also allows multiple portal sites to be associated with each other, enabling a hierarchical search environment to be implemented. We cover this in more detail in Chapters 6 and 8.

Once you have created a portal site, you then organize its contents through portal areas. In SPS 2001 terms, an area is akin to a category in that you would group similar content together in an area. However, in SPS 2001, a category was merely a view on documents within the single document library of the SPS workspace, whereas a portal area is a far richer place for storing and organizing content. This is where the WSS site framework comes into play. Each portal area is actually a WSS-based site that can contain document libraries, lists, views and Web Part Pages, which you would typically use to maintain content relevant to a particular subject matter. I use the term *WSS-based site*, since there are some subtle differences between a native WSS site and a site that is created for use by an SPS portal area. For example, the security model for a portal area does not allow list- or item-level permissions, whereas these are allowed in a WSS site.

So, as required, we will use the terms *portal area* and *team site* in order to differentiate between an SPS and WSS site. You will also encounter the term *My Site*. SPS introduces the ability for each user to have his or her own personal Web site, known as "My Site"; beneath the covers this is just a WSS site with a public and private view.

4.4   Portal areas

You can create as many portal areas and subareas as you like within your portal site, and area templates are used to ensure consistency of information presentation across all portal content. Area templates are implemented using site configurations and site definitions, as discussed in Chapter 2, which should not come as a surprise given that an area is basically a WSS site beneath the covers. By default a portal site consists of the special area called Home (which uses the SPS template) and three other portal areas called Topics, News, and Sites (which use the SPSTOC, SPSNHOME, and SPSSITE template, respectively).

Just as the two site configurations delivered with WSS (STS and MPS) enable you to choose a site template when creating a team site, SPS delivers another 10 configurations that represent the different types of sites that it supports (portal areas, personal sites, etc.). Six of these are for portal areas. Each portal area has associated settings that allow you to specify the area template that should be used when a subarea is created. You can force a subarea to use the same template as the parent area or allow creators to choose from one of the six templates. The six area templates are Contents, Topic, News, News Home, Site Directory, and Community. These can be augmented with your own area and custom templates, and you can also change the template that is currently being used by an area. (As an aside, you can tell which template was used to create a site or area by looking at the Web-Template column on the Webs table for your portal site—the value here relates to the ID of the template as defined in the WEBTEMP*.XML files found in C:\Program Files\Common Files\Microsoft Shared\web server extensions\60\TEMPLATE\<lcid>\XML.) You can also save custom list templates from a portal area, but as with team sites, the custom list can only be used in other portal areas that have been instantiated with the same area template from where the list originates.

As we know, templates define the initial content of a site in terms of libraries, lists, Web Part Pages, navigation, and so forth. The six area templates mentioned here are contained within the folders called SPSTOC, SPSTOPIC, SPSNEWS, SPSNHOME, SPSSITES, and SSPCOMMU. To the naked eye these templates are very similar, and indeed the only discernible difference between them is in the SPSTOC template. It is designed as a table-of-contents-type area and thus has a predefined Web Part on its Home page that allows you to browse all the subareas that have been created from the parent area. The other templates all allow you to add content directly to the area—to add a listing or person or to upload a document—from the *Actions* section of the left navigation bar.

As mentioned previously, each portal area is essentially a WSS team site; therefore, content in terms of libraries, lists, and Web Part Pages can be created. Just as with a team site, you use libraries and lists to store content, and then you use Web Parts to expose this content on different pages within your portal area. Thus, when a portal area is provisioned using these templates, three storage locations are instantiated for you—one for portal listings (which is a specific list to SPS and doesn't exist in team sites), a library for documents, and a library for pictures. Only the default Home and Sites areas instantiate any other lists, but of course you have the flexibility to create as many lists and libraries as you like using the *Manage Content* option from the Action menu. Now, when you use the *Add a listing*, *Add a person*, or *Upload a document* options, all you are doing is placing content into the appropriate list or library (person items are stored in the portal listings library). Each portal area's Home page then uses Web Parts to display information from these locations. For example, most templates just use two Web Parts, called Area Detail and Grouped Listings. The former shows contact information and a description of the portal area, and the latter shows items from the portal listings list.

When you upload a document from the portal area's Home page, you are placing a physical copy in the default document library (<portal area>/Document Library), and you are also given the option of adding an entry for it to the portal listings. In such a case, you will then expose the link to the document via the Grouped Listings Web Part on the Home page of the portal area. We can see this in Figures 4.2 and 4.3. Here I have created a brand new portal area and added a listing, a person, and a document library. Note how we now have two items in the portal listings and one in the document library and how the Grouped Listings Web Part exposes the three portal listings. Incidentally, Figure 4.2 shows the design mode, thus revealing the names of the Web Parts and also revealing the *Create SubArea* option on the top menu bar. In a team site the **Modify Shared Page** link at the top right of the page is always available, whereas in a portal area you

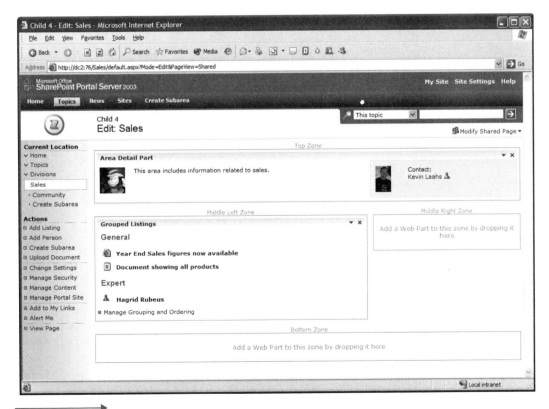

Figure 4.2   *Portal area Home page in design mode showing two Web Parts.*

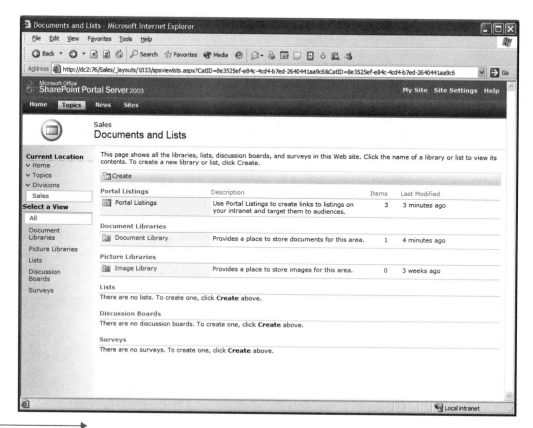

Figure 4.3   *Items in the portal listings and document library of a portal area.*

first have to toggle the page from View Page Mode to Edit Page Mode using the menu option from the *Actions* section of the left navigation pane.

Each portal area has multiple settings that affect how it behaves. The *Change Settings* option on the Actions menu opens a tabbed dialog that allows you to manage the general, publishing, page, display, and search settings for the portal area.

The *General* section allows you to specify the title, URL, description, and contact details that appear in the Area Detail Web Part, as shown in Figure 4.2. Contact details can be manually entered, or you can look up details from the Active Directory (AD), which are then written into the contact details. This is a one-off lookup, and any changes to the AD object will not be reflected in the portal area contact unless you redo the setting. Note the picture that appears here—the Settings page asks for the URL of the image to display. Now you can either type in an absolute URL to a remote image, or, if you so choose, you can load your images into the image library (or indeed any other library!) that is provisioned with the portal area. In the latter case, you can use a relative URL to point to the image, which, in this case, was `/sales/image library/kal.jpg` after having added `kal.jpg` to the image library in the sales portal area.

You can also change the URL for the area and its location—both of which are discussed later. Finally, you can see the creation and last-modified dates for the portal area.

The *Publishing* section allows you to control a date range for when a portal area is shown in the portal site. This would typically be used when you want to publish information associated with a forthcoming event and have it gracefully "die" after the event has passed. Note that the appearance and expiration dates affect whether the portal area appears when users are navigating through the different portal locations. It does not render the area inaccessible, since you can still directly access it if you know its URL or by navigating to it via a network share or Web Folders. Similarly, content from the portal area will still be returned in search results regardless of these date settings.

You can also control whether portal listings need approval before they will be displayed through a Web Part and whether content-area managers also need their listings approved before they can be published.

The *Page* section allows you to specify the template that should be used for any subareas that are created and also allows you to specify which template the current area should use.

The *Display* section allows you to manually control whether the area appears in site navigation (as opposed to doing this through the appearance/expiration dates mentioned earlier) and how portal listings are sorted when displayed in the area. Also, you can specify two images to be associated with the area—one that is displayed in the Area Details Web Part (as shown in Figure 4.2) and one that is used next to a link to the area (e.g., in the portal site map, as discussed later).

The *Search* section allows you to control whether the contents associated with a portal area are indexed and also whether the Topic Assistant includes this area when automatically categorizing content.

4.5   A word about SPS URLs

Just as with a team site, each portal area has a URL that will take you to its home page, and this Web address has to be unique. The formation of a team site's URL is different from that of a portal area, however.

As we discussed in Chapter 2, a site collection consists of a top-level Web site plus any number of subsites. When you create a team site, you are effectively creating a site collection. For the top-level Web site in this collection you specify the right-most part of the URL, and the system will check for uniqueness. Then, as you create subsites, you similarly specify the right-most part of the URL, but the path of your URL grows to reflect each subsite level. Thus, if I create a site collection called "projects" and create, say, three subsites, then a URL to the lowest-level subsite would be of the form `http://vserver/sites/projects/subsite1/subsite2/subsite3`. Thus, the URL to a team Web site reflects its hierarchical position in the site collection.

Now, portal areas and subareas can also be organized hierarchically, so you would think that their URLs would be constructed hierarchically, but they are not! And there is a good reason for this, since SPS allows you to change the hierarchy and drag and drop portal areas around to suit your navigational needs, as we discuss shortly. Additionally, you could have many levels to your portal areas, which could result in some very long and unwieldy URLs.

So how is the URL constructed? First, the URL is rooted from the virtual server that is hosting the portal site. From here the first 20 portal area URLs are constructed using the name of the area, irrespective of where the portal area is in the overall hierarchy. If two areas have the same name within this 20, a unique number is inserted at the end of the right-most part of the URL. This URL can be overridden by the portal-area creator, but it must be unique within the 20 portal areas. So, for the first 20 portal areas the URLs are of the form `http://vserver/<portal area>/`, resulting in something like `http://myserver/topics`, `http://myserver/divisions`, and `http://myserver/topics0` (assuming I had two areas called "topics").

Once we reach 20 portal areas, a new level is inserted into the URL using C0 to C19 as the name for the level. Therefore, the 21st portal area will be of the form `http://vserver/C0/<portal area>/`, the 22nd will be `http://vserver/C1/<portal area>`, and so on. Again, the `<portal area>` part of this URL must be unique within the current level. Once we have 20 areas in each sublevel, we then introduce another level and so on.

This naming keeps the URLs "shallow," irrespective of the depth of the portal content hierarchy. Additionally, if a hierarchical naming convention were used to generate the original URL, users may be confused, since the

URL may not actually reflect the position of the content within the portal site. Now, it's arguable whether this naming convention is any less confusing for users, since they effectively have no clue as to where the content exists based on its URL, and, certainly, in my experience, users do not like to see terms such as `/C1` in URLs that they may send around to others!

There is also a subtle difference in the way that portal areas are created compared with team sites. Each portal site is a single-site collection, and all portal areas are subsites from this collection. Furthermore, if you have more than 20 portal areas, then you will have multiple levels of subsites. So, if we have a portal area with a URL of `http://vserver/C1/projects`, then behind the scenes, we have one top-level Web site created (`http://vserver`), one first-level subsite (`http://vserver/C1`), and one second-level subsite (`http://vserver/C1/projects`).

4.6   Portal content navigation

SPS provides a hierarchical structure that aids navigation and discovery of content within your portal site. The hierarchy is used to group content together that deals with the same subject matter. As you create portal areas to host portal content, you assign the area a relevant position within the hierarchy. There is a simple and effective user interface that allows you to manipulate and move areas around the structure, and the hierarchy is exposed to end users through various portal site Web Part Pages. This flexibility allows you to effectively restructure the portal content to suit your business requirements.

For example, you may have a portal site for all your company-based information—with some portal areas specifically for the products your company produces. These areas may be positioned at a low level within the hierarchy and are discovered by users drilling down through the hierarchy. Well, what if one of your products won a prestigious award and you wanted to highlight it for a short period within your portal? In this case, you would only need to move the particular portal area to the top level of the hierarchy, thus exposing the area within the navigation elements on the top-level page of your portal.

If you refer to Figure 4.2, you can see that, by default, we have Topics, News, and Sites at the top level of the hierarchy (Home is a special case and is always present at all levels of navigation), and any top-level portal area will appear. As you navigate through the hierarchy, the vertical navigation bar on the left-hand side will show you a bread-crumb trail of where you

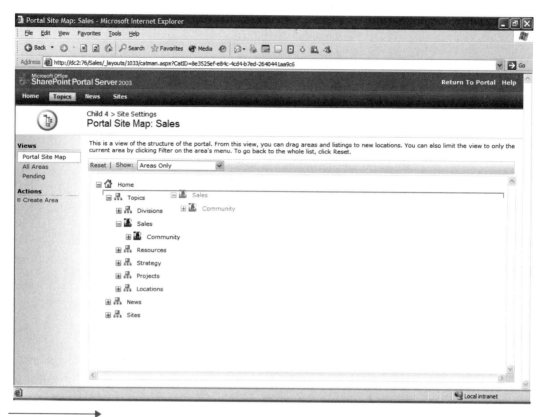

Figure 4.4   *Dragging and dropping a portal area to a different place in the hierarchy.*

are, including any immediate subareas from your current location. In this example, we are browsing the Sales area, which has a Community subarea (the extra *Create SubArea* option is present because we are viewing this page in edit mode as opposed to view mode).

To reorganize our content, we only need to choose the *Manage Portal Site* option from the Actions menu, which then presents us with a filtered view of all the portal areas in the portal site map. It also shows us the current portal area's position within the hierarchy. (As an aside, note here how the icon we associated with the portal area is used alongside the area itself.) Figure 4.4 shows the portal site map with a drag and drop in action! Here I am taking the Sales area and moving it to the top level of the hierarchy. The net result here is that the Sales area is prominently placed with a direct link from the top menu bar, as shown in Figure 4.5.

Not only can portal areas be dragged and dropped using the portal site map, but portal listings can as well.

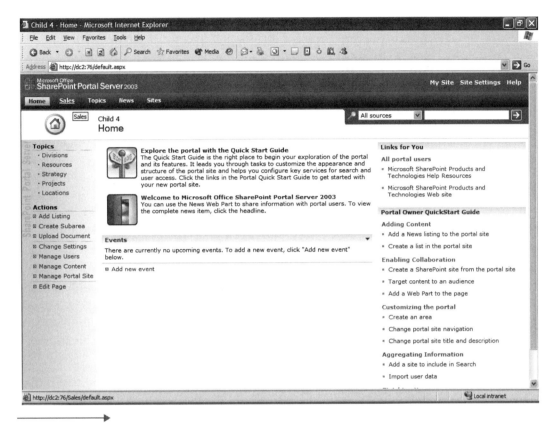

Figure 4.5   *Sales area now moved to top level.*

4.7   **Portal listings and news**

A portal listing is a piece of information that is made available somewhere within your portal site. The contents of a listing can be manually entered at the point of creation (e.g., an announcement) or can be a link to any other piece of information, including links to information about people and external information. Therefore, a listing could point to a Web page on the Internet, a custom list within a team site, or a document that is published in a portal area's document library. Note that there is no ongoing relationship between a listing and the associated source link—in other words, if the source link disappears, then the listing will merely point to an invalid location. This can be an issue if you use the inbuilt functionality to associate documents held in a team site's document library with a portal area, since moving the original document from the team site will not update the link in the listing.

Listings are initially created as items in a portal area's Portal Listings list. As you mange your portal site through the portal site map, you can drag and drop listings from one area to another, in which case they are moved between the Portal Listings lists. Now, while you create a listing from within an area, there are multiple ways to publish the listing such that it reaches the desired audience. First, listings can be linked to more than one location within the portal hierarchy. Thus, you can create a listing and associate it with multiple portal areas. This allows you, for example, to highlight an individual item in a prominent position in multiple places. Given the earlier example about highlighting a product area on the top-level navigation, you could, in theory, highlight a particular product specification directly on the home page of the portal by creating a listing for the specification in your product portal area and associating it with the location of the top level of the hierarchy.

Once a listing is associated with one or more areas in the hierarchy, it is exposed on a page within a portal area via the Grouped Listings Web Part. You can create as many groupings as you like in order to categorize listings. One implicit grouping called "Highlights" groups together all listings that have the Highlights flag set on them and allows for a prominent display position with the area's portal page.

You can associate publishing dates with listings such that they expire gracefully and an area content manager must approve the publishing of a listing. The managers do this by manipulating the list called Portal Listings within their area—this list has multiple views, such as Pending, Rejected, and Expired. This allows users to submit suggested listings for publishing that may be of relevance to the area's content, while letting the content manager make the final decision on publication.

Note that when you do associate a listing with more than one location, you are effectively creating multiple independent listings. Thus, if you delete the listing in one area, it will not be deleted from the other areas—this is clearly less than optimal, and we can only hope Microsoft will improve this in the future, along with the issue mentioned earlier in this section about the source link of a listing. You can, however, see related listings for those that contain a link; so, for example, if you have multiple listings that all point to the same remote Web page, and the remote page's address changes, then at least you can identify all of the listings that point to this remote Web page in one operation. You do this by editing the listing, which then allows you to manipulate general, publishing, display, and search settings for the listing.

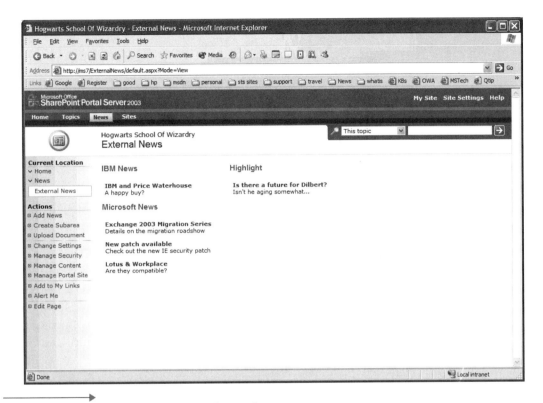

Figure 4.6   *News listings grouped in a subarea.*

Listings can also appear in search results and can be targeted to appear on particular users' personal Web sites, as we will discover shortly.

News is an example of listings in action—SPS provides a News area (and subareas) into which news listings can be published and displayed through various Web Parts. Furthermore, you can also target news listings to desired audiences (see later). Figure 4.6 shows an example of listings grouped for display on a News subarea of the portal.

4.8   Security

Before we go any further, let's talk about security, since we have already mentioned area content managers and approving items, and these fall under the security umbrella.

In Chapter 2, we discussed how authorization works in WSS in terms of rights and site groups (a.k.a., roles). SPS has its own rights and site groups, which are very similar to the WSS ones but are used for SPS-specific operations. Permissions can be set on a per-area basis or can be inherited from the parent area; by default, all permissions are inherited from the root portal site. The rights generally affect how the user can manipulate listings, content, and Web pages within a portal area. As we have already discussed the basics of rights and site groups, we'll just concentrate on the more interesting ones that SPS uses. For full details on all rights and site groups, please refer to the SPS Administrators Guide. Note that SPS does not support the concept of cross-site groups and neither does it support list-level permissions. If you require different access to different content, then you must create it in a separate portal area.

SPS has a role called Content Manager that allows the holder to create portal areas and manage the rights on an area. A Content Manager can create listings and content (in the form of libraries and lists) within an area and is also responsible for approving any content that has been put forward for publishing. Recall earlier how we discussed changing the area settings such that listings required approval before being published. The Contributor role lets a user add listings and content but not create areas or manage area rights. Thus, a Content Manager has the final say for whether listings and content actually appear on a portal area.

Another interesting right is Search, which can be used to restrict users from using the *Search* functionality. Why you would ever want to do this I don't know, but it is possible! Indeed, if the user does not have this right, then the *Search* option is removed from the user interface. Other rights allow users to manage indexing and search settings, as well as control audience targeting, personal sites, and alerts.

4.9   Site directory

To highlight how portal areas leverage the standard WSS functionality, consider the following. When you create a portal site, a few initial portal areas are created for you—one of these being the site directory. Each of these portal areas has its own associated lists, libraries, and Web Part Pages, which are effectively created from site templates. The portal area for the site directory maintains a list holding details of all team sites that have been created and associated with the portal site. In addition, it can hold details of any other Web site you want to have associated with your portal site. This is a standard customizable WSS list allowing you to gather relevant metadata about sites such that end users can make informed decisions about their content.

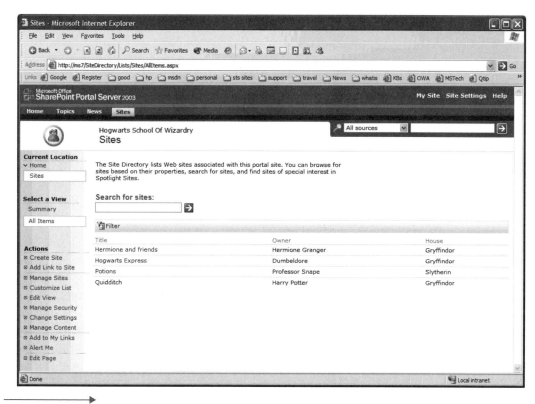

Figure 4.7   *Sites directory.*

As it's a standard list, items can be added to it, allowing you to include details of other Web sites that may be of interest to the portal site's community.

Figure 4.7 shows the Sites list from the Sites portal area, whose unique URL is `SiteDirectory` (the full URL is `http://<server>/SiteDirectory/Lists/Sites/allitems.aspx`)—this list is stored and processed in exactly the same way as any list that you would create in a team site. Note how the metadata (i.e., columns) of items within the list has been customized in order to gather details that are relevant to the overall portal site—any site details entered must specify the Hogwarts house it is associated with.

The site directory also assists in categorizing the sites, and various Web Parts (such as Newest Sites and Spotlight Sites) display site details. You can also add a portal listing for sites that you add to the site directory and associate them with multiple portal areas, thus allowing users to discover them as they browse other areas of the portal site.

4.10   Connecting team sites to a portal site

When you create a team site through the portal, it is by default connected to the portal site. Owners of team sites can disconnect and reconnect their sites to any portal site using the site-administration option *Configure connection to portal site*. This option allows the user to enter a URL to the portal site and give it a friendly name. A portal-connected team site benefits from the following:

- Navigation aids from the team site to the portal site. Each Web page on a top-level team site has a link at the right of the top horizontal navigation bar to the home page of the portal site. Team subsites link back to their parent team sites.

- Connections to profile and personal sites. On a stand-alone team site, minimal information is available about people when you link to them (e.g., through the author attribute of a document). Indeed, the only information available on a stand-alone team site is the details held in the UserInfo table, as discussed in Chapter 2 (i.e., the user's display name, e-mail, and any notes that were added when the user was added as a member of a site). In a connected team site, people links take you to the public view of that person's My Site, enabling you to glean much richer information about the user. Chapter 5 discusses My Sites.

- Links to portal enterprise search. The results of a standard team-site search are limited to the team site. If WSS search is enabled, an extra option appears under the Search dialog that allows the search to be performed on the portal site rather than through WSS. Note that WSS search can be disabled, in which case users would need to follow the link to the portal site in the top navigation bar in order to use its search capabilities. Portal search, as described in Chapter 6, can include many sources and can be scoped to search over all team sites, which is clearly a big benefit over WSS search. It is also more flexible in its search options, supporting property and Boolean searches.

- Document portal listings and links for My Links. Links to documents stored within a team-site document library can be submitted to a portal area as a listing or added to the My Links Web Part, which is displayed on a user's My Site. The portal listings are just links to the underlying team-site document library item and suffer from the same issues as detailed earlier. These options surface in the drop-down menu that appears when you hover over an item in a library.

None of these options actually changes anything in the portal site itself. They all basically add some navigational links to the team site, enabling a simpler way of linking to the portal site. Indeed, there is no check made when users connect their team sites that the portal site is even valid or that the users have rights to access it. These types of discoveries are only made at run time when users take the links!

4.11 Alerts

In line with connecting people to relevant information, users can set up alerts for portal content. Alerts can be set at many levels: a portal area, a library or list, individual items within the list, or search results. Users can indicate that they want to be notified via the My Alerts Web Part on their personal sites or via e-mail whenever a change occurs.

We previously discussed how WSS supports alerts, and there are some differences that you need to be aware of. First, the aggregating of Alerts inside Outlook, as discussed in Chapter 3, works for both SPS and WSS alerts. The only difference happens behind the scenes, with SPS alerts calling the `outlookadapter.asmx` Web service to enumerate the users' alerts (as opposed to WSS alerts, which call the `alerts.asmx` service).

Second, SPS alerts are triggered via the indexing engine, whereas WSS alerts are triggered as content is created. Indexing is an asynchronous task; thus, it may take a lot longer for an SPS alert to reach you via e-mail than a WSS alert. Details such as which content source and search-content index the content is in can affect the overall elapsed time between an event occurring and your being notified. The benefit of alerts being tied to the indexing engine is that you can effectively search the future! What I mean is that you can perform a search on your portal site and set up an alert on the search results. This means that in the future, as content is generated that matches your original search, you are alerted! The mechanism that is performing this, the Persistent Query Engine, is built into the indexing engine.

So, as an example, you may have performed a search for anything authored by Kevin Laahs and got an interesting result set returned. You might then say to yourself: You know, this guy writes some interesting stuff—I'd like to make sure I read all his stuff (alternatively you may say nothing of the kind to yourself ☺!). You can then set an alert on this search so that when any new content authored by Kevin Laahs is found, you are alerted.

Third, although both WSS and SPS alert notifications can be delivered by e-mail, only SPS alerts can be rolled up and displayed via the My Alerts Web Part on a user's My Site.

Fourth, the format of alert e-mail messages is significantly different between SPS and WSS, as you can see in Figure 4.8. You can, however, change the format of these e-mails. SPS alerts are constructed using the following XSL stylesheets, which you can find in the `C:\Program Files\ SharePoint Portal Server\DATA\Alerts\<lcid>` folder on your SPS server (as always, best practice dictates that you copy these files before making any modifications):

```
AlertAutoDeactivationNotification.xsl
AlertCreationConfirmation.xsl
AlertNewsLetterNotification.xsl
AlertResultNotification.xsl
```

WSS alerts are constructed using the following templates, which are stored in `C:\Program Files\Common Files\Microsoft Shared\web server extensions\60\TEMPLATE\<lcid>\XML`:

- `NotifItem.xml`: Defines the section that specifies the item that was changed in an e-mail alert about changes to a list or item

- `NotifListHdr.xml`: Defines the section that specifies the name of the list in an e-mail alert about changes to a list or item

- `NotifSiteFtr.xml`: Defines the footer section in an e-mail alert about changes to a list or item

- `NotifSiteHdr.xml`: Defines the header section in an e-mail alert about changes to a list or item

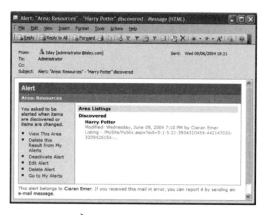 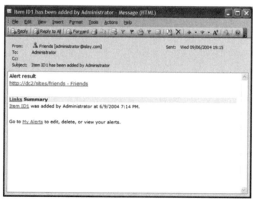

Figure 4.8   *Alert notifications.*

4.12 Enterprise application integration

Web Parts are the key to providing an aggregated view of information from many different data sources. As we know, Web Parts can basically expose any kind of information as long as someone manages to code them to do so! So, does this mean that all applications that a user ever uses should be delivered via a Web Part? And, if so, what challenges and opportunities would this bring? In this closing section of this chapter we take a brief look at how you might go about connecting enterprise applications (such as SAP and Siebel) to SharePoint and the features that SPS delivers to assist in such scenarios.

The first thing to understand is that there is no one-size-fits-all method for exposing and integrating data from a line-of-business (LOB) application into the portal platform. You need to understand who the audience is and what degree of integration is needed in order to make the effort beneficial. It may be that you want to provide employees with human resources self-service capabilities, such as viewing their pay slips, to give a CEO an overview of the pulse and key indicators of the business, or to make available to a salesperson an aggregated view of customer sales data alongside personal contacts, calendars, and tasks.

This results in different integration scenarios, ranging from infrequent read-only access, interactive read/write access, and the reusing of portions of enterprise application data to create new composite applications. And it is really the integration of portal services (such as search and collaboration) with portions of LOB applications that fits best into the overall portal design paradigm. By this I mean that if you only want to run the LOB application in its entirety, then using the portal as an access point to the application does not bring much value. Indeed, you may even reduce the value of the LOB application if you tried to run it from within a Web Part, since, by definition, you would be reducing the real estate that the LOB application has to work with and may therefore end up using those scroll bars more often than you'd like!

So basically you need to build composite applications that take their data from multiple LOB applications, aggregate the view of this data through multiple Web Parts, and join this data through Web Part connections. As a result, selecting a piece of data coming from one application causes other data from another application to be refreshed in its Web Part. And this has to be developed in a matter of months and not years! SPS is not the panacea for such a scenario, but it is part of an overall application-integration strategy that involves .NET at the foundation; building blocks

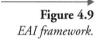

Figure 4.9
EAI framework.

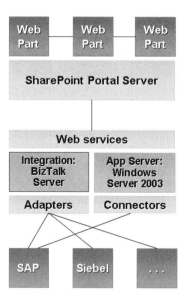

such as Web Services and Web Parts; rapid-development tools and services such as Visual Studio .NET, Office, and FrontPage 2003; application-management services built into Windows 2003; and a spectrum of integration models with a full Enterprise Application Integration (EAI) framework leveraging BizTalk for orchestration, messaging, and connectivity services. Such a framework is depicted in Figure 4.9.

There are typically four models for integrating data from an LOB into a Web Part: Web capture, point to point, data cache, and application-integration server. Any overall solution is likely to use a combination of all four models.

Web capture refers to the ability basically to screen scrape or clip parts of an existing Web application and merely display this portion in a Web Part. A Web Part available through the Office Components download uses a client-based tool to allow you to map out the regions of a Web page that you want displayed inside the Web Part. You can also use the Page Viewer Web Part and just point it at your Web application.

Point to point is where the Web Part directly calls an application on the back end through its native APIs. This is a reasonable approach for smaller and relatively simple applications, but inefficiencies of scale develop once you have a large number of point-to-point connections everywhere. Tools such as the FrontPage Data View with ADO.NET as the data source would fall into this category, and common APIs such as the SAP .NET Connector and Siebel DCOM Connector would also be used.

Data cache is where you don't access the back-end application directly, since you don't want to put any unnecessary extra load on it. Instead, you build some form of data warehouse that can extract and cache a subset of data from multiple applications into, say, a SQL server and then use the many Web Parts that can read data directly from this source. This is important if you have, for instance, a worldwide application in one region, and you want to enable read access to it from other regions, but you do not need up-to-the-second data. Storing it locally will allow better performance than accessing the application directly in a point-to-point fashion.

In application-integration server, you employ a middle tier and require orchestration, transactions, transformations, and so forth. In this model you use a common API from your Web Parts, and they all talk to the application server, which then controls access to the LOB application. All four models are depicted in Figure 4.10.

So, what value does SPS bring to this environment? Well, first, certain characteristics of Web Parts help significantly. Obviously, being able to combine multiple Web Parts on one page means data from multiple LOB applications can be viewed together. Personalization—the ability to decide where and which Web Parts appear—is another key piece. Being able to target Web Parts at audiences is another important area. Once I have a piece of data from an LOB application in a Web Part, I can then make that Web Part available only to relevant audiences. Web Part connections are clearly very beneficial since, again, you can take data from one application and have it drive the display of data from another application. Finally, being

Figure 4.10
EAI models.

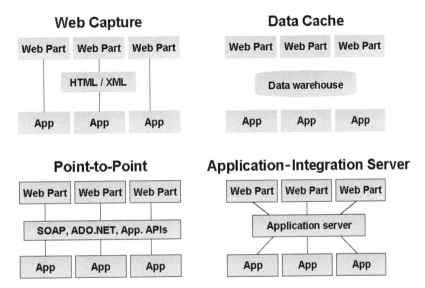

able to add Web Parts to site templates means that you can easily have multiple sites draw on the same tools and techniques for integrating.

Now these features are generic to all Web Parts and not specifically designed to aid the EAI problem—but they do help! SPS does, however, deliver a specific service that is designed to aid a certain aspect of the EAI problem and that is the Single Sign-On Service.

4.12.1   Single sign-on

If you are integrating multiple LOB applications through multiple Web Parts, then it's likely that you will have multiple, different credentials that you have to use to authenticate yourself to the different LOB applications. Being prompted for all these credentials would swiftly remove any benefit of having done the EAI in the first place.

The term *single sign-on* (SSO) doesn't accurately reflect the service that SPS brings to the table. It is more of a secure credential cache rather than a full-blown SSO system that would support password changes and the like. Also, it is only used by Web Part Pages. In other words, I cannot cache my credentials for my LOB application and then run my application outside of the portal and have it read the cache. The cache can be used in any of the previous four EAI models we described, since all of these ultimately present the LOB application through a Web Part.

The credential cache is stored in a mapping database and can store per-user and per-group credentials. Per-group credentials allow you to map

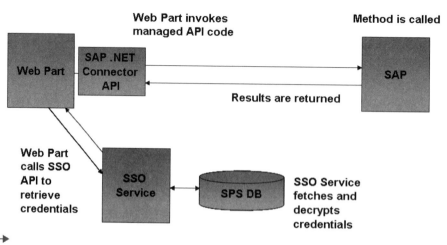

Figure 4.11   *Single sign-on in action.*

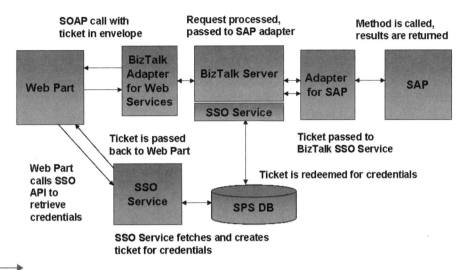

SOAP call with
ticket in envelope

Request processed,
passed to SAP adapter

Method is called,
results are returned

Ticket is passed
back to Web Part

Ticket passed to
BizTalk SSO Service

Web Part
calls SSO
API to
retrieve
credentials

Ticket is redeemed for credentials

SSO Service fetches and creates
ticket for credentials

Figure 4.12   *BizTalk adapter and distributed ticketing.*

several NT accounts to a single set of credentials for some back-end LOB applications. Credentials can be stored using username/password combinations, and there is also support for storing certificates. The credential store allows you to store multiple pieces of information to cater to those systems that require more than just a username and password for identification.

Web Parts have to be developed to utilize the cache, and there is full programming support. Thus, you can, for example, utilize the cache along with APIs such as the SAP.NET Connector to provide seamless access to SAP-based data from within a Web Part. This is shown in Figure 4.11. You can also use the distributed ticketing model that's built into the service if you are using an application-integration model. This is designed to allow you to effectively use constrained delegation à la Kerberos without requiring all the back-end LOB applications to support Kerberos. The Share-Point folks have worked with the BizTalk folks to come up with a BizTalk Web Services adaptor that can utilize the distributed ticketing system and, thus, pass the ticket to BizTalk. BizTalk itself then has the ability to call the SSO service to redeem the ticket for user credentials. This scenario is shown in Figure 4.12.

5

People and Personalization

So, as mentioned in Chapter 4, people are first-class objects; therefore, SharePoint needs to meet some challenges to ensure that the intellectual property held within your documents and lists is fully exploited by connecting it to people.

Three major challenges spring to mind here. The first is to ensure that users can discover more than just document information. For example, I may find an interesting document through search, but I want to be able to find the people who know something about the contents of the document. The second is to connect people together and to be able to discover rich details about other people—in other words, more than just their telephone number and location. The third is to ensure that personally relevant information can be highlighted to users in such a way that it is not lost in the sea of available information. A portal, after all, is all about having a relevant view of the world for the task at hand.

WSS, SPS, and Office 2003 combine to support the needs of people. WSS, for example, ships a Members Web Part, which allows you to view instantly the online status of the members of your team site. Similarly, this status is shown in the SharePoint task pane delivered by Office 2003. And both of these features rely on an ActiveX control that installs with Office 2003 to allow other applications to call upon either MSN or Windows Messenger to find out about folks' status. SPS also allows you to post listings to people such that portal areas can have a quick link to information about the experts in that area's subject matter.

For the rest of this chapter we are going to focus on the following areas:

- Site personalization, delivered by WSS
- Profiles, delivered by SPS
- Personal sites, delivered by SPS

- Audience targeting, delivered by SPS

- IM integration, delivered by Office 2003 and Messenger

5.1   Site personalization

WSS supports personalization of Web Part Pages, resulting in the page having a personal or shared (a.k.a., public) view. The level of personalization is controlled via user rights, and users can be allowed to update personal Web Parts and add private Web Parts to a page. Personal Web Parts are those whose developers have determined that they can be personalized by the end user. It is entirely possible for developers to not allow a Web Part to be personalized, and this can lead to a Web Part Page with some parts allowing personalization and others not.

The right to add a private Web Part to a page is dependent upon having the right to update personal Web Parts. Adding a private Web Part allows the user to browse and search for Web Parts in the various available galleries or to import a Web Part. Clearly, the code for the Web Part will have to have been installed previously on the server by a suitably authorized individual.

If a user has the right to update personal Web Parts, then a **Modify My Page** link appears near the top right of each Web Part Page. This link invokes a drop-down menu, which will have two options, *Design This Page* and *Modify My Web Parts*, as well as a third option, *Add Web Parts,* if the user has the right to add private Web Parts. This can be seen in Figure 5.1.

The *Design this Page* option allows the user to move Web Parts around the various zones and modify any properties of the part the developer has marked as modifiable in a personal view of the page.

So, end users can be allowed to modify their own personal view of a Web Part Page, but there is also the ability to modify the shared view of the page. Users with the Add and Customize Pages right can toggle between the shared and personal view of the page in order to customize either view, as can be seen in Figure 5.2.

A view of a library or list is essentially just a Web Part Page, and so the ability to create and maintain personal views is also supported. To create and maintain personal views of documents and lists requires the Manage Personal Views right. Any list view marked as being personal is rendered via the `PersonalViews.aspx` page.

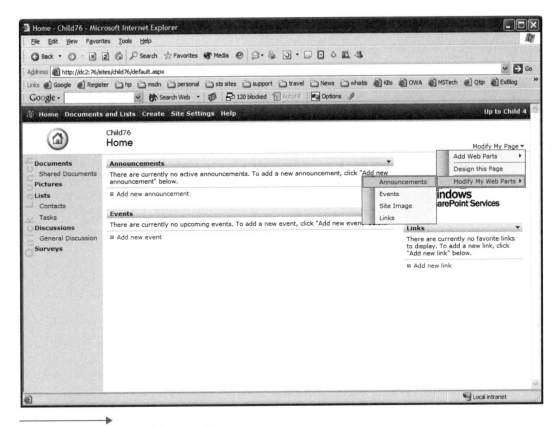

Figure 5.1 *Modify My Web Parts page.*

Behind the scenes, a couple of important SQL tables inside the site content database control how a Web Part Page looks to a user. First, a row exists in the Web Parts table for every Web Part that is on every Web Part Page. Columns such as `tp_ZoneId` control the physical location of the Web Part on the Web Part Page. Another couple of columns control the properties associated with the Web Part—these are `tp_AllUsersProperties` and `tp_PerUserProperties`. As a Web Part is added to a Web Part Page, its properties (such as `title`, `framestate`, etc.) are included in the `tp_AllUsersProperties` column. If any changes are made to the shared view of this Web Part on this Web Part Page, then the changed properties are written to the `tp_AllUsersProperties` column.

There is also a table called Personalization that controls the personal view of a Web Part Page. Any Web Part that has been personalized by a user has its changes logged into this table. As with the Web Parts table, the same

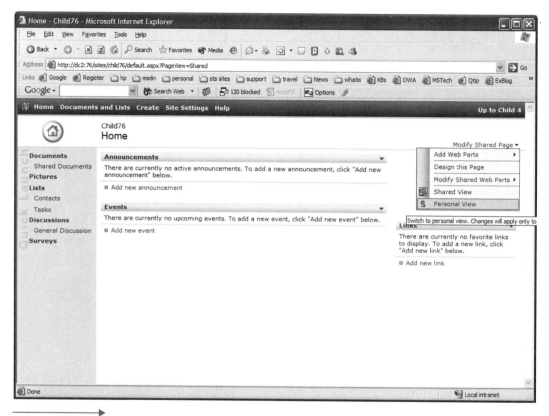

Figure 5.2   *Modify Shared Web Parts page.*

columns that determine the position of the Web Part and any customized properties exist in the Personalization table.

As each page is requested, several stored procedures combine to fetch the page. The normal mode of operation calls the main procedure, `proc_FetchDocForHttpGet`, which subsequently calls `proc_GetAllWebParts-Internal`. The latter coalesces the properties from the Personalization table with the properties from the Web Parts table to produce the desired personal view of the Web Part Page.

5.2   Profiles

In an attempt to facilitate linking people and information, SPS maintains its own profile database, which other features build upon. For example, audience targeting and personal sites all leverage the profile, and searches for people are performed against it. You may question why SPS has its own profile rather than using something like the Active Directory (AD). Well, while you can use the AD to import data into the SPS profile, there is no actual requirement to even have an AD for SPS to run; SPS only requires Windows 2003 and can quite happily run in an NT4 domain environment.

It may also be that the AD does not contain all the people in your organization. It is not uncommon for large enterprises to have a separate master enterprise directory that feeds other directories such as the AD. Finally, it may well be that the people in charge of the AD may not want any extra stress placed on it by SPS.

The profile is effectively just another WSS list. Thus, it is extensible, allowing you to create your own properties (metadata) about people, and you can, if you so wish, associate these properties with attributes of user objects in the AD. You may want to do this if the AD is your master directory and other processes are in place to keep these attributes up-to-date.

In actual fact, importing from the AD is controlled via the SPS indexing mechanism, with the AD being just another content source that uses a protocol handler called `spsimport`; thus, for example, if I am importing from a domain controller called `dc1`, the content source has a URL of `spsimport://dc1`. You can configure this source and specify details such as whether to import from the whole forest or a single domain. Additionally, you can specify the base root for the LDAP search and an LDAP filter either to include or to exclude particular objects. Finally, you can set up a schedule for full and incremental imports.

There is also an object model for maintaining the profile, should you not wish to use the AD as your master source or should you have supplementary data that is stored in some other form of directory. Regardless of how you populate the profile database, you can only add entries to it that have a corresponding NT account somewhere. This is because one of the primary keys to the profile is the NT account, and it is used to match up a logged-on user with that user's own profile entry. Indeed, as the profile is populated, other details, such as the user's security identifier (SID) and the globally unique identifier (GUID) of his or her AD user object, are also stored in the profile, and these properties can be used to retrieve the user's individual profile entry.

Note that accessing AD data is a one-way operation, and there is no out-of-the-box way to write details back to the AD (of course, you could write your own code to perform this task). The AD is basically used as a source that can bootstrap the population of your SPS profile database and, optionally, keep your profile in synch as changes are made to the underlying AD objects.

By default, the profile contains 24 properties, 13 of which are associated with the AD (even though it says 14 in the user interface!). You can define each property's position in the profile, whether it is linked to an AD attribute, whether users can edit its value. and whether it is a public (e.g., appears in public views of a user's personal site) or private property. Note that you cannot link a profile property to a multivalued AD property. The default profile properties that are linked to an AD property are shown in Table 5.1.

It is important if you are going to benefit fully from the profile data that it is kept up-to-date and consistent. For example, profile data is shown when you view a person's public page. Therefore, if the Manager entry is kept up-to-date for all user profiles, then direct reports are shown when you view the public page of the manager.

Similarly, several profile properties play a large part in the ability to discover information about people. For example, the link to a user's personal site is held in the profile. Also, profile properties can be marked as aliases, which means they are treated as equivalent to the username and account

Table 5.1 *Profile Properties Linked with AD Properties*

Profile Property Name	AD Property
SID	objectSID
ADGuid	objectGuid
AccountName	distinguishedName
FirstName	givenName
LastName	sn
PreferredName	displayName
WorkEmail	mail
WorkPhone	telephoneNumber
Office	physicalDeliveryOfficeName
Department	department
Title	title
Manager	manager
UserName	samAccountName

name when searching for items authored by a user, targeting items to a user, or displaying items in the My Documents Web Part of the personal site for a user.

5.3   Personal sites (My Site)

There are two aspects to personal sites. First, there are two Web Part Pages that act as the public and private Home pages of a user's personal site. The public page is `MySite/public.aspx`, and it is shown when you link to any user's details from, say, the *Author* field of a document that has just been returned to you as a search result. There is no personal view available for this page; thus, users cannot control which Web Parts appear on the page. By default the following Web Parts appear on this page:

- Profile Details

- Shared Links

- Recent Documents

- Shared Workspaces Sites

There is also another page, called `MySite/default.aspx`, which always shows the personal (or private) view. There is, in effect, no public view of this page. Now links to this page will only appear on `public.aspx` for the currently logged on user if that user has the Use Personal Features right on the portal site. If a user without the said right tries to open `MySite\default.aspx` directly, then he or she will receive an Access Denied error.

Furthermore, users who do possess the right to see the page can modify their personal view of it in the same ways described in section 5.1, if they possess the Update Personal Web Parts and the Add/Remove Personal Web Parts rights at the portal site level. By default, the personal view of the user's Home page contains the following Web Parts:

- My Calendar

- My Alerts Summary

- My Links Summary

- Links For You

- News For You

The second aspect of personal sites is whether users actually have a full-blown WSS site for their own personal use in addition to the Home pages mentioned previously. In order to create a personal site, the user must possess the Create Personal Site right. If this is the case, most portal pages will render with a **My Site** link at the top right of the page.

If this is the first time a user has taken this link, a new WSS site is created for him or her, and the link to this site is entered into the `Personal-Site` property in the profile database. If a current entry does not exist for the user in the profile, it is automatically created at this time. Now the private Home page (`MySite/default.aspx`) renders many more options, such as the ability to manage documents and lists and to add pages, as you would expect in a normal WSS team site. Essentially, the user now has a full-blown WSS team site to use for his or her specific needs and can control the security on it as he or she sees fit, create subsites, and so forth.

Now, as users create content in the portal and populate their personal sites, some information is revealed in the public view of that user's Home page (i.e., in `MySite\public.aspx`). For example, as content is added to

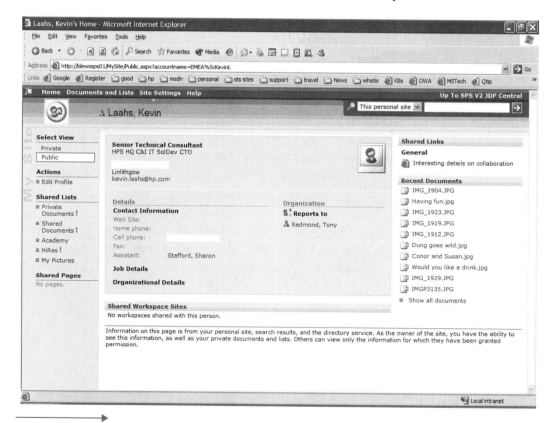

Figure 5.3   *Public view of a personal site.*

the My Links Web Part on the personal site, the user can choose whether the link should be published in the Shared Links Web Part on the public page. Similarly, as the current user authors content in the portal, this is displayed in the Recent Documents Web Part. When a personal site is provisioned, a private document library and a shared document library are created. A link to the shared document library is rendered in `public.aspx`, allowing the user to publish documents for everyone to see.

Also, as users create lists in their personal sites, they can choose to mark the views associated with the lists as shared, which means links to them will appear in the left navigation bar of the public page. Finally, the Shared Workspace Sites Web Part on the `public.aspx` page will show those subsites created within the personal site to which the user viewing the public page has read access.

We can see this type of information discovery in Figures 5.3 and 5.4.

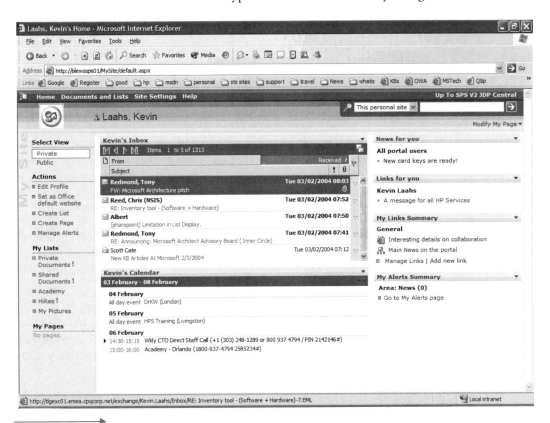

Figure 5.4   *Private view of Home page of a user's personal site.*

If you are using Office 2003, you also have the ability to have your personal site added as a convenient location on the File Open and Save As dialogs for all Office applications. Recall that we discussed in Chapter 3 how Office applications can deal directly with SharePoint sites via WebDAV. The existence of My Site in the dialog avoids your having to remember and type the URL to your personal site.

In a shared services environment, all links to My Site (`MySite/default.aspx`) are replaced with the page called `portalapi.aspx` in all portal sites except the portal site that is physically hosting the personal sites. This page has to do some more special processing in order to make sure that the shared profile (the profile is shared in a Shared Services environment, as is search) is updated correctly and that the personal site is physically created on the portal site that is defined for personal sites. `Portalapi.aspx` then redirects the link to the `MySite/default.aspx` page on the site that hosts personal sites.

Personal sites have two other very important uses: They are a place where specific content can be targeted at a user and also where alerts can be aggregated and displayed.

5.4   Audience targeting

Audience targeting can be used to ensure that the right information is delivered to the right people. You can target content (news, listings, Web Parts) to appear in special audience-targeted Web Parts such as Links For You. These Web Parts typically appear on a user's personal site (as discussed previously) but can also appear on any main portal page.

There are three steps to ensuring that targeted content is displayed in the appropriate place. First, you have to define your audiences. Audience membership is controlled via rules, and these rules can either be based on Windows accounts (such as membership in a security group, being on a distribution list, or reporting to a particular person) or on properties in the SPS profile. Once you create a rule, it has to be "compiled." This is the process that determines the actual membership of the audience. Ultimately, the members of an audience must exist in the profile database regardless of the rule. So, for instance, if your rule is that the audience comprises the membership of a security group in the AD, the actual membership will only include those members who are actually present in the profile. And the compilation process does not create profile entries for missing users, so you have to ensure that your profile is up-to-date.

Membership of the audience is ultimately held in a SQL table called `Orgle_List` in the `<portal>_PROF` table. You may think that "Orgle" is a strange name, but in actual fact the whole audience-targeting component of SharePoint was known by the working term of Organizational Role (OrgLe) during development! Thus, you could in theory use alternative mechanisms to populate the membership of an audience, but, as always, best practice would suggest not doing this directly into the SQL tables!

Second, you have to associate some portal content with an audience. This is done through portal listings at the point of creation or, subsequently, by editing the display properties of a listing through the portal site-navigation hierarchy (there is a filter available on the hierarchy that allows you to reveal all content rather than just portal areas). Associating a listing with an audience means you are targeting that particular item to certain users.

Finally, you have to show the targeted item to the desired audience by associating it with an audience-targeted Web Part. By default there are three such Web Parts: News and Links on personal sites and Links on the main portal page. As these Web Parts gather their content, they filter out items where the current user is not a member of any associated target audiences.

5.5   Smart Tag and Presence information

Office 2003 installs an ActiveX control that is used in conjunction with Windows Messenger or MSN Messenger in order to show you information about users as you come across their names in portal- or team-site content—for example, the Members Web Part or looking at the author of a document or a list item. In addition to having Office 2003 and Windows or MSN Messenger, you also have to enable the Smart Tag and Presence feature on a virtual server basis using SharePoint Central Administration.

If everything is enabled, a pawn icon appears next to users and, when you hover over this pawn, you get a pop-up menu that can show you many details about the user, including phone numbers and calendar information. If the user is a contact in your Windows or MSN Messenger list, his or her presence information is also shown.

But how does SharePoint know how to look for a particular contact in Messenger? Well, the answer is that the e-mail address associated with the SharePoint user has to match that of the contact in Messenger. This may or may not be the case, depending on how your organization supports Messenger! For example, many organizations allow MSN Messenger to be used, and there is no guarantee that users will create their Passports with the same e-mail address as their internal e-mail address.

However, if the two do match, then you are shown the online status of the contact, assuming you are actually online yourself and running Messenger!

The ability to show information about a user prevails through the whole of Office, and the context menu that appears is also known as the Name menu (indeed, the control itself is housed in Name.DLL). Thus, the Name menu also appears in Outlook in the recipient controls of an e-mail message, in meeting requests, in the preview pane, and so forth.

As well as requiring the ActiveX control, SharePoint also has some supporting Java script that calls the control. Now, the interesting thing here is that you can call the same controls from within your own Web Parts very simply. A function called IMNRC takes an e-mail address as a parameter and

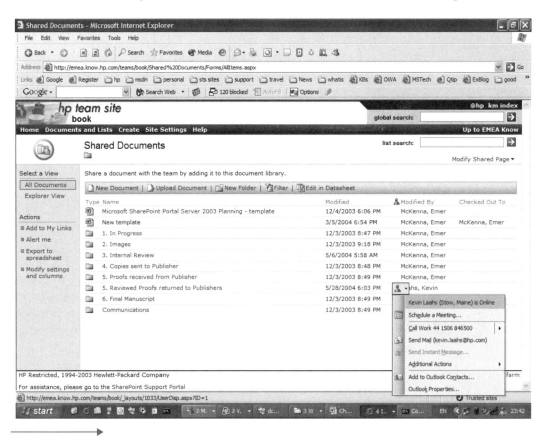

Figure 5.5   *Smart Tag and Presence in action.*

does all of the magic for you! Some pseudo HTML code is shown here, and you can see the control in action in Figure 5.5.

```
<span>
<A href="http://ms7/mysite/default.aspx">Kevin Laahs</A>
<img border="0" valign="middle" height="12" width="12"
src="/_layouts/images/blank.gif"
onload="IMNRC('kevin.laahs@hp.com')" id="imn8" />
</span>
```

Search

Given the amount of information that is likely to be stored in any WSS/SPS deployment, a reliable and performant search function is mandatory. In this chapter, we look at the major components of search and how they can affect the features available to end users. The first thing to note is that out of the box WSS and SPS use different mechanisms for the indexing and retrieval of content and, as a result, the end-user experience can differ significantly. Of course, this may seem strange at first, but there are a couple of points to note here. First, WSS is a separate product from SPS designed for team-based collaboration. Thus, it provides a basic search experience that should be adequate for the needs of small teams. SPS is targeted at much more than just small teams and is focused on making the right information available to the right people. Thus, it has to have a much larger investment in search technology, since it needs to target a much larger corpus (and wider variety) of information. It therefore must provide a highly scalable and manageable search system. I guess the biggest confusion for end users is that SPS can index the content of WSS team sites, and this ultimately results in two different ways to retrieve information from team sites.

6.1   Terminology

In this chapter, we refer often to different places where content that we want to index for retrieval purposes can be stored. The majority of these places are merely Web sites, so, in order to avoid confusion, the following terminology is used to define the different types of sites that you will encounter in a typical SPS/WSS implementation:

- **Team site**: A site controlled by WSS that can be used by ad hoc teams and generally has a closed membership. It can be created using the self-service creation option from within a WSS deployment or from the sites option in an SPS portal site. Many thousands of team sites can be supported within a single IIS virtual server. A team site may or may not be associated with a portal site.

- **Portal site**: An SPS portal controlled by SPS; a centralized point for finding and managing information. Membership is generally open. You can have one portal site per IIS virtual server.

- **Portal area**: A site controlled by SPS and used to group content of common subject matter within a portal site. Portal areas basically provide the navigation for the content within a portal site. You can have many portal areas per portal site.

- **My Site**: A site controlled by SPS. Each user can have his or her own personal site. You can have one My Site per user per portal site unless you have a Shared Services deployment, in which case you can have one My Site per user for all the portal sites that share the services. See Chapter 7 for details on implementing Shared Services.

- **Web site**: Any other Web site not controlled by SPS or WSS. For example, this includes sites on the Internet or in-house application sites.

6.2   Major search components

A full-text index exists to support the efficient retrieval of relevant information from a collection of sources in response to user queries. If an index is to be truly useful, then it must be able to support the content sources that users are interested in, the type of data held within those content sources, and rich retrieval capabilities. Many Microsoft server and client products offer full-text search, and several of them share common technology. The Microsoft Search Service (MSSearch) provides support to other products by creating full-text indexes on content and properties of structured and semi-structured data and allowing fast linguistic searches on this data.

Now, while MSSearch supports the actual index, it is up to the consumers of this index to provide the content to be indexed, to format user queries, and to return the results of searches to the requesting clients. As such, the consumers effectively control the overall search experience, and different products (i.e., consumers) do much better in this space than others. As an example, consider that SPS can provide content to be indexed from many sources, such as Exchange public folders and Lotus Notes databases, whereas SQL Server full-text indexing can only provide content from SQL tables.

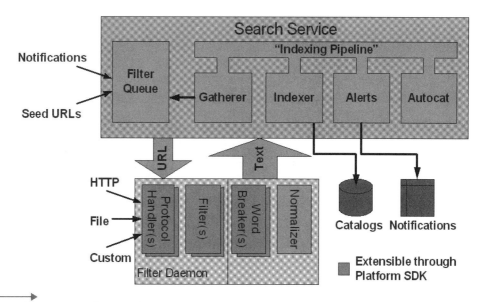

Figure 6.1   *SPS indexing architecture.*

The following list describes the major components upon which MSSearch relies to support full-text indexing. Individual products contribute to these areas in order to ensure that searching is adequately supported for that product's needs. For example, it is SPS that adds the Persistent Query Engine to the architecture and protocol handlers, and IFilters can be built by third parties. Also, note that not all consumers benefit from all the components—for example, SPS is the only product that uses the Persistent Query Engine, but any product that uses the MSSearch architecture will benefit from IFilters. You can see the architecture of MSSearch as it would be in an SPS environment in Figure 6.1.

- **Protocol handlers**: A protocol handler can access data over a particular protocol or from a particular store. Common protocol handlers include the file protocol for file shares, HyperText Transfer Protocol (HTTP), Messaging Application Programming Interface (MAPI), and HTTP Distributed Authoring and Versioning (WebDAV). The protocol handler processes URLs passed to it by the gatherer. Protocol handlers know how to open up a particular type of data store and extract the individual items that will subsequently be indexed.

- **Gatherer**: The gatherer maintains the queue of URLs to be accessed across protocols. For example, a Web site crawl may include hundreds of pages and create network traffic by accessing each Web page one at a time. To be more efficient, the gatherer interleaves URLs from a remote Web location with URLs from other Web locations or with access to file-system documents or other stores. For each document accessed, the gatherer fetches the stream of content from the protocol handler and passes it on to the appropriate filter.

- **Filters**: Filters (also known as IFilters) extract textual information from a specific document format, such as Microsoft Word documents or text files. For example, Microsoft provides the Microsoft Office filter, which can extract terms from Microsoft Word, Microsoft Excel, and Microsoft PowerPoint files, as well as from newer formats such as Microsoft OneNote. Other filters work with HTML, XML, or e-mail messages. There are also third-party filters, such as the PDF filter provided by Adobe. The filter's task is to extract a stream of textual information from a document, discarding all nontextual and formatting information. The filter produces strings of text and property/value pairs, which are passed in turn to the indexing engine.

- **Word breakers and stemmers**: A word breaker is a component that determines where the word boundaries are in the stream of characters in the query or in the document being crawled. A stemmer extracts the root form of a given word. For example, "running," "ran," and "runner" are variants of the word "run." In some languages, a stemmer expands the root form of a word to alternate forms.

- **Indexing pipeline**: The pipeline is a series of functions that want to do something based on the text that eventually comes from the data source. The indexer prepares an inverted index of content. An inverse index is a data structure with a row for each term. In this row, there is information about the documents in which the term appears and the number of occurrences and relative position of the term within each document. The inverse index provides the ability to apply statistic and probabilistic formulas to quickly compute the relevance of documents.

   Alerts is the Persistent Query Engine, and its job is to figure out whether the new content matches any queries that are stored for user alerts and issues notifications of such events.

   AutoCat is the process that determines whether the new content should be automatically categorized.

- **Catalogs**: Full-text indexes are stored in one or more catalogs within the file system on the server running the MSSearch service. Applications interact with MSSearch to maintain the indexes and the catalogs.

- **Query languages/search engine**: MSSearch supports three different query languages: Query Dialect 1, Structured Query Language (SQL) full-text extensions, and Query Dialect 2, which allows varied forms of client queries to be performed. For example, a client search could be scoped only to indexes contained within a particular catalog.

Now that we understand a little about the search architecture, let's see how WSS and SPS differ in the way that they use the architecture and how this results in different features for the end user.

6.3   Searching with WSS

STS v1.0 relied on the Windows base service called Microsoft Indexing Service for building full-text indexes. This service is limited to indexing files on the file system or in Web sites (by analyzing the IIS metabase to find the underlying files associated with a Web site). In STS v1.0 documents were stored on the file system, but lists and lists items were stored inside the SQL database. This combination resulted in only documents being available for search and retrieval. WSS, on the other hand, has been redesigned so that the contents of lists and libraries can be indexed.

WSS relies on SQL Full-Text Indexing, which in turn interacts with MSSearch. Thus, the search capabilities WSS offers to team sites are limited by what SQL full-text indexing can do. As such, one prerequisite for enabling search within a team site is that WSS be using SQL Server 2000 rather than WMSDE as its storage engine. In other words, searching directly from a team site is not supported on a stand-alone WSS configuration.

SQL full-text indexing provides a protocol handler for MSSearch that understands the content of SQL databases and tables. This protocol handler is responsible for providing content to the gatherer. It does not provide any other protocol handlers; therefore, the results of a native search initiated from a team site can only include content that is held inside SQL. Of course, all team-site content in terms of document libraries and lists is stored inside SQL, so this is not a major problem, but it is a difference from SPS search.

SQL full-text indexing supports catalogs at the database level. You can have more than one catalog per database, but each table within the database can only have a full-text index contained in one catalog. Thus, indexing itself occurs at the table level, and there is no way to index only specific rows within the table. Thus, when you enable searching from WSS, it is enabled for all team sites, since there is no separation of WSS content from different team sites into different tables. For example, the Docs table in a content database contains documents stored in all libraries within all team sites that use that content database.

By default, full-text indexing is switched off on a native WSS installation and is enabled through the SharePoint Central Administration utility; search links do not appear on team sites until indexing has been enabled. It is enabled per-server farm, which means that all team sites within all virtual servers on that farm are enabled for search. Behind the scenes a full-text catalog is created for each WSS content database associated with the farm. Each catalog is a separate set of files managed by MSSearch that, by default, are located at `C:\Program Files\Microsoft SQL Server\MSSQL\FTDATA`. You can see the name of the catalog that is associated with a content database and which tables it holds indexes for by viewing the Full-text Catalog Properties dialog with SQL Enterprise Manager, as shown in Figure 6.2.

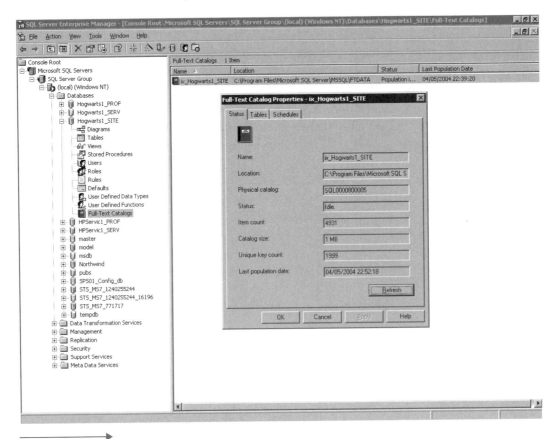

Figure 6.2   *Full-Text Catalog Properties dialog.*

Within each catalog four indexes are initialized. These indexes correspond to the database tables listed in Table 6.1, which also shows a description of the columns that are indexed. A full-text index definition includes a column that uniquely identifies each row in the table (a key value) and one or more character string columns that are covered by the index. The full-text index is populated with the key values. The entry for each key has information about the significant words (noise words or stop words, such as "in," "a," "the," and the like are stripped out) that are associated with the key, the column they are in, and their location in the column. Thus, only words that are contained within an indexed column will generate a match in any query. From a team-site point of view, the indexed columns allow searching on list items, documents, and user details, but there is no support for any attachments to list items. Filters for .doc, .xls, .ppt, .txt, and .htm are supported out of the box, and other file types can be indexed by installing the appropriate IFilters.

SQL full-text indexing supports different methods for ensuring that an index is kept up-to-date. It can do full, incremental, and change-tracking updates. After full-text search is initially enabled, a full update is performed for all content databases. Thereafter, change-tracking population is enabled. This option stores the changes that have been made to the various tables in a system table and then subsequently delivers these changes to the indexing engine. There are three methods in which these changes can be delivered—background, on-demand, or schedule. In the case of WSS, a background method is used, which effectively means that changes are processed as soon as they occur. From an end-user point of view, this means that any search results should include list additions fairly soon after the change is made. I say "fairly soon," as it clearly depends upon how busy the SQL server is, but on a normal working system you would expect to see changes appearing within a couple of minutes. If you don't, then there is cause for further investigation.

Table 6.1   *Tables Included in Full-Text Indexing*

Table	Key Value	Indexed Columns	Description
UserInfo	Tp_GUID	`Tp_Login, tp_Title, tp_Email`	Details of users that have visited a site collection
UserData	Tp_GUID	`nvarchar1` to `nvarchar64` `ntext1` to `ntext32`	Text-based custom columns for items in a list or library
Lists	Tp_ID	`Tp_Title, tp_Description`	Title and description of lists
Docs	Id	`LeafId, Content`	Filename of document and its content

Obviously, the catalogs take up some disk space and, as a rule of thumb, you should allow 30 to 40 percent of the total size of all documents and items stored in all libraries and lists within the server farm for the catalog's storage. See Chapter 8 for details on planning your disk-space requirements.

SQL full-text search extensions are integrated into the T-SQL language and the CONTAINS and FREETEXT predicates are supported (as are CONTAINSTABLE and FREETEXTTABLE). A search from a team site uses the FREETEXT statement, which supports stemming and inflectional forms of the supplied query terms. Thus, searching for "drink" also returns matches on "drinking," "drank," "drunk," and so forth.

The Search Results page returns individual list items and documents where a match has occurred with the supplied search query terms (as we will see later, SPS returns the list itself rather than individual list items when a match occurs anywhere in the list). The search terms you can supply are exceptionally basic. There is neither phrase nor Boolean searching (if you supply multiple words in your search, they are treated as an OR). Nor can you narrow a search to within a previous result set and get an indication of the number of hits. Also, note that you can scope a search to the contents of an individual list. However, the search is performed against the current view of that list; therefore, any items that are being filtered out of that view will not appear in the search results. Security settings, although not included in the index as with SPS, are honored in search results. Thus, the query engine returns all the items within the team site that contain the search term, but the page that displays the results filters out those to which the user does not have read access—including per-list security settings.

This will doubtless come as a surprise to many folks, but a WSS search from a team site is limited in scope to that particular site. No subsites are included in the search. Why? Well, obviously anything is technically possible, so one can only guess at why this functionality has not been included out of the box. Content from subsites is always stored within the same content database as the parent, so it can't be an issue with having to execute multiple searches across multiple indexes and aggregating the result set. More likely it has to do with the fact that once empowered, users can create as many subsites as they like; thus, a result set of a cross subsite search could be very large. Furthermore, subsites need not have the same permissions as the parent, so it could be that not all content in all subsites will be readable by the requesting user. And, with subsites some user interface would have to be provided to allow scoping of a search to only those subsites the user had access to. These are not excuses for why subsite searching is not available—

just some reasons that might be used in defense of such a stance! Of course, another reason might be that subsite searching is possible with SPS, but that would be cynical of me given that WSS is free and SPS is not!

If you really felt it necessary to have subsite searching, then you could build your own Web Part that called custom SQL stored procedures to do so. The out-of-the-box search uses two stored procedures called `proc_ExecDocSearch` and `proc_ExecListItemSearch` for the main processing. These procedures specifically search using the current `WebId` as an input parameter, so a subtle change could result in all webs within a site collection being searched instead. Figures 6.3 and 6.4 show the search link on a team site and the results of a search.

In closing this short discussion on the search capabilities within WSS, it is fair to say that it is fairly inflexible and not designed to be an Enterprise-strength search. It allows for a basic search experience that does full-text retrieval on the body of documents and the column values of items in a list.

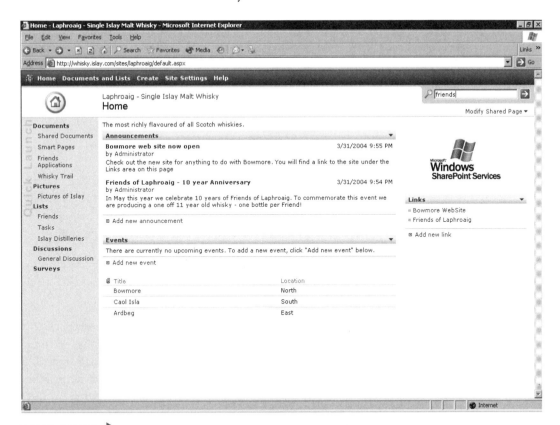

Figure 6.3   *Search dialog exposed at top right corner; full-text search is enabled.*

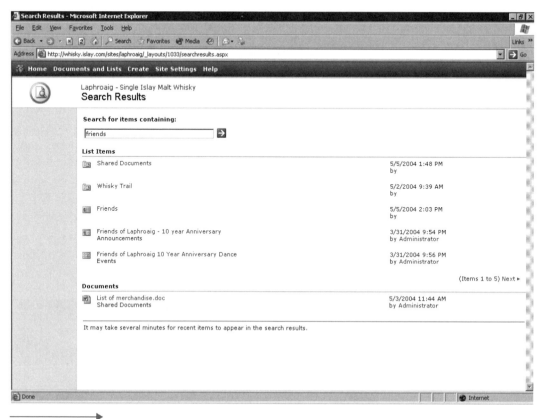

Figure 6.4   *Search results from a team site using WSS search.*

The user interface does not allow for any advanced search that would allow users to retrieve information based on individual column values. Furthermore, it has some scaling limitations that would severely restrict its use in large server-farm deployments, which could conceivably contain millions of documents across many thousands of team sites.

6.4   Searching with SPS

If WSS search is limited in terms of its scalability and functionality, SPS is designed to be Enterprise strength. Although the underlying indexing architecture delivered with SPS 2003 has not changed that much since SPS 2001, its scalability, performance, manageability, usability, and accessibility have changed significantly. SPS still uses the basic MSSearch architecture, but it is significantly extended when SPS is installed. In fact, SPS now delivers its own search service in order that SQL search and SPS search can coexist on the same server. The executable is still called `mssearch.exe`, but a different Windows service, Microsoft SharePointPS Search, is created.

We discussed the core search features of SPS 2001 in our first book, *Microsoft SharePoint Portal Server 2001: Building Knowledge Sharing Applications*, and these are still there in SPS 2003. Thus, technologies such as the Okapi probabilistic ranking algorithm, property weighting, Persistent Query Engine, adaptive crawling, support vector machine categorization, and configurable Thesaurus all combine to ensure that relevant and up-to-date results are returned in response to end-user queries.

Possibly the biggest change underneath the covers is the move toward storing everything, bar the index catalogs, in SQL rather than a mixture of registry entries and the Web Storage System, as was the case in SPS 2001. Additionally, managing the various pieces of the jigsaw is done through a Web interface rather than the MMC console and Web Folders interface used in SPS 2001. Most of the management of indexing components is done via the *Search Settings/Index Content* section on the Site Settings page of the portal site.

Out of the box, SPS 2003 provides protocol handlers for any kind of SharePoint site, file shares, Exchange 5.5 2000/2003 public folders, Lotus Notes, and any Web site. The support for any type of SharePoint site includes documents and list data from team sites and portal areas, the Site Directory, and information about people stored in the SPS profile.

SPS includes filters for Microsoft Office documents (including OneNote), HTML and XML files, Tagged Image File Format (TIFF) files, and text files. The TIFF filter enables SPS to crawl the textual content of saved fax data based on Optical Character Recognition (OCR) technology. SPS uses the Multipurpose Internet Mail Extensions (MIME) filter that ships with Windows 2000 when filtering messages from Exchange public folders.

As well as indexing the textual content of an item, SPS also indexes properties associated with the item. Properties can be associated with source content in different ways and are generally used to describe the content further. For example, Office documents have inbuilt properties and custom properties, HTML files use <META> tags, and SharePoint sites use columns in lists. Indexing properties allows you to perform much more refined searches than are available with just a full-text search of the content, as is the case with WSS.

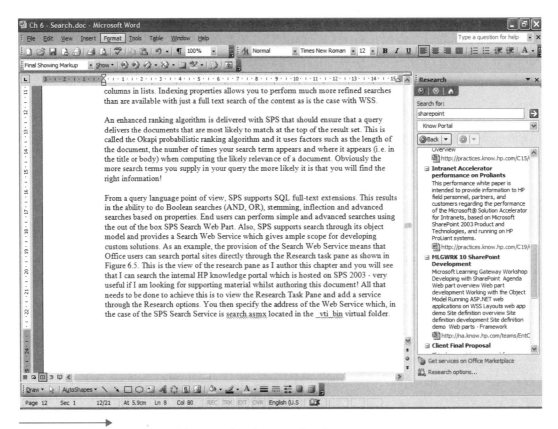

Figure 6.5   *SPS search being used in the Research task pane.*

An enhanced ranking algorithm is delivered with SPS that should ensure that a query delivers at the top of the result set the documents that are most likely to match. This is called the Okapi probabilistic ranking algorithm, and it uses factors such as the length of the document, the number of times your search term appears, and where it appears (i.e., in the title or body) when computing the likely relevance of a document. Obviously, the more search terms you supply in your query, the more likely it is that you will find the right information!

From a query language point of view, SPS supports SQL full-text extensions. This results in the ability to do Boolean searches (AND, OR), stemming, inflection, and advanced searches based on properties. End users can perform simple and advanced searches using the out-of-the-box SPS Search Web Part. Advanced search allows you to search by property, date range, and multiple keywords. Note that the use of AND and OR are mutually exclusive in a single search through the user interface and that you are limited to three expressions for the WHERE part of the search.

Also, SPS supports search through its object model and provides a Search Web Service, which gives ample scope for developing custom solutions. As an example, the provision of the Search Web Service means that Office users can search portal sites directly through the Research task pane, as shown in Figure 6.5. This is the view of the research pane as I write this chapter; you see that I can search the internal HP knowledge portal that is hosted on SPS 2003—very useful if I am looking for supporting material while writing this document! To do this you need only view the Research task pane and add a service through *Research options*. You then specify the address of the Web Service, which in the case of the SPS Search Service is search.asmx located in the _vti_bin virtual folder. This folder is usually physically located at C:\Program Files\Common Files\Microsoft Shared\web server extensions\60\ISAPI. So, for example, if my search server is called SPSSearch, then I would point the service at http://SPSSearch/_vti_bin/search.asmx.

6.5 Implementation and management options

Many implementation and management options ultimately influence the effectiveness of the end user's search. First, administrators have to decide what content they want to index, how often they want it indexed, where they want to store the index for different content sources, and how to partition the overall index such that searches can be scoped to suitable content. Furthermore, they have to decide which properties from crawled content should be indexed and whether these are usable through the *Advanced Search* option. Additionally, for large farm scenarios, decisions must be made about where index and search servers will be located to ensure a highly scalable and available solution.

SPS uses four concepts to manage and partition indexed content effectively—content indexes, content sources, content source groups, and search scopes.

6.5.1 Content indexes

Multiple content indexes can be created to store indexes from one or more content sources. Note that a content index is just a catalog in MSSearch terms and therefore exists on the file system of the indexing and search servers. A difference from other, normal catalogs is that a separate property store database is also maintained. By default the catalogs and property store are located from the root folder `C:\Program Files\SharePoint Portal Server\DATA`. From here each content index inhabits a unique folder. You can choose your own unique name at the creation time of a new content index should you wish to.

Searches can be scoped to only search over certain content indexes; therefore, consideration has to be given to the number of content indexes and the number of content sources they contain. For example, you may decide to have one content index per department if you felt that most searches were scoped at the department level. Another reason for dedicating an index to a particular type of content could be that you always want the content to be as up-to-date as possible; therefore, you want to gather content held within the index on a more frequent basis than other content. A word of caution here—if you do have many content indexes and a user wants to search the whole corpus, then behind the scenes multiple searches must actually be performed with the results aggregated, resulting in longer search times. In fact, another issue with a search being performed over multiple content indexes is that the ranking of results is swayed somewhat. Ranking relies heavily on the size of a corpus; therefore, hits against a small content index will have a different ranking from the same kind of hit on a large content index.

Out-of-the-box SPS uses two content indexes—one for content physically inside the portal site (called portal content) and one for content physically stored elsewhere (called nonportal content), such as team sites' and external Web sites' content. Each content index can be configured in terms of its update frequency and rules that can be used to include or exclude specific URLs within the content sources being indexed. The frequency of update is a good reason for the portal versus nonportal indexes you get out of the box, since the portal content index is updated more frequently than nonportal content, the argument being that content posted directly into the portal site is of more importance than that stored elsewhere.

Ultimately, a search request is made against one or more content indexes. The search request itself will indicate the properties it wants returned and the criteria to use for a match, plus any ordering information. The following example shows the basic search that is actually performed on an out-of-the-box installation via the Search Web Part when searching for the word "islay" in "All sources." Pretty complex for a basic search, huh? But the premise here is that the search engine is trying to find anything that might possibly be related to what you are looking for—a person, document, item, link to a Web page, and so forth. Note how each content index results in a UNION within the actual query that is performed.

```
SELECT "DAV:href," "DAV:displayname," "DAV:contentclass,"
"DAV:getlastmodified," "DAV:getcontentlength,"
"DAV:iscollection," "urn:schemas-microsoft-
com:sharepoint:portal:profile:WorkPhone," "urn:schemas-
microsoft-com:sharepoint:portal:profile:WorkEmail,"
"urn:schemas-microsoft-
com:sharepoint:portal:profile:Title," "urn:schemas-
microsoft-com:sharepoint:portal:profile:Department,"
"urn:schemas.microsoft.com:fulltextqueryinfo:PictureURL,"
"urn:schemas.microsoft.com:office:office#Author,"
"urn:schemas.microsoft.com:fulltextqueryinfo:description,"
"urn:schemas.microsoft.com:fulltextqueryinfo:rank,"
"urn:schemas.microsoft.com:fulltextqueryinfo:sitename,"
"urn:schemas.microsoft.com:fulltextqueryinfo:displaytitle,"
"urn:schemas-microsoft-com:publishing:Category,"
"urn:schemas-microsoft-com:office:office#ows_CrawlType,"
"urn:schemas-microsoft-com:office:office#ows_ListTemplate,"
"urn:schemas-microsoft-com:office:office#ows_SiteName,"
"urn:schemas-microsoft-com:office:office#ows_ImageWidth,"
"urn:schemas-microsoft-com:office:office#ows_ImageHeight,"
"DAV:getcontenttype," "urn:schemas-microsoft-
com:sharepoint:portal:area:Path," "urn:schemas-microsoft-
com:sharepoint:portal:area:CategoryUrlNavigation,"
"urn:schemas-microsoft-com:publishing:CategoryTitle,"
"urn:schemas.microsoft.com:fulltextqueryinfo:sdid,"
"urn:schemas-microsoft-com:sharepoint:portal:objectid" from
( TABLE Portal_Content..Scope() UNION ALL TABLE Non_Portal_
Content..Scope() UNION ALL TABLE Three..Scope() ) where
WITH
("DAV:contentclass":0,"urn:schemas.microsoft.com:fulltextqu
eryinfo:description":0,"urn:schemas.microsoft.com:fulltextq
ueryinfo:sourcegroup":0,"urn:schemas.microsoft.com:fulltext
queryinfo:cataloggroup":0,"urn:schemas-microsoft-
com:office:office#Keywords":1.0,"urn:schemas-microsoft-
com:office:office#Title":0.9,"DAV:displayname":0.9,"urn:sch
emas-microsoft-com:publishing:Category":0.8,"urn:schemas-
microsoft-com:office:office#Subject":0.8,"urn:schemas-
microsoft-com:office:office#Author":0.7,"urn:schemas-
microsoft-com:office:office#Description":0.5,"urn:schemas-
microsoft-
com:sharepoint:portal:profile:PreferredName":0.2,contents:0
.1,*:0.05) AS #WeightedProps (("urn:schemas-microsoft-
com:publishing:HomeBestBetKeywords"= some array ['islay']
RANK BY COERCION(absolute, 999)) OR (FREETEXT("urn:schemas-
microsoft-com:sharepoint:portal:profile:PreferredName,"
'islay') RANK BY COERCION(multiply, 0.01)) OR
```

```
FREETEXT(#WeightedProps, 'islay') ) ORDER BY
"urn:schemas.microsoft.com:fulltextqueryinfo:rank" DESC
```

Configuring and updating content indexes

When configuring a content index, you identify which source group it belongs to. You can also specify exclusion and inclusion rules (see section 6.5.2). The source group is used during the definition of search scopes that are ultimately displayed to the end user via the Search Web Part.

Also, you can specify logging options that can help in troubleshooting problems. By default the gatherer log only holds details of any indexing failures, but you can choose to have it log successes and any URLs that have been excluded. While it is interesting to watch what is going on, remember to switch these back to the defaults or you will end up with rather large gatherer logs.

While you can trigger an update of an individual content source, you also indicate a schedule for updates for each content index. When the schedule fires, all content sources within the index are updated. There are four different types of updates that can be performed on a content index—full, incremental, incremental (inclusive), and adaptive. SPS 2001 employed the notion of notification updates for content held within the workspace, and this resulted in almost instantaneous search results on new workspace content. This is no longer the case in SPS 2003, and the Portal_Content index runs an incremental update on a schedule of every 10 minutes. You can, of course, change this schedule to suit your own needs. Similarly, the Non_Portal_Content index runs an incremental update once a day at 0100 hours, although if you remove a site from the Site Directory, then a notification is sent to this content source such that an immediate update is performed (see Figure 6.6).

SPS 2003 introduced the inclusive update option to cater to SharePoint sites (team sites, portal areas, My Sites). By default only the contents of SharePoint lists and libraries is indexed during a normal crawl. However, a SharePoint site has many more objects associated with it, such as custom Web Part Pages and default.aspx, but these do not change as frequently as the contents of lists and libraries. Therefore, the inclusive update, which runs once a day at 0300 hours, will also crawl the supplementary contents of SharePoint sites.

Adaptive updates are just what they were in SPS 2001—a way of learning which pages within a Web site change most frequently to avoid having to check every single page of a Web site to see if it has been changed since the last update.

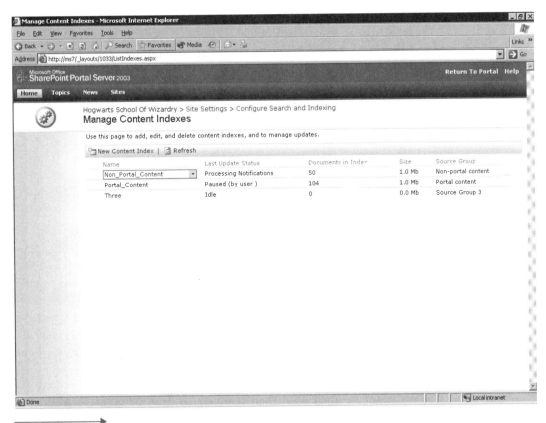

Figure 6.6   *Processing notifications after a change to the Site Directory.*

6.5.2   **Content sources**

As you define content sources, you indicate which content index they should live in and allocate them to a search group for scoping purposes. Out of the box, SPS defines three content sources: This Portal and People, which both live in the `Portal_Content` index, and the Site Directory, which lives in the `Non_Portal_Content` index. Each content source can be configured in terms of update frequency, whether it participates in adaptive updates, where to begin its search (e.g., `http://www.hp.com`), and how it should follow links from there to other sources. The page-depth limit and site-hops limit can be specified, thus ensuring, for example, that only top-level pages of an external Web site are crawled and that you don't follow links to any other Web sites referenced therein.

You can add any number of content sources to suit your needs. As you do, you allocate the index in which they will be contained and the type of content that will be crawled—Exchange public folders, file shares, Web sites, or the sites listed in another portal site's Sites to Be Crawled list (see the discussion on the Site Directory content source at the end of this section). A Web site type allows you to specify the URL to the target site and, from there, the crawling engine will determine the actual type of Web site that it is. This simplifies adding WSS and other portal sites to your index, as SPS itself will determine the type of content and use an appropriate protocol handler. You can actually see this in action if you look at a gatherer log, since team sites ultimately use an `sts2://` protocol, portal sites use `sps://`, and normal Web sites use `http://`.

Content sources: This Portal

The This Portal content source lives inside the `Portal_Content` content index. It defines the URL to the portal site as its starting point, an unlimited page depth (ensuring that any URL that begins with the portal site URL is crawled), and a site hop of 1 (ensuring that only the Home page of any external links found is crawled). This means that all portal content in terms of lists and libraries residing in all portal areas is crawled as part of this source. Furthermore, if any item has a link to a URL outside of the portal site itself, then the page at that link is also crawled. However, no links from the external page are crawled. The exception to only crawling a site's Home page from a link found in a portal areas is for those sites that are listed in the Site Directory. See later for a discussion about how the contents of these sites are indexed.

Content sources: People

The People content source lives inside the `Portal_Content` content index. It defines a URL of `sps://<server>/site$$$people` as its starting point. This type of content source is a hybrid type in that it crawls the user profile and the My Sites that are associated with entries in the profile. By default, the locations of the My Sites are relative to the portal site. That is, the My Sites are normally hosted on the same server as the portal site. However, in a Shared Services scenario (see section 6.9), the physical location could be on another portal site. Indeed, if you provision your own My Sites, then they could also reside at a different location from the default. If this is the case, then you need to enable this content source to allow a site hop of 1, or the content of the My Sites will not be indexed.

On the contrary, you may not want the contents of My Sites to be indexed at all. One way of achieving this is to add an exclusion rule for the default location of My Sites (which is `/personal/*`).

Content sources: Site Directory

The name of this content source is confusing due to conflicting terminology. Let me first explain what the Site Directory content source isn't! SPS provides a yellow pages–type list for storing links to Web sites that may be of interest to your community. You can place anything you like in this list, and typically you would store links to team sites and other Web sites. From the user interface point of view, this list is known as the Site Directory—users navigate to it through the *Sites* menu option, which takes you to the portal area called "SiteDirectory." On this portal area, there is a Sites list, which has multiple views available. Also, from this portal area there is an action available to create a new team site. During creation you are given the option to have the site listed in the Site Directory. This list of sites lives in the SiteDirectory portal area, and the items held in the list are indexed as part of the This Portal content source. Note, it's the list of sites that is indexed and not the contents of the Web sites that the list items point to.

The Site Directory content source does not refer to the Site Directory list! Rather, the Site Directory content source contains the list of team sites and other Web sites whose contents you want to index. And, although this is a completely separate list in architectural terms, the user interface allows you to add sites to both the yellow pages Site Directory and this list in one operation, serving to confuse even further. Thus, as you add a site to the yellow pages Site Directory, you can choose also to have its contents indexed, in which case it also gets added to the Sites to Be Crawled list (note, users do not get this option in a child portal within a Shared Services deployment). Additionally, if you add a site to the Sites to Be Crawled list, it is automatically added to the yellow pages Site Directory as well. Note, this is a one-off operation, and there is no ongoing link between the two lists. Thus, you can quite happily (and easily!) remove a site from the yellow pages Site Directory but still have its content indexed. Additionally, you can remove a site from the Sites to Be Crawled list (via *Site Settings/Manage crawls of Site Directory*) but still have its listing in the Site Directory indexed.

It would have been less confusing if the content source were called something like "Sites to be indexed" rather than "Site Directory." However, that aside, the content source lives in the `Non_Portal_Content` index and specifies a starting URL of `sps://ms7/site$$$site/scope=$$$default$$$`. The content source is basically locked down, and no changes can be made to it other than changes to its name!

6.5.3 Content source groups and search scopes

Each content index and content source can be allocated a content source group. The idea here is to group similar content types together in order to present a simplified way for users to scope their searches to relevant content. Ultimately, the end user sees the search scopes in the Search Web Part; a scope consists of one or more portal areas and one or more content source groups. Out of the box you only have the All sources search scope, but it is simple enough to create others. For example, in Figure 6.7 I have created a search scope called "Employees," which only includes the People content source, and you can see the results of a search against this scope. Additionally, some dynamic scopes are generated depending upon where the user is issuing a search from—for example, "This Topic" or "This personal site." This allows you plenty of scope (pardon the pun) for ensuring that users can search for information based on its type rather than where it is physi-

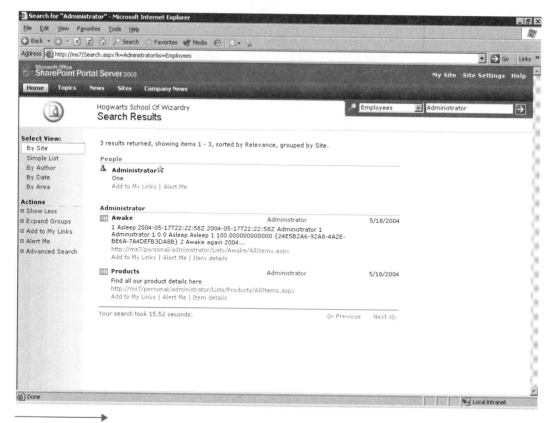

Figure 6.7 *Scoped search.*

cally stored. Combining portal areas and source groups allows internal and external content to be searched in one operation.

An example here would be if you had a portal site that was designed for company product information, and you had a top-level portal area with each individual product's details contained in a subarea. It is also conceivable that you might have other Web-based resources that all have product type information in them—perhaps a product-pricing resource and a product-schedule resource. You could allocate each external content source to a source group called "Products." Then you could create a search scope called "All product information," which contained the Products source group and the top-level portal area.

Behind the scenes, two properties, `urn:schemas.microsoft.com:fulltextqueryinfo:cataloggroup` and `urn:schemas.microsoft.com:fulltextqueryinfo:sourcegroup`, control search results when source groups are specified as part of a search scope. As content is crawled and inserted into the index, the values of these properties are set to the source group that is associated with the content index and the content source, respectively. As search scopes are selected, the underlying queries are tweaked accordingly to include the `cataloggroup` for any content indexes that are part of the scope and the `sourcegroup` for any content sources. This results in multiple WHERE clauses OR'd together, ensuring that content is only returned from the correct locations. By default, the All sources scope does not include these properties in a WHERE clause, ensuring that all content locations are searched.

If a search scope includes a portal area, then the property called `urn:schemas-microsoft-com:sharepoint:portal:IDPath` comes into play. This property contains a comma-separated list of IDs corresponding to the hierarchical location of the area within the portal—each area has a unique ID. Thus, when you specify a portal area as being part of a search scope, a CONTAINS clause for the ID of the portal area is added to the search. This ensures that only content contained in the portal area and any subareas is returned. Content in subareas is returned since it's IDPath will contain that of the parent area. If you specify multiple portal areas in a search scope, multiple CONTAINS clauses will be added.

The dynamic search scope called "This Topic" also uses a CONTAINS clause on the IDPath for the ID of the current portal area.

Finally, the dynamic search scope called "This personal site," which is made available on My Site, augments the search with a check for the property `urn:schemas-microsoft-com:sharepoint:portal:profile:`

`UserProfile_GUID`. Each user has a unique GUID, which is stored in the profile database for the portal site, and the property is checked against the GUID of the user performing the search.

Managing indexed properties

Although it was possible to control which properties were indexed in SPS 2001, this was not a straightforward task by any means. SPS 2003 offers a big improvement in this area, giving you a management interface to control properties and how they influence search.

SPS supports indexing content and properties, and the property index is actually stored in a separate file called `sps.edb`. It may well be that your corpus includes a vast quantity of properties that are never actually used in search queries or would never be influential in the result set returned from a query. You can, therefore, decide which properties from crawled content are actually indexed, whether they appear as a selectable property for an advanced search, whether they appear when users look at the details of an item that was returned in a search, and whether a change to such a property is to be treated as a change from an alert point of view. The latter is very important if you are going to mass change certain properties associated with content in your corpus, since you wouldn't want to start an alert storm for people who had set up alerts for other normal changes to the underlying item.

As content is crawled, any properties that are found are added into the Manage Properties from Crawled Documents Web page. This page is very useful when it comes to building your own search utilities, as it shows the schema for all the properties known to the search engine. This page groups together properties from the same namespace, allowing you to drill down and look at individual properties. From here you can select an individual property and define how it should be treated—such as displaying in advanced search. Among other things, this page also allows you to see if any items or documents within the index are currently using the property, which can be very useful if you are looking to remove indexed properties.

A word of caution: If you are going to be using properties seriously in any of your applications, be aware that property definitions are per portal site, and there is no policing of schema whatsoever. Therefore, if I change how a property is handled, I change it for every source in which the property is present. A simple example will help here. As you add custom columns to a WSS list, a new property is generated under the `urn:schemas-microsoft-com:office:office` namespace. The name of the property is set to be `OWS_<name>`, where `<name>` is the column name you provide. So let's say you add a custom column called "Price" to a WSS list in a team site that is being crawled by a portal site. The property `urn:schemas-microsoft-com:office:office#ows_price` is added to the properties page. As an administrator I can then control whether this property appears in advanced searches or, indeed, in the index at all.

A problem occurs, however, if someone else creates a custom column that is also called "Price" in a separate WSS list that is also indexed. I only have one definition of the property, and it may be that I want the property indexed for one list but not for another. There is no easy solution here, given that WSS empowers end users to create their own lists. If this is deemed a big problem, then a convention for naming custom columns would have to be designed and adhered to so that only unique names were used.

You can see the effect of adding a custom column to a list, indexing the list, and then setting the property to be selectable in an advanced search in Figure 6.8. In this case I have added a column called "Price" to a document library. Note that only text-based columns can be used for retrieval purposes through the Advanced Search page.

Indexing lists and libraries

Consideration has to be given to the way that the contents of lists and libraries are indexed. In any SPS implementation you could have lists and libraries that are hosted within portal areas and team sites. Furthermore, the team sites could be on the same server farm as the portal site or on a separate farm. There are some issues in the area of property management and alerts that may mean you have to change the default indexing behavior. Let's explain how the basic indexing works by default and then explain what this means for alerts and property management.

Let's deal with lists first. By default a list is treated as a single document for indexing purposes. In other words, the entire content of the list can be considered as if it were the body of a document. If in your search queries a term matches any column of any item within the list, then the list itself is returned as a hit. If you compare this to what happens on a normal document, then this make sense—as a hit on a word anywhere in the body of a document would return that document.

For document libraries the story is slightly different. In this case each document, plus its metadata (i.e., the columns in the library and any inbuilt properties such as Office properties, HTML <META> tags, etc.), is treated as a single unit and indexed as a separate document in the index. This means

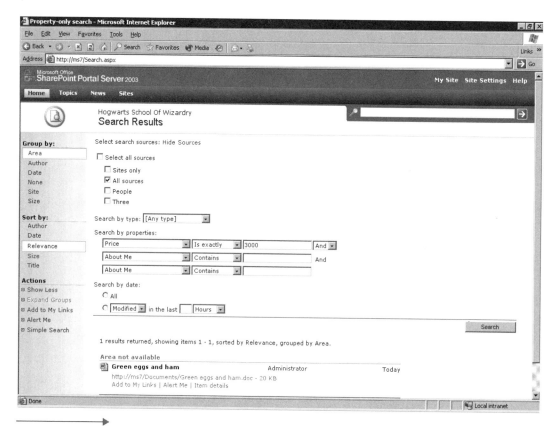

Figure 6.8   *Using a custom property in an advanced search.*

that any searches that match either a word in the document or its metadata will return a link to the actual document and not to the library, as is the case with lists.

Now, when the gatherer performs an incremental update to gather changes to lists and libraries, it is only told by WSS that something has changed. It is not told which item caused the change to occur, as this would only be possible if WSS had some form of incremental change system, which it doesn't (at this time anyway—we can only hope for this change in the future!). For lists, since they are treated as a single document, this is not an issue; we don't need to know which item caused the change, since the whole list content is reindexed anyway. However, for document libraries this means that every item in the library has to be checked to see if its modified date has changed since the last index run. The modified date is held in the property called `ows_modified`, which is updated when a column is changed in the document library or the document itself is modified. Now, there is only one `ows_modified` property per item, which means that the gatherer does not know whether a column or the document has changed; therefore, it has to reindex both the document and its metadata.

This is not really a major issue if you have a dedicated index server, but it may well influence your designs in terms of the number of items in document libraries and lists and how you set up your content indexes and search scopes. This is particularly so if you have large lists or libraries that change frequently and you always want to keep your index as up-to-date as possible. In this case, partitioning these lists and libraries into a separate content index may well be a good idea.

Now, let me try to confuse you slightly here and talk about how alerts are handled. Even though lists are treated as a single document, individual items are actually indexed by default for lists that reside within the portal site. Although they are indexed, they are not retrieved via a search; they are only indexed in order to allow any alerts that have been set up on the item to fire. Remember that it is the fact that an item is indexed that causes the Persistent Query Engine to wake up and determine whether anyone needs to be notified with an alert. For lists that reside outside of the portal site (e.g., remote team sites in the Sites to Be Crawled content source), individual items are not indexed by default. You can, however, set up a site rule to enable this so that individual items can be retrieved via a search and a subsequent alert can be set on the item from the search results. A word of caution here, however: Obviously your index size could grow significantly if you index every single item in every list!

Finally, there is an issue involved in allowing users to use a column from a list as part of an advanced search. The previous example of adding a column called "Price" to a document library was carefully selected! If I add the column to a list, I am not able to retrieve the list using only a property search because the list items are indexed as a whole and the individual property values from each list item are therefore not indexed separately or associated with the list as a whole.

Configuring inclusion and exclusion rules

You can specify inclusion and exclusion rules that can control the resources that should be included in or excluded from the content index and which complex URLs (URLs that contain question marks) can be included in the index. Rules are associated with particular URLs and apply to the content index as a whole (indeed, they can also be set from the content index menu itself). However, given that URLs define the starting point for a content source, it makes sense to be able to set rules from content sources as well.

The rules apply to particular URLs, and as links to content are discovered during a crawl, they are checked against the rules to see if they should be included or excluded. An example of where this is used is with supporting files for a typical Web site. Most standard Web sites would have a particular folder that contains supporting images, client-side Java script code, and the like. Rather than have the content of these files polluting your index, you can explicitly exclude these folders or even certain file types. For example, the `Portal_Content` index has an exclusion rule to exclude `*.aspx` files.

Other rules exist to allow you to specify a different access account to be used when crawling a particular location, whether individual Share-Point list items are indexed (as opposed to the whole list), and whether alerts can be set for individual items within a SharePoint list (as discussed earlier).

6.6   What does it all mean to the end user?

I mentioned earlier about SPS 2003 providing a much more usable index-ing and search experience than SPS 2001, and I've already discussed how administrators can control the scoping of searches through search scopes and making properties available to the Advanced Search page. The biggest improvement from the end user's point of view, aside from faster search results, is how search results are displayed using the out-of-the-box Search Web Part Pages `search.aspx`. This is a Web Part Page and three Web Parts combined to provide all types of searches. These Web Parts are the Search Box, Advanced Search Control, and Search Results.

Several dynamic canned views allow the user to easily manipulate the result set, enabling smart groupings and sorting. Additionally, several actions are available, such as showing more or less information and setting up an alert to the search query that generated the result set. It is the `Group-ByList` property on the Search Results Web Part that controls how the results are rendered. Thus, as users select a particular view, this property is set accordingly, such that the Web Part regenerates the appropriate view. You can see a result set grouped by author in Figure 6.9.

There is also the opportunity to look at the details of an item that was returned in a result set. This is very useful, since, from the resulting view, you can also see other items that have been authored by the same person (see Figure 6.10). Note that the properties about the item that are displayed on this page can be controlled as discussed earlier using the *Manage proper-ties of crawled documents* option.

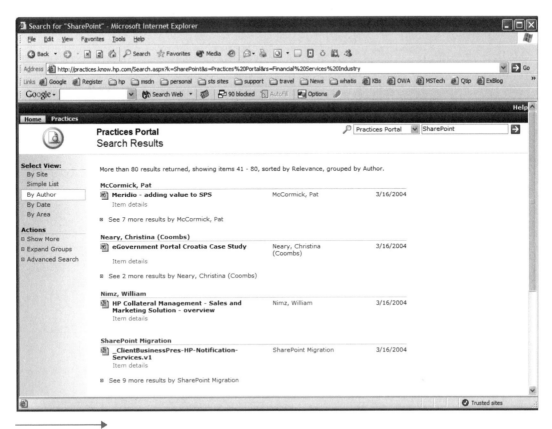

Figure 6.9   *Result set grouped by author.*

6.7   Combining WSS and SPS search

In a default SPS deployment, full-text indexing is enabled for team sites, assuming you are using a SQL back end. This means that the Search user interface will appear on any team site that is provisioned from the portal site. Additionally, team sites provisioned in this way are automatically associated with the portal; note, however, that you can break this association and reassociate to any portal site you like. Similarly, team sites created on a stand-alone WSS farm can also be associated with any portal site. Now, you might expect that since team sites can be created from the portal site and since that portal search is much richer, any search performed from the team sites will somehow execute against the associated portal site with a suitable scope; this is not the case. Rather, the team site just uses the WSS search mechanism as it would have if the team site were provisioned on a stand-

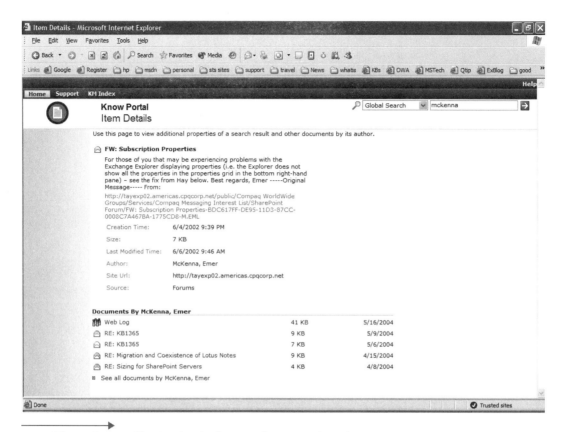

Figure 6.10   *Viewing details of an item from a search result.*

alone WSS deployment. Thus, the limitations of this search, as discussed previously, are still in force.

To avail him- or herself of the SPS search, the user must somehow execute the query against the portal site. For an associated team site, this is achieved by providing a link in the local search results that redirects the user to the portal site with which the team site is associated and that issues the same search criteria—against the All sources search scope. There is also a navigation aid placed on the team site to allow the user to navigate up to the portal site. If you compare Figures 6.4 and 6.11, you will see these links after connecting the Laphroaig WSS team site to the Scottish Whisky SPS portal. This redirection leverages the ability to pass query strings to the SPS search page, and it is called using the "k" (keyword) string. So, in our example in Figure 6.11, the link for "Search for 'friends' on Scottish Whisky Portal" results in a redirection to the URL `http://<portal    site>/ search.aspx?k=friends`.

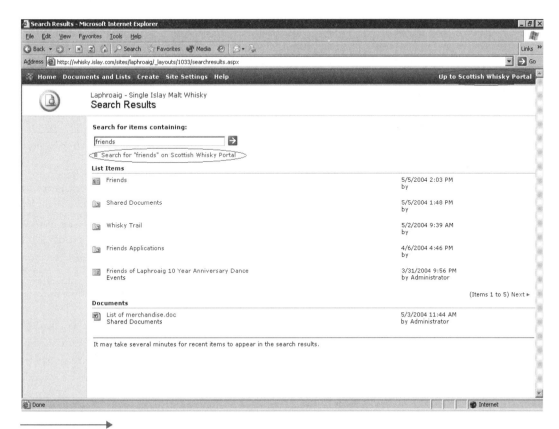

Figure 6.11   *Team site connected to a portal site.*

If the team site is not associated with the portal site, or if full-text index-ing has been disabled, then there is nothing in the team site that aids the user in getting to the portal site to do a search.

Of course, this is not ideal, but there is plenty of scope for customiza-tion; for example, you could design a WSS site template that included a Search Web Part that automatically performed a search to a suitable search scope on the portal—perhaps scoped to the team site and all its subsites? The trick here is not actually in how to execute a search against the portal site index, it's more in ensuring that you can organize your SPS index such that search scopes exist that can return the desired content.

When a team site is associated with a portal site, you also have the option of selecting a portal area for team site lists and document libraries. This option actually allows you to create a portal listing that points back to the team site list or library. You have exactly the same options when creating any listing and so can post the listing to any portal area. Does this, therefore, affect the search experience on the portal site? Does it perhaps offer opportunity for having, say, a team document library automatically searched as part of a portal area search using This topic? Unfortunately, the answer is no for two reasons. First, only the portal listing is indexed, not the contents of where it is pointing to. Second, even if the content were indexed, the This topic search scope only looks for items that have the property `urn:schemas-microsoft-com:sharepoint:portal:IDPath` set, as discussed earlier, and this property is only set for content that is physically stored in a portal area.

A workaround is to have a content source for each team site that you want to associate with the portal area and then build a search scope that includes the area and the relevant content sources. This is not ideal, and we can only hope that we see better integration between team sites and portal areas in the future.

6.7.1   Two indexing engines = two lots of resources

There is one last thing I want to mention about combining WSS and SPS indexing. You have to remember that they are indeed two different processes and therefore consume two lots of resources in terms of catalogs and CPU cycles. Thus, you have to plan for this, especially in terms of catalog disk space, which is discussed in Chapter 8.

Remember that all content is stored in content databases and, on a default implementation, team sites and portal area content will share the same content databases. Furthermore, recall that WSS full-text indexing is enabled serverwide on an SPS installation; thus, all content databases are configured for full-text indexing. So, even if you were to have two separate virtual servers (one for WSS and one for SPS), it would appear that the SPS content is still indexed by the WSS full-text indexing (see Chapters 8 and 11 for ways to ensure that SQL indexing can be switched off on a per–virtual server basis). And, as we know, team sites can also indexed with the SPS indexing engine through the Sites to Be Crawled content source.

Therefore, on larger-scale implementations it is a best practice to ensure that your team sites are created on a separate server farm from that of your portal sites. That way at least the SPS content is not indexed unnecessarily by the WSS full-text indexing. Note that some anecdotal evidence suggests that there is a way for portal content that is in the same content database as WSS content not to be indexed by the WSS full-text indexing, but at the time of writing I haven't yet discovered how!

6.8   Monitoring and customizing the search experience

If you want either to customize the search experience or to build search into your own applications, then there are three basic approaches. You can pass query strings to the search page, call upon the Search Web Service, or build your own Web Parts using the SPS object model.

There are also some tweaks you can make to the existing Web Parts in order to do things such as set the starting search scope and enable full logging so that you can monitor and analyze the queries performed against your index.

6.8.1   Tweaking the Search Web Parts

If you use FrontPage 2003 to edit the search page, you will find three Web Parts lurking inside. Each of these Web Parts has various properties associated with it that control its behavior. These properties are defined in XML, and you can change and add other properties. Of course, you need to know what the properties do so that you don't break the search experience completely! Some, but not all, of the properties are documented in the SPS SDK; for example, if you look at the Search Results Web Part you will see a `SortByList` property that defines how the canned views should be sorted in the results page.

There are two interesting properties on the Search Results Web Part that can help in monitoring the type of searches being performed. The first is `EnableQueryLogging`, which is switched on by default and results in the search terms from queries being logged in the IIS log files. The second, which is not present by default, is `EnableSQLCommandLogging`. If you add this property to the Web Part, then the full SQL query is logged. While this can obviously help you see what is going on, be aware that your IIS logs will grow significantly in size; please use this with caution and remember to revert to normal logging after you have finished.

Logging the full queries can be very useful if you are writing your own queries, since it lets you discover the syntax that is required for typical search operations. For example, I discovered that you can pass functions to the WHERE clause when calculating dates as the following snippet shows (it's URL encoded, but you should get the drift!):

```
where++(+(%22DAV%3agetlastmodified%22+%3e+DateAdd(Day%2c
+-7%2c+GetGMTDate())))
```

6.8.2   Using the Search page: search.aspx

A simple, quick, and effective way of consuming the search service is to post queries to the search page. You merely encode your query in a URL using query strings and then post it to the Search page. This can be done programmatically or merely by including a hyperlink to the correct URL. The use of a hyperlink means the search service can be called from just about anywhere—be it inside an application, an Office document, an e-mail, or a Web site. As mentioned previously, this is the method used when you link a WSS team site to a portal site and want to execute a query against the portal site.

The URL parameters are documented in the SPS SDK, and you can control things such as the search scope to use, the keywords to use, and the types of items that should be returned.

In fact, you can get great examples of how to call the `search.aspx` page by just looking at what some of the links inside SharePoint do. For example, when you look at the details of an item that has been returned to you from a search, an option at the bottom of the page allows you to see other items authored by the same person. So, assuming you are looking at an item that was authored by Kevin Laahs, this link merely calls the following:

```
http://<server>/Search.aspx?db=Kevin+Laahs&wd=Recent+
documents+by+Kevin+Laahs
```

6.8.3   Calling the Search Web Service

The Search Web Service (`http://server_name/_vti_bin/search.asmx`) can be called when you need to embed search into a remote application and process the results yourself rather than being redirected to the Search Results page. The search results can be returned in XML form or in a data set. The Query Service is documented in the SPS SDK, and you can basically send a list of keywords or a full SQL query to the service—this is where logging the full query commands in IIS becomes helpful!

At the time of writing, the details in the SDK are fairly limited, but you can find details on the request and response schema at `http://msdn.microsoft.com/library/default.asp?url=/library/en-us/rssdk/html/rsxsdResposnse.asp`.

6.8.4   Using the SPS Object Model

If you want to write your own Web Parts that consume the search service, you typically call upon the SPS object model. Many available objects and

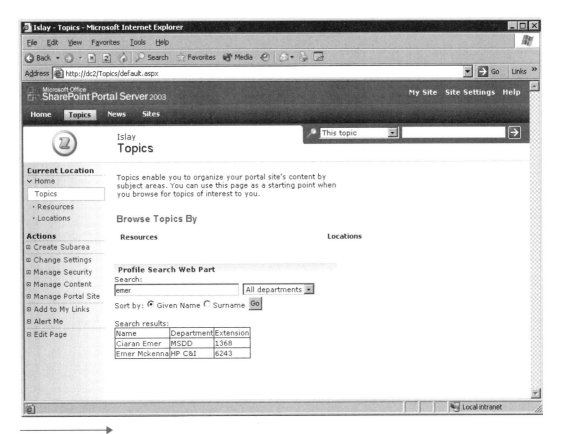

Figure 6.12   *A custom Search Web Part.*

methods allow you to call the service in a multitude of ways. As an example, see Figure 6.12. This is a Web Part that uses the object model to perform a search on the SPS profile, using it much as you would a phone directory. This Web Part was actually based on some code made available by Anders Rask at `http://www.msd2d.com/content/Tip_viewitem_03.aspx?ID=6dba612f-bd30-4e19-ad99-d3975f2d71eb`.

6.9   Shared Services considerations

6.9.1   Deploying a hierarchy of portal sites

You can deploy multiple portal sites in a Shared Services scenario. This environment results in one portal site being the parent portal and others being child portals. One of the main reasons for deploying a Shared Services environment is to avoid multiple portal sites, each needing its own index, and all the management (and resources) it entails. In a typical large organization, you could have a portal site for each division but want to have a single profile and search experience across all the portal sites. In this instance you would perhaps create a corporate portal site that offers Shared Services to the divisional portal sites. Thus, only the corporate portal site has to do any indexing, and searches from the divisional portal sites are executed against its index. Behind the scenes the child portal finds out from the Topology Manager which portal site is the parent and connects directly to its SQL database in order to initiate searches.

Microsoft envisioned, when designing Shared Services, a hierarchy of portal sites, with search being aggregated the further up the tree you went. Thus, if I am searching at the divisional level, I should only see results from my division and any portal sites that are below that level. Similarly, if I search from the corporate portal, I should be able to see results from all divisions.

With this in mind, we can now talk about how this has been implemented and what you need to do to enable such a hierarchy where one portal site is associated with the next portal site up the tree. In a Shared Services environment, you have one parent portal site, and all other portal sites on the same server farm or any other farm that has been associated with the parent farm are known as child portal sites. There is no topological association between the child portal sites at creation time, so you can consider them all as being at the same single level of a tree. In order to turn them into a logical tree of child portal sites, you have to use the unbelievably confusingly named *Use a search scope from another portal site* option. This option, available on any portal site, only makes sense when executed on a child portal within a Shared Services environment.

Taken literally, you would think that the option would merely take the search scopes that were defined on another portal site and make them available on the child portal site. But this is not the case. In fact, this option effectively adds the child portal to the All sources search scope on another child portal site. Thus, you can build a hierarchy of sites from a search point of view, because when you assign a child portal site to another child portal site, any sites that were associated with the original child are also automatically included in the All sources scope on the newly associated child site. Note, you only have one association in effect for each child portal site, so you couldn't, for example, have a divisional portal site associated with two different regional sites.

The All sources scope from the parent site will always contain all of the child sites without having to perform this operation. But you do have to configure content sources on the parent portal site that crawls the child's portal areas and any sites (team or Web) listed in the child's Sites to Be Crawled list. (When you create a team site from a child portal site, you are not given the choice to include it in the Sites to Be Crawled list, as you are on a stand-alone portal site. It is automatically added into this list, so administrators of the child portal site may need to modify the list using the *Manage crawls of Site Directory* option if they do not want the content from particular team sites to appear in search results.)

You create a content source of type "Web site" to cover the child portal areas and one of type "SharePoint Portal Server Site Directory" for the sites to be crawled. In both cases you point the starting URL to the child portal site. Once this is done, you can have an aggregated search that can span a hierarchical tree and implement topologies such as Corporate, Region, Division, and Group.

In a Shared Services environment, any management option that has anything to do with the index has to be executed on the parent portal site, since this is where the content sources live. In fact, you are given a message if you attempt to take an option, such as *Manage properties from crawled documents*, from a child portal site where the operation is invalid and offered the choice to go directly to the parent portal site. Search scopes can, however, be defined and maintained on a child portal site, and we will see later why you might need to do this due to an anomaly in the use of the All sources search scope on a stand-alone portal site versus a Shared Services child portal site. The anomaly is that content from external sites in the Sites to Be Crawled list are not returned in an All sources search on a child portal, whereas they are on a stand-alone portal site search. We need to understand how scoping works in a Shared Services environment before we can describe why this anomaly exists.

The trick behind the aggregated search is the use of the `urn:schemas-microsoft-com:sharepoint:portal:IDPath` property in the SQL query that is issued from a child portal site against the All sources scope (this property is not checked when the search is performed on the parent portal site). As when searching within the This topic scope, items are checked to see if this property contains the ID of the child portal itself (each portal, like the portal area and subareas, has its own unique ID). If the item being searched does not include this property with this value, it is not returned in the search results. If the search query wasn't augmented with this check, then all content from all portals that were sharing the shared index would be returned when the All sources scope was used. Now, recall that this property is a multivalued property, and as content is crawled in a child portal site, its `IDPath` property gets set to include all other child portal sites to which it is associated (including all transitive associations). This is the key to why aggregated searches work!

The `IDPath` property is only present on content that physically resides in a portal area or team site. Any external content that is indexed does not have the `IDPath` property set on it. This is why we have the anomaly between an All sources search on a stand-alone portal site and a child portal site. An All sources scoped search on a parent portal site or stand-alone portal site is not augmented with any check on the `IDPath`. Thus, content in all content indexes is returned, including external content indexed through the Sites to Be Crawled content source. However, with a child portal the search is augmented with a check for `IDPath`; therefore, external content is not returned in search results since it does not have an `IDPath` property.

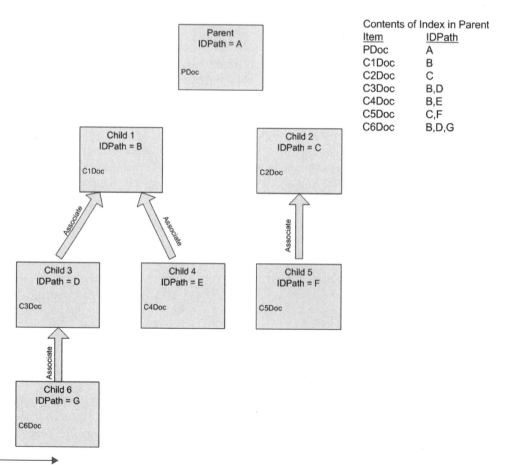

Figure 6.13   *Shared Services search architecture.*

Hence, if you do want external content referenced in the Sites to Be Crawled source to be returned in an All sources search in a child portal, then you must modify the All sources search scope to include the Sites to Be Crawled source explicitly. Additionally, if you want to maintain the hierarchical search experience, then you will need to do this manually for all portal sites further up the tree.

Figure 6.13 is a very simplified view of a Shared Services setup and will help explain what goes on behind the scenes. Here we have six child portals and one parent portal. All the indexing is done by the parent portal, and the child portals perform their search against this index. To create the hierarchy as in the diagram, we need to take the *Use search scope from another portal site* option on some of the child portals and associate them with their immediate parent. Thus, on Child 6 we would set this to Child 3, and on Child 3 to Child 1. Note that there is no need to associate the first-level child portal sites with the parent portal. Now, as content is crawled in the child sites, the index gets built as shown in the top right of the diagram. Note how the IDPath of each item gets set to include the IDs of those sites further up the hierarchy.

Now, when an All sources scoped search is performed, we get different results depending upon where we do the search from. If we are on the parent portal, the search is performed against the full index with no WHERE clauses; thus, all content from all child portals is returned. However, if we do a search from any of the child portals, a WHERE clause is added to the query. This WHERE clause checks for the IDPath property containing the IDPath of the portal from which we are issuing the search. Thus, a search from Child 1 would only return items that had "B" in their IDPath. Looking at the index, you can see that this would only return those items that were in portal sites Child 1, Child 3, Child 4, and Child 6. However, the same search performed on Child 3 would only return those items contained in Child 3 and Child 6.

Part II

Planning, Deployment, and Operations

7

SharePoint Products and Technologies Architecture

The *Merriam-Webster Dictionary* defines the word "architecture" as "the manner in which the components of a computer or computer system are organized and integrated." In this chapter, when we talk about architectures, we talk about the building blocks that you must put together to assemble the final end product, your SharePoint Products and Technologies deployment.

Specifically, this chapter introduces you to software and hardware architecture concepts that you should familiarize yourself with, since they will give you the context for the other chapters in Part II and beyond.

7.1   Windows Server 2003 and IIS

SharePoint Products and Technologies are inherently tied to the Windows Server 2003 platform, specifically IIS 6.0, which is part of the core Windows Server 2003 platform. Microsoft made a design decision early on to leverage key architecture components and security features provided by the new Windows Server 2003 platform; thus, you cannot install SharePoint on any previous version of the Windows Server operating system.

7.1.1   Windows Server 2003 editions

As with many other Microsoft platform products, Windows Server 2003 comes in different editions targeted at specific scenarios and numbers of users. Since licensing costs are tied to the Windows Server 2003 editions, it's good to familiarize yourself with the different editions to make an informed decision when selecting the base operating system for your SharePoint Products and Technologies deployment. While many organizations have standard configurations of the Windows Server 2003 platform for particular tasks, such as a Web server, you need to keep in mind that SharePoint Products

Table 7.1   *Windows Server 2003 Editions*

Windows Server 2003 Edition	Edition Highlights	SharePoint Notes
Web Edition	Up to 2 processors Up to 2 GB of RAM Network load balancing	Interesting Web front-end alternative Cannot run SQL Server Cannot act as an Active Directory Domain controller
Standard Edition	Up to 4 processors Up to 4 GB of RAM Network load balancing	Standard single-server configuration Good Web front-end server No clustering support
Enterprise Edition	Up to 8 processors Up to 32 GB of RAM Up to eight-node server clustering Network load balancing	Standard SQL Database back-end server with clustering support Good single-server choice with future scale-out and clustering support
Data Centre Edition	Up to 32 processors 64 GB of RAM Up to eight-node server clustering Network load balancing	High-end SQL back-end server

and Technologies is much more than just a Web application. SharePoint products are highly integrated applications that depend on core operating system features; thus, you should consider them more similar to Exchange than custom Web applications.

Table 7.1 introduces the Windows Server 2003 editions with highlights and a few notes on each edition's relevance to SharePoint. Don't worry if all the terms don't make sense just yet; we'll cover the particulars and why they matter later on in the chapter. For now, just be aware of the edition titles and the differences in functionality. Of course, if licensing is not an issue in your organization, the choice might be simple, since the Enterprise Edition has all of the features without any cons except cost.

7.1.2 Introduction to IIS 6.0

IIS 6.0 is a significant upgrade from previous releases. In fact, it has been completely redesigned and rewritten from the ground up to provide security, scalability, and reliability features fit for an enterprise. Tightly integrated into the core operating system, IIS 6.0 is only available on the Windows Server 2003 platform.

IIS 6.0 utilizes a new HTTP protocol stack, called HTTP.sys, provided by Windows Server 2003 to listen for HTTP queries. HTTP.sys is part of the operating system network subsystem and thus runs in kernel mode, just like device drivers for hardware components and other core operating system code. By moving the HTTP listener into kernel mode from previous Winsock User Mode implementation, IIS 6.0 benefits from performance enhancements gained by kernel-mode caching and request queuing. The HTTP protocol stack is responsible for listening for queries and queuing them up to the correct IIS virtual server process queues, which the IIS worker process in turn picks up. In addition, the HTTP protocol stack is responsible for text-based logging and ensuring that SSL traffic is decrypted and encrypted appropriately by the SSL provider.

Due to the extensive redesign, it was inevitable that Microsoft had to design a backward-compatible mode to ease Web application migrations from Windows 2000 and IIS 5.0. Thus, IIS 6.0 features two request-processing modes, also known as application isolation modes, which ensure backward compatibility while allowing organizations to migrate to the new processing model and make use of the new reliability features.

When you upgrade a Windows 2000 Server to Windows Server 2003, IIS 6.0 is by default configured to run in IIS 5.0 Isolation Mode, which mirrors the processing model used by IIS 5.0. While the IIS 5.0 Isolation Mode does use the same base kernel-mode HTTP processing provided by the HTTP.sys provider, it still features the old low-, medium-, and high-processing options that IIS 5.0 used. Since SharePoint Products and Technologies is engineered around the new IIS 6.0 features, you *cannot* run SharePoint with the backward-compatible IIS 5.0 Isolation Mode, and, thus, we will focus on the Worker Process Isolation Mode for the rest of this book.

Worker Process Isolation Mode is the native processing mode, which has been engineered to make use of the redesigned IIS 6.0 architecture. In Worker Process Isolation Mode, the Web applications, including ISAPI filters and Extensions, are run in application pools, which provide process segregation for all the code executed when users request Web pages from the server, as shown in Figure 7.1. IIS 6.0 allows several application pools to be configured and thus allows you to run applications in virtual silos without incurring a performance penalty, as in IIS 5.0 high-processing mode. In addition to being able to run each virtual server in its own application pool, thus segregating ISAPI filter and extension processes from other virtual servers, you can also define application pools at the virtual directory level, giving you more manageability options.

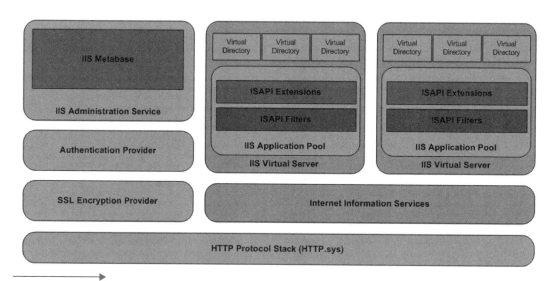

Figure 7.1   *IIS 6.0 architecture in Worker Process Isolation Mode.*

Each application pool is allocated its own user-mode worker process (`W3wp.exe`), which allows you to effectively "reboot" the Web applications running in the application pool by recycling the worker process. While you were able to stop and start each virtual server individually in IIS 5.0, the actual process used to execute custom code was shared across multiple virtual servers. Thus, you regularly had to restart IIS, which affected all of the virtual servers hosted on the physical server. In addition to application pool recycling, the worker processes can be recycled automatically without application downtime, since an application pool can consist of more than one worker process, thus allowing a new worker process to take over instantly as the old process is terminated. Since the HTTP protocol stack is in charge of queuing requests, when an application pool terminates unexpectedly, IIS will automatically start a new worker process and pick up in the queue where the old process left off.

Since each application pool is run in its own worker process, each application pool incurs a memory overhead depending on the application it runs. For example, each application pool running a SharePoint server can take up to 150 MB of RAM per pool. Since it would not be feasible to run every piece of code in its own application pool, IIS 6.0 allows you to share application pools across virtual servers or virtual directories to reduce memory overhead.

As shown in Figure 7.2, with IIS 6.0 all user queries are intercepted by the new kernel-mode HTTP protocol stack provided by Windows Server

Figure 7.2
*Request processing
in IIS 6.0.*

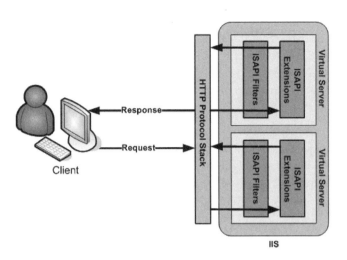

2003, which is responsible for placing the requests in the correct IIS virtual server queue from where the application pool's worker process picks them up.

Once the worker process for the virtual server has picked up a request, it is passed through all ISAPI filters registered for the virtual server in order of priority defined by the filters. ISAPI filters are compiled DLL libraries, which are registered for IIS events and execute code once a matching event passes by. Since ISAPI filters are able to examine and modify HTTP headers and content for both incoming requests as well as outgoing responses, they can be used to create powerful applications that, for example, provide authentication and data encryption. ISAPI filters can be registered either for a particular virtual server or for all virtual servers.

Once through the ISAPI filters, IIS passes each request to an ISAPI extension based on the file extension registration. Although ISAPI extensions might at first sound unfamiliar, they are at the core of IIS request processing. All common application pages served by IIS are in fact processed by ISAPI extensions, including, for example, ASP and ASP.NET pages. Once the ISAPI extension processes the requests, the response is passed back through the ISAPI filters and the HTTP protocol stack to the end users.

7.1.3   ASP.NET processing in IIS 6.0

Although ASP.NET has been around since .NET Framework 1.0 release in January 2002, the version of .NET Framework 1.1 ASP.NET that ships with Windows Server 2003 is now "baked in" to the product and has been engineered to fully utilize the new IIS 6.0 architecture and the new Worker Process Isolation Mode. Thus, all ASP.NET applications running on the Windows Server 2003 and IIS 6.0 platform enjoy the performance and reliability benefits of the new platform.

As Figure 7.3 illustrates, ASP.NET is called from an ISAPI extension, `aspnet_isapi.dll`, which is registered in IIS to process file extensions such as `.aspx`, `.ashx`, and `.asmx`. Since ASP.NET is called from an ISAPI extension, all the managed code is now executed in the application pool worker process assigned to the virtual server or virtual directory that the ASP.NET application resides in. ASP.NET also registers a serverwide ISAPI filter in order to process, for example, the session state for ASP.NET applications.

When running ASP.NET in IIS 6.0 Worker Process Isolation Mode, ASP.NET process modes are set to mirror those of IIS 6.0, and, thus, most `machine.config` file parameters, with few exceptions, do not affect ASP.NET processing. As seen in Figure 7.3, ASP.NET now reads most of its configuration information from the application pool settings and application-specific `web.config` file, which we will cover in Chapter 15.

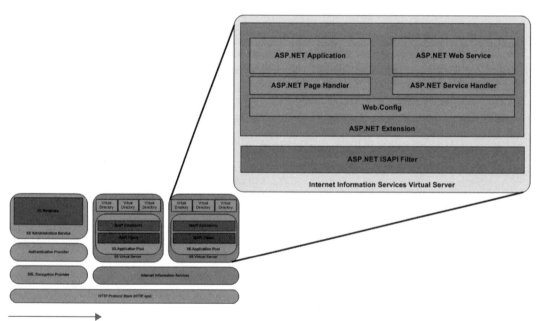

Figure 7.3   *ASP.NET architecture in IIS 6.0 Worker Process Isolation Mode.*

The core ASP.NET processing engine resembles IIS to a fine degree, which was a conscious design decision, as Microsoft wanted to provide developers with an easy-to-use yet powerful development platform without having to resort to complex, unmanaged C++ ISAPI filters and extensions.

The ASP.NET rendering process can be seen in Figure 7.4. As you can quickly deduct from the figure, ASP.NET HTTP modules are essentially ISAPI filters that have been registered for events in the ASP.NET processing pipeline and can investigate and modify packets as they pass by. ASP.NET handlers, on the other hand, are just like ISAPI extensions that have been registered to handle certain file extensions. For example, the Page Handler is registered for `.aspx` files, while the Service Handler executes `.asmx` Web Services.

The difference, of course, is that it's incredibly easy to create HTTP modules and handlers in Visual Studio.NET with any of the managed languages, including VB.NET, while ISAPI filters, for example, can only be created with unmanaged C++.

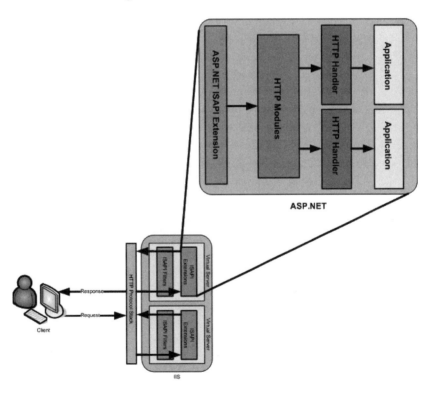

Figure 7.4   *Request processing with IIS 6.0 and ASP.NET.*

7.1.4   **Network load balancing**

Windows Server 2003 includes a feature-rich software network clustering and load-balancing driver, which allows inexpensive, fault-tolerant connections to be established without additional hardware components. Since the load balancing is done at the device driver level, applications such as IIS 6.0 and SharePoint are unable to distinguish user queries made to the load-balanced addresses from those made directly to the servers.

Network Load Balancing (NLB), illustrated in Figure 7.5, works by assigning a new virtual IP address to all the servers participating in the cluster. The virtual IP address is a standard static IP assigned to each of the clustered servers in addition to their own IP addresses. Normally, if you assigned the same IP address to multiple hosts, the network traffic sent to the IP address would collide with the other hosts, since they have no way of knowing which one of the hosts should respond the query. It would be like shouting "Hi there, Paddy!" in a crowded Irish pub (Paddy is a very popular name in Ireland) and having dozens of strange heads turning around at the same time.

To combat this issue, an NLB driver is installed before the TCP/IP stack on each of the clustered servers to filter traffic and ensure that only one of the clustered servers is responding at any given time. The NLB driver communicates with the other clustered servers, assigns queries to them, and fails over traffic in case one of the servers does not respond within a predefined time period.

Figure 7.5
*NLB in Windows
Server 2003.*

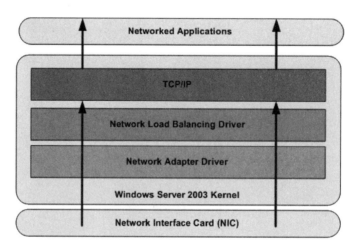

While NLB does work with only one network adapter in each of the clustered servers, it is recommended to have two per server when working in the default Unicast Mode. With two network adapters, the primary interface is left to deal with the network traffic, while the secondary card communicates with the other servers in the clusters, thus reducing the overhead on the primary network. Alternatively, as long as the network infrastructure supports multicasting, you can enable Multicast Mode with a single network adapter and reduce overhead with the Internet Group Management Protocol provided by IPv4.

For more details on NLB, please refer to the Windows Server 2003 Help.

7.2   SharePoint Products and Technologies architecture

As we've already covered in Part I of this book, SharePoint Products and Technologies builds on the foundation provided by Windows Server 2003, IIS 6.0, and ASP.NET. WSS is both a product and an enabling technology; in fact, SPS 2003 builds on that foundation provided by the technology framework. Figure 7.6 illustrates the high-level architecture for SharePoint Products and Technologies. Both products use Microsoft SQL Server 2000 technology to store configuration data, metadata, and binary files.

Figure 7.6
*SharePoint
Products and
Technologies high-
level architecture.*

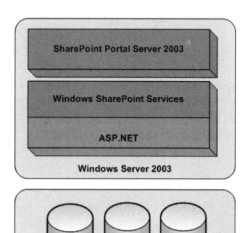

7.2.1   Building on top of IIS and ASP.NET

Since SharePoint Products and Technologies are architected around the new IIS 6.0 Worker Process Isolation Mode and ASP.NET, all the architecture components provided by the Windows Server 2003 foundation are utilized to their full potential. When a virtual server is extended on a WSS server, several components are injected to the IIS 6.0 and ASP.NET processing model, as illustrated in Figure 7.7. While the underlying processing model is not changed, both IIS 6.0 and ASP.NET are extended with custom functionality—hence, the terminology.

While Figure 7.7 might at first seem much more complex than the stand-alone ASP.NET laid out in Figure 7.3, most of the complexity is due to the dual-path execution model SharePoint extended Web sites must be able to support, since organizations might want to deploy other ASP.NET applications on the same server. In order to distinguish which virtual directories can contain other ASP.NET applications, WSS/SPS maintains a list

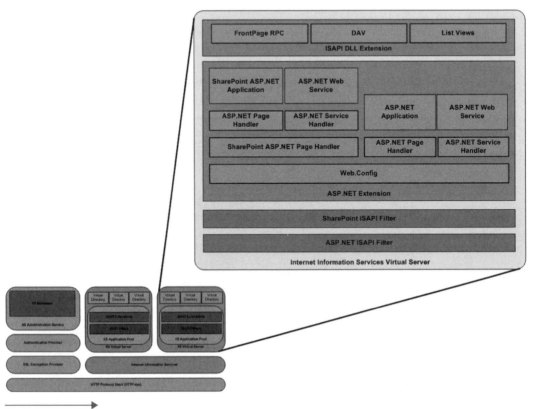

Figure 7.7   *Virtual server processing model extended by WSS.*

of managed paths, which can contain any number of path inclusions and exclusions. Managed paths are configured on the WSS Virtual Server Administration page, and we'll cover them in more detail in Chapter 10.

In order to maintain backward compatibility with older FrontPage releases, WSS also installs a number of unmanaged ISAPI DLL extensions that provide the FrontPage RPC, DAV, and URL protocol support. One of the ISAPI DLLs you will run into quite often is the OWSSVR.DLL, which was used to provide the bulk of STS's rendering capability in the past. Even today, the OWSSVR.DLL is heavily used, for example, for view rendering and CAML support.

To control how requests should be handled, WSS installs an ISAPI filter to each of the extended virtual servers. The ISAPI filter intercepts requests and routes them to their rightful owners based on settings defined in the managed path's configuration. The ISAPI filter also controls a number of other aspects regarding how requests are handled and what the end users get back. Thus, if you're planning to deploy a custom ISAPI filter, for example, for Web Single Sign-On or custom authentication, the WSS filter might affect the functionality of the custom code. For example, ISAPI filters that need to know the virtual directory a user is requesting will need to be registered to intercept the requests before the WSS IFilter, since WSS will rewrite URLs for internal processing.

Figure 7.8 details the process flow for SharePoint Products and Technologies. As we already covered, the ISAPI filter examines each request and checks the requested path against the managed paths list of the virtual server in order to route the request to the SharePoint Page Handler or to

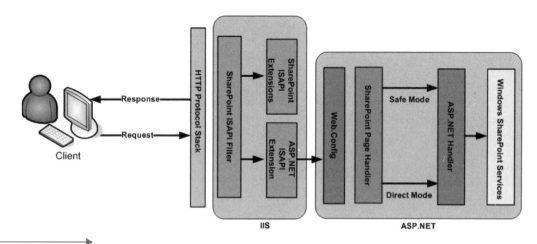

Figure 7.8   *WSS request processing.*

send it to the ASP.NET Page Handler. The filter also has a hard-coded exclusion for the `/_vti_bin/` directory, since it contains the ISAPI extensions used by SharePoint to provide FrontPage RPC and DAV support.

In order to provide restricted Web Part Page Execution Mode, WSS modifies the default ASP.NET process by swapping the `.aspx` pages to be executed by a "shimmy" page handler provided by WSS. I say "shimmy," because the handler doesn't actually take over rendering of ASP.NET pages completely; it still calls the default page handler in either Direct or Safe Mode to execute the pages.

Direct Mode is the ASP.NET default, where the pages are compiled into DLLs and thus benefit from compiled-code execution performance. All of the content in `/_layouts/` directory are executed in this manner, including, for example, all of the administration pages. The `/_layouts/` IIS virtual directory in a default installation maps to `C:\Program Files\Common Files\Microsoft Shared\web server extensions\60\TEMPLATE\ LAYOUTS` directory.

On the other hand, ASP.NET pages executed in Safe Mode are compiled on the fly for the user in a more restrictive mode. Pages rendered with Safe Mode have active scripting disabled and only allow server controls that have been marked as safe to be executed. As we've covered earlier in the book, Web Parts are server controls, and thus the Safe Mode rendering applies to all pages that users are allowed to edit. The SharePoint Page Handler is also in charge of building the ASP.NET pages based on information fetched from the database prior to passing to the ASP.NET Page Handler for execution. Each Web Part Page can exist in ghosted or unghosted format.

Ghosted pages are fetched from the front-end server file system, and the SharePoint Page Handler will simply retrieve the Web Parts included on the page to compile the ASP.NET page. Unghosted pages, on the other hand, have been modified with an HTML editor such as FrontPage and, thus, need to be stored fully in the database and fetched for execution, leading to a slight performance penalty. We'll discuss the performance impact of Web Part Page ghosting in Chapter 9 and deal with support impact in Chapter 12.

7.3   WSS architecture

It's easy to consider WSS a simple Web application that can be installed in 15 minutes to provide collaboration functionality for a small user audience. Microsoft makes installations very easy—a few clicks of a mouse and you're done. However, this might give you an overly simplified picture of what's actually going on behind the scenes and of all the possibilities that are available. So, while WSS is provided as a free add-on to Windows Server 2003, it is a fairly complex environment that has multiple software-configuration and extensive hardware-platform topology options.

In order to provide flexible platform options, WSS uses Microsoft SQL Server to store all information about configuration as well as actual content. By storing everything, including the file binaries, on the SQL back end, WSS completely separates the information-processing layer from the data storage, enabling stateless application-server architectures. When installed, WSS creates a central configuration database to store information about the physical hardware configuration, as well as information about every virtual server that has been extended. In addition, every extended virtual server creates a content database for storing virtual server information and team site content. Administrators can define more than one content database for each virtual server in order to break up content into more manageable sizes for backup and restore purposes.

As seen in Figure 7.9, most of the functionality is encapsulated within IIS, as we discussed earlier. ASP.NET provides the Web page rendering, while ISAPI extensions provide View, FrontPage RPC, and WebDAV support.

Figure 7.9
WSS software architecture.

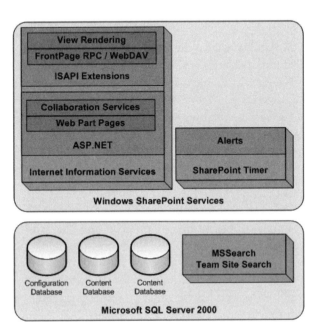

However, WSS is not a pure Web application; it relies on Windows Services to provide part of the functionality. The SharePoint Timer Service is in charge of executing timed events (i.e., actions that need to occur at specific times or predefined periods). Alerts are a good example of a timed action. When creating alerts, users can choose to receive notification, either immediately or as a daily or weekly summary, when an item is changed. In order to provide alerts, the SharePoint Timer Service checks for changes every five minutes for immediate notifications that need to go out. For daily and weekly summaries, checks are run every night and at the end of the week, respectively, by the Timer Service. The SharePoint Timer Service also runs other timed events, such as the Public Folder integration for enabling attachments to be e-mailed directly to document libraries.

7.3.1   Physical architecture components

One of the major design goals for WSS was scalability, Microsoft wanted to ensure that both the scale-up and scale-out scenarios were fully utilized. Scale-up essentially means that the software should be able to squeeze every bit of CPU, memory, and I/O performance out of the hardware it's being hosted on and allow organizations to add more capacity by, for example, adding an extra CPU to the server. Scale-out, on the other hand, means the ability to add additional servers to the architecture and share the load between them, thus enabling organizations to add extra servers to add capacity when scale-up options have been explored.

Scalability wasn't the only design goal, however, especially since STS V1.0 already performed extremely well. Reliability and fault tolerance are key features of the new WSS platform and are achieved by using a familiar, tried-and-tested Web farming approach. In a Web farm, *multiple front-end Web servers* are load-balanced, or clustered, to provide a fault-tolerant Web rendering capability, while all the data is stored in a *back-end database*, as seen in Figure 7.10. An additional benefit of Web farms is the scale-out capability by adding more Web front-end or additional back-end database servers to the farm.

Since WSS front-end Web servers are effectively stateless (all the data, including configuration, is stored in the back-end SQL database), WSS provides an extremely robust Web farm capability. Adding new Web front ends is straightforward, since the software simply needs to register itself to the back-end configuration database. In fact, WSS supports up to 10 front-end Web servers to be able to respond to even the most challenging performance and reliability requirements.

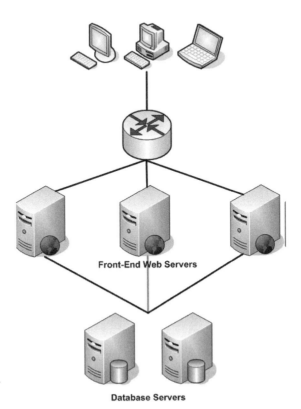

Figure 7.10
WSS server topology options.

Front-End Web Servers

Database Servers

WSS supports Microsoft SQL Server 2000 SP3 database back-end servers in a Web farm configuration, but, importantly, WSS doesn't know or care how these SQL servers have been configured. Thus, you can freely create multinode SQL clusters, and, since WSS supports separate SQL servers configured for each content database, you can even use multiinstance SQL clusters and load balance the back-end databases.

Load balancing for the front-end Web servers can be achieved by the software-based NLB we discussed earlier in the chapter. However, since the software load balancing does include a small performance penalty, as well as additional network traffic, WSS fully supports hardware-based load-balancing abilities provided by physical network devices. While the hardware-based NLB has little impact on performance, larger enterprises often include hardware devices in their data center design in order to provide a shared load-balancing capability.

We'll cover the performance scalability options further in Chapter 9; for now it's important to be aware of all the possibilities and the terminology.

7.4   SPS architecture

Building on top of WSS, SPS 2003 leverages all of the functionality and adds a number of customized templates and services to provide enterprise portal capabilities. Perhaps the most significant of these added services is the Enterprise Search, provided by SPS.

SPS uses the presentation and collaboration layer provided by WSS and simply installs its own templates, from which the portal sites and areas are created. In order to provide hierarchical navigation, while also being able to reorganize the areas, SPS installs a number of server controls that provide the navigational elements and hide the underlying site structure from the users. Underneath the hood though, it's still the same plumbing provided by WSS.

As seen in Figure 7.11, SPS adds a number of services to the software architecture on top of WSS. While the SharePoint Timer Service is still used to provide alerts for WSS sites, SPS installs its own SharePoint Portal Alert Service for items stored in portal areas. Since portal alerts can be created for search results as well as item modifications, Microsoft had to archi-

Figure 7.11
SPS 2003 software architecture.

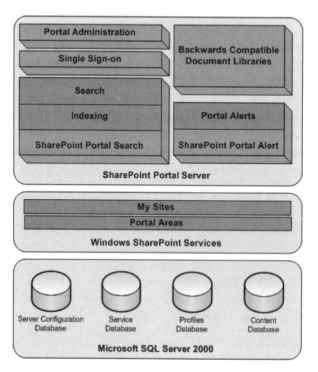

tect a portal alert service that understood the search engine and the persistent query interface.

As we discussed in Chapter 5, SharePoint Portal Search is based on the same MSSearch core shared by several Microsoft products, including SQL Server. The Portal Server MSSearch is the latest generation specifically engineered to provide large-scale indexing and extensive management possibilities to provide Enterprise Search capabilities. However, due to this shared heritage, the Portal Search Service still ships with its own database technology, which is installed on all search and indexing servers and thus does not rely on SQL Server as does WSS.

In order to provide backward compatibility, SPS allows the previous version of the document libraries to be installed as a separate service. The legacy Document Store is based on the same database storage as Exchange 2000 and Exchange 2003 but features a few differences in implementation that prevent the Legacy Store from being clustered. While new implementations are unlikely to install the backward-compatible document library components, organizations upgrading from SPS 2001 might run with the legacy library until the data has been migrated fully to the new SQL-based document libraries.

As with any Enterprise portal, SPS provides features to enable Enterprise application integration, and a core part of these services is Single Sign-On, which allows Web Parts to map users' NT credentials to legacy application-authentication schemes.

Since the number of services and components has been increased, Portal Server uses the Portal Administration Service to keep all of the component settings synchronized. Being able to synchronize, for example, the service accounts and proxy settings across multiple servers in a farm eases management considerably. The Portal Administration Service is also responsible for starting and stopping services according to the configuration information stored in the database. For example, it would not make sense to run the Portal Search Service on the stateless Web servers if they have not been configured with that role.

7.4.1   **Physical architecture components**

Being built upon WSS, SPS inherits all of the platform options for building reliable and scalable server topologies. The noticeable difference between the WSS and SPS server topologies is the availability of extra services, which can be separated to run on their own server instances, as Figure 7.12 shows.

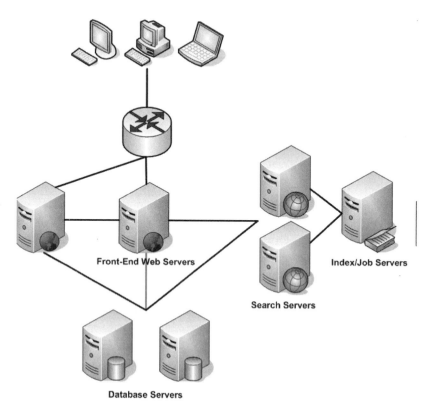

Figure 7.12
*SPS 2003 server
topology options.*

Front-End Web Servers

Index/Job Servers

Search Servers

Database Servers

One of Microsoft's design goals for Portal Server was to provide enterprise-strength search capabilities. Thus, the SPS server topology allows the search servers to be separated and load-balanced in order to provide high-availability and scale-out options. Portal Server allows up to four load-balanced search servers to be installed, which should provide enough capacity for most organizations, while allowing them to continue operations even if a server is down for maintenance.

Indexing content is highly CPU intensive, since the Index Service has to break down the document and pull the full-text content out of it for inclusion in the search database. In addition, all of the text is passed through filters to drop "noise words" such as "the" and "of," which might otherwise skew the search results due to their frequent use in the language. Since the load generated by indexing is unpredictable, Portal Server allows the Index Service to be run on its own physical server in order to eliminate the possibility of affecting the user's experience. Since no one will connect to the index servers directly, it doesn't matter if they are running at 100 percent CPU during an index update. Given that in large organizations there will be an extensive amount of content to index, Portal Server allows up to four index servers to be included in a farm.

Once an index server has compiled its indexing results, it propagates the new search index to all of the search servers in the farm. The search servers merge the new content indexes with the online copy without affecting the service to users. However, in order to facilitate an online index merger, the search servers require double the space for the index. We hope Microsoft will address this in the next product release, since incremental index propagations would significantly cut the amount of time and space required for larger search indexes.

The job server, which is typically assigned on one of the index servers, handles timed events on Portal Server, just as the SharePoint Timer Service does for WSS. The job server is in charge of portal alerts, Active Directory user-profile imports, audience calculations, and the Single Sign-On Service. The job server is the only component in an SPS farm that cannot be made redundant; thus, the mentioned services will be affected in case of software or hardware issues.

Given the number of possible Portal Server configuration combinations, Microsoft was unfortunately unable to test every one of them within the product-release schedule. Thus, Microsoft supports a number of "prescribed architectures" for SPS 2003, which have been fully tested and are therefore fully supported by Product Support Services. The Central Administration Component Assignment process has built-in logic, preventing you from configuring the servers to operate in an unsupported configuration (although the error message when you try such a configuration is not very helpful!).

As seen in Figure 7.13, although the configuration options have been somewhat restricted, they are by no means limited. Obviously, SPS supports cramming everything onto the same server, as well as a number of variations, including using a separate SQL server for storage. Even with the small farm, you could add a separate index server to the mix in order to separate the crawling to a separate server.

The minimum highly available configuration is the medium farm, which includes two load-balanced Web servers that also act as search servers, an index server that also includes the job component, and, of course, a SQL Server 2000 cluster. You might wonder why the Index Service has to be run on its own server, and this is where the restrictions I mentioned earlier come into play. Unfortunately, the Index Service cannot propagate to itself and other search servers at the same time, ruling out the possibility of

Single Server Configuration

Small farm

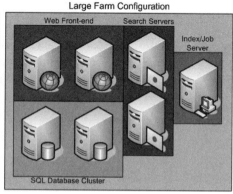

Figure 7.13   *Server topology options.*

using one of the search/Web servers as an index server as well. While running indexing on one of the Web servers would imbalance the resource requirements, an organization without a large user base and looking for high availability would have surely welcomed the option to do so.

Unfortunately, another restriction is related to the SQL servers. Microsoft allows you to either run everything on the same server (including SQL) or to run nothing but SQL on the database server. Thus, in a farm environment, you cannot have any portal components installed on the SQL back-end server. For operational purposes this makes a lot of sense, especially as SQL database administrators are often extremely wary of running any other services than SQL on their servers. By limiting the configuration options, Microsoft just might have saved the operations team from having some arguments, although, again, having the option to run, for example, the index component on a standby SQL node would have been nice.

You can extrapolate the large-farm configuration to up to 10 front-end Web servers, 4 search servers, and 4 index servers for the full scale-out capability offered by SPS 2003. While it is unlikely you would ever need to do so (as you will discover in Chapter 9), we do appreciate knowing that the option is available. In addition, Portal Server allows WSS to run on separate Web front ends, bringing the maximum farm configuration to 10 SPS Web front ends, 10 WSS Web front ends, 4 search servers, and 4 index servers. On the SQL Server side, as we noted earlier, anything goes, since Share-Point does not know or care how the services are configured.

7.5   SPS Shared Services

SPS Shared Services aim to provide centrally managed, core portal services, which can be utilized by all of the portal sites defined within a deployment (even across different portal farms). While Shared Services were originally created for enabling extensive farm configurations without the additional overhead, you can enable Shared Services on a single-server setup as well. In addition to enabling services within a server or a farm, Shared Services also allow geographically displaced farms to be integrated and to share core services, reducing duplication in a global deployment.

While we already covered the impact of Shared Services on Search in Chapter 5, several other core services are also shared between the portals, including My Sites, Alerts, Audiences, Profiles, and Single Sign-On. While it certainly makes sense to share all of these core services across portals, some business organizations might want to run autonomous portals with their own set of audiences for targeting content.

It's important to note that Shared Services can be enabled at any time, regardless of how many portal sites have already been created and what the physical server configuration looks like. However, importantly, Shared Services *cannot be turned off* once enabled. Thus, it's extremely important to know the impact before turning on the service.

Shared Services aim to consolidate resources and reduce duplication of processing—for example, the work required to index external content or import a large number of people profiles from the Active Directory. You can enable Shared Services by picking an existing portal site that is to become what's known as a parent portal. The parent portal controls all of the Shared Services and provides them for all of the child portals. You do not need to have any child portals actually created at the time you enable Shared Services, although there is no good reason to enable the Shared Services if there are no other portals present yet. Remember that once you flick the switch, the only way back is by reinstalling the software.

7.6   **Database services**

As with any product that provides capabilities beyond storing files for large numbers of users, SharePoint Products and Technologies requires the functionality of a database back end to store various properties and data. WSS supports Microsoft SQL Server 2000 SP3, as well as Microsoft SQL Server Desktop Engine 2000 for Windows (WMSDE) as its database product. Since Microsoft provides WSS free as part of Windows Server 2003, the installation kit ships with WMSDE so that the product can be provided without additional license costs.

WMSDE is essentially a cut-down version of Microsoft's enterprise-strength SQL 2000 database platform. WMSDE can be easily confused with Microsoft SQL Server Desktop Engine 2000 (MSDE), which developers can include with their products free of charge. The WMSDE version of the data engine does not include the size and scalability limits associated with the more common MSDE release. However, in order to prevent users from using this unrestricted data engine for purposes other than hosting WSS data, WMSDE will only execute scripts signed by Microsoft. Therefore, if custom applications/customizations that require a separate SQL database are planned, you must switch to SQL 2000.

To add some more confusion for us all, Microsoft decided to ship SPS 2003 with the MSDE engine instead of WMSDE. Thus, WSS instances hosted on a server installed using the SPS 2003 kit are more restricted than a WSS-only deployment. An SPS 2003 deployment with MSDE features a 2-GB database and five concurrent job restrictions, thus limiting the usefulness of this database technology even further. With only a maximum of five concurrent jobs in the execution queue, server performance hits a bottleneck much earlier than with the unlimited execution queue featured in WMSDE and SQL 2000.

WSS provides search capabilities out of the box for users to be able to find information stored within lists or libraries in their team sites. It's important to note that WSS Search is based on the MSSearch full-text technology, which is *not* included in WMSDE. WMSDE is also very limited from a manageability and operational perspective—for example, limiting your backup and restore strategies to only what WSS command-line utilities provide.

Due to these limitations with WMSDE and MSDE, most deployments outside of the lab or, perhaps, a small single-server deployment will need to move to one of the SQL 2000 versions offered by Microsoft. As with Windows, SQL 2000 ships in different "flavors" targeted at different audiences. SQL 2000 Standard is the basic version that most organizations would use for their applications, including SharePoint Products and Technologies. The SQL 2000 Enterprise and SQL 2000 Datacenter editions are targeted for large, clustered environments where high availability, standby servers, and more backup options are part of everyday life.

SharePoint Products and Technologies do not know or care which of the SQL 2000 flavors you are deploying. Microsoft leaves the decision completely up to you or your capable SQL 2000 database administrators, who might have standards based on requirements, such as expected database size. If you wish to enable Search functionality in WSS though, you must enable and configure the MSSearch Service for your SQL deployment. Some database administrators are not very keen on MSSearch, since it is a fairly old implementation that does not scale well and has in the past been particularly troublesome in a clustered environment.

Clustered SQL configurations are absolutely supported, and log shipping can be used to keep an offline standby environment ready to come online in a short time. For deployments requiring standby systems to be placed in a remote data center, in case of a disaster such as a fire occurring in the production data center, log shipping provides a means of restoring database services within minutes, rather than the hours or days it would take if offline backup media were the only means of business continuity.

7.6.1   Database communication

Both WSS and SPS use the .NET SQL Provider for connecting to the back-end database, and, as with the SQL Provider, both products support communicating over a variety of protocols and ports.

Ever since the SQL Slammer Worm, which affected numerous servers all around the Internet and company internal networks, SQL administrators prefer to set up nonstandard ports to dwarf, or at least slow down, future attacks. WSS and SPS fully support nonstandard TCP/IP ports for communication with the SQL Server, although neither product requests the information during installation. Luckily, both products use the settings defined with the SQL Client Configuration utility, as seen in Figure 7.14. You can find the tool from \Windows\System32\cliconfg.exe and configure each server to use the protocols and protocol options you prefer.

Figure 7.14
*SQL Client
Configuration
utility.*

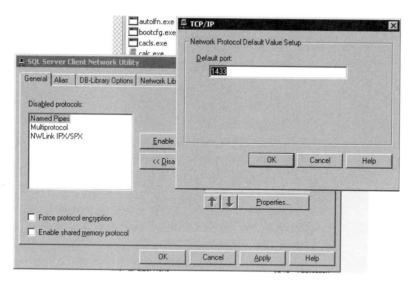

7.6.2   Database security options

SQL Server supports two access control mechanisms—SQL Authentication and Windows Authentication. SQL Authentication provides a username and password that is stored on the SQL Server. Windows Authentication, on the other hand, uses the domain user credential token provided as part of the connection against an authorization list stored on the SQL Server. Since Windows Authentication does not pass credentials over the connection, it is inherently more secure then SQL Authentication. During installation the SQL Server prompts for the Authentication Mode, although you can switch the modes later on in the Enterprise Administration Server Properties console, as shown in Figure 7.15. Although today Windows Integrated Authentication is prevalent with SQL Server 2000 installations, there are still instances where the use of the older SQL Authentication protocol might be preferred.

WSS fully supports the use of SQL Authentication, although Microsoft suggests using Windows Integrated Authentication instead due to added security benefits. However, SPS decided against implementing SQL Authentication within its data access libraries. In order to protect the communication path between the front-end Web servers and the SQL server, Microsoft supports TCP/IP encryption mechanisms such as IPSec for SQL traffic. For more information on securing SQL traffic with IPSec, please refer to the Microsoft Knowledge Base Article 276553.

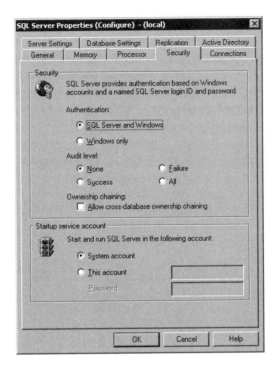

Figure 7.15
*SQL Server
authentication
options.*

Microsoft recommends that the SharePoint Products and Technologies should have at least the database creator and security administrator server roles on the SQL Server. In addition, SharePoint grants itself Database Owner (DBO) privileges on all configuration and content databases provisioned for the environment. Granting an application DBO rights is enough to make any SQL database administrator queasy, let alone allowing the service to provision databases and configure their security rights. While it is not documented, SharePoint Products and Technologies do operate in Restricted SQL Privileges Mode, although Product Support Services are not happy providing support for such an environment. We hope that Microsoft will address this gap in support policy in the future.

7.7   Security architecture

Instead of building its own security model, SharePoint Products and Technologies leverage the authentication and security services provided by the underlying Windows Server 2003, IIS 6.0, and ASP.NET architectures. Therefore, all the best practices that apply to Windows Domain Account security, IIS 6.0 configuration, and ASP.NET code access security apply to SharePoint Products and Technologies.

Since every organization has its own security policies for Domain Account lockouts and password length and expiration, we'll focus on the security aspects configurable in SharePoint Products and Technologies instead. Code access security and other ASP.NET security options relating to Web Parts are covered later in Chapter 15.

7.7.1 Authentication and authorization

SharePoint Products and Technologies rely solely on Windows Domain Authentication provided by IIS 6.0; SharePoint must be able to identify users as valid domain principals. If you are planning to use a Web Single Sign-On (SSO) product, such as Netegrity SiteMinder or HP SelectAccess, the SSO agent must be able to translate the user account into domain principals and provide the identity to IIS.

IIS out of the box supports Integrated Windows, Digest, Basic, and .NET Passport authentication, as Figure 7.16 shows. In addition, IIS has the ability to map X.509 client certificates to user accounts. SharePoint Products and Technologies support three of these authentication mechanisms: Integrated Windows, Basic, and X.509 certificate mapping. SharePoint *does not* support Digest or .NET Passport authentication at this time, although we hope this will be remedied in the future.

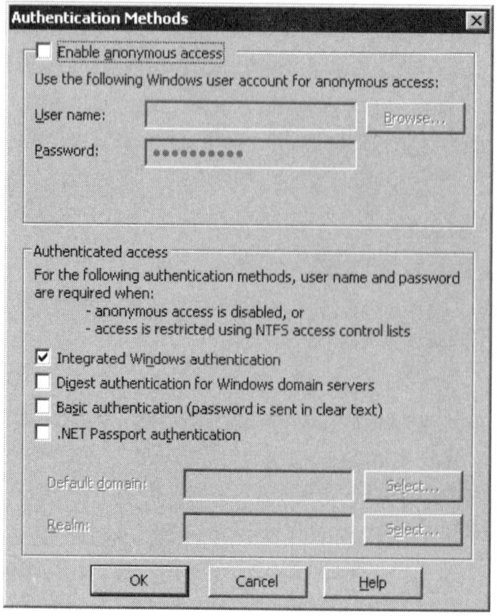

Figure 7.16
IIS authentication protocols.

SharePoint Products and Technologies compare the user credentials provided by IIS against the user identities and groups granted access to the resource the user is attempting to access in order to verify the user authorization.

WSS provides team site access via site groups, which can also be described as roles for all intended purposes. Each user can belong to one or more site groups, and the permissions are rolled up from each site group to form which actions the user is authorized to perform on the site. Each site group can contain both user principals as well as domain groups. WSS also allows lists to have unique rights, either based on site groups, individual users, or domain groups.

Since creating domain groups can be cumbersome and resource intensive without additional tools or domain privileges, WSS provides a mechanism to create domain group–like user lists, which can be used across team sites that are part of the same site collection without having to create a domain group. These lists are called cross-site groups and can be created and managed from each WSS site collection and used across the subwebs within the site collection.

SPS also authorizes users in a manner similar to WSS and uses the same concepts of site groups. In addition, the Backward Compatible Document Library features a role-based security model that is separated from the site group approach in the new SQL-based document libraries. Unlike WSS, SPS does not support the concept of cross-site groups, although you can still use cross-site groups within WSS sites created from SPS.

A difference in authorizing access to portal sites and areas is that security in portals is defined at the site and area level, while list-based authorization cannot be uniquely set, as with WSS. Microsoft thought that enabling list-based access control would likely result in confusing security control and, thus, decided to always inherit the permissions from the hosting area. It is very unfortunate that the list-based security is not supported in Portal Server, and we can only hope Microsoft will rectify this later on. By limiting the security-control possibilities, Microsoft has also limited the information-architecture consolidation options areas provide.

In addition to authenticated access, both SPS and WSS also support limited anonymous access to information resources. Since many organizations want to prevent users from being able to use anonymous access, IIS must first be configured to allow anonymous access, as Figure 7.16 shows. As anonymous is by default disabled in virtual servers extended by WSS, server administrators must consciously decide to provide the functionality.

Furthermore, turning on anonymous access in IIS will not immediately allow unauthenticated users to access WSS sites or portal areas. Each site or portal administrator must configure the WSS or portal site to allow anonymous users.

7.7.2 Data communication security options

HTTP traffic is suspect to eavesdropping, just like the traffic of any other communication protocol. While eavesdropping might not be such an issue in an intranet setup, it is still always important to take at least basic steps to secure important information, such as user credentials, from plain view. For Internet-accessible extranet setups, however, encrypting the client session is highly recommended for data integrity and protection.

The standard for the HTTP protocol includes a challenge-response mechanism that the server can use to request the client to authenticate. The Web server uses tokens to identify the supported authentication schemes for the requested resource. Tokens are embedded in the 401 (unauthorized) response headers sent to the browser. RFC 2617 states that more than one authentication scheme token can be sent to the client to allow the browser to select the most appropriate scheme. The RFC also states that the browser must use the strongest authentication scheme it supports. The browser sends back a response to the server with an authorization field containing the authentication information. The server can refuse the authorization and send back another challenge, possibly using new authentication information.

In a perfect world, there would be a standard way to authenticate securely across operating system, Web server, and browser boundaries. Unfortunately, the only widely supported cross-browser authentication mechanism is Basic Authentication, which is notoriously insecure.

Basic Authentication responds to a server challenge by sending the username and password information in a Base64-encoded string. Potential hackers can very easily capture and decode this data, and then use it to compromise accounts. Figure 7.17 shows the HTTP header and encoded authentication string ("Authorization: Basic ZG9tYWluXHVzZXJuYW1lOnBhc3N3b3Jk"), which you can decode, for example, using the tools on the `http://www.opinionatedgeek.com/dotnet/tools/Base64Decode/` Web page.

IIS 6.0 and SharePoint Products and Technologies support the secure Windows Integrated Authentication for intranet systems. Windows Integrated Authentication negotiates the actual protocol with the client, based on the server configuration and client support. Windows Integrated

Figure 7.17
*Captured Basic
Authentication
header.*

```
0x0000    00 00 0C 07 AC 0C 00 D0-59 64 41 4F 08 00 45 00    ....¬..ÐYdAO..E.
0x0010    00 8E B9 13 40 00 80 06-09 E1 10 D1 0D A8 10 D1    .Ž¹.@.€..á.Ñ.¨.Ñ
0x0020    08 2C 0C 60 00 50 1B 3B-F2 F6 81 5F A7 A0 50 18    .,.`.P.;òö□_§ P.
0x0030    44 70 BD 4D 00 00 47 45-54 20 2F 20 48 54 54 50    Dp½M..GET / HTTP
0x0040    2F 31 2E 31 0D 0A 48 6F-73 74 3A 20 63 67 73 64    /1.1..Host: cgsd
0x0050    65 76 30 31 0D 0A 41 63-63 65 70 74 3A 20 2A 2F    ev01..Accept: */
0x0060    2A 0D 0A 41 75 74 68 6F-72 69 7A 61 74 69 6F 6E    *..Authorization
0x0070    3A 20 42 61 73 69 63 20-5A 47 39 74 59 57 6C 75    : Basic ZG9tYWlu
0x0080    58 48 56 7A 5A 58 4A 75-59 57 31 6C 4F 6E 42 68    XHVzZXJuYW1lOnBh
0x0090    63 33 4E 33 62 33 4A 6B-0D 0A 0D 0A                c3N3b3Jk....
```

Authentication is sometimes also referred to as Negotiate Authentication, given challenge-response phase before the authentication protocol is agreed upon. The two protocols include Kerberos Authentication, which was first introduced with Windows 2000, and the older NTLM authentication protocol.

With Kerberos Authentication, clients obtain tickets from the Active Directory Kerberos Key Distribution Center (KDC), which they then pass to IIS to gain authorization. NTLM authentication, which is also referred to as Windows NT Challenge-Response Authentication, uses an algorithm to generate a one-way hash of the user's password. The client sends the hash to the server as the response to the authentication request.

In order to provide a straightforward installation on Web farm configurations, WSS and SPS turn off Kerberos Authentication by default. In order to reenable Kerberos Authentication, you must manually configure all of the Web servers to accept the Kerberos protocol again, which we will cover in Chapter 10.

Unfortunately, both NTLM and the Windows Server 2003 implementation of Kerberos Authentication are notoriously specific to Microsoft browsers, although lately Mozilla Foundation (www.mozilla.org) has included a cross-platform support for NTLM authentication on their Mozilla and Firefox browsers. Since older browsers and other browser families do not yet uniformly support Microsoft's NTLM, Basic Authentication is still the only out-of-the-box solution to connect most non-Microsoft browsers to Web sites hosted by IIS.

In order to heighten the security of Basic Authentication and the data communication, you must enable SSL encryption for the virtual server. SSL secures all information sent between the browser and the server with strong certificate-based encryption and host authentication. (See Figure 7.18.)

Unfortunately, performance suffers when you enable SSL encryption, since the server must authenticate SSL sessions, encrypt information before sending it to the client, and then decrypt the data before passing it on to the

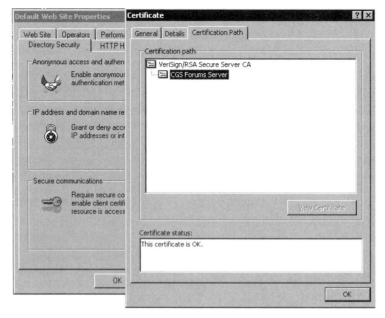

Web application. Hardware solutions that offload the server exist, but these are often expensive.

Browsers always send Basic Authentication information as part of the authorization challenge, regardless of the browser type and access method,

Figure 7.19
*Forcing SSL
encryption for all
clients.*

which opens up a security risk because non-IE users can enter the site through unsecured `http://` URLs. Potentially, IE users can also authorize with Basic Authentication if NTLM or Kerberos fails for any reason. For example, most proxy servers do not support Windows Integrated Authentication, forcing IE to fall back on Basic Authentication.

Fortunately, you can enforce SSL per virtual host or virtual directory, shown in Figure 7.19, but this will cause additional server load, since the server will have to process each query with added authorization, encryption, and decryption of the information.

8

Planning SharePoint Features

As you have undoubtedly come to realize by this stage of the book, Share-Point Products and Technologies provide a rich and extensible framework for collaboration. The rich feature set and scalable architecture provide endless options for all manner of implementation scenarios across an enterprise. Whether you're planning to deploy WSS or SPS 2003, thoroughly planning the solution and its architecture is the key to a successful implementation for your particular business requirements. Before server hardware is ordered, a well-thought-out architecture plan ensures a smooth implementation, and planning the features that will be utilized from the framework ensures that you will hit the ground running after deployment.

In this chapter, we will take a brief look at the core server products you may want to integrate with your deployment and then focus on planning the features you can enable for SharePoint Products and Technologies. Finally, this chapter sets the scene for Chapter 9.

8.1   Getting to know the requirements

Before even thinking about SharePoint configuration or hardware specifications, you should spend time understanding the usage scenario thoroughly. What is the environment going to be used for, and how is it going to be used? These seem simple enough questions to ask, right? But, often as not, the answers are not well thought out in advance of any deployment!

When buying a second car for your drive to the office every morning, you might decide on that sporty two-seater. However, after discussing it over with your partner and realizing that the car also needs to be used for weekend drives to the countryside with the family, your shiny new two-seater has less chance of ever pulling into the driveway. What you planned to use the car for was affected by how the family expected it to be used, thus tipping the scales on your choice to go for that comfortable people carrier instead.

The same rules apply to a SharePoint deployment. Thus, although the environment might primarily be designed for use as an enterprise search portal, end users, after discovering the collaborative features of WSS, might mainly use the environment for team collaboration. We learned this lesson in the HP Services Knowledge Management Team early on when we simply "turned on" SharePoint Team Services (the previous version of WSS), thinking no one would really use it. You can imagine our surprise one year later when we discovered that country business units depended on the service being available 24/7, with estimated downtime costs of $100,000 per hour for the business.

Spend time finding out the answers to what and how by talking not only to the deployment champions and the company management but also to the future end users. Often, you will find end-user expectations to be quite different from management's vision. Managing end-user expectations and balancing them with management's priorities will help adoption and user acceptance once the system goes into production. Talking to users is especially important if you are planning to migrate from an existing legacy system, since users often have novel ideas about how to apply the technology to their particular business problems.

8.2   Solving your deployment jigsaw puzzle—which core server products might you need?

There is a suite of tools and products available from Microsoft to address the collaboration needs of an organization. By integrating these products, compelling end-to-end solutions can be created to reduce manual work and increase information-worker productivity. Now, while the out-of-the-box integrations between the various products may not be complete enough today to solve all your needs, Microsoft does seem to be heading in the right direction, and we can expect to see tighter integrations with future product releases that build upon the core technologies provided today.

8.2.1   WSS or SPS 2003?

Perhaps one of the most burning questions for anyone planning to implement SharePoint Products and Technologies is which one of the two products to choose. When does WSS provide the functionality required, and when do the business requirements justify choosing SPS?

A concise description of these products is that WSS enables teams to collaborate on team-specific information, while SPS enables publishing and discovery of relevant information to a wider audience. The best advice is to consider WSS as the baseline collaborative framework for an organization and SPS as the glue that brings personal information, team-collaboration, and divisional information sites together with enterprise-strength search capabilities. WSS is an extendable and scalable platform, as proven by the fact that SPS builds on top of technology provided by WSS. However, even if you are just looking for team-collaboration capability for an organization, you should consider deploying SPS to host the team sites for the following major reasons.

- On top of the base collaborative environment, SPS enables abilities beyond team collaboration, such as People Directory, Enterprise Search, and Team Site Directory, thus acting as the collaboration aggregation point within an enterprise. The SPS Site Directory enables organizations to collect more information about the team sites, which might otherwise become information silos that are only visible to, used by, and accessible to people who know about them. From the end user's point of view, one of the most compelling reasons to use SPS is the comprehensive search capability, which enables users to search across team sites while still honoring the security settings for each site.

- SPS creates an end-to-end model for collaboration and personal-information storage by allowing users to create My Sites, personal Web sites that individuals can tailor to their own liking. My Sites also offer a public view, which lists people information, such as the telephone number, address, and organizational structure, as well as any other publicly available fields the portal administrator has added. The public view to My Site also shows files or lists that the owner has made available to others and a list of recently published items by the user.

- WSS information-architecture options are limited, since it has been tailored for small and ad hoc team collaboration where taxonomy considerations do not usually come into play. For example, out of the box with WSS you cannot build a comprehensive category structure with a consistent navigation pane that spans all team sites without getting into FrontPage 2003 customizations. For information repositories targeted for thousands of users, taxonomy and information architecture play a big part in users' ability to discover relevant information easily. SPS organizes information through a nested area structure to allow information to be categorized according to subject matter. WSS document libraries allow portal area listings to be created within the parent SPS portal via a File/Edit shortcut, thus allowing team sites to publish their material in a common taxonomy. (Unfortunately, the link between WSS items and SPS listings is not automatically kept up-to-date, leading to broken links due to files being deleted or renamed in WSS. Microsoft is said to be working on resource kit tools to identify broken listings, but for the time being, the usefulness of this feature is severely restricted if the underlying team-site information is changed regularly!)

- In a large corporation with disparate knowledge systems, the only way to provide a cohesive front end to knowledge workers is through an enterprise search facility, which brings all the knowledge silos together into a single discoverable index. SPS includes a robust Indexing Service and Search Service, designed to meet the needs of a global enterprise. Arguably, Enterprise Search is the most compelling reason to choose SPS over WSS.

In the end, cost is an inevitable consideration, and since WSS comes free of charge as an optional download for Windows Server 2003, choosing between the two products can be challenging, since SPS requires both a server as well as client-access licenses.

8.2.2 Microsoft Content Management Server 2002

Microsoft Content Management Server 2002 (MCMS) is Microsoft's Enterprise Web-content management offering, which aims to increase Web content publishers' productivity by separating the HTML and script coding from the content that is delivered to site users. This allows Web developers to focus on other challenges rather than creating static Web pages. MCMS dynamically creates the Web pages for end users by combining content objects stored in SQL Server databases with templates to come up with the final page delivered to the user's browser. In short, MCMS is for building and managing Web sites, with an ability to scale incredibly well beyond millions of Web site users.

You can use MCMS to publish content both internally within an enterprise as well as externally to partners and customers. Since the content is dynamically created for every user, MCMS has an ability to swap templates based on the user's browser client or operating system. Being able to facilitate multiple form factors, be it a Pocket PC or a TV set-top box, is especially important for Internet-facing portals.

Branding and publishing approval are important when publishing content on the Internet. MCMS can make sure all of the Web pages have a common look and feel and enforce an editorial process to ensure that only the right content is being made available to the Web site users. In order to facilitate content approvals, MCSM offers capabilities to manage content publishing with a multistep role-based workflow process, which can be tailored to suit business needs. Figure 8.1 displays the Microsoft XBOX Web site, which is managed by MCMS and showcases the adaptability and power of the dynamic templates for multiple browser technologies and languages.

There are two very obvious connect points with MCMS and SharePoint Products and Technologies. First, since WSS is geared for collaborative doc-

Figure 8.1   *MCMS-managed Web site utilizing dynamic templates.*

ument creation within a team, you typically need a place to publish files once they are complete. For an externally facing business, being able to publish content, such as technical papers or product descriptions, directly from a WSS team site to an MCMS content workflow system makes a lot of sense and saves manual steps, thus boosting productivity.

Second, since MCMS does not come with search features, SPS offers obvious benefits to an MCMS deployment through its enterprise-strength search capabilities. Because MCMS pages end up as HTML content after they are dynamically compiled, the SPS indexing engine can be set up to crawl the MCMS environment with very little effort. By exposing the Search Service as a Web Service, Microsoft also allows third parties to integrate the SPS search-query and result-handling capabilities into their products. A good example of this is the MCMS integration pack, which provides a set of ready-made components that call the SPS Search Service remotely and render the results within the MCMS-generated pages. The MCMS and SPS Integration Pack is downloadable from Microsoft and also features a number of Web Parts that can be used in situations such as a divisional SPS portal managing content stored in an MCMS system.

MCMS is part of the Microsoft.NET server family and features an extensive object model enabling easy customization and extendibility. By combining the collaboration features of SharePoint Technologies with strong Web-content publishing capabilities, you can create innovative content-management solutions. By adding SPS Search to the mix, you also ensure that users are able to find what they're looking for on the managed Web site.

MCMS has the makings of a great product for both internal and external Web site management; it is, therefore, surprising to note that the underlying product technology is totally different from the now apparent Microsoft go-forward strategy for portals and collaboration. The Microsoft story is that since MCMS was on a different product release cycle, it wasn't possible to synchronize it with the new Windows 2003 Web Part Framework delivered by WSS. It is unfortunate that the integration packs are all that exist to tie these two very different technologies together today, since the possibilities would have been endless. Microsoft has assured us that this gap will be bridged with the next release cycle of both products, finally combining the two portal-technology frameworks. However, today we're left with the add-on packs and software development kits for custom integration.

8.2.3   **Microsoft Office Project Server 2003**

As everyone who has been involved in a large project at one time or another can testify, any project needs proper planning and project management to be successful. Since most project managers are overseeing completion of more than one project at any given time, they need tools to manage timelines, tasks, resources, and deliverables effectively. Microsoft Office Project 2003 is an extensive product for project managers to maintain an end-to-end view on timelines, resources, and deliverables with dependencies that automatically adjust schedules if any given task goes over the time allocated for completion.

However, a project plan stored on the project manager's personal hard disk is not much use to the rest of the project members or the project sponsors. Thus, in most organizations the need to implement a server-based, collaborative project environment surfaces, and Microsoft Office Project Server 2003 is a natural option, given that it was built to do exactly that. Project Server allows organizations to standardize the way projects are delivered, utilize central resources, and provide high-level reporting on all projects under way and resources being utilized.

In any project, the team members must collaborate to achieve a common goal; thus, it is only natural that Project Server 2003 integrates heavily with WSS. Although Project Server is a centralized repository in its own right, integrating with WSS gives users features such as Issue and Risks lists and document libraries, which enable a whole new level of functionality for the Project Server Web-access server. Project Server can be set to automatically provision WSS sites for each new project created, thus reducing the manual steps required and standardizing the way WSS spaces are created for projects.

Project Server communicates with the WSS service via XMLHTTP to fetch data from lists and document libraries for rendering within the Project Server Web-access server. An administrative URL protocol provided by WSS is used for routine site administrative tasks from within Project Server, and, finally, a synchronization protocol called Object Link Provider (OLP) is used to keep Project Server in sync with the changes made in WSS. Since Project Server features an object model, you can achieve more extensive integration through customization.

8.2.4   Microsoft BizTalk Server 2004

BizTalk Server 2004 is the latest release of Microsoft's business-process integration product, which enables applications to communicate in a standards-based, cohesive manner while ensuring message delivery and integrity. In today's increasingly service-oriented architecture, where no application is an island, it's hard to find an IT consultant who has not at least heard about BizTalk. BizTalk Server 2004 can be described as a significant upgrade and introduces a host of new services, including Human Workflow Services, Business Activity Services (BAS), and Business Activity Monitoring (BAM).

Since BizTalk is an application-integration product, the integration (no pun intended) points with SharePoint Products and Technologies are endless. WSS and SPS both provide virtually everything over Simple Object Access Protocol (SOAP) Web Services, thus providing endpoints for virtually any operation to and from BizTalk.

Out of the box, BizTalk integrates with WSS via the new BAS and BAM features. In fact, BAS is a new WSS site definition you can install on a WSS server, thus providing users with an option to create a BAS Web site when provisioning a new site, which you can then register with a BizTalk server. BAS allows you to effectively manage and monitor partner relationships and associated data from a WSS site and create BAS-enabled orchestrations, which provide e-mail-server-like communication channels with partners within WSS. BAM, on the other hand, provides a business-process tracking framework with analytical services that provide real-time data views from any content source, including WSS sites, for business users to react to.

BizTalk integrates with different applications through BizTalk Adapters, which provide a communication layer with the native language of the remote application. Provided as an add-on download, the BizTalk 2004 Adapter for SharePoint Libraries allows BizTalk to send and receive messages from SharePoint document libraries. The Document Library Adapter allows BizTalk developers to create orchestrations that can integrate directly with WSS or SPS libraries—for example, for business-process workflow purposes.

SPS has always been a natural choice for Enterprise Application Integration (EAI), given the extensive dashboard platform delivered by Web Parts. In SPS 2003, Microsoft introduces a number of specific EAI enhancements, including out-of-the-box integration with Microsoft BizTalk Server for Web Part SSO services, which can be passed the SSO credentials for data adapters—for example, when connecting to payroll information stored within a SAP database. By utilizing BizTalk as the integration framework instead of directly fetching data from a remote system, you can take advantage of the hundreds of existing adapters already in existence today instead of creating the code yourself. BizTalk processes can also be configured to format information they are routing according to the destination, thus reducing the effort involved to create Web Parts to integrate with third-party systems. For example, the same pay-slip Web Part could be used against both SAP and custom SQL payroll applications, as long as the messaging format is common and converted according to the end application in the integration layer BizTalk provides.

8.2.5   Live Communications Server 2003

Live Communications Server (LCS) delivers an extensible, real-time communication platform and a standards-based, enterprise-ready Instant Messaging (IM) solution. It provides presence information that integrates into Microsoft Office and SharePoint Products and Technologies, allowing users to see immediately who is available to collaborate and communicate with, as shown in Figure 8.2. The IM service is delivered to the end user using Windows Messenger V5.0 and includes logging, multiparty messaging, message archiving, file transfer, audio and video conferencing, and application sharing. LCS also features a rich API for custom integration and application development, and I would not be surprised if Web Parts specifically targeted for LCS/SharePoint integration around real-time collaboration were to appear from Microsoft in the form of an integration pack or resource kit downloads.

Note that the ability to integrate presence information into SharePoint does not actually require LCS as the IM server. Rather, it requires an integration with the running version of the Windows Messenger or MSN Messenger client, and this integration is provided by Office 2003. Thus, you can, for example, integrate presence information into SharePoint even if you are just using the commercial MSN Messenger.

Type	Name	Modified	Modified By	Checked Out To
	New Document	Upload Document	Up	New Folder	Filter	Edit in Datasheet			
	Ch 1 - From whence we came	3/5/2004 7:36 PM	McKenna, Emer	
	Ch 1 - From whence we came_vv quick comments	3/3/2004 12:18 AM	Vanamo, Veli-Matti	
	CH 16 - Customizing SharePoint using FrontPage 2003	5/17/2004 3:26 PM	ahs, Kevin	
	Ch 2 - Windows SharePoint Services	4/5/2004 10:46 AM	Kevin Laahs (Vacation) is Not Online	
	Ch 3 - Office Integration	5/7/2004 2:55 PM	Laahs, Kevin	

Figure 8.2   *Presence information from LCS can be integrated with SharePoint sites and libraries.*

8.3   Choosing the right account mode for WSS

WSS integrates with an existing NT or Active Directory domain infrastructure, or it can work in Active Directory Account Creation Mode. Active Directory Account Creation Mode is mainly targeted for application or Internet service providers, although it also has its merits when considering an extranet deployment. When configured with Account Creation Mode, WSS will automatically create new accounts for users invited to participate in a team site if they have not been issued with an account beforehand in a predefined Active Directory organizational unit (OU).

Choosing either normal domain authentication or Account Creation Mode is a one-time operation for a deployment; you cannot reverse it without uninstalling and reinstalling WSS, since these settings are written to the configuration database. It is, therefore, extremely important to plan ahead and choose the right account mode for your deployment. In most cases, it's safe to say you will always want to choose the default domain account mode, which uses existing accounts from trusted domains and does not allow WSS to provision new accounts.

If you do not have an NT domain or Active Directory infrastructure deployed within your organization, Account Creation Mode may provide an interesting alternative to account management. In typical enterprises, a number of people resources are dedicated for user account support. Allowing WSS site administrators to manage accounts and reset passwords for their site users reduces the administrative burden required from the IT organization and allows them to direct resources at more interesting tasks.

However, from a risk-management perspective, allowing any business user to create as many accounts as he or she wishes may be an unacceptable legal and information-security risk, especially when deploying an extranet environment. In an intranet deployment, users need first to have physical access to the network, which in itself provides a layer of security, whereas in an extranet setup that physical perimeter does not exist. Therefore, when considering the Account Creation Mode for your deployment, you should first check with the legal and information-security representatives for existing guidelines for user account creation and management within your organization.

8.4   Performing site-usage analysis

Being able to identify how a team site is being used is not only important for system administrators, but it also provides an invaluable tool for business users managing the team site and provides critical usage data for business sponsors paying for the up-front and ongoing deployment costs of the SharePoint environment. Administrators need the usage data to plan proactively for scaling up the deployment infrastructure for future growth and to better understand the user patterns.

Administrators can, for example, track usage growth over a long period and plot it against performance counters, thus allowing for more accurate predictions of how the infrastructure needs to be grown in six months' time. This leaves plenty of time to seek the necessary approvals and, perhaps more importantly, to justify expenses. In a regionally distributed organization, administrators can track usage from different parts of the enterprise and make informed decisions on server placement or perform proactive network upgrades based on a region's usage patterns. Some administrators might also find usage figures useful for identifying information that is no longer being consumed and therefore eligible for archiving.

Team-site administrators and owners find usage data useful as an indication of whether their target audiences find the material they provide useful and whether all the effort associated with managing and contributing content is valuable. Without usage data, administrators have to rely on those few who comment rather than being able to view information consumption across the board. Site administrators can also make informed decisions when cleaning up old data and make sure they are not deleting content that the users still find useful.

All solutions have an ongoing support cost, and if future investments are planned, business management bearing the costs often needs information on how the solution is being used. I'm sure any manager, having decided to invest in a brand new SharePoint environment, would feel much more at ease if he or she were handed monthly usage adoption reports that demonstrated to the company management how the new collaboration capabilities were being used within the enterprise. If the reports showed slow adoption rates, appropriate communication plans could be put together to reinforce the need to collaborate and share data within the organization.

To address the basic requirements, WSS comes with a usage-analysis feature, which allows team-site administrators to generate reports for daily and weekly site usage. System administrators can create scripts that use the object model to gather data from all team sites and generate serverwide reports. It's unfortunate that Microsoft did not include serverwide usage statistics to be viewed out of the box, but I expect there will be many free community tools to bridge the gap.

When enabled, the WSS ISAPI filter writes a text log file of important user actions on each of the front-end servers. The log directory can be configured to reside on any drive you wish, although even in a large deployment, the log files don't grow very large. The ASCII text log file on its own means very little, as you can see from Figure 8.3; therefore, WSS must schedule a log-analysis process that inserts the key analyzed-log results into the site content database once per day.

Site-usage analysis is not enabled by default, and since usage information is only available from the time you first turn it on, it is important to plan in advance if this is something you want to provide to the users. The impact of turning on usage analysis is minimal, although in a large enterprise deployment you should consider timing the log analysis to occur dur-

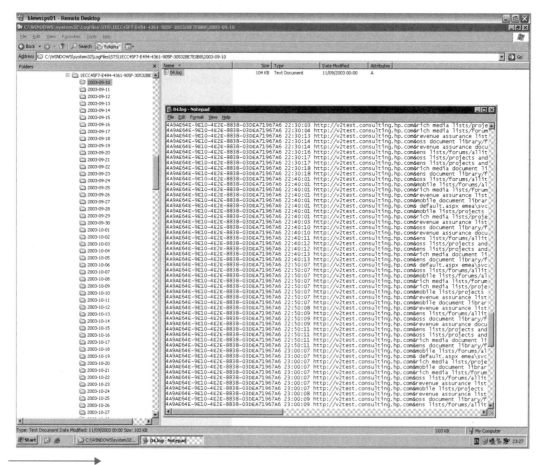

Figure 8.3   *WSS log files on their own have very little value without analyzing tools.*

ing off-peak hours. WSS stores the monthly usage data for 31 months, while daily usage details are kept for 31 days.

Site-usage data is stored as a binary column in the Webs SQL table, as shown in Figure 8.4, but since an object model interface to this information is provided, there should be no need to go directly to the SQL database. Although the data is stored in the database, it has little impact when sizing your database servers. For example, in a real-world deployment, after 12 months in production with over 5,500 team sites, the average size of a monthly data column was 7.7 KB, while daily data columns averaged at 4.2 KB. Although the largest monthly column was a sizable 1 MB, the overall size taken by the usage data was only 33 MB for monthly usage and 18 MB for daily usage. By taking the 100 most active sites in our example deployment, the average monthly and daily column sizes rose to 139 KB and 56 KB, respectively.

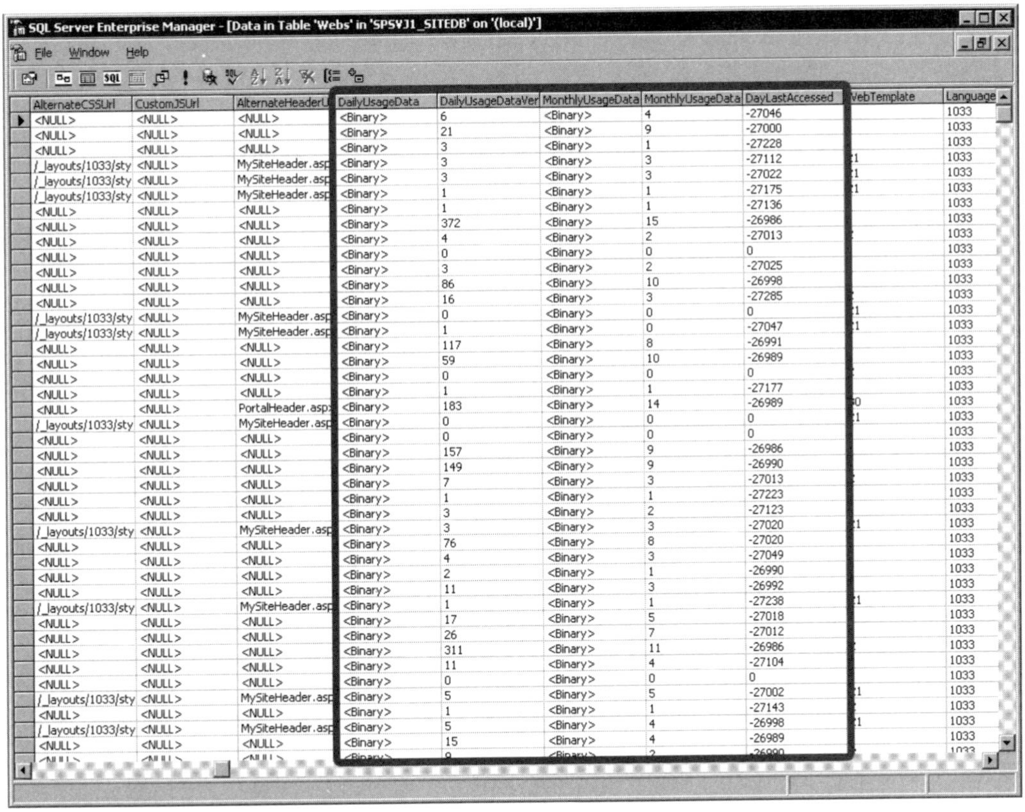

Figure 8.4   *WSS stores daily and monthly usage data in the SQL database as binary columns.*

8.5   Retiring old sites with site-collection use confirmations

As we discussed in Chapter 2, WSS aims to empower users to create and manage their own team Web sites without requiring help or intervention from IT support. However, the self-service nature of WSS often leads to site owners forgetting to delete the team site after it has served its purpose. Luckily, for this very reason, WSS comes with a site-usage confirmation option, which polls site owners after a predetermined time to see if they still require the site.

Shown in Figure 8.5, site-collection use confirmation and auto-deletion can be enabled to send e-mail notifications after a configurable period after the site was first created or last confirmed to be still in use. Use-confirmation settings are virtual-server specific, thus allowing different policies to be

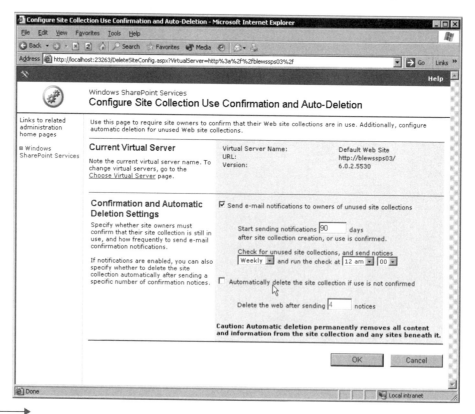

Figure 8.5   *WSS site-use and automatic-deletion settings can be configured for each virtual server.*

Table 8.1   *Notification Frequency Also Affects the Automatic Site Deletion Feature*

Notification Frequency	Minimum Notices Allowed	Site Deleted After ...
Daily	28	30 days with 29 e-mails sent
Weekly	4	6 weeks with 5 e-mails sent
Monthly	2	4 months with 3 e-mails sent

applied for multiple virtual servers. Notices can be configured to be sent daily, weekly, or monthly to the primary and secondary site owners.

If frequent e-mail reminders are not enough, site-collection use confirmation can be configured to automatically delete the site collection and all subwebs beneath it. The period after which the site collection is deleted depends on the use-confirmation frequency and the number of notices the site owner is given before auto-deletion, thus allowing organizations to create flexible policies for site deletion. For example, if the default notification period of 90 days is used, with unused sites checked weekly and deletion set to occur after four notices, the service will send the site owners an e-mail for five weeks in a row; finally, on the sixth week, the site will be deleted. In order to reduce the possibility of the owner's being on a long vacation, minimum notice periods are enforced for each of the notice frequency options, as listed in Table 8.1.

Unfortunately, since the use confirmation does not base notifications on actual usage data, many active team-site owners are asked to confirm that the site is still being used. It might seem like a trivial task to confirm that a site is used, for example, every 90 days; however, because the confirmations are sent per site collection rather than per owner, users who have created a number of team sites will find themselves bombarded by a regular e-mail storm. It's not uncommon to see site administrators receive tens, if not hundreds, of use-confirmation e-mails such as the one shown in Figure 8.6, and clicking through each site confirmation link individually will undoubtedly frustrate end users. Thus, you should weigh the benefits with the added site owner administrative tasks and headache when deciding on a notification frequency for your organization.

It appears that under certain circumstances the use-confirmation e-mails can be interpreted by Microsoft Outlook 2003 as junk mail and filtered to another folder or even deleted on receipt (see Figure 8.7). Therefore, you should use an e-mail address that your Outlook 2003 deployment considers a safe sender or plan to include the e-mail address in the user's safe senders

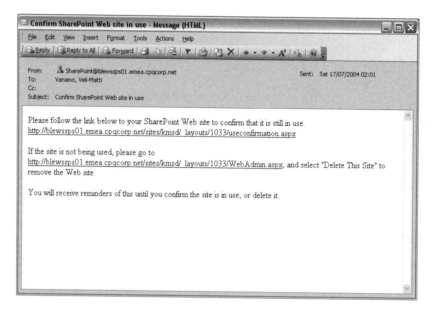

list. Hopefully, Microsoft will address these issues in a service pack or a future release, but for now we'll discuss in Chapter 11 some alternative methods to clean up sites no longer being used.

Although enabling auto-deletion might at first sound like a good idea, its downfall is its reliance on the correctness of the site owner's e-mail data

when the site collection was first created. Since the e-mail field is not validated in any way when the site collection is created via the self-service option, there is a margin for error. To alleviate the possibility of mistyping, you can set the self-site creation to enforce entry of a secondary owner. However, in longer-running team sites the people involved inevitably change, and unfortunately it is not apparent to the site administrators who the site owner actually is, which increases the likelihood of incorrect ownership data being used for use confirmations. Site-collection auto-deletion is still an important feature, and as long as backup and restore plans allow a single site collection to be restored, it is worth considering.

Even with the shortcomings, site-collection use confirmation and auto-deletion are very good tools to free up resources. By planning upfront for this feature and including it in user training, you can lower the risk of sites having incorrect ownership information. By requiring secondary owners to be entered from the start, the chance of both administrators being away for over 28 days at the same time is minimal. By planning backup and restore processes so that a site deleted by auto-deletion can still be restored afterward, the risk of critical data loss suddenly becomes very small; thus, out-of-the-box functionality can be turned on as another successful feature of your SharePoint deployment.

8.6   Setting site quota limits

As file sizes are getting larger and larger, the storage requirements of collaborative spaces are also rocketing skyward. Anyone involved in trying to restrict File Share or Exchange Public Folder growth is no doubt painfully aware that most users treat these central resources as personal filing cabinets for a myriad of files, some dating back more than six or seven years. Digital audio and video files certainly occupy a fair amount of space, but still, in most of the cases I've been involved with, the largest piece of the hard disk pie is still taken over by Microsoft Office files. Nowadays, it's not uncommon to see 6- or 7-MB Microsoft PowerPoint presentations, and Microsoft Word file sizes also seem to be 3 or 4 MB and upward, largely due to embedded image content. At the same time, the size of personal computer hard disks has multiplied to keep pace, and the data center has seen the introduction of Storage Area Network (SAN) devices, which provide shared disk space on demand for servers at more cost-effective prices. However, it's good to look at past lessons learned and take steps to ensure that adding disk space is not the only answer to the growing storage problem.

WSS introduces a proactive method of restricting storage growth beyond the boundaries of designed architecture in the form of site-collection quota limits. As we discussed earlier in the chapter, site-collection use confirmations can ensure that old information doesn't use valuable resources other active spaces could benefit from, but it is still very important to restrict the few eager adopters from using an unfair chunk of the resources for their spaces.

Personally, I always recommend setting the quota limits to as small as possible while taking into account the usage scenario. I know this is a somewhat strange recommendation coming from an employee of a company that manufactures a large array (no pun intended) of storage solutions to fit any need under the sun. Nevertheless, quota limits of just 150 MB for team sites and 100 MB for My Sites have been well received by users in many large enterprises after some initial rumblings from both the user and management sides of the table. It might be surprising to note that in the 5,500 team-site production deployment mentioned earlier, the average size of a team space is just over 50 MB, although the largest site collection is over 9 GB in size.

Each site quota template defines the storage limit of the site collection it is applied to and the threshold for sending a storage-level warning e-mail message to site owners, as seen in Figure 8.8. WSS allows you to create as many quota templates as you like and to define different default quota templates for each virtual server. Common practice is to define a larger quota for "premium users," for example, company executives, while leaving a more restricted, generic quota in place. System administrators can

Figure 8.8
E-mail warnings are sent to site owners when the set quota-limit warning threshold is reached.

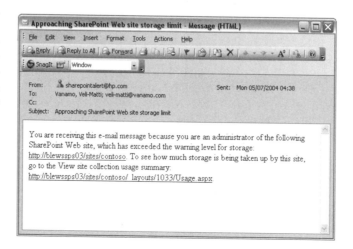

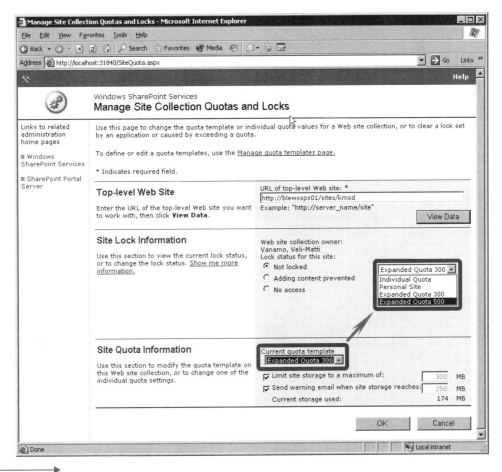

Figure 8.9   *Quota templates can be changed for each site if a higher storage limit is required.*

change the active quota template on a site afterward, thus allowing users with genuine business requirements to request higher quota limits, as shown in Figure 8.9.

It's said that history keeps repeating itself, but hopefully enough of us have been burned by unrestricted storage space offerings in the past to find ourselves caught up once again in storage growth issues.

8.7   **Considering SPS Shared Services**

Although we covered Shared Services in Chapter 7, I must stress how important it is to consider this feature carefully before turning it on. As

I've stated before, the only way to turn off Shared Services is to uninstall and reinstall SPS or to restore from a backup made before turning on the feature.

To refresh on the main points: When enabled, Shared Services hosts key functions for all child portals from a single parent portal in order to reduce service duplication. Shared Services enables you to create portals that have a lower resource cost, thus allowing substantially more portal spaces to be hosted on the same hardware. Shared Services provided from the parent portal are Search and Indexing, My Site and Alerts, Audience Targeting, People Profiles, and Single Sign-on. Due to limitations with the number of portal search catalogs SPS supports, without Shared Services you can only host a maximum of 15 SPS portal sites per farm. In a Shared Services–enabled deployment, this jumps to 100, since the search catalogs are hosted on a single portal site and shared by all the child-portal sites.

Therefore, perhaps the most important question to ask yourself when considering enabling Shared Services is whether you are going to create multiple portals right away. If the answer is no, you can proceed without worrying about Shared Services and plan to come back to the topic when the business requirements demand that a second portal be created. Remember that Shared Services can be enabled at any point, even when multiple portals exist, but it can never be turned off once enabled.

For most organizations planning an enterprise SPS deployment, the answer, no doubt, is yes. For example, by creating multiple portals in a Shared Services deployment, each business unit can maintain its own identity and data ownership while still being tied to a corporate parent portal for cross-business services, such as People Profiles, My Sites, and Search. However, since in a Shared Services environment the child portals cannot create or manage search indexes and audiences, you must plan to deal with the operational limitations of search management on child portals. It's likely that the child-portal owners have expectations as to which search content sources they want to include when users search for information on their portal. Luckily, Shared Services allows child portals to define their own search scopes, thus enabling portal owners to narrow down the information resources. From an IT-management perspective though, every time a child-portal owner wishes to add a new content source to be crawled, it must be added on the parent portal—thus, likely requiring action by the system administrator.

We'll cover search and audience planning in more detail later on in this chapter.

8.8   Using SPS user profiles

As we've mentioned before, people in SPS 2003 are "first-class objects," and SPS aims to ensure that your intellectual property, held within your documents and lists, is fully exploited by connecting it to people.

User profile fields are fully customizable, allowing you to define exactly which data you wish to store as part of a user profile. Each field definition allows you to define whether the field should be hidden from users or displayed on users' My Site information pages and whether or not users are able to edit the field values. You can import existing user information from Active Directory and map Active Directory fields to User Profile fields, in case your organization has, for example, extended the schema. Realizing that in many organizations Active Directory might not be the people directory of choice, the profile administration object model allows custom tools to be developed to synchronize people profiles from other sources, such as an LDAP directory or a custom database.

When planning, you should first get clarity as to which profile fields your organization wants to collect and which ones should be visible to everybody via the public view of My Sites (see Figure 8.10). You can also define fields that the users can edit themselves, although they will not be synchronized back to the Active Directory unless you create a custom write-back synchronization tool. If possible, you should consult your organization's privacy officer to verify that data-protection regulations are adhered to with respect to the personal data that is stored in the user profiles. Since regulations differ drastically from country to country, data-protection considerations are especially important when planning a global deployment. Once all the stakeholders agree on the data fields to be stored, you should map where, if anywhere, the information should be synchronized from, while keeping in mind that synchronization will always override user-editable fields.

If you plan to synchronize information from either Active Directory or a custom source, you should plan in advance the schedule and method of updating. The built-in Active Directory import supports both full and incremental updates, allowing you, for example, to schedule incremental updates during weekdays in order to cut down on both the time it takes to synchronize and the load placed on the system. It still makes sense to schedule periodic, full updates to catch items that the incremental crawl may have missed for one reason or another. A good approach is to schedule weekly, or even monthly, full updates with a daily incremental update to guarantee an up-to-date people directory.

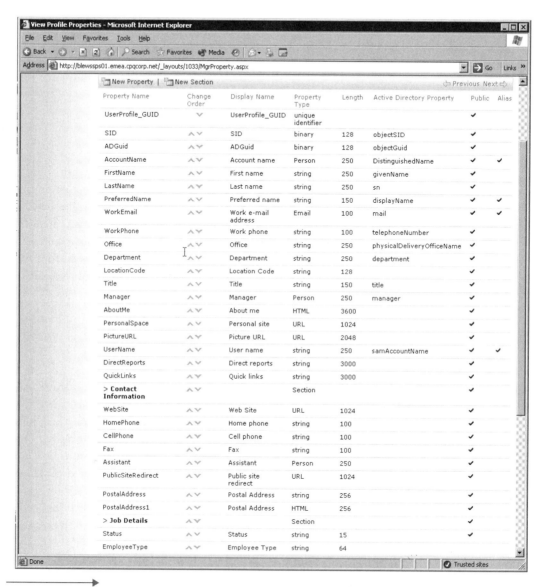

Figure 8.10   *An extensive list of profile fields can be created and organized by sections for grouped display in the My Site public view.*

With custom directory synchronization, incremental updates might not be possible if the source directories do not support retrieving modifications based on a time stamp. Also, it's not uncommon for people information to be stored in disparate systems around the enterprise; thus, a single source for updates may not be available. There are third-party metadirectory synchronization solutions that provide a middle layer and thus allow incremental updates regardless of the data source. These third-party solutions typically support exporting to a definable XML format, thereby allowing more freedom when creating a custom profile importer using the object model.

8.9   Planning SPS search architecture

In large corporations with disparate knowledge systems, the only way to present a cohesive front end to the knowledge workers is through an enterprise search facility, which integrates all the knowledge silos into a single discoverable index. Microsoft SPS 2003 provides an extensive search framework to allow enterprises to break down knowledge silos and facilitate effective knowledge reuse within the corporation. However, without effective planning, an enterprise search portal can quickly become unusable, as aging and uninteresting content is included in the search results. It is extremely important to prevent information avalanches and to carefully plan the content sources to include in the search catalogs. With selective use of search scopes, organizations can drive user behavior to be more exclusive when searching for content, thus returning more relevant search results.

The SPS is based on the MSSearch architecture, which we explained in Chapter 6 and will quickly recap here. From a systems architecture perspective, the SPS Search components can be condensed to the high-level diagram shown in Figure 8.11. Users execute searches from the portal interface

Figure 8.11
High-level search architecture.

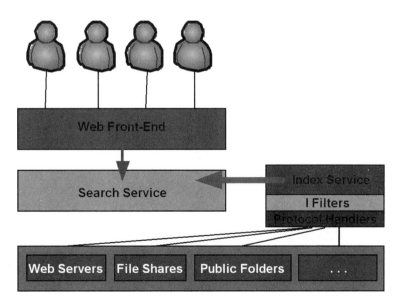

or from applications such as the Microsoft Office Research pane. These user queries are executed by the Web front-end components. These, in turn, query the Search Service using search dialect syntax, which returns query results for rendering out to the users. The search engine itself does not index the content it provides for users to search on. Instead, it relies on the indexing engine to crawl the content and break it down into searchable keys. The indexing engine uses protocol handlers, such as SharePoint Site or File Share, to fetch items that the IFilters can break down and add to the search index.

8.9.1 **Which content types to index**

Out of the box, the SPS Indexing Service is able to generate full-text indexes of Microsoft Office Word, Excel, PowerPoint, Visio, and Publisher files; HTML, text, and TIFF files; and MIME content. As you can quickly see, at least one major content type most organizations want to include is missing: Adobe PDF.

Since the SPS Search Service uses the standard IFilter interface to index document content, there are a host of filters available for content types ranging from MP3s to Adobe PDF files. Some of the IFilters, such as Adobe PDF, are available free of charge, but some, such as the ZFilter for ZIP files,

Table 8.2   *Content Filters*

Content Extension	Description	Cost at Time of Writing
.PDF	Adobe PDF files (www.adobe.com/support/downloads/detail.jsp?ftpID=1276)	Free of charge
.ZIP	Compressed ZIP files (www.4-share.com/content/products.htm)	$75
.DWG	AutoCad files (www.cad-company.nl/ifilter)	$250
.RTF	Rich-text files (www.microsoft.com/sharepoint/server/techinfo/reskit/RTF_Filter.asp_)	Free of charge
.XML	eXtensible Markup Language files (www.microsoft.com/sharepoint/server/techinfo/reskit/XML_Filter.asp)	Free of charge
.ONE	Microsoft Office OneNote files (http://support.microsoft.com/default.aspx?scid=kb;EN-US;832289)	You must install licensed copy of OneNote on the index server

come with a cost attached. Table 8.2 describes some of the typical IFilters you might want to consider, their cost, and where to get them.

In addition to purchasing and installing the IFilter on the index server, you must also add the file extension to the included file-type extension on the SharePoint Portal Search configuration page.

Since each IFilter must process the files into a form the word breaker is able to process, certain IFilters will apply more load on the index system than others. For example, TIFF image OCR is far more process intensive than indexing Microsoft Word files. If you plan to index large numbers of TIFF, PDF, or ZIP files, you should consider moving processing of these content types to a dedicated index server.

8.9.2   Planning content indexes and content sources

To refresh your memory from the previous chapter, there are three layers used to partition indexes in SPS 2003: content indexes (see Figure 8.12), content sources, and content source groups.

Content indexes, also called search catalogs, are the physical databases that store the full-text data. By default, there are two content indexes, Portal Content and Non Portal Content, which do exactly what their names indicate. For further granularity, content indexes can be set to include or exclude certain content based on filter strings defined in the content index settings. From a planning perspective, it might be tempting to create several content indexes to keep the catalogs to manageable sizes for disaster recovery and index rebuild, but remember that the search queries must be executed separately against each content index and ranking is done per index. Thus, you must weigh the higher query resource cost and longer search query execution times against the benefits for operational management. On a positive note, in a farm setup, by separating content to multiple content indexes, you decrease the time it takes to propagate search catalogs from the index servers to the search servers, since files are smaller in size. I recommend keeping the number of content indexes to three or four in a typical deployment, or, if you plan to index millions of documents, to one index for every million items, although there are no hard-coded limits on the number of items per content index.

Content sources define the location of the content you'd like to crawl for content and allow you to set up rules, such as site hops, page depth, and update frequency, to name a few. Each content source is assigned to a content index and a content source group. Content source groups provide a

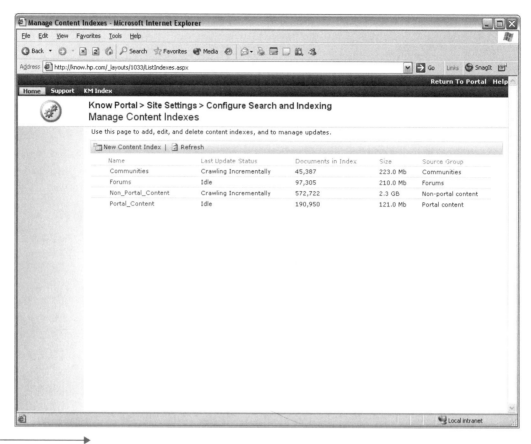

Figure 8.12   *Managing content indexes.*

mechanism to allow the creation of search scopes (which we will cover shortly), so end users can target their searches against specific content.

You should plan well ahead when considering which external and portal-hosted content you wish to index, since it's easy to be too specific when creating content sources and in time end up with a management nightmare. Also, remember that content sources are not the only way to limit what gets indexed from the target source; you can also utilize content index filters, as well as other supported methods, such as the robot exclusions (www.robot-stxt.org/wc/exclusion.html) on the target Web server. A good rule of thumb is to try to keep the number of content sources below 80.

The old adage "Garbage in means garbage out" is also good to keep in mind when planning content sources. So, although it might appear like a good idea to let SPS index every server in an enterprise, you will quickly find that the valid content gets lost in the avalanche of information users are presented with when querying the search portal.

8.9.3   Planning search scopes

Search scopes are visible to end users, who do not know what's going on under the hood with content indexes and content sources. Search scopes allow users on the portal to target their searches to avoid having to wade through information they're not interested in. Properly used, search scopes can significantly improve knowledge-worker productivity and help to ensure a positive user experience.

You can define as many search scopes per portal as you like and choose to include any number of content groups within the scope, thus providing

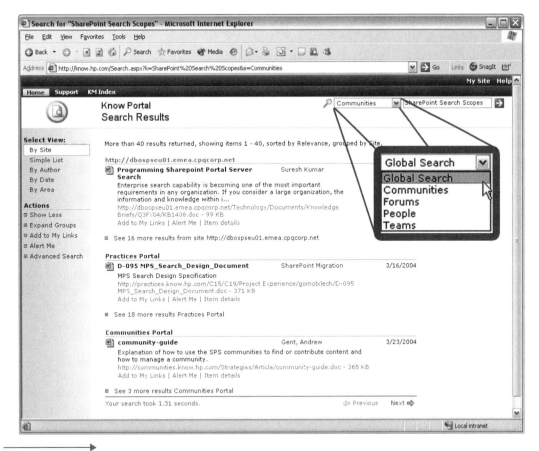

Figure 8.13   *Search scopes allow users to target searches against the content they are interested in.*

flexibility to include a particular content group in more than one search scope. For example, you can create one content group that includes all the products a company produces and another for all services-related material. You would likely want to give end users the option to search only products or services independently or allow them to choose a *Products & Services* option, which would cover both content groups.

It is perhaps even more important to plan well ahead when creating search scopes than content groups, since you can change content groups behind the scenes, while search scopes are visible to the end users from the start. User habits are hard to change; thus, you want to ensure as little change as possible in search scopes to avoid user confusion. Also, resist the temptation to create tens, if not hundreds, of search scopes, and focus instead on top-level subject matters. Too many search scopes are just as bad as the information avalanche we described earlier, since users might not find what they are looking for if searching in the wrong "bucket." I recommend that you keep the number of scopes to fewer than 10, if possible, to avoid burying content through scopes that are too specific. Remember that even in a Shared Services setup, search scopes are specific to a portal site, allowing you to vary scopes for each portal site according to business objective. For example, as Figure 8.13 shows, HP keeps the search scopes down to a bare minimum.

8.10   Impact of Web Parts

WSS and SPS 2003 both ship with dozens of Web Parts that Microsoft provides out of the box for users to adapt sites to their own particular business needs. However, the true power of adaptability and systems integration can be realized with the help of custom Web Parts that you create to perform specific tasks. It is, therefore, likely that sooner or later every enterprise deployment will include some custom Web Parts developed by third parties or in-house programmers as part of the architecture.

8.10.1   Review of out-of-the-box functionality

As we discussed earlier, WSS (and thus SPS, which is built on top of WSS) consists of a number of Web Parts that build a page for end users to view. By encapsulating the site into manageable views, SharePoint provides an easily extendable and customizable platform without users ever having to resort to HTML editing tools, such as Microsoft FrontPage. Since site administrators are allowed to add any number of Web Parts to their sites, they can quickly build an application specific to the business problem.

Figure 8.14   *Team site built with standard Web Parts.*

The out-of-the-box List View Web Part, together with custom lists, provides an extensible and customizable vehicle for building information display and storage databases, while the Content Editor Web Part allows users to enter rich HTML content anywhere on the page. Since the built-in Web Parts, such as the Image Web Part, support Web Part connections, users can build dynamic interactive Web applications without even having to worry about coding HTML or .NET managed languages. Figure 8.14 shows a typical team-site Home page composed of a number of out-of-the-box Web Parts organized to accomplish effective cross-business team planning. By using custom lists and utilizing the List View controls, you can create simple, yet robust, lines of business applications with little effort—for example, for project management tasks.

8.10.2   Overview of custom Web Parts

When functionality provided by out-of-the-box Web Parts, FrontPage Data View Web Parts, and customizations doesn't address the business problem, an organization can choose to deploy custom functionality encapsulated in Web Parts. Web Parts are compiled .NET server controls that are executed on the server and can thus access a wide array of .NET system classes and external COM components. Therefore, your imagination is the only limit to the functionality you can create to add value to your SharePoint deployment. Later on, in Chapters 13 and 14, we will cover Web Part development in depth and recommend best practices for custom Web Parts.

The SharePoint community has already created a wide variety of Web Parts available free of charge or for a small fee to accomplish various tasks. Other Web Parts are available from third-party solution providers and Microsoft. A good example of add-on Web Parts is the Microsoft Office add-on Web Part Package that ships on the SPS CD. Microsoft Office Web Parts allow users who have Office 2003 deployed on the desktop to access a wide array of functionality normally only available within an Office application, such as Excel. Some good examples include the Office Pivot View Web Parts, which you can connect to SharePoint lists; OLEDB data sources, such as Microsoft SQL Server; or Excel spreadsheets to render data from the connected data source. The Web Capture Web Part, shown in Figure 8.15 allows users to take data from external Web sites and display it on the SharePoint site as a Web Part. In fact, the Web Capture Web Part is the easiest way to integrate line-of-business application data into a SharePoint site, since it works against most Web applications.

Microsoft maintains a Web Component Directory for the Share-Point community to submit components, including Web Parts, at www.microsoft.com/sharepoint/downloads/components/default.asp. Although at first it might seem like a good idea to download and provide all of these Web Parts for end users, in an enterprise deployment you will quickly realize that the support and operational concerns of running third-party-provided components without support, adequate documentation, or even source-code access often poses an unacceptable risk for operational stability. Although some of the Web Parts are provided by reputable companies, including Microsoft, they come with no guarantees. By installing a third-party component, you are explicitly trusting that the developer has "done the right thing" and developed a Web Part that doesn't waste resources and handles errors in an appropriate way.

8.10.3   Impact of Web Parts on the deployment

All applications that execute code to accomplish a task have a resource cost, and since Web Parts are essentially small applications, they too require proc-

Figure 8.15   *Using the Web Capture Web Part to display information from external Web applications.*

essing power and computer resources. Therefore, it is very important in an enterprise deployment, with thousands of users accessing the environment every day, to test each new component properly to make sure it does not exhaust resources, thus affecting end-user perceived performance.

You can get very sophisticated when developing Web Part test procedures, using various tools and performance analyzers, but one should balance the effort it takes to test Web Parts with the effort it takes to create and modify them. So, although you could run load tests on each new component with sophisticated performance analysis tools such as Segue Silk-Performer (www.segue.com/products/load-stress-performance-testing/silkperformer.asp) and ensure that every Web Part complies with .NET managed code best practices and FXCop (www.gotdot-net.com/team/fxcop) recommendations, the effort expended is usually double the time it takes to create and debug a Web Part in the first place.

Middle ground can be found with a robust performance test tool called Microsoft Application Center Test (ACT) (`http://msdn.microsoft.com/library/default.asp?url=/library/en-us/act/htm/actml_main.asp`), which ships with Microsoft Visual Studio.NET 2003 Enterprise Developer and Enterprise Architect. ACT is shown in Figure 8.16. It is perfect for lightweight tests on Web-based applications' overall throughput and can be directly called from within the Visual Studio user interface when you are developing new components. Even without setting up complicated, variable-based tests and realistic models, you can detect significant performance issues with Web Parts using ACT.

We will cover SharePoint capacity planning and performance analysis in more depth in Chapter 9, but to illustrate the impact that Web Parts can have on system performance, I created a simple custom Web Part. The custom Web Part has a straightforward task; it calculates π to a decimal pro-

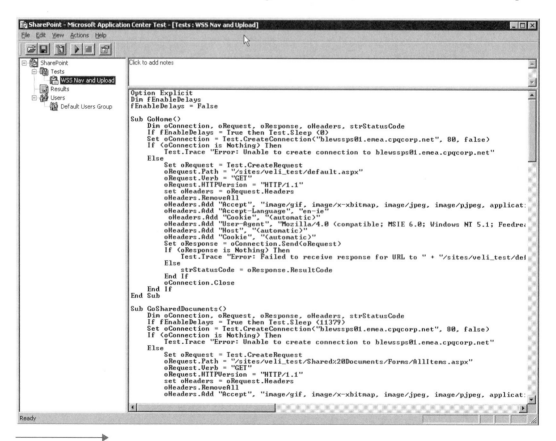

Figure 8.16 *Microsoft Application Center Test.*

vided as a custom property of the Web Part. Since the number of system resources required to calculate π increases exponentially with the number of decimals to calculate, we can see a linear decrease in the operations per second our server can process, eventually causing the application to take too long to execute the ASP.NET page, resulting in an error message. This is shown in Figure 8.17.

At the beginning of the test, the 10-MB LAN network in the test lab was a limiting factor, but as the CPU requirements for calculating the value of π increased, server throughput suffered. As time to render the Web Part grew, the team site that hosted the custom Web Part eventually became unresponsive, and requests started to time out. Unfortunately, with more than 300 simultaneous threads executing the custom Web Part, calculating 1,000 decimals of π, it was too much for the quad processor server to handle; IIS became deadlocked, requiring a service restart—so, hopefully, such

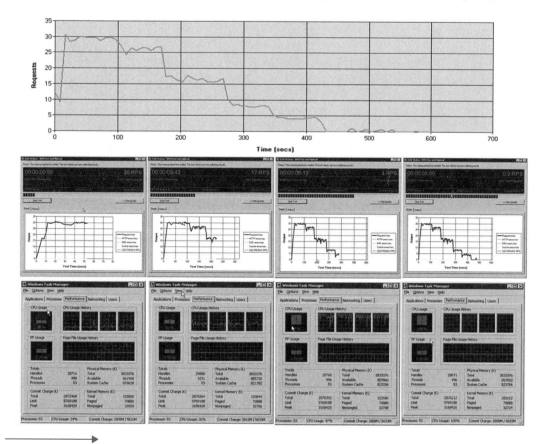

Figure 8.17   *SharePoint Server performance grinding to a halt due to a custom Web Part.*

an operation won't be required in your business! Repeating the same test with 10 simultaneous users also produced 100 percent CPU loads, but, importantly, other portals and team sites continued to function with only slightly noticeable delays.

While it is possible to bring a server to a halt with custom Web Parts, the likelihood of making 300 simultaneous connections to a page with a resource-intensive Web Part is slim to none, unless the custom part is deployed on every team site. However, although the sample shown here is far from realistic, its main goal is to illustrate the need for performance testing on any add-on Web Part, be it custom-made or third-party purchased, to avoid possible performance issues down the line.

8.10.4   Managing and supporting custom Web Parts

Upfront performance testing during development and testing can ensure that no surprises are hidden in the new whiz-bang Web Part ready for production. However, often enterprise deployments are managed by dedicated operations and support teams, who are in charge of day-to-day management and responding to end-user queries. Operations groups typically do not have development experience; therefore, handing over a CAB or even a compiled MSI install package is likely to be inadequate, especially given the strict code-access security settings. Proper install documentation, installation packaging, and functional description prepare the operations and support groups for deployment and end-user queries and should, therefore, be required for all add-on Web Parts in an enterprise deployment.

In a larger deployment with multiple servers running SharePoint, version control on all aspects of the deployment, including Web Parts, prevents servers, becoming out of sync and thus avoids risking issues with incompatible software versions or bug fixes that have only been installed on part of the overall deployment. Since Web Part assemblies support version numbering, it is recommended that every new revision get an incremental version number that allows operation teams to verify common deployment quickly in case of doubt.

Perhaps the main challenge with add-on Web Parts is support, and, more precisely, the question of who to call in case of problems. Contracted custom development might not include a support agreement, possibly putting the operations team in a difficult position when troubleshooting issues that might have something to do with custom Web Parts. Support issues are especially problematic with Web Parts provided to the Microsoft community free of charge, since usually the only solution left for the operations team when trying to find a root cause is to uninstall these Web Parts temporarily.

Even if the source code is provided as part of the submission, debugging someone else's code without knowing exactly what to look for is a nightmare for any developer. It is, therefore, imperative that a clear support and change-management responsibility be established before going into production with add-on functionality. When possible, for in-house or contract-developed code, a business group or another entity, instead of the original developer, should be assigned as the primary owner, since people come and go and Web Parts might therefore be left orphaned.

8.11   Impact of customizations

By default, every site administrator and member of the Web Designer site group is allowed to open Web Part Pages in FrontPage, permitting you to accomplish a whole other level of customizations with basic HTML and FrontPage knowledge. We will cover FrontPage Data Views later on, in Chapter 16, and show how users can integrate external data sources to SharePoint pages and build interactive applications by utilizing the Web Part connections.

As illustrated in Figure 8.18, ASP.NET data-retrieval services, together with FrontPage 2003 Data View Web Parts, can integrate a variety of line-of-business applications without having to involve system administrators. FrontPage even allows applications to be built directly on WSS, such as Web logging sites (a.k.a., "blogs") or expense-reporting applications.

While FrontPage 2003 does not prevent you from writing server-side code directly onto your Web Part Page, the Web Part Framework prevents the code from executing and displays an error when you try to access the page. The error states, "The page contains server script, which is not supported on this server." Therefore, from an administrative point of view, no special planning or operational procedures need to be invoked to protect your server from malicious code.

However, support organizations will quickly find that sites edited with FrontPage can become their worst nightmare. Although editing sites might appear easy and straightforward from a developer's perspective, normal users who are not well acquainted with HTML and scripting technologies can very easily render the page they are customizing unusable. For example, a simple deletion of a </TABLE> or </DIV> end tag can lead to unpredictable results for users browsing the site, not to mention that users are able to

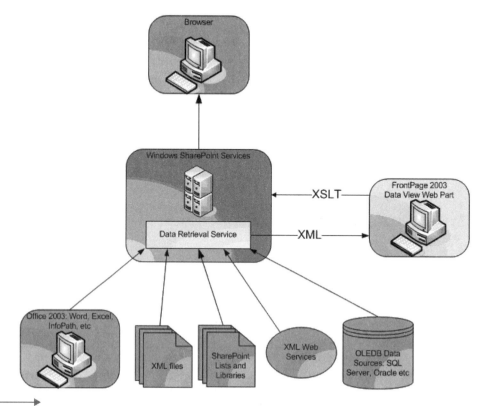

Figure 8.18   *Integrating line-of-business applications via SOAP and OLEDB.*

permanently delete core site files such as the default.aspx from
FrontPage.

Therefore, most large SharePoint implementations, including those
within HP and Microsoft, make it a policy not to support any team spaces
edited with FrontPage beyond a best-effort basis. Organizations can take
steps to prevent users from opening SharePoint sites with FrontPage, which
we will cover later in Chapter 16. With the millions of variations and
minute changes possible within FrontPage, it's simply impossible for support and operations teams to know everything that could go wrong. In
addition, every page that is saved with FrontPage or a compatible editor is
"unghosted" from the default system templates and stored in the SQL database, thus incurring a small performance penalty and disconnecting it from
the default SharePoint templates. It is also unclear how well future upgrades
will affect FrontPage customized sites. For example, the Version 1 (STS) to
Version 2 (WSS) upgrade dropped all FrontPage modifications.

9

Planning the Deployment Architecture

9.1   Overview of deployment sizing

In traditional client/server applications, such as Microsoft Exchange, emphasis for server sizing is on the number of users and type of clients they are using. Typically, the types of actions users are able to perform are limited, and, thus, the performance impact of each user can be precisely estimated. Often the resource cost of each client connection, which is maintained throughout the session, is the limiting factor due to memory usage per connection. In a high-availability Exchange deployment, there are well-defined numbers of users a specific hardware configuration can support. Although sizing an Exchange environment is still an art form due to various storage options available today, planning typically centers on the number of users the environment should be able to handle.

Since SharePoint Products and Technologies are a Web application, there are no constant connections between the users and the server. A browser requests a page, the server responds, and the connection is closed, regardless of how long the user spends looking at the returned information. In addition, the performance impact of each request varies, depending on the type of action performed. Since each action type has a different resource cost, to be able to accurately devise the overall resource requirements, you must be able to predict the way the environment will be used. When sizing a SharePoint Products and Technologies deployment, your emphasis should be on trying to understand the types of actions your users are likely to perform and how often they will perform them.

If, after reading this chapter, you want to delve further into capacity and hardware planning for SharePoint Products and Technologies, you can find some sizing tools and performance white papers on the HP ActiveAnswers

Web site (www.hp.com/solutions/activeanswers), as well as on the Microsoft
Web site.

9.1.1 Performance-testing methodology

As you've undoubtedly found out by now, SharePoint Products and Technologies' range of functionality is far too extensive to even try to come up
with a model that replicates all the possible things that a knowledge worker
can do in the course of a typical day. Thus, generalizations must be made
when performance testing by combining key functions, such as Browse,
Search, and Document Upload, into batches, which are called *workloads*.
The workload defines the types of operations and the frequency of their
occurrence for a simulated user. In order to simulate real-life conditions
slightly more accurately, typically a randomize function is added to each
type of action, since users do not perform the same sequence of actions on
every visit.

Every platform has its limit on the number of actions it can simultaneously perform, which is called *system throughput*. The selected performance testing suite applies the workloads on the application at an ever-
increasing volume, until the throughput levels off or starts to decline, indicating that one of the system components is not able to keep up with the
pace. This is called a *bottleneck*, since the combined result of the system
hinges on the component's performance. Think of running the water at full
force in your bathroom sink; eventually the drain hole is not able to keep
up, thus becoming a bottleneck, and the water will overflow.

SharePoint Products and Technologies offer you two ways to combat the
ever-increasing throughput: scale-up and scale-out. Scaling up means adding more processors, memory, or disks to the server you have deployed, but
obviously you can only upgrade so far before you have to upgrade to a
whole new server platform. Alternatively, you can scale out by adding more
servers to the deployment and distributing the load between them. In performance testing, the goal is to find a way to predict system performance in
both scale-up and scale-out scenarios. Thus, a good number of different
configurations are typically tested in order to try to find a formula that can
be applied to various scenarios.

With SharePoint Products and Technologies, the throughput is measured in the number of operations per second (ops/s) the system is able to
perform. An operation is a sequence of physical events, such as opening a
Web site Home page, which appears to the end users as a single operation,

but in reality actually consists of numerous transactions behind the scenes, such as fetching an included JavaScript or StyleSheet file. Each Web Part also adds to the complexity of the operation, since the server must do more work to be able to provide the end result to the user.

Operations per second don't equate to simultaneous connections in terms of, for example, Exchange, since the connection is stateless; the number of operations per second is typically considerably higher than the number of users currently visiting the SharePoint Products and Technologies deployment. It's not uncommon to see thousands of users simultaneously visiting a portal, for example, and only generating fewer than 10 ops/s. Don't confuse the number of *simultaneous users* with the number of *actual users* in the company either; they are drastically different unless you plan to integrate a line-of-business application that all people in the company must have open on their desktops at the same time. Typically, the number of active users per day is around 40% in a very active corporation; personally, we've typically found most organizations to be around 15% to 20%.

9.1.2   Estimating required throughput for SharePoint Products and Technologies

Why are we talking about all of these weird and perhaps uninteresting terms? Well, later on in the chapter, when we get down to sizing hardware, the estimated throughput requirements for your deployment are derived from all of the things we've just mentioned.

Microsoft has devised a formula that you can use to calculate the estimated throughput volume based on generalizations and estimations. The formula has proved to be quite accurate but requires you to estimate the number of users, the percentage of those users who are active on a given day, the estimated number of operations per active user, and the number of hours in a workday, in order to calculate the average operations-per-second requirements. Obviously, the accuracy of the average operations-per-second figure derived depends on the accuracy of the provided estimates.

In organizations where previous implementations do not exist, determining accurate figures to feed to the formula is often an educated guess at best. However, existing environments such as eRoom or Lotus Notes can provide detailed logs for you to analyze usage figures and patterns, such as average users and operations per day. Even analyzing existing File Shares might give you some idea of typical active users to operations per day in your enterprise.

The formula used to calculate required operations per second for a SharePoint Product and Technologies deployment, which you can use to estimate the required hardware topology for your enterprise, is as follows:

$$\frac{\text{Number of users} \times \dfrac{\text{Percent of active}}{\text{users per day}} \times \dfrac{\text{Number of operations}}{\text{per active user per day}} \times \text{Peak factor}}{360{,}000 \times \text{Number of hours per day}}$$

"Number of users" is the possible number of users who might connect to the system at any given time; if you're planning to deploy SharePoint Products and Technologies across the enterprise, it is obviously the number of NT or Active Directory accounts that exist and, as such, usually covers all the employees and contractors. If the environment is going to be accessible by external parties, such as partners or customers, be sure to include them in the figure. "Percent of active users per day" requires you to estimate how many of the potential users will actually visit the deployment on any given day. As noted earlier, 40% is a safe bet in a typical usage scenario. The "number of operations per active user per day" might be even harder to predict, since it requires you to consider how the environment will be used. Again, a safe bet is 10, which has been determined as average in a typical enterprise. Obviously, there will be power users and content authors who will perform considerably more operations, but they are typically balanced out by the significantly larger reader population who might only visit the Web site Home page and download a couple of the latest files.

"Peak factor" is a bit of a dark horse; it's a multiplier typically from 1 to 10, which is used to indicate the peak-hour extra throughput requirements. For example, consider a factory that opens at 9:00 A.M. and closes at 5:00 P.M. Between 8:45 A.M. and 9:00 A.M., when the employees arrive, the coffee vending machines are typically under significantly increased throughput demands. Thus, to be able to meet requirements, the vending machines have likely been sized for this peak capacity. Similarly, with SharePoint Products and Technologies, it's only natural that there will be peaks in the usage pattern, although in a global or cross-regional deployment, these peaks will be averaged by the time differences. A safe bet is to go with 5 to 7 in a typical enterprise deployment, but if you know that there will be a considerable peak during specific hours of the day, you should apply a higher peak factor.

Finally, you must divide the figure by the "number of hours per day," which is the time span during which most of the users will utilize the environment. This is typically the average working day for the user population the environment is targeted for. However, as with the peak factor, cross-regional and global deployments will have to account for the time zone differences. The hours per day are multiplied by 360,000, which is derived from:

$$
\underset{\text{(percent conversion)}}{100} \quad \times \quad \underset{\substack{\text{(number of minutes} \\ \text{in an hour)}}}{60} \quad \times \quad \underset{\substack{\text{(number of seconds} \\ \text{in a minute)}}}{60}
$$

As an example, let's take an Enterprise portal deployment for a 10,000-user organization across the United States. Since the portal is targeted at every employee, there will be 10,000 potential users with a reasonable estimate that 40% of them will visit the environment on a given day. A typical operations-per-day sum of 10 is used with a relatively low peak factor of 5, given the time zone impact cross the country. We'll use a 12-hour working day, again given the cross-country time zone impact. The end result, as shown here, is an average throughput requirement of 4.629 ops/s (we'll talk about what that means in hardware terms in just a while):

$$
\frac{10,000 \times 40 \times 10 \times 5}{360,000 \times 12} = 4.629 \text{ ops/s}
$$

Not only are the formulas generalized, but they are also based on a number of assumptions about how the environment is utilized by the end users. Next, we'll look at some of those assumptions, since regularly exceeding the recommended application limits will result in unpredictable performance characteristics.

9.1.3   Recommended application limits

Every product has practical and technical reasons to recommend certain limits on how the application should be used. Microsoft has made several recommendations for both WSS and SPS 2003 feature utilization, which give you guidance as to how you should structure your deployment and information architecture. While hardly any of these recommended limits are enforced, and as such referred to as *hard limits*, in the application, typically, the recommendations have been made for a good reason. In SharePoint's case, by exceeding the limits, you will find that performance starts to decrease with longer response times for end users.

Table 9.1 details the recommended limits for Windows SharePoint Services and, as such, applies to WSS sites hosted from SPS as well.

Table 9.2 lists SPS-specific recommended limits and includes a few hard limits as well, which cannot be exceeded. Since a Portal site is created as a

Table 9.1   *Recommended Limits for Windows SharePoint Services Components*

Feature	Recommended Limit	Notes
Site collections	50,000	Although it is not a hard limit, Microsoft recommends splitting site collections across virtual servers if you plan to create more than 50,000 site collections, since performance has been shown to decrease steadily after 10,000 site collections.
Web sites per site collection	250,000	Several sites can be created within a site collection by utilizing subweb hierarchies.
Subwebs per Web site	1,000	Due to limitations with subweb enumeration routines, you should limit subwebs to less than 1,000 per Web site.
Security principals per Web site	2,000	We recommend that users utilize Windows Security Groups (Active Directory or NT4) to grant access to a Web site if there are more than 200 users. Technically, though, you could add up to 2,000 security principals before the enumeration and rendering start to get too slow to become useful.
Lists per Web site	2,000	Once again, we would suggest that you will face usability limitations far before the technical-rendering-related issues catch up. Presenting 2,000 lists without a hierarchical navigation to end users will undoubtedly result in a lot of confusion.
Items per list	2,000	While we have seen many Web sites with more than the recommended number of items in production, unfortunately the rendering times have been borderline unacceptable, with 10-to-20-second rendering times on a LAN connection. This is one recommended limit that you will likely come across on your WSS deployment, as users start to create line-of-business applications on the team Web sites.
Documents per library	2,000,000	WSS allows a significant number of files to be stored in a document library as long as you observe the per-folder recommendation.
Documents per folder	2,000	As with a few of the previous items, enumeration and rendering are likely reasons for recommending a 2,000-document limit in a given folder. Once again, though, usability and the ability to find the information in a large flat structure will likely become a limitation well before the technical limit is reached. Thus, this point is likely moot, since most users are familiar with creating information structures with subfolders, allowing a considerable numbers of files to be stored in a WSS library.

Table 9.1   *Recommended Limits for Windows SharePoint Services Components (continued)*

Feature	Recommended Limit	Notes
Maximum document size	50 MB–2 GB	The Index process has issues breaking up large Office files; thus, you should seriously consider limiting the file upload size to about 50 MB. If your users must be able to store large files, such as CD images or video files, it is possible to raise the limit to 2 GB.
Web Parts per page	100	Once again, usability will likely be a limiting factor, since no one is interested in sifting through lots and lots of information presented on a single page. Thus, the recommended limit is unlikely to be approached in a typical usage scenario.

Table 9.2   *Recommended Limits for SPS 2003 Components*

Feature	Recommended Limit	Notes
Portal sites	15 full portal sites 100 with Shared Services (hard limit)	As noted before, Shared Services significantly reduce overhead for portal sites; thus, you can create up to 100 child portal sites when Shared Services are enabled.
Portal areas	10,000	Although, from an information architecture point of view, creating more than 1,000 areas might be considered excessive, you could create elaborate taxonomies if you wanted to.
Area nesting depth	20 levels (hard limit)	If you were creating 10,000 areas, you might run into this issue. For most of us, though, burying information down to this extent might be considered hiding, since it's unlikely anyone would find his or her way to these depths.
User profiles	1,000,000	Million-user portal was Microsoft's target for SPS 2003; thus, all aspects have been scaled to ensure this, including profiles.
Audiences	10,000	We're fairly sure that although it's technically possible to create 10,000 audiences, content publishers would give up using the feature since it would be too difficult to find the right audience to target content to.
Audience membership	5,000,000	If you were deploying a million-user portal, rest assured that you could create audiences to target content to subsections of your user base.

Table 9.2   *Recommended Limits for SPS 2003 Components (continued)*

Feature	Recommended Limit	Notes
SSO credentials	100,000	Single Sign-On credentials limits might become an issue for larger enterprise deployments. Then again, in a large enterprise typically there are identity-management solutions already deployed to meet the enterprise's needs.
Search indexes	32	Although you can technically create several content indexes, remember that each query is executed per content index, thus adding to the time it takes to resolve queries. You should consider keeping the maximum number of indexes to around four to six.
Content sources	250	When crawling a significant amount of external content sources, the 250-cap recommendation might seem like a limiting factor. However, there are many ways around this if it really becomes an issue, including, for example, building a Web page that simply links to all of the thousands of content sources you'd like to index. As long as you set the site hops above 1, you'll be able to index various smaller content sources.
Search scopes	250 (hard limit)	From a usability point of view, search scopes should be kept to as few as possible; otherwise, users might have difficulty picking the right one from the extensive list. Consider keeping the number below 25 for usability's sake.
Indexed documents per search index	5,000,000	Microsoft states that, while 5 million is not a hard limit, performance will start decreasing. Thus, it's recommended to distribute indexed content over a few search indexes.
Indexed documents overall	20,000,000	Overall, the recommended indexed documents limit is set to 20 million across at least four content indexes.
Alerts	1,000,000	One million alerts might sound like a considerable amount, but you should take steps to ensure that you will not go over the limit in an enterprise deployment. For example, 10 alerts per person is not unheard of, and, in a 100,000-user organization, that's all that users would be allowed to create. Consider limiting alerts per person in a larger deployment to a number that ensures you won't go above the recommended limit.
Personal sites	250,000	While 250,000 personal sites should be enough, it is, of course, possible to create more, spanned over several portals or farms, if you are planning that million-user portal.

WSS site collection, the Web site's limit within a site collection applies to portal areas as well. In addition, recommendations with lists and libraries and the number of items they should contain also apply to portal areas.

While the recommended limits detailed in the two tables are not surprising, it's good to remember a few of them for future reference—for example, the list-items recommended limit, which you are likely to see an end user exceed.

9.2   Global deployment considerations

We live in an exceedingly globalized world; thus, it's not surprising that most of us work in distributed work environments emphasizing the need for good collaboration. For example, this chapter is being written in Finland, while Kevin is going to review it in Scotland and pass it on to Emer in California. In order to work efficiently, we must utilize the collaboration tools to work across time zones and great distances.

It's not surprising, therefore, that enterprise deployments of SharePoint Products and Technologies must consider how best to serve the collaboration requirements of the global workforce. This might include simply hosting the services in a centralized network hub and ensuring that latency and bandwidth meet the needs of the remote users. However, today we must also consider the language requirements a global deployment dictates.

9.2.1   Addressing multiple languages

If you are considering hosting services for multiple regions from a centralized deployment, you will likely have to provide regionalized services for different countries. Regionalizing SharePoint Products and Technologies ranges from time zone and character set modifications all the way to fully translated site templates.

WSS allows any number of the languages supported by Office to be installed on the same server with downloadable language packs. Users will be able to select the language when first provisioning the site, although once the language templates have been applied, there is no easy way to change them. In addition, the language is set per site; therefore, multinational spaces will have to agree upon a common dialect. The only cautionary note with language templates relates to template customizations, which we cover in Part III of the book. Since each language template essentially adds its own site-definition templates, all base template customizations (e.g., corporate look and feel) must be applied separately to every language pack. If you're considering using the out-of-the-box look and feel, language packs are a great way to provide multinational users with an ability to apply a regional identity to the sites.

SPS users are not as fortunate. SPS 2003 still supports only one language per server for portal areas, although you can install as many WSS language packs as you like and provision multilanguage team sites from the portal. Still, if you need to provide regionalized SPS portals, the only way to do this out of the box is to deploy multiple servers. We certainly hope Microsoft addresses this in the future, since users—for example, from Japan, China, and France—would certainly appreciate local language portals in a centralized SPS deployment. Today, you must factor in additional servers or consider server virtualization if you need to provide regionalized portal user interfaces.

9.2.2 Distributed or regionalized server deployment

In a global deployment, one of the fundamental questions is always how best to serve the regional users. From an IT management and cost perspective, a centralized deployment is often the favored option, since you can deploy one large farm that is able to scale to any enterprise requirements. The placing of that one central farm, though, often becomes a company political issue, especially if there is a strong presence on multiple continents. Placing the hardware near the largest user base might not always be wise, if most of the content readers, for example, are based on another continent. Of course, deploying hardware at each of the major sites would resolve any disputes and provide users with fast connectivity all around. However, if high availability is a requirement for these environments, it quickly becomes prohibitively expensive to put up farms in multiple sites.

An issue with regional deployments of SharePoint Products and Technologies is often content replication, or, more specifically, the lack of it. Placing the server near the end users will do little good if the content is still stored remotely or, worse yet, if document authors have to remember to post an extra copy of each file on the regional platforms. There is no silver bullet for regional-deployment server-placement planning, but we can offer two major approaches that we have been involved with, as well as the pros and cons of both.

A valid approach, both technically and from an information-architecture perspective, is to go with a centralized deployment of SharePoint Products and Technologies, even with the difficulty added by SPS's inability to host more than one portal language per server. With a centralized deployment, you don't have to worry about duplicating content or about users going to the wrong URL; you have one place to bookmark, and you can find everything from that one central location. The IT staff doesn't have to worry about supporting multiple platforms and the infrastructure they rely on.

Unfortunately, the problem with centralized deployments is speed for remote users. WSS typically requires good network connectivity since, due to the nature of the application, you are actively working on information such as documents and presentations, which today can be rather large in file size. While, because it is a Web application, SharePoint is not as dependent on network latency, there's not a lot one can do about uploading a 4-MB file to a team site. Document management is slow over a low-bandwidth wide area network (WAN) link, and there's not much you can do about that. Well, that's not exactly true. If you have the ability to do so, you can request that remote links be upgraded to a certain standard latency and bandwidth, thus making the centralized server deployment a serious architecture contender. Obviously, another issue with centralized deployments is that you are effectively placing all your eggs in one basket, thus placing demands on your business-continuity planning. Business-continuity planning should detail the plan to continue operations in the shortest available time when a disaster strikes and the primary server farm cannot be quickly brought back online. Data-center fires are not unheard of, and other natural and manmade disasters are also possible. If you must be able to continue operations in these exceptional circumstances, you must plan for a disaster-recovery environment in another data center.

The second option is to deploy regional instances in the user-population centers across the enterprise. While technically this is an easy fix, it does cause headaches for the knowledge-management and information-architecture planners. By distributing sites across servers, you are effectively creating information silos in these regional environments. Operations overhead is also increased, since there are now more servers to look after. The cost is likely higher, given the extra hardware and operational requirements, especially if high availability is still a requirement in these regional instances.

Even with all these negative points, regionalized infrastructure is often the best solution for end-user productivity; end users don't have to wait around and become frustrated with upload and download times. Frustration often leads to abandonment, which is exactly what the business sponsors likely want to avoid. Thus, we architects often find ourselves just biting the bullet and designing a regionally distributed architecture, typically based around the network diagram.

One lesson learned that we can offer with regard to regional architectures is to attempt to at least agree on a centralized SPS architecture while maintaining regional WSS and My Site services. Information posted in a portal site is often "ready" for consumption; after all, that's the reason for posting it on a portal. Since there's little need to work continuously on the copy published on the portal, slightly slower response times do not typically matter as much. However, when first writing the document or later, when collaborating on an update, there is a need for constant revision control, for which the extra bandwidth of a local environment definitely helps. If you can drive users to collaborate on creating or modifying the documents in WSS and, when finished, publishing on SPS, you're likely to be able to provide portal site services from a central location, thus addressing the knowledge-management concerns about information silos. You might also be able to reduce hardware and maintenance costs, as long as you do not need any portal services such as My Site on the regional environments.

9.3   Sizing Windows SharePoint Services

We've found that some people have preconceptions about Windows SharePoint Services performance, given that the product is offered by Microsoft free of charge, while SPS 2003 is not. Perhaps the fact that WSS is a free product makes people think that it is only suitable for small deployments and that you must pay for the enterprise-scale product, namely SPS. Undoubtedly, since you've made it this far in the book, you know that such misconceptions couldn't be farther from the truth. Rest assured; WSS scales, and it scales very, very well, as you're about to find out.

9.3.1   Web front-end scalability

The roots for Windows SharePoint Services scalability can be traced back to its predecessor, STS, which, back in its day, was able to perform a staggering 50 ops/s on a typical server platform of its time. Microsoft increased functionality considerably in the new release with Windows SharePoint Services, but was able to keep up and increase throughput performance.

Microsoft's WSS capacity-planning white paper quotes 65 ops/s on a dual 1-GHz server, which is slightly higher than HP's testing on a dual-processor 2.8-GHz server, which also yielded 65 ops/s. The differences in performance can be explained by slightly different workload configurations: HP's test used the internal implementation's proven metrics as a basis for constructing the workload.

Whether you take the Microsoft figure or the HP result, it doesn't really matter; 65 ops/s is an enormous throughput result for any application. Recall the 10,000-user example we calculated earlier on in the chapter. We calculated that in a typical workload configuration, the throughput requirements would only be 4.69 ops/s, which is easily within reach of a typical server platform today. To put things in perspective, the laptop on which this chapter is being written performs approximately 11 ops/s and would, thus, be able to respond to the raw throughput requirements of the example company twice over.

A single-server deployment of Windows SharePoint Services is, without a doubt, CPU bound, at least with today's typical memory configurations in a data-center network environment. As we discussed earlier, this means that in theory you can increase performance by adding additional CPUs or by adding additional Web servers. We're happy to confirm that the theory holds true with reality, and WSS has been shown to be an excellent example of both scale-up and scale-out performance.

Scale-up performance can be demonstrated with a modern dual 3.06-GHz server platform yielding 105 ops/s, which is 1.6 times the performance of a dual 2.8-GHz platform. HP's testing has also shown WSS to scale up by adding more processors with approximately a 1.88:1 ratio. This means that a single CPU 3.06-GHz server is able to perform approximately 58 ops/s; theoretically it also means that a quad CPU 3.06-GHz server would be able to perform approximately 197 ops/s in ideal conditions.

Scale-out, as expected, doubles the effective throughput performance on any given platform, thus yielding 130 ops/s on a 2x dual CPU 2.8-GHz platform and 210 ops/s on a 2x dual CPU 3.06-GHz platform. Both HP's and Microsoft's testing have shown the trend to continue for as long as the database server can keep up the pace.

9.3.2 SQL server impact

Since all of the WSS data is stored on the SQL server, it plays a crucial role in scalability. As we've covered earlier, WSS ships with WMSDE in order to be able to be used out of the box without additional server licenses. However, most installations out of the development and testing environments will likely use the SQL Server 2000 platform instead for added management and scalability options.

Since WMSDE does not have the five-concurrent-jobs restriction of MSDE, from a scalability perspective deployments with WSS and WMSDE running on the server do perform very well, largely due to WSS

Web front end's stellar performance. Microsoft has clocked a modest single-server installation at 34 ops/s, which will likely translate to considerably higher throughput on modern 2.8/3.06-GHz platforms. From a performance perspective, therefore, you do not need to look to SQL Server 2000 as your database engine. However, if you need to provide Search capabilities or would like to utilize enterprise management and reliability options, you need to move to SQL Server 2000.

You can, of course, install SQL Server 2000 and WSS on the same physical server, although your performance is likely to be the same as that of WMSDE and quite possibly even lower due to added Search features. For full scale-out options now or in the future, we highly recommend separating the SQL server role from the Web server role. Even if you are not going to deploy a full-fledged farm immediately, a future transition, should you ever need to make one, will be considerably more straightforward when you don't have to worry about the SQL server services. It seems that most database administrators (DBAs) are sworn never to allow other applications to be installed on their precious database servers, though personally we have not seen any operational reasons not to do so. Still, best practices are formed over time, and we tend to recommend running SQL on a separate server in order to put database administrators at ease and make the operational model slightly more straightforward.

HP's testing has shown that with a separate SQL server running on a dual CPU 2.8-GHz server, the previous 2x dual CPU 2.8-GHz server Web front ends were only utilizing 35% of CPU capacity on the SQL server. This indicates that you could scale-out the Web front ends up to 4 before you needed to add capacity on the SQL side. We have to note, though, that the 4:1 ratio is highly dependent on the number of Search operations being performed as part of the workload. In fact, Microsoft's capacity-planning white paper notes the Web front end to SQL server ratio to be closer to 3:1, which could be due to higher probability of search operations (frequency was not noted in the test).

The Search Service is without doubt a very resource-intensive operation on Windows SharePoint Services. Unlike SPS, SQL Search Service, which WSS utilizes, cannot be delegated to a dedicated server, thus affecting the main SQL platform throughput. The Search operation resource is also dependent on the number of items in the index, making it hard to draw conclusive patterns for WSS deployments. For larger deployments, consider only enabling WSS Search for part of the team sites or integrating, for example, the SPS search engine, which performs significantly better and can be load-balanced to up to four servers.

9.3.3   Network impact

All the figures we've noted before have been tested in data-center network conditions (i.e., 100-Mbps switched LAN). HP's workload, modeled after an internal SharePoint Products and Technologies deployment, utilized the 2x dual CPU 2.8-GHz platform an average of 9,300 Kb (1,162.5 KB) per second total network traffic for the simulated users on full 130 ops/s throughput. This throughput translates to an average of approximately 72 Kb (9 KB) per operation. As you can see, the network throughput requirements exceed that of the typical effective speed of a 10-Mbps network, thus definitely requiring at least the 100-Mbps network connection. It needs to be pointed out, though, that the bandwidth requirements vary based on the file sizes and frequency of updates. The figures here are generalizations that have been found to be accurate in one particular deployment scenario but might not fit in every environment.

In real life, we don't always have the luxury of 100-Mbps connections to the office networks, especially when planning a centralized deployment for a geographically distributed organization. You should work with your network team to ensure that adequate network capacity is at hand for your estimated throughput requirements and work with them on an ongoing basis to adapt the estimates based on your deployment workload characteristics.

Even though the tested network capacity was not close to saturating the 100-Mbps data-center network, separate network cards were utilized for back-end connectivity. It's not uncommon for today's servers to include at least two embedded NICs, thus allowing you to dedicate one of them for traffic related to back-end SQL and network load balancing, not to mention backups.

9.3.4   Choosing the right hardware topology

So, with talk of all of these operations-per-second figures, you might be slightly confused as to which hardware topology you should choose for your deployment of Windows SharePoint Services. First, let's remind ourselves of the formula to estimate the required throughput requirements:

$$\frac{\text{Number of users} \times \frac{\text{Percent of active}}{\text{users per day}} \times \frac{\text{Number of operations}}{\text{per active user per day}} \times \text{Peak factor}}{360,000 \times \text{Number of hours per day}}$$

Perform a quick calculation for your environment and compare it with the hardware platform options shown in Table 9.3.

Table 9.3   *Example WSS Hardware-Platform Throughput Figures*

Server Topology	Estimated Server Throughput	Estimated Client Network Traffic
Laptop with SQL 2000 (Virtual PC) 2.2 GHz with 1 GB RAM	11 ops/s (load tool on the same "server")	792 Kbps (99 KBps)
Single server with WMSDE Dual 2.8 GHz with 1 GB RAM	~40 ops/s (estimated)	2,880 Kbps (360 KBps)
1 Front-end + 1 SQL Server Dual 2.8 GHz with 1GB RAM (all)	65 ops/s	4,680 Kbps (585 KBps)
1 Front end + 1 SQL server Dual 3.06 GHz with 1 GB RAM (all)	105 ops/s	7,560 Kbps (945 KBps)
2 Front ends + 1 SQL server Dual 2.8 GHz with 1 GB RAM (all)	130 ops/s	9,360 Kbps (1,170 KBps)
2 Front ends + 1 SQL server Dual 3.06 GHz with 1 GB RAM (all)	210 ops/s	15,120 Kbps (1,890 KBps)
4 Front ends + 1 SQL server Dual 3.06 GHz with 1 GB RAM (all)	420 ops/s	30,240 Kbps (3,780 KBps)

Okay, so the first option is meant as comic relief, which you no doubt need after getting this far. All joking aside though, we have a feeling that even if you're approaching an enterprise deployment of Windows Share-Point Services, your throughput requirements might not even be as high as 11 ops/s, let alone 65 ops/s with the standard enterprise server platform today (dual 2.8 GHz).

Personally, we have recommended the dual 2.8-GHz server platform to several large corporations with over 10,000 estimated users without a doubt that the platform is able to meet the throughput requirements for some time to come. In our opinion, there is absolutely nothing wrong with starting small and growing the environment as the requirements and the usage grow. We do suggest, however, choosing to separate the SQL server from the WSS server for easy future growth and a move to a highly available platform.

So why would you even consider selecting a topology with more than one front-end server? The answer can be summed up in two words: high availability.

9.3.5 High-availability considerations

Without a doubt, for most organizations the only reason to even consider a farm deployment is not throughput requirements; it's because the environment must be highly available. When that single server is down due to software, hardware, or administrator failure, the environment is down, and it will stay that way until the problem has been addressed.

Windows SharePoint Services supports load-balanced Web front ends, which provide not only increased throughput but also fault tolerance in case one of the front ends is no longer responding. Both the hardware- and software-based Network Load Balancing Service automatically directs all traffic to a working server in case one of the servers is not responding within a pre-defined period. While Network Load Balancing determines the status of the nodes participating in the cluster via heartbeats, hardware-based solutions can be configured to examine the HTTP result codes for lower-level fault tolerance.

In addition to load-balanced and fault-tolerant Web front ends, WSS also supports SQL clusters for back-end database fault tolerance. You can install SQL Server 2000 in single- and multiinstance mode, which previously used to be referred to as active/passive and active/active configurations. Essentially, in a multiinstance SQL cluster, both of the nodes run separate SQL server instances, which can have any number of databases configured, thus effectively allowing you to manually load-balance the SQL server load. Some SQL database administrators do not like to run SQL in multiple-instance mode, since it gives you a false sense of capacity. When one of the SQL cluster nodes needs to fail over for one reason or another, the second node must have enough capacity to take on the load of the failed-over instance. For example, if both nodes were running at 60% capacity, there would suddenly be 120% capacity requirements put on the single cluster node. Thus, most people prefer to run single-instance SQL, because at least you can be sure that the second node can take on the load of the server failing over. SQL Server 2000 also supports $N + 1$ clusters, which are effectively multiinstance SQL clusters with an extra standby node ready to take over the load of a failing instance. $N + 1$ clusters are a good way to reduce cost for larger SQL deployments, since the standby server can be shared between two active SQL servers. Of course, if two servers fail in an $N + 1$ cluster . . .

9.4   Sizing SPS 2003

Perhaps the throughput performance of STS was one of the reasons SPS 2003 is now built on top of Windows SharePoint Services. As some of you may remember, SPS 2001 was able to only perform between 5 and 8 ops/s due to the extensive dashboard-rendering requirements and the Web storage system WebDAV communication protocol.

SPS 2003, having been built on the foundation provided by Windows SharePoint Services, definitely dusts off the past concerns and emerges as a scalable and reliable platform for enterprise portals. SPS takes the underlying technology infrastructure provided by WSS and extends it with its own services, such as Search and Single Sign-On, which have been engineered to be on par with the underlying page-rendering scalability options.

Since SPS 2003 is built firmly on WSS, all of the sizing guidelines discussed earlier also apply to SPS, with slight variances and a few added services. Thus, we will list the major differences and proceed to the portal-component sizing considerations.

9.4.1   Differences with Windows SharePoint Services

While the page-rendering framework still remains essentially the same in portal sites, the workload definition is slightly different. After all, the intended use of portal sites is considerably different from WSS collaboration team sites, although a certain percentage of WSS site usage is also included in the SPS workload, given that most organizations would choose to use the same farm for both WSS collaboration and SPS portal publishing. Portal-site workload focuses more on browsing, document downloads, and Enterprise Search activities, with slightly reduced emphasis on document management and team collaboration. Given that the Portal Search component, which ships with SPS, is significantly different from the SQL Server MSSearch counterpart, issues with search scalability are far reduced. In fact, the Portal Search is perhaps the most scalable component of SPS, but let's not jump ahead of ourselves.

Since the workload is different, the throughput results you will see in white papers are slightly different as well, although there are only 5 to 10 ops/s differences between SPS and WSS on the same platform. SPS capacity planning focuses on predefined so-called prescribed architectures, which have been well documented by Microsoft and partners. As we discussed in Chapter 7, the prescribed architectures include a single-server, small-farm, medium-farm, and a large-farm setup, shown in Figure 9.1.

Figure 9.1
Microsoft-prescribed SPS architectures.

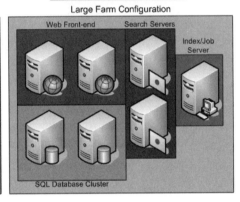

Since the MSDE data-engine version is much more restricted than the WMSDE version, which ships with WSS, HP did not conduct performance testing on this platform. Given the reduced 2-GB storage limit and five-concurrent-job limit, the MSDE data engine will not likely attract many larger production users. It's likely that an SPS deployment utilizing an MSDE data engine is able to perform 15 to 20 ops/s on a typical server platform, this time restricted by the concurrent-job queue limit.

The prescribed small-farm SPS configuration, which in reality is a single-server deployment with a separate SQL back end, is able to perform roughly the similar number of operations per second as its WSS counterpart with 50 ops/s on a dual 2.8-GHz server. The difference here is that in a single-server configuration the Search and Indexing services add slightly to the required server capacity, resulting typically in results reduced by 5 to 10 operations.

A medium-farm prescribed architecture, on the other hand, is able to reach to 110 ops/s on a 2x dual 2.8-GHz Web front-end configuration. By utilizing the latest 3.06-GHz and 3.2-GHz servers, the throughput increases to 172 ops/s and 210 ops/s, respectively. In a medium farm, the

Search Service is still hosted on the same physical server as the Web front end, although the CPU-hungry indexing service has been moved to a dedicated server.

It's clear that a medium farm is able to meet the needs of most enterprises, but just in case there's any doubt, Microsoft also included a large-farm configuration in the prescriptive architectures. The large farm sees the Search component moved to dedicated, load-balanced servers and, as such, is able to provide increased throughput of 125 ops/s with 2x dual CPU 2.8-GHz servers. The workload used for the performance test included only moderate Portal Search usage, as was found to be the case in HP's own internal deployment of SharePoint Products and Technologies. In an Enterprise Search Portal deployment, it's likely you would see a considerably larger divide between the medium and the large farm, since the Search utilization is directed to dedicated servers in a large-farm configuration.

The large-farm prescribed architecture also includes a large farm + WSS configuration, which adds two WSS Web front ends to the large farm in order to separate team collaboration usage from portal site usage. In a typical workload configuration, this increases the throughput to 175 ops/s for the large farm + WSS configuration, thus making the configuration an interesting possibility for large organizations considering extensive portal site deployment with large-scale WSS team collaboration.

Of course, you can choose to keep out of the prescribed architectures, within the limits discussed in Chapter 7. As a guideline, you should consider 50 ops/s per Web front end for a dual CPU 2.8-GHz server and a 4:1 Web front-end to SQL server ratio when utilizing identical SQL Server platforms. By increasing the SQL server to a quad processor configuration, you can achieve a 6:1 ratio instead, just like with WSS.

9.4.2   Choosing the right hardware topology

The WSS formula used to estimate throughput requirements for your organization applies to SPS as well. Thus, let's remind ourselves once again of the formula to estimate required throughput requirements for SPS and use it for some calculations:

$$\frac{\text{Number of users} \times \frac{\text{Percent of active}}{\text{users per day}} \times \frac{\text{Number of operations}}{\text{per active user per day}} \times \text{Peak factor}}{360,000 \times \text{Number of hours per day}}$$

As with WSS, perform a quick calculation for your environment, and compare it with the hardware-platform options shown in Table 9.4.

Table 9.4   *Example WSS Hardware-Platform Throughput Figures*

Server Topology	Estimated Server Throughput
Single server with MSDE Dual 2.8 GHz with 1 GB RAM	~20 ops/s (estimated)
Small farm Dual 2.8 GHz with 1 GB RAM (all)	50 ops/s
Medium farm Dual 2.8 GHz with 1 GB RAM (all)	110 ops/s
Large farm Dual 2.8 GHz with 1 GB RAM (all)	125 ops/s
Large farm + WSS Dual 2.8 GHz with 1 GB RAM (all)	175 ops/s
Medium farm Dual 3.06 with 1 GB RAM (all)	168 ops/s
Medium farm Dual 3.2 GHz with 1 GB RAM (all)	200 ops/s
Extended large farm (6 + 1) Dual 3.2 GHz with 1 GB RAM (all)	600 ops/s

This time around, the last row in the table is not comic relief, but it is, in fact, a six Web front-end, large-farm configuration utilizing a quad processor SQL server, which is the quad CPU SQL back-end scalability limit (6:1) we discussed earlier. It is unlikely that your organization will require such throughput; but rest assured, if the need be, it is there.

Most organizations will likely consider the small-farm, single-server configuration with separated SQL server or the medium-farm configuration, which is the minimum requirement for high-availability SPS 2003 deployment.

So, why would you ever consider a large farm, if your throughput requirements are unlikely to ever justify one? That question is not as easy to answer as the single-server versus load-balanced issue we discussed earlier. If you know that there will be significant demands put on the Search component, you should consider going for the large-farm configuration in order to immediately scale-out for Search performance. However, in a typical enterprise, even with relatively high Search utilization, as you're about to find out, the Search Service scalability far exceeds the need for dedicated Search servers due to scalability. Let's explore the Search Service scalability a little bit further.

9.4.3   Search Service scalability

From a performance perspective, separating Web and search servers isn't necessary for most organizations. HP's testing shows that the core Search Service can respond to queries at a staggering rate of 200 queries per second on a modern dual CPU 2.8-GHz server. Thus, even a typical medium-farm configuration, where Search and the Web front end are hosted on the same server, is able to process more than 110 user ops/s, which in a typical usage scenario translates to hundreds of thousands of users.

In fact, given that the core Search Service can handle 200 queries per second/per server, you will be hard pressed to find a usage scenario where you have enough Web operations per second to be able to reach anywhere near the Search Service throughput (in a typical enterprise deployment only every tenth request is a search query). Extending this math a bit further, in a large-farm deployment with two search servers performing 400 queries per second, you would have to be able to process 4,000 ops/s on the front-end Web servers. This would likely require the maximum 10 Web servers you can operate in a farm and the fastest available quad/eight processor servers around. Obviously, if the usage scenario dictates a higher than average number of search queries, then you will be more likely to hit the Search Service throughput limits. With four servers you can easily perform 800 queries per second, which should be enough capacity to meet the needs of even the largest global enterprises.

Although the indexer performance is largely dependent on the location of the content crawled and the type of files the indexer has to break up, tests have shown the indexer to process typical enterprise content at a rate of approximately 33 documents per second. Given the different crawling options, ranging from full to adaptive, a single index server should be able to keep well up-to-date with a reasonable amount of external content. Consider adding an extra index server for every 5 million items you plan to index, which corresponds with the maximum recommended index size of 20 million items using the maximum supported four index servers.

9.5   Disk subsystem planning

SharePoint Products and Technologies disk subsystem planning is slightly trickier than most applications, due to the database disaster-recovery options and various content indexes that are generated outside the database. Especially in a farm configuration, you should carefully plan the I/O capacity requirements and ensure ample space for future growth. Luckily, today's copious storage-technology options have brought down the per-gigabyte cost of storage, and you have many choices when deciding upon your storage platform.

Shared storage-area networks (SANs) are becoming ever more popular in the enterprise data centers, providing cost savings and easy upgrade paths. Since SQL fully supports SAN storage, you can take advantage of this technology across your SharePoint Products and Technologies deployment. Still, even with a SAN, you have to define a slice from the shared storage pie that should be allocated to you in the beginning. If you're choosing to use directly attached storage instead, it's even more important to consider all future requirements beforehand, since adding capacity might not be as straightforward on a directly attached storage device.

With disk subsystem planning, the easy part is to tell you what Microsoft recommends for your SharePoint Products and Technologies deployment: 200% of content stored for the database server, 50% of all indexed content for the SPS index server, and double the index server's storage capacity for the SPS search servers.

The hard part is trying to come up with an accurate estimate of the "content stored" part for an enterprise with thousands of users. Personally, we've been bitten by this in the past, and it appears we did not learn any lessons. Thus, from bitter experience, we recommend that you think of the worst possible scenario and *double* it. That just might get you through the first 12 months and establish more accurate storage-growth patterns for your enterprise.

9.5.1   Database sizing

First and foremost, database sizing should be your primary concern. Although it's easy to add additional data files to SQL Server 2000, you should try to anticipate usage well in advance, since sometimes the order process might take a while. With directly attached storage devices, you might also need to plan for system downtime, unless the devices support adding capacity online, which SANs, at least, typically do.

The 200% for SQL Server is slightly high, although it is a good recommendation. SQL transaction logs will easily gobble up a large amount of storage, and the SQL MSSearch Index will take up to 25% of the stored content size as well. Still, we've seen the figure typically average around 150% with aggressive transaction log backups and sizing.

9.5.2 Search index sizing

Microsoft recommends that you size the Search Service with 50% of all indexed content for the index server, which is also slightly high. We've seen it be around 20% to 25%, which is possibly explained by the high graphic content of today's increasingly large files (the graphic content is not indexed). However, it pays to be extra safe, since the content index databases cannot be spread across volumes. Every content index is its own database stored in a location that can be changed with command-line tools, but as such is slightly tricky to execute. You should instead follow Microsoft's recommendation and reserve the full 50% for the index servers.

Since the index server will always propagate the full content index database to the search servers after finishing an update, the search servers have to be able to receive a full copy of the index database, along with the currently running database. Microsoft wanted to provide online index updates; thus, the running search index is not replaced but merged as an online operation on the search servers. Therefore, you should plan for double the capacity of the index server on each of the search servers, which is effectively 100% of all the content indexed if you follow Microsoft's recommendations. Again, we've seen this to be lower, but you should follow the safe recommendations if at all possible.

Of course, if you are not planning a server-farm deployment, the previous guidelines are slightly different. In a single-server environment, Microsoft recommends 2.75 times of the total content stored for disk capacity, while in a small-farm deployment, you should follow the previous SQL Server recommendations and prepare for 0.75 times the content stored for Portal Index.

9.6   Planning backup and restore

Part of your overall deployment planning exercise should be considerations for disaster recovery, especially since all of the out-of-the-box options require a significant amount of storage space. The backup-and-restore plan is important in order to prepare for disasters such as database corruption; most of the lost data is typically deleted by end users, albeit accidentally. Therefore, most of the restore requests you're likely to face in ongoing operations are due to accidental file deletes, since SharePoint Products and Technologies do not include trash-bin functionality.

Unfortunately, we must plan for exceptional circumstances when planning our deployment architectures. What if there were a fire in the building hosting the servers, and all of the servers were burned to the ground? Most organizations require a business-continuity plan for such exceptional circumstances that details a plan to continue operations as soon as possible in another location.

9.6.1 Out-of-the-box backup options

Out of the box, SharePoint Products and Technologies ship with tools for both products that allow you to take online backups to disk of production portals and WSS site collections. Of course, you can also utilize all of the disaster-recovery options provided by SQL Server, except, of course, for SPS search indexes, which are stored in another database engine. You can use the Spsbackup tool, discussed in the following text, to back up the search indexes in conjunction with SQL Server disaster-recovery methods. Alternatively, you could choose not to back up the index at all and accept an increased recovery period for the Search component as the content is being reindexed from scratch.

Windows SharePoint Services backups can be performed from the command line with the STSADM tool, which effectively takes a full-fidelity copy of a WSS site collection to a specified backup file. Unfortunately, out of the box, STSADM does not include a command to automatically back up all of the site collections hosted on a virtual server, let alone all of the site collections on all of the virtual servers. Luckily, it is straightforward to create a simple script that batches the tool and even includes an option to schedule backups only of sites that have been modified since the last date a backup was taken. These tools are provided as part of the SharePoint Resource Kit, released on the Microsoft Web site.

SPS ships with a Windows Form application, called SPS 2003 Backup and Restore, with a command-line interface (Spsbackup.exe), shown in Figure 9.2. The Spsbackup tool essentially enumerates the Portal Server structure to provide a nice user interface for backing up and restoring SQL databases. In fact, behind the scenes, Spsbackup uses the SQL Client Tools to execute the SQL backup and restore commands; thus, the SQL Client Tools must be installed on the Web front-end server on which you are executing Spsbackup. In addition to the SQL databases, Spsbackup also backs up the search indexes to disk. To keep track of all the backup files,

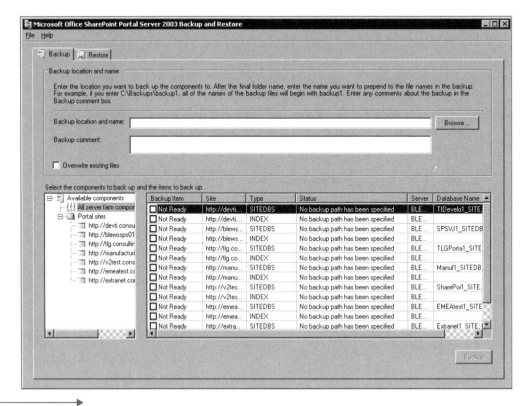

Figure 9.2   *SPS 2003 Backup and Restore utility.*

spsbackup creates an XML manifest file in the directory, where you back up the portals in order to restore the portals with all the previous settings, including the search indexes.

In addition, you can use the Smigrate.exe import/export tool to export spaces and, at a later stage, import them back in using a different site name. Unfortunately, Smigrate exports are not full-fidelity copies of the sites, and you will lose, for example, user rights and permissions when importing the files back to WSS. Still, the tool can be used for providing scripted per-site backup jobs in order to be able to restore accidentally deleted files and sites.

9.6.2   Backup-disk subsystem impact

Since all of the out-of-the-box backups stream the backup files to disk, you must plan for additional disk capacity for backups, unless you plan to use a third-party tool that is capable of streaming backups directly to tape.

To make matter worse, in addition to the disaster-recovery copy you're likely to take directly from SQL or with the `Spsbackup` tool, you should consider how to respond to accidental delete-restore requests. The only out-of-the-box method to perform this is to schedule batched daily `Stsadm` or `Smigrate` exports for all of the team sites and to restore the sites with deleted content using a different name, thus allowing users to manually copy back the files. Unfortunately, this is often done on top of the disaster-recovery backup also performed to disk. Thus, in a worst-case scenario, you must plan for 400% of disk capacity for expected content (200% for SQL, 100% for disaster recovery, and 100% for `Stsadm` or `Smigrate` copies).

9.6.3 Third-party backup solutions

Of course, there are a number of third-party solutions from various providers that offer per-site and even per-document backup and restore capabilities for a cost. The first one to market was AvePoint (`www.avepoint.com`) with a product called Doc Ave 2.5, offering both site- and document-level backup and restore capabilities. There are a number of other products from various vendors also planned, so keep an eye on the Microsoft Partner Solutions Directory for updates on these tools (`http://directory.partners.extranet.microsoft.com/advsearchresults.aspx?productscsv=14`).

10

Deploying SharePoint Technologies

The hard part in your deployment is now behind you, as long as you've set your deployment plans in stone and prepared the underlying infrastructure, as discussed in the first three chapters of Part II. In this chapter, we cover the major aspects of deploying SharePoint Products and Technologies and walk you through a few example installation scenarios for both products.

You know what you're going to deploy, which features you want to enable, and how you're going to use it. So now let's go ahead and do it!

10.1 Preparing for deployment

Before installing the products, you should take a moment to review some up-front tasks that will help streamline the deployment process and, thus, save you time and effort. Since certain infrastructure configuration changes, such as adding DNS aliases and pointers, can take a while to synchronize across the organization, it's good to plan and execute them in advance.

10.1.1 Preparing service accounts

SharePoint Products and Technologies support the new network service local account, which has only minimal rights to the server resources compared with the local system account, which was previously used for running services. However, since the network service account is a local system account, it is recommended that in a farm configuration and when using a remote SQL server, you elect to use a domain service account instead, since authentication between the components must be based on commonly recognized credentials. Built upon Windows Server 2003, SharePoint Products and Technologies support using domain service accounts for authentication across components and technologies utilized by SharePoint.

Service accounts are straightforward domain user identities; however, in order to reduce operational overhead, they are often configured with security policies different from normal user accounts. Typically, service accounts are, for example, set to never expire and are sometimes created without interactive logon rights. While SharePoint does not require anything special from the domain service accounts, I would recommend setting the service accounts to never expire to avoid periodic service reconfiguration. Changing the service account password does require system downtime, limiting the change execution to occur after hours or during weekends.

As you can see from Table 10.1, SharePoint Products and Technologies offer a multitude of possibilities for segregating different components to run under their own individual accounts, even down to the virtual server level. Thus, it's very easy to overarchitect the service account model for a

Table 10.1   *SharePoint Products and Technologies Service Accounts*

Service Account Type	Account Purpose
Configuration database administrator account	This is the main service account for SharePoint that is used for all services and the central administration service application pool.
Application pool account	Each application pool can be configured to run with a different account. By default SharePoint Products and Technologies create two application pools, one for the central administration virtual server and one that can be shared between all extended virtual servers.
Default content access account	SPS Search Service requires a default indexing account used to access resources that require authentication and authorization.
Content source access account	Instead of using the default content source account, each content source can be configured with a separate account for accessing protected resources.
User profile import account	SPS user profile import from the Active Directory by default uses the default content access account but can be configured with a separate identity, which has Active Directory Read permissions.
Single Sign-On Service account	This account is used to run the Single Sign-On Service.

deployment, causing overhead account management down the line. While certain segregation is certainly advisable in order to reduce downtime caused by account lockouts, for example, it's good to find a middle ground between over- and underarchitecting the service account model.

Unless you are running a single-server configuration and elect to use the network service local identity, you will need to create at least the configuration database administration service account, regardless of which SharePoint product you are deploying. The question is: How many other accounts are required for your deployment scenario? Of course, you can choose to use a single service across resources. However, by separating different components to run under separate identities, you can mitigate the impact of an account lockout and security impact in case the service account is compromised.

Although in some scenarios running IIS application pools under different accounts might mitigate security risks, for typical intranet setups, you should consider the security compartmentalization benefits against added management overhead for both SharePoint and SQL. Each application pool account needs to be part of the Power Users group and have *Replace a process level token*, *Adjust memory quotas for a process*, and *Log on as a service* local security policy rights, as shown in Figure 10.1. These security settings are automatically configured for the configuration database administration account, but if you choose to create additional service accounts, these steps must be manually executed for each account. Additionally, you need to ensure that the extra service accounts have at least read, write, and execute privileges on the SQL databases they will be accessing. While Microsoft documents that database owner rights are required, it is not a technical requirement.

For SharePoint Portal Server, you should seriously consider using a dedicated default content access account to reduce the risk of compromising the service account during indexing operations. However, if you trust the resources you will be indexing or if you will only index local content, it is possible to use the same service account you use for other services. Microsoft recommends that the content source access account for Windows SharePoint Services content sources should be granted administrator privileges on the target server in order to ensure that all the content is indexed properly. If you plan to index a lot of external content sources in addition to local SharePoint Sites, you should consider using a separate content access account for external content sources in order to prevent an account with administrative access from falling into the wrong hands.

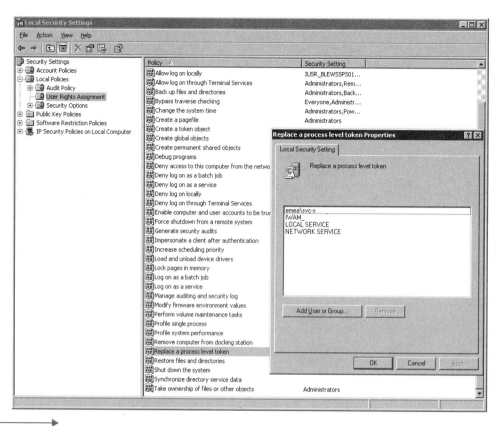

Figure 10.1   *Local Security Policy Editor.*

After choosing the right balance of convenience versus security compartmentalization for your deployment, you should document the accounts and their purposes and secure the passwords accordingly. In a disaster-recovery scenario, you do not want to lose time by having to hunt around for accounts and passwords.

10.1.2   Preparing the DNS architecture

While SharePoint Products and Technologies fully support WINS name resolution, fully qualified domain names (FQDN) are usually employed to ensure that everyone can access a service in an enterprise deployment. Since DNS changes usually take a while to replicate and process, depending on an organization's strategy, it's good to assign the DNS names well in advance and prior to installing SharePoint Products and Technologies.

Most organizations have standards for naming DNS pointers based on the region or business unit the servers belong to. While, for example, `dubwspro001.emea.company.com` is nice for IT organizations, since they can quickly deduct that the server is a production (`pro`) Web server (`ws`) node (`001`) located in Dublin (`dub`), it is unlikely that end users will have a clue as to how domain naming schemes work. Luckily, DNS architecture supports domain name aliases, which can point to existing records and provide much more user-friendly names for business applications. For example, a DNS alias for this server could be `teams.company.com`, which end users would certainly remember more easily than the complicated IT naming scheme.

There are three ways to create more than one virtual server on a single server (or farm). You can, for instance, assign each virtual server to operate on a specific TCP/IP port, such as port 88. Unfortunately, this method is the least obvious for end users, since they will need to append the port to the URL (`http://server.com:88`) when accessing the virtual servers; thus, I would not recommend using it unless it is the only available option.

Typically, most organizations elect to add additional IP addresses to the Web server, configuring each virtual server to use a dedicated IP address. This approach offers all IIS functionality without compromises but obviously adds a management overhead, since you have to worry about creating DNS pointers/aliases for various IP addresses and assigning them all to the servers. In a farmed environment, you will quickly have an IP address management problem on your hands, since, for example, two front ends would require a total of three IP addresses for each virtual server configured (one per front end and one for the load-balanced address). Unfortunately, at the time of writing, virtual servers assigned to IP addresses are not supported for SharePoint Products and Technologies, although we have successfully run several production environments using this type of IIS configuration. When troubleshooting any SharePoint issues, Microsoft Product Support Services will require that these configurations be changed in order to progress with the support case. We hope that this issue will be addressed in a future service pack. However, for now it's better to avoid the option altogether and instead use the next method described.

The far easiest method from an operational and user perspective is to use host headers, which allow several virtual servers to operate using the same IP address, as seen in Figure 10.2. Host headers are essentially DNS aliases, which resolve to the same IP address. However, since every browser provides the requested host name as part of the HTTP query, Windows Server

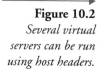

Figure 10.2
Several virtual servers can be run using host headers.

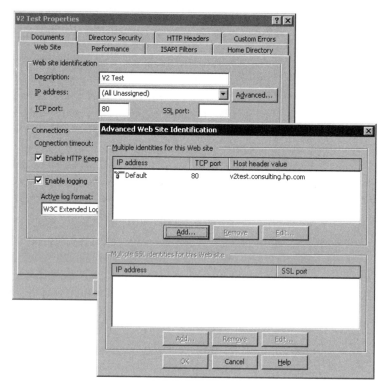

2003 is able to detect which virtual server the query is intended for and queue it up accordingly. Sounds perfect; minimal management overhead with pleasing URLs for end users! Unfortunately, as you might guess, there's a catch. Due to the way SSL-encrypted requests are processed, IIS cannot read the encrypted host headers and, thus, is unable to queue the requests to the correct virtual servers. SSL-encrypted requests are always forwarded to the default virtual server, which means that you can *only* provide SSL encryption for one virtual server with SharePoint Products and Technologies when using host headers. This can be a major concern for organizations requiring SSL encryption, and we hope Microsoft will allow IP-bound virtual servers to be used with a future service pack.

10.1.3   Configuring the operating system for SharePoint deployment

Windows Server 2003 does not by default install components such as IIS and ASP.NET. Thus, before installing WSS or SPS, you must make sure

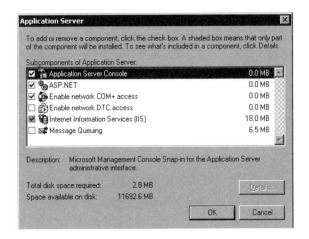

Figure 10.3
The easiest way to install components required by WSS and SPS is to install ASP.NET.

each application server is configured with the appropriate components beforehand.

The easiest way to install required components without services that conflict with SharePoint (FrontPage 2002 Extensions) is to install ASP.NET using the following method.

On each Web, application, search, and job server, you should execute the following:

1.   Go to **Start → Control Panel → Add or Remove Programs → Add/Remove Windows Components**.

2.   Select **Application Server.**

3.   Click on **Details**.

4.   Check **ASP.NET** (Figure 10.3).

5.   Click **OK**.

If IIS and ASP.NET were installed using a different method previously, you should ensure that FrontPage 2002 Extensions are not installed on the server, since they can conflict with WSS ISAPI Extensions.

To verify that FrontPage Extensions are not installed, do the following:

1.   Go to **Start → Control Panel → Add or Remove Programs → Add/Remove Windows Components → Application Server (Details)**.

2.   Select **Internet Information Services (IIS)**.

Figure 10.4
*Ensuring that
FrontPage 2002
Server Extensions
are not installed.*

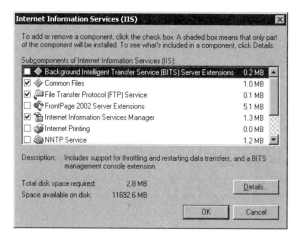

3.   Click on **Details**.

4.   Ensure that **Front Page 2002 Server Extensions** is *not* selected
(Figure 10.4).

5.   Click **OK**.

10.1.4 Changing SQL Server ports

As we discussed in Chapter 7, some database administrators prefer to run
SQL Server with a nonstandard TCP/IP port. For example, the Slammer
SQL Worm, which affected numerous systems all around the world,
exploited the fact that most SQL setups used the standard 1434 UDP and
1433 TCP ports. Thus, it's good to make life a little harder for malicious
users and viruses and to take steps at least to slow down attempts to exploit
services remotely. With SQL 2000 Server you can change the SQL ports by
opening the Server Network Utility and changing the default port 1433 to
something else, as long as the port is not reserved by another application
running on the server.

If you are planning to use a nonstandard TCP/IP port for SQL, Share-
Point requires that the SQL client options be configured prior to installation.

On each Web, application, search, and job server, you should execute
the following (replace port 2048 with your choice):

1.   Click on **Start**.

2.   Select **Run…**.

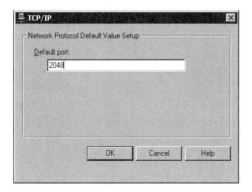

Figure 10.5
*Changing the
default 1433 port
to 2048.*

3.   Enter `cliconfg.exe` (the full path is `C:\WINNT\system32\`
      `cliconfg.exe`).

4.   Click on **OK**.

5.   Select **TCP/IP** from the Disabled protocols list.

6.   Click on **Enable**.

7.   Select **TCP/IP** from the Enabled protocols list.

8.   Click on **Properties**.

9.   Change the default port from `1433` to `2048`, as shown in Figure
      10.5.

10.   Click on **OK** twice to close the SQL Server Client Network Utility.

10.1.5   Configuring IIS for SharePoint Products and Technologies

Even if you are not planning to create more than one virtual server initially,
it's good to change a number of settings in IIS before proceeding to deploy
SharePoint Products and Technologies. Most companies today have best practices for securing IIS, which include making changes to the default IIS configuration. While most of these settings will not affect SharePoint deployments,
there are a few settings that might prevent proper functionality. Thus, it's
good to run through the IIS configuration before proceeding further.

   While it's not required, a widely accepted best practice is to change the
out-of-the-box default Web site to run under a random port and stop the
default Web site. All new virtual servers should also be configured to store
files on a disk partition different from the system drive (typically `c:`)—for
example, `d:\inetpub\wwwroot`. The less predictable your IIS configuration

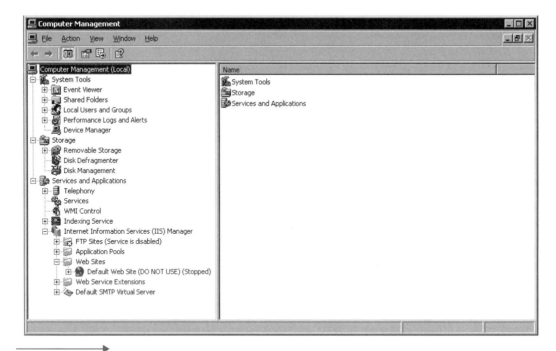

Figure 10.6   *IIS Manager.*

is, the harder it is for virus writers to make generic worms that propagate through potential security holes left behind by out-of-the-box configuration.

New virtual servers can be configured from the IIS Manager, shown in Figure 10.6. While you no longer need to have the actual directories created before proceeding to create a new virtual server, it's good to manually create the intended file-system structure for all new virtual servers hosted on the platform. Think about standardizing on the location and documenting it down for quicker disaster recovery and to avoid confusion when managing more than one SharePoint server.

Some organizations preconfigure IIS with their preferred settings to ensure secure IIS deployments. While most of these settings do not interfere with WSS, one setting in particular has been known to cause issues. NTLM Authentication, which is the default authentication method in SharePoint Products and Technologies, requires that HTTP keep-alives be turned on. This is the default in IIS, but if you suspect it might have been changed in your organization's deployment of Windows Server 2003, follow these steps to ensure that keep-alives are enabled.

1. Go to **Computer Management → Services and Applications → IIS Manager → Web Sites.**

2. Right-click on **Web Sites** and select **Properties**.

3. Check that **Enable HTTP Keep-Alives** is turned on, as shown in Figure 10.7. This is required for NTLM Authentication.

4. Click on **OK**.

5. Click on **Select All**.

6. Click on **OK**.

If you would like to disable the out-of-the-box default Web site, you can do so by following these steps:

1. Go to **Computer Management → Services and Applications → IIS Manager → Select Web Sites.**

2. Right-click on **Default Web Site** and select **Properties**.

3. Set **Web Site TCP Port** to a random number—for example, 56783.

4. Click **OK**.

5. Right-click on **Default Web Site** and select **Stop**.

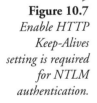

Figure 10.7
Enable HTTP Keep-Alives setting is required for NTLM authentication.

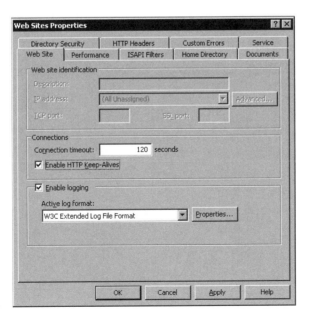

Once you have stopped the default Web site, you will need to create a
new virtual server that will be used for SharePoint Products and Technologies. Repeat these steps for as many virtual servers as you're planning to initially extend.

1.   Go to **Computer Management** → **Services and Applications** →
      IIS Manager → **Web Sites**.

2.   Right-click on **Web Sites** and select **New** → **Web Site...**, and
      enter a descriptive name in the *Description* field (this will not be
      visible to end users).

3.   Click on **Next**.

4.   Select (**All Unassigned**) for the Web Site IP address and ensure
      that Web Site TCP Port is set to 80 (Figure 10.8).

5.   When creating more than one virtual server with host headers,
      enter the appropriate host header for the Web site.

6.   Click on **Next**.

7.   Enter the path to the Web Site home directory (preferably not on
      the system drive).

8.   Click on **Next**.

9.   Click on **Next**.

10.   Click on **Finish**.

Figure 10.8
*Make sure All
Unassigned is
selected and enter
the appropriate
port and host
header.*

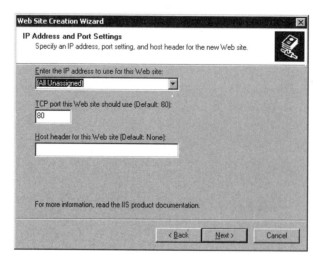

10.2 Deploying Windows SharePoint Services

Windows SharePoint Services is an extremely straightforward application to install, deceptively so sometimes. Microsoft has made even a large farm configuration easy to complete; installation is essentially a "click **Next**" type of affair with few configuration settings along the way. Since the actual installation steps are so straightforward, we won't cover each one of them down to the "click **Next**" level; instead, we'll point you to the important decisions to make during the deployment.

10.2.1 Installing Windows SharePoint Services

When installing WSS, there is only one critical choice to be made, and that's the database engine technology choice for your deployment.

If you are planning to use SQL Server 2000, regardless of whether you're going to use a remote SQL server or one that is installed on the same server, you need to indicate that you do not want WMSDE to be installed during WSS installation. This can be done by either selecting the *Server Farm* option during installation, as shown in Figure 10.9, or by executing the installer package with the `Setupsts.exe remotesql=yes` command-line switch.

Figure 10.9
Installing WSS.

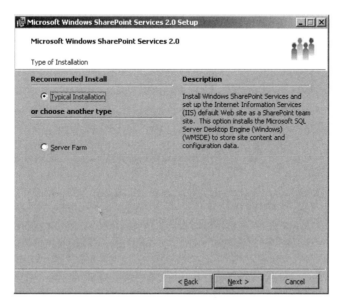

If you're wondering what the `setupsts.exe` file mentioned earlier is, it's likely you've downloaded the WSS Web Install Package (`stsv2.exe`). `Setupsts.exe` is the real WSS installer, which the Web Package `Stsv2.exe` automatically extracts to a temporary path and executes for you. On the other hand, if you have a CD with WSS included, it's likely that the package has been already extracted, leaving you with `Setupsts.exe` and a number of other files.

If you downloaded the Web package and want to perform a command-line installation, you can extract the files by executing `Stsv2.exe /T:c:\temp /C` and replacing `c:\temp` with the path where you want to extract the files to. For the full command-line reference available for the `Setupsts.exe` package, please refer to the `Setup.htm` file in the extracted directory. The most important switches are likely the previously mentioned `remotesql=yes` and `/qr` switch, which perform a quiet installation.

Regardless of whether you downloaded WSS from Microsoft.com or retrieved it from a CD, the installation steps are the same.

1.   Execute `Stsv2.exe` or `Setupsts.exe`.

2.   Accept the license agreement and click **Next**.

3.   If you want to use WMSDE, select **Typical Installation**. If you want to use SQL Server 2000, select **Server Farm**. Click **Next**.

4.   Click **Install**.

In approximately 10 minutes, WSS is installed, and, if you chose **Typical Install**, you're presented with a configured WSS Home page. However, if you chose **Server Farm** or ran the setup command with the `remotesql` switch, there's still a bit more to do, and you're instead presented with a Web page requesting SQL and IIS application pool details, which we will cover next.

10.2.2   Configuring account and database settings

As we discussed in Chapter 7, there are two authentication modes in SQL Server 2000 that you can use with Windows SharePoint Services. Windows Authentication is the preferred secure authentication method, while SQL Authentication is the legacy, which some organizations still prefer. Regardless of which authentication mode you have selected for your deployment, you need to make sure that appropriate credentials are granted for the account you use to connect to the SQL server.

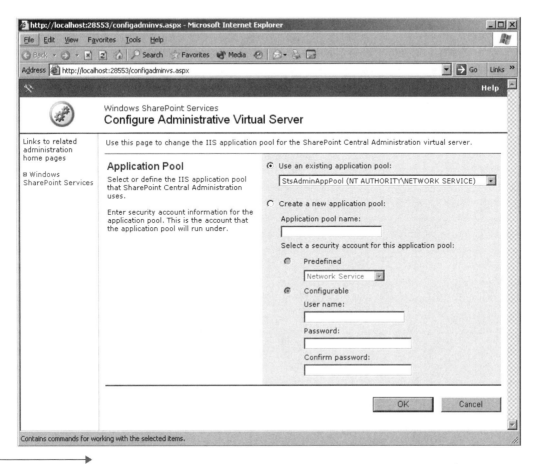

Figure 10.10   *Configuring WSS application pool settings.*

If you plan to use Windows Authentication to connect to the SQL server, the application pool identity settings (as shown in Figure 10.10) are very important, since WSS uses them to connect to the database server. Thus, you need either to create a new application pool with your preferred credentials or to open the IIS Services Manager and change the default StsAdminAppPool identity to your desired service account.

Once you have configured the application pool for the administration server and clicked **OK**, IIS must be restarted, which you can do by executing iisreset at the Start/Run prompt.

Next, you must provide the SQL server and central administration database names and whether you want to use Windows Authentication or SQL

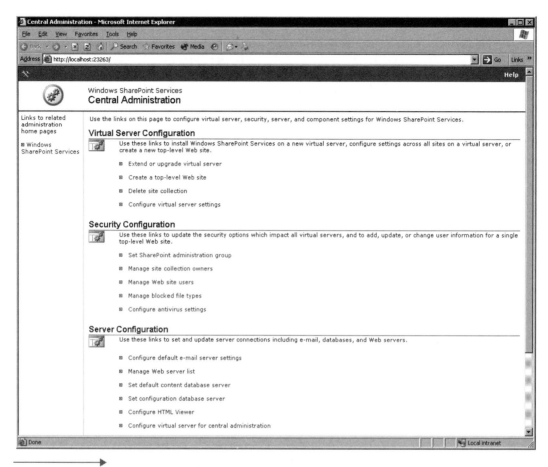

Figure 10.11   *WSS central administration pages.*

Authentication to connect to the SQL server. If you select Windows Authentication, which is the more secure of the two, WSS will connect to the SQL server with the credentials configured for the IIS application pool.

After configuring the relevant SQL details and clicking **OK**, WSS creates the central configuration database for your deployment and presents you with the central administration page shown in Figure 10.11, which means you're ready to extend virtual servers with Windows SharePoint Services.

10.2.3   Configuring server settings and defaults

Before extending virtual servers (as seen in Figure 10.12), it's good to define a few serverwide settings and defaults for new virtual servers. Blocked file

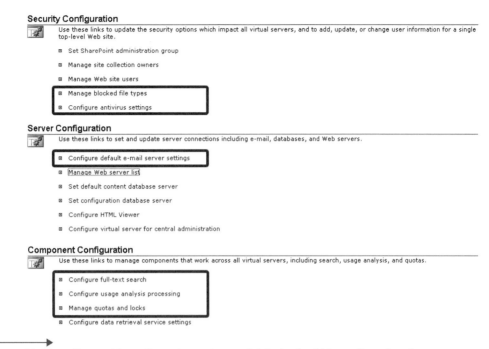

Figure 10.12 *Serverwide configuration options and defaults should be configured up front.*

types, antivirus settings, usage analysis settings, quota templates, and full-text search options are used across all virtual servers, while configuring the default e-mail server settings reduces the configuration needed after extending a virtual server.

10.2.4 Extending virtual servers with Windows SharePoint Services

Once server defaults have been set up, you're ready to proceed to extending a virtual server with Windows SharePoint Services. You can click on either **Extend or upgrade virtual server** or **Configure virtual server settings** to display a list of virtual servers configured in IIS. Click on the virtual server you configured previously (or the default Web site if you did not do anything), and you'll be presented with links to **Extend and create a content database** or **Extend and map to another virtual server**, as seen in Figure 10.13.

Each virtual server must create a content database for files and configuration data; thus, unless you're installing a WSS server farm, you will always select the first option to **Extend and create a database**. We'll come back to

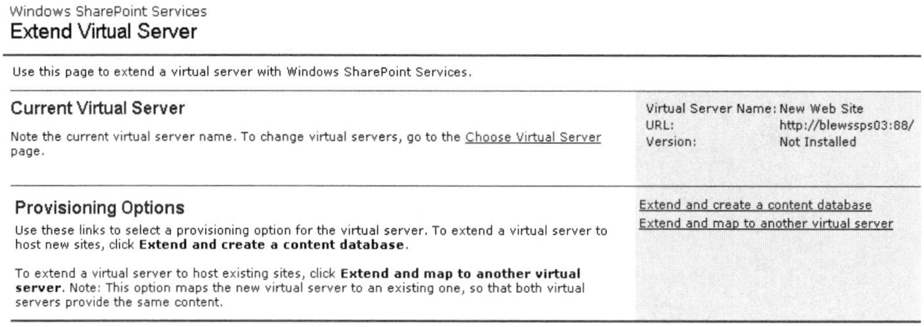

Windows SharePoint Services
Extend Virtual Server

Use this page to extend a virtual server with Windows SharePoint Services.

Current Virtual Server

Note the current virtual server name. To change virtual servers, go to the Choose Virtual Server page.

Virtual Server Name: New Web Site
URL: http://blewssps03:88/
Version: Not Installed

Provisioning Options

Use these links to select a provisioning option for the virtual server. To extend a virtual server to host new sites, click **Extend and create a content database**.

To extend a virtual server to host existing sites, click **Extend and map to another virtual server**. Note: This option maps the new virtual server to an existing one, so that both virtual servers provide the same content.

Extend and create a content database
Extend and map to another virtual server

Figure 10.13   *Extending a WSS virtual server.*

the server farm scenario in just a bit, but even when deploying a farm, you have to create a content database on one of the front-end Web servers.

Similar to configuring the first central administration Web site, you have to either use an existing application pool or create a new one with specific user credentials. When you extend a virtual server, WSS will automatically create a site collection for the top `http://server/` level, which is

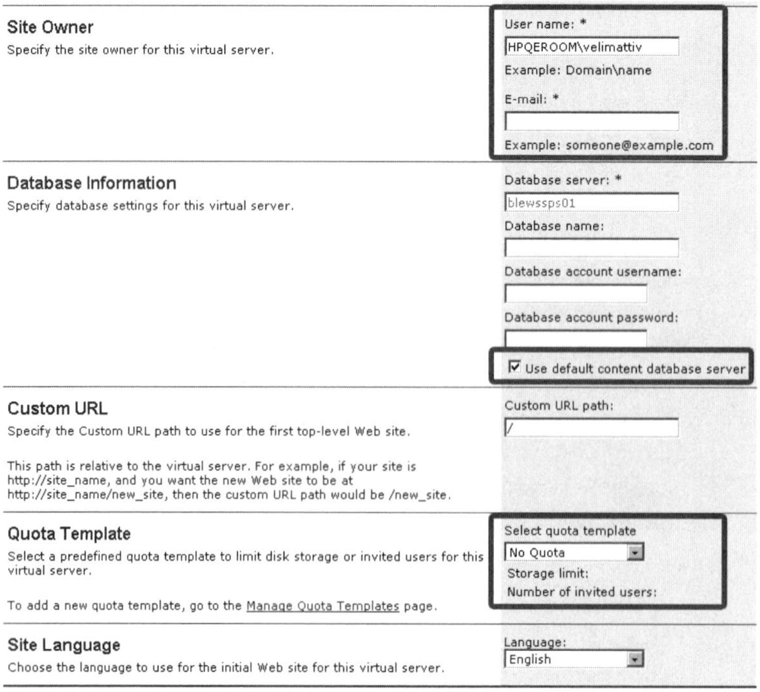

Site Owner
Specify the site owner for this virtual server.

User name: *
HPQEROOM\velimattiv
Example: Domain\name

E-mail: *

Example: someone@example.com

Database Information
Specify database settings for this virtual server.

Database server: *
blewssps01
Database name:

Database account username:

Database account password:

☑ Use default content database server

Custom URL
Specify the Custom URL path to use for the first top-level Web site.

This path is relative to the virtual server. For example, if your site is http://site_name, and you want the new Web site to be at http://site_name/new_site, then the custom URL path would be /new_site.

Custom URL path:
/

Quota Template
Select a predefined quota template to limit disk storage or invited users for this virtual server.

To add a new quota template, go to the Manage Quota Templates page.

Select quota template
No Quota
Storage limit:
Number of invited users:

Site Language
Choose the language to use for the initial Web site for this virtual server.

Language:
English

Figure 10.14   *WSS virtual server configuration.*

Windows SharePoint Services
Virtual Server Successfully Extended

The virtual server was successfully extended and a new, empty Web site has been created with the URL specified below. To view the Web site in a new browser window, click the URL. To return to the Virtual Server Settings page, click **"OK"**.

New top-level Web site URL: http://blewssps03:88

The virtual server has been extended, but the virtual server cannot be restarted. You must manually restart IIS. To restart IIS, open a command prompt window and type **iisreset**.

OK

Figure 10.15   *IIS must be restarted after a new virtual server has been provisioned.*

why you have to specify site ownership information, as shown in Figure 10.14. If you prefer, you can also define a quota template, which is applied to the top-level site collection.

When you select **Use default content database server** (the default), WSS will create a new content database automatically for you. However, if you wish, you can also use a different SQL server altogether in order to, for example, load-balance between two SQL Server 2000 instances on a cluster.

Once you have configured all of the options to your preference, click **OK**; WSS provisions the database and application pools options defined and indicates that the virtual server was successfully extended, as shown in Figure 10.15, requesting that you restart IIS manually if required.

10.2.5   Server farm considerations

When deploying a WSS farm, the installation steps for the first front-end Web server are exactly the same as for a single-server deployment. However, when installing WSS on any additional Web front-end servers, you have to choose **Extend and map to another virtual server** when extending a virtual server, as shown in Figure 10.16.

Windows SharePoint Services
Extend Virtual Server

Use this page to extend a virtual server with Windows SharePoint Services.

Current Virtual Server

Note the current virtual server name. To change virtual servers, go to the Choose Virtual Server page.

Virtual Server Name: New Web Site
URL: http://blewssps03:88/
Version: Not Installed

Provisioning Options

Use these links to select a provisioning option for the virtual server. To extend a virtual server to host new sites, click **Extend and create a content database**.

To extend a virtual server to host existing sites, click **Extend and map to another virtual server**. Note: This option maps the new virtual server to an existing one, so that both virtual servers provide the same content.

Extend and create a content database
Extend and map to another virtual server

Figure 10.16   *Additional front-end Web servers must choose to map to another virtual server.*

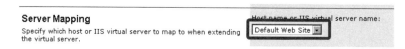

Figure 10.17 *Map additional Web front-end virtual servers to their corresponding hosts.*

To map to another virtual server, select the same virtual server as on the first Web front end, as shown in Figure 10.17, and specify application pool settings.

10.2.6   Configuring Windows SharePoint Services features

There are a few settings that apply only to the specific virtual server on which they have been configured—for example, self-service site creation. These settings have to be configured only once, even on a server farm, since changes are stored in the configuration database. Thus, the last step when deploying WSS is to make sure all of the virtual server–specific settings are configured as you previously planned.

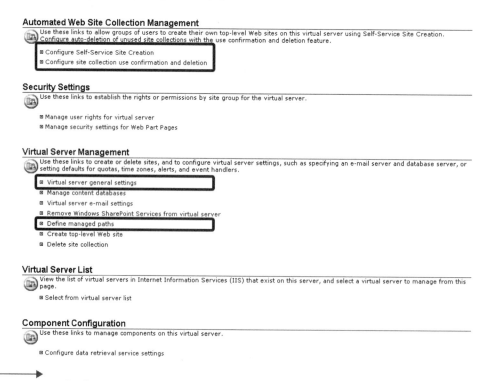

Figure 10.18 *Configuring virtual server–specific settings.*

As shown in Figure 10.18, in addition to settings for self-service site creation and site-collection use confirmation and deletion (covered in Chapter 8), you should make sure that virtual server general settings and managed paths are set before letting users loose on the system.

Virtual server general settings allow you to configure the default time zone and locality settings, quota templates, alert settings, and the maximum file upload site, as well as some security options. In addition you can enable event handlers and public folder integration by following the link for **Virtual server general settings**.

Managed paths, as we discussed earlier in Chapters 7 and 9, allow you to set exclusions for any custom ASP.NET applications and to set inclusions for URL paths that users can create new site collections to. While the default `/sites` path is a good choice, you could create any number of other paths for users to choose from or remove the default `/sites` path altogether.

And with that, you're ready for operations. Before sending out the URL though, I suggest you proceed to Chapter 12 for supportability and extra configuration suggestions.

10.3   Deploying SharePoint Portal Server 2003

Deploying SPS 2003 is almost as straightforward as WSS, although the product is much more complex. Unlike WSS installation, SPS gathers more details from the user during the installation in order to configure the various added components, such as Portal Search Service.

10.3.1   Installing SharePoint Portal Server 2003

As with WSS, during setup you must choose which database engine you're going to use for your SPS deployment. You have the option to install MSDE, which ships with the product, or to use SQL Server 2000 on a local or remote server. In addition, the SPS installation prompts you for the program data directories and the service account information.

By default, the SPS installation stores the program files and data files in the `\program files\SharePoint Portal Server` directory. In most cases, as we discussed in Chapter 8, you will want to change this so that the data files reside on a dedicated partition, since the Portal Search databases will be stored in this location by default. To reduce administrative overhead, you should change the default to the final intended location for SPS data files.

The service account prompted during the SPS install is added as the central administration application pool identity and is thus used for administrative operations that create, modify, or grant access to the configuration or portal site databases. Since the service account will also be used to run services, such as the Portal Alert Service, the account must be a member of the Power Users group on the server. The installation will automatically grant the defined account the following rights in order to be able to run the services: *Replace process level token*, *Adjust memory quotas for a process*, and *Log on as a service*. Note that if you change this account by using the Configure Server Farm Account Settings page, these rights are not revoked automatically for the previous account. However, you can remove these rights using Local Security Policy.

To start the SPS installation, double-click on `setup.exe`, located on the SPS 2003 installation CD (see Figure 10.19).

1. Click **Next** to start the setup.

2. Click on **OK** and wait until the binary installation completes (see Figure 10.20).

3. Once WSS binaries have been installed and configured, you are presented with the SPS install application. Click Next to start the installation (see Figure 10.21).

4. Accept the license agreement and click **Next** to continue.

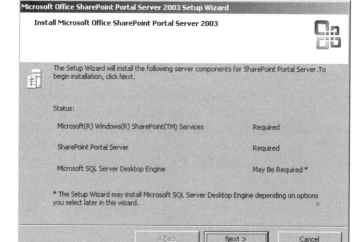

Figure 10.19
SPS 2003
`setup.exe`.

Figure 10.20
*SPS installs WSS
prior to proceeding
with portal setup.*

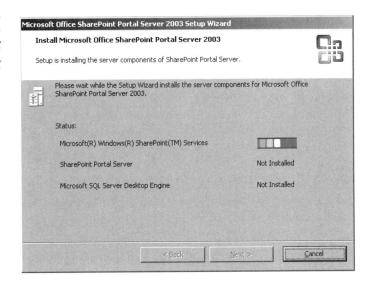

5.   Fill in your product key and click **Next**.

6.   Choose either to install the MSDE database engine or to use a SQL Server 2000 by selecting **Install without database engine** (see Figure 10.22).

7.   Change program binary and data locations by clicking **Browse**.

Figure 10.21
*The SPS part of the
installer starts after
WSS has been
installed.*

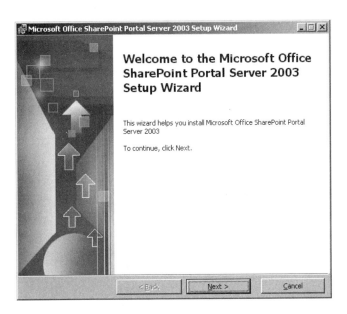

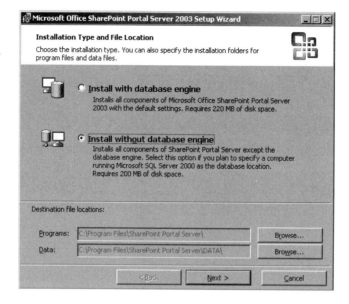

Figure 10.22
*SPS installation
will prompt you for
database engine
and data-file
location.*

8.   Once you have configured the database and program file loca-
      tions, click **Next** to continue.

9.   Enter your service account into the *Account name* field (see Figure
      10.23).

10.   Enter the password for this account and click **Next**.

11.   Click on **Next** and then **Finish** to end the installation.

Figure 10.23
*Service accounts
are configured
during SPS
installation.*

In approximately 30 minutes, SPS is installed on the server. Unlike WSS, regardless of whether you have chosen to install an MSDE data engine, there are some mandatory configuration steps you must still complete, which we will cover next.

10.3.2   Configuring account and database settings

Depending on whether you installed SPS with MSDE or without a data engine, the account configuration page looks slightly different. However, both pages ask you for the default content access account, which is used to crawl both internal and external content sources, as discussed earlier in the chapter. When installing without a data engine, you are additionally prompted for portal site application pool identity information, as shown in Figure 10.24.

When installed with MSDE, SPS creates the configuration database for you automatically on the local server and takes you directly to SharePoint

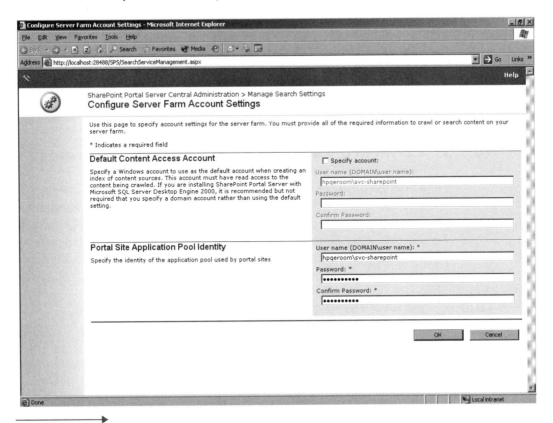

Figure 10.24   *Configuring service accounts for SPS.*

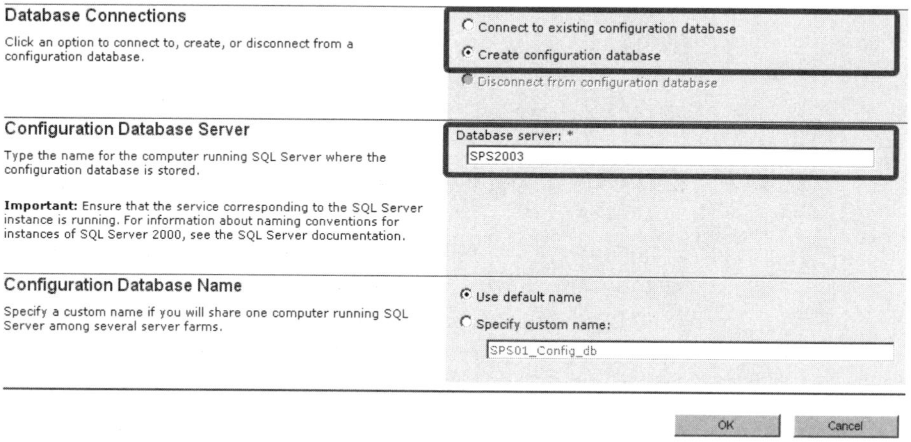

Database Connections

Click an option to connect to, create, or disconnect from a
configuration database.

- ○ Connect to existing configuration database
- ● Create configuration database
- ○ Disconnect from configuration database

Configuration Database Server

Type the name for the computer running SQL Server where the
configuration database is stored.

Important: Ensure that the service corresponding to the SQL Server
instance is running. For information about naming conventions for
instances of SQL Server 2000, see the SQL Server documentation.

Database server: *

SPS2003

Configuration Database Name

Specify a custom name if you will share one computer running SQL
Server among several server farms.

- ● Use default name
- ○ Specify custom name:

  SPS01_Config_db

OK   Cancel

Figure 10.25   *SQL connection information when installed without a data engine.*

Portal Server site creation, which is covered later in the chapter. Installations
opting to use SQL Server 2000 will need to define SQL connections, as
shown in Figure 10.25. If you are deploying a single server or the first node
of a server farm, you will need to select the *Create configuration database*
option and enter the database server name. You can also choose the *Specify
custom name* option for the configuration database, although the default
SPS01_Config_db is just as good a name as any, unless you are sharing the
same database server among multiple SPS installations.

10.3.3   Configuring SharePoint Portal Server topology

Once the configuration database is provisioned, you need to assign Web,
search, index, and job components to a server in order to create and host
ports. In a single-server setup, component configuration is straightforward,
since all of the components are assigned to the same server, as shown in Figure 10.26. After configuring the portal components, it is good to define the
e-mail server settings, although it is not mandatory.

10.3.4   Server farm considerations

When deploying an SPS farm, the installation steps for the first front-end
Web server are exactly the same as for a single-server deployment. However,
before proceeding with the component configuration, you should also
install SPS on all other servers participating in the farm. The only exception

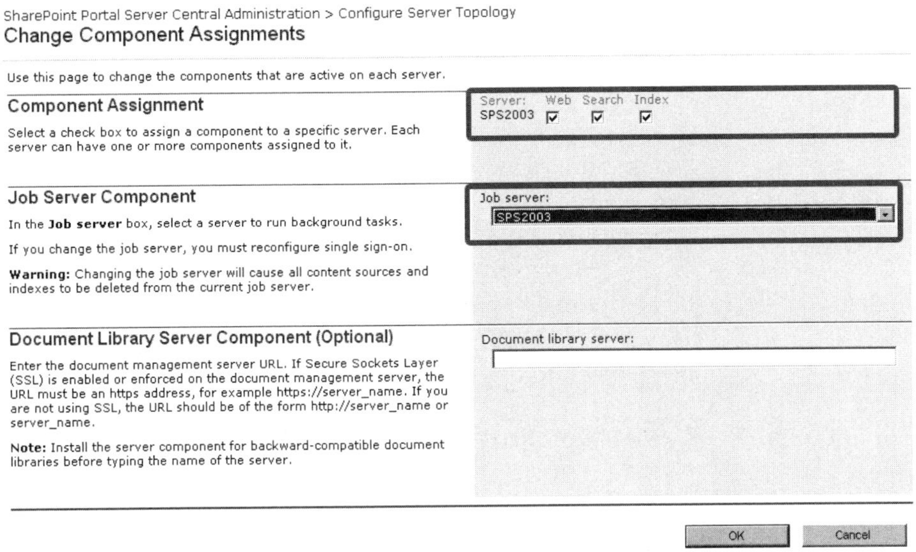

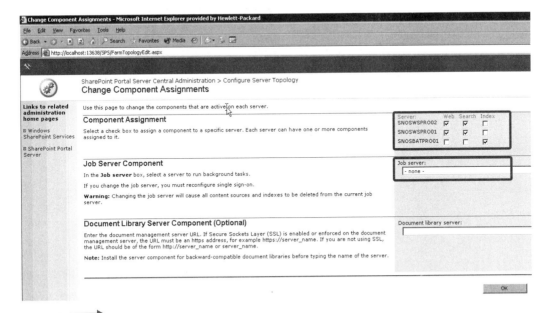

Figure 10.26   *Assigning portal components to their respective servers.*

Figure 10.27   *Assigning components in a farm deployment.*

during the installation process, as we noted earlier, is that you will only create the configuration database once and instead choose the *Connect to an existing configuration database* option for the rest of the farm servers.

Once you have joined all other servers to the configuration database and clicked the *Change components* option, you'll see all of the servers in the *Component Assignment* section, as shown in Figure 10.27. Proceed to assign components according to your server deployment plan and be sure to assign the job server role to one of the servers (as we covered earlier, the job role cannot be load balanced). Click **OK** and verify that the component assignment is correct; note that you can change the components at any time, even after going into production.

10.3.5 Creating SharePoint portal sites

Once the components are assigned, you are ready to create your first portal site, as shown in Figure 10.28.

1.   Navigate to the SharePoint Portal Server Central Administration Home page and click on **Create a portal site**.

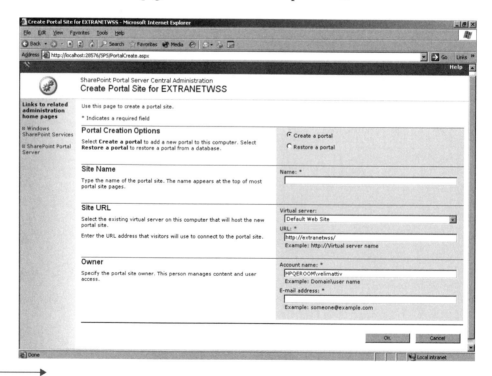

Figure 10.28   *Creating a portal site.*

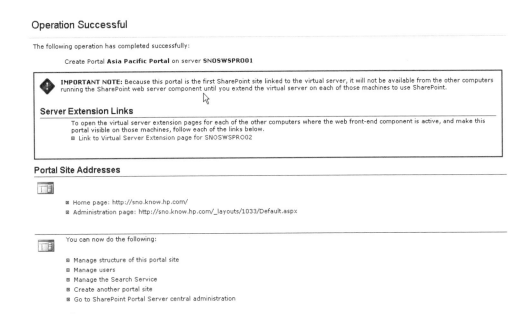

Operation Successful

The following operation has completed successfully:

Create Portal **Asia Pacific Portal** on server **SNOSWSPRO01**

IMPORTANT NOTE: Because this portal is the first SharePoint site linked to the virtual server, it will not be available from the other computers running the SharePoint web server component until you extend the virtual server on each of those machines to use SharePoint.

Server Extension Links

To open the virtual server extension pages for each of the other computers where the web front-end component is active, and make this portal visible on those machines, follow each of the links below.
- Link to Virtual Server Extension page for SNOSWSPRO02

Portal Site Addresses

- Home page: http://sno.know.hp.com/
- Administration page: http://sno.know.hp.com/_layouts/1033/Default.aspx

You can now do the following:

- Manage structure of this portal site
- Manage users
- Manage the Search Service
- Create another portal site
- Go to SharePoint Portal Server central administration

Figure 10.29   *SPS will detect all Web front-end servers and provide a link to extend them.*

2. Fill in the *Site Name* field and virtual server information, along with the URL users will use to connect to the portal site. On a farm setup, this would be the load-balanced DNS alias configured for the virtual server.

3. Provide the portal site owner account name and e-mail address. The account specified here will be given Portal Site Administrator access.

4. If you are deploying a farm configuration, you must map all remaining Web front-end servers to the portal site content databases after the portal has been created. SPS will detect the other servers participating in the Web front-end role and provide you with instructions and a link to each of the Web front-end-server central administration pages, as shown in Figure 10.29. As with WSS, you will simply select **Extend and map to another virtual server** on the other Web front ends in the farm deployment.

10.3.6   Configuring Portal Server settings

After creating a portal site, you should configure a few of the important SPS server settings shown in Figure 10.30. As with WSS, you should configure

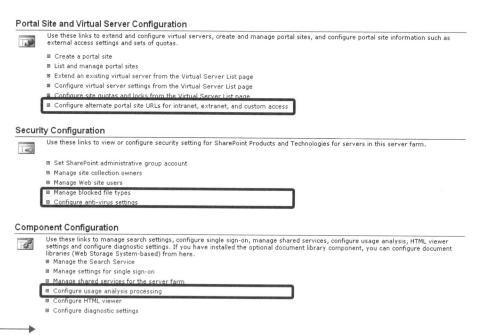

Figure 10.30   *Portal Server features can be configured from Central Administration.*

the serverwide blocked file types, antivirus settings, and usage-analysis features if you plan to use them in your deployment.

If you intend to create WSS sites within the newly created portal site, you should also follow the WSS virtual server configuration options we covered earlier in the chapter. In particular, the managed paths must be configured on the WSS administration pages if you intend to add managed paths other than the /sites path or if you plan to run custom ASP.NET applications on the server.

Your portal site is now ready for portal owners to add the data and define portal site settings, which we will cover in Chapter 12.

10.4   Service packs and hotfixes

This chapter covered the basic SPS and WSS installations. It is recommended that you regularly check the Microsoft Web site for the latest hotfixes and service packs and apply them as appropriate to your deployment. It's a good idea to apply all service packs prior to going live with the SharePoint deployment so that you do not need to worry about upgrading any databases or core files and, thus, having to test extensively prior to upgrade.

Migrating Data to SharePoint Products and Technologies

This chapter primarily focuses on cross-product and within-product migrations rather than the migration from SPS 2001 and STS. This decision was made since we feel there is a wealth of coverage out there on how to migrate from these products but less on migrating from other applications or moving your data around your SharePoint Products and Technologies deployments. That said, many of the techniques and thoughts documented here are equally applicable to a migration from any previous incarnation of SharePoint.

Even though migration from a legacy platform might not be part of your deployment plan, it is highly likely you will be faced with migrations sooner or later, be they migrations within your SharePoint Products and Technologies deployment or from other platforms. After all, maintaining and supporting disparate knowledge environments is not only costly from an operational and support perspective; disparate systems also create knowledge silos that prevent effective sharing of knowledge, experiences, and best practices within an enterprise.

In this chapter, we will cover some of the typical migration scenarios and tools available for you to perform them. While it is by no means meant to be a finite list of migration methodologies and technologies, we hope the chapter provides you with an insight on how to approach platform consolidation and migration efforts within your enterprise.

11.1 Migrating within SharePoint Products and Technologies

Although one might consider migrations as mainly taking data from System A to System B, a much more likely and common migration scenario is to actually move data within the same product. Having separate development, staging, and production environments is commonplace in any enterprise application deployment, and often moving data between these environments is part of a production deployment cycle. In regionalized deployments, moving production data is commonplace due to changing network conditions and users changing locations, not to mention consolidating infrastructures to a central farmed deployment from previous single-server configurations. Farther-reaching changes, such as mergers or divestitures, can also prompt the consolidation or separation of data.

Luckily, moving data around within the WSS environment is quite straightforward, and there are a few options that end users can execute without involving the system administrators, thus reducing the overhead of providing these services. Unfortunately, at the time of writing, SPS migrations are not as straightforward, and options are quite limited. There is hope, however, that in the near future this situation will be addressed by some community effort and support. In this section, we will cover the options available and point you toward additional resources, as well as indicate how to keep an eye out for future developments.

11.1.1   Tools and technologies to migrate between environments

Possibilities to move data within a SharePoint deployment range from manual copy/paste operations to custom tools written using the object model. Table 11.1 outlines the major options that are available out of the box to migrate data between environments or within a deployment.

In addition to the tools provided by Microsoft, there are third-party solutions, as well as free-of-charge community efforts for enabling a wide variety of migration scenarios. For a full list of third-party solutions, please refer to a product list on the MSD2D community site at `http://www.msd2d.com/Product_view_03.aspx?section=sharepoint` and the Microsoft migration resources page at `http://www.microsoft.com/office/sharepoint/prodinfo/migration.mspx`. Custom import/export tools, which we will cover in more detail later on in the chapter, have been created to primarily enable cross-product migrations and, thus, do not, at the time of writing, include tools to export from WSS or SPS.

As you can quickly deduce from Table 11.1, if you want to move data between WSS instances, you have several valid options available that can even be performed by end users with little assistance. FrontPage 2003 Package Web Wizard (Figure 11.1) in particular will appeal to end users, since it is fully integrated into the user interface.

Table 11.1   *Out-of-the-Box Tools for Moving Content*

Migration Method	Pros	Cons
Copy/paste (WSS and SPS)	End users are able to perform on their own Built into the user interface	Can only be used to move files Metadata will not be copied for non-Office files Has to be done per document library Network errors are likely when moving large amounts of data
Save as a template and select to include content (WSS and SPS)	Site administrators are able to perform on their own Built into the user interface Works at site or area level	Will only work for small sites (~3–5 MB) Users will need the rights to upload the template to the target system
STSADM (WSS)	Can migrate site collections Is effectively a backup/restore operation, thus moves everything Part of the product	Has to be run by the system administrators Intended for restoring content within the same deployment Can only move site collections and is not able to move subsites
Smigrate (WSS)	Can be used to migrate site collections or individual subsites Site administrators are able to perform on their own	Will not migrate security Will not migrate personalization settings You have to create a new site without applying a template before importing the site
FrontPage 2003 Package Web Wizard (WSS)	Effectively a front end to the Smigrate process Can be used to migrate site collections or individual subsites Site administrators are able to perform on their own Exported files are compatible with Smigrate	Will not migrate security Will not migrate personalization settings You have to create a new site without applying a template before importing the site
Database backup and restore (WSS and SPS)	Moves everything, including configuration data	Can only be performed at the virtual server level Intended for restoring content within the same deployment In a Shared Services scenario, the parent portal must exist before child portals are restored

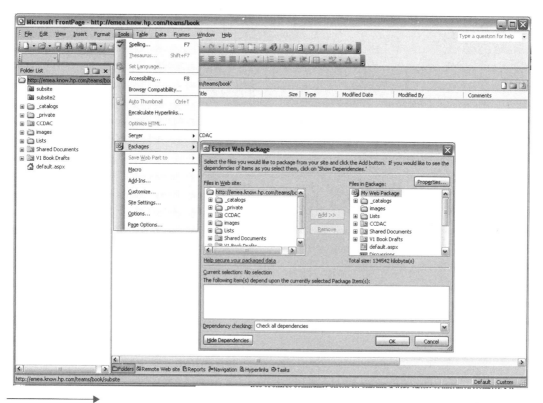

Figure 11.1   *Exporting sites with FrontPage 2003.*

Unfortunately, the same can't be said for SPS, and at the time of writing, the only option for moving SPS content between servers is via copy/paste or database backup/restore. Hopefully, by the time the book reaches you, a custom exporter for SPS 2003 will be available on the GotDotNet space at `http://workspaces.gotdotnet.com/spimport`. For Portal Server migrations, the backup and restore methods covered in Chapter 12 are valid as long as the target environment is in a trusted domain.

While copy/paste is a valid way of moving content, it is unlikely to be useful for larger migrations. On the other hand, full database backup and restore operations are too resource intensive for most migrations, leaving you with only a few viable methods, which we'll cover next in greater detail.

11.1.2   Using Smigrate to move WSS spaces

WSS Migration Tool, better known simply as Smigrate, or `Smigrate.exe`, is a command-line executable that uses the FrontPage RPC protocol to

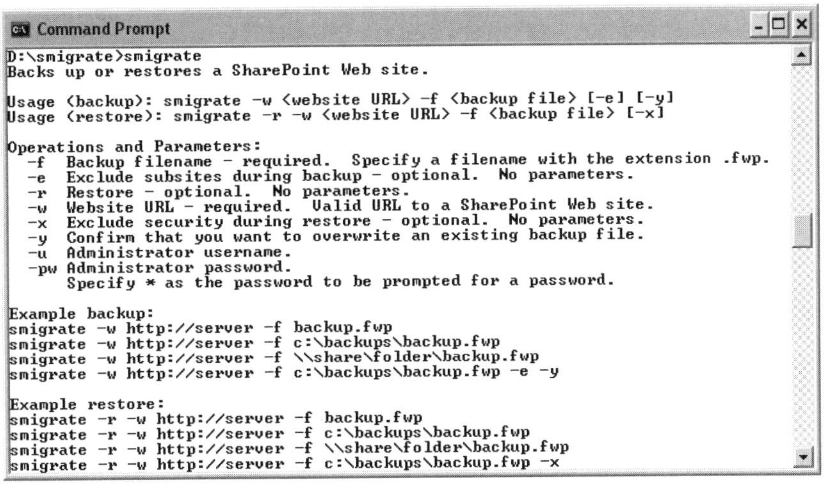

```
Command Prompt                                                          - □ ×
D:\smigrate>smigrate
Backs up or restores a SharePoint Web site.

Usage (backup): smigrate -w <website URL> -f <backup file> [-e] [-y]
Usage (restore): smigrate -r -w <website URL> -f <backup file> [-x]

Operations and Parameters:
   -f   Backup filename - required.  Specify a filename with the extension .fwp.
   -e   Exclude subsites during backup - optional.  No parameters.
   -r   Restore - optional.  No parameters.
   -w   Website URL - required.  Valid URL to a SharePoint Web site.
   -x   Exclude security during restore - optional.  No parameters.
   -y   Confirm that you want to overwrite an existing backup file.
   -u   Administrator username.
   -pw  Administrator password.
        Specify * as the password to be prompted for a password.

Example backup:
smigrate -w http://server -f backup.fwp
smigrate -w http://server -f c:\backups\backup.fwp
smigrate -w http://server -f \\share\folder\backup.fwp
smigrate -w http://server -f c:\backups\backup.fwp -e -y

Example restore:
smigrate -r -w http://server -f backup.fwp
smigrate -r -w http://server -f c:\backups\backup.fwp
smigrate -r -w http://server -f \\share\folder\backup.fwp
smigrate -r -w http://server -f c:\backups\backup.fwp -x
```

Figure 11.2   *WSS migration tool.*

fetch and upload files. The tool is essentially an export and import tool that copies information from a team site to an intermediate export format, which can then be imported back to another URL. It was mainly created to enable migration from STS (Version 1) to WSS (Version 2), but since the FrontPage RPC protocol is backward compatible, Microsoft also enabled the tool to migrate content within WSS with a few exceptions. When using Smigrate to copy content between WSS spaces, the tool will not migrate any security and personalization information, including Web Part modifications created using the *Modify My Web Part* option.

Smigrate, as seen in Figure 11.2, can be found by default in `C:\Program Files\Common Files\Microsoft Shared\Web Server Extensions\60\Bin` on the Web front-end server, but end users can also download it directly from Microsoft at `http://www.microsoft.com/downloads/details.aspx?familyid=3df85705-5635-40db-adbe-e13ab8684a60&displaylang=en`.

The straightforward and self-explanatory command syntax for the tool can be seen in Figure 11.2 with example operations—simply run the tool without any command parameters to generate this output. Both the export and import (-r) require Internet Explorer (IE) to be correctly configured and able to access the supplied URLs. This is due to the fact that Smigrate uses the same mechanisms as IE to access the URLs; therefore, you should ensure that you do not have any configurations such as proxy settings that prohibit access to the URLs in question.

The only required parameters are the Web site address and the backup file location. The *Exclude security* option is only relevant for migrations from STS to WSS; thus, it will not have any effect on the WSS-to-WSS migrations we're covering in this chapter. If you do not provide a username and password, Smigrate will attempt to use the currently logged-on user's credentials to perform the backup/restore operation. The complete set of functions of the Smigrate tool is documented further in the SharePoint Products and Technologies Administrator's Guide.

The FrontPage Web Package (FWP) format created by the Smigrate tool is in fact a renamed `.cab` (cabinet file), enabling users to view the exported files or modify the `manifest.xml` file before importing the information. Unfortunately, the manifest XML format is not documented, thus making changes to the file a trial-and-error exercise and limiting the usefulness of being able to see it in the first place!

Smigrate can only restore sites to an existing WSS site, that do not currently have a template applied to them. Administrators can create such "nontemplated" sites with the STSADM tool, but end users can most easily create sites able to receive Smigrate/FrontPage 2003 restores by following the normal self-site creation process and canceling out of the Template Selection step seen in Figure 11.3. Since there is no actual **Cancel** button on this page, possibly the safest and least confusing way to proceed correctly is just to close the browser at this point.

For larger migrations, individually creating the sites either with the STSADM tool or the Web interface is likely to be too resource intensive. Luckily, the object model supports creating sites and site collections that allow the creation of custom tools. For sample code and compiled applications, please refer to the custom import/export tools GotDotNet space at `http://workspaces.gotdotnet.com/spimport`. HP's STS-to-WSS migration tools collection released on the site, for example, includes a tool and source code to create WSS team sites using a text file with desired WSS site names. The tool collection also includes a Windows Form application to batch the Smigrate tool process and migrate any number of sites in one go.

11.1.3   Using STSADM to move content

As with Smigrate, STSADM is a command-line-only tool that allows you to manage all aspects of a WSS environment without ever going near the Central Administration Web pages. Since WSS can be installed using the WMSDE or MSDE data engines, which do not include the SQL tools,

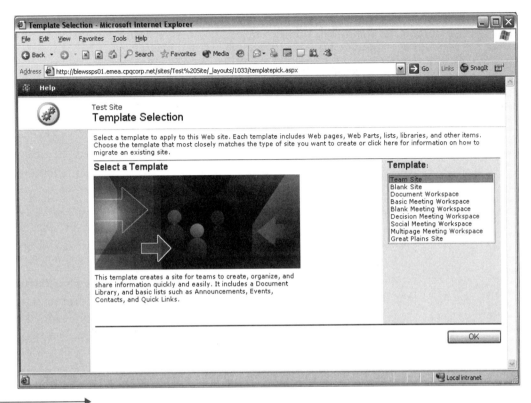

Figure 11.3 *Users can create sites without applying a template by stopping on the Template Selection page.*

Microsoft had to include a way for system administrators to back up and restore WSS sites without requiring the SQL tools. Hence, STSADM includes command-line parameters to perform backup (-o backup) and restore (-o restore) operations.

As with Smigrate, STSADM only requires two parameters: the URL to the site collection (-url) and the path to a file (-filename) with an optional overwrite switch (-overwrite), making backup and restore operations easy to execute. Unlike the Smigrate tool, however, STSADM must be run on the physical WSS Web server by a system administrator. STSADM does take a full fidelity backup of the WSS site collection and, thus, is able to restore site collections with all the user information and personalization changes included.

Since STSADM was created for administrating and configuring a WSS on a single server or a farm installation, it's not surprising that the backup/restore operations are not meant to be performed across servers or farms.

Having said that, there are no hard-coded limitations to prevent you from using the tool to migrate content between environments. Since STSADM backup includes security settings, the target server must be in the same or another trusted domain in order for users to be able to access the restored site collection. For cross-domain migrations, you should use the Smigrate tool instead, since it will strip security settings during the migration.

For detailed information on the STSADM tool, please refer to the SharePoint Products and Technologies Administrator's Guide.

11.1.4   When a company's structure changes

Many of us have been involved in bringing the IT landscape of an enterprise into steady harmony after a merger, but we suspect few of us have also been involved with figuring out how to separate enterprise systems after a divestiture. Out of experience, we can vouch that mergers can even occur while deploying a technology only to find that your new colleagues are in the process of doing the same. While neither merger or divestiture is without challenges for an enterprise deployment of SharePoint Products and Technologies, a merger is typically more straightforward to plan out and execute than a divestiture.

Since SharePoint Products and Technologies depend on Windows Active Directory or NT Domain Authentication, the first step to providing interoperability during a merger is to ensure that the two domain infrastructures trust each other and that network connectivity exists between the two companies. When HP and Compaq underwent the largest IT merger in history, we talked about "Day 1" interoperability, which included both network bridges and domain trusts. Thus, on Day 1 of the merger, both companies' SharePoint environments were fully accessible to all employees. A few days later, the new color schemes had also been applied; thus, both environments at least looked identical to end users.

While at first it might appear that there's very little to be done to enable WSS/SPS interoperability, typically the longer-term merger goals for IT systems include a consolidation of duplicate environments, including the domain infrastructure. To consolidate two SharePoint environments, migrations between servers are a valid way to proceed with an "adopt-and-go" approach (i.e., choose one of the deployed infrastructures and move data across). Alternatively, if the usage patterns and new capacity planning dictate, the infrastructures can be integrated in a similar way to that discussed in Chapter 9 with multiregional deployments. We will also cover integrating existing WSS deployments to new SPS portals, which is also a viable alternative to data migration, in Chapter 12.

Domain account consolidation, on the other hand, will always cause headaches, since neither WSS nor SPS supports the SID History property, which is typically used in Active Directory migrations to enable applications to automatically transition to the new user identity while still being able to access legacy resources using the old user identity. Thus, from SharePoint's perspective, the new migrated domain account is a new user and will not have access to those resources whose permissions were granted via the old account. What's worse, all alerts are tied to the old account and will continue to fire after the account migration. The only difference is that the newly migrated user will not have permissions to change or delete the alerts.

Divestitures are slightly trickier, since they can include such situations as needing to break up an existing SharePoint deployment or migrating domain accounts for at least one of the new companies. As in consolidations, data can be moved from server to server with one of the migration methods we discussed earlier. Additionally, the migrated spaces and data belonging to the divested entity need to be cleaned up from the "old" environment after the data separation, but this can easily be accomplished by scripting the STSADM tool or via a custom application using the object model. However, authentication will prove more challenging, since this time around trusts are being broken, not forged.

Typically in a divestiture, one of the new entities will create a new domain infrastructure for the employees and recreate or migrate accounts to that domain infrastructure. A straightforward backup/restore method of moving data will therefore result in portals and sites being inaccessible to these new accounts. Thus, a custom tool to map accounts between old and new identities needs to be run after the data migration to enable access once again and to remove identities belonging to employees of the divested entity.

Unfortunately, Portal Server divestitures today are problematic, since, as we mentioned earlier, no tool for data migrations exists (at least not at the time of writing). An option would be to back up the environment, restore to a newly created infrastructure, and manually delete the portals and data belonging to the divested entity; however, since the new infrastructure would more than likely be in another domain that doesn't trust the old one, you would need once again to fix the domain identities after restoring the portals.

11.2 Approaching migrations from other platforms

While migrations within the SharePoint Products and Technologies deployments are commonplace, when approaching a new deployment, you will more likely be given an opportunity to consolidate other technologies to the new SharePoint environment. Given today's feature-rich environments and multitude of possibilities for deploying and structuring those environments, there's no silver bullet for migrations. Approaching migration projects requires extensive planning and careful study of the existing environment.

Having been involved in discussing, planning, and even on one occasion executing migrations from enterprise implementations of LiveLink, eRoom, and Windows File Shares, we can say that the basic approach to these projects has been similar. In a nutshell, you must map out and address the functionality differences, decide where to move the data, agree how the migrated data will be structured, and find a way to map the user identities. Unfortunately, the best-laid plans often cannot cover every eventuality, so you should also be prepared to adapt along the way.

Users often hate change; just as they've gotten comfortable using a system, the rug is yanked from beneath them, and they must learn a new way of working. We technologists often forget that typical business users don't usually care about which product they use, as long as it does what they need it to do. Users are too busy to learn about cool new functionality, and rightly so—it's not their job. Trying to justify migrations with "but you'll get this, this, and this new functionality" is often a lost battle, since the disturbance to business is not only in downtime during migrations (careful planning can minimize downtime, but it is unlikely that you will achieve zero downtime during any migration!). The major disturbance to the business is undoubtedly employees having to learn the new technology and, more importantly, trying to apply past experience with the old way of working to the new.

Migration planning is not only about the tools and technology; it's about making the experience as seamless to the users as possible. We've often heard users still using an old legacy product's name to refer to a new SharePoint environment they've been migrated to—and we've left such conversations without comments or corrections. Personally, we think the less change people notice, the better; thus, that is one of the goals we like to apply when planning any migrations. A good example of a transparent migration is shown in Figure 11.4. Can you spot the difference?

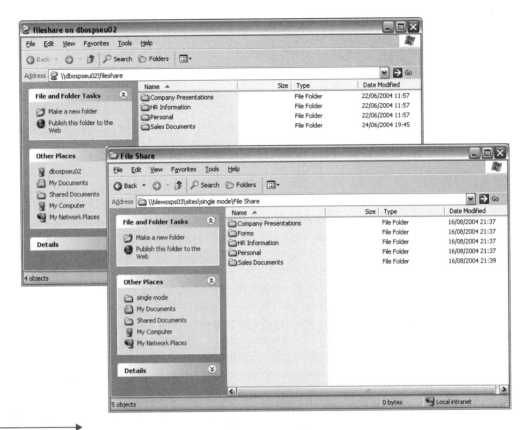

Figure 11.4   *Can you spot the difference in the migrated user experience?*

11.2.1   Addressing functionality gaps and the user experience

The user interface and the functionality that is presented by that interface are without a doubt the first things users will notice after migration, and thus, they are the highest-priority items to address early on. While user experience can be changed with customizations to the user interface, which we will cover in Part III, addressing functionality gaps between two products is much harder.

Unless you are prepared to address gaps by developing additional functionality on the platform, your only other option is to recognize the differences and advise users how to deal with the loss of functionality. However, first you must know what the functionality gaps are and then find out how important those features are to the end users. Therefore, perhaps the first task in any migration project should be to create a functionality matrix for the two products. Unfortunately, this is often much harder than it at first appears, and most matrixes we've seen have been biased toward one product or the other, depending on the personal opinion of the author. We've compiled such biased lists as well, not intentionally mind you, and we've seen enough that we can honestly say such lists should not be a part of the process of deciding which product should be deployed. They do, however, serve a useful purpose after the decision has been made and the migration project gets under way.

By creating a functionality matrix, you will also learn a great deal about the product you're deploying, since you'll likely have to investigate features such as security and document-management capabilities in depth. Personally, while mapping out the differences between SharePoint and LiveLink, although we had deployed and managed several servers in various stages of the SharePoint beta cycle, we still picked up new tricks and features of the product. It's like Microsoft Word—how many of us can honestly say we know exactly what the product can do? But if we were to get 1,000 users to the same room and ask them to write down which features they use, we're sure we'd get quite a comprehensive list by merging the answers. Thus, it is very important to spend the time and effort to list both products' functionalities and come up with the gaps and their impact on the users.

Personally, we like to pass on the functionality gap list to a few power users and ask them to rate each gap with "Must have," "Nice to have," or "Don't care" labels, since, let's be honest, none of us knows exactly what the users consider important. On the other hand, a business is not a democracy, and in the end the buck stops with the business sponsor. So, while we can map out the gaps and ask users to rate them, whether they will be addressed depends on time, effort, and cost to the overall project.

Since SharePoint Products and Technologies offer a highly customizable platform to build upon, there are very few, if any, functional gaps between products that cannot be met with custom development or third-party add-ons. Thus, the important question to ask is: Which of the gaps are important enough to address and which are left for future SharePoint versions to hopefully add? Obviously, cost has a major impact on decisions, making up-front planning and research even more important when presenting the migration plan to the business sponsors. For example, let's take workflow, since several widely deployed products out there already have differing levels of functionality in this area. Since neither WSS nor SPS has out-of-the-box workflow designers, you are left with a choice of either developing custom workflow processes using the provided event handlers or buying one of the many third-party products out there. On the other hand, given that many of Microsoft's competitors already offer workflow capabilities out of the box, it is likely that the functionality gap will be addressed in one of the future releases of the product.

Another example is file- or folder-level security, which you will undoubtedly face with most cross-product migrations. In WSS, security is set at the list or library level, while in SPS it can only be set at the portal area level, thus leaving a sizable gap with products that offer per-item security. At the time of writing, there are no third-party add-ons that we know of that can provide granular security control, although at least one Microsoft partner is working on a solution. It's impossible to say how well a custom solution or third-party product would work, however, given that users can access data stored in SharePoint via a variety of user interfaces. Thus, today this is one of those functionality gaps that might just be too difficult and expensive to address, leaving you to address it with user training and information design instead.

While workflow and file-level security are two very common examples of functionality gaps, they will by no means be the only ones. Some of these gaps you can easily address with customizations, while others you will accept as lost functionality and work around by training users to work differently. The important thing is to know and prepare for the differences up front, not after the migration.

11.2.2   Data structure

When moving data to SharePoint Products and Technologies, you obviously have a choice in where the data will be placed and how it is organized. Your options are slightly different when moving data to SPS areas as opposed to WSS sites, given the slight differences in information design and security options, as we covered earlier in Part I. Not to worry if you jumped over Part I; we will cover the major differences in just a bit.

Portal Server areas give you a hierarchical navigation structure that allows users to navigate the migrated data while retaining the ability to apply security on each level and create several lists for other content types, such as documents, announcements, and links, as shown in Figure 11.5. When migrating data to portal areas, you have to be mindful that security can only be set at the area level, not individually for each list or library as in WSS. Thus, in order to retain per-folder security, you have to create each

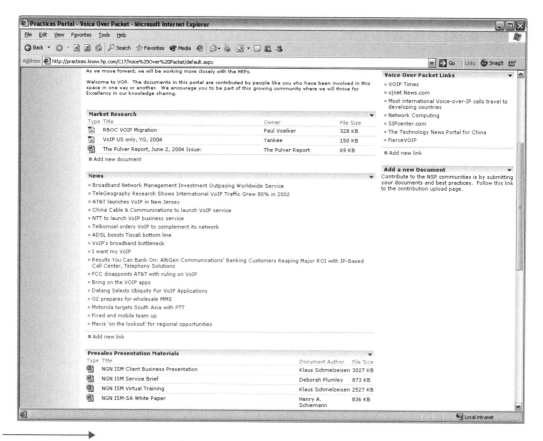

Figure 11.5   *Data migrated to portal areas can include content types other than just files.*

migrated subfolder as a subarea in SPS, significantly increasing the navigation complexity. Personally, we're huge fans of simple navigation structures that require as few mouse clicks as possible to access the data we're looking for. As always, information design is a compromise between convenience and control.

After deciding upon the hierarchy to which the data will be migrated, you have an option to choose between displaying the data on the portal area pages via Web Parts or creating portal listings to the portal areas, which link to the stored content. Portal listings allow you to separate the data management from the end-user navigation structure and link to the same content from several different portal areas. For those familiar with SPS 2001, this is exactly the paradigm with categories and documents structure. Authors in SPS 2001 went to the documents tree, created a structure they were comfortable with, and when publishing documents assigned them to one or more categories, which end users were familiar with. A problem with this paradigm, of course, often was that categories simply ended up being a mirror copy of the documents structure, since the authors didn't want to learn the dual-structured information design. SPS 2001 isn't the only product to function in this way; thus, it is likely you will face this issue when migrating from other legacy products as well.

Unfortunately, portal listings are not without issues; they do not contain any metadata about the item to which they link, and, what's worse, the listing is completely disconnected from the item it is linked to. Thus, if the source data is renamed or deleted, the portal listing will *not* reflect the change, resulting in a broken link. Given enough time, this will become an annoying, if not serious, issue, which we hope Microsoft will address in the future. Due to the issues with portal listings, you should carefully consider the impact and plan to create processes and tools to address the broken links. Personally, we highly recommend avoiding portal listings for now and accepting the loss of multiple categorization functionality. This might come as a shock to information architects, but again, by tackling this early on, the users can be trained to work differently.

Since WSS was designed to be a team-collaboration tool, it does not include the hierarchical navigation or multiple categorization possibilities of SPS portal areas. That doesn't mean you don't still have options when planning a data structure for the migrated data. Again, security is likely to have a major effect on how the data should be structured, since security can only be set at the library or site level. Thus, in order to retain security, you need to create subsites or libraries for each container that requires a different access control list (ACL).

For the data that is migrated to the sites, you have the option to show the library contents via List Web Parts on the Home page, to list the library in the Quick Launch bar, or only to display it in the Documents and Lists area. The actual files can be placed in a folder hierarchy within the library or left to the top level. We'll cover these options in more detail later on in the chapter when we cover options for file-share migrations.

11.2.3 Versions and metadata

Many of the products today include some form of versioning and metadata storage ability. Luckily, both of these features are supported, making the transition essentially a mapping exercise. For metadata, migration is often a rare opportunity to "clean the house" and enforce a common set of fields across all migrated information. You can choose to drop, rename, or add metadata fields and adopt your migration process accordingly.

For versioning, you might find that the numbering scheme in Share-Point Libraries is slightly different from the legacy platform, since versions are kept in a straightforward 1, 2, 3, … format and cannot be changed. Thus, the important decision to make is how to handle versions. You can choose to leave a version history behind and only bring the last one across, cutting down on the storage space needed, as long as there are no reasons to require the revision history to be preserved. On the other hand, you could limit the number of revisions to bring over or, of course, just migrate everything, depending on the requirements.

11.2.4   Identity mapping

Not all environments use domain accounts to grant access to resources; thus, often you will be faced with the task of mapping user credentials from the legacy system to domain accounts. Usually it's as simple as using something like the e-mail address stored in the legacy system user database that hopefully maps directly to an Active Directory account, allowing Share-Point to look up the account information without any custom tools. Unfortunately, you might not be so lucky and may need to develop custom tools that look up the information from a repository, such as an LDAP directory, and convert user credentials into domain accounts.

Users might not be the only identities requiring conversions though, and often the real challenge comes with user groups. Many products, for example, allow groups to be provisioned in LDAP and used to grant access rights across various parts of the infrastructure, thus reducing the administrative overhead. SPS portal areas support NT and Active Directory groups, while WSS, in addition to NT/AD groups, also allows site owners to create WSS-specific cross-site groups, which can be used across spaces on the server. Both NT/AD and cross-site groups have their pros and cons, but if there is a good method of managing NT/AD groups within your organization, we would go for NT/AD groups due to their ability to secure resources beyond just the SharePoint server that the spaces are being migrated to. On the other hand, cross-site groups can be created within the SharePoint environment without any rights to the NT/AD infrastructure, and site users can manage them from within their SharePoint spaces, making this option appealing for the end user, as long as the groups are not required outside the deployed server.

11.3   Migration tools and technologies

As always, you have a wide variety of options available when choosing how to move the data across to your new SharePoint environment. Out of the box, Microsoft only provided the Smigrate tool for importing data, but, unfortunately, the tool uses an undisclosed XML format, limiting, if not negating, its usefulness in product-to-product migrations. Slightly more useful is the SPIn tool, released as part of the SPS 2001 to SPS 2003 toolkit free of charge. It includes a fully documented XML format, allowing custom exporters to be developed for other environments. Unfortunately, at the time of writing, SPIn only supports migrating data to Portal Server, restricting the usefulness of the tool in many migration scenarios. Additionally, SPIn only supports files to be imported to the portal areas and, thus, cannot be used to import list data types such as Calendar, Contacts, and Announcements.

Luckily, there is light at the end of the tunnel, and later on in the chapter, we will cover a project to create custom import/export tools with shared source code for customizations. Let's not get ahead of ourselves though. Table 11.2 lists the major migration options you have at your disposal. Although you can't really consider copy/paste and Smigrate realistic options for cross-product migrations, they are still listed, since they are options at your disposal nevertheless.

11.3.1   Building a migration framework

Since SharePoint Products and Technologies feature an extensive object model, which you can use to do pretty much anything you like, a valid option to consider, in addition to the various tools provided by Microsoft, the community, and third parties, is to create your own tools for extracting and importing data. While being the most time-consuming, not to mention likely the most expensive, option, it does provide you with full control of the migration process. You can export only the data needed and import it in exactly the way it makes sense for your organization.

Having had the pleasure of developing part of the custom import/export tools, you will find that importing data to SharePoint in exactly the way you want is not without challenges. In particular, version history is difficult to maintain during the migration process, especially if metadata needs to be taken across as well. In order to bring over the metadata without affecting the *Modified By/Modified At* fields and keeping the right version order, you must call an unmanaged FrontPage RPC service and post the document content over HTTP. In addition, you have to programmatically deal with the URL length restrictions, since SharePoint enforces a 260-character URL

Table 11.2 *Migration Tools and Strategies*

Migration Method	Pros	Cons
Copy/paste (WSS and SPS)	End users are able to perform on their own Built into the user interface	Can only be used to move files Metadata will not be copied for non-Office files Has to be done per document library Network errors are likely when moving large amounts of data
Smigrate (WSS)	Can be used to migrate site collections or individual subsites Site administrators are able to perform on their own Can import any list type	Document format is not documented Will not migrate security Will not migrate personalization settings You have to create a new site without applying a template before importing the site
SPIn (SPS)	Created and supported by Microsoft Product Group Can migrate data to existing areas and libraries	Able to import only to SPS portal areas Can only import document libraries Has to be run on the Web server
Custom SharePoint import/export tools (WSS and SPS)	Can be used to migrate individual portal areas, site collections, sites, libraries, and lists Can migrate data to existing areas, lists, and libraries Shared source code allows organizations to customize according to particular user scenarios	Is only supported as a community effort, not officially by Microsoft or HP As a community effort, provides no formal quality assurance Has limited documentation at the time of writing
Various third-party tools (WSS and SPS)	Created and supported by a third-party provider	Additional license cost
Custom-developed tools per project (WSS and SPS as required)	Fully custom created for a particular migration scenario	High development cost

limit for any content stored within the environment. Additionally, in order to be allowed to import data into SPS portal areas, you must first set a registry key containing the credentials of the user who is running the import tool and restart IIS. Luckily, all of these challenges are solved in the custom import/export tool for which full source code is available.

So, from personal experience, we recommend considering all other options before embarking on the custom development route. Compare the cost and options carefully before making a decision either way.

11.3.2 Community effort: Custom SharePoint import/export tools

Development of the custom SharePoint import/export tools started in June 2003 in order to create an open framework for cross-product migrations. The project was sponsored and staffed by HP and Microsoft due to the close relationship that the two companies share and the internal requirements for platform consolidation at the time within HP. The tools are planned for release on MSDN after sufficient maturity and feature set is reached. Meanwhile, volunteers are invited to participate in development and testing at the GotDotNet workspace at `http://workspaces.gotdotnet.com/spimport`.

At the time of writing, both the importer and all of the exporters are still in beta, although feature set and data file formats are nearly finalized. The GotDotNet space, shown in Figure 11.6, also allows community participation by a way of message boards, a Bug Tracker, and the ability for anyone to apply to join the project and be automatically notified of announcements and changes to the project.

As the name implies, the process includes an export from a legacy product to a well-documented, intermediate format, which is then imported into WSS or SPS, depending on the options defined in XML. At the time of writing, there are three exporters in beta: Windows File System, Exchange Public Folders, and Lotus QuickPlace. In addition, the eRoom tool is under development, and various others are in the planning stages. All of the tools are provided free of charge but, as such, come without warranty or support, as can be expected. Full source code for all the tools is freely available on the GotDotNet space, however, allowing changes to be made or bugs to be fixed during the migration process.

The custom importer is able to import data to all list types supported by SharePoint and can be run against both Portal Server as well as a standalone WSS installation, due to the use of satellite assemblies that allow the

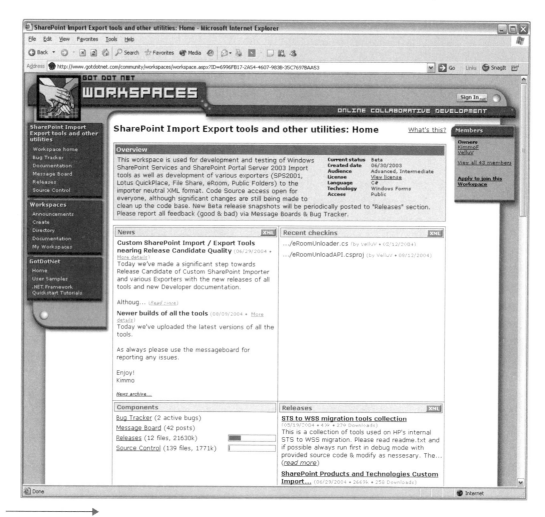

Figure 11.6   GotDotNet *community development site for custom import/export tools.*

program to be created without a dependency on the Portal Server assembly files. In addition, the importer supports all security options, as well as creation and mapping of portal listings and alerts. Full support for version history and metadata are also included, along with custom list and site template creation. In fact, the end goal of the importer is to support virtually every data type and configuration option possible in order to eventually support migrations within the product itself or from WSS to SPS and vice versa.

Using the custom importer is very straightforward, since one of the design goals was to include almost everything about how the data should be imported in the intermediate XML file instead of in the user interface. Thus, as Figure 11.7 shows, the only required fields on the user interface are the location of the XML manifest file and the URL to which the data should be imported. Optionally, users can select to include security, create custom list templates, and allow import to existing sites, areas, or libraries. Everything else must be set in the XML manifest prior to import. Due to the two-step process, you have an opportunity to affect the way the data is imported by modifying the XML manifest files before the import, thus, for example, enabling the data structure to be consolidated or reorganized in a way that makes sense for your scenario.

Although modifying the XML manifest files might sound like a daunting task at first, a full format documentation XSD file, as well as a .NET Assembly for reading and writing the XML files, is provided, significantly reducing the effort involved with either writing a custom exporter or creating a tool to modify the exported XML files. For a full, up-to-date copy of the documentation and assembly files, simply log on to `http://workspaces.gotdotnet.com/spimport` and download the relevant files from the *Release* section of Source Control.

Figure 11.7
Custom SharePoint
importer.

11.3.3   Commercial offerings

There is a wide variety of third-party solutions available, and the list is growing by the day. Thus, a listing of products available during the writing of this book will be outdated by the time the book reaches you. You can view an up-to-date list at `http://www.msd2d.com/Product_view_03.aspx?section=sharepoint`.

In addition to third-party tools, you also have an option to engage a Microsoft-certified solution provider to plan, develop, and execute your migration scenario. For a list of registered solution providers, you can refer to the Microsoft Office Systems Solutions Directory at `http://directory.partners.extranet.microsoft.com` or the Microsoft Resource Directory at `http://directory.microsoft.com/MPRD`.

11.4   Migrating from legacy environments with the custom import/export tools

In addition to the feature-rich custom importer, the community project also offers ready-made custom export tools for various legacy environments. As with the custom importer, these custom export tools are provided free of charge but, as such, come without warranty or support. Development, quality assurance, and feature planning are done by the community itself on the GotDotNet workspace at `http://workspaces.gotdotnet.com/spimport`. Although still in beta at the time of writing, several successful production migrations have already been performed by various organizations, using the custom import/export tools. The end goal of the project is to provide stable and feature-rich tools for organizations to move data into a SharePoint Products and Technologies deployment. Since the source code is also provided free of charge, organizations can choose to migrate as is, with the tools provided, or to customize the code to fit their particular migration scenario.

11.4.1   What data to move across

Unfortunately, environments that allow users to store data without enforcement of archival policies eventually become burial grounds for vast numbers of files that have served their useful purpose and no longer hold any value to the enterprise. It's only natural, after all, and we can all think of items we keep around that have outlived their purpose, like that Windows 95 Service Pack 1 CD still sitting in the back of the drawer. At least we can visualize the problem at our office or home when items start to pile up and storage space becomes limited. The problem, of course, with network-connected electronic-data storage is that we often forget where the storage lockers are, thus leaving the files to gather cyber dust for years to come.

So, before proceeding to simply move all of the data, you should pursue opportunities to limit the amount of data that needs to be migrated. Migrations are a great opportunity to perform a "spring cleaning" on the digital filing cabinets; it's usually one of the rare opportunities to be able to spend time on analyzing which data is actually stored on the infrastructure and how much of it is really needed. Although storage space is cheap today, the more data you store, the longer your backup and restore cycles become, thus affecting disaster-recovery plans. Since it's likely that the migrated information is also indexed and made searchable, end users will probably notice deterioration in the search abilities due to large amounts of old and irrelevant data inundating the search index.

Obviously, the best way to ensure that only the relevant data is brought across to the new environment is by inspecting every file manually and determining its usefulness before flagging it for migration. Since the person making the call needs to be able to determine usefulness of the data in the business context, it's unlikely that any central IT resources can make a call whether a file is still useful or not. Thus, the burden of manual inspection often falls on the business users instead, since they are the experts in the field to which the data relates.

Still, many IT organizations' dream would be to perform migrations using this "tough love" approach. We've been involved in numerous conversations where the proposed migration strategy in a nutshell has been, "Tell users they have two months to move important data from System A to System B if they really need it." We've yet to see one of these proposals approved by the business organizations due to the huge inconvenience and disturbance to business it would cause. We do not even believe that the end result would be much better than an automated migration strategy, since people are still likely to bring over data that is not relevant anymore. After all, users often take the easy path and simply drag and drop everything across rather than take the time to weed through old files.

A far more realistic, limited migration strategy is to define criteria for files that should be migrated across and to perform automated migration of data with these rules. After automated migration, the business users would have a predetermined time frame in which to move any necessary files across that did not meet the automated data-migration criteria. The challenge, of course, is to define a mutually agreeable set of criteria with the business that would migrate most of the valuable data without bringing across any of the junk. All of the custom exporters support filtering content by modified date, file size, and content type. Thus, the business and IT can agree upon migration criteria such as, Export all content modified in the last 12 months that is under 50 MB in size and is not an `.mp3`, `.avi`, `.iso`, or `.wav` file.

Obviously, every migration scenario is different, since many organizations are required to follow data-retention policies for legal reasons. Nevertheless, analysis of the stored content and detailed plans for data inclusion should be a top priority for any migration project.

11.4.2   Migrating from Windows File Shares

Perhaps one of the most common migration scenarios to consider is Windows File Shares, especially since WSS could be considered a replacement for this very, very old technology. File Shares–to–WSS migrations are particularly attractive for group file shares, since WSS offers far superior collaborative capabilities for user groups. Enhanced document-management capabilities, new data-container types, such as calendars and contacts, and alert functionality will likely attract the end users. File Shares are notoriously slow, high-latency connections, which lead to file servers being placed near the end users in many decentralized organizations. The sheer number of servers in a large organization can lead to significant support costs and create a cost timebomb due to the aging infrastructure, which will eventually need to be replaced with hardware that is still serviceable.

WSS lends itself extremely well to high-latency and low-bandwidth connections, as we discussed in Chapter 9. File share migrations present a case for infrastructure consolidations, since users can access the data far more efficiently from the centralized servers over HTTP than they could with File Shares. On the other hand, SharePoint will by no means replace all File Shares, since the product was not designed to host large files or executables. There are very valid usage scenarios in any organization for software kits and other larger files that will require an ongoing File Shares deployment and support. But at the very least, by migrating Office files and group shares to SharePoint, the number of servers can be reduced, and teams can collaborate more effectively.

However, cost will likely not be the main justification for migrating content from File Shares. Since the technology has been around for eons without major developments, the technology has matured to the point that it requires very little operational or support effort. Given the scale of deployments and the amount of data stored on relatively low-spec hardware, the cost per gigabyte is likely to be far cheaper on File Shares compared with WSS. Of course, it's all relative, since the majority of the content would likely be filtered during the migration or cleaned up by the users due to more restrictive quotas and site-collection use confirmations. Still, the main reasons for migrating from File Shares are undoubtedly the collaborative features, Search, and the knowledge-management capabilities that WSS and SPS provide. It's far easier to discover information on a SharePoint Products and Technologies deployment through its extensive search and rich navigation capabilities.

Custom exporter for Windows File System, shown in Figure 11.8, is a straightforward command-line application (a Windows Form version is being planned at the time of writing). While an output path (-out) is required, the tool does not actually copy the files from the exported folder (-folder). Instead, the tool will create relative links to the content using a Uniform Naming Convention (UNC) locator, which the importer will fetch during the import phase. While this will significantly reduce the amount of temporary storage required during a migration, there might be scenarios where the importer is unable to access the UNC paths due to firewalls or network segmenting. Thus, an overwrite switch can be specified (-copy) to take duplicate copies of the content intended for migrating. As with all other custom exporters, File System Exporter is able to target content either against SPS (-type Area) or WSS (-type Site). The data itself can be structured in one of three ways (-mode).

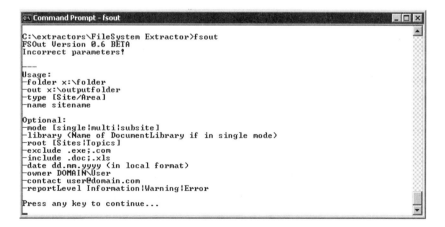

Figure 11.8   *Command-Line File System export tool syntax.*

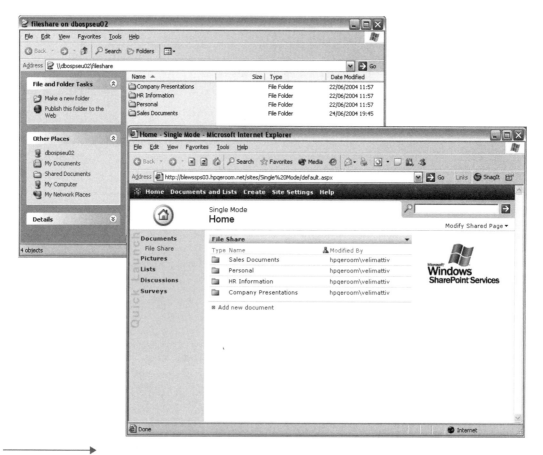

Figure 11.9   *File Shares exported in Single Library Mode.*

The Single Library Mode (-mode single) adds a single document library and creates each File Shares subfolder as a subfolder in the document library, as seen in Figure 11.9. The Single Folder Mode will, by default, take the security settings from the specified path and ignore any unique security rights specified in subfolders, since security can only be set at the library or portal area level in SharePoint. Single Folder Mode is best suited to migrating group shares one at a time to WSS, as well as to migrating simple folder structures to SPS topic areas.

Multiple Document Library Mode (-mode multi) creates a document library for each folder in the extracted path and applies unique security for each document library. Subfolders are created as document library subfolders, and security is omitted, just as in Single Folder Mode. Since security for subfolders is still largely ignored, Multiple Document Library Mode,

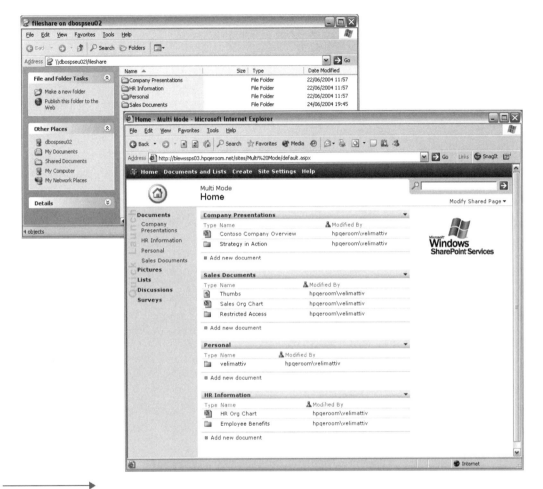

Figure 11.10   *File Shares exported in Multiple Library Mode.*

similar to Single Folder Mode, is also mostly suited to migrating group shares one at a time. The difference between it and the Single Folder Mode is mainly cosmetic, as Figure 11.10 shows, although it presents a far more attractive view when migrating content to Portal Server topic areas.

The only way to ensure that security settings are correctly brought across is to use the Subsite Mode (-mode subsite), which will create a new sub-site or topic area for each migrated subfolder. In order to maintain the folder hierarchy in Subsite Mode, the tool will create a Links list to each site created and place links to all subsites hosted, as Figure 11.11 shows. Since the Subsite Mode supports maintaining per-folder security in WSS and SPS, it is suited to migrating a large number of group shares at once or the

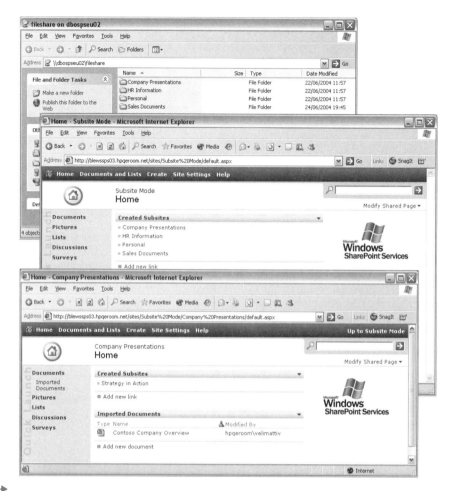

Figure 11.11   *File Shares exported in Subsite Mode.*

migration of deeply nested directory structures to SPS portal areas. Unfortunately, the Links lists are created as a one-time operation; thus, any subsequent changes to the structure, such as deletion of a site, will not be automatically reflected in the Links lists. Therefore, you should consider creating or downloading a Web Part that dynamically renders the list of subsites if you're going to move considerable amounts of data with the subsite mode.

11.4.3   Migrating from Exchange Public Folders

Exchange Public Folders is another aging technology that has been used for group-collaboration capabilities in the past. Although the functionality is by no means equivalent, WSS does offer potential as a replacement for public folders, which were created to host collaborative spaces or applications. However, as with File Shares, Exchange Public Folders have not outlived their purpose just yet for every conceivable usage scenario. In fact, the e-mail-in ability of WSS document libraries depends on public folders to provide a mail-enabled, temporary storage location. Thus, careful planning and study of usage patterns is just as important as in any other migration.

The Public Folder Extractor, shown in Figure 11.12, supports limiting the exported content with the usual folder path, as well as with date and size filters. As with the File Share Exporter, the tool is straightforward to use and requires very little up-front configuration. The tool uses MAPI to connect to the Exchange servers and, as such, requires a version of Outlook to be installed on the workstation it is run on. This was done, by design, to be able to support Exchange 5.5, 2000, and 2003 servers without duplicating logic and complicating the program design. On a bright note, the application can be run from any workstation as long as it has the .NET Framework 1.1 and a version of Outlook installed.

The exporter was designed to migrate public folder content into document libraries or threaded discussion lists. When targeting content to document libraries, you have an option to select one of four supported export

Figure 11.12
Exchange Public Folder Extractor.

formats for the messages. Messages can either be saved as native Outlook Message (MSG) files or converted into Rich-Text Format (RTF), plain text (TXT), or HTML (HTM) files. When exporting content into discussion lists, the message attachments are included as attachments of the Discussion items.

11.4.4   Migrating from Lotus QuickPlace

Lotus QuickPlace is a team-collaboration tool built on the Lotus Domino platform with a feature set broadly similar to WSS, thus providing a great example case for platform consolidation.

QuickPlace organizes data in rooms, which in turn can contain document folders, calendars, discussion folders, and, of course, subrooms. Documents are stored in folders as compound documents (if you are not familiar with the context of compound documents, just consider them as e-mail messages). While an e-mail message usually has embedded content, it can also contain arbitrary and unstructured data as attachments. In WSS the items stored in document libraries can contain the file itself and any number of custom properties, but you cannot add an attachment to a file, which means that when migrating data from QuickPlace, the information must be stored differently in WSS. The extractor solves this problem by breaking up the compound documents and storing the individual files in document libraries, with extra metadata fields that tie the files together.

Compound documents are a perfect example of a functionality gap between these two products, which must be solved during a migration by organizing the information differently in SharePoint Products and Technologies deployment. Since end users are familiar with the functionality in the previous environment, part of the migration should be a crash-course training exercise, which not only introduces the new environment but also addresses these functionality gaps head on.

An up-to-date documentation and setup kit for Lotus QuickPlace Custom Extractor, which can be seen in Figure 11.13, can be found along with the other import/export tools at `http://workspaces.gotdotnet.com/spimport`. Since QuickPlace data is stored in a Lotus Domino database, the QuickPlace Extractor uses the Lotus Notes C++ API to connect to the QuickPlace server and extract data. Therefore, the workstation running the exporter must have the Lotus Notes R5 client installed and configured with appropriate settings to programmatically access the QuickPlace server. Once Notes has been configured, you can run the tool and export spaces

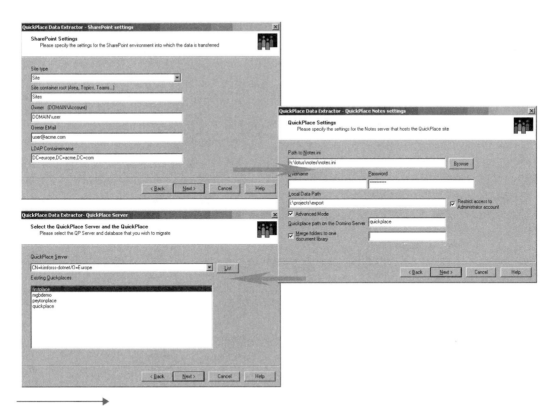

Figure 11.13   *Lotus QuickPlace Custom Extractor.*

one at a time or in batch mode. Content can be filtered based on modified time stamps or file sizes, as with other export tools mentioned earlier.

QuickPlace can either store user accounts locally or integrate with an external LDAP directory, Notes directory, or NT domain. Thus, you must be able to resolve user accounts somehow to NT domain identities in order to retain ACLs for migrated rooms. The custom extractor can either attempt to resolve SMTP e-mail addresses automatically against an LDAP server or prompt the user to enter domain account details manually. For a larger migration, the ability to tie e-mail addresses to NT domain accounts is crucial in order to ensure a speedy export of data. Unfortunately, at the time of writing, the custom extractor does not provide support for automatically translating groups into corresponding NT/AD security groups or cross-site groups in WSS. Therefore, groups must be created in NT/AD before running the extractor, and the identity mapping must be entered manually for each group.

11.4.5 **Migrating from Documentum eRoom**

Documentum eRoom is another team-collaboration platform with functionality similar to Lotus QuickPlace and WSS, making it our second example case for platform consolidation. eRoom organizes data in folders, which in turn can contain files, other folders, calendars, discussions, and custom databases, such as contacts and user-defined tables. Due to its folder-based approach, shown in Figure 11.14, users will likely find the WSS user interface quite different at first, although functionality differences are very small. At the time of writing, the Custom eRoom Extractor is still in the prototype stages. Thus, you will find the most up-to-date documentation and install package on the GotDotNet Space at `http://work-spaces.gotdotnet.com/spimport`.

Since folders in eRoom can contain other data containers, such as calendars, some design decisions need to be made in order to present the data in a meaningful manner after migration to SharePoint. SharePoint lists and libraries cannot contain other data containers, so you must decide whether

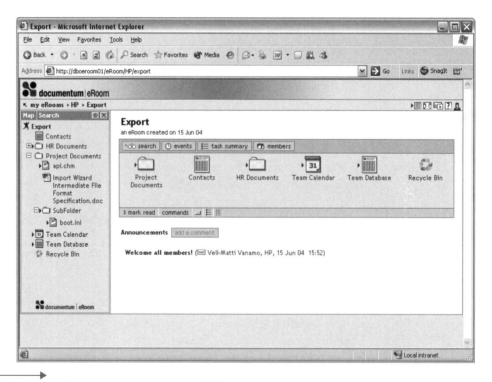

Figure 11.14   *Documentum eRoom team collaboration space.*

to create each data container as a list on the top site or to create subwebs for each folder in eRoom.

The Custom eRoom Extractor includes full support for translating all data-container types in eRoom to their respective list types in WSS. In addition, eRoom databases are converted to WSS custom lists, and eRoom notifications are successfully translated into WSS alerts. Security is supported at the library level, which means that item and subfolder ACLs are dropped during the migration, unless you choose to export eRoom folders as WSS subwebs. At the time of writing, per-item security is not supported, although future plans include the ability to create document workspaces for each item that does not inherit security from the parent folder.

As we discussed earlier, there will sometimes be feature gaps that can be very important to the business users and, thus, must be addressed somehow in the new SharePoint environment. One such example is eRoom *Inbox* functionality, which allows users to copy eRoom e-mail addresses and archive correspondence within the eRoom space. While WSS offers functionality to enable document libraries to receive e-mail attachments via

Figure 11.15   *Custom eRoom Extractor.*

public folder integration, the typical use of eRoom Inbox requires the complete message to be archived for further reference. Since the e-mail correspondence archival functionality is not included in WSS, you need to find out how critical the feature is to the end users and choose to either accept the loss of functionality or address it with custom development or a third-party add-on product.

The custom extractor itself is a very straightforward application, not unlike the other extractors we've already covered. The custom extractor, as shown in Figure 11.15, allows you to export one eRoom at a time or many at once in batch mode. Filters for excluding content based on modified date, file size, and content type are also available, giving you the ability to restrict which content is brought over to the new environment.

Since the custom extractor tool uses the eRoom COM API, you must run the tool on the eRoom server, although the data can be exported to a network share. Since the tool was created using Visual Studio.NET 2003 C#, you must have .NET Framework 1.1 installed on the server before proceeding to install the Custom eRoom Extractor.

12

Supporting and Managing a SharePoint Deployment

12.1   Supporting SharePoint Products and Technologies

Although SharePoint is a Web application, we've repeatedly compared it more with Exchange, which is an integrated platform full of features that need constant monitoring and can fail independently of other components. As with Exchange, SharePoint relies heavily on the stack of cards it's built upon: Windows Server, Domain Authentication, Microsoft .NET Framework, and IIS. If any one of these cards falls, most, if not all, of the stack comes down with it. We've made this point before, but it's important to stress it, especially when we talk about support and operations. Having an application support an operations team that doesn't understand the underlying infrastructure will severely restrict the team's ability to think laterally in a critical situation, thus lengthening the process. If the support team must go to another team for advice after all other avenues have been explored, valuable time passes as your environment is having problems.

We're not saying the SharePoint operations team must be a master of all trades; that would be unfeasible and restrictively expensive. What we are suggesting is that the operations team should have a reasonable understanding of the architecture on top of which SharePoint Products and Technologies is built to be able to think outside the box and consider other elements that make up the total solution. We've seen many unfortunate hours spent on issues that could have been resolved more quickly if the big picture were clearer to everyone involved.

12.1.1   Planning a support strategy

It's important to decide upfront on a clear support strategy, since there's nothing worse than having to "play as it goes" when dealing with issues. Be

Figure 12.1
Staging process is key for high-availability enterprise applications.

clear about what you support and who is in charge of what, and make sure the end users know the support policy and how to get in contact. We'll discuss some of the more important topics for a support strategy, such as operational models and service level agreements (SLAs), shortly, but first let's discuss some of the higher-level points you should consider.

First of all, let's emphasize the importance of a staging process, or making sure that all changes go through a testing environment that mirrors the production setup (see Figure 12.1). While this might be a moot point, we have seen deployments that did not include this step for budgetary reasons. We've also seen these deployments cost dearly later on, with downtime due to various operating system changes that changed the environment in an unforeseeable manner, causing the application to fail. You don't have to mirror the production environment exactly; it's enough to have a similar configuration without all the latest and greatest hardware. Note, though, that when the staging environment isn't a perfect match, there can be situations, such as updating device drivers, where you will have to perform without prior testing. Thus, we would recommend getting as close as you can to the production environment, if high availability is absolutely key for your deployment.

Although determining what you support might sound simple, you should consider this carefully for SharePoint Products and Technologies. Even the out-of-the-box capabilities are extensive, putting a burden on the support organization for having to learn everything to be able to support it. If you add on top of that the customizations possible with FrontPage, your task just got a whole lot more complicated. Given that WSS and SPS are not only applications, but that they are a technology framework to build line-of-business applications upon as well, supporting absolutely everything will become a daunting task.

We recommend that support organizations draw the line to customizations that are possible with Internet Explorer and come up with a model for custom Web Parts and applications that give most of the support tasks to the developers. Supporting FrontPage customizations is too wide a field to tackle; the training alone for operations staff would need to be extensive.

we're not recommending that FrontPage modifications should be banned altogether, but we would recommend deciding on a strategy that will not offer support, defined in the SLAs, for FrontPage-modified webs. While this can be a controversial view, and is one that has been widely debated in the Web logs and community forums around the Internet, we've seen the support calls generated and would never sign off on a support strategy for an organization that included SLA for FrontPage customizations. We have recommended and implemented a support strategy that included end-user education and clear statements that FrontPage-modified webs are allowed but only supported on a best-effort basis.

Custom Web Parts and other applications can become an issue for operations staff, unless the new Web Part deployment process includes steps to ensure that the staff is informed about the customizations and aware of their intended functionality. Since it is unlikely that the operations staff possess developer skills, you should ensure that the developers accept responsibility for their work and commit to ongoing support of the customizations. While developers might change, properly documented code can be modified and supported by their replacements. Therefore, one key point for a support strategy is to take steps to ensure that the code is properly documented, instead of relying on developers to do this out of the kindness of their hearts.

The operational model shown in Figure 12.2 has been used successfully for Web Parts and other custom code on several large enterprise deployments of SharePoint Products and Technologies. While it can, at first, look quite complicated, and the figure has already been significantly generalized from the "live" versions, the basic thinking behind the process is straightforward. As with any development, the requirements must first be defined and documented; then, the application is designed and developed. Ensuring that the requirements are documented up front helps the operations team support the end result better, since they understand what the usage scenario

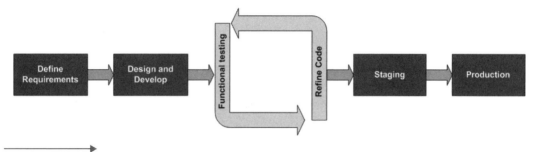

Figure 12.2   *Custom development process.*

is. As we've already shown in Chapter 8, badly coded Web Parts can, in the worst possible scenario, bring the environment to a halt. While this is extremely unlikely, we would still recommend making sure that the functional testing phase of the custom-code deployment process includes a performance benchmark. Finally, once the code has been verified and modified as necessary, all changes should go through a staging process to ensure that the production environment does not introduce any surprises.

One often-forgotten, important point to remember when developing a support strategy is to properly document it once done and to make it available for the end users. While most end users will likely not care to read the documents, there will be key business-process owners who will benefit from the gained insight and make use of the documentation effort. Of course, you can always point people to the documentation when complaints are voiced on some of the more controversial points—for example, the FrontPage modifications mentioned earlier. A condensed support-policy presentation should also be compiled for users who do not care to wade through the full documentation.

12.1.2 Planning an operational model

Most organizations have well-established and preferred operational models in place for various applications, such as Exchange. Thus, choosing the operational model will likely just be an exercise to find out your organization's preferred model and adopting it. However, if there are no established methods in your organization, you might need to spare some thought for this point as well.

Typically, in an enterprise environment with a shared infrastructure, the application-support team relies on other teams to perform at least the hardware, power, and network support and operations. It's natural that the support for these shared infrastructure and physical components be delivered from a centralized resource, since the application-support team might not be on site at all the data centers where SharePoint Products and Technologies have been deployed. While this introduces reliance on other teams and their ability to meet SLAs, the benefit is reduced cost, especially if you are considering a geographically distributed deployment. On the other hand, today it would be completely possible for a remote support team to be able to support a remote deployment, given that most high-end servers ship with integrated remote-control hardware, which allows support to perform everything from a local console, including powering the server on and off. You would still have to contract someone to perform hardware replacements and other tasks that require physical presence.

Today, more often than not, the operating system is considered part of the underlying shared infrastructure, and support for it is also delivered by a dedicated team. Given the frequency of operating system security updates these days, sourcing operating system support externally certainly reduces the management overhead for the application-support team. IT organizations might, in fact, require this in order to have the operating environment managed in a secure and accountable model.

For the actual application support, most enterprise applications are run in a tiered operational model, especially if 24/7 operations capability is required. A tiered model establishes a number of operations teams with varying levels of knowledge and sometimes access to systems. A tiered operational model often also includes an escalation step outside of the operations team to a subject-matter expert or external consultant. For example, in a four-tiered operations model, shown in Figure 12.3, tiers 1 through 3 are in house, while tier 4 can be reached via an escalation to the subject-matter experts.

In the four-tier model, the first level is really the help desk. The help-desk function is usually outsourced to a lower-cost center, which handles a number of technologies and, thus, does not comprise experts in any given application. The first-level help desk typically gathers information from the end user and checks it against a known-issues-and-resolutions list to attempt to resolve the case immediately. However, if the error does not sound familiar, the first level will transfer the case to the second-level help desk, which is often run from the same low-cost center. In order to deal with these filtered calls, the second-level help desk staff has usually been trained to understand the application quite well and is thus able to troubleshoot the issues with the end users. If the issue cannot be solved by the second-level help desk, the case is transferred to the third-level help-desk staff,

Figure 12.3
Tiered operational model.

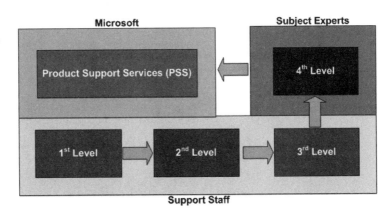

who typically double as the application administrators for the environment. Thus, the third-level staff consists of application experts, since they are in charge of the day-to-day administration and change management. If the issue is too complex for the third-level staff to solve, it can be transferred to the subject-matter experts, who might be you if you're planning to deploy SharePoint Products and Technologies in your organization. The fourth level typically consists of architects and other key knowledgeable staff within the organization. The fourth level typically also works with Microsoft Product Support Services to troubleshoot and resolve serious issues that might require a hotfix.

Obviously, the model shown in Figure 12.3 can be adapted to your organization by dropping the levels that are not required. It would be advisable to have at least two levels so that the application administrators do not need to spend their time helping trivial cases when they could be off doing something much more productive.

12.1.3   Planning Service-Level Agreements

The SLA is the key contract signed by the business and the operations team that defines the support services delivered for an application. SLA is not only a percentile number for availability, such as 99.8%, but it includes the agreed-upon availability goal as well. An SLA should cover the whole support strategy, expectations, and metrics for the environment. An SLA should address at least the following key points:

- Services provided

- Roles and responsibilities

- Priority service levels and handling expectations for different levels

- Communication and escalation paths

- SLA measurement and reporting

Most support organizations prioritize cases and, thus, commit to different response times based on the issue priority. For example, system downtime would no doubt be a priority 1 issue, which should be dealt with immediately, whereas a user asking how to upload a batch of files at the same time will no doubt be put toward the back of the queue and handled when more critical issues are out of the way. In the SLA you should clearly define what the different priority levels are and what lead time the end users should expect when there are more important issues to deal with. Table 12.1 shows an example prioritization breakup with issue severity descriptions and

Table 12.1   *Example Prioritization Levels*

Issue Severity	Description	First Response
Priority 1 (critical)	Application is down, or major business is process impacted; end users are critically impacted.	15 minutes
Priority 2 (serious)	Major functions are not working or business processes are impacted. However, end users are not critically impacted but do notice the issue.	1 hour
Priority 3 (important)	The application is functioning, but there are issues with some components. End users experience minor nuisance; however, they can continue to use the system.	6 hours
Priority 4 (low impact)	There are "how to" questions and requests for more information.	24 hours

how soon the users should expect someone to get back to them on the issues they logged.

Unfortunately, sometimes the defined response times cannot be kept; thus, you should clearly define the escalation path that the users can take to raise the priority of their case. Escalations should go through a function in the business to prevent the support organization from becoming burdened with users requesting escalations just because they think the case is just that much more important. Some kind of filter must be applied to adjust the levels and ensure fair treatment. Business contacts should also be listed somewhere so that the end users know who to call when they do not feel they are receiving adequate support for their case. In case of system downtime or other serious issues, the business contacts should also be kept up-to-date at all times so that they know how to respond to user questions.

The SLA should also include a definition of roles and responsibilities of all entities involved one way or another with the SharePoint Products and Technologies deployment. It's good to know who to contact, but it's also important not to knowingly step on someone else's toes. Usually the roles and responsibilities are defined in a responsible, accountable, consulted, and informed (RACI) chart for different tasks in the environment.

And, of course, the SLA should include the all-important commitment to certain availability targets. Availability is a percentile number that is derived from the period the application has been down in any given time span—for example, if your application was down for 15 minutes during a 24-hour period, your availability was 98.96% $[(24 \times 60 - 15/(24 \times 60)) \times 100]$.

Coming up with the availability target is somewhat of a refined art form, since you are dealing with a number of unknowns. Typically, you have to calculate the availability target from the hardware, network, power, operating system, and the application availability commitments to come up with a single magic number for the business. For example, even if you can guarantee 99.9% availability for the SharePoint application, it doesn't matter much if the data center can only provide you with a network link rated with a 97% availability target. Sure, the application is up, but since end users can't access it, you're out of luck. Thus, you should study the full picture carefully before committing to an availability target that you will be measured against. As a rough guideline, your availability should be the number of hours per year the least resilient infrastructure has been rated for, minus the planned downtime for the application itself. For example, if your network is rated for 98% availability and you plan to perform 32 hours of application maintenance that requires complete downtime, your total availability will be 97.63%.

Finally, you should agree on a set of criteria that you will be measured against. Undoubtedly, one of them will be the availability of the environment, but support issue–resolution times should also form part of the overall measurement. The "traffic light" approach for measurement works here just as well as it does in a number of other situations for indicating how well you've done. There should be thresholds agreed upon for green, yellow, and red, with green obviously being above or at the agreed-upon service levels. The yellow and red are up for discussion though, so you should agree on these with the business funding the environment and provide a monthly summary of support performance and events, as well as explanations for when things did not go as planned and an action plan to remedy issues for the next reporting period.

12.1.4   Expected support-call volume

Estimating the support-call volume is very hard to generalize; every organization is different, and the culture affects how the users behave. For example, in a technology company, users are tech-savvy and are often used to things breaking every now and then. They are therefore unlikely to complain right away. Tech-savvy employees will also typically prefer self-help methods, such as a support portal with known issues and FAQs, as well as the Internet with monster search engines such as Google. On the other hand, a less-knowledgeable user base is more likely to use the company's support help desk for smaller issues.

Luckily, it's highly unlikely that SharePoint will be the first application deployed within an organization. Thus, you can go to the other application-support teams to get a feel for the user base. The desktop support team, for example, is a good gauge for per-person call rates within your organization. So, prepare for at least the same per-user case volume in the beginning and adjust accordingly as time goes on. Nobody expects you to get it right on the first go.

As a rough guideline, we've seen call volumes of approximately one call for every 230 users per day after six months in production. By using that guideline, for a 20,000-user organization with 40% (very high) of the users visiting the environment every day, you should expect 34 calls per day. Obviously, in the beginning the volume is likely to be higher, as the users are coming to grips with the tools.

12.1.5   Staffing an operational team

Unfortunately, some support managers might interpret the outsourcing of operating system and other infrastructure support as one less skill set the operations staff has to possess. While it is true that the SharePoint operations staff doesn't have to worry about security patching and service pack updates, it would be a mistake to think that you can run a successful SharePoint operation without having skills in the various infrastructure components on which SharePoint Products and Technologies is built.

We've had numerous discussions with various support managers on the subject and still maintain that the operations team must be able to quickly analyze the problem and consider outside factors without having to go back to the team responsible for the component. Otherwise, you'll quickly find yourself in a position where the system is down, and the application-support staff simply note that it's not SharePoint's fault and get another team involved. Of course, this takes time, and application support often has to prove that the fault is indeed with the underlying infrastructure, not the application, thus adding to downtime.

We highly recommend seriously considering including operating-system and basic network skill sets in the higher-tier support-personnel requirements. Understanding how DNS works, being able to do light network-traffic analysis to make sure that authentication is properly working, and understanding how IIS responds to user queries can save valuable minutes when the application is down without an immediately identifiable cause. While this certainly adds to the support delivery cost, given the additional training and technical-level requirements of the staff, it all comes down to how important the environment is to the business. Ask the business sponsors if they would be willing to spend $10,000 more per year on support, if they would be able to save 10 hours of application downtime, for example.

Once you understand the operations-staff technical-level requirements and expected call volume, you can put in plans to staff the team appropriately. Even in a smaller deployment, if application availability is a key requirement, you need to ensure extra staff for the operations team in order to provide adequate cover for holidays, sick days, and so forth. Higher-tier levels can provide assistance for lower tiers, but this does not work the other way around. Thus, you should assign extra funds to the higher-tier staffing so that when required, they can cover holidays and sick leaves for tier 1 help desk staff.

12.2   Proactive support strategy

Part of your overall support strategy should be how to avoid issues that cause support calls in the first place. If you know in advance that, for example, an operating system patch causes issues, you can take proactive measures to minimize the impact on the production environment. On the other hand, you should try to be one step ahead of users in detecting issues, such as application faults. If you rely solely on users coming back to you when there's an issue with an application, you risk lengthened downtime and end-user impact, since users might not immediately report issues as they come across them.

12.2.1   Pathway to production

One of the best ways to prevent issues is to try to make sure they never get to the production platform in the first place. Having a change-management process is key for limiting issues caused by customizations, configuration changes, and system patches. Although we already covered the staging process in the beginning of this chapter, we cannot stress enough its importance with enterprise deployments of SharePoint Products and Technologies.

While the staging process does add considerable overhead to the operations, especially if the environment is only serving a few thousand users, it's still good to adopt at least some form of change-management process for your deployment. If the requirements do not justify the expense of maintaining a complete shadow environment, consider using smaller, single-server deployments to at least be able to test service packs and other patch upgrade processes on a platform you can afford to make mistakes on.

Complete shadow environments have other benefits, aside from being a staging environment; they can also act as a disaster-recovery platform and take on the production role in case the production farm has to be reconfigured for some reason. Storage reconfiguration is one such case that many of you might face in the next 12 to 24 months of production, unless you've taken steps to ensure high storage-growth possibilities. It's often prohibitively expensive to scale up the storage infrastructure right away, especially if you're deploying a new service to the enterprise without knowing how popular it will become. Thus, Storage Area Network (SAN) storage might be out of bounds, and you might be faced with a directly connected storage to SAN/fiber-connected storage migration in the future. Having an environment you can fail over to, reconfigure, and test new hardware architectures on in peace is a luxury worth fighting for.

Especially when opening cases with Microsoft Product Support Services, being able to demonstrate a reproducible error condition is worth its weight in gold when dealing with a critical issue. Like all of us, Product Support Services do not hold the key to unlocking every mystery just by hearing the problem description. They have to debug, test, and capture logs and network traces in order to solve a difficult case they haven't faced before. Having to do this on a production environment is unnerving at best, so for your support managers' continued good health and the reliability of the delivered service to end users, do include a staging environment in your organization's budgetary plans.

We will get off the soapbox now, hoping we've illustrated the need for seriously considering a change-management process that includes a staging-environment testing process.

12.2.2   Active monitoring

It would be naive to think that all possible issues could be filtered with planning and change management. SharePoint Products and Technologies are just as likely to encounter a software or hardware fault that causes system downtime for end users. There's no way around it; it's going to happen to your environment as well sooner or later.

So, as you accept that downtime will occur, you should take proactive steps to catch it as soon as it happens and in a best-case scenario deal with it before the end users even notice it. Therefore, having an automated monitoring and alerting infrastructure that will keep an eye on the application operation 24 hours a day, 7 days a week, and 365 days a year should be a key priority for the operations team.

There are numerous product offerings from various vendors available—for example, from Microsoft Operations Manager (MOM) to SiteScope to HP OpenView, which all provide SharePoint-specific modules that keep an eye on hardware alerts, event log errors, and application-specific services, along with URL monitoring. Some of the tools even offer automated tasks to perform based on the error context, such as restarting the Portal Search Service when a database memory-fragmentation warning event appears in the application event log. Typically, every organization has an existing license to a monitoring product, since it's very likely most organizations already monitor their Exchange and Web Server environments. If there is no infrastructure in place, however, evaluate the different service offerings and make your decision based on functionality criteria and cost.

The monitoring service should at least be able to poll SharePoint-specific service status from Windows (such as the Portal Alert Service) and, most importantly, to perform a content match for URL queries. Being able just to report that the service is responding with an HTTP status quote of 200 is by no means enough for SharePoint Products and Technologies, since the product now reports with "friendly" error messages when SQL connectivity, for example, is having problems. Thus, if you do not check that the actual HTML content returned matches expected values, many problems will go unnoticed until end users complain.

Remember that SharePoint Products and Technologies rely heavily on SQL being available and performing up to standards. Therefore, it's important to include SQL services and databases in the monitoring and ensure that you fully follow SQL-management best practices. You should, for example, set up alerts to ensure that databases and transaction logs never run out of space and schedule various management jobs that keep the databases healthy and at peak performance. Please refer to the extensive documentation in the SQL Online Books for more information on SQL management and monitoring.

Last, but not least, you should make sure that the alerts don't simply go to an e-mail inbox that is rarely checked. If possible, you should try to put in place an alert-management plan that uses different means of communication to ensure that critical alerts are dealt with even at 4:00 A.M. on Saturday night within a reasonable period, obviously defined beforehand in the SLA. Use pagers and other devices, since your e-mail infrastructure, just like your SharePoint deployment, is subject to service availability.

12.2.3 Passive analyzing

In addition to monitoring that the service is responding to user queries, you should take proactive steps to seek possible clues for trouble down the line. Periodically analyzing the event logs, for example, for warnings and errors can save you time and effort, since you can deal with the issues before they become serious cases, possibly causing system downtime.

In addition to event logs, you should analyze the IIS log files for usage patterns to better understand the user scenario and adapt the architecture to the way the users are really using the infrastructure. You might discover, for example, that users are performing more searches than you had expected and can thus prepare well ahead of time, even before the performance analysis catches the extended resource usage. SQL Server logs should also be periodically analyzed for possible issues with index fragmentation and other database events that might cause problems in the future.

12.3 Performance monitoring

Of course, the most important passive analysis method is system performance monitoring, which can be set up to continuous log and alert based on predefined thresholds. Most of the monitoring products mentioned earlier also record performance information and, thus, can report on trends and send alerts. In addition, Windows Server 2003 ships with Perfmon, which gathers and logs data from performance counters. Perfmon also allows alerts to be set up with thresholds, although you must have a program that does something more intelligent than logging the alert to system log to make this feature useful. (See Figure 12.4.)

12.3.1 Monitoring strategy

It's important to consider exactly which counters you should capture and how often they need to be recorded. In order to establish a system baseline, for example, you will need sampling data over several days to be able to draw conclusions. With hundreds of counters available for both system and application components, it doesn't make sense to capture everything, thus allocating a lot of space and resources for just recording performance. Instead, it's better to continuously monitor key aspects of system performance, which give you clues to what's going on and indicate when you should pay closer attention and add a number of specific counters for deeper analysis.

Figure 12.4
*Perfmon
performance-
monitoring tool.*

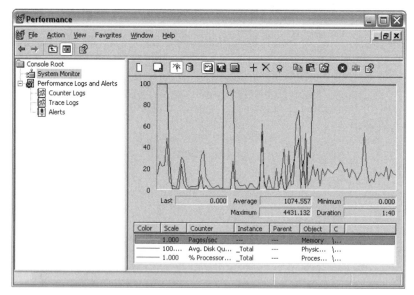

Additionally, you should ensure that your monitoring strategy includes sending out alerts when key thresholds are exceeded, such as available disk space. You should also make sure that key performance counters, such as processor utilization and system queue, also generate alerts if their thresholds are exceeded for a period of time. Peaks will obviously occur; thus, you need to take steps to ensure that you do not generate false alarms for peaks.

It's important to be able to establish growth patterns and trends, which will guide you through the production phase and ensure that any given component is never allowed to become a bottleneck for usage growth in your enterprise. You should be able to predict capacity requirements six months ahead of time, giving you plenty of time to process necessary funding approvals, purchase the needed hardware, and plan for deploying it in the least-obtrusive manner for the end users. If you find out that you've got 1 GB of disk space left, there's very little time to plan for anything but turning off site creation and effectively freezing the environment while you scramble to source more disk space for the environment. A monitoring strategy with periodic reviews ensures you never have to duck for cover when the growth pattern exceeds earlier estimations.

12.3.2   Identifying future bottlenecks

There are three main utilization areas, which you should frequently monitor and use to establish growth patterns: processor, memory and disk.

Typically, network is also included in this, but we've yet to see a full-duplex 100-Mbps network card become saturated with SharePoint Products and Technologies before one of the other components has reached a limit, so we've left it on the list of items to monitor less frequently. However, if you are operating on a 10-Mbps link, you are likely to reach a network bottleneck much sooner there than on another component.

As we discussed in Chapter 9, 100-Mbps network speeds are rarely realistic in enterprise deployments, given that it's unlikely all of the employees are in one central location. Unfortunately, monitoring wide area network (WAN) routes is not possible from the physical servers and must be done by the network administrators, who typically are in charge of upgrading links as thresholds creep closer. Thus, in this book we focus on things you as an administrator can control and monitor. However, you should talk with your network team about your organization's WAN links and thresholds and ask if it's possible to get a report from them on network usage of the SharePoint Products and Technologies in order for you to identify possible WAN bottlenecks. Armed with this knowledge, you can keep the end users informed of the situation and involve management as necessary if the situation needs to be addressed. Now, let's get back to the bottlenecks we can monitor and control.

Table 12.2 lists the key system-performance counters that you should monitor to establish a performance trend and to set up alerts when utilization creeps near to the thresholds. You should establish the alert margins based on how long it takes in your organization to source required extra capacity.

Please see Microsoft Knowledge Base Article Q300237 for more information on setting up alerts on key system components.

Table 12.2 *Important System-Performance Counters*

Counter Name	Description	Threshold
Processor: % Processor Time _Total	Combined average CPU utilization. SharePoint, as with many other applications, will not perform consistently after 80% constant CPU utilization. Use in conjunction with the Processor Queue Length to identify a processor bottleneck.	80%
System: Processor Queue Length	Number of execution threads in the processor queue. Typically, when the queue goes over six, the server is not able to process requests quickly enough, indicating a processor performance bottleneck	6

Table 12.2   *Important System-Performance Counters (continued)*

Counter Name	Description	Threshold
Memory: Pages/sec	"Hard" pages/sec. When a page is not in memory, it has to be fetched from the page file, which is also referred to as a "hard" page fault. This is arguably the most important indicator for memory bottlenecks and should not get close to 20. Use in conjunction with other memory counters to verify that paging is really an issue.	20
Memory: Available bytes	Memory available for applications and the operating system to use. Use in conjunction with Pages/sec to identify a memory bottleneck, since SharePoint Search Service will happily use as much memory as is available. Low available bytes on its own doesn't necessarily mean you have to add more memory, but low available bytes together with a high Pages/sec count indicate the need to add some RAM.	128 MB
LogicalDisk: % Disk Time (for each volume)	Indicates if the disk is busy performing operations. If the disk time is high for a period of time, it does not necessarily indicate an I/O bottleneck, but it does warrant a more in-depth investigation utilizing the Disk Average Read/Write Queue Lengths. High I/O can also be caused by excessive paging, so remember never to read the values in isolation and to keep other factors in mind as well.	50%

Table 12.3   *Interesting Counters for SharePoint*

Counter Name	Description	Threshold
ASP.NET applications: Requests/sec	The number of requests the ASP.NET engine is executing. This is only interesting on the Web front-end servers and can be used in conjunction with the CPU utilization for usage-pattern analysis and predicting future capacity demands.	—
Search catalogs: Number of documents (select all of your catalogs)	The number of items the search catalog (index) contains. Microsoft recommends up to 5 million items per catalog with 20 million overall for SPS 2003 spanned over four search catalogs.	5 million
Search: Query rate	The number of search queries executed every second. If both CPU utilization and the Search query rate is high, you should consider moving Search onto a dedicated server, which can be load-balanced for further scalability.	—

In addition to these basic system counters, which are relevant for all servers in a SharePoint farm, there are a number of application-specific counters that can give you indications of how well the environment is performing. Table 12.3 lists the main application counters you should pay attention to and gives a short description of how to interpret them. As always, don't use the counters in isolation, and keep an eye on the system counters as well.

12.4   Managing SharePoint Products and Technologies

After having planned, designed, and deployed SharePoint Products and Technologies, managing the environment is quite straightforward. Most of the management tasks will likely be triggered by end-user support queries and business change-management requests.

Of course, exceptional circumstances cannot be planned for. Everyone involved with managing a SharePoint Products and Technologies deployment will likely have to deal with troubleshooting downtime issues and, unfortunately, sometimes even performing disaster recovery. Thus, it's good to prepare for the unplanned and make sure the operations team knows what to do in case of a disaster.

Before jumping to disasters, let's cover the more common, although less exciting, occurrences in a daily operations-staff work schedule.

12.4.1   Managing sites and portal areas

Although in most cases team-site and even portal-site management tasks are executed by the space owners, there are circumstances in which the operations staff is called for assistance. Thus, it's good to get to know the functionality of the products thoroughly in order to best be able to assist users in their management tasks.

You should familiarize yourself with creating and maintaining list, site, and portal-area templates, since you will undoubtedly face questions on this topic. Business sponsors might also request new site definitions or templates to be added to the root portal or WSS site in order to provide users top-level line-of-business templates on which to create their sites quickly. You will no doubt also face requests to add Web Parts and other customizations, which are covered in Part III.

While SPS areas can easily be restructured to follow a new information architecture mode, WSS sites cannot. Portal owners will quickly catch on to the handy `drag&drop` portal-area restructuring method available behind the **Manage Portal Site Structure** link on the portal. However, you will no doubt receive requests to move WSS sites from one place to another, for which the `smigrate.exe` tool we discussed in Chapter 11 is ideally suited.

There are numerous other settings, such as regional settings and alerts. Thus, the best way to get to know each one of them is to click on every possible link on the Portal Server administration pages and the WSS site settings.

12.4.2   Managing Search

Perhaps the most common change request for a SharePoint Portal Server deployment has to do with the Search service. Both business sponsors and end users will undoubtedly want to include various systems both internally and externally as a content source for the SPS deployment. Instead of blindly accepting every request, you should establish a procedure and a clear strategy for Search to prevent it from becoming unmanageable and bloated with useless information. Still, adding content indexes and content sources, which we already covered in Chapter 8, will no doubt be part of the operation team's task list.

SPS 2003 Portal Search can be slightly temperamental in its operation, requiring some close attention and, sometimes, hands-on management. It's not uncommon for the search catalogs to lose touch with reality, requiring a hard wake-up call in the form of an index reset. By resetting the index, you are effectively purging the database and initiating a full content update. Thus, it's not a step to be taken lightly, especially if you are reindexing an amount of external content that might take hours, if not days, to complete fully.

12.4.3   Other common management tasks

The operations team will most likely need to help end users with user management, especially when the site owner wants to add a good number of users to the site. We would recommend creating an NT/AD security group for any member list that's larger than 100 users, since adding that number of users would not be a task to take lightly. Although you could certainly pick every user from Outlook's global address list (GAL) easily enough, SharePoint will likely time out when attempting to resolve tens of e-mail addresses to account names, especially when there is more than one domain to check e-mail addresses against.

A number of automated features, such as site-collection use confirmations, depend on the site ownership information being correct. Thus, if you plan to enable these features, you should ensure that the ownership information is properly kept up-to-date. Out of the box, even site owners themselves are not able to change this information without involving the system administrators. Therefore, you should make sure end users understand the procedure to follow to request that their space ownership information be changed in case the original owner is reassigned to another team or leaves the company. You should also make sure they understand the possible consequences of failure to follow the process.

12.4.4   Common support issues

The most common support query we've seen in a few different enterprise implementations has had to do with authentication, or, rather, the browser configuration for authentication. NTLM authentication, which is the default authentication method, does not work with most proxy servers, which strip the unknown authentication headers from the requests in transit. The result is an IIS permission-denied error message, adding to end-users' confusion, since the first thing that comes to mind is that the site owner forgot to grant them access. Therefore, you should take steps to ensure that your organization's autoconfiguration servers do include exclusions for the SharePoint servers.

Accidental file deletions often cause headaches for the support teams, since SharePoint Products and Technologies do not provide a wastebasket, or per-item restore capabilities. As we discussed in Chapter 9, there are a number of third-party products out there that do cover this functionally. As we also discussed in Chapter 9, for WSS you can schedule the `stsadm` tool to take backups of each site collection in order to be able to at least recover one site with a different name to facilitate end users' manually copying back the accidentally removed files.

Part III

Customizing and Extending SharePoint

13

Introduction to SharePoint Development

13.1 Development architecture overview

Chapter 1 provides us with information on the evolution of Microsoft SharePoint Products and Technologies (SharePoint). From a development standpoint, much has changed since the initial release of SPS 2001 and STS. This chapter looks briefly at the architectures of both SPS 2001 and STS and how they evolved into the current SharePoint platform. We examine the various components making up the current version and highlight areas of particular interest to developers and Web designers who wish to customize and extend its functionality. Subsequent chapters in this section elaborate on many of the concepts discussed in this chapter.

SPS 2001 is based on the Digital DashBoard architecture and provides a set of customizable dashboards designed to act as a collaborative Web portal for a company's intranet. Each dashboard comprises a number of Web Parts that enable users to manage, share, and filter important information. The SPS 2001 document store, previously known as the Web Storage System, stores the dashboards and Web Part items in addition to the dashboard factory responsible for page rendering. Figure 13.1 illustrates the dashboard architecture implemented by SPS 2001.

STS, on the other hand, is based on the Microsoft FrontPage Extensions 2002 architecture, which includes a database component, either SQL Server or the Microsoft Data Engine (MSDE). The database component supports STS features such as document libraries, lists, and discussions. The architecture includes a set of Internet Server Application Programming Interface (ISAPI) applications that run in process with the IIS Web server (Figure 13.2).

STS clients communicate with IIS using HTTP. All content is returned to the client in HTML form. STS uses a combination of SQL Server and

Figure 13.1
SPS 2001 dashboard architecture.

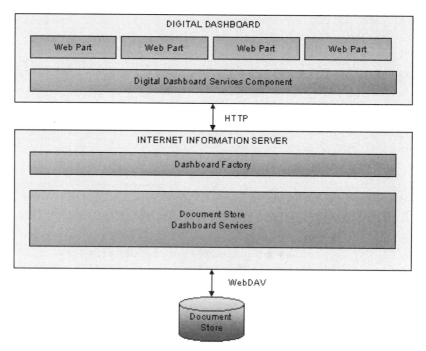

the local file system as its storage mechanism and ISAPI as the mechanism for running pages within the application.

The release of SharePoint has brought us the best of both worlds with the complete rearchitecturing and convergence of both SPS and STS into a common platform. This version of SharePoint leverages the Microsoft

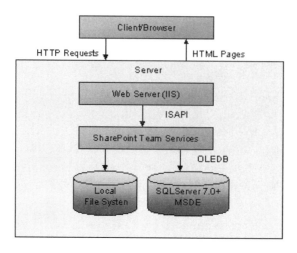

Figure 13.2
STS architecture.

.NET Framework, Web services, Microsoft Visual Studio .Net, and Windows Server 2003 and provides a scalable, flexible, and secure environment on which to build, deploy, and manage enterprise Web applications.

Microsoft's long-term strategy from a storage perspective for products such as SharePoint and Exchange is to leave behind the Web Storage System model and to take advantage of SQL Server's relational database and XML data-storage technology. While the plans for Exchange to leverage SQL Server may not be realized for quite a while, SharePoint uses SQL Server as its storage platform today. With the exception of the search indexes created by Microsoft Search technologies, all configuration, content, site, and profile information is stored in a SQL Server database.

From a scalability perspective, SharePoint provides an architecture that consists of stateless Web servers and stateful data servers. Stateless Web servers are basically front-end servers that run code but do not store any local data. Stateful servers hold all user, site, profile, and configuration data and are partitioned by site collection. When you type in a request to a SharePoint site, the request first hits the Web server. The Web server handles this request through a number of components, namely an ISAPI

Figure 13.3
SharePoint
architecture.

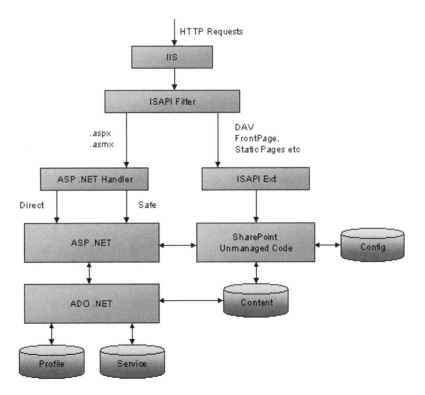

filter, an ISAPI extension ASP.NET handler, and, finally, ASP.NET. Figure 13.3 illustrates the Web server components in addition to the database components.

13.1.1   IIS

While IIS's involvement in the SharePoint product has been significantly reduced from previous versions, it still performs a vital role in running the application. IIS acts as the HTTP listener on port 80 and handles all the IP packets. Requests are resolved using the domain name, the port, and the IP address of the virtual server the request is targeting. In addition, IIS handles authentication to the virtual server; SharePoint is not involved in actually authenticating who the user is. SharePoint leverages the IIS 6.0 Application Pools, which allow virtual servers to run in different application pools. SharePoint uses application pools for three reasons:

1. *Process identity:* When SharePoint connects to SQL Server, it connects as the Application Pool identity.

2. *Process isolation:* If you have two virtual servers on the same physical server and you want to prevent the virtual servers from sharing database connectivity, you can isolate them from one another by allowing them to run with different accounts.

3. *Application recycling:* Previous versions of IIS allowed a process to run eternally, resulting in even the slightest memory leak causing a system crash. IIS 6.0 has the concept whereby application processes are recycled on a fixed basis. The SharePoint process is recycled by default every 24 hours, between 1:00 A.M. and 2:00 A.M. With application recycling any small leaks in resources will not result in the server going down in an uncontrolled fashion. This functionality is native to IIS 6.0; SharePoint does not add any additional code to make this happen.

13.1.2   Internet server API

Once the user has been authenticated, the ISAPI filter processes the URL. The ISAPI filter examines the URL and determines if it is requesting a SharePoint managed path. The ISAPI filter uses the list of inclusions and exclusions maintained by the administrator to make its decision. If the ISAPI filter sees that the URL contains a path listed in the exclusions list, it does not intercept the request. From an application development perspective, this is important. If you want an application to coexist with Share-

Point, you need a way of telling SharePoint not to process the URL; this is achieved by adding your application path to the exclusion list. All requests using paths listed in the exclusion list are ultimately processed by IIS.

If the request is for a SharePoint managed path, the ISAPI filter passes the request to either the ASP.NET handler or handles the request through a SharePoint ISAPI extension call. The ISAPI extension calls are used to process legacy protocols, FrontPage protocols, the DAV protocol, and any requests for static pages, such as a .doc or .htm file. The request for dynamic pages, such as .aspx pages, passes to the ASP.NET handler. The ASP.NET handler handles ASP.NET pages (Active Server Pages or ASPX pages).

13.1.3   ASP.NET handler

SharePoint uses ASP.NET pages throughout its application. For example, the Contacts list uses an ASP.NET page named AllItems.aspx to display all the contacts in the Contacts list on a single Web page. These pages can be customized, and you can add additional ASP.NET pages to run custom solutions on top of SharePoint. ASP.NET pages are served in one of two ways: direct mode or safe mode.

Direct mode

Direct-mode pages live in the Web server's file system and are processed with the standard ASP.NET processing model. Direct-mode pages are available to all sites on the server. SharePoint uses direct mode for all the ASP.NET pages in the _layouts directory. This directory contains a fixed set of the SharePoint application pages, such as the Site Settings and Create List pages, and any modifications to them may result in breaking Share-Point. In fact, modification to pages in the _layouts directory is unsupported by Microsoft. While direct-mode pages appear to live in the user's web, they are actually considered to be outside of the Web site and are processed by ASP.NET just like a regular ASP.NET page. To verify this, if you open up a site in FrontPage 2003, you will see that the _layouts directory does not exist in the site. In essence, the ASP.NET pages in the _layouts directory are shared application pages, running managed code that accesses the SharePoint Object Model (OM).

Safe mode

If the ASP.NET pages are in the Web—that is, they are not in the _lay-outs directory—they run in safe mode. The Contacts AllItems.aspx is

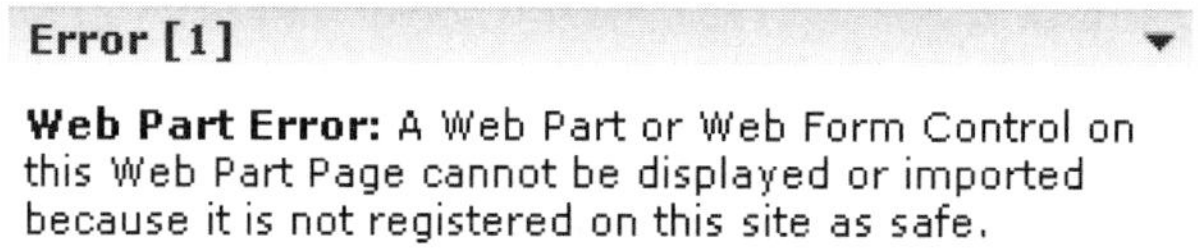

Figure 13.4
*Unsafe control
error.*

Error [1]   ▼

Web Part Error: A Web Part or Web Form Control on
this Web Part Page cannot be displayed or imported
because it is not registered on this site as safe.

an example of an ASP.NET page running in safe mode. Safe mode only
allows the Web Form Controls that the administrator defines as safe to run
on the page. The virtual server's Web.Config file contains the list of controls considered safe to run. Custom controls can be stamped as safe by
simply adding them to the list. Behind the scenes SharePoint actually
builds the ASP.NET page object and then hands that page object to
ASP.NET for processing. If you place an unsafe Web Form Control on the
page, SharePoint does not include the control in the page object that it
hands to ASP.NET; instead, it replaces the control with formatted text
informing the developer of the error (Figure 13.4). Safe mode has the
advantage of increasing both SharePoint's safety and scalability. From a
safety perspective, it allows end users to customize the site without the risk
of unauthorized code running on the server. From a scalability perspective,
it saves resources. With STS having 1,000 sites in your deployment used to
mean having 1,000 copies of the Contacts AllItems.aspx running in
your environment. This was an enormous waste of resources if the page
was not customized. With the current release of SharePoint, safe-mode
pages are shared using the concept of ghosted pages. Only one copy of the
page is stored in SharePoint's setup directory. The logic behind the concept
of ghosted pages is that until you customize the page, you do not need
your own copy of it. Sharing resources in this way improves scalability,
since IIS and SQL Server do not have to serve multiple copies of the same
information.

Managed and unmanaged code

ASP.NET has the concept of managed and unmanaged code. Managed
code executes under the control of the Common Language Runtime
(CLR). For example, any code that is written in C# or Visual BASIC
.NET is managed code. Unmanaged code runs outside the control of the
CLR, such as COM components, ActiveX components, and Win32 API
functions.

The core logic of SharePoint lives in unmanaged code. This logic
includes the FrontPage 2003 API, DAV support, the rendering of CAML
views, the retrieval of static documents, and the database I/O. In previous
versions of SPS and STS, Web Parts used the ASP-based Web Part model,

resulting in unmanaged code. This story has changed for the current release of SharePoint, and Web Parts now live in managed code, with the exception of View Web Parts. A View Web Part is merely a wrapper around the unmanaged CAML code.

Authorization and authentication

It is important to stress that the database does not enforce security. As far as the database is concerned, the Web server is one user running as the Application Pool account. Authorization as to who gets to see what is enforced on the Web server. SharePoint reads the metadata out of the database, and that metadata includes an access control list (ACL) defining who gets to see what. From a security perspective, a fundamental aspect of SharePoint is that end users do not have direct access to the database; instead, the Web server brokers all the security.

13.2   Enabling ASP.NET applications to coexist with SharePoint

There may be times when you require the ability to run an external ASP.NET application on a SharePoint-enabled virtual server. As previously mentioned, the ISAPI filter, by default, intercepts all requests to access the virtual server. In order to prevent SharePoint from processing your ASP.NET application, you need to perform a number of steps. First, you must inform the ISAPI filter that your application is not a SharePoint application by entering the path to your ASP.NET application in the exclusions list for the virtual server. In addition you may also need to make sure that the SharePoint ASP.NET handler does not process your pages. Full details of this process can be found in Microsoft's knowledge base article 828810. For convenience the steps are shown in the following list.

To configure the excluded path for your application:

1.   From the SharePoint server, click the **Start** button on the task pane.

2.   Click **Administrative Tools**.

3.   Click **SharePoint Central Administration**. The SharePoint Central Administration page appears in your browser.

4.   From the *Virtual Server Configuration* section, click the **Configure Virtual Server Settings** link. The Virtual Server List page appears.

5.   Click the virtual server where you would like your application to run. The Virtual Server Settings page appears.

6.   From the *Virtual Server Management* section, click the **Define Managed Paths** link.

7.   From the *Add a New Path* section, enter the path within the URL namespace to exclude. For example if you specify "myapp," this will exclude any paths to `http://servername/myapp` (Figure 13.5).

8.   Click the **Excluded path** type.

9.   Click **OK.**

To specify the default ASP.NET handler for all pages:

1.   From the server that hosts your application, navigate the path to where your application resides; for example, `c:\inetpub\wwwroot\myapp`.

2.   Make a backup copy of the `Web.Config` file so that you always have it to revert to should you need to roll back your changes. In addition, once you are happy with your modifications, it is best practice to make a backup copy of the modified `Web.Config` file, since this file may be overwritten with any service packs or patches.

3.   Open the `Web.Config` file.

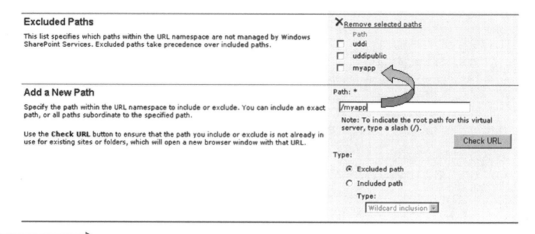

Figure 13.5   *Excluding the application path.*

```
<httpHandlers>
 <clear />
 <add verb="*" path="*.aspx" type="System.Web.UI.PageHandlerFactory, System.Web,
Version=1.0.5000.0, Culture=neutral, PublicKeyToken=b03f5f7f11d50a3a"/>
</httpHandlers>
<httpModules>
 <add name="UrlAuthorization" type="System.Web.Security.UrlAuthorizationModule"/>
 <add name="Session" type="System.Web.SessionState.SessionStateModule"/>
</httpModules>
<!-- Enable Session for the pages in your application -->
 <pages enableSessionState="true" enableViewState="true" enableViewStateMac="true"
validateRequest="true" />

<trust level="Full" originUrl="" />
```

Figure 13.6   *Web.Config changes.*

4.   Navigate to the `<system.web>` tag and modify the entry to include the changes shown in Figure 13.6.

5.   Save the file.

13.3   SharePoint page rendering and Web Part overview

Even though the dashboard architecture has been abandoned, parts of it, such as Web Parts, still remain a vital component of SharePoint. The Web Parts available in SharePoint are much more scalable and secure and are easily developed with development tools such as Visual Studio .NET. The concept of dashboard pages has been replaced by Web Part Pages. Web Part Pages are basically ASP.NET pages comprising zone containers that host Web Parts. The Web Parts themselves are based on ASP.NET Form Controls saved as `.dwp` files that contain metadata describing the instance of the part.

From a page-rendering perspective, two types of pages are handled by SharePoint—the ASP.NET pages in the `_layouts` directory of the site and ASP.NET pages inside a Web site containing Web Parts. As previously mentioned, the ASP.NET pages in the `_layouts` directory for a SharePoint site run in direct mode and are basically fixed SharePoint application pages. They are rendered as normal ASP.NET pages.

ASP.NET pages, such as Web Part Pages running inside a Web site, run in safe mode. In safe mode the ASP.NET page is handled by the Web Part Framework, and only a predefined set of controls is considered safe to run

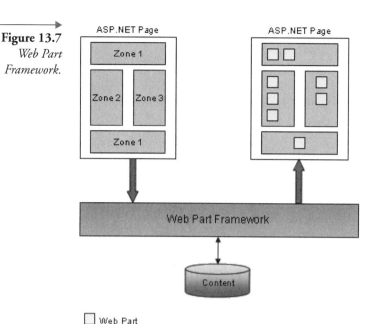

Figure 13.7
*Web Part
Framework.*

in the Web site for a virtual server. So, in essence, the Web Part Framework is the component responsible for performing the safe-mode handling. In SharePoint terminology, a page whose controls are determined by the database is referred to as a SmartPage. SmartPages only operate in safe mode. If you examine the content of the Home page of a Web site (`default.aspx`), you will find that the page itself is really just made up of a number of Web Part zones; there are no actual controls on the page other than the zone controls (Figure 13.7). The zone controls are basically container objects for other controls on the page.

When a request is made for `default.aspx`, SharePoint retrieves the source of the page. If the page has not been customized using FrontPage, the source is retrieved from the SharePoint setup directory on the Web server; if the page has been customized with FrontPage, it is retrieved from the content database. SharePoint also accesses SQL Server to retrieve the list of Web Parts that appear on the page. For the Home page of a SharePoint team site, this includes the Announcements, Events, Links, and Site Image Web Parts. The Web Part Framework builds the ASP.NET page object by inserting the controls onto the page. Once all the controls have been added to the page, the page object is allowed to run. Designers have the ability to add any type of control, including unsafe controls, on the page during design time. Safe-mode security is enforced at run time, so SharePoint will prevent any unsafe controls from actually running at that stage of the rendering process. Allowing the Web Part Framework to build the pages at run time is fundamental to the personalization experience, since users are able to view only the Web Parts that are of interest to them.

Chapters 14 and 15 provide more detail on building and deploying Web Parts for SharePoint.

13.4 SharePoint site definitions and templates

The templating aspect of STS provided one site template from which sites were created. This concept has been refined and carried forward in Share-Point, creating a very flexible platform for customizing look and feel. Share-Point now supports multiple server templates; Team Collaboration, Meeting Workspaces, and Document Workspaces templates all live on the Web server side by side.

SharePoint provides two very different but related mechanisms for pro-viding consistent presentation and functionality to your site: site definitions and custom templates.

Site definitions are similar in content to the STS site template in that they comprise XML files that live in the Web server and define what actu-ally make up the site (Figure 13.8). The site definition determines the navigational structure, list definitions, zone layout, and Web Parts that appear in the default site. All the default SharePoint sites and SPS areas are site definitions. For example, the Document Workspace site and SPS News Area each have an associated site definition on the Web server. Site definitions can host multiple configurations; for example, the Basic Meet-ing Workspace configuration is actually defined by the MPS site defini-tion, which also defines the Blank Meeting Workspace, Decision Meeting Workspace, Social Meeting Workspace, and Multipage Meeting Work-space configurations.

The configuration information is stored in the *Configuration* section of the ONET.XML file associated with the site definition. Chapter 17 details the XML files that make up a site definition.

Custom templates are a user interface–driven mechanism that allow you to save a site or list as a template for reuse (Figure 13.9). For example, if you have a list in SharePoint that you think could be leveraged on other sites, you can point and click and save that list as a template for reuse. In addition to being able to save the customizations that you may have applied to the list, such as custom columns, you can also save the content of the list. The same applies for saving complete sites as templates—you can save the cus-

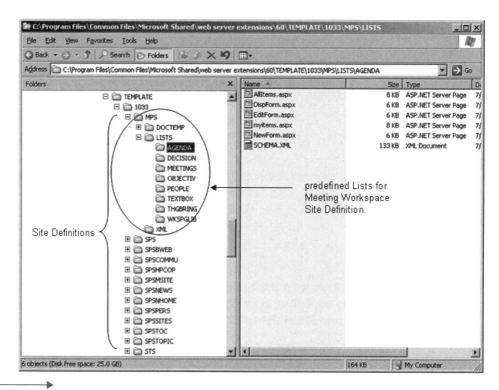

Figure 13.8   *Site definitions.*

My New Site
Template Selection

Select a template to apply to this Web site. Each template includes Web pages, Web Parts, lists, libraries, and other items. Choose the template that most closely matches the type of site you want to create or click here for information on how to migrate an existing site.

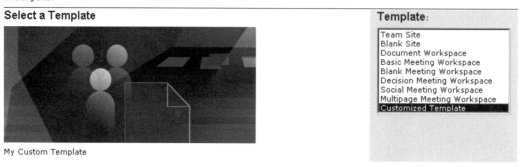

Figure 13.9   *Custom templates.*

tomizations, such as the Web Parts that appear on the Web Part Pages, and the contents of any lists and document libraries that exist in the site.

Custom templates can be thought of as a customization that has been applied to an existing site definition; unlike site definitions, they are stored as content in the SharePoint database. A custom template cannot exist by itself, because it effectively references a site definition. For example, a site definition such as the WSS Team Site site definition can be customized and saved as a custom template. Only the differences between the custom template and the site definition are saved to the database. Custom templates are made available through the central template gallery or through the template gallery for the current site collection.

Chapter 17 further examines the concepts of site definitions and custom templates and shows how to apply customizations to your site.

13.5   SharePoint OM

WSS and SPS offer a managed-code OM from which you can access data stored in SharePoint. The OMs are implemented in C# and can be accessed through ASP.NET or any .NET Framework process. The WSS OM provides an easy mechanism for navigating through the various components that make up your WSS deployment. The `Microsoft.SharePoint` and `Microsoft.SharePoint.Administration` namespaces provide access to the various types, members, and methods for working with and managing SharePoint data, such as lists, sites, subsites, and WSS servers. Each namespace contains many classes for working with SharePoint; however, four deserve special attention, since they are the classes that provide the most functionality:

1. **SPWeb:** The `SPWeb` class represents the top-level object for an individual Web site and provides access to all its lists, files, folders, Web Parts, and any additional objects.

2. **SPSite:** The `SPSite` class represents the top-level object for a SharePoint site collection and provides access to its collection of subsites and templates.

3. **SPVirtualServer:** The `SPVirtualServer` class represents the top-level object for a virtual server and is used to implement serverwide configuration settings. This class can be used to create, delete, and access sites under a specific virtual server.

4.   **SPGlobalAdmin:** The `SPGlobalAdmin` class represents the top-level object for administering a SharePoint deployment. This class can be used to install and enable a Web Part Package and add it to the Web Part Gallery.

The `SPWeb` object is of paramount importance, as it acts as the entry point for accessing the SharePoint objects such as lists, items, documents, users, and alerts for your Web site. Figure 13.10 shows the `SPWeb` class through the Visual Studio .NET Object Browser. As you can see, the `SPWeb` object contains numerous properties and methods. For example, the `CurrentUser` property returns the current user of the site, and the `SaveAsTemplate` method saves the site as a template.

The SPS 2003 OM builds on top of the WSS OM and provides access to the portal objects, such as user-profile objects and single sign-on objects. Most of the new portal functionality is written in ASP.NET managed code with the exception of legacy aspects of the portal. The document-management functionality that was available in SPS 2001 and accessible through the Publishing and Knowledge Management Collaboration Data Objects

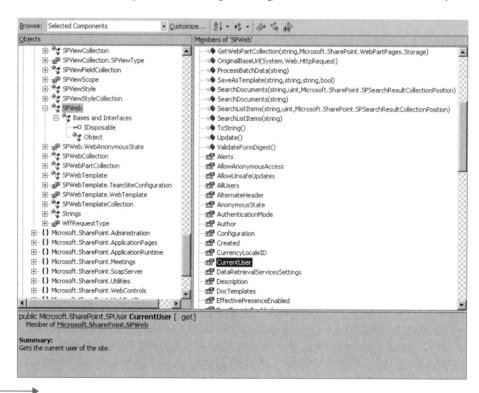

Figure 13.10   *SPWeb class viewed in Object Browser.*

(PKMCDO) OM is still available in SPS 2003 for backward compatibility. Additionally, some of the advanced search features such as protocol handlers and IFilters still use essentially the same old COM-based OM used in SPS 2001.

SPS 2003 introduces two new assemblies that you can use if you want to reference the portal functionality programmatically: `Microsoft.SharePoint.Portal.dll` (`Portal.dll`) and `Microsoft.SharePoint.Portal.SingleSignOn.dll` (`SingleSignOn.dll`). `Portal.dll` hosts the vast majority of the portal functionality, whereas `SingleSignOn.dll` hosts user and password information implemented by the single-sign-on functionality. If you examine each component through the Visual Studio .NET Object Browser, you will see the namespaces, classes, properties, and methods accessible. The `Portal.dll` component introduces a large number of subnamespaces for each set of objects. Chapter 17 provides more detail on both the WSS and the SPS 2003 OMs.

13.6 SharePoint Web services

You use the server OM if you are writing code on the server. If you are writing code that is remotely connecting to SharePoint, you use Web services. For example, if you are writing a client application or an application that performs server-to-server communications, then Web services would be the mechanism to accessing SharePoint. The general rule of thumb is: If you are writing code on a server running SharePoint, then use the server OM; if you can't use the server OM, then use the Web services layer. The Web services layer is built on top of the server OM, so the Web services layer actually calls the OM methods.

The basic functionality is similar to that described for the server OM; you can work with SharePoint data, including lists, webs, items and views, user profiles, and areas. Office 2003 is a prime example of an application that makes extensive use of the Web services layer in SharePoint. For example, Excel, Outlook, and FrontPage use Web services to access data from SharePoint. Many different types of methods are available for accessing SharePoint data both in WSS and SPS. Chapter 17 also provides more detail on the Web services layer.

13.7 Developing SharePoint applications

There are a number of ways to start developing SharePoint applications. One method is to build a Web Part. Web Parts are a great way to create application components that run within a SharePoint site. The advantage of using Web Parts as your application-distribution mechanism is that they are reusable and can be easily managed using the Web Part tools and browser interface. Developers need to be aware when writing Web Parts that Share-Point has security built into the product. If you want code to run and execute within the context of SharePoint, it needs to be precompiled and preregistered code. In order for code to run within the SharePoint site, you have to build a custom control or Web Part and install it in the set of safe controls and place the control on your page.

Another method is to build an ASPX page. If you want to write code that functions in a full ASPX page instead of using the Web Part Framework, the code needs to live in the `_layouts` directory of the Web server. As previously mentioned, SharePoint uses direct mode for all the ASP.NET pages in the `_layouts` directory. While direct-mode pages appear to live in the user's web, they are actually considered to reside outside of the Web site and are processed by ASP.NET just like a regular ASP.NET page. Placing your page in the `_layouts` directory means that it is accessible from any SharePoint Web site and can run in the context of that site much like the Create page. For example, if you create `myCode.aspx` in your own subdirectory of the `_layouts` directory, it is accessible from the following URLs:

```
http://myweb/_layouts/myapp/mycode.aspx
```

```
http://myweb/sites/mysite/_layouts/myapp/mycode.aspx
```

If your code only uses the `Microsoft.SharePoint.Administration` namespace for working with global settings in a SharePoint deployment, Microsoft recommends that the application be created on the administrative port. You can build and store ASPX pages and Web applications for the administrative port in the following directory:

```
\Program Files\Common Files\Microsoft Shared\Web Server
Extensions\60\TEMPLATE\ADMIN\1033
```

Pages in this directory are accessible through a URL in the following format:

```
http://localhost:Port_#|Your_File.aspx
```

Finally, you can build a Windows executable or any other type of application that has access to the OM. For example, you could create a standalone application for adding users to a site.

Web Part Development

Throughout this book we have touched on the concept of Web Parts and Web Part Pages; by now you should understand that Web Parts are the cornerstone of SharePoint Products and Technologies in that they provide much of the functionality to the user. For example, the announcements that appear on the Home page of a WSS site are presented to the user through a Web Part. This chapter examines the concept of Web Parts and Web Part Pages and where they fit into the overall SharePoint architecture. More importantly, we show you how to increase the functionality and appropriateness of your site by building your own custom Web Parts.

14.1 What is a Web Part?

SPS 2001 and STS use differing technologies when presenting functionality to their users. SPS 2001 uses the Web Storage System in conjunction with Digital DashBoard and Web Part technologies, whereas STS uses Microsoft FrontPage and Office Web Server technologies. SharePoint Products and Technologies combine these two products into a suite that shares the same architecture based on the .NET Framework and ASP.NET. The Digital DashBoard is superseded by the Web Part Page. A Web Part Page is an ASP.NET page that presents the user with information derived from a variety of sources. The information is served through the use of Web Parts. Web Parts themselves are ASP.NET server controls, also known as Web controls. An ASP.NET server control is basically a control tag in an `.aspx` page that is understood by the server and contains the `runat=server` attribute. With traditional ASP-based Web pages, events were initiated and handled by the client (browser), and the browser then posted the form to the server. The `runat=server` attribute associated with ASP.NET controls now allows events to actually be processed on the server. ASP.NET handles all the mechanics of capturing the event, transmitting it to the server, and processing the event. From a development perspective, all you have to do is develop the appropriate event handlers.

A Web Part Page consists of one or more Web Part Zones, which in turn contain one or more Web Parts. Web Part Zones are ASP.NET controls, whose sole function is to provide a home for Web Parts. Web Parts that live in a zone are referred to as dynamic Web Parts. Dynamic Web Parts and their associated properties, such as the title of the Web Part, are stored in the SharePoint database and can be customized and personalized by users with the appropriate permissions. Figure 14.1 shows the zone layout on the default Web Part Page of a WSS site. Note there are only two zones, named Left and Right, on this Web Part Page, and each zone contains two Web Parts. The zone layout and naming can differ between Web Part Pages. For example, the Web Part Page of the main portal site contains four zones by default, named `TopZone`, `MiddleLeftZone`, `MiddleRightZone`, and `BottomZone`. The Web Part Zone layout is viewable in design mode, which is accessible from the *Design This Page* command on the Modify Shared Page and Modify My Page menus. In addition, you can add and remove Web Part Zones from a Web Part Page by customizing the site templates, using tools such as FrontPage 2003 or through code.

Web Parts that do not live within a Web Part Zone are referred to as static Web Parts. Static Web Parts are added to the Web Part Page by developers at design time. Web Parts added to the Web Part Page at run time using the browser must be placed in a Web Part Zone. In addition, static Web Parts and the properties associated with the Web Parts are stored directly in the Web Part Page and not in the SharePoint database.

Figure 14.1
WSS site default zone layout.

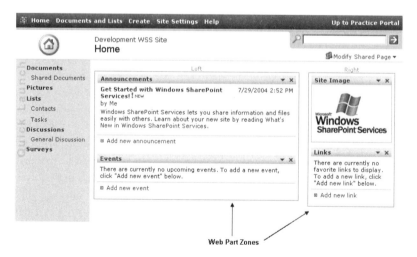

14.2   Creating a Web Part Page

SharePoint sites come equipped with Web Part Pages hosting multiple Web Parts that provide the functionality of the site. You can easily extend and customize this out-of-the-box functionality by adding, removing, and rearranging Web Parts. In addition to this, you also have the ability to extend your site by creating your own Web Part Pages. The steps to create a new Web Part Page are as straightforward as creating a SharePoint list or document library:

1.   Navigate to the WSS site on which you wish to add a new Web Part Page.

2.   From the horizontal navigation bar, click the **Create** link. The Create page appears.

3.   Scroll to the bottom of the page and in the *Web Pages* section, click **Web Part Page**. The New Web Part Page page appears.

4.   Type the file name of the Web Part Page—for example, `mypage.aspx`.

5.   Select the layout template that you wish to apply to the page. For example, the Header, Left Column, Body layout template creates a Web Part Page with three Web Part Zones, named Header, Left Column, and Body.

6.   Select the document library in which you wish to save the Web Part Page, for example, Shared Documents.

7.   Click **Create**.

Once you click the **Create** button, SharePoint creates the new Web Part Page in the specified location and automatically opens the page in design mode so that you can start adding Web Parts to the page (Figure 14.2).

Notice that the new Web Part Page already has a lot of functionality, such as the horizontal navigation bar, the Web Part Page Title Bar Web Part, the **Modify Shared Page** link, and the Web Part Zones. This allows you to focus on the real functionality of the page.

To create a Web Part Page in an SPS site, simply replace steps 1 and 2 with the following:

1.   Navigate to the SPS site in which you wish to add a new Web Part Page.

Figure 14.2   *Creating a Web Part Page.*

2.   From the vertical navigation bar, click on the **Manage Content** link. The Documents and Lists Web Part Page appears. Click the **Create** link. The Create page appears.

14.3   Adding, modifying, and arranging Web Parts

Adding, modifying, and arranging Web Parts on a Web Part Page is also very straightforward. SharePoint comes equipped with a number of task panes that host many of the design features for the site. For example, you can drag and drop Web Parts from the Add Web Parts task pane to your Web Part Page. The design task panes are accessible from the Web Part menu or the Modify Shared Page and Modify My Page menus.

A subtle, yet important, point to keep in mind is that with a WSS site, the **Modify Shared Page** and **Modify My Page** links appear in the upper right region of the Web Part Page. SPS displays the links in the same place; however, you must first click the **Edit Page** link in the vertical navigation bar to access them.

14.3.1   Adding Web Parts

There are versions of the Add Web Parts task pane that provide the ability to add Web Parts to a Web Part Page. The first Add Web Parts task pane has browsing functionality and provides access to the available Web Part Galleries. A Web Part Gallery is basically a location that hosts Web Parts that you can import to your SharePoint site. Adding Web Parts to a Web Part Page from this task pane is a simple matter of dragging and dropping the Web Part from the selected gallery to a specific zone in the Web Part Page.

The steps to add a Web Part from the current site's Web Part Gallery to a Web Part Page in shared view are as follows:

1. Navigate to the Web Part Page to which you wish to add a new Web Part.

2. If you are adding Web Parts to an SPS page, click the **Edit Page** link from the vertical navigation bar on the left side of the page.

3. Click the **Modify Shared Page** link. A shortcut menu appears (Figure 14.3).

4. Click **Add Web Parts**. Another shortcut menu appears.

5. Click **Browse**. The Add Web Parts task pane appears on the right with browse functionality (Figure 14.2).

6. From the *Browse* section, select the current site's Web Part Gallery (this should be selected by default).

7. From the *Web Part List* section, select the Web Part to add to the Web Part Page, for example, the Shared Documents Web Part.

Figure 14.3
Adding a Web Part menu.

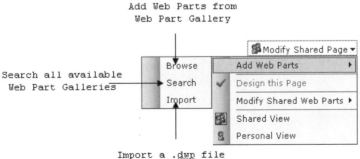

Figure 14.4   *Web Part Page with Shared Documents Web Part added.*

8. Drag the Web Part from the Web Part List and drop it into the chosen zone on the Web Part Page. For example, drag the Shared Documents Web Part and drop it into the Body zone. Alternatively, you can select the zone from the *Add To* section at the bottom of the task pane and click the **Add** button.

9. Once you have added all the Web Parts, click the **X** on the top right-hand corner of the Add Web Parts task pane to close the task pane. The Web Part Page displays the newly added Web Part (Figure 14.4).

10. If you are adding Web Parts to an SPS page, click the **View Page** link from the vertical navigation bar on the left side of the page to return to the Web Part Page.

The second Add Web Parts task pane has *Search* functionality. The search function provides the ability to search all of the available Web Part Galleries for a Web Part that contains specific text. Both the Web Part title and the Web Part description are included in the search; so, if the text appears in the description of a Web Part, the Web Part will be returned in the search results. For example, if you search the galleries for the text "content," the Page Viewer Web Part and the Content Editor Web Part appear in the search results (the description of the Page Viewer Web Part contains the word "content"). The search results appear in the task pane sorted by gallery (Figure 14.5). Adding Web Parts to a Web Part Page from this task pane is a simple matter of dragging and dropping the Web Part from the Search Results section to a specific zone in the Web Part Page.

Figure 14.5
Searching for a Web Part.

The steps to search the available Web Part Galleries for a Web Part and apply the Web Part to the page are as follows:

1. Navigate to the Web Part Page on which you wish to add a new Web Part.

2. If you are adding Web Parts to an SPS page, click the **Edit Page** link from the vertical navigation bar on the left side of the page.

3. Click the **Modify Shared Page** link. A shortcut menu appears (Figure 14.3).

4. Click **Add Web Parts**. Another shortcut menu appears.

5. Click **Search**. The Add Web Parts task pane appears on the right with *Search* functionality (Figure 14.5).

6. Type in the text you would like to search for.

7. Click **Go**. Web Parts with a title or description containing the search text will appear in the *Search Results* section of the task pane and are sorted by the Web Part Gallery.

8. Click the Web Part Gallery links until you find the Web Part that you want to add to your Web Part Page.

9. Drag the Web Part from the *Search Results* section and drop it into the chosen zone on the Web Part Page. For example, drag the Content Editor Web Part and drop it into the Header zone. Alternatively, you can select the zone from the *Add To* section at the bottom of the task pane and click the **Add** button.

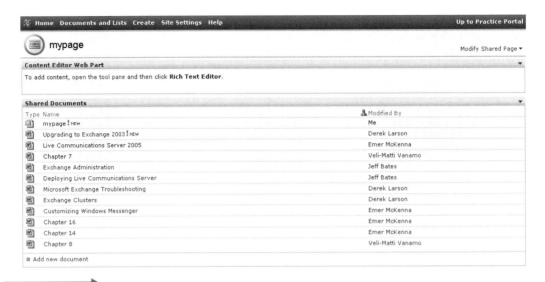

Figure 14.6   *Web Part Page with Content Editor Web Part added.*

10. Once you have added all the Web Parts, click the **X** on the top right-hand corner of the Add Web Parts task pane to close the task pane. The Web Part Page displays with the newly added Web Part (Figure 14.6).

11. If you are adding Web Parts to an SPS page, click the **View Page** link in the vertical navigation bar on the left side of the page to return to the Web Part Page.

The third Add Web Parts task pane has *Import* functionality. The import function provides the ability to upload a Web Part definition file to the Web Part Page Gallery and add it to the current Web Part Page. Once the file is uploaded, the Web Part that it represents is accessible from the Browse task pane.

The steps to upload a Web Part to the Web Part Page Gallery and apply it to the page are as follows:

1. Navigate to the Web Part Page to which you wish to add a new Web Part.

2. If you are adding Web Parts to an SPS page, click the **Edit Page** link in the vertical navigation bar on the left side of the page.

3. Click the **Modify Shared Page** link. A shortcut menu appears (Figure 14.3).

Figure 14.7
*Uploading a
Web Part.*

4.   Click **Add Web Parts**. Another shortcut menu appears.

5.   Click **Import**. The Add Web Parts task pane appears on the right with *Import* functionality (Figure 14.7).

6.   Type in the filename, including the path, of the .dwp file, or click **Browse** to navigate to the Web Part.

7.   Click **Upload**.

8.   The Web Part appears in the *Uploaded Web Part* section of the task pane.

9.   Drag the Web Part from the *Uploaded Web Part* section, and drop it into the chosen zone on the Web Part Page. For example, drag the imported Web Part and drop it into the Body zone directly above the Shared Documents Web Part. Alternatively, you can select the zone from the *Add To* section at the bottom of the task pane and click the **Import** button.

10. Once you have imported the Web Parts, click the **X** at the top right-hand corner of the Add Web Parts task pane to close the task pane. The Web Part Page displays with the newly added Web Part (Figure 14.8).

14.3.2   Modifying Web Parts

Once you have the Web Parts added to your page, you can begin to tailor them to suit your needs. For example, the title of a Web Part Page is actually hosted in the Web Part Page Title Bar Web Part and can be changed by simply modifying this Web Part with the Web Part Editor task pane. Each Web Part has a set of base properties, such as height and width, and any number

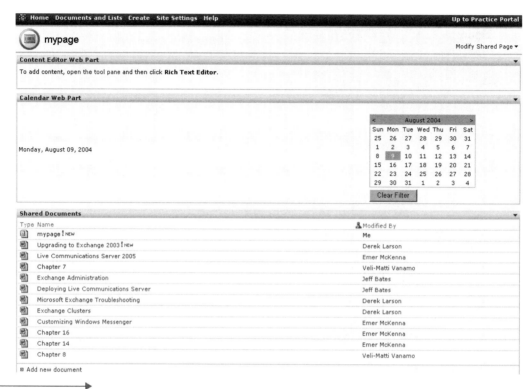

Figure 14.8   *Web Part Page with Imported Calendar Web Part added.*

of custom properties. Depending on how the Web Part was developed, these properties may appear in the Web Part Editor task pane for customization. You can access the Web Part Editor task pane by clicking on the **Modify Shared Web Part** link or the **Modify My Web Part** link from the Web Part menu. Alternatively, you can access the Web Part Editor task pane by clicking the same links from the **Modify Shared Page** and **Modify My Page** links, respectively, from the Web Part Page. Accessing the editor task pane using the latter method gives you access to the Web Part Page Title Bar Web Part.

The steps to modify the Web Part Page Title Bar Web Part are as follows:

1.   Navigate to the Web Part Page whose title you wish to modify.

2.   Click the **Modify Shared Page** link. A shortcut menu appears (Figure 14.3).

3.   Click **Modify Shared Web Parts**. Another shortcut menu appears.

Figure 14.9
*Web Part Page
Title Bar Web
Part Editor.*

4.   Click **Web Part Page Title Bar**. The Web Part Page Title Bar Web
      Part Editor task pane appears (Figure 14.9).

5.   Type the new page title.

6.   Type a caption for the page. The caption appears directly above
      the title in a smaller font.

7.   Type a description for the page. The description appears as a tool
      tip when you hover over the title.

8.   Click **Apply** to view the changes in the browser.

9.   If you are happy with the changes, click **OK**. The Web Part Page
      displays with the new title (Figure 14.10).

Note: This method only applies to WSS Web Part Pages created using the
Create pages function—default WSS pages cannot be changed in this manner. The Web Part Page title and description of an SPS site can be set using
the **Change Settings** link on the vertical navigation bar.

The Web Part Page Title Bar Web Part Editor task pane is a heavily customized task pane and not representative of the Web Part Editor experience
that you get from most other Web Parts. For example, if you modify the
Content Editor Web Part, you can customize a whole host of properties and
settings to change the default behavior.

In the following example, we customize the Content Editor Web Part to
display a set of hyperlinks, resize the width of the Web Part, and remove its
title bar.

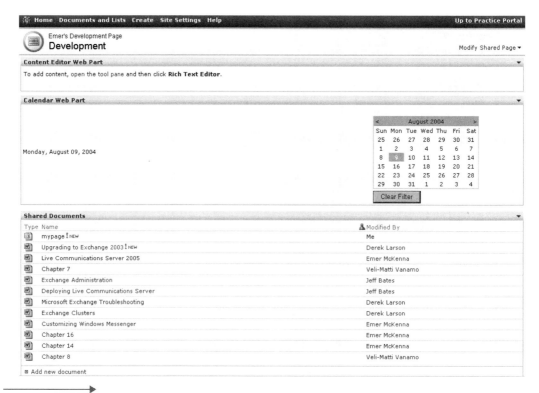

Figure 14.10   *Customized Web Part Page title.*

The steps to modify the Content Editor Web Part are as follows:

1.   Navigate to the Web Part Page that contains the Content Editor Web Part.

2.   From the Content Editor Web Part, click the down arrow. The Web Part menu appears.

3.   Click **Modify Shared Web Part**. The Content Editor Web Part Editor task pane appears.

4.   Click **Source Editor**. The Web Page dialog appears (Figure 14.11).

5.   Enter the HTML code for the Web Part. Alternatively, instead of writing HTML, you can enter rich text directly using the Rich Text Editor.

6.   Click **Save** to save the HTML code.

Figure 14.11
*Web Part Page
Title Bar Web
Part Editor.*

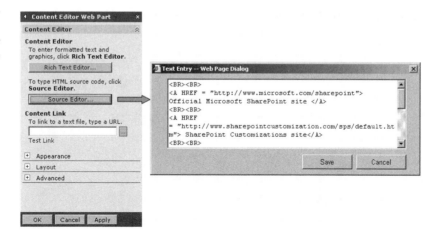

7.   Expand the *Appearance* section of the task pane (Figure 14.12).

8.   Set the Width property to 200 pixels.

9.   Set the Frame Style property to None.

10.   Click **Apply** to view the changes in the browser.

11.   If you are happy with the changes, click **OK**. The Web Part Page
        displays with the customized Web Part (Figure 14.13).

Figure 14.12
*Appearance section
of editor task pane.*

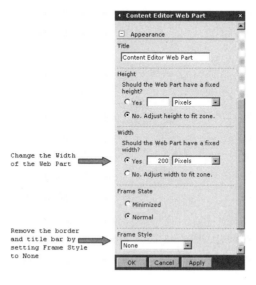

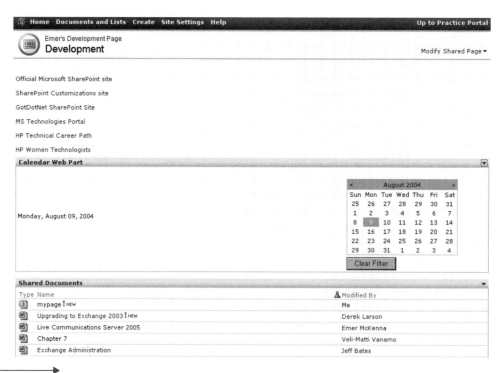

Figure 14.13   *Customized Content Editor Web Part.*

14.3.3   **Arranging Web Parts**

The zone layout of a Web Part Page adds versatility to the page, since you can easily drag and drop Web Parts from one zone to another until you are satisfied with the layout. As previously mentioned, you can add and remove Web Part Zones from a Web Part Page by customizing the site templates, using tools such as FrontPage 2003, or through code.

In our previous example, we added the Content Editor Web Part to the Header zone of the Web Part Page; however, the resultant look is quite cluttered. This can easily be changed in design mode by dragging the Content Editor Web Part from the Header zone to another, more suitable zone on the page, such as the Left Column zone. The zone in which a Web Part resides is actually stored as a property of the Web Part. Consequently, another method for moving a Web Part from one zone to another is to modify the Web Part and change the zone property using the Web Part Editor task pane. In addition to moving a Web Part between zones, SharePoint also provides the ability to reorder Web Parts within a zone (Figure 14.14). For example, we could easily move the Shared Documents Web Part above

Figure 14.14
*Arranging Web
Part position by
modifying
properties.*

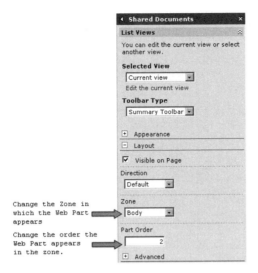

Change the Zone in
which the Web Part
appears

Change the order the
Web Part appears
in the zone.

the Calendar Web Part. The order in which a Web Part appears within a
zone is also stored as a property of the Web Part and can be changed by
modifying the Part Order property using the Web Part Editor task pane.

The steps to rearrange a Web Part in design mode are as follows:

1.   Navigate to the Web Part Page that contains the Web Part you
     want to move.

2.   If you are adding Web Parts to an SPS page, click the **Edit Page**
     link in the vertical navigation bar on the left side of the page.

3.   Click the **Modify Shared Page** link. A shortcut menu appears
     (Figure 14.3).

4.   Click the **Design this Page** link. The Web Part Page appears in
     design mode, displaying the zone layout.

5.   Select the Web Part to move and drag it to the zone of choice. For
     example, drag the Content Editor Web Part from the Header
     zone to the Left Column zone.

6.   Click the **Modify Shared Page** link. A shortcut menu appears.

7.   Click the **Design this Page** link to return the page to normal
     view.

8.   If you are adding Web Parts to an SPS page, click the **View Page**
     link in the vertical navigation bar on the left side of the page to
     return to the Web Part Page.

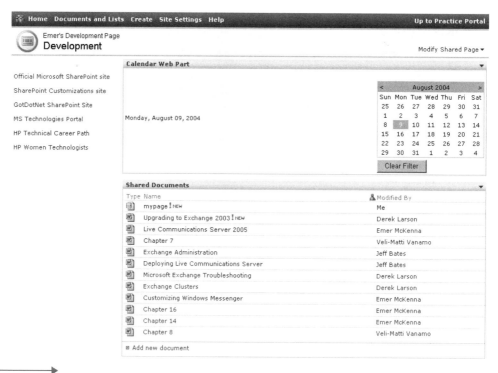

Figure 14.15   *Moving Web Parts between zones.*

Figure 14.15 shows the outcome of moving the Content Editor Web Part to another zone.

14.3.4   Removing a Web Part from a Web Part Page

Removing a Web Part from a Web Part Page is a simple process that involves accessing the Web Part menu and clicking **Close**. The Web Part is still available in the Web Part Gallery and can be readded at any time. Web Parts can also be removed from a Web Part Page by clicking the Delete command from the Web Part menu in Design view.

14.4   Creating a simple Web Part

SharePoint comes equipped with many useful Web Parts out of the box, and many more are available from the Microsoft online gallery and through third-party vendors. However, there will be times when you need a Web Part that is not available from these sources and is very specific to your business needs. Fortunately, SharePoint is highly extensible and allows you to develop your own custom Web Parts using industry-standard development tools such as Visual Studio .NET.

The following section steps you through the basics of how to create two simple Web Parts. The main purpose of this section is to walk you through creating your first Web Part as quickly as possible. We introduce many concepts and code specifics that are explained in detail later in the book, so don't panic if you don't understand everything right away.

If you have experience developing Web Parts in SPS 2001, you would be correct in thinking that Web Part development has become more complex. This complexity is not intended to frustrate the developer—quite the opposite in fact. Microsoft's goal is to improve the entire development-and-deployment experience by providing developers with a platform that is integrated with the .NET Framework. Developers familiar with .NET Framework development, database tools, and, in particular, building ASP.NET Web pages and controls can use this knowledge when developing solutions for SharePoint Products and Technologies.

14.4.1   Web Part component files

Before we delve into creating a Web Part, it helps to understand the actual components that make up a Web Part. A Web Part basically comprises a Web Part description file, a Web Part Assembly, resource files, and property values.

- The Web Part description file (.dwp) describes the properties associated with the Web Part. These properties are used to define the appearance and behavior of the Web Part, such as the height and width of the Web Part and whether the title bar is displayed. Once again, those readers who have experience with SPS 2001 Web Part development will recognize the .dwp file. However, there is one significant difference in the .dwp file used by the current version of the product: the code associated with the Web Part does not live with the Web Part itself. The .dwp file in SPS 2001 was able to contain code that could run on the server. Trustworthy computing was a major design goal for the release of SharePoint Products and Technologies, and Microsoft achieved this goal by providing SharePoint administrators with an environment they can lock down to the level that best suits their needs. From a security standpoint, the only way to execute inline script code directly on a Web Part Page is to code it as a server control and register the control as safe. Web Part security is discussed later in this book.

■ The Web Part Assembly is a dynamic link library file (.dll) that contains the Web Part code. In order for the Web Part to function, the assembly must be installed on all SharePoint front-end Web servers.

■ The Web Part resource files are any files that are required to support the Web Part and are stored on the SharePoint server.

■ The values of the Web Part's associated properties are stored in the SQL Server database. The Web Part infrastructure references the database to determine the values.

14.4.2   Getting started

Since Web Parts are ASP.NET controls, you can use Visual Studio .NET to perform all Web Part development. To make Web Part development easier, Microsoft has provided Web Part Library templates that can be downloaded from MSDN. These templates provide skeleton code and the appropriate files required for a basic Web Part and are available in Visual Basic .NET and C#. Once you have downloaded the templates, you can begin creating your Web Part by starting Visual Studio .NET and creating a new project using the Web Part Library template. If you would rather develop your Web Part from scratch, you can create a new project using the Web Control Library template instead.

The following example leverages the Web Part Library template. The Web Parts we are about to create simply display some text in a large font. As you will see, the code is very basic, and the setup and deployment of the Web Part requires the most work. The steps assume that you are running Visual Studio .NET on a server running Windows SharePoint Services or SPS 2003.

Step 1: Create the project

1.   Start Visual Studio .NET.

2.   From the File menu, click **New** and then click **Project**. The New Project dialog appears.

3.   Select the language of your choice, either Visual Basic .NET or Visual C#.

4.   From the *Templates* section, click the **Web Part Library** template.

5. Enter the name of the project in the Name text box, for example, `MyWebParts`.

6. Enter the location where you want the project to be created.

7. Click **OK**.

Notice that the Web Part Library template automatically adds the required references, such as `Microsoft.SharePoint.dll` and `System.Xml`, and also adds the appropriate namespace directives to the code, such as `Microsoft.SharePoint.WebPartPages` (Figure 14.16).

If you are not using the Web Part Library template to create your Web Part, you must add a reference at least to the `Microsoft.SharePoint` assembly (`Microsoft.SharePoint.dll`) and the `System.Xml` assembly (`System.Xml.dll`). Also ensure that the following namespace directives are added to your code:

```
Microsoft.SharePoint.WebPartPages
System.Xml.Serialization
System.Web.UI.HtmlControls
```

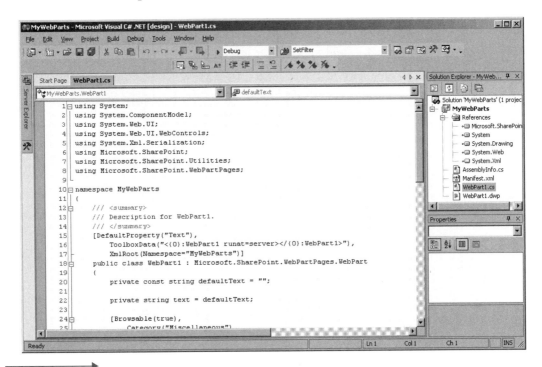

Figure 14.16   *Web Part Library C# project.*

Step 2: Specify the build output path

All the files that make up a Web Part, or for that matter a .NET application, are packaged into an assembly. Assemblies appear to the user as a single dynamic link library (`.dll`) or executable file (`.exe`). In order for your Web Part or assembly to run, it must be physically located in one of two specific locations on the server: the Global Assembly Cache (GAC) or the Web server's `\bin` directory. The GAC is used to store assemblies that need to be available to all applications on the server and is typically located at `c:\winnt\assembly`. If you want to place your Web Part Assembly in the GAC, you do not need to change the build output for your project. Instead, manually copy the assembly to the GAC or use the Visual Studio .NET GAC command-line utility (`gacutil.exe`), located in the `\bin` directory of the Framework SDK.

If you are developing your Web Part on the same computer that your SharePoint site is running, you can set the build output path to point to the Web server's `\bin` directory (`inetpub\wwwroot\bin`), which is the same location from which the Web Part will run on the server. If you are developing your Web Part remotely, you can simply copy the Web Part Assembly to the Web server's `\bin` directory after it is built.

Set the build output path as follows:

1.   From the Project menu, click **MyWebParts Properties**. The Property Pages dialog box appears.

2.   Expand the Configuration Properties folder.

3.   Click **Build**. The Build property page appears in the right pane.

4.   From the *Outputs* section, set the output path to `c:\inetpub\wwwroot\bin`.

5.   Click **OK**.

Step 3: Set the version number

In addition to classes and methods, assemblies also contain versioning information so that multiple versions of the same code can run side by side without conflicts. A Web Part Page uses the version number specified in the `web.config` file to identify a Web Part. Therefore, you must ensure that when you recompile your Web Part the `AssemblyInfo` contains the same version information specified in the `web.config` file; otherwise, the Web Part will not run. The easiest way to do this is to manually control the version information stored in the `AssemblyInfo` file. Setting the version to "1.0.*" means the project will automatically increment the version of your

Figure 14.17
*VB.NET assembly
version code.*

```
<Assembly: AssemblyVersion("1.0.0.0")>
```

Figure 14.18
*C# assembly
version code.*

```
[assembly: AssemblyVersion("1.0.0.0")]
```

Web Part. Setting the version to "1.0.0.0" will ensure that the version numbering is static. If you want to release a new version, simply increment the version number (e.g., "1.0.0.1") and update the `web.config` file.

If you use the Web Part Library template to create your Web Part, the version number is already static.

Set the version number as follows:

1.   From the Solution Explorer, open the `AssemblyInfo` file. This will be named `AssemblyInfo.cs` in C# and `AssemblyInfo.vb` in VB.NET.

2.   Ensure that the assembly version is set to manually increment. Figures 14.17 and 14.18 show the required VB.NET and C# code.

3.   Save your changes to the `AssemblyInfo` file.

Step 4: Strongly name the assembly

A strong name consists of the assembly's identity, a public key, and a digital signature. In order for a Web Part to run in a SharePoint site, it needs to have a strong name, which basically informs SharePoint that the Web Part can be trusted. The Strong Name tool (`sn.exe`), available with the .NET Framework SDK, allows you to easily create a key pair file. Once you have generated your strong name using the tool, you must create a reference to it in your Web Part's assembly file.

The steps to strongly name the assembly are as follows:

1.   Open up a command prompt.

2.   Navigate to the `\bin` directory of the .NET Framework SDK. For example:

```
cd \Program Files\Microsoft Visual Studio .NET 2003\
SDK\v1.1\Bin
```

Figure 14.19
*VB.NET strong
name reference.*

```
<Assembly: AssemblyKeyFile("c:\keypair.snk")>
```

Figure 14.20
*C# strong name
reference.*

```
[assembly: AssemblyKeyFile("c:\\keypair.snk")]
```

3.   Create a key pair file by executing the following command:

     ```
     sn.exe -k c:\keypair.snk
     ```

     Note: You can use any path as long as the reference in the AssemblyblyInfo file points to the same location.

4.   In Visual Studio .NET open the AssemblyInfo file.

5.   Scroll to the bottom of the file and add a reference to the key file
     by editing the AssemblyKeyFile. If you are using VB.NET, you
     will need to create the AssemblyKeyFile reference. Figures
     14.19 and 14.20 show the required VB.NET and C# code.

6.   Save your changes to the AssemblyInfo file.

14.4.3   Coding the Web Parts

Now that we have the appropriate setup information defined, we can generate the code for our Web Parts.

Step 1: Name the assembly and namespace

The first thing we need to do is specify the name of the assembly and
namespace that we want to use for our project. When naming your
assembly, keep in mind that the assembly can house many Web Parts. In
our example, the assembly will house two Web Parts, named WebPart1
and WebPart2. Consequently, it makes sense to apply a more generic
name to the assembly, and it is good practice to provide a descriptive
name that applies to all the classes in the assembly—for example, "Book-
WebParts." For illustrative purposes, our example uses the assembly name
of "MyAssembly." While this name is not particularly descriptive, it does
help illustrate the places where the assembly name appears in code. It is
very easy to get confused between the assembly and the namespace when
developing Web Parts.

When naming your namespace, keep in mind that Web Parts within the same assembly can have different namespaces. For example, the SharePoint assembly is represented by the file `Microsoft.SharePoint.dll` and contains many classes that derive from many namespaces, such as `Microsoft.SharePoint.WebPartPages`, `Microsoft.SharePoint.Web-Controls`, and `Microsoft.SharePoint.SoapServer`.

The steps required to rename your assembly and namespace differ depending on the language you are using to develop your Web Parts.

The following steps are specific to VB.NET.

1.   Open your project in Visual Studio .NET.

2.   From the Project menu, click **MyWebParts Properties**. The Property Pages dialog box appears.

3.   Expand the Common Properties folder, and click **General**. The General property page appears in the right pane.

4.   In the *Assembly name* field, enter the name of your assembly, for example, `MyAssembly`.

5.   In the root namespace field enter the name of your namespace, for example, `MyNamespace`.

6.   Click **OK**. The output `.dll` file will update to reflect the new name of your assembly.

7.   Open the Web Part class file (`WebPart1.vb`) and update the namespace sections of the code. Line 9 of Figure 14.21 shows where the changes need to occur.

8.   Save the project.

The following steps are specific to C#.

1.   Open your project in Visual Studio .NET.

2.   From the Project menu, click **MyWebParts Properties**. The Property Pages dialog box appears.

3.   Expand the Common Properties folder, and click **General**. The General property page appears in the right pane.

4.   In the *Assembly* field in the *Applications* section, enter the name of your assembly, for example, `MyAssembly`.

5.   In the *Default Namespace* field in the *Applications* section, enter the name of your namespace, for example, `MyNamespace`.

```
1.   Imports System
2.   Imports System.ComponentModel
3.   Imports System.Web.UI
4.   Imports System.Web.UI.WebControls
5.   Imports System.Xml.Serialization
6.   Imports Microsoft.SharePoint
7.   Imports Microsoft.SharePoint.Utilities
8.   Imports Microsoft.SharePoint.WebPartPages

9.   <ToolboxData("<{0}:WebPart1 runat=server></{0}:WebPart1>"), XmlRoot(Namespace:="MyNamespace")> _
10.  Public Class WebPart1
11.      Inherits Microsoft.SharePoint.WebPartPages.WebPart

12.      'Render this Web Part to the output parameter specified.
13.      Protected Overrides Sub RenderWebPart(ByVal output As System.Web.UI.HtmlTextWriter)
14.          output.Write("<h1>This is my first Web Part.</h1>")
15.      End Sub

16.  End Class
```

Figure 14.21   *VB.NET code for WebPart1.*

6. Click **OK**. The output `.dll` file will update to reflect the new name of your assembly.

7. Open the Web Part class file (`WebPart1.cs`) and update the namespace sections of the code. Lines 9 and 12 of Figure 14.22 show where the change needs to occur.

8. Save the project.

Step 2: Rename the Web Part

For the purposes of our example, we will keep the default Web Part name applied by the Web Part Library template: WebPart1. However, if you wish

```
1.   using System;
2.   using System.ComponentModel;
3.   using System.Web.UI;
4.   using System.Web.UI.WebControls;
5.   using System.Xml.Serialization;
6.   using Microsoft.SharePoint;
7.   using Microsoft.SharePoint.Utilities;
8.   using Microsoft.SharePoint.WebPartPages;

9.   namespace MyNamespace
10.  {
11.      [ToolboxData("<{0}:WebPart1 runat=server></{0}:WebPart1>"),
12.                  XmlRoot(Namespace="MyNamespace")]
13.      public class WebPart1 : Microsoft.SharePoint.WebPartPages.WebPart
14.      {
15.          protected override void RenderWebPart(HtmlTextWriter output)
16.          {
17.              output.Write("<h1>This is my first Web Part</h1>");
18.          }
19.      }
20.  }
```

Figure 14.22   *C# code for WebPart1.*

to change the Web Part name, all you need to do is replace all occurrences of the text "WebPart1" with your new name. This can be easily achieved using the *Find and Replace* functionality in Visual Studio .NET, with the search scope set to Current Project.

Step 3: Insert the Web Part code

Now that we have the environment set up correctly, we can add our Web Part code. The Web Part code is very basic and overrides the RenderWeb-Part method to display some HTML in the browser. The HTML code is a single line of text with the H1 style applied.

Figures 14.21 and 14.22 show the required code. Open the Web Part class file (e.g. WebPart1.vb), and update the code to reflect the example.

Step 4: Build the solution

We are now ready to compile the assembly. This creates the assembly in the location specified in the output build path (inetpub\wwwroot\bin).

1.   Save your project to make sure you have the latest updates.

2.   From the Build menu, click **Build Solution**.

Step 5: Extract the public key

Once the solution is built, you can extract the public-key token from the key pair sink file using the Strong Name tool. This value is needed in order to register your Web Part as a safe control for the site.

The steps to extract the public-key token are as follows:

1.   Open up a command prompt.

2.   Navigate to the \bin directory of the .NET Framework SDK—for example:

```
cd \Program Files\Microsoft Visual Studio .NET 2003\
SDK\v1.1\Bin
```

3.   Extract the public-key token by executing the following command:

```
sn.exe -T c:\inetpub\wwwroot\bin\MyAssembly.dll
```

4.   Copy the token from the command-prompt window, and paste it into notepad for future use. An example of what the token looks like is d823bd75ba8558df.

```
<?xml version="1.0" encoding="utf-8"?>
<WebPart xmlns="http://schemas.microsoft.com/WebPart/v2" >
        <Title>Web Part A</Title>
        <Description>A simple Web Part that displays some text</Description>
        <Assembly>MyAssembly, Version=1.0.0.0, Culture=Neutral, PublicKeyToken=d823bd75ba8558df</Assembly>
        <TypeName>MyNamespace.WebPart1</TypeName>
        <!-- Specify initial values for any additional base class or custom properties here. -->
</WebPart>
```

Figure 14.23   *WebPart1 Web Part definition.*

Step 6: Modify the Web Part definition file (`.dwp`)

The next step in developing our Web Part is to modify the Web Part definition file (`.dwp`). The `.dwp` file is the actual file that is imported to the SharePoint site. It is an XML file containing the property settings for a single Web Part. Two properties are required in the `.dwp` file: `Assembly` and `TypeName`. It is also good practice to include a display name and description for the Web Part, so also add the Title and Description properties.

The Web Part Library template automatically creates the `.dwp` file; however, there are still some modifications required, such as updating the assembly and namespace names and including the public-key token. Figure 14.23 shows the updated `.dwp` file for `WebPart1`.

Notice that the `<Assembly>` element includes the updated assembly name, the version of the assembly, and the `PublicKeyToken` value. When updating your `WebPart1.dwp` file, paste the public-key-token value copied in the previous step into the `PublicKeyToken` parameter value. Also, the `TypeName` value reflects the updated namespace name.

Step 7: Create the second Web Part

We'll create a second Web Part that performs the same function, but displays different text.

The steps to create the second Web Part are as follows:

1. From the Solution Explorer, copy the Web Part class file (either `WebPart1.cs`, or `WebPart1.vb`).

2. From the Solution Explorer, right-click the project name and click **Paste**.

3. Rename the newly created file to `WebPart2.cs` or `WebPart2.vb`, depending on the language you are using.

4. Open the newly created Web Part class file and replace each occurrence of "WebPart1" with "WebPart2." If you use the *Find*

and Replace functionality, make sure you have the search scope set to the current document only.

5.   From the Solution Explorer, copy the Web Part definition file (`WebPart1.dwp`).

6.   From the Solution Explorer, right-click the project name and click **Paste**.

7.   Rename the newly created file to `WebPart2.dwp`.

8.   Open the newly created Web Part definition file and replace each occurrence of "WebPart1" with "WebPart2." If you use the *Find and Replace* functionality, make sure you have the search scope set to the current document only.

9.   In the same file, change the `<Title>` property to "Web Part B."

10. Save the project and rebuild the solution.

14.4.4   Deploying the Web Part

At last, we are now close to seeing our newly created Web Parts in action. The Web Parts are ready to import into your SharePoint site; however, in order for them to be able to run successfully, we need to register the Web Part Assembly as a safe control.

Step 1: Register the Web Part as a safe control

Since the Web Parts share a common assembly and namespace, only one entry in the `web.config` is needed. Figure 14.24 shows the entry to add to the `<SafeControls>` block of the `web.config` file. The `web.config` file is located in the `inetpub\wwwroot` directory.

In order for the Web Parts to run successfully, the assembly name and namespace name must be consistent between the Web Part class file, the Web Part definition file, the `web.config` file, and the project settings within Visual Studio .NET.

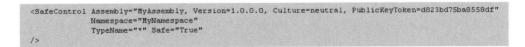

```
<SafeControl Assembly="MyAssembly, Version=1.0.0.0, Culture=neutral, PublicKeyToken=d823bd75ba8558df"
        Namespace="MyNamespace"
        TypeName="*" Safe="True"
/>
```

Figure 14.24   *Registering the assembly as a safe control.*

Figure 14.25   *New Web Parts imported to SharePoint.*

Step 2: Import the Web Part definition file (.dwp)

All that remains is for the Web Parts to be imported into the SharePoint site. The steps to import a Web Part are detailed in section 14.3.1.

Figure 14.25 shows the imported Web Parts.

14.5   Web Part infrastructure

Standard ASP.NET controls inherit their properties and methods from the `System.Web.UI.WebControls.WebControl` class, which in turn inherits from the `System.Web.UI.Control` class. Web Parts, on the other hand, inherit their properties and methods from the base `Microsoft.Share-Point.WebPartPages.WebPart` class, and this class also inherits from the `System.Web.UI.Control` class. Any custom Web Parts that you create must derive from the `WebPart` class (Figure 14.26).

14.5.1   Web Part rendering process

The Web Part Framework is at the heart of SharePoint's rendering process. When a request is made for a Web Part Page, SharePoint retrieves the page source. If the code has not been customized using FrontPage, it is considered a ghosted page, and the source is initially retrieved directly from the SharePoint setup directory on the Web server. If the page has been customized, the source is retrieved from the content database. SharePoint also accesses SQL Server to retrieve the list of Web Parts that appears on the page. The Web Part Framework processes Web Part Page requests using a custom ASP.NET handler. The SharePoint handler is responsible for retrieving the necessary data from the content database, including the Web

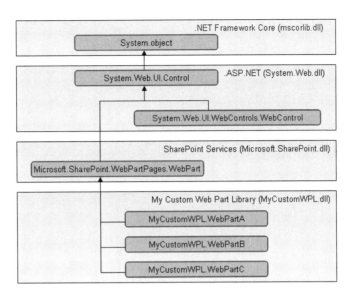

Figure 14.26
`WebPart` *class*
inheritance.

Part Page defining the zone layout and any customization and personalization information. The Web Part Framework then builds the ASP.NET page object by inserting the controls onto the page. Once all the controls have been added to the page, the page object is allowed to run.

The rendering process for an individual Web Part can be broken down further by examining the sequence of ASP.NET events executed (Figure 14.27). When a Web Part Page is requested, the `OnInit` event is triggered. The `OnInit` event launches the initialization phase for the Web Part. During the initialization phase, the Web Part Framework retrieves the property values associated with the Web Part from the database, such as the title of the Web Part and its height and width. If your custom Web Part needs to perform any additional initialization steps, you can subscribe to the `OnInit`

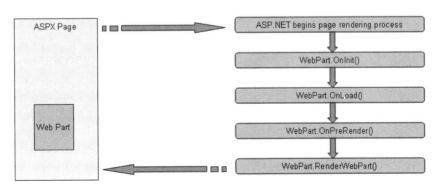

Figure 14.27
Web Part rendering
process.

event. If this is the first time the Web Part is loaded, it proceeds to the OnLoad event, which sets the Web Part properties with the values retrieved in the initialization phase. If the Web Part has been loaded previously, the System.Web.UI.Control.LoadViewState method is invoked to load the state information previously serialized into the Web Part, after which the OnLoad event proceeds and updates the properties. You can leverage the OnLoad event to retrieve information from various data sources, such as a database, that you want to display in the Web Part. If your Web Part uses any ASP.NET controls, the EnsureChildControls and CreateChild-Controls events are launched to ensure that all the appropriate server controls are initialized and created in the control tree.

Once the Web Part has finished creating the required server controls and has handled user-generated events, it is ready to render the output to the browser. The rendering phase commences with the OnPreRender event. Developers can use the OnPreRender event to change Web Part properties before the output is rendered to the browser. On completion of the OnPre-Render event, the view state information of the Web Part is serialized and saved to a hidden variable on the Web Page for future load requests. At this stage of the rendering process, the output can actually be rendered to the browser. Two rendering methods, or events, are responsible for producing the final output. The first event is the standard Render event, which is responsible for rendering the chrome of the Web Part. The chrome encompasses the header style aspects of the Web Part, including the title bar and border. Although this method is overrideable in code, this is not advisable, since you would have to manually generate the chrome, including the Web Part menu options, such as the Modify Shared Web Part menu. Any modifications to the rendering can be implemented by overriding the Render-WebPart event. The RenderWebPart event renders the HTML for the body of the Web Part to the browser.

14.6   Web Part properties and methods

So far, we know that a Web Part is an ASP.NET control that inherits its properties and methods from the WebPart class. The properties determine the appearance and behavior of the Web Part, and each property typically has a get and set accessor method defined. The get accessor enables you to retrieve the value of a property, and the set accessor enables you to set the value of a property. Figure 14.28 shows sample C# code to define a custom Web Part property.

Figure 14.28
Defining a property using C#.

```
private string _wpintro;
const string _defIntro = "Modify the Web Part to change the introduction";

[Browsable(true)]
[DefaultValue(_defIntro)]
[WebPartStorage(Storage.Personal)]
[FriendlyName("Web Part Intro")]
[Description("Text to display at the top of your Web Part")]
[XmlElement(ElementName="_WPIntro")]

public string _WPIntro
{
    get
    {
        return _wpintro;

    }

    set
    {
        _wpintro = value;
    }
}
```

If you have experience developing Web Parts for SPS 2001, many of the properties will be familiar. For example, an SPS 2001 Web Part had a schema property named `FrameState`, which determined whether a Web Part displayed as minimized or maximized on the page. The current version of SharePoint includes the `FrameState` property in the base `WebPart` class. When you use the `Microsoft.SharePoint.WebPartPages.WebPart` class to create a Web Part, it automatically inherits all the base-level properties and methods. If you examine the `WebPart` class using the object browser that comes with Visual Studio .NET, you can see a list of the available properties (Figure 14.29).

Figure 14.29
`WebPart` *class properties viewed using object browser.*

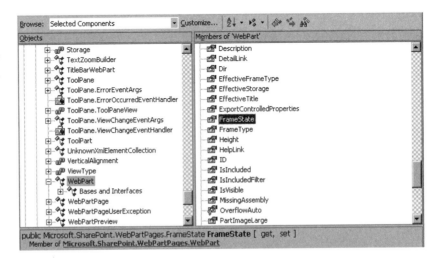

Figure 14.30
*Setting Web Part
properties
programmatically.*

```
public class MyClass : Microsoft.SharePoint.WebPartPages.WebPart
{
  ...

  public MyClass()
  {
    this.Load += new EventHandler (myLoadHandler);
  }

  private void myLoadHandler(object sender , System.EventArgs e )
  {
    this.Title = "My New Title";
    this.Description = "Setting Web Part Properties";
  }

  ...

}
```

The default settings for the Web Part properties are defined when the
Web Part is loaded onto the page. If you want to control the settings for
your Web Part using the object model, your changes should be applied in
the OnLoad event. Figure 14.30 shows sample C# code used to set the
Title and Description properties of the Web Part.

In addition to properties, Web Parts have a number of methods defined
that provide functionality to the Web Part. For example, the base WebPart
class includes a RenderWebPart method, which is called by the Web Part
Framework to render the HTML for the body of the Web Part to the client.
When building your Web Parts, you will most likely override the Render-
WebPart method to render custom HTML for the Web Part. More specifically, it is the HtmlTextWriter class provided by the RenderWebPart
method that allows you to create any HTML output you desire for your
Web Part. If you do not override the RenderWebPart method, then you
will not have control over how the ASP.NET controls that you create in
your code will render. Figure 14.31 illustrates how to create a very basic

Figure 14.31
*C# code
implementing the*
RenderWebPart
method.

```
1.   using System;
2.   using System.Web.UI;
3.   using System.Web.UI.WebControls;
4.   using Microsoft.SharePoint;
5.   using Microsoft.SharePoint.WebPartPages;
6.   using System.Xml.Serialization;

7.   namespace BookWebParts
8.   {
9.        [XmlRoot(Namespace="BookWebParts")]
10.       public class BasicWebPart : Microsoft.SharePoint.WebPartPages.WebPart
11.       {
12.
13.            protected override void RenderWebPart(HtmlTextWriter output)
14.            {
15.                output.Write("<BR><B>Today's date and time is: </B>" +
                         DateTime.Now.ToLongDateString());
16.            }
17.       }
18.  }
```

Figure 14.32
*Basic Web Part
rendered in
browser.*

Web Part using C#. Lines 13 through 16 show how to override the `RenderWebPart` method using the `HtmlTextWriter` object named `output`. The `Write` method of the `HtmlTextWriter` class, shown in line 15, writes a string to the HTML text stream. In this case the string we are providing includes some special HTML tags, some text, and the string output of the `DateTime` ASP.Net function. Any HTML-embedded tags are rendered in the browser as HTML elements. If you want the HTML-embedded tags to render as text, or even to ensure that any input properties are rendered as text, use the `SPEncode.HtmlEncode` method.

The outcome of this code is illustrated in Figure 14.32. The Basic Web Part displays the current date in long format.

14.6.1   Implementing child controls

If you have developed ASP.NET server controls using Visual Studio .NET, you are already aware that implementing child controls within your control, such as a text box or a drop-down list box, is *not* just a simple matter of dragging and dropping the control onto your page; you actually have to create the control in code. The same holds true when developing Web Parts; because the `WebPart` class derives from the `System.Web.UI.Control` class, the user interface for a Web Part must be generated through code.[1]

From a user interface perspective, the typical sequence of events when developing a Web Part involves first creating the ASP.NET controls that you need in code, then adding these controls to the controls collection by

---

1.   There are a number of workarounds for this restriction available on the Internet. Some involve creating a Web Part container that hosts the user controls; others rely on a separate virtual directory to host the user controls. The viability of such workarounds greatly depends on your production deployment and security policies.

overriding the `CreateChildControls` method of the base class. Figure 14.33 shows sample C# code that creates a Web Part with a Calendar control and a Label control. The basic premise of the Web Part is that when the user selects a date on the Calendar control, the Label control is populated with the selected date in the format of: "Day, Month DD, YYYY," for example, Wednesday, June 18, 2004. When the Web Part initially loads, we want both the Calendar control and the Label control to reflect the current

Figure 14.33
Creating child controls in a Web Part using C#.

```
1.   using System;
2.   using System.Web.UI;
3.   using System.Web.UI.WebControls;
4.   using System.Xml.Serialization;
5.   using Microsoft.SharePoint;
6.   using Microsoft.SharePoint.WebPartPages;

7.   namespace BookWebParts
8.   {
9.       /// <summary>
10.      /// This Web Part shows how to override the CreateChildControls method
11.      /// </summary>
12.      [XmlRoot(Namespace="BookWebParts")]
13.      public class ChildControlWP : WebPart
14.      {

15.          // Declare variables for ASP.NET controls user interface elements.
16.          Calendar _mycalendar;
17.          Label _mylabel;

18.          public void _myselection_change (object sender, EventArgs e)
19.          {
20.              // When the user selects a date update the text on the
21.              // label control to reflect the currently selected date

23.              _mylabel.Text = _mycalendar.SelectedDate.ToLongDateString();
24.          }

26.          // Override the CreateChildControls method to create the objects
27.          // for the Web Part's controls.
28.          protected override void CreateChildControls ()
29.          {
30.              // Create the calendar control and select today's date.
31.              _mycalendar = new Calendar();
32.              _mycalendar.SelectedDate = _mycalendar.TodaysDate;

33.              // Create the label control and set the text to today's date
34.              _mylabel = new Label();
35.              _mylabel.Text = _mycalendar.TodaysDate.ToLongDateString();

36.              // Add the new controls to the controls collection
37.              Controls.Add(_mylabel);
38.              Controls.Add(_mycalendar);

40.              // When the user selects a date on the calendar
41.              // call our custom selectionchange handler
42.              _mycalendar.SelectionChanged += new EventHandler (_myselection_change);
43.          }

45.          protected override void RenderWebPart(HtmlTextWriter output)
46.          {
47.              RenderChildren(output);
48.          }
49.      }
50.  }
```

date. As you can see by the sample code, the aforementioned functionality is easily achieved. Lines 16 and 17 declare the variables used for the ASP.NET controls. The Calendar control comes equipped with an event, named `SelectionChanged`, which handles when a user selects a date on the control. When this event fires, we want to invoke a custom handler that updates the `Text` property of the `Label` control. Lines 18 through 24 represent the custom handler _myselection_change.

The `CreateChildControls` method, represented by lines 28 through 43, is responsible for instantiating the controls and capturing the appropriate events. Lines 31 and 32 create a new instance of the Calendar control and set the currently selected date equal to today's date. Lines 34 and 35 create a new instance of the Label control and set the display text equal to today's date. Lines 37 and 38 add the controls to the controls collection.

Figure 14.34
Creating child controls in a Web Part using VB.NET.

```
1.   Imports System
2.   Imports System.Web.UI
3.   Imports System.Web.UI.WebControls
4.   Imports System.Xml.Serialization
5.   Imports Microsoft.SharePoint
6.   Imports Microsoft.SharePoint.Utilities
7.   Imports Microsoft.SharePoint.WebPartPages

8.   <XmlRoot(Namespace:="BookWebParts")> _
9.   Public Class ChildControlWP
10.     Inherits Microsoft.SharePoint.WebPartPages.WebPart
11.     ' Declare variables for ASP.NET Controls user interface elements.
12.     Private _mycalendar As Calendar
13.     Private _mylabel As Label

14.     ' Event handler for _mycalendar control that sets the
15.     ' Label text to the value selected in the Calendar control.

16.     Public Sub _mycalendar_selection_changed(ByVal sender As Object, _
                    ByVal e As EventArgs)
17.         _mylabel.Text = _mycalendar.SelectedDate
18.     End Sub

19.     ' Override the ASP.NET Web.UI.Controls.CreateChildControls
20.     ' method to create the objects for the Web Part's controls.

21.     Protected Overrides Sub CreateChildControls()
22.     ' Create _mycalendar control and trigger its event handler.
23.         _mycalendar = New Calendar
24.         _mycalendar.SelectedDate = _mycalendar.TodaysDate
25.         AddHandler _mycalendar.SelectionChanged, AddressOf _
                        _mycalendar_selection_changed
26.         Controls.Add(_mycalendar)

27.         ' Create _mylabel control
28.         _mylabel = New Label
29.         _mylabel.Text = _mycalendar.TodaysDate.ToLongDateString()
30.         Controls.Add(_mylabel)
31.     End Sub

32.     Protected Overrides Sub RenderWebPart(ByVal output As HtmlTextWriter)
33.         RenderChildren(output)
34.     End Sub
35. End Class
```

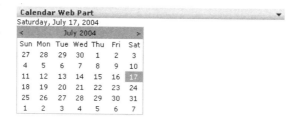

Figure 14.35
*Calendar
Web Part.*

Line 42 invokes the custom event handler, _myselection_change, if the selection changes on the Calendar control, such as when the user selects a date.

Finally, line 47 invokes the RenderChildren method, which outputs the content of the Web Part's child controls to the HtmlTextWriter object, which subsequently writes the content to be rendered on the client. Figure 14.34 shows the same Web Part using VB.NET, and Figure 14.35 shows the Calendar Web Part rendered in the browser.

Notice in Figure 14.35 how tightly packed the controls appear in the Web Part; they are literally on top of one another, causing the Web Part to look cluttered. The RenderChildren method provides little control over how the controls actually appear within your Web Part. One way to overcome this problem is to encapsulate your ASP.NET controls in a table and render the controls one at a time. Figure 14.36 shows the updated code for the RenderWebPart method, and Figure 14.37 shows the results in the browser interface.

14.6.2   Customizing the Web Part menu

Each Web Part that you create automatically inherits a default Web Part menu, which, depending on the property settings of the Web Part, includes commands such as Remove, Minimize, Close, Modify Shared Web Part,

Figure 14.36
*Rendering child
controls in an
HTML table.*

```
44.        ...
45.        protected override void RenderWebPart(HtmlTextWriter output)
46.        {
47.            output.Write("<table border=0 Width=100%>");
48.            output.Write("<tr>");
49.            output.Write("<td Width=70%>");
50.            _mylabel.RenderControl(output);
51.            output.Write("</td>");
52.            output.Write("<td>");
53.            _mycalendar.RenderControl(output);
54.            output.Write("</td>");
55.            output.Write("</tr>");
56.            output.Write("</table>");
57.        }
58.        ...
```

Figure 14.37   *Calendar Web Part rendered in an HTML table.*

and `Export`. You can customize this menu by overriding the `CreateWeb-Part` method. Customizations include the ability to add your own custom menu items, remove existing menu items, or even change the state of existing menu items. Figure 14.38 shows our previous Calendar Web Part with a custom menu. Three menu items have been added to the Web Part menu. The three menu items include a parent menu item with the caption "Calendar Style," and two submenus with captions "Toggle Show Day Header" and "Toggle Show Grid Lines." When you click on the *Toggle Show Day Header* menu option, the day header that appears at the top of the Calendar control will appear or disappear, depending on the previous setting. If you click on the *Toggle Show Grid Lines* menu option, the grid lines will appear or disappear from the Calendar control, depending on the previous setting. Figure 14.38 shows the results of clicking the *Toggle Show Grid Lines* menu option when the grid lines were previously hidden. Notice that the Calendar control now displays the grid lines.

The code required to implement the three menus is very basic and involves declaring the menu item variables, instantiating the menu items, creating the appropriate event handlers, and correctly positioning the menu tree.

Figure 14.39 shows sample C# code required to implement the custom Web Part menu. Of the three menu items we want to generate, only two actually trigger an event. Each event requires a custom event handler to handle the event when it is triggered. Lines 1 through 6 define the event

Figure 14.38
Custom Web Part menu.

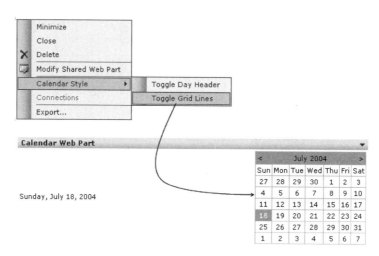

handler for the *Toggle Show Day Header* menu option. The code sets the value of the Calendar control's `ShowDayHeader` property to the opposite of its current value. For example, if the `ShowDayHeader` property is set to `true`, the `_item1handler` event will reset the value to `false`, which in turn hides the day header from the top of the Calendar control. Lines 7 through 12 define the event handler for the *Toggle Show Grid Lines* menu option. The code sets the value of the Calendar control's `ShowGridLines` property to the opposite of its current value. For example, if the `ShowGrid-Lines` property is set to `false`, the `_item2handler` event will reset the value to `true`, which in turn displays the grid in the Calendar control (Figure 14.38). Lines 13 through 40 represent the `CreateWebPartMenu` method that the Web Part implements. Lines 15 and 16 declare the variables to be used for the menu items in the remainder of the code. Line 23 creates the *Calendar Style* menu item. This item is the parent menu item and as such does not require event handlers. Line 25 creates the *Toggle Show Day Header* menu item and links it with the `_item1handler` event handler. Line 27 creates the *Toggle Show Grid Lines* menu item and links it with the `_item2handler` event handler. If you want to invoke a client event when a user clicks on the menu item, use the second parameter to define the script code to run. Lines 19 and 30 add the last two menu items as submenu items to the *Calendar Style* menu item. All that remains is to add the *Calendar Style* menu item to the default Web Part menu. First, we need to pick a location on the menu where we would like our new item to appear. In our example, we have decided that we would like our menu item to appear directly below the *Modify Shared/Personal Web Part* menu item, and include a separator. Once we have determined where we want our menu to appear,

Figure 14.39
Creating a custom Web Part menu using C#.

```
1.   public void _item1handler (object sender, EventArgs e)
2.   {
3.       //When the user click the Toggle Day Header menu option
4.       //Show or Hide the Grid Lines depending on the previous state
5.       _mycalendar.ShowDayHeader = !(_mycalendar.ShowDayHeader);
6.   }

7.   public void _item2handler (object sender, EventArgs e)
8.   {
9.       //When the user click the Toggle Grid Lines menu option
10.      //Show or Hide the Grid Lines depending on the previous state

11.      _mycalendar.ShowGridLines = !(_mycalendar.ShowGridLines);
12.  }

13.  public override void CreateWebPartMenu()
14.  {
15.      // Declare variables for menu items.
16.      MenuItem ParentItem;
17.      MenuItem Item1;
18.      MenuItem Item2;
19.
20.      // Create Calendar Style menu (parent) and two submenus:
21.      // Toggle Day Header and Toggle Grid Lines
22.      // Create the parent item.
23.      ParentItem = new MenuItem("Calendar Style", "", "ParentItemID");

24.      // Create the first submenu with a server event on click
25.      Item1 = new MenuItem("Toggle Day Header", "Item1ID", new
                  EventHandler(_item1handler));

26.      // Create the second submenu with a server event on click
27.      Item2 = new MenuItem("Toggle Grid Lines", "Item2ID", new
                  EventHandler(_item2handler));

28.      // Add the submenu items to the parent item.
29.      ParentItem.MenuItems.Add(Item1);
30.      ParentItem.MenuItems.Add(Item2);

31.      // Add the parent item after the "Modify Shared/Personal Web Part"
32.      // command in the default menu.

33.      // Retrieve the index of the "Modify Shared/Personal Web Part" command.
34.      int EditIndex = this.WebPartMenu.MenuItems.IndexOf
                  (this.WebPartMenu.MenuItems.ItemFromID("MSOMenu_Edit"));

35.      // Insert the parent item after "Modify Shared/Personal Web Part item
36.      this.WebPartMenu.MenuItems.Insert(EditIndex + 1, ParentItem);

37.      // Add a separator above the parent item.
38.      ParentItem.BeginSection = true;
39.  }
```

we need to find the index value of that location. Line 34 shows how to retrieve the index of the `Modify Shared/Personal` Web Part command using the `IndexOf` and `ItemFromID` methods. The `MSOMenu_Edit` identifier represents the *Modify Shared Web Part* menu item, and Table 14.1 shows the identifiers for additional SharePoint built-in menus.

Once we retrieve the index of the menu item that we want our menu item to follow, we simply use the `Insert` method to place the menu item at the location of our previous index incremented by one. Line 36 shows this code in action. Line 38 shows how to add a separator between the *Modify*

Table 14.1   *Built-in Menu Identifiers*

Built-in Menu	Identifier
Close	MSOMenu_Close
Connections	MSOMenu_Connections
Delete	MSOMenu_Delete
Export	MSOMenu_Export
Help	MSOMenu_Help
Minimize	MSOMenu_Minimize
Modify Shared Web Part	MSOMenu_Edit
To Computer	MSOMenu_ExportCatalog
To Personal	MSOMenu_ExportPersonalCatalog
To Site Catalog	MSOMenu_ExportSiteCatalog

Shared Web Part menu item and our new *Calendar Style* menu item using the BeginSection method.

14.6.3   Tool Panes and Tool Parts

If you refer back to Figure 14.28, notice that in addition to the get and set accessors that control the value of the property, there are attributes associated with the actual property itself, such as the Category attribute and the WebPartStorageAttribute. These attributes control how the Web Part property appears through the browser interface when in design mode. When you modify a Web Part in design mode using the browser interface known as the Web Part Task Pane, the Tool Pane appears to the right (Figure 14.40).

The Tool Pane is analogous to the Web Part Settings customization page in SPS 2001 and allows you to modify the properties associated with the currently selected Web Part. The Tool Pane is divided into various sections, or Tool Parts, determined by the Web Part itself. For example, the News Web Part has a Custom Properties Tool Part, a Miscellaneous Tool Part, an Appearance Tool Part, a Layout Tool Part, and an Advanced Tool Part. The Web Part infrastructure provides two basic types of Tool Parts associated, by default, with each Web Part. The first derives from the WebPartToolPart class and handles all of the properties associated with the WebPart base

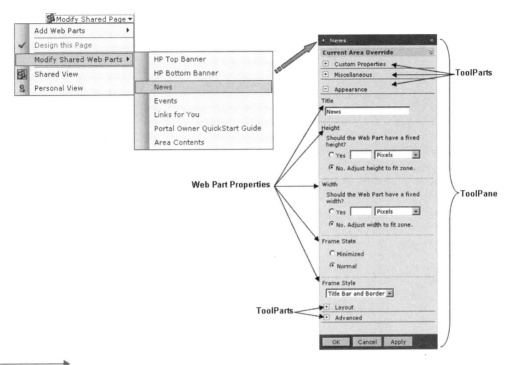

Figure 14.40   *Web Part Properties Tool Pane.*

class, such as the `Height` and `Width` properties and the `FrameState` properties. Examples of Tool Parts derived from the `WebPartToolPart` class include the Appearance Tool Part, the Layouts Tool Part, and the Behavior Tool Part. The second type of Tool Part objects are those derived from the `CustomPropertyToolPart` class. The `CustomPropertyToolPart` object handles all custom properties based on supported types such as `String`, `Integer`, `Boolean`, `DateTime`, and `Enum`. The base type of the custom property determines the control rendered in the Tool Part. For example, if your custom property is of type `String`, the Web Part infrastructure renders a text box to store the property's contents. Table 14.2 shows the property types and their associated controls.

If you want to leverage the default Tool Pane and Tool Parts when developing your Web Parts, you will typically want any custom property that you create to appear in its own custom Tool Part. The simplest way to achieve this is by specifying the name of your Tool Part in the `Category` attribute of your property code definition. By doing so, the Web Part infrastructure automatically creates a custom Tool Part based on the `CustomProperty-ToolPart` class and applies the name that you defined in the `Category`

Table 14.2 *Controls Created for Specific Data Types*

Type	Control
Boolean	Check box
DateTime	Text box
Enum	Drop-down menu
Int	Text box
String	Text box

attribute. Figure 14.41 shows how a custom Tool Part derived from the `CustomPropertyToolPart` class is implemented using C#.

If you do not specify a custom Tool Part, or specify `Default` for the `Category` attribute, then your custom property appears in the Miscellaneous Tool Part. Additionally, if you try to assign your custom property to the Appearance, Layouts, or Behavior Tool Parts, SharePoint ignores this command and displays it in the Miscellaneous Tool Part instead.

The default property pane provided with SharePoint can be further extended to provide custom functionality, including additional ASP.NET controls. In fact, the Tool Part in and of itself is basically a Web Part hosted on the Tool Pane instead of a Web Part Page. You can create your own cus-

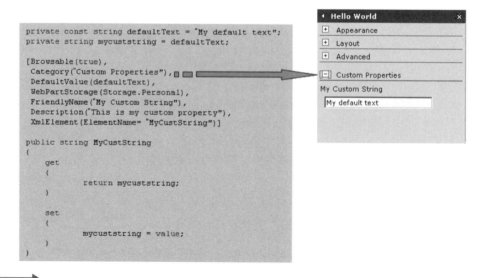

Figure 14.41 *Tool Part derived from the* `CustomPropertyToolPart` *class.*

tom Tool Part by creating an instance of the `ToolPart` class and overriding the `GetToolParts` method. The `ToolPart` class is the base class used for all custom Tool Parts, and, as with most classes, it contains a set of properties and methods. The `GetToolParts` method is a member of the `ToolPart` class and determines the Tool Parts that appear in the Tool Pane in design mode. As previously mentioned, if your Web Part implements one or more custom properties and does not override the `GetToolParts` method, then the custom properties are added to the default Tool Part derived from the `CustomPropertyToolPart`, assuming the properties are of a supported data type.

If you create a Web Part with custom properties that do not match one of the supported data types listed in Table 14.2, then you must create a custom Tool Part to manage the property value by overriding the `GetTool-Parts` method. To demonstrate the `GetToolParts` method, we will modify our previous example by replacing the *Menu Item* functionality with two custom Boolean properties that represent the current setting of our `ShowDayHeader` and `ShowGridLines` properties. We will then override the `GetToolParts` method and create a custom Tool Part that will host our newly created properties.

Step 1: Creating custom properties

The first step is to create our custom properties. Earlier in the chapter, we saw that the creation of a custom property involved creating `get` and `set` accessors for the property. In addition to the accessors, we need to define the attributes that control how the Web Part property appears in design mode. Table 14.3 shows the attributes available for a given Web Part.

Figure 14.42 shows the C# code used to create our two custom properties. Notice that in addition to the attributes listed in Table 14.3, each property has an `XmlElement` attribute that maps to the public custom property. The `XmlElement` property is used by the .NET `XmlSerializer` to write the properties in XML and persist the Web Part's data.

Lines 1 and 2 of the code define the default values for each of the properties. We want the calendar to initially show with the day header enabled and grid lines off. Therefore, we define two default Boolean constants: one representing `true`, the other representing `false`: `c_mybooldefT` and `c_mybooldefF`, respectively. Lines 3 and 4 declare the private variables used in the `get` and `set` accessors later in code. Lines 5 through 22 define the `_MyShowHeader` custom property, with the `XmlElement` mapping to the property so we can persist the value. The fact that the `Browsable` attribute is set to `false` may seem strange at first, since you would expect that if you want to browse the attribute in your custom Tool Part, it would require a setting of `true`. However, setting the `Browsable` attribute to `false` merely prevents the custom property from appearing in the default Tool Part derived from the `CustomPropertyToolPart` class. This is an

Table 14.3   *Web Part Property Attributes*

Attribute	Purpose
Browsable	The `Browsable` attribute determines whether the Web Part property appears in the Tool Pane. If it is set to `false`, then the custom property will not appear in the Tool Pane. Also, if the `WebPartStorage` attribute is set to `Storage.None`, the custom property will not display in the Tool Pane. If you create a custom Tool Part for your custom properties and the `Browsable` attribute is set to `false`, the custom properties are still visible in your custom Tool Part; however, they will not appear in any Tool Part derived from the `CustomProperty-ToolPart` class.
Category	The `Category` attribute determines the Tool Part in which you would like the custom property to appear. If the `Category` attribute is not set or is set to `Default`, the custom property appears in the *Miscellaneous* section of the property pane. *Note:* If one of the default categories, such as `Appearance`, is specified, the `Category` attribute setting is ignored, and the custom property appears in the *Miscellaneous* section.
DefaultValue	The `DefaultValue` attribute determines the default value of the custom property. Specifying the default value minimizes the Web Part's storage requirements by storing the property's value only if it is different from the default.
Description	The `Description` attribute determines the contents of the tool tip that appears when you hover the mouse pointer over the custom property in the Tool Pane.
FriendlyNameAttribute	The `FriendlyNameAttribute` determines the text that appears for the custom property in the Tool Pane. If this attribute is not set, the actual custom property name appears in the Tool Pane.
ReadOnly	The `ReadOnly` attribute is set to `true` if the custom property needs to be read-only in the Tool Pane.
WebPartStorage	The `WebPartStorage` property determines whether the custom property is personalizable. If the attribute is set to `Storage.Shared`, the custom property appears in the shared view of the page. If it is set to `Storage.Personal`, the custom property appears in the Tool Pane when the user is in shared or personal view of the page. If it is set to `Storage.None`, the setting for the custom property does not persist. The custom property does not appear in the Tool Pane.
HtmlDesignerAttribute	The `HtmlDesignerAttribute` is used to associate a property builder with the custom property.

```
1.    const bool c_mybooldefT = true;
2.    const bool c_mybooldefF = false;
3.    private bool _myshowdayheader = c_mybooldefT;
4.    private bool _myshowgridlines = c_mybooldefF;

5.    [Browsable(false)]
6.    [DefaultValue(c_mybooldefT)]
7.    [WebPartStorage(Storage.Personal)]
8.    [FriendlyName("Show Day Header")]
9.    [Description("Check to display day header on the top row of the Calendar")]
10.   [XmlElement(ElementName="_MyShowDayHeader")]
11.
12.   public bool _MyShowDayHeader
13.   {
14.       get
15.       {
16.           return _myshowdayheader;
17.       }

18.       set
19.       {
20.           _myshowdayheader = value;
21.       }
22.   }

23.   [Browsable(false)]
24.   [DefaultValue(c_mybooldefF)]
25.   [WebPartStorage(Storage.Personal)]
26.   [FriendlyName("Show Grid Lines")]
27.   [Description("Check to display grid lines on the Calendar")]
28.   [XmlElement(ElementName="_MyShowGridLines")]
29.
30.   public bool _MyShowGridLines
31.   {
32.       get
33.       {
34.           return _myshowgridlines;
35.       }
36.
37.       set
38.       {
39.           _myshowgridlines = value;
40.       }
41.   }
```

advisable practice, since it avoids confusing the user by having the custom property accessible from two places and also avoids the developer having to synchronize the changes between the Tool Parts. Since we want the Calendar Web Part to initially show with the day header enabled, we set the DefaultValue attribute of our custom property to c_mybooldefT (true). The WebPartStorage attribute is set to Storage.Personal, which means that the custom property will appear in the design mode of both the shared view and personal view. Users will be able to personalize the setting for the Web Part. The FriendlyName attribute is set to ShowDayHeader, which appears in the Tool Pane and, since the property is of type Boolean, the Web Part infrastructure by default renders it as a check box. The Description attribute defines the tool tip associated with the property. Lines 14 through 21 define the get and set accessors for the property. The get accessor allows you to retrieve the current value of the custom property, and the set accessor allows you to set its value.

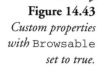

Figure 14.43
*Custom properties
with* Browsable
set to true.

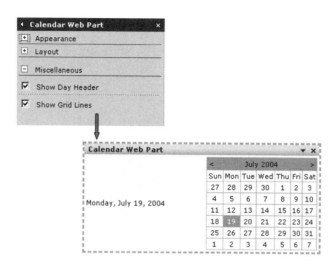

Lines 23 through 41 similarly define the _MyShowGridLines custom property, with the XmlElement mapping to the property so we can persist the value.

From a development-and-testing perspective, it is sometimes useful to set the Browsable attribute to true to test the functionality of your custom properties before you implement the custom Tool Part. Once you are happy that the custom properties are behaving as expected within your Web Part, you can then reset the Browsable attribute to false. If you build the solution at this stage with the Browsable attribute set to true, the custom properties appear in the Tool Pane under the Miscellaneous Tool Part, and you can check and uncheck the property values (Figure 14.43). Opening and closing the browser will show you that the values persist in the Tool Pane; however, the properties lack functionality. When you check or uncheck the custom properties, the Calendar control does not reflect the property changes, because we have not added logic to render these changes.

Figure 14.44 shows the code added to the RenderWebPart method that applies the changes to the custom properties to the Calendar control. The code is very straightforward; it basically sets the Calendar control's ShowDayHeader to the value stored in the _MyShowDayHeader custom property

Figure 14.44
*Rendering the
custom property
settings using C#.*

```
1.   protected override void RenderWebPart(HtmlTextWriter output)
2.   {
3.       _mycalendar.ShowDayHeader = this._MyShowDayHeader;
4.       _mycalendar.ShowGridLines = this._MyShowGridLines;
5.       ...
6.   }
```

and sets the Calendar control's `ShowGridLines` property to the value stored in the `_MyShowGridLines` custom property.

Step 2: Creating the custom Tool Part

Now that we have the appropriate functionality applied to our Web Part, all that remains is to create the custom Tool Part. The creation of the custom Tool Part is separated into two parts. First, we need to create the class that we will use for our custom Tool Part, and then we must override the `Get-ToolParts` method in the main `WebPart` class. Figures 14.45 and 14.46 show the code required to create our custom Tool Part class: `customTool-Part`. The `customToolPart` class derives from the base `ToolPart` class; so, before we delve into the sample code, let's take a closer look at this class.

As with any ASP.NET class, the `ToolPart` class has a number of properties and methods that affect the presentation, behavior, and functionality of its instantiated objects. It comes equipped with the `ToolPart` constructor, which allows you to create an instance of the `ToolPart` class. As you will

```
1.    using System;
2.    using System.Web.UI;
3.    using System.Web.UI.WebControls;
4.    using Microsoft.SharePoint;
5.    using Microsoft.SharePoint.WebPartPages;
6.    using Microsoft.SharePoint.Utilities;

7.    namespace BookWebParts
8.    {
9.        public class customToolPart:Microsoft.SharePoint.WebPartPages.ToolPart
10.       {
11.           // declare checkboxes
12.           CheckBox _mycheckA;
13.           CheckBox _mycheckB;

14.           // an event handler for the Init event
15.           private void customToolPart_Init(object sender, System.EventArgs e )
16.           {
17.             //instantiate the checkbox controls and set their labels
18.             _mycheckA = new CheckBox();
19.             _mycheckB = new CheckBox();
20.             _mycheckA.Text = "Show Day Header";
21.             _mycheckB.Text = "Show Grid Lines";

22.             //get a reference to the parent Web Part
23.             ChildControlWP wp1 = (ChildControlWP)this.ParentToolPane.SelectedWebPart;

24.
25.             //set each checkbox equal to the current value of the
26.             //corresponding custom property
27.             _mycheckA.Checked = wp1._MyShowDayHeader;
28.             _mycheckB.Checked = wp1._MyShowGridLines;

29.             //add the controls to the controls collection
30.             Controls.Add(_mycheckA);
31.             Controls.Add(_mycheckB);
32.           }
```

Figure 14.45   *Creating* `customToolPart` *class using C# (part A).*

```
33.        public customToolPart()
34.        {
35.          // Set default properties for the class
36.          this.AllowMinimize = false;
37.          this.FrameState = FrameState.Normal;
38.          this.Title="Calendar Style";

39.          // Invoke the custom event handler for the init event
40.          this.Init += new EventHandler(customToolPart_Init);
41.        }

42.        public override void ApplyChanges()
43.        {
44.          ChildControlWP wp1 = (ChildControlWP)this.ParentToolPane.SelectedWebPart;

46.          // Update the custom properties to match the values in the checkboxes
47.          wp1._MyShowDayHeader = _mycheckA.Checked;
48.          wp1._MyShowGridLines = _mycheckB.Checked;
49.        }

50.        protected override void RenderToolPart(HtmlTextWriter output)
51.        {
52.          //Render the custom Tool Part
53.          output.Write("<BR>");
54.          _mycheckA.RenderControl(output);
55.          output.Write("<BR>");
56.          _mycheckB.RenderControl(output);
57.        }
58.      }
59.  }
```

Figure 14.46 *Creating* customToolPart *class using C# (part B).*

see in the sample code, the `ToolPart` constructor is the ideal place to set the default properties of the class and override the `init` event to perform initializations of the Tool Part variables. For example, if you want your custom Tool Part always to appear in expanded view, you can set the `FrameState` and `AllowMinimize` properties in the `ToolPart` constructor. Table 14.4 lists the properties associated with the `ToolPart` class.

The `ToolPart` class has four basic methods, listed in Table 14.5, but you will probably find the `ApplyChanges` method and the `RenderTool-Part` method the most useful. The `ApplyChanges` method launches when a user clicks the **OK** or the **Apply** button in the Tool Pane. Any custom properties and objects that you want your Tool Part to affect can be handled by overriding the `ApplyChanges` method. The `CancelChanges` method launches when a user clicks the **Cancel** button on the Tool Pane; it is ideally suited for any cleanup you need to perform for the Tool Part. The `Sync-Changes` method is invoked when all other Tool Parts call the `Apply-Changes` method. If there are other Tool Parts on the Tool Pane that have the potential to modify custom properties that your Tool Part uses, then you will need to synchronize those changes with your Tool Part by overriding the `SyncChanges` method. In the code sample, we do not need to invoke the `SyncChanges` method, since the custom properties we are inter-

Table 14.4   `ToolPart` *Class Properties*

Property/Data Type	Description
AllowMinimize Boolean	The `AllowMinimize` property determines whether the Tool Part can be minimized by the user. If this property is set to `true`, then the Tool Part can be minimized. You can use this property in conjunction with the `FrameState` property to force the Tool Part to appear in expanded view at all times.
FrameState FrameState	The `FrameState` property determines whether the Tool Part appears in expanded view or minimized. Possible values include `FrameState.Minimized` and `FrameState.Normal`. The default value is `FrameState.Normal`. If the AllowMinimize property is set to `false`, then setting the `FrameState` property to `FrameState.Minimized` is ignored.
FrameType FrameType	The `FrameType` property determines the type of frame that surrounds the Tool Part. Possible values include `FrameType.None`, `FrameType.Standard`, and `FrameType.TitleBarOnly`.
ParentToolPane ToolPane	The `ParentToolPane` property retrieves the Tool Pane that contains the Tool Part.
Qualifier String	The `Qualifier` property retrieves a unique identifier for the Tool Part.
Title String	The `Title` property determines the title of the Tool Part. If the `FrameType` is set to `FrameType.Standard` or `FrameType.TitleBarOnly`, then the value of the `Title` property appears in the title bar of the Tool Part.
UseDefaultStyles Boolean	The `UseDefaultStyles` property determines whether the Tool Part uses the default themes and styles for its body.

Table 14.5   `ToolPart` *Class Methods*

Name	Description
ApplyChanges	The `ApplyChanges` method is invoked when a user clicks the **OK** or the **Apply** button in the Tool Pane.
CancelChanges	The `CancelChanges` method is invoked when a user clicks the **Cancel** button in the Tool Pane.
SyncChanges	The `SyncChanges` method is invoked when all other Tool Parts call the `ApplyChanges` method.
RenderToolPart	The `RenderToolPart` method sends the content for the Tool Part to the `HtmlTextWriter` object, which then writes the content to be rendered on the client.

ested in are not affected by any other Tool Part in the Tool Pane. Finally, the
RenderToolPart method is analogous to the RenderWebPart method in
the WebPart class and is basically responsible for the Tool Part content that
is rendered to the client. As with the RenderWebPart method, you must
override the RenderToolPart method in order to present a custom view of
the Tool Part.

Now let's examine the sample code for the customToolPart class. The
entire code for the customToolPart class spans Figures 14.45 and 14.46.
Lines 9 through 59 actually define the class. The first thing to notice is the
class declaration in line 9. The customToolPart is derived from the
Microsoft.SharePoint.WebPartPages.ToolPart class, which means
that it inherits the properties and methods previously discussed. With the
customToolPart class, we want to represent each of our custom properties,
_MyShowDayHeader and _MyShowGridLines, with a check box that con-
trols whether the Calendar control's day header and grid lines appear. To do
this, we must first create our check box child controls. Lines 12 and 13
declare the variables we use to instantiate the Check box controls, and lines
15 through 32 actually build the controls. The customToolPart_Init
function handles the Init event associated with the custom Tool Part.

The Init event is the first event in the Tool Part's life cycle and is the
ideal place to instantiate controls or initialize variables for your Tool Part. If
you want to leverage the Init event in this way, you will need to provide a
custom event handler, such as the customToolPart_Init. In the
customToolPart_Init event, we want to set the values of the controls
equal to the values stored in the custom properties. To do this, we need to
have some way of referencing the custom properties created in our WebPart
class. Line 23 shows how the ParentToolPane property provides us access
to our WebPart class ChildControlWP. Now that we have a reference, we
can access the custom properties of that class, namely, the _MyShowDay-
Header and _MyShowGridLines custom properties.

Lines 33 through 41 show the code for the custom Tool Part's constructor, named customToolPart. We use the constructor method to set the
default properties of the Tool Part and to trap the Tool Part's Init event.
Lines 36 through 38 ensure that the Tool Part always appears in expanded
view with a title bar and a border and set the text to appear in the title bar.
Line 40 invokes the custom event handler, customToolPart_Init, for the
Init event.

Lines 42 through 49 show how to override the ApplyChanges method.
Line 47 sets the _MyShowHeader custom property equal to the value in the

Show Day Header check box, and line 48 sets the _MyShowGridLines custom property equal to the value in the Show Grid Lines check box. This ensures that the settings in the custom Tool Part are reflected in the actual Web Part. Finally, lines 50 through 57 show how to override the Render-ToolPart method and create your own output for your custom control. One thing to note is that with a custom Tool Part, you are not restricted to a specific set of data types and controls to render your properties. So, for example, instead of using a Check box control, you could just as easily implement the CheckBoxList control instead.

Now that we have created the code for our customToolPart class, we need to implement that code in our Web Part. To do this we need to override the GetToolParts method. The GetToolParts method returns an array of references to the new ToolPart objects that appear in the Web Part's Tool Pane. The ToolPart objects are rendered by the Tool Pane in the order they appear in the array. By controlling the array sequence, you can control where your custom Tool Part appears in the ToolPane. If you override the GetToolParts method, the default ToolPart objects, Web-PartToolPart and CustomPropertyToolPart, are *not* generated automatically. Consequently, if you want the default Tool Parts to appear in the Tool Pane, in addition to your custom Tool Part, you must include them in the code.

Figure 14.47 shows the code to override the GetToolParts method in our sample. Line 3 creates an array of Tool Parts named toolparts. Lines 4 and 5 generate the WebPartToolPart object and the CustomProperty-ToolPart object. Line 6 adds the WebPartToolPart object as the first Tool Part item in the toolparts array, line 7 adds the CustomProperty-ToolPart object as the second Tool Part item in the toolparts array, and line 9 creates a new instance of the customToolPart class and assigns the customToolPart object as the last Tool Part item in the toolparts array. The Tool Parts appear on the Tool Pane in the order they are represented in

```
1.   public override ToolPart[] GetToolParts()
2.   {
3.        ToolPart[] toolparts = new ToolPart[3];
4.        WebPartToolPart _defWPTP = new WebPartToolPart();
5.        CustomPropertyToolPart _defCPTP = new CustomPropertyToolPart();
6.        toolparts[0] = _defWPTP;
7.        toolparts[1] = _defCPTP;
8.        // This is the custom ToolPart.
9.        toolparts[2] = new BookWebParts.customToolPart();
10.       return toolparts;
11.  }
```

Figure 14.47   *Overriding the* GetToolParts *method with* CustomPropertyToolPart.

```
1.    public override ToolPart[] GetToolParts()
2.    {
3.        ToolPart[] toolparts = new ToolPart[2];
4.        WebPartToolPart _defWPTP = new WebPartToolPart();
5.        toolparts[0] = _defWPTP;
6.        // This is the custom ToolPart.
7.        toolparts[1] = new BookWebParts.customToolPart();
8.        return toolparts;
9.    }
```

Figure 14.48   *Overriding the* GetToolParts *method without* CustomPropertyToolPart.

the Tool Part array. In our example, the custom Tool Part appears as the last Tool Part in the Tool Pane.

As previously mentioned, you can use the GetToolParts method to hide or modify the default Tool Parts. Given that all the custom properties associated with our Web Part are represented in the custom Tool Part *and* that the custom properties' Browsable attributes have been set to false, there's really no need to include the CustomPropertyToolPart object in the Tool Part. To hide CustomPropertyToolPart, we simply remove it from the toolparts array (Figure 14.48).

Figure 14.49 shows the final result of our custom Tool Part.

As you will note, it's very similar to the way our custom properties are handled by the default Tool Part (Figure 14.43), but that's just because we chose to code it this way. Figure 14.50 shows a variation on the same Tool Part with a Panel control and two Image controls added. The main point is that you can use your own code to build your Tool Part to suit your needs.

Figure 14.49
Custom Tool Part.

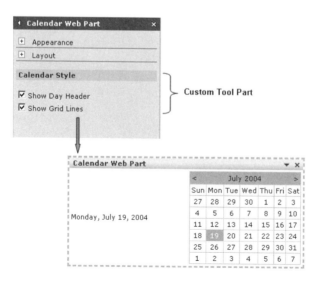

Figure 14.50
Custom Tool Part with additional controls.

There are many more methods and properties that you can leverage when building your Web Parts. Full details on the various methods and properties can be found in the SharePoint Products and Technologies Software Development Kit. Many of the methods listed focus on the serialization and deserialization process. Serialization is the process of converting an object, or objects, into a linear sequence of bytes for storage. Deserialization is the process of consuming this stored information and then recreating the objects based on the stored data. Any custom properties created by your Web Part are serialized using the System.Xml.Serialization namespace.

14.7 Web Part connections

Web Parts themselves are excellent vehicles for providing users with relevant information, but their true potential lies in their ability to communicate with each other. SPS 2001 provided Web Part communications via the Digital DashBoard Services Component (DDSC). The DDSC is basically an ActiveX control that provides objects, methods, and properties for use when developing Digital DashBoard–based Web Parts.

The current version of SharePoint provides more options with respect to Web Part communications, now referred to as connections. A Web Part connection typically has a provider and a consumer. The provider represents the Web Part initiating the communication by providing some form of information that is of interest to the consumer Web Part. For example, we have a simple Form Web Part connected to a Shared Documents Web Part on the Home page of our site. The Form Web Part has the role of the provider for the connection, so that when the user enters a name in the form, the text is sent to the consumer Web Part, which in this scenario is the Shared Documents Web Part. In the role of the consumer, the Shared Documents Web Part then consumes the name and filters the Shared Documents Document Library to display only those documents modified by the user that matches the name (Figure 14.51).

Figure 14.51
Form Web Part
Filtering Shared
Documents
Web Part.

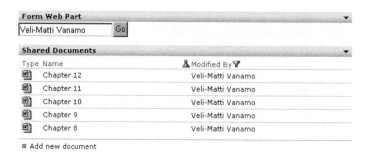

When a Web Part is created, it does not automatically support connections; in order to provide this functionality, the Web Part itself has to implement a number of interfaces, which we'll cover shortly. You can determine if an existing Web Part supports connections by navigating to the Web Part menu when in design mode. If the Connections menu is enabled (i.e., not grayed out), then the Web Part supports connections. The actual type of connection that a Web Part supports depends on a number of factors, including the type of Web Part it is (i.e., whether it's a server-side Web Part or a client-side Web Part), the location of the Web Part (i.e., whether it is on the same Web Part Page as its connection Web Part), and whether it has exceeded the maximum number of connections permissible for the Web Part. If your Web Part is a client-side Web Part (i.e., it contains script code that runs on the client as opposed to the server), then a similar component to the DDSC is available, namely, the Web Part Page Services Component (WPSC). The WPSC is implemented in JavaScript as opposed to ActiveX and allows developers to create Web Parts that connect through interfaces on the client. The WPSC acts as a router to broker event communication. It receives the event and passes it to each part that has a registered event handler and a connection between the sending and receiving Web Part. In order for a Web Part to be able to connect to another Web Part, it must be of the same type. In other words, client-side Web Parts can only connect to other client-side Web Parts, and server-side Web Parts can only connect to other server-side Web Parts.

14.7.1   Connection interfaces

The Web Part Framework provides a standard set of interfaces, known as connection interfaces, that allow Web Parts to communicate with one another at run time. The great thing about this is that Web Parts can be developed independently of one another and can ultimately share information if they both support the appropriate interfaces. Web Part developers need only be concerned with their own Web Part implementation. The interfaces derive from the `Microsoft.SharePoint.WebPartPages.Com-munication` namespace and are implemented in a provider/consumer interface pair used to complete the communication sequence. For example, the `ICellProvider` interface allows communication with another Web Part that implements the `ICellConsumer` interface. Table 14.6 shows the supported connection interface pairs.

Table 14.6   *Connection Interface Pairs*

Connection Interface Pair	Description
`ICellProvider, IcellConsumer`	The `ICellProvider` interface provides a single item value to a connected Web Part that implements the `ICellConsumer` interface. The `ICellConsumer` interface retrieves a single item value from a connected Web Part that implements the `ICellProvider` interface.
`IRowProvider, IRowConsumer`	The `IRowProvider` interface provides a single/multiple row of values to a connected Web Part that implements the `IRow-Consumer` interface. The `IRowConsumer` interface retrieves the row values from a connected Web Part that implements the `IRow-Provider` interface.
`IListProvider, IListConsumer`	The `IListProvider` interface provides an entire list (rowset) of data to a connected Web Part that implements the `IList-Consumer` interface. The `IListConsumer` interface retrieves an entire list (rowset) from a connected Web Part that implements the `IListProvider` interface.
`IFilterProvider, IFilterConsumer`	The `IFilterProvider` interface provides filter information to connected Web Parts that implement the `IFilterConsumer` interface. The `IFilterConsumer` interface retrieves filter information from a connected Web Part that implements the `IFilter-Provider` interface.
`IParametersInProvider, IParametersInConsumer`	The `IParametersInConsumer` interface defines a parameter list it can retrieve from connected Web Parts that implement the `IParametersInProvider` interface. This differs from the `IParametersOut` interfaces where the `IParametersOut-Provider` interface defines the parameter list to be used by the connected Web Parts.
`IParametersOutProvider, IParametersOutConsumer`	The `IParametersOutProvider` interface defines a parameter list it can send to connected Web Parts that implement the `IPa-rametersOutConsumer` interface. This differs from the `IParametersIn` interfaces where the `IParametersIn-Consumer` interface defines the parameter list to be used by the connected Web Parts.

Table 14.7   *Interfaces Supported with Transformers*

Transformer
`IRowProvider` to `ICellConsumer`
`IRowProvider` to `IFilterConsumer`
`IParametersOutProvider` to `IParametersInConsumer`
`IRowProvider` to `IParametersInConsumer`

Certain interfaces can communicate with interfaces outside of their interface pair using a *transformer*. The Web Part infrastructure provides a set of transformers that allow Web Parts that implement different connection interfaces to communicate with one another. The Web Part infrastructure automatically detects that the Web Parts can communicate via a transformer and displays a dialog box from which users can map values from one interface to another. For example, if we have a Web Part that implements the `IRowProvider` interface, and we want to connect it to a Web Part that implements the `ICellConsumer` Web Part, a dialog box appears from which we can select an individual column from the `IRowProvider` Web Part to send to the `ICellConsumer` Web Part. Table 14.7 shows the possible interface combination using transformers.

The ability for a Web Part to be connected using the browser or using FrontPage 2003 depends on the interfaces used in the communication. Additionally, certain interface combinations support cross-page connections, meaning that a Web Part on one page can connect to a Web Part on another page. Table 14.8 shows all of the supported interface combinations, where they can be connected, and whether they support cross-page connections.

14.7.2   Connection processing

Each interface combination requires its own set of events and methods in order to function; however, there is a common sequence of events and methods processed by the Web Part infrastructure when connecting Web Parts. The Web Part infrastructure gathers connection information from all the Web Parts on the page when the page is viewed in design mode. The Web Part infrastructure queries the Web Parts to determine the interfaces they support and whether they support client-side connections, server-side connections, or both. The Web Part infrastructure then uses this information to build the design time Web Part Connections menu, presenting users with compatible Web Parts and interfaces to which they can connect.

Table 14.8   *Interface Combinations*

Source Interface	Target Interface	Browser Support	FrontPage 2003 Support	Cross-Page Connection Support
ICellProvider	ICellConsumer	Yes	Yes	No
IRowProvider	IRowConsumer	Yes	Yes	No
IListProvider	IListConsumer	Yes	Yes	No
IFilterProvider	IFilterConsumer	Yes	Yes	Yes
IParametersInProvider	IParametersInConsumer	No	Yes	Yes
IParametersOutProvider	IParametersOutConsumer	No	Yes	No
IRowProvider	ICellConsumer	Yes	Yes	No
IRowProvider	IFilterConsumer	Yes	Yes	Yes
IRowProvider	IParametersInConsumer	No	Yes	Yes
IParametersOutProvider	IParametersInConsumer	No	Yes	Yes

So, how does the Web Part infrastructure get this information? Figure 14.52 shows the common methods deployed by a connectable Web Part to inform the Web Part infrastructure of its connectability. Each connectable Web Part informs the Web Part infrastructure of the interfaces it supports by overriding the EnsureInterfaces method. The EnsureInterfaces method is a member of the base WebPart class and is called by the Web Part infrastructure before rendering the Web Part. Consequently, this method is responsible for ensuring that the appropriate interfaces for the Web Part are registered using the RegisterInterface method. The RegisterInterface method is also a member of the WebPart base class and notifies the Web Part infrastructure of the interfaces to be used by the Web Part. Once all the interfaces are successfully registered, the Web Part infrastructure calls the Web Part's CanRunAt method to determine where the Web Part can run: whether it can run on the client, server, or both. Next, the Web Part infrastructure calls the Web Part's PartCommunicationConnect method to notify the Web Part that is has been successfully connected and to deliver relevant information, such as the Web Part to which it is connected and the connecting Web Part's interface used to complete the communication.

Once the connections have been established, the Web Part infrastructure calls the PartCommunicationInit method to see if there's any information that the Web Part needs to initialize or broadcast to connecting Web Parts.

Figure 14.52
*Connection
life cycle.*

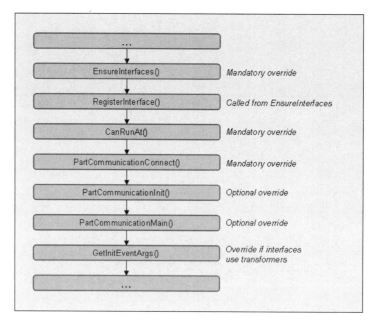

For example, if you connect a List Web Part to a Form Web Part, the List
Web Part should inform the Form Web Part of its fields so that it can render its user interface accordingly. When developing connectable Web Parts,
overriding the PartCommunicationInit method is optional, as is overriding the PartCommunicationMain method, which is the next method to be
called by the Web Part infrastructure. The Web Part uses the PartCommunicationMain method to communicate data values between connected
Web Parts by invoking other events from its interface. For example, if you
want your Web Part to communicate the data values when a user changes or
selects a cell within your Web Part, you would invoke the CellReady event
of the ICellProvider interface. Finally, if the Web Part provides or consumes data using a transformer, then the Web Part infrastructure calls the
GetInitEventArgs method to retrieve the mapping information. For
example, if we have a Web Part that implements the IRowProvider interface, and we want to connect it to a Web Part that implements the
ICellConsumer Web Part, the GetInitEventArgs of the provider Web
Part informs the Web Part infrastructure of the columns available for mapping to the consumer Web Part. The Web Part infrastructure uses this
information to create the visual mapping dialog to display to the user.

From a development perspective, the tasks that need to be completed
when coding a connectable Web Part depend on the interfaces the Web Part

supports and where the Web Part can run. Each interface implements its own set of methods and events. For example, the `IRowProvider` interface supports two events: `RowProviderInit` and `RowProviderReady`. The `RowProviderInit` event is an initialization event responsible for sending the names and display names of the fields in a specific row. The `RowReady` event fires when the selected row in a provider Web Part changes, either when the row is updated or selected.

To better illustrate the connection process, lets take the Calendar Web Part from our previous example and make it connectable. We want the date selected by the users to be communicated to the connected Web Parts. For this example, we are particularly interested in filtering the contents of the Shared Documents Web Part. Specifically, when you change the date in the Calendar Web Part, it passes this date to the connected Shared Documents Web Part, which in turn filters its list to display the documents modified on the selected date.

When you are creating connectable Web Parts, you need to answer a number of questions before you can actually implement this functionality.

1. What information do I want my Web Part to be able to share and communicate?

2. Do I want to be able to support cross-page connections?

3. Does my Web Part run on the client or the server?

4. What interfaces do I need to implement in order to send/receive the appropriate information?

The answers specific to our example are as follows:

1. We want to send the currently selected date to the Shared Documents Web Part. When connected, the Shared Documents Web Part will consume the date provided by the Calendar Web Part and filter on the *Modified* field.

2. We do not need to support cross-page connections, since both Web Parts exist on the same page.

3. The Web Part runs on the server and supports server-side connections.

4. Since our Web Part is basically providing a filter value to the Shared Documents Web Part, it is appropriate to implement the `IFilterProvider` interface.

```
Imports Microsoft.SharePoint.WebPartPages.Communication
```

Figure 14.53   *VB.NET* IfilterProvider *(step 1).*

```
using Microsoft.SharePoint.WebPartPages.Communication;
```

Figure 14.54   *C#* IFilterProvider *(step 1).*

When implementing the IFilterProvider interface, the following development tasks need to be performed:

1.   Reference the Microsoft.SharePoint.WebPartPages.Communication namespace.

As previously mentioned, the connection interfaces are derived from the Microsoft.SharePoint.WebPartPages.Communication namespace. Consequently, in order to implement these interfaces, your Web Part code must include a reference to this namespace. Figures 14.53 and 14.54 show the necessary code.

2.   Implement the IFilterProvider interface.

The next step is to create a new class that implements IFilterProvider. Since we are using the existing Calendar Web Part from previous examples, all we need to do is implement the IFilterProvider interface for that class. The IFilterProvider interface can be used to set or clear the filter values of a Web Part that implements the IFilterConsumer interface. In our example, we only pass the currently selected date to the *Modified* field of the Shared Documents Web Part; however, you can pass a filter value to all the fields of the consuming Web Part if you wish. Figures 14.55 and 14.56 show the code to implement the IFilterProvider.

```
Public Class ChildControlWP
        Inherits WebPart
        Implements IFilterProvider
```

Figure 14.55   *VB.NET* IFilterProvider *(step 2).*

```
public class ChildControlWP : WebPart, IFilterProvider
```

Figure 14.56   *C#* IFilterProvider *(step 2).*

3.   Declare the `IFilterProvider` events.

Each interface has its own set of events that help fulfill its function. The `IFilterProvider` interface comes equipped with three events: `ClearFilter`, `SetFilter`, and `NoFilter`. The Clear-Filter event notifies the consumer Web Part to clear the current filter. The `SetFilter` event provides the filter expression for the consumer Web Part. The filter expression informs the consumer Web Part which fields and corresponding field values to filter. The filter expression is in the form of a sequence of `FieldName` and `FieldValue` pairs assigned a unique number—for example:

```
FilterField1=FieldName1&FilterValue1=FieldValue1&Filt
erField2=FieldName2&FilterValue2=FieldValue2
```

The `NoFilter` event notifies the consumer that no filter will be provided.

In this step, we are only concerned about declaring the events that we are going to use. The handling of the events happens in step 7, when we override the `PartCommunicationMain` method. Figures 14.57 and 14.58 show the code required to declare the `IFilterProvider` events.

4.   Override the `EnsureInterfaces` method, and call the `RegisterInterface` method.

In order to ensure that all the appropriate interfaces for your Web Part are registered successfully, you need to override the `EnsureInterfaces` method and call the `RegisterInterface` method. The `RegisterInterface` method accepts a number of parameters, which are listed in Table 14.9. In fact, there are actually two implementations of the `RegisterInterface` method that you can override; the difference between the implementations

```
Public Event SetFilter As SetFilterEventHandler Implements IFilterProvider.SetFilter
Public Event ClearFilter As ClearFilterEventHandler Implements IFilterProvider.ClearFilter
Public Event NoFilter As NoFilterEventHandler Implements IFilterProvider.NoFilter
```

Figure 14.57   *VB.NET* `IFilterProvider` *(step 3).*

```
public event SetFilterEventHandler SetFilter;
public event ClearFilterEventHandler ClearFilter;
public event NoFilterEventHandler NoFilter;
```

Figure 14.58   *C#* `IFilterProvider` *(step 3).*

Table 14.9   `RegisterInterface` *Parameters*

Parameter	Type	Description
interfaceName	String	Represents the friendly name for the interface and should be unique within the Web Part.
interfaceType	String	Represents the type of interface that you wish to register, which in this case is the `IfilterProvide`.
maxConnections	Int	Determines how many connections can be made for the interface; it can be set to either `WebPart.LimitOneConnection` (-1) or `WebPart.UnlimitedConnections` (1).
runAtOptions	Connectionrunat	Defines where the interface can run; possible values include: `ConnectionRunAt.Client` `ConnectionRunAt.None` `ConnectionRunAt.Server` `ConnectionRunAt.ServerAndClient`
interfaceObject	Object	Refers to the object that implements the interface; for example, in VB.NET you would most likely set this parameter to Me, and in C# you would set it to `this`.
interfaceClientReference	String	Represents the string that will be used as the identifier for the client-side object that implements the interface. To ensure that the name is unique, you can use the Web Part qualifier token (_WPQ). The Web Part architecture replaces _WPQ_ with a unique value when rendering the Web Part. If the interface does not support client-side connections, then you can pass an empty string instead.
menuLabel	String	Represents the string that appears in the Connections menu when a user connects to your part—for example, "Provide Filter To."
description	String	Further describes the interface (does not appear on the menu).
allowCrossPageConnection	Boolean	Determines whether to expose the connections interface to allow cross-page connections using authoring tools such as FrontPage 2003. You only need this parameter if you want your Web Part to support cross-page connections; otherwise, you can omit the parameter from the `RegisterInterface` call completely.

```
Public Overrides Sub EnsureInterfaces()
    Try
      RegisterInterface("MyFilterProviderInterface_WPQ_", _
              InterfaceTypes.ICellProvider, _
              WebPart.UnlimitedConnections, _
              ConnectionRunAt.Server, _
              Me, _
              "", _
              "Provide Filter To", _
              "Provides a filter to a consumer Web Part.")

    Catch se As SecurityException
          _registrationErrorOccurred = True
    End Try
End Sub
```

Figure 14.59   *VB.NET* IFilterProvider *(step 4).*

is that one contains an additional parameter (allow-CrossPageConnection). If you want your Web Part to be able to connect to Web Parts on other pages, then you will call the RegisterInterface method that accepts the allowCross-PageConnection parameter.

If the Web Part infrastructure cannot register the interface successfully, it will raise an exception. Therefore, when calling the RegisterInterface method, it is a good practice to call it within a try/catch block so that any exceptions that occur are handled appropriately. Figures 14.59 and 14.60 show the code to override the EnsureInterfaces method and call Register-Interface.

```
public override void EnsureInterfaces()
{
    try
    {
        //Registers an interface for the Web Part
        RegisterInterface("MyFilterProviderInterface_WPQ_",
        InterfaceTypes.IFilterProvider,
        WebPart.UnlimitedConnections,
        ConnectionRunAt.Server,
        this,
        "",
        "Provide Filter To",
        "Provides a filter to a consumer Web Part.");
    }
    catch(SecurityException se)
    {
        _registrationErrorOccurred = true;
    }
}
```

Figure 14.60   *C#* IFilterProvider *(step 4).*

```
Public Overrides Function CanRunAt() As ConnectionRunAt
    Return ConnectionRunAt.Server
End Function
```

Figure 14.61   *VB.NET* IFilterProvider *(step 5).*

```
public override ConnectionRunAt CanRunAt()
{
    return ConnectionRunAt.Server;
}
```

Figure 14.62   *C#* IFilterProvider *(step 5).*

5.   Override the CanRunAt method.

The Web Part infrastructure checks the CanRunAt method to determine whether the Web Part can run on the client, the server, or both. You can code your Web Part so that the user's client configuration dictates where the Web Part runs. For example, if the user has the appropriate ActiveX control downloaded, then run the Web Part on the client; otherwise, run it on the server. For the purposes of our example, we choose to run the Web Part on the server. Figures 14.61 and 14.62 show the code to override the CanRunAt method.

6.   Override the PartCommunicationConnect method.

The Web Part infrastructure calls the PartCommunication-Connect method to notify the Web Part that it has been connected and to pass relevant information, such as the title of the connecting Web Part. The PartCommunicationConnect method has several parameters, which are listed in Table 14.10.

Figures 14.63 and 14.64 show the code to override the PartCommunicationConnect method.

7.   Override the PartCommunicationMain method.

The PartCommunicationMain method is where the interface events, such as the SetFilter event, are launched. It is also during this method that the actual data exchange between the connected parts takes place. In our example, we use the PartCommunication method to fire the ClearFilter, SetFilter, and NoFilter events when necessary.

Table 14.10   `PartCommunicationConnect` *Parameters*

Parameter	Type	Description
interfaceName	String	Represents the friendly name of the interface for the Web Part that is being connected
connectedPart	Webpart	Represents the `WebPart` object of the Web Part that is being connected to
connectedInterfaceName	String	Represents the interface name of the Web Part that is being connected to

runAt	ConnectionRunAt	Defines where the interface should run; possible values include:
		
		`ConnectionRunAt.Client`
		`ConnectionRunAt.Server`
		`ConnectionRunAt.ServerAndClient`

```vbnet
Public Overrides Sub PartCommunicationConnect( _
    interfaceName As String, _
    connectedPart As WebPart, _
    connectedInterfaceName As String, _
    runAt As ConnectionRunAt)

    ' Keep track of whether the Web Part is connected.
    If interfaceName = "MyFilterProviderInterface_WPQ_" Then
        _connected = True
        _connectedWebPartTitle = SPEncode.HtmlEncode(connectedPart.Title)
    End If
End Sub
```

Figure 14.63   *VB.NET* `IFilterProvider` *(step 6).*

```csharp
public override void PartCommunicationConnect(
    string interfaceName,
    WebPart connectedPart,
    string connectedInterfaceName,
    ConnectionRunAt runAt)
{
    //Keep track of whether the Web Part is connected
    if (interfaceName == "MyFilterProviderInterface_WPQ_")
    {
        _connected = true;
        _connectedWebPartTitle = SPEncode.HtmlEncode(connectedPart.Title);
    }
}
```

Figure 14.64   *C#* `IFilterProvider` *(step 6).*

As previously mentioned, the `ClearFilter` event notifies the consumer Web Part to clear the current filter. If you want your Web Part to be able to invoke the `ClearFilter` event, you need to provide some mechanism to launch it. In our example, we create a simple **Clear Filter** button for the Web Part. When the button is pressed, the `ClearFilter` event is launched, which subsequently clears the current filter from the connected Shared Documents Web Part. So, before we actually code the `PartCommunicationMain` method, we need to create the Button control and a handler for the button's `click` event. When the user clicks the button, we can tell the Web Part that it has been clicked by setting the `_clearFilterClicked` Boolean property to `true`. Figure 14.65 shows the C# code for the **Clear Filter** button and the code for the button click handler.

The `SetFilter` event provides the filter expression to the connected Web Part. We want to send the currently selected date from our Calendar control to filter the *Modified* field in the Shared Documents Web Part. For document library Web Parts, the *Modified* field is actually named `Last_x0020_Modified`; *Modified* is just the display name. As a result, the filter expression passed to the Shared Documents Web Part should reference `Last_x0020_Modified`. You can find out the name of fields in the default SharePoint lists by examining the `ONET.XML` and `Schema.XML` files. More information on `ONET.XML` and `Schema.XML` can be found later in subsequent chapters. The filter expression sent to the Shared Documents Web Part consists of

```
protected override void CreateChildControls ()
{
    ...
    //Create clear filter button
    _clearFilterButton = new Button();
    _clearFilterButton.Text = "Clear Filter";

    ...
    Controls.Add(_clearFilterButton);

    ...
    //Create a handler for the button
    _clearFilterClicked = false;
    _clearFilterButton.Click += new EventHandler (_myClearFilterButton_click);
}

private void _myClearFilterButton_click(object sender, EventArgs e)
{
    _clearFilterClicked = true;
}
```

Figure 14.65   *C# code to create the **Clear Filter** button.*

```
FilterField1=Last_x0020_Modified&FilterValue1=8/8/2004 12:00:00 AM
```

Figure 14.66   *Filter expression sent to the Shared Documents Web Part.*

one field name and field value pair, where 8/8/2004 12:00:00 A.M. is representative of the date selected from the Calendar Web Part (Figure 14.66).

Figure 14.67 shows the C# code to override the `PartCommunicationMain` method. The first thing we do in the code is check to see if the Web Part is connected; only if it is connected do we need to fire the filter events. If the Web Part is connected, then we check to see if the user has clicked the **Clear Filter** button. When the user clicks the **Clear Filter** button, the property

```
1.   public override void PartCommunicationMain()
2.   {
3.       //Check if connected
4.       if (_connected)
5.       {
6.           //Check if the user has clicked the Clear Filter button
7.           if (_clearFilterClicked == false)
8.           {
9.               if (SetFilter != null)
10.              {
11.                  //Create the SetFilterEventArgs data structure for the SetFilter event
12.                  SetFilterEventArgs setFilterEventArgs = new SetFilterEventArgs();

13.                  //Create filter expression
14.                  string filterExpression = string.Empty;
15.                  for (int index =0; index < _fieldList.Length; index++)
16.                  {
17.                      if (_fieldList[index] == "Last_x0020_Modified")
18.                      {
19.                          filterExpression += FieldLabel + "1=" + _fieldList[index] + "&";
20.                          filterExpression += ValueLabel + "1=" + _mycalendar.SelectedDate;
21.                      }
22.                  }
23.                  setFilterEventArgs.FilterExpression = filterExpression;
24.                  //fire the SetFilter event
25.                  SetFilter(this, setFilterEventArgs);
26.              }
27.              else if (NoFilter !=null)
28.              {
29.                  //fire the NoFilter event
30.                  NoFilter(this, new EventArgs());
31.              }
32.          }
33.          else
34.          {
35.              if (ClearFilter != null)
36.              {
37.                  //fire the ClearFilter event
38.                  ClearFilter(this, new EventArgs());
39.                  _clearFilterClicked = false;
40.              }
41.          }
42.      }
43. }
```

Figure 14.67   *C#* `IFilterProvider` *(step 7).*

_clearFilterClicked is set to true; otherwise, it is false. If the **Clear Filter** button has not been clicked, then we need to handle the other two events: SetFilter and NoFilter. Line 9 checks if there is a consumer Web Part listening for the SetFilter event. Line 12 creates the appropriate data structure to send to the SetFilter event, which includes the FilterExpression property. Lines 14 through 22 construct the filter expression, and line 23 applies this value to the FilterExpression property of the SetFilterEventArgs data structure. Then line 25 fires the event that passes the filter to the listening Web Part. The listening Web Part then applies the filter to its data.

Line 27 handles the NoFilter event, which isn't used in our application since the SetFilter will always be raised first. The code is listed for illustrative purposes. You could easily create another button that fires the NoFilter event. Lines 35 through 40 fire the ClearFilter event when the user clicks the **Clear Filter** button. The effect of this is that the consumer Web Part removes the filter from its Web Part view.

Figure 14.68 shows the same code implemented in VB.NET.

```
Public Overrides Sub PartCommunicationMain()
        ' Check if connected.
    If _connected Then
        ' Check if the Clear Filter button was clicked
        If _clearFilterClicked = False Then
            ' Create the SetFilterEventArgs object for the SetFilter event.
            Dim setFilterEventArgs As New SetFilterEventArgs
            Dim filterExpression As String = String.Empty
            Dim index As Integer
            For index = 0 To _fieldList.Length - 1
                If _fieldList(index) = "Last_x0020_Modified" Then
                    filterExpression += FieldLabel + "1=" + _fieldList(index) + "&"
                    filterExpression += ValueLabel + "1=" + mycalendar.SelectedDate
                End If
            Next index

            ' Set the FilterExpression property on the SetFilterEventArgs object.
            setFilterEventArgs.FilterExpression = filterExpression

            ' Fire the event.
            RaiseEvent SetFilter(Me, setFilterEventArgs)

        ElseIf _clearFilterClicked = True Then
            RaiseEvent ClearFilter(Me, New EventArgs)
            _clearFilterClicked = False
        Else
            RaiseEvent NoFilter(Me, New EventArgs)
        End If
    End If
End Sub
```

Figure 14.68   *VB.NET* IFilterProvider *(step 7).*

```
Public Sub FilterConsumerInit(sender As Object, _
                   filterConsumerInitEventArgs As FilterConsumerInitEventArgs) _
                   Implements IFilterProvider.FilterConsumerInit
    If Not (filterConsumerInitEventArgs.FieldList Is Nothing) Then
        _fieldList = filterConsumerInitEventArgs.FieldList
    Else
        _fieldList = Nothing
    End If
        If Not (filterConsumerInitEventArgs.FieldDisplayList Is Nothing) Then
            _fieldDisplayList = filterConsumerInitEventArgs.FieldDisplayList
        Else
            _fieldDisplayList = Nothing
        End If
End Sub
```

Figure 14.69   *VB.NET* `IFilterProvider` *(step 8).*

8.   Implement the `FilterConsumerInit` method.

The consumer Web Part calls the `FilterConsumerInit` method during its `PartCommunicationInit` phase and passes initialization information to the Web Part, such as the field names available in the Web Part. When the Shared Document Web Part is the consumer Web Part, the fields passed depend on the view selected for the Web Part. For example, the default view for the Shared Documents Web Part results in only two fieldsbeing passed in the `FilterConsumerInit` method: `DocIcon` and `Editor`. Modifying the Shared Documents Web Part and changing its view to All Documents results in four fields being passed during the `FilterConsumerInit` method: `DocIcon`, `Last_x0020_Modified`, `Editor`, and `LinkCheckedOutTitle`. For the purposes of our example, we simply modify the current view of the Shared Documents Web Part to include the Modified column.

Figures 14.69 and 14.70 show the code to implement the `IFilterConsumerInit` method. The code basically populates

```
public void FilterConsumerInit(object sender,
                    FilterConsumerInitEventArgs filterConsumerInitEventArgs)
{
    if(filterConsumerInitEventArgs.FieldList != null)
        _fieldList = filterConsumerInitEventArgs.FieldList;
    else
        _fieldList = null;

    if(filterConsumerInitEventArgs.FieldDisplayList != null)
        _fieldDisplayList = filterConsumerInitEventArgs.FieldDisplayList;
    else
        _fieldDisplayList = null;
}
```

Figure 14.70   *C#* `IFilterProvider` *(step 8).*

Table 14.11   FieldList *and* FieldDisplayList *Values*

FieldList	FieldDisplayList
DocIcon	Type
Last_x0020_Modified	Modified
Editor	Modified By
LinkCheckedOutTitle	Checked Out To

the provider Web Parts FieldList and FieldDisplayList arrays with the values from the consumer Web Part. The Field-List array contains the field names, and the FieldDisplayList array contains the corresponding display names for each field in the FieldList. The display name is the field name that appears in the user interface. Table 14.11 shows the values of the Field-List and FieldDisplayList arrays for the Shared Documents Web Part when the Web Part view is set to All Documents.

To see the results of the Web Part connections code, you need to deploy the Web Part and import it into your site. Once the Web Part is imported

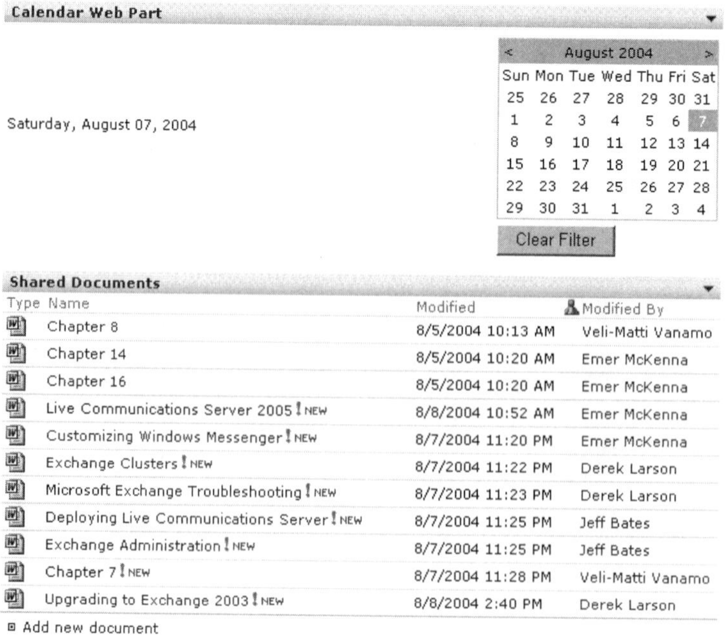

Figure 14.71
Web Parts before connection.

successfully, add the Shared Documents Web Part to the same Web Part Page. Modify the Shared Documents Web Part and add the Modified column to the current view. Finally, connect the Calendar Web Part to the Shared Documents Web Part. Figure 14.71 shows the Web Parts before they are connected.

The following steps outline how to connect the two Web Parts.

1.   Navigate to the shared view of the Web Part Page that hosts your Calendar Web Part and the Shared Documents Web Part.

2.   Click the **Modify Shared Page** link. A shortcut menu appears.

3.   Click **Design this Page** from the shortcut menu.

4.   Click the down arrow on the Calendar Web Part. The Web Part menu appears.

5.   Click **Connections**, then click **Provide Filter To**, and then click **Shared Documents**.

The Calendar Web Part and Shared Documents Web Part are now connected. To verify that the connection is working, click on a date on the calendar. The Shared Documents Web Part only displays documents that have a modified date that matches the currently selected document (Figure 14.72).

Figure 14.72
Connected Web Parts with filter applied.

15

Deploying and Debugging Web Parts

This chapter introduces the concept of Web Parts and shows how easy it is to extend the functionality of your site by building your own custom Web Parts. It also shows the basics of how to deploy a simple Web Part by ensuring that the Web Part is registered as a safe control. This chapter expands upon the topic of deployment and explains the security framework surrounding Web Parts. In addition, we show you how to debug your Web Parts using Visual Studio .NET.

15.1 Code Access Security

Before the introduction of ASP.NET 1.1, developers were accustomed to writing code with role-based security in mind. This provided us with the assumption that resources such as the file system, printers, the registry, and environment variables were accessible to our applications as long as the user had the appropriate permissions. Unfortunately, the world being what it is today, this type of role-based security led to malicious code wreaking havoc within corporations. ASP.NET 1.1 alleviates this problem with the introduction of Code Access Security (CAS). With ASP.NET the Common Language Runtime (CLR) is responsible for executing programs, or assemblies, on the Web server. CAS is basically an integrated security model that grants permissions based on information gathered from the assembly that the CLR is attempting to execute. The information gathered from the assembly is referred to as evidence in CAS terminology and includes such things as where the assembly originates and whether it is a strongly named assembly. The CLR uses this evidence to assign the assembly into a specific code group. Code groups are explained later in this chapter.

Figure 15.1
*Default trust level
for SharePoint.*

```
<system.web>
  ...
  <trust level="WSS_Minimal" originUrl="" />
  ...
</system.web>
```

15.1.1   Trust level

The trust level determines the access granted to an application. There are five ASP.NET trust levels defined by the .NET framework: full, high, medium, low, and minimal. Full trust grants applications unrestricted code-access permissions. By default, Web applications built using the .NET Framework version 1.0 run with full trust. Web applications built using the .NET Framework version 1.1 also run with full trust by default; however, the trust level is configurable. If the trust level for an application is set to anything other than full, then it is referred to as a partial-trust application. SharePoint is an example of such an application, since its trust level, by default, is set to WSS_Minimal. The WSS_Minimal trust level is a custom trust level defined by SharePoint that applies a specific set of permissions using a custom policy file.

Each trust level maps to a specific XML policy file, which lists the set of permissions and code groups defined for a specific trust level.

The default policy files are located in %windir%\Microsoft.NET\ Framework\<version>\CONFIG directory.

SharePoint-specific policy files are located in the <local drive>\Program Files\Common Files\Microsoft Shared\web server extensions\60\CONFIG directory.

The <trust> element of the machine.config or the web.config files controls whether CAS is enabled for a Web application. Figure 15.1 shows

Table 15.1   <trust> *Element Attributes*

Attribute	Description
Level	Specifies which security level is selected from among the security levels listed in the <trustLevel> elements.
originUrl	Used in medium-trust settings where code on the server needs to make Web Service calls to another server. The originUrl attribute provides the value for the $OriginHost$ substitution parameter in the WebPermission class.

```
<system.web>
    ...
    <securityPolicy>
        <trustLevel name="WSS_Medium" policyFile="C:\Program Files\Common Files\Microsoft Shared\Web Server
Extensions\60\config\wss_mediumtrust.config" />
        <trustLevel name="WSS_Minimal" policyFile="C:\Program Files\Common Files\Microsoft Shared\Web Server
Extensions\60\config\wss_minimaltrust.config" />
    </securityPolicy>
    ...
    <trust level="WSS_Minimal" originUrl="" />
    ...
</system.web>
```

Figure 15.2   *Trust-level mapping to policy files.*

the `<trust>` element of the `web.config` file on a SharePoint server. The `web.config` file is located in the SharePoint virtual server's `Inetpub\wwwroot` directory.

Table 15.1 describes the attributes associated with the `<trust>` element.

Trust levels are mapped to policy files using the `<trustLevel>` element in the `machine.config` or `web.config` configuration files. The `<trustLevel>` element is defined as part of the `<securityPolicy>` element, which is located above the `<trust>` element in the configuration file. Figure 15.2 shows the `<trustLevel>` element setting in the `web.config` file.

Table 15.2 describes the attributes associated with the `<trust>` element.

15.1.2   Policy files

CAS policy is hierarchical and can be administered at multiple levels. By default, a security policy can be created for the enterprise, machine, user, and application domain levels. The user security policy is specific to an individual user on a specific machine, the machine security policy applies to all users on a specific machine, and the enterprise security policy applies to

Table 15.2   `<trustLevel>` *Element Attributes*

Attribute	Description
name	Specifies a named security level that is mapped to a policy file. The default setting for SharePoint is WSS_Minimal.
policyFile	Specifies the policy file that contains security policy settings for the named security level. In SharePoint, these files are stored in C:\Program Files\Common Files\Microsoft Shared\web server extensions\60\CONFIG.

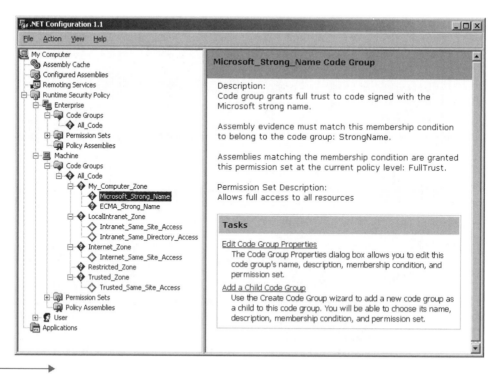

Figure 15.3   *Microsoft .NET Framework Configuration Tool.*

all machines in an Active Directory deployment. ASP.NET CAS is an example of an application domain–level policy. The settings associated with a specific policy are stored in an XML-based file. The settings associated with enterprise, machine, and user policy files can be viewed and modified using the Microsoft .NET Framework Configuration Tool (Figure 15.3). This tool loads information from and updates information to the appropriate configuration file.

Unfortunately, ASP.NET policy files cannot be viewed or modified using the configuration tool; instead, the settings must be manipulated manually using an XML or text editor. The actual policy is evaluated from the enterprise level down to the ASP.NET application level, and consequently permissions may only be revoked at this level. In order to add permissions at the ASP.NET level, they must first be granted at a higher level. The benefit of this approach is that the enterprise administrator ultimately controls the permissions hierarchy.

The security policy files define the code groups and their associated permission sets. Figure 15.4 shows the basic structure and elements that comprise a policy file.

Figure 15.4
Policy file structure.

```
<configuration>
    <mscorlib>
        <security>
            <policy>
                <PolicyLevel version="1">
                    <SecurityClasses>
                        <SecurityClass..../>
                        <SecurityClass..../>
                        ...
                    </SecurityClasses>
                    <NamedPermissionSets>
                        <PermissionSet ...>
                            ...
                            <IPermission
                                ...
                            />
                            <IPermission
                                ...
                            />
                            <IPermission
                                ...
                            />
                        </PermissionSet>
                        <PermissionSet .../>
                    </NamedPermissionSets>
                    <CodeGroup...>
                        ...
                        <CodeGroup...>
                        ...
                        </CodeGroup>
                    </CodeGroup>
                </PolicyLevel>
            </policy>
        </security>
    </mscorlib>
</configuration>
```

The main elements in the policy file can be grouped into three base elements: the `<SecurityClasses>` element, the `<NamedPermissionSets>` element, and the `<CodeGroup>` element.

Security Classes

The `<SecurityClasses>` element defines the individual `<SecurityClass>` elements required to handle specific security permissions. The `<SecurityClass>` element is to CAS what setting an assembly reference and a using statement is to a C# program. Essentially, the `<SecurityClass>` element defines the connection to an assembly that handles security permissions. Figure 15.5 shows the SharePoint-specific `<SecurityClass>` elements as defined in the `WSS_Medium` policy file. The attributes in the `<SecurityClass>` element specify the assembly, version, culture, and public key token.

The `SharePointPermission` security class provides access to the Share-Point object model, and the `WebPartPermission` security class provides the ability to create Web Part connections. The `WSS_Minimal` policy file does not include the `SharePointPermission` security class, which means

```
<SecurityClasses>
    ...
    <SecurityClass
        Name="SharePointPermission"
        Description="Microsoft.SharePoint.Security.SharePointPermission,
        Microsoft.SharePoint.Security, Version=11.0.0.0, Culture=neutral, PublicKeyToken=71e9bce111e9429c"
    />
    <SecurityClass
        Name="WebPartPermission"
        Description="Microsoft.SharePoint.Security.WebPartPermission,
        Microsoft.SharePoint.Security, Version=11.0.0.0, Culture=neutral, PublicKeyToken=71e9bce111e9429c"
    />
    ...
</SecurityClasses>
```

Figure 15.5   *SharePoint-specific* `<SecurityClass>` *elements.*

that Web Parts running under `WSS_Minimal` cannot access the SharePoint object model.

Named Permission Sets

The `<NamedPermissionSets>` element contains all of the detailed security policies that can be applied to a server. The `<NamedPermissionSets>` element may host a number of `<PermissionSet>` elements. For example, a typical ASP.NET policy file will have three `<PermissionSet>` elements nested within the `<NamedPermissionSet>` element: `FullTrust`, `Nothing`, and `ASP.NET`. The `ASP.NET` named permission set lists the permissions that are configured for the application at the current trust level. Figure 15.6 shows the `ASP.NET` named permission set as defined in the `WSS_Minimal`

```
<NamedPermissionSets>
    ...
    <PermissionSet
        class="NamedPermissionSet"
        version="1"
        Name="ASP.Net">
        <IPermission
            class="AspNetHostingPermission"
            version="1"
            Level="Minimal"
        />
        <IPermission
            class="SecurityPermission"
            version="1"
            Flags="Execution"
        />
        <IPermission
            class="WebPartPermission"
            version="1"
            Connections="True"
        />
    </PermissionSet>
    ...
</NamedPermissionSets>
```

Figure 15.6   *ASP.NET named permission set.*

Table 15.3   WSS_Minimal *Permissions*

Permission	**WSS_Minimal** Setting
AspNetHostingPermission	Minimal
SecurityPermission	Flags="Execution"
WebPartPermission	Connections="True"

policy file. Each <PermissionSet> element may host a number of <IPermission> elements, which define the permission at its most basic level. For example, an <IPermission> element can declare whether access to the SharePoint object model or SQL client connections is permitted. All permissions implement the class and version attributes. The class attribute references the class and assembly that implement the custom permission. In addition, developers can define other attributes or child elements. For example, the WebPartPermission class has a custom attribute named Connections associated with it that informs SharePoint whether to allow Web Part connections. This attribute can be set to True or False.

The policy files defined by SharePoint are based on the default policy files defined by ASP.NET. Consequently, they address many of the same permissions and add the two previously mentioned SharePoint-specific permissions: SharePointPermission and WebPartPermission. Tables 15.3 and 15.4 show the permission settings for the WSS_Minimal and WSS_Medium trust levels, respectively.

Table 15.4   WSS_Medium *Permissions*

Permission	**WSS_Medium** Setting
AspNetHostingPermission	Medium
DnsPermission	Unrestricted=True
EnvironmentPermission	Read="TEMP;TMP;USERNAME;OS;COMPUTERNAME"
FileIOPermission	Read="$AppDir$" Write="$AppDir$" Append="$AppDir$" PathDiscovery="$AppDir$"
IsolatedStorageFilePermission	Allowed="AssemblyIsolationByUser" UserQuota="9223372036854775807"
PrintingPermission	Level="DefaultPrinting"

Table 15.4   `WSS_Medium` *Permissions (continued)*

Permission	`WSS_Medium` Setting
`SecurityPermission`	`Flags="Assertion, Execution, ControlThread, ControlPrincipal, RemotingConfiguration"`
`SharePointPermission`	`ObjectModel="True"`
`SqlClientPermission`	`Unrestricted="true"`
`WebPartPermission`	`Connections="True"`

`WebPermission`	`<ConnectAccess>`
	`<URI uri="$OriginHost$"/>`
	`</ConnectAccess>`

Notice that the `FileIOPermission` and `WebPermission` defined for the `WSS_Medium` policy contain substitution parameters (`$AppDir$`, `$OriginHost$`). These parameters allow you to configure permissions to the assemblies that make up your Web application but reside in different locations. Each substitution parameter is replaced with an actual value the first time your Web application assembly is loaded. The `$AppDir$` parameter represents the root application directory for a given application. The `$OriginHost$` parameter is replaced by the `OriginUrl` attribute defined in the `<trust>` element of the `web.config` file.

SharePoint Permission Attributes

The `SharePointPermission` and `WebPartPermission` classes have additional attributes that control access to SharePoint resources. These attributes are detailed in Table 15.5.

Code Groups

Each policy level has a code group tree. This tree consists of a root code group that may have child code groups, which in turn may have their own child code groups. The `<CodeGroup>` element maps an assembly referenced by a `<SecurityClass>` element to a named permission set. This mapping is done using the `PermissionSetName` attribute when defining the code group. Figure 15.7 shows the code groups defined for the `WSS_Minimal` policy. As previously mentioned, the CLR uses the evidence gathered from an assembly to assign it to the appropriate code groups. The code groups in turn reference the named permission sets, which detail the permission settings for the assembly. A code group is assigned a specific membership condition that defines the criteria an assembly must meet in order to be

Table 15.5   *SharePoint Permission Attributes*

Permission Class	Attribute	Description
SharePointPermission	ObjectModel	Set to True to access the SharePoint object model
SharePointPermission	UnsafeSaveOnGet	Set to True to save data on HTTP-GET requests
SharePointPermission	Unrestricted	Set to True to enable all rights associated with this permission
WebPartPermission	Connections	Set to True to participate in Web Part–to–Web Part communications
WebPartPermission	Unrestricted	Set to True to enable all rights associated with this permission

assigned to that code group. Table 15.6 lists the IMembershipCondition classes used by SharePoint.

There are basically two types of code groups: FirstMatchCodeGroup and UnionCodeGroup. The FirstMatchCodeGroup only applies when the assembly's evidence matches the code group's membership condition. If a match is found, the membership condition of each child code group is

```
<CodeGroup class="FirstMatchCodeGroup" version="1" PermissionSetName="Nothing">
   <IMembershipCondition class="AllMembershipCondition" version="1" />
   <CodeGroup class="UnionCodeGroup" version="1" PermissionSetName="ASP.Net">
      <IMembershipCondition class="UrlMembershipCondition" version="1" Url="$AppDirUrl$/*" />
   </CodeGroup>
   <CodeGroup class="UnionCodeGroup" version="1" PermissionSetName="FullTrust">
      <IMembershipCondition class="UrlMembershipCondition" version="1" Url="$CodeGen$/*" />
   </CodeGroup>
   <CodeGroup class="UnionCodeGroup" version="1" PermissionSetName="FullTrust">
      <IMembershipCondition class="UrlMembershipCondition" Url="$Gac$/*" version="1" />
   </CodeGroup>
   <CodeGroup class="UnionCodeGroup" version="1" PermissionSetName="Nothing">
      <IMembershipCondition class="ZoneMembershipCondition" version="1" Zone="MyComputer" />
      <CodeGroup class="UnionCodeGroup" version="1" PermissionSetName="FullTrust"
         Name="Microsoft_Strong_Name"
         Description="This code group grants code signed with the Microsoft strong name full trust. ">
         <IMembershipCondition class="StrongNameMembershipCondition" version="1"
            PublicKeyBlob="00240000048000...."
         />
      </CodeGroup>
      <CodeGroup class="UnionCodeGroup" version="1" PermissionSetName="FullTrust"
         Name="Ecma_Strong_Name"
         Description="This code group grants code signed with the ECMA strong name full trust. ">
         <IMembershipCondition class="StrongNameMembershipCondition" version="1"
            PublicKeyBlob="00000000000000000400000000000000"
         />
      </CodeGroup>
   </CodeGroup>
</CodeGroup>
```

Figure 15.7   WSS_Minimal *policy code groups.*

Table 15.6 `IMembershipCondition` *Classes*

`IMembershipCondition` Class	Description
`AllMembershipCondition`	Represents a membership condition that matches all code
`StrongNameMembershipCondition`	Determines whether an assembly belongs to a code group by testing its strong name
`UrlMembershipCondition`	Determines whether an assembly belongs to a code group by testing its URL
`ZoneMembershipCondition`	Determines whether an assembly belongs to a code group by testing its zone of origin

tested until the first match occurs. So, the result of the `FirstMatchCode-Group` is ultimately the union of the policy statement of the root code group and the policy statement of the first child code group matched. The `UnionCodeGroup` is the most common type of code group, and if you examine the `WSS_minimal` policy file, you will see that there are six code groups of this type. The `UnionCodeGroup` is a child code group of the root code group. If a match is made on the membership condition of a `Union-CodeGroup`, then the policy statement of the parent root code group combines with the policy statement of the matching child code group, including any matches that are made with its child code groups.

15.2 CAS implementation

Out of the box, SharePoint implements a trust level of `WSS_Minimal` for all sites. Any Web Parts that are deployed to the `\inetpub\wwwroot\bin` directory are affected by the trust level set in the `web.config` file. As a result, any Web Parts deployed to this directory operate with significant limitations. For example, they do not have access to the SharePoint object model. If your Web Part attempts to access an unauthorized resource, the CLR will throw an exception error; therefore, it is best practice when developing Web Parts to ensure that adequate error handling is applied when accessing resources.

What happens if you want certain Web Parts to be able to access resources that require a higher trust level? Basically, you have three options:

1. Raise the trust level for all SharePoint sites.

2. Deploy your Web Parts to the GAC.

3. Create your own custom policy.

Figure 15.8
*Raising the trust
level to*
WSS_Medium.

```
<system.web>
  ...
  <trust level="WSS_Medium" originUrl="" />
  ...
</system.web>
```

15.2.1 Raising the trust level for all SharePoint sites

You can raise the trust level for all SharePoint sites by simply editing the
<trust> element in the web.config file to apply the WSS_Medium trust
level. Raising the trust level in this manner is appropriate and very convenient for development environments but is not recommended for production. Access to resources in your production environment should be limited
to only those Web Parts and applications that require access. The WSS_
Medium trust level applies the appropriate permissions for debugging Web
Parts, which is very useful when developing and testing your Web Parts.
That said, when your Web Part is ready for deployment, you will want to
test it against the same trust-level settings that will apply in production to
ensure that your Web Part will run.

To raise the trust level from WSS_Minimal to WSS_Medium, edit the
web.config file, search for the <system.web> section, and modify the
code in the <trust> element (see Figure 15.8). Once you have raised the
trust level, reset IIS to have the changes take effect.

15.2.2 Deploying Web Parts to the GAC

The GAC is a place that houses assemblies and grants them full-level trust.
The GAC resides in the \windows\assembly directory on the server, and
any assemblies that are placed in this directory are available to all virtual
servers and applications running WSS. As you can see, this is not a viable
option for a production environment, since assemblies may have higher
access to resources than necessary. Assemblies that are in the GAC are not
affected by the trust level of the assemblies installed in the \inetpub\
wwwroot\bin directory.

To deploy your Web Part assembly to the GAC, you can copy the assembly file from the location where it was compiled and drop it into the \
%windir%\assembly directory. Each time you recompile your assembly,
you will need to reset IIS. Another method of deploying an assembly to the
GAC is to use the gacutil.exe command-line tool. The tool can be
found in the %windir%\Microsoft.NET\Framework\<version> directory. The syntax required is Gacutil.exe /i myassembly.dll.

Finally, yet another method for deploying an assembly into the GAC is to use the `stsadm.exe` tool with the `-globalinstall` switch. The `stsadm.exe` tool is discussed further in the section 15.3.

15.2.3   Create a custom policy file

The recommended and most secure method for raising the level of trust for your assembly is to create your own custom policy file. Creating a custom policy file will ensure that your Web Part can run on the destination server. For example, if you have a Web Part that requires access to the SharePoint object model but want to keep the trust level set to the minimum for all other Web Parts, you could create a custom policy file that assigns the `SharePointPermission` with the `ObjectModel` attribute set to `True` to those Web Parts that match the `StrongNameMembershipCondition`.

Figure 15.9 shows the rendering of a simple Web Part that accesses the object model to display the name of the current site. If the Web Part cannot display the site name, it displays the error raised by the CLR. Since the trust level for the server is set to `WSS_Minimal`, the CLR complains that it does not have the necessary permissions to access the SharePoint object model.

The following steps show how to create a custom policy file that raises the trust level of the `WSS_Minimal` policy to provide additional access for an assembly to the SharePoint object model.

1.   Navigate to the directory that contains the SharePoint policy files:
      `<local drive>\Program Files\Common Files\Microsoft Shared\web server extensions\60\CONFIG`.

2.   Copy the `wss_minimaltrust.config` file.

3.   Rename the new file—for example, `wss_mysecurity.config`.

4.   Edit the new file with an editor such as Notepad.

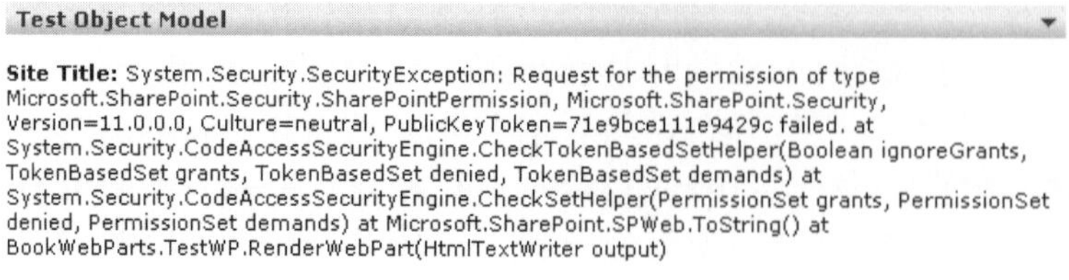

Test Object Model   ▼

Site Title: System.Security.SecurityException: Request for the permission of type
Microsoft.SharePoint.Security.SharePointPermission, Microsoft.SharePoint.Security,
Version=11.0.0.0, Culture=neutral, PublicKeyToken=71e9bce111e9429c failed. at
System.Security.CodeAccessSecurityEngine.CheckTokenBasedSetHelper(Boolean ignoreGrants,
TokenBasedSet grants, TokenBasedSet denied, TokenBasedSet demands) at
System.Security.CodeAccessSecurityEngine.CheckSetHelper(PermissionSet grants, PermissionSet
denied, PermissionSet demands) at Microsoft.SharePoint.SPWeb.ToString() at
BookWebParts.TestWP.RenderWebPart(HtmlTextWriter output)

Figure 15.9   *Web Part before custom policy is applied.*

```
<SecurityClasses>
    ...
    <SecurityClass Name="SharePointPermission"
                   Description="Microsoft.SharePoint.Security.SharePointPermission,
                   Microsoft.SharePoint.Security,
                   Version=11.0.0.0,
                   Culture=neutral,
                   PublicKeyToken=71e9bce111e9429c"
    />
    ...
</SecurityClasses>
```

Figure 15.10   `SharePointPermission` *class reference.*

5.   Locate the `<SecurityClasses>` element and add a reference to the `SharePointPermission` class (Figure 15.10).

6.   Locate the `<NamedPermissionSets>` element and create a new permission set that grants all the rights you want to define for the new policy, including permission to access the SharePoint object model. The simplest way to achieve this is to make a copy of the ASP.NET permission set and paste the copy directly below. Then rename the `<PermissionSet>` element to your new filename—for example, `wss_mysecurity`. Finally, add the `SharePointPermission` as an `<IPermission>` node of the new permission set. The newly created permission set should resemble that shown in Figure 15.11.

```
...
<PermissionSet
    class="NamedPermissionSet"
    version="1"
    Name="wss_mysecurity">
    <IPermission
        class="AspNetHostingPermission"
        version="1"
        Level="Minimal"
    />
    <IPermission
        class="SecurityPermission"
        version="1"
        Flags="Execution"
    />
    <IPermission class="WebPartPermission"
        version="1"
        Connections="True"
    />
    <IPermission class="SharePointPermission"
        version="1"
        ObjectModel="True"
    />
</PermissionSet>
...
```

Figure 15.11   *New permission set.*

```
<CodeGroup
    class="FirstMatchCodeGroup"
    version="1"
    PermissionSetName="Nothing">
    <IMembershipCondition
        class="AllMembershipCondition"
        version="1"
    />
    <CodeGroup
        class="UnionCodeGroup"
        version="1"
        PermissionSetName="wss_mysecurity">
        <IMembershipCondition
            class="StrongNameMembershipCondition"
            version="1"
            PublicKeyBlob="0x00240000048000009400000006020000002400000
                           52534131000400000100010053E1AEDB865E404F1EE36654868142
                           5A6E1E646CDB667CF8D513A99A94BF6A1BE8C9F287CAECECEE0927A190
                           4BB29B7DD422C419695E12BE268DC12ED18181D71090395
                           A63E27C140D82839464ECAC625C8D3C302D3791B058AAF06DEFBB7BD1B9
                           CF24EDEEB52B2DFF6607F3B3B5C2DA7231253AF20A2D5516E8098F0C14FAC2"
            Name="BookWebParts"
        />
    </CodeGroup>
    ...
    <!-- the ASP.NET code group follows -->
    ..
</CodeGroup>
```

Figure 15.12   *New code group mapping to new permission set.*

7.   Create a code group to notify the CLR when it should apply the new permission set. Remember, the root code group is a `First-MatchCodeGroup` type, and, as such, the CLR will not assign permissions after the first match to that code group. The permissions include all child code groups of the `AllCode` code group. Therefore, in order for the CLR to apply our new permissions, we must create the new code group as the *first* child code group of the root code group. The child code group must be a `UnionCodeGroup` type. To match the code group to our assembly, we can base it on the strong name membership (Figure 15.12).

8.   To ensure that a match is made against your Web Part, use a `StrongNameMembershipCondition` and set the `PublicKeyBlob`

```
<securityPolicy>
    ...
    <trustLevel
      name="WSS_MySecurity"
      policyFile="C:\Program Files\Common Files\Microsoft Shared\Web Server Extensions\60\config\wss_mysecurity.config"
    />
</securityPolicy>
```

Figure 15.13   *New trust level.*

```
<trust level="WSS_MySecurity" originUrl="" />
```

Figure 15.14   *New trust level applied.*

attribute equal to the public-key blob for your assembly. You can retrieve this key using the `secutil.exe` tool, which can be found in the `\Bin` directory of the .NET Framework SDK. The syntax required is `Secutil.exe -hex -s myassembly.dll`.

9.   Save and close the policy file.

10.   Navigate to the `\inetpub\wwwroot` directory.

11.   Edit the `web.config` file with an editor such as Notepad. It is recommended that you make a backup copy of the `web.config` file before you make any changes.

12.   Locate the `<SecurityPolicy>` element, and add a new trust level that maps to your new policy file (Figure 15.13).

13.   Modify the `<trust>` element to reference the new trust level (Figure 15.14).

14.   Save and close the `web.config` file.

15.   Reset IIS. You can reset IIS using the `iisreset` command from the command prompt or using the IIS Manager snap-in.

Figure 15.15 shows how the Web Part appears with the new custom policy applied. Notice that the CLR no longer raises an exception; instead, the SharePoint object model is accessed successfully and displays the title of the current site.

15.3   Deploying Web Parts

Now that we have an understanding of the security aspects surrounding SharePoint, let's revisit the steps required to deploy a Web Part. In Chapter 14, we stepped through the process of creating and deploying a simple Web

Test Object Model   ▼

Site Title: Development Site

Figure 15.15   *Web Part with custom policy applied.*

Part. No matter how complex the Web Part code is, the basic deployment requirements are the same:

1. Compile the Web Part assembly to the `\inetpub\wwwroot\bin` directory or to the GAC.

2. Register the Web Part as a safe control.

3. Import the Web Part into a Web Part Page.

Registering a Web Part as a safe control requires information about the Web Part assembly, such as its name, version, culture, public key, namespace, and the type name. The assembly name maps to the name defined in the code, the version maps to the version number assigned in the `AssemblyInfo` file when building the assembly, the namespace maps to the namespace defined in the code, and the type name maps to the Web Part class that you want to make safe. If you want to make all the classes in a specific assembly safe, set this attribute to "`*`". In order for a Web Part to run in a SharePoint site, it needs to have a strong name, which informs Share-Point that the Web Part can be trusted. A strong name consists of the assembly's identity, a public key, and a digital signature and can be assigned to a Web Part assembly using the strong name tool (`sn.exe`). The public key generated by the strong name tool is specified when registering a Web Part as a safe control. See Chapter 14 for steps on how to strongly name an assembly and to extract the public key from an assembly to use when registering the control as safe. The strong name tool generates the public-key blob required when using the `StrongNameMembershipCondition` to match an assembly with a code group.

To register a Web Part as a safe control, simply edit the `web.config` file and add a `<SafeControl>` element to the `<SafeControls>` section. Figure 15.16 shows an example of the `<SafeControl>` entry for a Web Part.

Once a Web Part has been compiled in the `\inetpub\wwwroot\bin` directory or the GAC, and it has been registered as a safe control, it is ready to be imported into a SharePoint site. Once again, the steps required to import a Web Part into a SharePoint site are detailed in Chapter 14.

```
<SafeControl
    Assembly="BookWebParts, Version=1.0.0.1, Culture=neutral, PublicKeyToken=0b6be9364fd482d7"
    Namespace="MyNameSpace"
    TypeName="TestWP"
    Safe="True"
/>
```

Figure 15.16   *Register the TestWP Web Part as a safe control.*

15.3.1   Packaging Web Parts

When deploying Web Parts to a production environment, you can package all the necessary files that make up the Web Part into a deployable unit, such as a cabinet (.cab) file. A Web Part Package typically contains a manifest.xml file, one or more Web Part assemblies, any class resource files, and Web Part definition (.dwp) files for each Web Part assembly. The manifest.xml file is a mandatory configuration file that describes the structure and contents of the cabinet file. One of the many functions of the stsadm.exe tool that ships with SharePoint is the ability to deploy the content of the cabinet file (excluding the manifest.xml) to a SharePoint site. The manifest.xml consists of several nodes and subnodes, listed in Table 15.7. Stsadm.exe uses the contents of the manifest.xml to determine which assemblies to deploy along with their class resources. It also retrieves the SafeControl entries that need to be added to the web.config file to register the Web Part(s) as safe, as well as imports the Web Part definition file into the appropriate location in SharePoint.

If you create your Web Parts using the Microsoft Visual Studio .NET Web Part templates, then the manifest.xml file is automatically generated for you. Care must be taken, however, to ensure that the Assembly, Namespace, and TypeName references map those used in the code. Figure

Table 15.7   Manifest.xml *Nodes*

Node	Description
WebPartManifest	Defines the schema and is the parent node of all subnodes
Assemblies	Contains the definitions for each assembly being deployed
Assembly	Defines an individual assembly, including class resources and the definition to be used in the SafeControls list
ClassResources	Contains the definitions for each class resource for the parent assembly
ClassResource	Defines an individual class resource
SafeControls	Contains the definitions for each line of the SafeControls list for the parent assembly
SafeControl	Defines each line of the SafeControls list, which will ultimately be populated into the web.config file on deployment
DwpFiles	Contains definitions of each Web Part definition file being deployed
DwpFile	Defines an individual Web Part definition file

```
<?xml version="1.0"?>
<!-- You need only one manifest per CAB project for Web Part Deployment.-->
<!-- This manifest file can have multiple assembly nodes.-->
<WebPartManifest xmlns="http://schemas.microsoft.com/WebPart/v2/Manifest">
  <Assemblies>
    <Assembly FileName="MyAssembly.dll">
            <!-- Use the <ClassResource> tag to specify resources like image files
                 or JScript files that your Web Parts use. -->
      <!-- Note that you must use relative paths when specifying resource files. -->
      <!--
      <ClassResources>
        <ClassResource FileName="Resource.jpg"/>
      </ClassResources>
      -->
      <SafeControls>
        <SafeControl Namespace="MyNamespace" TypeName="*"/>
      </SafeControls>
    </Assembly>
  </Assemblies>
  <DwpFiles>
    <DwpFile FileName="WebPart1.dwp"/>
    <DwpFile FileName="WebPart2.dwp"/>
  </DwpFiles>
</WebPartManifest>
```

Figure 15.17   Manifest.xml *file.*

15.17 shows a simple manifest file for a package that deploys a single assembly containing two Web Parts. Even though this manifest file does not include any class resources, a placeholder comment shows where the class resources would be defined.

15.3.2   Creating a cabinet file

There are two basic methods available for creating a cabinet file: using Microsoft Visual Studio .NET or using a command-line tool called Make-CAB.exe. MakeCAB.exe ships with Windows 2000 or later and can be found in the %windir%\system32 directory. If your .cab file requires internal directories, for example, if you want a separate image directory for all image resources associated with your Web Part, then you must use the MakeCAB.exe tool, since Microsoft Visual Studio .NET does not support creating cabinet files with internal directories. Otherwise, the decision to use one method over the other really depends upon personal preference.

Using Visual Studio .NET

1.   Open Visual Studio .NET and click **New** from the File menu.

2.   Select **Setup and Deployment Projects** from the Project Types pane.

3.   Click **Cab Project** from the Templates pane.

4. Type the name of your cabinet file and the location where you want the cabinet file created.

5. Click **OK**.

6. From the Solution Explorer, right-click on the new solution.

7. Click **Add**, and then click **Existing Project**.

8. Select the Web Part project that you want to deploy, and click **Open**.

9. From the Solution Explorer, right-click on the cabinet project.

10. Click **Add**, and then click **Project Output**.

11. From the drop-down list, select the Web Part project that you added in step 8.

12. Select the file categories you want from the list, making sure that you select **Primary output** and **Content files**.

13. Click **OK**.

14. Save and build the solution to create the cabinet file.

The cabinet file is now ready for deployment.

Using MakeCAB.exe

1. Create a diamond directive file (.ddf) to be used with make-cab.exe and save it with the .ddf extension. The .ddf file contains information required to compress your files into a cabinet file; the .ddf file itself is not placed in the .cab file. Figure 15.18 shows a sample directive file.

2. Copy all the files that you want to include in your .cab file to the same folder that hosts the .ddf file. The files should match the

Figure 15.18

Sample .ddf *file.*

```
;*** MakeCAB Directive file example
;
.OPTION EXPLICIT                          ; Generate errors on variable typos

.Set CabinetNameTemplate=MyCab.cab  ; Name of cabinet file
.set DiskDirectoryTemplate=CDROM          ; All cabinets go in a single directory
.Set CompressionType=MSZIP                ; All files are compressed
.Set UniqueFiles="OFF"
.Set Cabinet=on
.Set Compress=on
.Set DiskDirectory1=MyCabFolder
manifest.xml
WebPart1.dwp
WebPart2.dwp
MyAssembly.dll
;*** <the end>
```

Figure 15.19
`Makecab.exe`
command.

```
makecab.exe /f myddf.ddf
```

files listed at the end of your `.ddf` file. In our example, these include `manifest.xml`, `WebPart1.dwp`, `WebPart2.dwp`, and `MyAssembly.dll`.

3.   From the command prompt, navigate to the directory that hosts your files, including the `.ddf` file, and then enter the command shown in Figure 15.19.

Based on the directive file shown in our example, the `makecab.exe` command creates a folder called `MyCabFolder`, which houses the new cabinet file `MyCab.cab`. This Web Part Package is now ready for deployment.

15.3.3 Deploying a Web Part Package

As previously mentioned, the `stsadm.exe` tool is used to deploy Web Part Packages to SharePoint. The `stsadm.exe` is a command-line tool that can be used to administer a server running WSS and can be found in

Table 15.8   `AddWPPack` *Switches*

Switch	Description
`-url`	Specifies the URL of the virtual server where the Web Part Package is to be installed. If this switch is not specified, then the package is installed on all SharePoint-enabled virtual servers on the current server.
`-name`	Installs a Web Part Package to a virtual server from the configuration database. The first time a Web Part Package is installed on a server, `stsadm.exe` makes a copy of the `.cab` file and stores it in the configuration database. This is very convenient in a server farm deployment, because once the administrator installs the Web Part Package on the front-end server, the `.cab` file is available for installation on subsequent Web servers without requiring a local copy of the `.cab` file.
`-globalinstall`	Installs the Web Part Package to the GAC. `Stsadm.exe` only installs strongly named assemblies to the GAC; all other assemblies are installed into the `/bin` directory of the virtual server.
`-force`	Forces `stsadm.exe` to overwrite an existing, installed Web Part Package.
`-filename`	Defines the path to the `.cab` file for `stsadm.exe` to use.

Figure 15.20
*Installing a Web
Part Package.*

```
stsadm.exe -o addwppack -filename "c:\My App\mycab.cab"
```

the `C:\Program Files\Common Files\Microsoft Shared\web server extensions\60\BIN` directory. There are three options specific to Web Part Package deployment: `AddWPPack`, `DeleteWPPack`, and `EnumAP-Packs`. Each option has a number of associated switches. To list the required parameters for each option, enter the following command: `stsadm.exe -help` *option*.

Installing a Web Part Package

The `AddWPPack` option adds a Web Part Package to a specified location, such as a specific virtual server or the GAC. Table 15.8 shows the switches available with this option.

Figure 15.20 shows an example of the command used to install a Web Part Package to all the SharePoint-enabled virtual servers on a server.

Once this command has completed successfully, the Web Parts defined in the `manifest.xml` file are available in the Virtual Server Gallery (Figure 15.21). We discuss Web Part Galleries later in this chapter. In addition, if you examine the `web.config` file, you will see that a new entry has been made in the `SafeControls` section of the file, registering the assembly as a safe control. Once the Web Parts are registered as safe, they can be successfully added to a Web Part Page.

Figure 15.21
*Web Parts added to
Virtual Server
Gallery.*

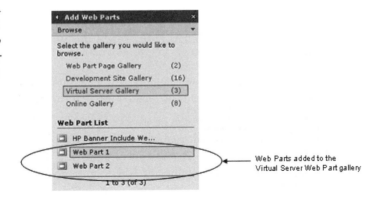

Table 15.9   `DeleteWPPack` *Switches*

Switch	Description
-name	The name of the Web Part Package to remove.
-url	Specifies the URL of the virtual server from which the Web Part Package is to be removed. If this switch is not specified, then the package is removed from all SharePoint-enabled virtual servers on the current server.

```
stsadm.exe -o deletewppack -name "mycab.cab"
```

Figure 15.22   *Removing a Web Part Package.*

Deleting a Web Part Package

The `DeleteWPPack` option removes a Web Part Package from a specific virtual server. Table 15.9 shows the switches available with this option.

Figure 15.22 shows an example of the command used to remove a Web Part Package from all SharePoint-enabled virtual servers on a server.

Once this command has completed successfully, the Web Parts are no longer available on the Virtual Server Gallery. In addition, the `SafeControl` entry is removed from the `web.config` file. The same command also removes Web Part Packages installed to the GAC.

Enumerating Web Part Packages

The `EnumWPPacks` option lists all the Web Part Packages installed on a specific virtual server. Table 15.10 shows the switches available with this option.

Figure 15.23 shows an example of the command used to list all the Web Part Packages installed on the SharePoint-enabled virtual servers on a server.

If you'd rather not use `stsadm.exe` from the command prompt, there is a basic Windows-based user interface to the tool (Figure 15.24) available from the Microsoft site. At the time of writing, it can be found in the SharePoint Products and Technologies Web Component Directory.

Table 15.10   EnumWPPack *Switches*

Switch	Description
-name	The name of the Web Part Package to check for installation. If you do not use this switch, the command lists all the Web Part Packages installed on the specified virtual server.
-url	Specifies the URL of the virtual server from which you want to list the installed Web Part Packages. If this switch is not specified, then the packages are listed from all SharePoint-enabled virtual servers on the current server.
-farm	Lists all the Web Part Packages that are installed on a SharePoint server farm deployment.

```
stsadm.exe -o enumwppacks
```

Figure 15.23   *Enumerating all Web Part Packages.*

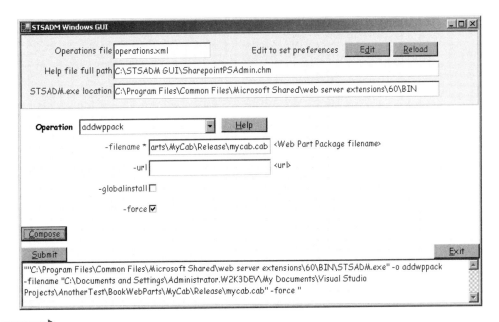

Figure 15.24   STSADM *Windows GUI.*

15.3.4 Web Part Galleries

A Web Part Gallery, also referred to as a Web Part Library, is a central location from which users can retrieve Web Parts and add them to the Web Part Pages in their SharePoint site. Web Parts deployed to the galleries must be registered as safe controls in order to be successfully loaded onto a Web Part Page. Out of the box, SharePoint supports four types of Web Part Galleries:

1. Virtual Server Gallery: The Virtual Server Gallery lists the Web Parts that are available to all the sites on the server. As discussed in the previous section, Web Part Packages can be deployed to the Virtual Server Gallery using the `stsadm.exe` tool.

2. Site Gallery: The Web Parts that appear in the Site Gallery are available to a specific top-level site and all its subsites and are also referred to as a site collection. The name of the Site Gallery matches the top-level site. For example, the name for the Site Gallery of a site named "Development" is "Development Site Gallery" (Figure 15.25). A number of Web Parts appear in the Site Gallery upon creation; the types of Web Parts depend on the site template applied. For example, by default, a site created using the Team Site template contains a Content Editor Web Part, an Image Web Part, a Members Web Part, a Page Viewer Web Part, a Simple Form Web Part, and an XML Web Part. In addition, there will also be a Web Part representing each list or document library in the site (Announcements, Events, Shared Documents, etc.). The site administrator controls the Web Parts that appear in the Site Gallery and can easily add or remove Web Parts using the Manage Web Part Gallery site-administration page (Figure 15.25).

3. Online Gallery: By default, the Online Gallery maps to a site that contains Web Parts provided by Microsoft. Currently, this site contains several MSNBC Web Parts that display stock, news, and weather information; however, as time goes by Microsoft may add additional Web Parts to this site.

    If the Online Gallery does not appear in your list of Web Part Galleries, and access to the Online Gallery has not been disabled on the virtual server, chances are that your proxy server is preventing access to the Microsoft Online Gallery. Resolving this problem requires editing the `web.config` file and including the proxy server settings for the virtual server. More details on this issue and

Figure 15.25
*Web Part
Site Gallery.*

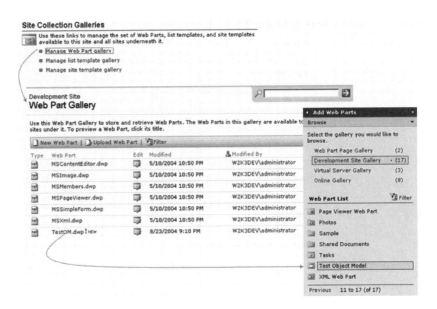

how to resolve it can be found in Microsoft Knowledge Base Article 823375.

If you would prefer that this gallery point to a custom online Web Part Gallery, you can easily redirect the default location to your location of preference. Simply replace the URL referenced in the `<OnlineLibrary>` element of the `web.config` file with a URL that points to your custom online Web Part Gallery.

4. Web Part Page Gallery: The Web Part Page Gallery contains Web Parts that have been added to the current Web Part Page but are not currently visible; the contents of this gallery are added dynamically. If you remove a Web Part from the page using the **Close** button, the `IsIncluded` property of the Web Part is still `True`, which means that even though the Web Part is no longer visible (`IsVisible=false`), it appears in the Web Part Page Gallery so that you can reload the Web Part on the page. Once the Web Part is readded to the Web Part Page, it disappears from the Web Part Gallery.

In order to completely remove a Web Part from the Web Part Page Gallery, you must select the *Delete* option on the Web Part menu. This option is only available in design mode (*Design this Page*).

15.4   Debugging Web Parts

Have you developed a Web Part that compiles successfully only to find that when you load it onto your Web Part Page, you receive a generic error indicating that your Web Part "appears to be causing a problem"? Fortunately, there are a number of options available that allow you to debug your Web Part, the most useful of which is the ability to step through your code line by line as your Web Part runs on the page. Achieving this level of debugging requires a number of preparatory steps before you can actually step through the code. At a high level, these steps include the following:

1. Ensure that your Web Part is registered as a safe control.

2. Set the project configuration options to *Debug* and ensure that the build path maps to the `\inetpub\wwwroot\bin` directory.

3. Set up the project debugging options, such as enabling ASP.NET debugging.

4. Turn debugging on by modifying the `<compilation>` element in the `web.config` file.

5. Modify the level of trust from `WSS_Minimum` to `WSS_Medium`. `WSS_Minimal` does not allow debugging. Alternatively, you can create a specific policy file that applies the necessary permissions for debugging.

The following steps show how to set up debugging in C#. These steps assume that you are developing on the same server running SharePoint.

1. Open your Web Part project in Visual Studio .NET.

2. From the Build menu, click **Configuration Manager**. The configuration manager dialog appears.

3. From the Active Solution Configuration drop-down list, select **Debug**.

4. Click **Close**.

5. From the Project menu, click **Web Part Properties**. The Property Pages dialog appears.

6. From the Configuration Properties folder, click **Build**.

7. Ensure that the output path maps to the `\inetpub\wwwroot\bin` directory.

8. From the Configuration Properties folder, click **Debugging**.

9.   Set **Enable ASP.NET Debugging** to **True**.

10.   Set **Start URL** to the URL of the Web Part Page from which you wish to debug your Web Part.

11.   From the Solution Explorer, right-click your Web Part assembly and click **Set As Startup Project**.

12.   Save and build your project.

13.   Set the breakpoints in your project.

Once you have made the necessary modifications to the `web.config` file (see next steps), you can click the **Start** button to start debugging your Web Part and step through your code.

The following steps show the necessary modifications to the `web.config` file required to enable debugging.

1.   Open the `web.config` file in a text editor, such as Notepad.

2.   Locate the `<compilation>` element and change the debug attribute to `True`.

3.   Locate the `<trust>` element and change the current trust level to `WSS_Medium` or to a policy that has the necessary permissions required for debugging.

4.   Save and exit the file.

5.   From a command prompt, type `iisrest` to restart IIS.

Instead of setting up the start URL and debugging options, you can simply attach your project to the ASP.NET process (`w3wp.exe`); however, using this method requires that you reattach to the process after you have stopped debugging. So, for example, if, while debugging, you find an error that you want to correct, you terminate the process, modify and save the code, and reattach the process to step through your changes.

The following steps show how to implement debugging by attaching to the ASP.NET process:

1.   From the Build menu click **Configuration Manager**. The Configuration Manager dialog appears.

2.   From the **Active Solution Configuration** drop-down list, select **Debug**.

3.   Click **Close**.

4.   Open a Web Part Page that contains the Web Part you wish to debug.

5.   Open your Web Part project in Visual Studio .NET.

6.   From the Project menu, click **Web Part Properties**. The Property Pages dialog appears.

7.   From the Configuration Properties folder, click **Build**.

8.   Set the breakpoints in your project.

9.   Ensure that the output path maps to the `\inetpub\wwwroot\bin` directory.

10.   From the Debug menu, click **Processes**. The Processes dialog appears.

11.   Ensure that the **Show system processes** and the **Show processes in all sessions** check boxes are checked.

12.   From the available processes list, select the **w3wp.exe** process.

13.   Click **Attach**.

14.   Choose **Common Language Runtime** as the program type you want to debug.

15.   Click **OK**.

16.   Click **Close**. You can now step through the Web Part code.

If you are developing Web Parts on a remote computer, there is a slight variation to setting up debugging. First, you must ensure that the server that hosts SharePoint is configured for debugging, and then you need to configure your remote computer for debugging. The following steps show how to set up remote debugging.

15.4.1   Configuring SharePoint Server

1.   Share the directory that hosts the SharePoint virtual server. By default, the SharePoint virtual server maps to the `inetpub\wwwroot\bin` directory.

2.   Ensure that your Web Part developers have read and write access to the directory shared in step 1.

3.   Share the directory that contains the SharePoint assembly (`Microsoft.SharePoint.dll`). By default the assembly is located in the `\Program Files\Common Files\Microsoft Shared\Web Server Extensions\60\ISAPI` directory.

4.   Ensure that your Web Part developers have read access to the directory identified in step 3.

5.   If it isn't already, ensure that your Web Part assembly is registered as a safe control.

6.   Set the trust level to `WSS_Medium` or an equivalent level that permits debugging.

7.   Set the `debug` attribute of the compilation element in the `web.config` file to `True`.

8.   Ensure that remote debugging services are installed and configured on the server.

15.4.2   Configuring a remote computer

The only real difference from a Visual Studio .NET perspective between debugging an application from a remote computer and debugging on the actual server running the application is the output path where the application will be built.

1.   Open your Web Part project in Visual Studio .NET.

2.   From the Project menu, click **Web Part Properties**. The Property Pages dialog appears.

Request Details

Session Id:		Request Type:	GET
Time of Request:	8/23/2004 11:51:34 PM	Status Code:	200
Request Encoding:	Unicode (UTF-8)	Response Encoding:	Unicode (UTF-8)

Trace Information

Category	Message	From First(s)	From Last(s)
aspx.page	Begin Init		
aspx.page	End Init	0.000266	0.000266
aspx.page	Begin PreRender	0.001482	0.001216
aspx.page	End PreRender	0.015016	0.013534
aspx.page	Begin SaveViewState	0.016390	0.001374
aspx.page	End SaveViewState	0.016511	0.000120
aspx.page	Begin Render	0.016542	0.000031
aspx.page	End Render	0.022031	0.005489

Control Tree

Control Id	Type	Render Size Bytes (including children)	Views Size I (excl childr
__PAGE	ASP.default_aspx	38251	24
_ctl0	Microsoft.SharePoint.WebControls.ProjectProperty	16	0
_ctl1	Microsoft.SharePoint.WebControls.Theme	0	0
_ctl2	Microsoft.SharePoint.WebControls.ProjectProperty	16	0
_ctl3	Microsoft.SharePoint.WebControls.Navigation	607	0
_ctl4	Microsoft.SharePoint.WebControls.PortalConnection	72	0
_ctl5	Microsoft.SharePoint.WebControls.ProjectProperty	16	0
L_SearchView	Microsoft.SharePoint.WebControls.ViewSearchForm	1101	0
_ctl6	Microsoft.SharePoint.WebPartPages.SettingsLink	423	0
_ctl7	Microsoft.SharePoint.WebPartPages.AuthenticationButton	0	0
_ctl8	Microsoft.SharePoint.WebControls.Navigation	341	0
_ctl9	Microsoft.SharePoint.WebControls.Navigation	319	0
_ctl10	Microsoft.SharePoint.WebControls.Navigation	588	0

Figure 15.26   *Web Part Page with tracing enabled.*

Figure 15.27
<trace> *element.*

```
<trace enabled="true" pageOutput="true"/>
```

3. From the Configuration Properties folder, click **Build**.

4. Ensure that the output path maps to the \inetpub\wwwroot\
    bin directory of the SharePoint server—for example, \\SPDEV\
    wwwroot$\bin.

5. Follow the previously listed debugging steps to begin debugging.
    The set of steps you follow depends on whether you want to
    attach directly to the ASP.NET process or to use the Debugging
    menu options.

ASP.NET has a tracing feature that provides you with a snapshot of the
steps and processes your code went through after the page has been rendered in the browser. The tracing information appears at the bottom of the
page (Figure 15.26).

To enable tracing, simply edit the web.config file and add the code
shown in Figure 15.27 to the <system.web> element.

16

Customizing SharePoint Using FrontPage 2003

16.1   Microsoft Office FrontPage 2003

Microsoft Office FrontPage (FrontPage) is Microsoft's product for Web site creation and management and includes all of the necessary design, authoring, data, and publishing tools to create dynamic, sophisticated Web sites. The FrontPage team has done a tremendous job of providing a wonderful medium for designing, coding, and extending your SharePoint site. FrontPage 2003 is, in fact, Microsoft's recommended product for advanced customizations of both Windows SharePoint Services and SPS sites, and this comes as no surprise, because FrontPage 2003 is noticeably SharePoint aware. For example, when you use the Page Templates dialog to create a new page on a SharePoint site, you'll see an additional tab for Web Part Pages.

FrontPage itself is a huge topic; if you take a walk through any bookstore, the computer section is usually overflowing with books targeted at FrontPage users and developers. Because we only have one chapter to devote to FrontPage, we'll focus on the aspects of FrontPage and SharePoint integration that have the most impact.

16.2   Editing a SharePoint site with FrontPage 2003

There are two methods of opening a SharePoint site in FrontPage 2003—open the site directly from FrontPage 2003 by specifying the URL or directly from your browser using the *Edit with Microsoft Office FrontPage* option available on both the File menu and the button bar.

To open a SharePoint site from FrontPage 2003, do the following:

1.   Open FrontPage 2003.

2.   From the File menu, click **Open Site**.

3.   Type the URL of the SharePoint site in the Site text box.

4.   Click **Open**.

To open a SharePoint site from Internet Explorer, do the following:

1.   Using your browser, navigate to the Home page of the SharePoint site you would like to edit.

2.   From the File menu, click **Edit with Microsoft Office FrontPage**.

16.3   Features of FrontPage 2003

FrontPage 2003 offers many tools and features out of the box that significantly ease the process of designing and customizing your Web site. To start with, the actual layout of the FrontPage environment is very intuitive and lends itself to both the novice user and experienced developer. Figure 16.1

Figure 16.1   *FrontPage editor.*

shows the default layout of FrontPage 2003. The left pane displays one of two types of information: the list of folders in the Web site or the site's navigational structure, the folder list being the default. Double-clicking on an item in either the Folder List pane or the Navigation pane displays its content in the editor window.

16.3.1   WYSIWYG editing

The editor window has a number of views associated with it: Design, Split, Code, and Preview (Figure 16.2). The Design view provides a What You See Is What You Get (WYSIWYG) editor that allows you to design your Web page using graphical tools and formatting.

The Design view closely matches the appearance of the Web page in the browser while still providing information on the structural components of the page. For example, if you compare the Design and Preview views in Figure 16.2, you will see they are very similar; however, the Design view shows

Design View

Split View

Code View

Preview View

Figure 16.2   *Editor views.*

the Web Part zone layout of the page and the table structures present. When customizations are made through the Design view, FrontPage automatically generates the appropriate HTML code behind the scenes.

The Split view allows you to see the code generation in action. When the editor is in Split view, two panes appear within the editor window. The top pane displays the code behind the Web page, and the bottom pane displays the Design view of the Web page. As you select items in one pane, the other pane scrolls to and highlights the item in that pane. In addition, any changes you make in the bottom Design pane appear instantly in the top Code pane. However, the reverse is not true; changes made directly into the Code pane only appear in the Design view once the Web page is refreshed or saved or if you switch to the Preview view. You can refresh the page by pressing F5. The reasoning behind this is that FrontPage needs a way of knowing when you have finished typing your code before it can interpret the HTML and present it in the Design pane.

The Code view is the same as the Code pane that appears in Split view, but instead of splitting into two panes, it displays the code of the Web page in the entire editor window.

The Preview view gives you an idea of how the Web page will appear once it is published to your site, which is very useful for viewing customizations prior to saving the page. When you switch to Preview view, FrontPage saves the current Web page to a temporary disk area, then starts Microsoft Internet Explorer and informs it to display the saved page in the editor window.

16.3.2   Quick Tag tools

To make code navigation easier, FrontPage provides a Quick Tag Selector and a Quick Tag Editor. The Quick Tag Selector appears in the form of a toolbar at the top of the editor window (Figure 16.3) and is available in the Code, Design, and Split views. When you click an area of the page, the Quick Tag Selector automatically displays a tag selector presenting the underlying HTML tag for that area. For example, if you click on the page title of the Home page of a SharePoint site, the `<td>` tag selector appears in the Quick Tag Selector. If you hover over the tag selector, a ScreenTip appears displaying the complete tag—for example, `<td ID=onetidPage-Title class="ms-pagetitle">` (Figure 16.3).

An arrow appears next to the tag selector. Clicking this arrow displays the Quick Tag shortcut menu, which lists the edit and selection options for the tag, also shown in Figure 16.3.

- *Select Tag* selects the start and end tags and content in between. For example, if you click the *Select Tag* option for the tag associated with the SharePoint page title, FrontPage will select the following code in the Code pane:

```
<td ID=onetidPageTitle class="ms-pagetitle">Home</td>
```

If you are in Split view, it selects both the code in the Code pane and the corresponding area in the Design pane.

- *Select Tag Contents,* as its wording suggests, selects the content between the start and end tags. Using this option against the previous example would result in the word "Home" being selected.

- *Edit Tag* displays the Quick Tag Editor window and populates the window with the start tag, end tag, and contents ready for editing. You can use the Quick Tag Editor to change the complete tag, including the tag type.

- *Remove Tag* removes the start and end tags but leaves the content intact.

- *Insert HTML* adds HTML code to the page.

- *Wrap Tag* places a wrapper tag around the current tag. The current tag becomes nested inside the tag you define.

- *Tag Properties* displays the properties dialog associated with the selected tag. For example, if you select a paragraph tag (`<p>`), the Paragraph dialog box appears, from which you can change the alignment, indentation, spacing, and line spacing; whereas, if you selected a table tag (`<table>`), the Table dialog box appears, from which you can change the table layout, size, borders, and background.

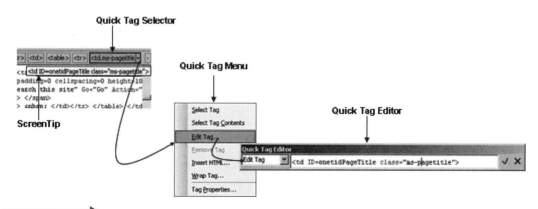

Figure 16.3   *Quick Tag tools.*

16.3.3   Image tracing

When designing a Web page, people commonly create a draft of the layout and structure of the site. Some designers find a pencil and paper to be the perfect media for creating this draft; others like to use more advanced graphical solutions such as Adobe Photoshop. Regardless of your preferred method, you can leverage your design when creating your Web page with FrontPage by using the *Tracing Image* option on the View menu. The *Tracing Image* functionality allows you to take an image, such as a scanned sketch saved as a GIF file, and use it as the background for your Design view (Figure 16.4). This gives the effect of working on a light table, where you can trace the image to produce the final Web page.

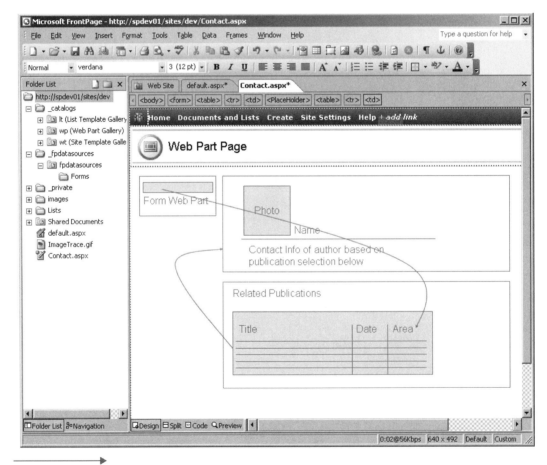

Figure 16.4   *Image tracing.*

You can adjust the transparency of the image to the level that best suits your needs. You can also choose whether to display or hide the image by checking and unchecking the *Show Image* option on the Tracing Image menu. FrontPage keeps track of which image belongs to which page in your Web site. If the tracing image associated with your Web page does not reside in your site, FrontPage will prompt you to save it the next time you save your Web page. Once the page is in the site, other Web designers responsible for the site will have access to the tracing image.

16.3.4   Table and cell layout

FrontPage 2003 includes a framework for defining the layout of tables and cells in a Web page. The Layout Tables and Cells task pane (Figure 16.5) presents a list of options with which you can define such things as table alignment, layout style, and cell width. The task pane appears on the right-hand side of the FrontPage window.

FrontPage provides a number of table layout styles from which to choose; however, if none of the options presented meets your needs,

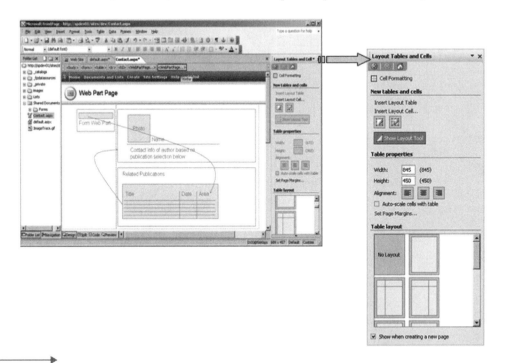

Figure 16.5   *Layout Tables and Cells task pane.*

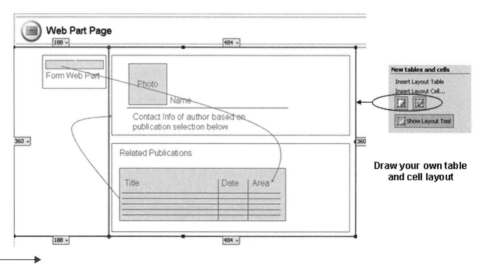

Figure 16.6   *Drawing a table and cell layout.*

FrontPage also provides the ability to draw the table and cell layout directly onto the page. Figure 16.6 shows a custom table and cell layout that has been drawn over a tracing image.

16.3.5   Themes

Designing a Web page so that it is both visually appealing and effective is of paramount importance to the ultimate success of the site. Not all Web sites are created by professional Web designers who know all of the intricacies and design techniques such a post entails. Microsoft helps to produce a professional look and feel to a site quickly through the use of themes. Themes are basically professionally designed style packages that define the color, fonts, and graphical page elements of Web pages within a site. You can apply a theme to a single page or to the entire site with a single click.

FrontPage comes equipped with numerous themes out of the box and lists them in the *All available themes* section of the Theme task pane (Figure 16.7).

In addition to being able to select a ready-made theme, you can create your own custom theme using the Customize Theme dialog, accessible via the **Create new theme** link on the task pane.

When you have selected your theme, you can apply it as the default theme for the site, which applies it to all newly created Web pages in your site, or you can apply it to a selected number of Web pages. The whole purpose of themes is to help provide a consistent look and feel to your Web

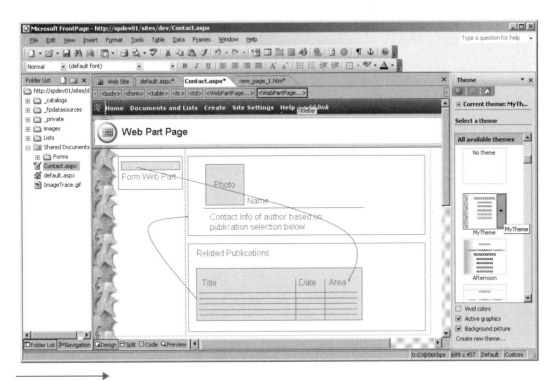

Figure 16.7   *MyTheme applied to a Web page.*

pages. If you apply different themes to different pages, the Web site has the potential to become awkward and confusing to users.

While themes are an excellent way to provide a consistent look and feel to a site quickly, they are designed not to be overridden; therefore, once you apply a theme, it controls a predefined set of elements within that page. You cannot remove or add the elements controlled by the theme, and if you make a change to the theme, it affects all of the pages that use the theme.

For WSS sites, themes can be applied using both FrontPage and the browser; however, building or applying custom themes requires FrontPage. The following steps show how to apply a theme to the Home page of a WSS site through the browser (Figure 16.8):

1.   Using your browser, navigate to the Home page of the SharePoint site to which you would like to apply the theme.

2.   Click the **Site Settings** link on the horizontal navigation bar at the top of the page.

3.   From the *Customization* section of the page, click the **Apply theme to site** link. The Apply Theme to Web Site page appears.

Figure 16.8
*Applying a theme
through the
browser.*

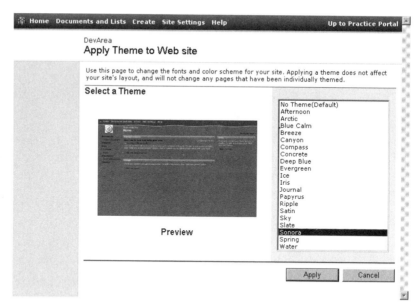

4.   Select the theme to apply to the site from the list box on the right
        of the page. A preview of the theme is shown.

5.   Click **OK**.

Note: If you edit an SPS 2003 site with FrontPage 2003, themes are disabled by default. The logic behind this restriction is that some of the Web
Parts within the portal site do not respond well to the application of a
FrontPage theme. Consequently, if you want to apply a theme to your portal site, you must do it through the Site Settings page in your browser.

16.3.6   Dynamic templates

Chapter 17 introduces the concept of site definitions and Custom Templates that SharePoint can leverage to provide a consistent look and feel to
the site. To summarize, site definitions comprise a set of XML files stored in
the file system that determine the site's navigational structure, lists, libraries,
and Web Parts that appear in the site. Custom Templates are UI-based templates stored in the database that can be used as the model for a new list or
site, and they are ultimately applied to an existing site definition. Although
a site definition has the advantage of improved performance—due to the

XML files being stored in the file system—it has some noticeable disadvantages. For example, it is lacking a UI and is therefore more difficult to customize, and once you deploy a site definition, it is difficult to modify, because anything other than an add operation has the potential to cause disruption to the site. While Custom Templates are very easy to create, they are basically static templates; therefore, any future changes made to the Custom Template will not apply to existing sites or lists.

FrontPage 2003 introduces the concept of Dynamic Web Templates. Dynamic Web templates are similar to Custom Templates and site definitions in that they allow you to provide Web pages with a consistent visual design and to preposition page elements. Unlike Custom Templates they have the added benefit of remaining attached to the pages they create; therefore, any updates made to the template will propagate to all attached pages. In addition, Dynamic Web Templates allow you to define editable and noneditable regions, which allows you to control specific areas of the Web pages within a site. For example, if you want to prevent users from modifying the corporate header and footer on a page, you can define these elements as noneditable regions of the template. Furthermore, once the Dynamic Web Template is deployed, it is easily modifiable without causing disruption to existing sites.

Leveraging Dynamic Web Templates is a two-step process. First you create and save the template file (.dwt), next you attach the template to the pages in your site. The following example shows how to add a banner and footer to the top and bottom of the pages within a SharePoint site.

Creating a Dynamic Web Template

Dynamic Web Templates start out as regular Web pages. It is only when you save the Web page as a .dwt file that the page itself is transformed into a Dynamic Web Template. Once you have saved the template as a .dwt file, you can define editable regions on the page. Editable regions are basically the areas on the page that may be modified. All other regions are marked as noneditable, meaning that their content cannot be modified or deleted in any way by users.

If you want to apply a Dynamic Web Template to the pages in a SharePoint site, it is recommended that you use a Web Part Page as the base for the .dwt file. Doing so ensures you have all of the necessary SharePoint styles defined in the header section, such as ows.css. Having access to the SharePoint styles also means that you can update them to reflect the desired look and feel of your site.

If you want to apply a Dynamic Web Template to SPS 2003 pages, you may run into similar problems where the template rewrites the header section of the page and removes references to the cascading stylesheet (sps.css), ultimately affecting the appearance of your page. To resolve this ensure that your template includes the header information necessary for application to the portal. Given that the header information for SPS pages differs from that for WSS pages, it may be better to define a separate template for each.

To create a Dynamic Web Template, do the following:

1.   From FrontPage, open the SharePoint site that you wish to customize.

2.   From the File menu, click **New**.

3.   From the New task pane, click the **More Page Templates** link.

4.   From the Page Templates dialog, click the Web Part Pages tab.

5.   Select the page template that best suits your needs, for example the Full Page, Vertical template creates a blank Web Part Page, which is useful in our example because we only need to add a header and footer to the page.

6.   Click **OK**.

7.   Using the Code view editor, enter the code for your banner and footer in the appropriate place on the page—for example, the banner would go in the header section of the page directly above the Web Part Page header code, and the footer would be placed just before the closing body tag.

8.   Switch to the Split view editor.

9.   Select the area of the page that you want to allow changes. You can use either the Code pane or the Design pane in the Split view editor to choose the editable regions on the page.

10.   From the Format menu click **Dynamic Web Template**. An additional menu appears.

11.   Click **Manage Editable Regions**. The Editable Regions dialog appears.

12.   Enter the name of the new editable region (Figure 16.9).

13.   Click **Add**.

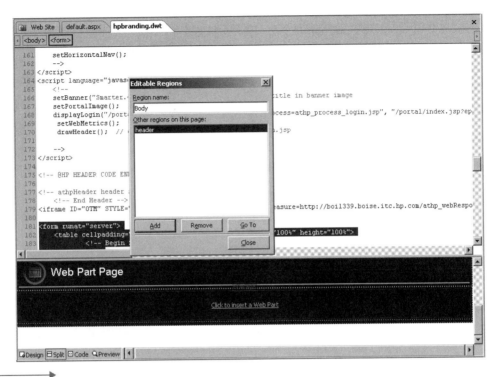

Figure 16.9   *Defining editable regions.*

14.   Repeat steps 9 through 13 for each editable region you would like
       to define.

15.   Click **Close**.

Attaching the template

Once you are happy that the template meets all your customization needs,
you can attach it to the pages in your site. To attach the template you simply select the pages you wish to update and click the **Attach Dynamic Web
Template** command from the *Dynamic Web Template* option on the Format
menu. To attach the template to all Web Pages in your site, select the parent
folder in the Folder List pane (e.g., http://myserver/sites/mysite)
and click the **Attach Dynamic Web Template** command from the *Dynamic
Web Template* option on the Format menu.

Figure 16.10 shows a SharePoint Team site with the Dynamic Web
Template attached. Note that the page now includes a corporate banner and
footer.

Figure 16.10
*Dynamic Web
template applied to
SharePoint
Team site.*

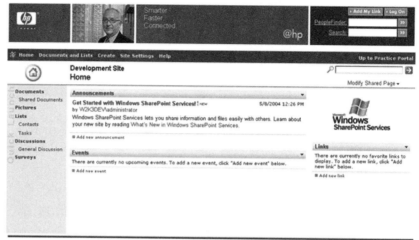

Handling script in Dynamic Web Templates

When defining editable regions on your page, you are restricted to using code within HTML elements. But what about script code defined between the `<head>` and `<body>` tags of a page, as is the case with the `Upload.aspx` file in the document library? Unfortunately, because you cannot define the space between two HTML elements as an editable region, the template will overwrite any existing code between them. If you create a Dynamic Web Template, attach it to all of the pages in the site, and find that certain functions generate errors on a page, it is most likely because the template has overwritten the original code. One workaround is to copy the script code from the affected file, such as `Upload.aspx`, and paste it into the template. This makes the script code noneditable in all pages to which the template attaches. Another alternative is to visit each affected page after the `.dwt` file is attached, reinsert the script code, and detach the page; but this really defeats the purpose of having Dynamic Web Templates in the first place!

To ensure the `Upload.aspx` page remains functional, do the following:

1. Open your Dynamic Web Template.

2. Copy the code shown in Figure 16.11 from the `<head>` section of the `Upload.aspx` file. You only need to do this if the code is not already included in the Dynamic Web Template file.

3. Insert the code into the bottom part of the `<head>` section of the Dynamic Web Template.

```
<meta name="WebPartPageExpansion" content="full">
<meta Name="GENERATOR" Content="Microsoft SharePoint">
<meta Name="ProgId" Content="SharePoint.WebPartPage.Document">
<meta HTTP-EQUIV="Content-Type" CONTENT="text/html; charset=utf-8">
<meta HTTP-EQUIV="Expires" content="0">
<title ID="onetidTitle"></title>
<link REL="stylesheet" Type="text/css" HREF="ows.css">
<script src="/_layouts/1033/owsbrows.js"></script>
<link type="text/xml" rel="alternate" href="../_vti_bin/spdisco.aspx">
<script><!--
if (browseris.mac && !browseris.ie5up)
{
    var ms_maccssfpfixup = "/_layouts/1033/styles/owsmac.css";
    document.write("<link rel='stylesheet' Type='text/css' href='" + ms_maccssfpfixup + "'>");
}
//--></script>
<meta name="Microsoft Border" content="none">
```

Figure 16.11   `Upload.aspx` *header code.*

4.   If you would like to be able to modify this header code at a later date, you should define an editable region for this part of the `<head>` section.

5.   Copy the script code found between the `<head>` and `<body>` HTML tags of `Upload.aspx`. Once again, you only need to do this if the code is not already included in your template file. The code starts and ends with `<script>` tags and contains four functions: `MultipleUploadView()`, `RemoveMultipleUpload-Items()`, `DocumentUpload()`, and `GetTreeColor()`.

6.   Insert the code between the `<head>` and `<body>` HTML tags of the Dynamic Web Template.

7.   Save your changes.

8.   When asked if you would like to update all of the attached pages, click **Yes**.

`Upload.aspx` should now function correctly. To test that the changes have been applied correctly, do the following:

1.   Using your browser, navigate to the Shared Documents document library in your site.

2.   Select *Upload Document* from the toolbar.

3.   From the Upload Document page, click the **Upload Multiple Files** link.

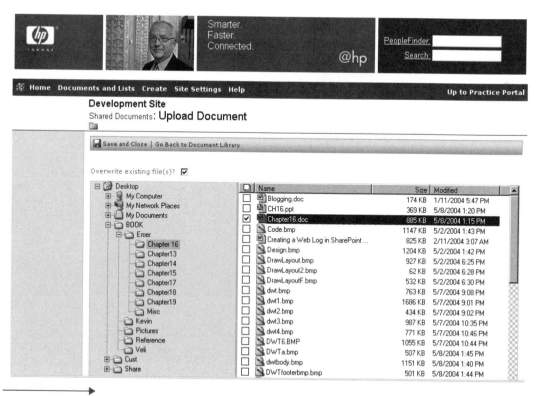

Figure 16.12   *Uploading multiple documents.*

If a document tree appears listing files on your file system in conjunction with whatever template changes you made, such as adding a banner (Figure 16.12), then the Dynamic Web Template is functioning correctly.

Updating changes

The great thing about Dynamic Web Templates is that you can make changes to the template and choose to apply the changes only to a select set of pages. This means that you can test the template to make sure that the updates behave as expected. Once you are satisfied with the template, you can propagate the changes to all attached pages using the **Update Attached Pages** command from the *Dynamic Web Template* option on the Format menu.

In addition, the **Update Selected Page** command applies template changes to the selected pages. The **Update All Pages** command applies template changes to all pages in the currently opened site. The **Update Attached Pages** command applies template changes to all pages in the current site attached to the current template. If you have other sites to which the template is attached, you will need to initiate the update from those sites using either the **Update All Pages** command or the **Update Attached Pages** command.

Before using any of the update commands, it is recommended that you recalculate the Web page. This ensures that all link information associated with the .dwt file is current and all attached pages are updated appropriately.

To recalculate the Web page, do the following:

1.   From the Tools menu, click **Recalculate Hyperlinks**.

2.   From the Recalculate Hyperlinks dialog box, click **Yes**.

3.   Wait until the synchronization process is complete.

Note: When you make changes to the pages of a SharePoint site using FrontPage 2003, these changes are written to the SQL database. As a result, there may be a delay before you see the changes appear in your browser.

Master template for multiple sites

Another great feature of Dynamic Web Templates is that other sites can attach the template to their Web pages if they know the URL of the Dynamic Web Template. This means that any changes and updates required need only be made once. However, the unfortunate part of this story is that you cannot force updates across sites from the site hosting the template. The update commands on the Dynamic Web Template menu only apply to the current site; even subsites of the current site are ignored. This means that if you have a master template applied to multiple sites within your organization, each site must initiate the update to reflect the template changes. If you deploy the self-service site-creation functionality and use Dynamic Web Templates to enforce corporate branding across all your WSS sites, then you must come up with some mechanism for pushing the template updates to your sites. This could be as simple as sending an e-mail to all of the site administrators informing them of the new template version and providing instructions on how to use the **Update Attached Pages** command.

Detaching pages

The **Detach From Dynamic Template** command on the Dynamic Web Template menu disconnects the selected pages from the template but leaves the template's content in place. The template's content is now editable within the page, and you can make changes as you see fit. This detachment process can be confusing, as you may have expected detaching the template to revert the page back to the way it was before the template was applied. Because this is not the case, it is important to remember that if your template overwrites content in the pages to which it is applied, your only method of recovering the page is to restore your page from a backup.

Combining Dynamic Web Templates with SharePoint Custom Templates

A limitation of Custom Templates is the fact that once the template is deployed you cannot easily update changes to the site. This story improves if you combine Dynamic Web Templates with Custom Templates. This combination results in the creation of a SharePoint site that is attached to a Dynamic Web Template containing the customizations to apply to the site. In order to take advantage of this functionality, you need to include the Dynamic Web Template in the Custom Template; you cannot use this method if the template to attach is located in another site, as in the previous section.

The basic premise of this technique is that you open the SharePoint site that you want to use as the Custom Template, create a Dynamic Web Template, apply it to all of the pages in the site, and then finally save the site as a Custom Template. You can save the site as a Custom Template through the browser interface by accessing the site-administration pages.

Once the Custom Template is created, you can create sites using that template. Figure 16.13 shows a site created using the Dynamic Web Template/Custom Template combination. Detailed information on Custom Templates and Site Definitions can be found in Chapter 17.

The Dynamic Web Template associated with a site created in this manner is completely independent of the template from which it was created. This means that in order to push updates to sites using the Dynamic Web Template, you will need to send the entire template to each site's administrator for application to the site, which is still better than having to change all of the site pages manually.

Limitations

Chapter 17 introduces some of the limitations that Custom Templates have with respect to customization possibilities. One such limitation is the fact that you cannot modify any of the pages stored in the _layouts directory, such as the Documents and Lists creation page. Dynamic Web Templates

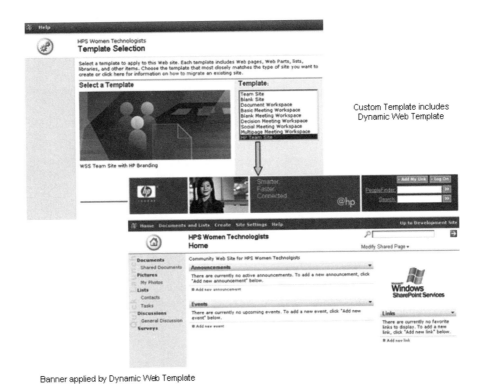

Figure 16.13   *Dynamic Web Template/Custom Template combo.*

suffer from this same limitation in that you cannot attach the template to files stored in the _layouts directory, because this directory is not accessible from the site when it is edited through FrontPage. As a result, several pages in your SharePoint site will not include your customizations. The only way to ensure that your customizations appear on all pages in the site, including administrative pages, is once again to step into the world of unsupported territory and modify the files in the file subsystem. This method is not entirely foolproof either, as you run into ghosting issues if you have edited sites using FrontPage 2003. We discuss the concept of ghosting at the end of this chapter.

16.4   Web Part and list integration

FrontPage 2003 was designed with SharePoint in mind and consequently has many explicit SharePoint integration points scattered throughout the product. The Data menu in particular is dedicated to SharePoint-based sites and contains SharePoint-aware commands such as **Insert Web Part** and

Insert Web Part Zone. Both the Page Templates and Web Site Template dialog boxes contain an additional tab that caters specifically to SharePoint sites, and the *Database* and *Form* options on the Insert menu contain custom SharePoint commands.

16.4.1   Web Part Pages

FrontPage 2003 provides a list of templates from which you can create Web Part Pages. There are eight templates included that match the templates provided in the browser UI. Figure 16.14 shows the Page Templates dialog from which you create new Web Part Pages. The SharePoint-specific templates are located on the Web Part Pages tab of the Page Templates dialog. The FrontPage UI provides more flexibility for creating Web Part Pages. With the browser UI you can only store the newly created Web Part Page in a document library, and once you have stored the Web Part Page, it is difficult to move it to another location within the site. FrontPage allows you to create, store, and move Web Part Pages using the Folder List view. This

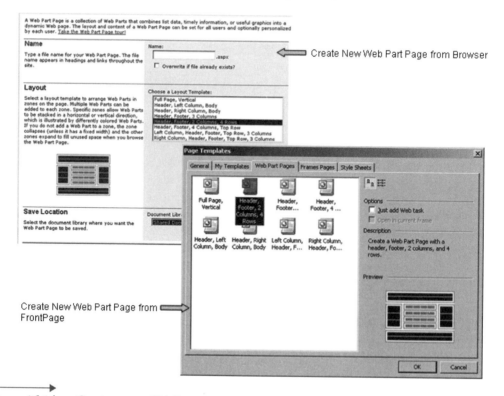

Figure 16.14   *Creating a new Web Part Page.*

means that you have access to all of the drag-and-drop functionality provided with the Folder List view. In addition, if there are any Dynamic Web Templates available, you can attach them once you have created the page.

To create a Web Part Page, do the following:

1. Select or create the folder where you would like to store the Web Part Page.

2. From the File menu, click **New**.

3. From the **Page Templates** dialog, click the Web Part Pages tab.

4. Select the Web Part Page template that best suits your needs; for example, Header, Left Column, Body creates a Web Part Page with a header, left column, and body section.

5. Click **OK**.

The Web Part Page will appear in the editor window.

16.4.2 Web Part zones

When you create a Web Part Page based on a template, the page comes preconfigured with zone areas. These zone areas are visible from both the Design view and Split view editor windows, but can be added using Design view, Split view, and Code view. You can add, remove, or reposition zones very easily from FrontPage. FrontPage provides a special command on the Data Menu for inserting Web Part zones onto your Web Part Page. Once you have added the zone to your Web Part Page, double-clicking on the zone area will display the Web Part Zone Properties dialog from which you can modify the properties of the zone.

To create a Web Part zone, do the following:

1. On the Web Part Page, click where you want the zone to be added.

2. From the Data menu, click **Insert Web Part Zone**. The Web Part zone will appear on the Web Part Page.

3. Double-click the new zone area. The Web Part Properties dialog appears.

4. Enter a name for your Web Part zone. This name appears in the Design view both in FrontPage and the browser.

5. Select the frame style you want to make the default for the Web Parts added to the zone. For example, if you select **Title Bar and**

Figure 16.15
Web Part zones.

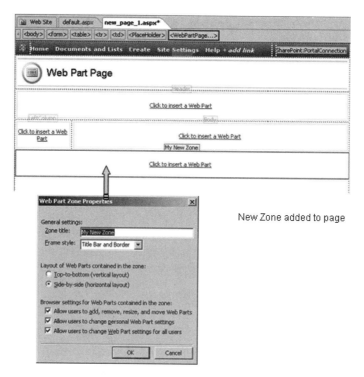

New Zone added to page

Border, each Web Part added to the zone will default to display a title bar and a border.

6.   Select the layout of Web Parts added to your zone. You can choose to display Web Parts top to bottom or side by side.

7.   Check the browser settings you would like to apply to the Web Parts added to the zone. Possible settings are as follows:

   ▪ Allow users to add, remove, resize, and move Web Parts.

   ▪ Allow users to change personal Web Part settings.

   ▪ Allow users to change Web Part settings for all users.

8.   Click **OK**.

Figure 16.15 shows a Web Part zone called "My New Zone" added to a Web Part Page and the properties associated with the zone.

16.4.3   Web Parts

Once you have created your Web Part Page and configured the necessary zones, you'll most likely want to add functionality to your page using Web

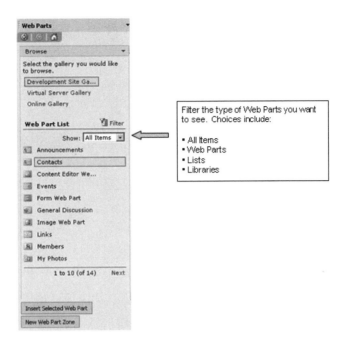

Figure 16.16
Web Parts task pane.

Parts. In addition to the **Insert Web Part Zone** command, FrontPage provides an **Insert Web Part** command on the Data menu. When you click the **Insert Web Part** command, the Web Part task pane appears (Figure 16.16) and provides you with a list of available Web Parts for the site. In addition, you can browse other Web Part galleries, such as the Virtual Server Gallery and the Online Gallery. You can apply a filter to the Web Part List that appears in the task pane. The following list describes the filter choices.

- **All Items** displays all Web Parts in the currently selected gallery.

- **Web Parts** filters out all Web Parts based on the `ListViewWebPart` class. For example, the Contacts and Shared Documents Web Parts both use the `ListViewWebPart` class. You can see this for yourself by clicking the Contacts Web Part on the Web Part Page and looking at its code in the Split view Code pane (Figure 16.17).

- **Lists** displays all Web Parts that present data from a SharePoint list, such as the Contacts Web Part.

- **Libraries** displays all Web Parts that present data from a SharePoint document library, such as the Shared Documents Web Part.

Similar to Web Part zones, Web Parts are visible from the Design and Split views, but can be added from all views with the exception of the Preview view. When you add Web Parts using FrontPage 2003, they are not

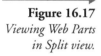

Figure 16.17
*Viewing Web Parts
in Split view.*

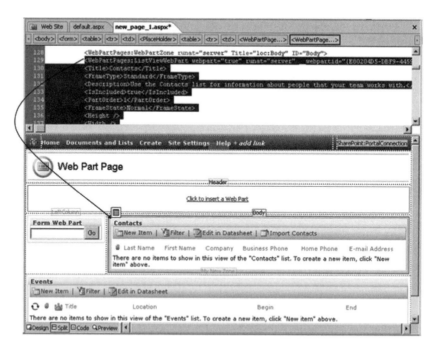

handled in the same way as if they were added using the browser interface.
The browser interface processes the Web Part through a set of ASP.NET
events. FrontPage 2003 requires a design-time view of the Web Part and, as
a result, needs to implement a special interface to retrieve the HTML for
the view. The design view, as expected, does not present a live view of the
Web Part. When a request is made for a page in FrontPage, SharePoint
sends a rendering of the part to FrontPage. Consequently, you will not be
able to see the true effect of your Web Parts until the Web Page is requested
by a browser. For example, the Contacts Web Part is not fully functional
even in the Preview view; clicking on the **New Item** link results in an error
in the Preview view and no response at all in the Design view. Figure 16.17
shows a Web Part Page populated with Web Parts in the Split view.

To insert a Web Part on the page, do the following:

1.   Click the zone area where you want to insert the Web Part.

2.   From the Data menu, click **Insert Web Part**. The Web Part task
      pane appears.

3.   Browse the Web Part galleries to find your Web Part of choice.

4.   Select the Web Part that you want to add to the page.

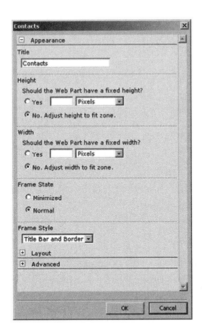

Figure 16.18
Contacts Web Part properties.

5.   Drag and drop the Web Part from the task pane onto the Web Part Page. The Web Part should appear on the page.

You can access the properties of a Web Part by double-clicking the part in the Design or Split views. A floating pane appears containing the Web Part Properties (Figure 16.18). This is very similar to the Web Part property pane shown in the browser interface. You can set all of the properties associated with the Web Part through the property pane, such as the Web Part's height, width, and frame style. You can also access the more advanced properties, such as the detail link.

Note: You may receive an `InitializeStrings` method error (see Figure 16.19) when you try to access the properties of a Web Part in FrontPage. This is a known problem that occurs when editing a WSS site located on an SPS server. Additional information, including a workaround, can be found in Microsoft Knowledge Base Article 829067 on the Microsoft Web site. This problem is resolved with SP1.

You can also access the properties of a Web Part directly from code using the Code view and Split view panes. Figure 16.17 shows the Contacts Web Part selected in the Design pane of the Split view window. The Code pane

Figure 16.19
*InitalizeStrings
Error.*

displays the code associated with the Contacts Web Part, and you can see a number of the Web Part properties, such as `Title`, `FrameType`, `Description`, `IsIncluded`, and so forth.

Web Part connections

Chapter 14 shows how easy it is to connect Web Parts to one another using the browser UI; however, you can only connect to Web Parts on the same page using this method. FrontPage 2003 enhances this functionality by allowing you to connect Web Parts over multiple pages and by introducing more provider/consumer interface pairs. Connecting Web Parts over multiple pages is only supported for server-side connections.

Two provider/consumer interface pairs are accepted when connecting Web Parts across pages: the `IParametersInProvider`/`IParametersInConsumer` interfaces and the `IFilterProvider`/`IFilterConsumer` interfaces. A Web Part that implements the `IParametersInConsumer` interface includes a set of parameters that can receive communications from a Web Part that implements the `IParametersInProvider` interface. In addition, if transformers are used, a Web Part that implements the `IParametersInConsumer` interface can also communicate with a Web Part that implements either the `IParametersOutProvider` or the `IRowProvider` interface.

While it is possible to author connections in FrontPage, the actual result of the connection can only be seen when requested by a browser.

To connect Web Parts on the same page in FrontPage, do the following:

1.   Right-click the Web Part that you want to use as your provider interface, for example, the Form Web Part.

2.   From the shortcut menu, click **Web Part Connections**. The Web Part Connections Wizard appears.

3.   Select **Provide Form Values To** as the action on the source Web Part.

4. Click **Next**.

5. Select **Connect to Web Part on this page**.

6. Click **Next**.

7. Select the target Web Part to which the data is to be sent—for example, the Contacts Web Part.

8. Select the action that you want the target Web Part to take.

9. Select a column from the provider Web Part and a matching column from the consumer Web Part.

10. Click **Next**.

11. Click **Finish**.

To connect Web Parts across pages in FrontPage, do the following:

1. Right-click the Web Part that you want to use as your provider interface—for example, the Form Web Part.

2. From the shortcut menu, click **Web Part Connections**. The Web Part Connections Wizard appears.

3. Select **Provide Form Values To** as the action on the source Web Part.

4. Click **Next**.

5. Select **Connect to Web Part on another page in this web**.

6. Click **Browse** and select the Web Part Page that hosts the Web Part you want to connect to. Alternatively, you can enter the relative address of the page—for example, `Lists/Contacts/AllItems.aspx`.

7. Click **Next**.

8. Select the target Web Part to which the data is to be sent—for example, the Contacts Web Part.

9. Select the action that you want the target Web Part to take.

10. Select a column from the provider Web Part and a matching column from the consumer Web Part.

11. Click **Next**.

12. Click **Finish**.

16.4.4 Lists and libraries

When you open a SharePoint site in FrontPage 2003, the contents of the site appear in the Folder List pane. The Folder List pane groups list items together under a single Lists folder. Each list is hosted as a subfolder and represented with a special icon. Each document library, on the other hand, has its own top-level folder represented with a special icon. Figure 16.20 shows the Folder List pane displaying the Lists and document libraries folder of a WSS site.

The forms used to display, edit, or create items in a list or document library use the List Form Web Part. FrontPage 2003 knows that this is a special Web Part type and provides a number of menu options accordingly. If you right-click on a List Form Web Part, you will notice that two menu items are dedicated to this particular Web Part type: *Customize SharePoint List Form* and *List Form Properties*. The *Customize SharePoint List Form* option allows you to add fields, edit the HTML markup applied to specific areas and fields on the form, insert rows and columns into the form, and even split cells. When you select this option, the List form switches to Design Mode (Figure 16.21). Parts of the form that are defined using HTML are sectioned and associated with an icon. If you double-click on this icon, you can edit the HTML. Once you are happy with the changes you have made, you can save the page and use your browser to view the results. The *Revert SharePoint List Form* option reverts the customized List

Figure 16.20
*Folder List pane:
lists and document
libraries.*

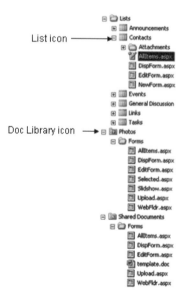

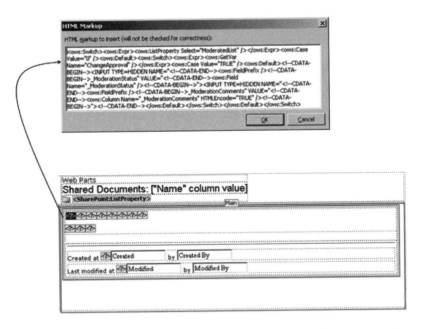

form to its original state, which is a nice option to have if you are not happy with your customizations.

The *List Form Properties* menu option displays the List or Document Library Form dialog. This dialog presents the properties associated with the List form, such as the name of the list or document library to which the form is linked, whether it is a display or edit form, and whether to display a toolbar with the form (Figure 16.22).

FrontPage also provides the ability to create *new* List forms via the *List Forms* option on the Insert menu. When you click this menu option, the List or Document Library Form dialog appears once again, and you can select the properties that you want to associate with your new form.

The contents of each list and document library are displayed in the `AllItems.aspx` page using a List View Web Part. FrontPage 2003 knows that this is a special Web Part type and provides a number of menu options accordingly. If you right-click on a List Form Web Part, you will notice that once again, two menu items are dedicated to this particular Web Part type: *List View Properties* and *Convert to XSLT Data View*. The *List View Properties* option displays the Data view task pane from which you can view the fields; style; and filter, sort, and group criteria associated with the view. You can use the Data View Details task pane to change any of these options. For example, if you want to add and remove columns appearing in the default

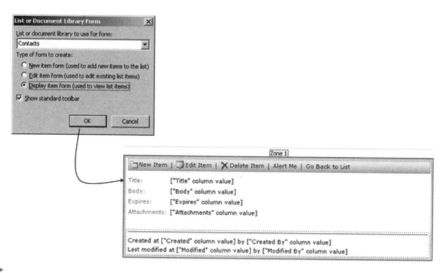

Figure 16.22   *Inserting display item form.*

view of the Contacts list, from the Data View Details task pane you simply
select the **Fields** link and, using the Displayed Fields dialog, add and
remove the relevant fields (Figure 16.23).

The *Convert to XSLT Data View* option converts the Web Part from a
List View Web Part to a Data View Web Part. A Data View Web Part is
more flexible when it comes to defining the presentation of data. We
describe the Data View Web Part in detail later in this chapter.

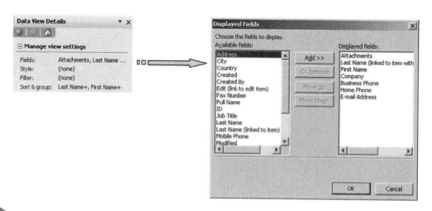

Figure 16.23   *List view properties.*

Inserting new lists, document libraries, and surveys

In addition to being able to customize existing lists, document libraries, and their associated Web Parts, FrontPage 2003 provides the ability to create new lists, document libraries, and surveys in your site. FrontPage 2003 provides a number of templates to use as the format for your list. If the standard templates do not meet your needs, each list type has an associated wizard that you can use to create a custom list.

To create a new document library, do the following:

1.   From the File menu, click **New**. The New task pane appears to the right.

2.   From the New task pane, click **SharePoint List**. The SharePoint List dialog appears.

3.   Click the Document Libraries tab.

4.   Select the Document Library template.

5.   Enter the name for the new document library.

6.   Click **Next**.

Creating a list, document library, or survey using the List Wizard allows you to add and remove fields from the list, enable versioning and content approval for the list, and define the security associated with the list. However, you can access these properties after list creation and make the necessary customizations.

To customize the document library settings, do the following:

1.   From the Folder List pane, right-click the document library you wish to modify.

2.   From the shortcut menu, click **Properties**. The Document Library Properties dialog appears.

3.   Click the Settings tab.

4.   Select the settings appropriate for your document library. For example, you can enable content approval and versioning of documents. You can also change the template associated with the document library.

5.   Select the Fields tab.

6.   Add, remove, or modify the fields of your choice. You can also change the display order of the fields using the *Move Up* and

Move Down options. The Security tab allows you to define whether authorized users can read or change all items in a given list or only their own items. However, you cannot define this level of security for document libraries, which results in the security functions being disabled under the Security tab.

7.   Select the Supporting Files tab.

8.   Select the file to display as the default page in the document library.

9.   Select the file to display when creating new items for the document library.

10. Select the file to display when editing the properties of a document in the library.

16.5 Data views

Microsoft put much effort into the development of its Office 2003 product suite to ensure XML support. This effort is apparent in the released product and makes the entire Office suite, including SPS 2003, an excellent vehicle for collaboration. For example, using Microsoft Word 2003 and Microsoft Excel 2003, you can store documents as XML documents and save them to a SharePoint site ready for consumption by other components on your site, such as a Web Part or a SharePoint list.

Out of the box, SharePoint uses column-based lists as its standard method for displaying data in a site and provides the ability to modify the column data, presenting different views of the list to the user. However, there are some scenarios where the underlying data does not lend itself well to column-based viewing. For example, Microsoft InfoPath 2003 allows you to create form libraries that reside on a SharePoint server and store form data within the library in XML format. Data from the form can be displayed as columns within the form library. If the form items contain a list of Web log postings, the data that you are interested in is the posting itself and any associated comments. This type of data does not lend itself to a column-style viewing format, because it is potentially large and does not have a consistent length. Therefore, we need to find a different mechanism for displaying this information to the user.

The SharePoint Products and Technologies architecture makes this task easy to accomplish, and the tools that ship with FrontPage 2003, in particular the Data View Web Part, make it effortless.

16.5.1   Data sources and Data views

FrontPage 2003, in conjunction with SharePoint, provides many features out of the box that make working with data an easy task. The Data Source Catalog and the Data View Web Part specifically use SharePoint to pull data into Web sites and provide live views of this data. Data can be extracted from a variety of sources, such as Microsoft Office documents, OLE databases, and Web services. An XML Web service known as the data retrieval service runs on the SharePoint server and enables consumers to retrieve and manipulate data from multiple data sources. SharePoint comes equipped with a default set of data retrieval service adapters for working with data in Share-Point lists, OLE databases, and XML data sources. Consumers communicate with these adapters by sending Simple Object Access Protocol (SOAP) requests to the adapter on the server, which returns data in the form of an XML document. The Data View Web Part is one such consumer; it consumes the XML data and formats it using Extensible Stylesheet Language Transform (XSLT) for final presentation in the browser (Figure 16.24).

The presentation layer is separated from the data itself; consequently, users receive a live view of the data. For example, if the data source were a SharePoint list and the content of the list changed, the changes would be reflected in the presentation of the data. The presentation is a view of the data stored in the data source and is referenced as a Data view in FrontPage 2003. The Data View Web Part is the vehicle by which Data views are displayed in SharePoint, and the terms *Data view* and *Data View Web Part* are synonymous. Data views and data sources are intrinsically linked.

You can insert a Data view onto a Web page in a SharePoint-driven site from a number of places within FrontPage 2003. You can use the *Insert Data View* option from the FrontPage 2003 Data menu and the Data Source Catalog drop-down menu associated with a data source. In addition, you also have the ability to insert a Data view from the Insert Database menu. The FrontPage Data view functionality leverages SharePoint's Web Part infrastructure and its underlying services. As a result, this functionality only applies to Web sites running SharePoint. If you attempt to insert a Data view on a site that isn't a SharePoint site, you are presented with a message informing you that this is not possible.

16.5.2   The Data Source Catalog

The **Insert Data View** command launches the Data Source Catalog task pane. The Data Source Catalog provides a single location to access and

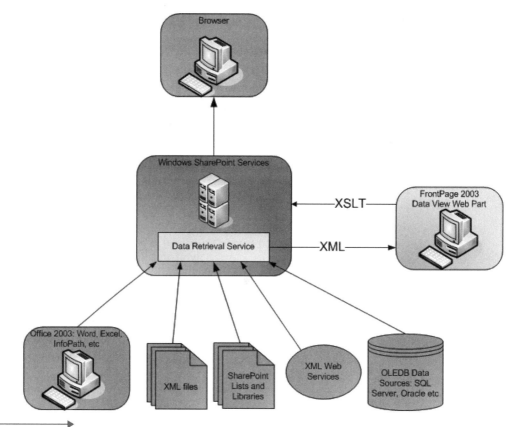

Figure 16.24   *XML data–driven SharePoint site using FrontPage 2003.*

manage data sources, whether they exist on your server or on an external server. You can define the sources of the data that you would like to leverage in your SharePoint site. These data sources can take a number of forms, including: SharePoint lists and SharePoint libraries. The Data Source task pane groups each data source into a corresponding category. Figure 16.25 shows the Data Source Catalog for a typical SharePoint Team Site. By default the catalog is divided into six categories:

1.   **SharePoint lists:** FrontPage automatically creates entries for the SharePoint lists based on the site contents. When you delete a list from the SharePoint site, it is automatically removed from the Data Source Catalog. You can create a new list to add to the Data Source Catalog using the **Create New SharePoint List** link.

- From the SharePoint Lists category in the Data Source Catalog task pane, click the **Create New SharePoint List** link.

- Select the type of list you want to create—for example, a Links list.

- If you haven't chosen to use the New List Wizard, type the name of the new list—for example, "My Links."

- Click **OK**.

The newly created list appears as a data source in the catalog under the SharePoint Lists category. It is important to note that you can also add lists from other sites as content sources; you are not restricted to the current site. To do this, instead of using the **Create New SharePoint List** link, use the **Manage Catalog** link (Figure 16.25). The **Manage Catalog** link allows you to specify additional SharePoint collections, such as lists, document libraries, and form libraries, to the Data Source Catalog. When adding the collection you specify its location in the form of a URL.

2. **SharePoint libraries:** FrontPage automatically creates entries for the SharePoint document libraries based on the site contents. In order to remove theses entries from the Data Source Catalog, you must delete the actual document library from the SharePoint site. However, you can create a new document library to add to the

Figure 16.25
*Data Source
Catalog.*

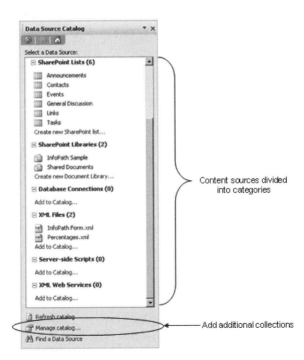

Content sources divided
into categories

Add additional collections

Data Source Catalog using the **Create New Document Library** link.

- From the SharePoint Libraries category in the Data Source Catalog task pane, click the **Create New Document Library** link.

- Select the type of document library you want to create—for example, a picture library.

- If you haven't chosen to use the New Document Library Wizard, type the name of the new document library—for example, "My Pictures."

- Click **OK**.

The newly created library appears as a data source in the catalog under the SharePoint Libraries category. Once again, using the **Manage Catalog** link, you can add document libraries from other SharePoint sites as content sources; you are not restricted to the current site.

3.   **Database connections**: The Database Connections category lists OLEDB data sources, such as Access, SQL Server, and Oracle, that have been added to the Data Source Catalog. The Database Connections category is empty by default, but you can easily add to it by clicking the **Add to Catalog** link (Figure 16.26).

- From the Database Connections category in the Data Source Catalog task pane, click the **Add to Catalog** link.

- Click the Configure Database Connection button.

- Type the server name of the database you want to connect to.

- Type the authentication information required to connect to the database; for example, use Windows authentication to use the currently logged on credentials.

- Click **Next**.

- Select the database and table, view, or stored procedure to use for this connection.

- Click **Finish**.

- Click **OK**.

The newly created database connection appears as a data source in the catalog under the Database Connections category.

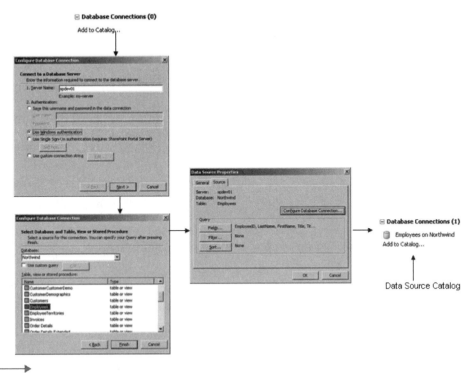

Figure 16.26   *Adding a database as a content source.*

4.   **XML files**: The XML Files category lists the XML files that have been added as data sources to the Data Source Catalog. These files include Word, Excel, and InfoPath documents that have been saved as XML documents. The XML Files category is empty by default, but you can easily add to it by clicking the **Add to Catalog** link.

-    From the XML Files category in the Data Source Catalog task pane, click the **Add to Catalog** link.

-    Type or browse to the location of the XML file.

-    Click **OK**.

The newly created XML file appears as a data source in the catalog under the XML Files category.

5.   **Server-Side Scripts**: The Server-Side Scripts category lists the server-side scripts that have been added to the Data Source Catalog. These scripts should return data in the form of XML so that consumers, such as the Data View Web Part, can use the Data

Retrieval Service to work with the data. The Server-Side Scripts category is empty by default, but you can easily add to it by clicking the **Add to Catalog** link.

- From the Server-Side Scripts category in the Data Source Catalog task pane, click the **Add to Catalog** link.

- In the *URL* field, type the path to the script.

- Select the method on which you want to run the script (HTTP Get or HTTP Post).

- Click **Add** to add parameters to use when running the script.

- Click **OK**.

The newly created server-side script appears as a data source in the catalog under the Server-Side Scripts category.

6. **XML Web services**: The XML Web Services category lists the XML Web services that have been added to the Data Source Catalog. The XML Web Services category is empty by default, but you can easily add to it by clicking the **Add to Catalog** link.

- From the XML Web Services category in the Data Source Catalog task pane, click the **Add to Catalog** link.

- Type the URL of the Web Service or browse its location using the Browse button.

- Click **Connect Now**.

- Modify the connection information to suit your needs; for example, if you are connecting to a Search Web service, you might modify the connection so that you assign a specific value to the query parameter.

- Click **OK**.

The newly created XML Web service appears as a data source in the catalog under the XML Web Services category.

16.5.3   Inserting the Data view

Once the data source has been defined, you are free to insert a Data view on your Web page.

1. Open the page you would like to add the Data view to, or create a new blank page by selecting **New** from the File menu.

2.   From the **Data Source Catalog**, select the data source that you would like to create a Data view for. A shortcut menu appears.

3.   From the shortcut menu, click **Insert Data View**.

The Data view automatically appears on the Web Part Page populated with the contents of the data source. For example, if the data source is a SharePoint list, the Data view will display the contents of this list. Also, if you switch to the code view, you will notice that the code for the Data view has been automatically generated. Modifications to the Data view can be made by directly modifying the code or through the Data View Details task pane. Obviously, the latter option is the least painful.

16.5.4 Selecting the table style

The Basic Table style is the default style used to display data in a Data view; this, of course, can be changed. You have numerous options from which to choose (Table 16.1). Additionally, once a style is chosen, you can continue to apply style modifications to the table using standard FrontPage formatting features or by modifying the XSL code directly.

1.   From the *Manage view settings* section of the Data View Details task pane, click the **Styles** link.

2.   Select the HTML view style to apply to your Data view.

3.   Click **OK**.

Table 16.1   *HTML View Styles*

Table Style	Description
	The basic table style shows a column for each field you choose and a new row for each item in the list.
	The repeating form style shows the title for an item in the list and the other fields on separate lines underneath the title. This layout is repeated for each item in the list.

Table 16.1   *HTML View Styles (continued)*

Table Style	Description
	The repeating form (centered) style shows the title for an item in the list and the other fields on separate lines underneath the title. This layout is repeated for each item in the list, and all of the information is centered.
	The repeating form with border style shows the title for an item in the list and the other fields on separate lines underneath the title. This layout is repeated for each item in the list, and each item appears in its own table cell.
	The two-column repeating form with border style shows a two-column table with each list item in its own table cell.
	The comma-separated style shows the titles for items in the list with all of the other field values separated by commas underneath the titles.
	The two-column comma-separated style shows a two-column view of the titles for items in the list with all of the other field values separated by commas underneath the titles.
	The bulleted list of titles style shows a bulleted list of the titles for all of the items in the list.

Table 16.1   *HTML View Styles (continued)*

Table Style	Description
	The numbered list of titles style shows a numbered list of the titles for all of the items in the list.
	The plain list of titles style shows the titles for all of the items in the list, each on a separate line.
	The horizontal list of titles style shows the titles for all of the items in the list separated by commas on a single line.
	The drop-down menu of titles style shows a drop-down menu that contains the titles for all of the items in the list.
	The page component style shows a bulleted list of the titles for all of the items in the list inside a box.
	The history list style shows the creation date for an item in the list, the title of the item, and the other fields on separate lines underneath the title. This layout is repeated for each item in the list, and items are shown in chronological order. All the information is centered.

Table 16.1 *HTML View Styles (continued)*

Table Style	Description
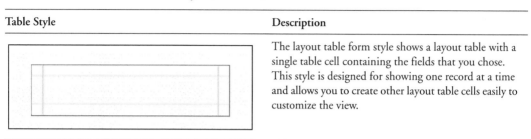	The layout table form style shows a layout table with a single table cell containing the fields that you chose. This style is designed for showing one record at a time and allows you to create other layout table cells easily to customize the view.

16.5.5   View style options

From the Options tab in the View Styles dialog you can specify additional display details such as whether to display a toolbar, a table header, and the number of rows to display per view (paging).

In the current version of the Data View Web Part, it is recommended that you turn on paging if the number of rows in your Data view exceeds 200. Failing to do so when large amounts of data are displayed results in poor performance when editing the Data view, and the performance decreases further as new columns are added. This is a known problem, and more information can be found in Microsoft Knowledge Base Article 820927.

To turn on paging, do the following:

1.   From the *Manage view settings* section of the Data View Details task pane, click the **Styles** link.

2.   Click the Options tab.

3.   In the *Record Sets* section, select the **Display items in sets of this size** radio button and type the number of items you would like to display per view.

4.   Click **OK**.

An item count and navigation links appear at the bottom of the view (Figure 16.27).

16.5.6   Adding fields to the Data view

When you insert the Data view onto your page, FrontPage automatically populates it with a number of fields that it thinks you may want to include.

Figure 16.27
*Data view with
paging turned on.*

For example, if you use a SharePoint Contacts list as your data source, FrontPage automatically includes the *Last Name, Modified By,* and *Modified* fields in the view. This automatic population is convenient when the fields included meet your needs, but what if you want to include a completely different set of fields for your view? The good news is that FrontPage provides a mechanism for you to pick and choose the data that you want to display, and it is a simple matter of dragging and dropping the appropriate fields onto your Data view.

Once you have selected the table style that best suits your needs, you can begin to define which data you want to appear. In addition to displaying formatting options, the Data View Details task pane displays the data associated with the data source. The data appears organized by rows and fields. Each row represents an individual record in the data source. The fields associated with each record appear vertically in the task pane. A toggle determines whether the pane also displays the data values for each field. You can traverse all of the records in a given data source by clicking the navigation arrows in the upper right portion of the *Work with Data* section (Figure 16.28).

To add fields to the Data view, do the following:

1.   From the *Work with Data* section of the Data View Details task pane, select the field you want to display in your Data view.

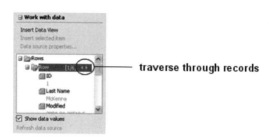

Figure 16.28
*Traversing records
in a data source.*

traverse through records

2.   Drag the field to the appropriate region in your Data view. For example, if you have opted for a table style and inserted a separate column to display the contact's e-mail address, drag the *Email Addresses* field and drop it in the first data row of the column. Dropping the field into the data row of the column will ensure that the data values for subsequent records appear in individual rows. Typically the first row associated with the Data view is a header row.

3.   Repeat steps 1 and 2 until you have chosen the appropriate fields for your view.

Adding fields by dragging and dropping from the task pane automatically inserts the data as text onto the page. However, there may be occasions when you want to specify other data formats when inserting data into the Data view. For example, if you have a URL to a photograph associated with a contact, you may want to display the actual image as opposed to the URL. In this case, instead of dragging and dropping the *URL* field from the task pane, use the **Insert As Picture** command from the shortcut menu.

To specify the format for the column data, do the following:

1.   From the Data view select a data row in the column to which you would like to insert the data.

2.   From the *Work with Data* section of the Data View Details task pane, right-click the field you wish to insert.

3.   From the shortcut menu, click the appropriate command. For example, click the **Insert As Picture** command to insert an image into the Data view.

If there are no records associated with your data source, you may want to provide the user with an appropriate message. Let's say, for example, you have created a site template that automatically populates the Home page with a customized view of the Contacts list associated with the site. When a user creates a site using this template, you will want him or her to know instantly which functionality is associated with the customized view and how to populate the view with data. In this instance, a simple message informing the user that he or she should create contacts in the Contacts list would suffice.

To configure the text that appears when there are no records to display, do the following:

1.   From the *Manage view settings* section of the Data View Details task pane, click the **Styles** link.

2.   Click the Options tab.

3.   In the *Record Sets* section, type the text you want to appear in the *Text to display if no matching items found* field.

4.   Click **OK**.

16.5.7   Formatting the Data view

Once you have selected the style and the data you want to display, you can finalize the look and feel of the view by applying additional formatting. There are a number of options available for formatting a Data view over and above selecting the HTML view. FrontPage provides the ability to format the data in a Data view using traditional FrontPage formatting commands. For example, to format the data in a specific column, you simply select a data cell in the column you want to apply the formatting to and then use the commands from the Format menu or the Formatting toolbar. If the cell is associated with repeating data, the same formatting is applied to the associated repeating data cells. Similarly, you can use the standard FrontPage table commands to insert and remove columns, rows, and cells to and from the Data view and to merge and split cell contents.

In addition to the traditional FrontPage formatting options, the Data View Details task pane provides other formatting commands, such as **Style**, **Filter**, **Sort**, **Group**, and **Conditional Formatting**. The **Style** command, previously discussed, provides the ability to associate a specific HTML view style with your data.

16.5.8   Filtering data

The **Filter** command on the Data View Details task pane allows you to determine which records to display depending on their content. For example, you could apply a filter to a contacts view so that it showed only U.S.-based contacts (Figure 16.29).

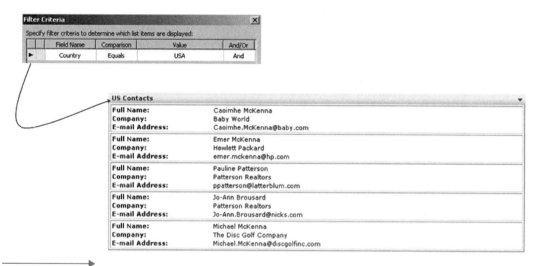

Figure 16.29   *Displaying only U.S. contacts.*

Clicking the **Filter** link in the Data View Details task pane displays the Filter Criteria dialog box. The Filter Criteria dialog box is a visual editor that allows you to create XML Path Language (XPath) expressions through a graphical user interface. XPath expressions are used to filter the elements and text of XML documents and can be edited directly through the code window.

To apply a filter to a Data view, do the following:

1.   From the *Manage View Settings* section of the Data View Details task pane, click the **Filter** link. The Filter Criteria dialog box appears.

2.   Click the **Click here to add new clause** link.

3.   From the Field Name drop-down list, select the field to which you would like to apply the filter—for example, the *Country* field.

4.   From the Comparison drop-down list, select the condition—for example, Equals.

5.   From the Value drop-down list, either type the value of the field that you would like to compare or select an option from the drop-down list. For example, you can check if a field matches the current user or the current date. In our current example we simply type "USA" as the field value.

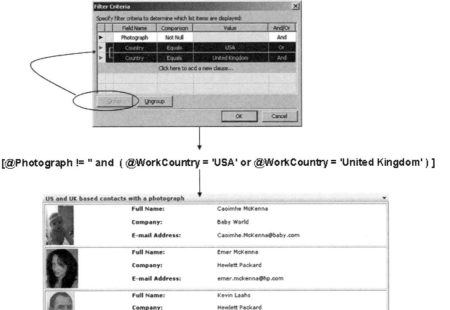

[@Photograph != '' and (@WorkCountry = 'USA' or @WorkCountry = 'United Kingdom')]

Figure 16.30   *Grouping expressions in XPath.*

6.   Click the And/Or drop-down list box to add an additional clause to your condition expression and repeat steps 2 through 6 until the filter criteria are complete.

The Filter Criteria dialog box allows you to group specific parts of a condition expression, much like adding parentheses to the query. For example, you could filter your view to show U.S.- *or* U.K.-based contacts with a photograph with the filter shown in Figure 16.30. Notice that the last two clauses in the expression are grouped, and the XPath expression has parentheses to illustrate the grouping.

16.5.9   Sorting and grouping data

The **Sort and Group** command on the Data View Details task pane allows you to sort and group data in the Data view. Clicking the **Sort and Group** link displays the Sort and Group dialog box. In order to group by a specific field, you must add it to the sort order because sorting and grouping are intrinsically linked. For example, if you wanted to sort and group the contacts list alphabetically by company, you need to add the *Company* field to

Figure 16.31   *Contacts grouped by company.*

the sort order first and then click the *Show Group Header* option. Displaying the group header basically displays all of the records in the group under a single header. In the previous example, the contacts of each company are collated and appear under the appropriate company header (Figure 16.31).

To apply a filter to a Data view, do the following:

1.   From the *Manage View Settings* section of the Data View Details task pane, click the **Sort and Group** link. The Sort and Group dialog box appears (Figure 16.32).

2.   From the Available fields list box, select the field(s) you would like to sort by and click the Add button. The selected fields appear in the Sort Order list box.

3.   From the *Sort Properties* section, click the sort order you wish to apply to the Data view. For example, selecting **Ascending** will sort text fields alphabetically starting with the letter "A."

4.   From the *Group Properties* section, click **Show Group Header**, then select whether to expand or collapse the group by default. Figure 16.32 shows the group expanded.

5.   From the *Group Properties* section, click **Show group footer** if you want to display the group title at the end of the group.

6.   From the *Group Properties* section, click **Hide Group Details** if you want to hide the content of a group. This setting effectively displays the group headers and does not provide a method for expanding the group to display its contents.

Figure 16.32
*Sort and Group
dialog.*

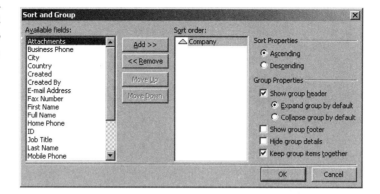

7.   From the *Group Properties* section, click **Keep group items together** if you want to display all records within a group on the same page regardless of paging settings defined for the view.

16.5.10 Conditional formatting

The **Conditional Formatting** link in the Data View Details task pane allows you to apply formatting based on the content of your data. For example, if you wanted to easily distinguish U.S.-based contacts from all other contacts in your list, you could achieve this by simply creating a conditional formatting expression. You can specify conditional formatting to show content, hide content, or apply formatting to content. In our previous example, we would create a Show Content condition that displays the American flag when a contact's country equals "USA." Alternatively, we could create a hide content condition, which hides the American flag when a contact's country data does not equal "USA." To further highlight the U.S.-based contacts, we can create a formatting condition that applies a border when the contact's country equals "USA." Figure 16.33 shows the result of a **Show Content** formatting condition applied to a Data view.

To apply conditional formatting to a Data view, do the following:

1.   From the *Manage View Settings* section of the Data View Details task pane, click the **Conditional Formatting** link. The Conditional Formatting task pane appears.

2.   Click the Create button. A shortcut menu appears.

3.   Click the option that matches the action you would like to take. For example, if you wish to display content based on a specific criterion, then click the **Show Content** command. Regardless of

Figure 16.33
*Data view grouped
by company.*

(Items 1 to 5) <u>Next</u>

which option you choose, the Conditional Formatting Criteria dialog box appears.

4.   Specify the condition expression. To do this follow steps 2 through 6 detailed in section 16.5.8.

5.   Click **OK**. If you chose to create an Apply Formatting condition, the Modify Style dialog box appears. Click the Format button and then select the appropriate Font, Paragraph, Border, Numbering, and Position formats to apply to your data.

6.   Click **OK**.

16.5.11   Web Part formatting

The Data View Web Part is, as its name suggests, a Web Part and, as such, inherits all of the features and standard properties of the Web Part infrastructure present in WSS. Consequently, you can apply additional formatting using standard Web Part customization. For example, you can change the title, height, width, and position of the Web Part through the browser-based interface.

16.5.12   Inserting subviews

If your view contains nested, repeating regions of XML data, the Data View Web Part allows you to insert a subview within your Data view. For example, if you have an XML file listing the details of employees and the documents they published, the Data view would contain a subview providing information on the published content (Figure 16.34).

To create a Data view subview, do the following:

1.   From the Data View Web Part click the area within your table where you would like to insert the subview. If you want the subview to appear directly below the current view for each record, then you can play about with the FrontPage table commands, such as **Insert Row** and **Merge Cells.**

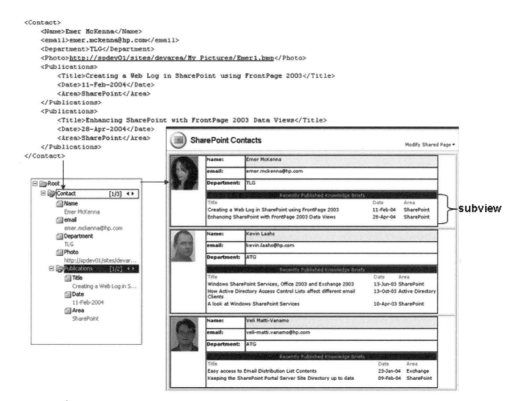

Figure 16.34   *Subviews.*

2.   From the *Work with Data* section of the Data View Details task pane, select the node you want to display in your Data view. Selecting the node will insert all fields in that node into the subview. If you only want to insert a select number of fields, then simply select the fields you want to include in the subview.

3.   From the *Work with Data* section of the Data View Details task pane click the **Insert subview** link.

16.5.13   Connecting Data views

As previously mentioned, the Data View Web Part is a Web Part and as such inherits all of the functionality of a Web Part, including the ability to connect to other Web Parts. For example, if you have a Web Part that receives input from a user, you can filter the results displayed in the Data view based on the text the user enters in the Input form. Figure 16.35 shows a simple Form Web Part mapped to a Data View Web Part via the *Name* field. Setting up a Web connection in this manner means that when a user enters a name in the Form Web Part, the Data View Web Part filters its results and displays details for the record matching the entered name.

If you connect a Web Part to a Data View Web Part containing a subview, you will not have access to the subview fields when it comes to choosing columns that contain matching data. In our previous example, if,

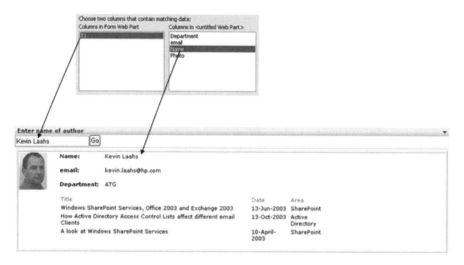

Form Web Part connected to Data View Web Part matched on Name field

Figure 16.35   *Connecting Web Parts.*

Figure 16.36   *Connecting to a subview.*

instead of entering the author name, we wanted to be able to enter a focus area, such as SharePoint, and filter results in the Data view based on that, then how would we achieve this? We would somehow need to have access to the *Area* field through the Web Part Connection Wizard. This can be achieved by extracting the subview into its own Data view, and modifying the XML file to include a field to map to the parent node.

In our previous example, we would remove the subview from the Contacts Data view, select the publication node, and insert it as a separate Data view on the Web Part Page, then update the XML file to include the *Name* field in the Publication node. Once this is achieved, we are able to set up a Web Part connection between the Form Web Part and the Publication Data view using the *Area* field as the mapping column. We can set up an additional Web Part connection between the Publications Data View Web Part and the Contacts Data View Web Part using the *Name* field on both Web Parts as the mapping column.

In Figure 16.36, when the user enters the area in the Form Web Part, all publications matching that entry appear in the Publications Data View Web Part. In addition, the Publications Data View Web Part highlights the articles written by the contact displayed in the Contact Data View Web Part. Clicking on an article that is not highlighted displays the author's contact details.

16.5.14   Converting lists to Data views

As previously mentioned, in addition to being able to insert Data views onto a Web Part Page, you can convert existing SharePoint lists, such as the Contacts list, to a Data view. Once you perform this conversion, you can format your list content as a Data view and edit the XSLT code directly.

To convert a list to a Data view, do the following:

1. Using FrontPage 2003 select the list you would like to convert.

2. Right-click the list.

3. From the shortcut menu, click **Convert to XSLT Data View.**

4. The Data View Details task pane appears, and you are now free to customize the list.

16.6   Customizing menus

FrontPage 2003 provides you with many options for customizing menus and the navigational structure of your site. This section highlights some of the areas in which you are likely to make customizations.

16.6.1   Customizing the navigational structure

The Navigation view and Navigation pane in FrontPage 2003 allow you to easily view the navigational structure and content layout of your SharePoint site. Figure 16.37 shows the Navigation view and Navigation pane for a WSS site.

The navigational structure is made up of a number of custom link bars, pages, and a Home page that indicates the starting point for the site. A link bar is basically a component that maintains a set of links that connect the pages in your site. Each page in a WSS site contains a link bar at the top, displayed horizontally, which, in turn, contains the main navigational menu for the site. Additional link bars are accessible by default in the Quick Launch area of each page and are displayed vertically. Custom link bars are not actual physical link bars, but a special type of object created through the Navigation view containing a list of links to one or more pages. Once a custom link bar is defined, it is available to insert as a link bar on your pages. Figure 16.37 shows the default custom link bars associated with a WSS site. These custom link bars are labeled SharePoint Top Navbar, Documents, Pictures, Lists, Discussions, and Surveys. Each link bar contains a list of links for use in one or more pages. For example, the list of links defined in the SharePoint Top NavBar custom link bar includes the `default.aspx` Home page, the Documents and Lists page, the Create page, the Site Settings page, and the Help page. A link bar appears at the top of each Web Part Page, providing navigational access to all other pages in the Links list.

Figure 16.37
*Navigation pane
and Navigation
view.*

Toolbar provides ability to add a new page, existing pages,
make custom link bars and include a page in a link bar.

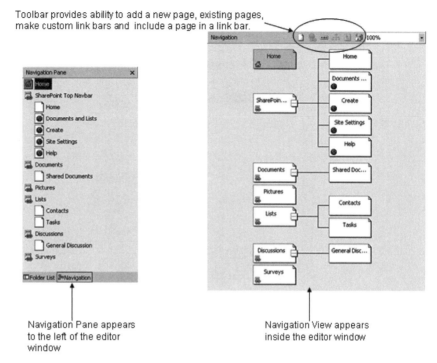

Navigation Pane appears
to the left of the editor
window

Navigation View appears
inside the editor window

If you double-click the link bar that appears at the top of the Home page of a WSS site, you are presented with the Link Bar Properties dialog (Figure 16.38). Using this dialog you can add and remove links from the link bar or change the order of how the links appear. In addition, you can change the style associated with the link bar. Adding, removing, and changing the order of a link bar in one page updates the link bar display on all connecting pages; however, style updates are not carried forward.

When you create a new Web Part Page in FrontPage 2003, the Share-Point Top Navbar link bar is conveniently inserted automatically at the top of the page. Changing the options defined on this menu results in changing the link bars for all connected pages. So how do you create a custom menu on a Web Part Page using the navigational structure? The answer lies in the ability to create and define your own custom link bars.

Once again, a custom link bar is a special type of object created through the Navigation view, which contains a list of links to one or more pages. Once created, this object is available to insert as a link bar from the Link Bar Properties dialog.

Figure 16.38
*Link Bar Properties
dialog.*

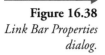

To create a custom link bar in your WSS site, do the following:

1.   From the View menu, click **Navigation**.

2.   Right-click the background area of the Navigation view.

3.   From the shortcut menu, click **New** and then **Custom Link Bar**. A custom link bar appears at the bottom of the first column in the Navigation view.

4.   Right-click the new custom link bar.

5.   From the shortcut menu, click **Rename** and enter a name that describes the custom link bar.

6.   Right-click the new custom link bar.

7.   From the shortcut menu, click **Add Existing Page** to add an existing page to the list of links maintained by the custom link bar. You can also create a new page to add to the list of links by clicking **New** and then **Page** from the shortcut menu. When you create a new page using this method, FrontPage creates a blank HTML file. You do not have the ability to create a page based on the Web Part Page template from this option.

8.   Repeat step 7 until you are satisfied that all your links are defined.

The custom link bar is now available for selection from the Link Bar Properties dialog. Modifying the existing horizontal navigational structure on your Web Part Page to use the links defined in the new custom link bar is a simple matter of double-clicking the link bar on your Web Part Page and selecting the custom link bar from the dialog.

To modify the existing navigation link bar on a Web Part Page, do the following:

1.   Open the Web Part Page you wish to modify in the Design view.

2.   Double-click the horizontal link bar at the top of the page. Alternatively, you can right-click the link bar and click the **Link Bar Properties** command from the shortcut menu. The Link Bar Properties dialog appears.

3.   From the drop-down list in the *Choose Existing* section of the dialog, select the custom link bar you previously created.

4.   If you want the Home page to appear in the link bar, check the *Home Page* option in the *Additional Links* section of the dialog.

5.   Click **OK**.

Your new menu appears in the horizontal navigation bar at the top of your Web Part Page.

16.6.2   Collapsing navigation bars

A common navigation technique employed by Web sites is the use of collapsing navigation bars. Collapsing navigation bars provide a list of items that users can expand to see associated links or collapse to hide the links from their view. This type of navigation bar can enhance the usability of your site, especially when used in conjunction with existing list and document library data. The following example will show how to create a collapsing navigation bar and how to leverage this functionality for navigating a large document library.

To create the collapsing navigation bar, do the following:

1.   Using your browser, create a new SharePoint list using the Custom List template.

2.   Modify the columns and settings of the new list.

3.   Add a new text field named *Area*.

4.   Add items to the list, entering the focus area in the *Area* field—for example, "SharePoint"—and a subject area in the *Title* field—for example, "FrontPage."

5. Navigate to the page that you want to add the collapsing menu to.

6. From the File menu, click **Edit with Microsoft Office FrontPage**.

7. From the Data menu, click **Insert Web Part**.

8. From the *Web Part List* section of the Web Parts task pane, drag the list that you created in step 1 onto the Web Part Page.

9. Right-click the Web Part and click **List View Properties** from the shortcut menu. The Data View Details task pane appears.

10. Click the **Fields** link. The Displayed Fields dialog appears.

11. Remove all fields and add the *Title* field to the Displayed fields list (Figure 16.39).

12. Click **OK**.

13. From the Data View Details task pane, click the **Style** link. The View Styles dialog appears.

14. Click the Options tab.

15. Uncheck the **Toolbar** check box. This hides the toolbar from the list view.

16. Click **OK**.

17. From the Data View Details task pane, click the **Sort & Group** link. The Sort and Group dialog appears.

18. Remove all fields from the Sort Order list, and then add the *Area* field.

Figure 16.39
Selecting the Area field for display.

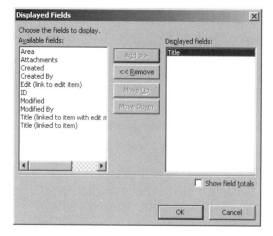

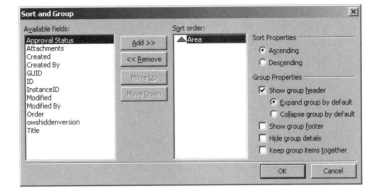

Figure 16.40
Sort and Group settings for menu.

19.   From the *Sort Properties* section, select the **Ascending** radio button.

20.   From the *Group Properties* section, select the **Show group header** check box, and select the **Expand Group by default** radio button (Figure 16.40).

21.   Click **OK**.

Figure 16.41 shows the list at this stage of customization. Further modifications can be made to remove the "Title" heading and the "Area:" reference. To do this we need to convert the list into a Data View Web Part.

1.   Right-click the list Web Part.

2.   From the shortcut menu, click **Convert to XSLT Data View**.

3.   Click the row that contains "Title."

4.   From the Table menu, click **Select** and then click **Row**.

5.   From the Table menu, click **Delete Rows**.

6.   In the first row that contains the Area header, select "Area:."

Figure 16.41
List menu.

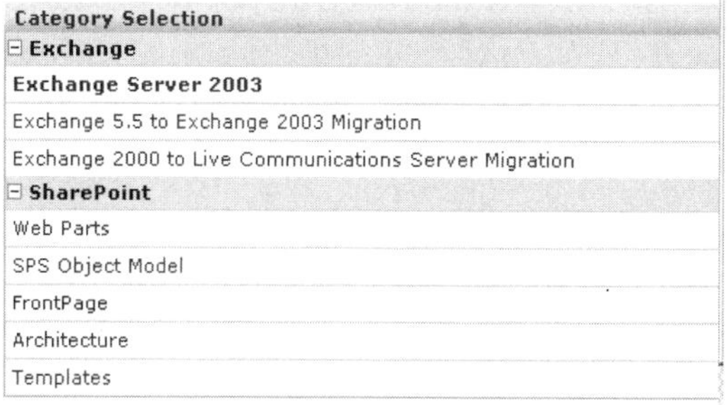

Figure 16.42
*Collapsing menu
with "Area" prefix
removed.*

Category Selection
⊟ **Exchange**
Exchange Server 2003
Exchange 5.5 to Exchange 2003 Migration
Exchange 2000 to Live Communications Server Migration
⊟ **SharePoint**
Web Parts
SPS Object Model
FrontPage
Architecture
Templates

7.   Press the Delete key.

8.   Save your Web Part Page.

The collapsible menu is now available for use. Figure 16.42 shows the menu with the "Title" and "Area:" prefixes removed.

Now we will link the menu to a document library on the same page and use Web Part connections to filter the view by the subject selected in the menu. The following example connects Web Parts on the same page; however, you can just as easily connect the menu Web Part to a Web Part on another page if that better suits your needs.

To link the menu to a Document Library Web Part, do the following:

1.   Use the browser interface to create a new document library. Alternatively, you can use an existing document library.

2.   Modify the columns and setting of the document library to include an additional field named *Subject*. Ideally, this would be a choice field and the list of choices would coincide with the subjects in the Menu list.

3.   Add documents to the document library and tag the documents appropriately. For example, a document about customizing SPS with FrontPage 2003 would map to the FrontPage *Subject* field.

4.   Navigate to the page that contains the collapsing menu.

5.   From the File menu, click **Edit with Microsoft Office FrontPage**.

6.   From the Data menu, click **Insert Web Part**.

7.   From the *Web Part List* section of the Web Parts task pane, drag the document library that you created in step 1 onto the Web Part Page.

8.   Right-click the collapsing menu Data View Web Part.

9. From the shortcut menu, click **Web Part Connections**. The Web Part Connections Wizard appears.

10. For the actions select **Provide Data Values To.**

11. Click **Next.**

12. Select **Connect to a Web Part on this page**.

13. Click **Next.**

14. Select the Document Library Web Part as the target Web Part for the connection.

15. Select **Get Sort/Filter From** as the target action.

16. Click **Next.**

17. From the left-hand list select **Title** as the column, and match it to the **Subject** column in the right list.

18. Click **Next.**

19. Select **Title** as the column to create a hyperlink that triggers the action on the consumer Web Part.

20. Select the **Indicate Current Selection using** check box and make sure it maps to the **ID** column.

21. Click **Next.**

22. Click **Finish.**

You now have a collapsing menu that filters the documents listed in a Document Library Web Part on your page (Figure 16.43).

Figure 16.43   *Collapsing menu working with Document Library Web Part.*

16.7 Web Packages

A Web Package is a set of files used to form the basis of a Web site. You can import a Web Package for use in a new Web site or export it as the foundation for other Web site projects. The packages are SharePoint aware and as such not only can import and export Web pages and their associated content, but also SharePoint lists, form libraries, document libraries and their content, and any associated link bars. In addition, the package can also identify file dependencies, such as stylesheets and images, and ensure that they are packaged so that the package itself can be deployed easily to other sites. This is very convenient if you have multiple lists, document libraries, and files that you want to share as one complete package instead of creating several list templates.

The package itself is a single file with a `.fwp` extension that contains a number of logical files in compressed format; as such it is similar in functionality to a CAB file.

To export a Web Package, do the following:

1. From the Tools menu, click **Packages**.

2. Click **Export**. The Export Web Package dialog appears (Figure 16.44).

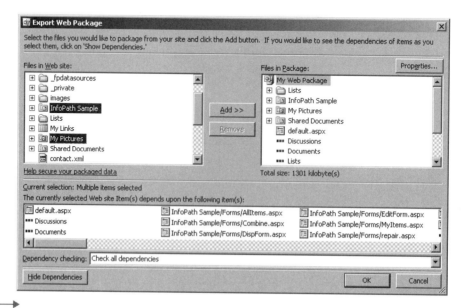

Figure 16.44   *Export Web Package dialog.*

3. From the Files in Web site list, select the files you want to include in the package. As you select files and folders, their dependencies appear in the bottom pane of the dialog.

4. Click **Add**. The files you selected appear in the Files in Package list.

5. Click **Properties**. The Web Package Properties dialog appears.

6. Enter the name of your Web Package, a description for the Web Package, the author of the Web Package, and the company that owns the Web Package.

7. Click **OK.**

8. Click **OK.**

9. Navigate to the location where you want to store the file and give the file a name—for example, "`mywebpackge.fwp`."

10. Click **Save**. Your Web Package is now ready for consumption by other sites.

To import a Web Package, do the following:

1. From the Tools menu, click **Packages**.

2. Click **Import**. The File Open dialog appears.

3. Select the `.fwp` file you want to import.

4. Click **Open**. The Web Package will be deployed to your site.

FrontPage 2003 provides two Web Package solutions for SharePoint sites out of the box: the Web Log Web Package and the News and Reviews Web Package. The Web Log Web Package creates a Web site containing Web Parts with blogging capability, and the News and Reviews Web Package creates a Web site containing Web Parts that are associated with news, such as a Headlines Web Part. Web Packages are not intended to be a complete solution; it is up to the user to customize the site with the styles and additional functionality needed.

16.8 Web Log Web Packages

The Web Log Web Package enables you to add blogging functionality to a Windows SharePoint Services site in a matter of minutes. The following section introduces the concept of blogging, discusses the features of this powerful add-on, and steps you through creating a blog with FrontPage 2003.

16.8.1   What is blogging?

Blogging is short for "Web logging" and is the term used to describe the journaling style of activity by an individual or group of individuals on a Web site. More specifically, a Web log, or blog, is a Web site containing entries listed in reverse chronological order so that the most recent entry appears at the top. Each entry is dated and most commonly contains textual information with links to content of interest or relevance; however, blogs that contain media formats such as photoblogs, videoblogs, and audioblogs are becoming more and more prevalent. This textual information is usually narrative in style and reflects the thoughts and opinions of the author. Blogs are an increasingly popular mechanism for individuals to publicly express opinions on topics of interest to them. For example, searching for the word "blog" on the Web returns links to various blog sites with topics ranging from humanitarian aid in Iran to how Joe's Christmas celebrations went.

There are many ways for readers to navigate to blogs. They can navigate directly to blog sites, where they can access the most recent posts; they can arrive at an older post via the results of a search; or they can access blogs via links to other Web sites. If the blog provides syndication, then they can read updates from their RSS reader. In addition, many blogs provide functionality to allow readers to comment on individual entries and as a result are often used as a discussion tool.

In a corporate environment blogging offers the capability for employees to collaborate and share their knowledge in a fashion that's relatively free from the strict publishing rules usually enforced on company Web sites. However, it should be noted that although blogs encourage freedom of speech, they are self-regulating because authors are ultimately responsible for what they write. If you have implemented the provisioning service within your organization, then SharePoint would be the ideal host for such a service. The SharePoint sites provide teams of individuals with a particular interest in common, such as a project they are working on, with an area in which they can collaborate and share information with one another. Providing blogging capabilities to these teams would allow them to easily share ideas, information, and progress on an ongoing basis. Readers interested in the same topics can provide feedback by adding comments to the blog posts. In addition to team blogs, individuals can add their own blogs providing details on what's going on in their daily lives, which can foster strong relationships with the virtual community.

16.8.2   Functionality overview

Before we delve into the structure of the Web log site, let's have a look at the functionality provided. The initial installation of the Web Log Web Package creates a site with blogging functionality based on SharePoint (Figure 16.45). The site has a WSS site look and feel, including a horizontal navigation bar that provides a link back to the parent site.

Out-of-the-box functionality includes content management, discussions, favorite links, Web log archives, search, and administration. The content-management pages of the site allow contributors to easily add and edit Web log posts and links to sites of interest (Figure 16.46). The editor used to add posts is the same rich-text editor used on other lists in WSS sites, such as the Announcements list. It provides basic formatting and allows hyperlinks. It does not provide the ability to insert images directly into a post, which is unfortunate because inline images are more prevalent in blog entries today. Of course, this functionality can be added by customizing the page to make use of a different editor, for example, an HTML editor.

Figure 16.45   *Web log Web site.*

When you a create a new Web log posting, the data is stored in a Share-Point list, and a data-driven Web Part on both the Home page and the New Web Log Posting page displays the contents of this list in chronological order, as shown in Figures 16.45 and 16.46. Each individual Web log post can have numerous comments associated with it. This functionality provides a vehicle for discussions on individual posts and consequently fosters collaboration between the author of the blog (blogger) and the audience. The comments are stored in another SharePoint list, and the same data-driven Web Part is used to display its contents.

Web log posts typically make extensive use of links, and readers of a blog may find themselves searching for previous posts to find a link that was of particular interest to them. The Links Web Part that appears on the Web log Home page attempts to alleviate this problem. It provides authors with an area to list the links that they feel are particularly relevant to the site and to the readers of that site. The actual links themselves are stored in yet another SharePoint list, and the Web Part on the default Home page simply displays a filtered view of the list contents.

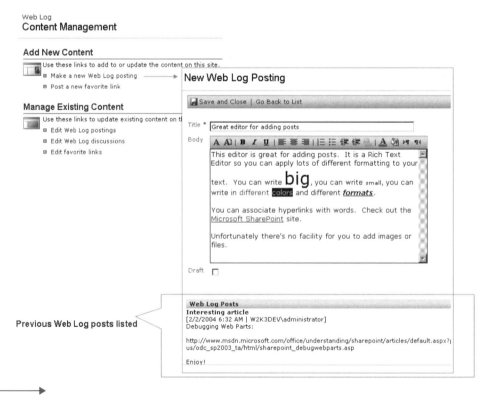

Figure 16.46   *Content-management pages.*

Figure 16.47
Admin document library.

The editing functions of the content-management pages direct the blogger to the AllItems Web Part Page of the actual lists used to store the Web log postings, discussions, and favorite links. Using these pages, also known as administration pages as they are stored in the Admin document library, bloggers can modify existing content on the site (Figure 16.47).

The Web Log Web Package provides users with the ability to view post archives. A Web Part on the Home page links the user to this month's posts, last month's posts, and the posts from two months prior (Figure 16.45). Each link launches the appropriate Web Part Page containing the same data-driven Web Part as used to display Web log posts and Web log discussions; however, this time the Web Part has a filter applied to it commanding the part to display results within a specific date range. The Web Log Web Part on the Home page displays the entire contents of the Web Log list because it does not have a date-range filter applied. If users want to see posts older than two months, they need to navigate to the Home page and scroll through the Web Log Web Part.

Search functionality allows users to search the contents of all the Web log postings and discussions stored on the site. Where you are in the site navigation determines the result set that appears. For example, if you enter a word to search on from the Home page, then the search is performed against the contents of the Web Log list. If you enter a word to search on from the Discussions View page, then the search is performed against the contents of the Web Log Discussions list. Returning results from both lists requires customization.

Administration pages allow the owner of the site to assign the necessary access and permissions to secure the data. For example, you may only want to be able to add Web log posts but willingly encourage comments from your audience. To facilitate this security approach the Web Part Pages that add content to the Web log are stored in a separate document library to which you can apply a set of permissions and access rights different from those granted on the lists.

The Admin document library also stores the Web Part Pages used to display the entire contents of each list in regular list format (Figure 16.47). Placing these files in the Admin document library and applying restrictions at the security level ensures that your audience can only view content in your site through the appropriate Web Parts, such as the Web Log Web Part.

When you first install your Web Log Web Package, the Home page displays instructions on how to secure your site. Security is applied using the site-administration pages of the Web log site. Because the Web Log Web Package creates a SharePoint-aware site, the features and functionality of the site-administration and site-settings pages are the same as those found on other WSS sites. Permissions on the Admin document library can be set. In WSS you can specify the actions specific groups of users can perform through the use of site groups. For example, the Reader site group allows users to read items in lists and document libraries, view pages in the site, and create a site using the Self-Service Site Creation Service. The Web Log security instructions advise you to remove the Contributor and Reader site groups, leaving the Web Designer site group intact. Consequently, only those users assigned the Web Designer site group will be able to create new postings and edit existing postings. Because the security functionality is the same as that found in any other WSS site, you can create your own site groups or customize existing ones to suit your needs. For example, if you want to give users the ability to create new postings, but do not want them to be able to delete or edit existing content, then you can create a specific site group and assign it to the appropriate users.

Web Log Web Packages—Behind the scenes

As previously mentioned, the Web Log Web Package is made up of a collection of SharePoint-aware files that include three lists, one document library, and several Web Part Pages (Figure 16.48). The Web Log list stores all Web

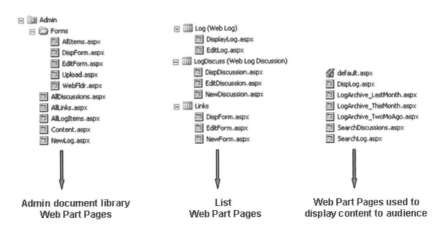

Figure 16.48
*Web Log Web
Package files.*

Admin document library   List   Web Part Pages used to
Web Part Pages   Web Part Pages   display content to audience

log postings, the Web Log Discussion list stores all discussion items related to the Web log postings, and the Links list stores favorite links entries. Notice that for each list, the default AllItems Web Part Page is located in the Admin document library instead of the actual list itself. This prevents readers of the Web log from being able to access the raw view of the data and edit its content.

Each document library in WSS has five default Web Part Pages, or forms, that provide the functionality of the document library. For example, the `AllItems.aspx` form displays the contents of the document library, and the `DispForm.aspx` form displays the contents of an individual item in the document library. These forms appear in the Forms subfolder in the document library. The Admin document library in the Web log site contains these forms, in addition to the content-management Web Part Pages. Table 16.2 describes the functionality of each of the Web Part Pages in the Admin document library.

Table 16.2   *Admin Document Library Files*

Web Part Page	Description
AllItems.aspx	Form used to display all of the items in the document library
DispForm.aspx	Form used to display the contents of an item in the document library
EditForm.aspx	Form used to edit an item in the document library
Upload.aspx	Form used to upload items to the document library

Table 16.2   *Admin Document Library Files (continued)*

Web Part Page	Description
Webfldr.aspx	Form used to display the contents of the document library in Windows Explorer format
AllDiscussions.aspx	Web Part Page used to display the contents of the Web Log Discussion list
AllLinks.aspx	Web Part Page used to display the contents of the Links list
AllLogItems.aspx	Web Part Page used to display the contents of the Web Log list
Content.aspx	Web Part Page used to display content-management options of the Web log site
NewLog.aspx	Form used to add a new item in the Web Log list (i.e., post a blog entry)

Each list in WSS typically contains four main Web Part Pages, or forms, that provide the functionality of the list: AllItems.aspx, Disp-Form.aspx, EditForm.aspx, and NewForm.aspx. Some lists, such as the Events list, contain additional Web Part Pages. The Web Log list contains just two Web Part Pages, DisplayLog.aspx and EditLog.aspx, which are modified versions of the DispForm.aspx and EditForm.aspx Web Part Pages. AllLogItems.aspx and NewLog.aspx are modified versions of the AllItems.aspx and NewForm.aspx Web Part Pages and are stored in the Admin document library to provide additional security. Table 16.3 describes the functionality of each of the files in the Web Log list.

The Web Log Discussion list contains three Web Part Pages, Dis-playDiscussion.aspx, EditLog.aspx, and NewDiscussion.aspx, which are modified versions of the DispForm.aspx, EditForm.aspx, and NewForm.aspx Web Part Pages. The AllDiscussions.aspx Web

Table 16.3   *Web Log List Files*

Web Part Page	Description
DisplayLog.aspx	Form used to display the contents of a posting in the Web Log list
EditLog.aspx	Form used to edit a posting in the Web Log list

Table 16.4 *Web Log Discussion List*

Web Part Page	Description
DispDiscussion.aspx	Form used to display the content of a discussion comment in the Web Log Discussions list
EditDiscussion.aspx	Form used to edit the content of a discussion comment in the Web Log Discussions list
NewDiscussion.aspx	Form used to add a new discussion comment to the Web Log Discussions list

Part Page is a modified version of the `AllItems.aspx` Web Part Page and is stored in the Admin document library to provide additional security. Table 16.4 describes the functionality of each of the files in the Web Log Discussion list.

The Links list contains three of the default Web Part Pages that provide the link functionality: `DispForm.aspx`, `EditForm.aspx`, and `New-Form.aspx`. The `AllLinks.aspx` Web Part Page is a modified version of the `AllItems.aspx` and is stored in the Admin document library to provide additional security. Table 16.5 describes the functionality of each of the files in the Links list.

The top level of the Web log site contains several Web Part Pages that provide visitors with the ability to view and navigate through the Web log. The Home page is represented by `default.aspx` and is the main Web Part Page of the site. It contains Web Parts that display the content of the Web log and allow you to navigate through the Web Log list via search functionality or archives. Table 16.6 describes the functionality of the files at the top level.

Table 16.5 *Links List Files*

Web Part Page	Description
DispForm.aspx	Form used to display the contents of a link entry in the Links list
EditForm.aspx	Form used to edit the contents of a link entry in the Links list
NewForm.aspx	Form used to add a new link entry to the Links list

Table 16.6   *Top-Level Files*

Web Part Page	Description
`Default.aspx`	Web Part Page that represents the Home page of the Web log site. It contains the Web Log Web Part, the Web Log Search Web Part, the Archives Web Part, and the Favorite Links Web Part
`DispLog.aspx`	Web Part Page that displays the discussion thread associated with a Web log posting. This page is invoked when a user clicks the comments icon in the Web Log Web Part.
`LogArchive_LastMonth.aspx`	Web Part Page that displays the previous month's Web log postings. It presents this information to the user via the Web Log Web Part with a filter applied on the date range.
`LogArchive_ThisMonth.aspx`	Web Part Page that displays the current month's Web log postings. It presents this information to the user via the Web Log Web Part with a filter applied on the date range.
`LogArchive_TwoMoAgo.aspx`	Web Part Page that displays the Web log postings from two months prior to the current date. It presents this information to the user via the Web Log Web Part with a filter applied on the date range.
`SearchDiscussions.aspx`	Web Part Page that displays the results of a search launched from the Search Discussions Web Part
`SearchLog.aspx`	Web Part Page that displays the results of a search launched from the Search Web Part on the Home page of the Web log site

Web Parts

The functionality of the Web log site is provided through the use of Web Parts. Table 16.7 lists the Web Parts involved at the top level of the site, the Web Part Page in which they are employed, the type of Web Part, and the function it provides. The table does not include the Web Parts found on the content-management, list, and document library pages.

Notice that the Web Part type used most often is the Data View Web Part (Figure 16.49).

Table 16.7   *Web Log Package Web Parts*

Web Part	Web Part Page	Web Part Page: Web Part Type	Description

`Web Log.dwp`	`Default.aspx,`
	`LogArchive_ThisMonth.aspx,`
	`LogArchive_LastMonth.aspx,`
	`Log_Archive_TwoMoAgo.aspx,`
		`DataViewWebPart`	A data-driven Web Part used to display the individual posts of a Web log in chronological order. The actual data presented in this Web Part is extracted from the Web Log list.

`Search.dwp`	`Default.aspx,`
	`SearchLog.aspx,`
	`LogArchive_ThisMonth.aspx,`
	`LogArchive_LastMonth.aspx,`
	`Log_Archive_TwoMoAgo.aspx,`
		`SimpleFormWebPart`	A simple Web Part that passes data to the target Data View Web Part via a Web Part connection. The actual result set returned depends on the Web Part Page from which the search was launched. For example, if the search was performed on `LogArchive_ThisMonth.aspx`, then only Web log postings from the current month will be returned.

`Archives.dwp`	`Default.aspx,` `LogArchive_ThisMonth.aspx`	`ContentEditorWebPart`	The Content Editor Web Part whose source properties contain HTML code that displays links to the archive Web Part Pages.
`Links.dwp`	`Default.aspx`	`DataViewWebPart`	A data-driven Web Part that displays the favorite links in basic table format. The actual data presented in this Web Part is extracted from the Links list.
`Log.dwp`	`DispLog.aspx`	`DataViewWebPart`	A data-driven Web Part that displays the individual posts of a Web log in chronological order. The actual data presented in this Web Part is extracted from the Web Log Discussion list.

Table 16.7 *Web Log Package Web Parts (continued)*

Web Part	Web Part Page	Web Part Page: Web Part Type	Description
Discussion.dwp	DispLog.aspx	DataViewWebPart	A data-driven Web Part used to display the individual comments associated with a Web log. The actual data presented in this Web Part is extracted from the Web Log Discussion list.
Search Discussions.dwp	SearchDiscussions.aspx	SimpleFormWebPart	A simple Web Part that passes data to the target Data View Web Part (Results List.dwp) via a Web Part connection.
Results List.dwp	SearchLog.aspx	DataViewWebPart	A data-driven Web Part that displays the results of the Refine Search and Search Web Parts. The data presented is extracted from the Web Log list.
Results List.dwp	SearchDiscussions.aspx	DataViewWebPart	A data-driven Web Part that displays the results of the Refine Search and Search Web Parts. The data presented is extracted from the Web Log Discussion list.
Refine Search.dwp	SearchLog.aspx, SearchDiscussions.aspx	SimpleFormWebPart	Data is passed from the Refine Search Web Part to the Results List Web Part via a Web Part connection.

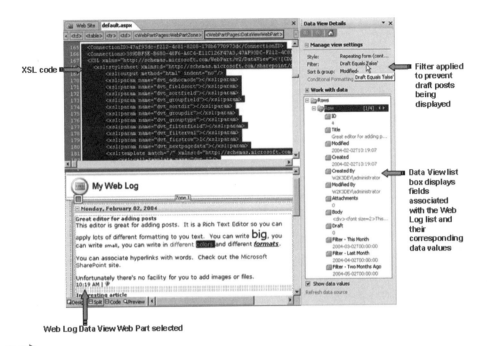

Figure 16.49   *Data View Web Part.*

16.8.3   Creating a Web log site

The following steps show you how to create a Web log site in WSS. The prerequisites are that you have FrontPage 2003 installed and have permissions on the selected site to create a new SharePoint site.

1.   Open your browser and navigate to the WSS site that you want to be the parent site of your Web log.

2.   On the File menu, click **Edit with Microsoft FrontPage**.

3.   On the FrontPage File menu, click **New**.

4.   In the New task pane, under *New Web site*, click **Web Package solutions**.

5.   From the Web Site Templates dialog box, click the Web Log Web Package.

6.   Type the URL of the SharePoint site to which you want to deploy the Web Log Package—for example, "`http://spdev01/sites/devSite/MyWebLog`." Alternatively, click **Browse** and navigate to the site.

Figure 16.50
*Default Web log
Home page.*

7. Click **OK**.

    The Import Web Package dialog appears. It presents the list of files included in the Web Log Package that are installed in the site. If you click on the Properties button, you can see the list of files that the Web Log Web Package relies on to exist.

8. Click **Import**.

9. When presented with the security warning, click **Yes**.

    The importing of the Web Log Package may take several minutes. Upon completion you are presented with a message indicating successful completion.

10. Click **OK**.

11. Exit FrontPage 2003 and, using your browser, navigate to the URL entered in step 6. You are presented with the default Web Log page shown in Figure 16.50.

16.8.4   Setting up your Web log site

Before you invite users to view your Web log, there are a few configuration steps to complete, such as securing your site, modifying the title, and adding content.

Securing your site

Clicking the **Ensure Your Security** link on the default Home page of your newly created Web log site presents you with a list of instructions on how to secure your site (see Figure 16.51). By following these instructions users will only be able to see the contents of your Web logs through the Web Log

Ensure Your Security
To protect your information, it is important for you to set permissions for your site.

1) *Protect Draft Postings:* With your Web Log it is possible to create 'draft' postings that only you can see. However, for this feature to be secure, you need to set access permissions for the **Admin** document library in this site.

To restrict access to the **Admin** document library, do the following:
1. Go to **Site Settings** page, click **Go to Site Administration**.
2. Click **Manage Permission Inheritance**, and then click **Use Unique Permissions**.
3. Click **OK**.
4. On the **Site Settings** page, click **Modify Site Content**.
5. Click **Customize Admin**, and then click **Change Permissions for this Document Library**.
6. Select **Contributor** and **Reader** users, and then click **Remove Users**.
7. Click **OK**.

Now, only authorized users will be able to see draft postings.

2) *Give Users Access:* For site visitors to visit your site, you need to add them to the Reader site group. For site visitors to be able to contribute postings, add them to the 'Contributor' site group.

To set user permissions:
1. Go to **Site Settings** and click **Go to Site Administration**.
2. Click **Manage Permission Inheritance** and then click **Use Unique Permissions**.
3. Click Ok.
4. On the **Site Settings** page, click **Manage Users**.

From there you can give access to users of your choice.

Figure 16.51   *Security instructions.*

Web Parts and will not be allowed to add content unless you have specifically granted them access.

Modifying the title

You will most likely want to replace the default title that appears on the Web Log page with your own title—for example, your own name.

1.   Click the **Modify Shared Page** link in the upper right corner of the Web Part Page (Figure 16.52).

Figure 16.52
Modifying the Web log title.

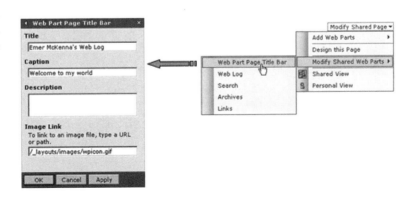

2.   Click the **Modify Shared Web Parts** link.

3.   Click the **Web Part Page Title Bar** link.

4.   Replace the contents of the *Title* field with your title.

5.   Enter a caption if you wish. The caption appears above the title in the Web Part Page.

6.   You can replace the default image that appears to the left of the title with an image of your choosing. I have chosen to keep the default.

7.   Click **OK** to see your changes.

Adding content

Your Web log is almost ready for consumption by the reader population. All that remains for you to do is to start adding content. The content-management pages of the Web log site provide the functionality for creating Web log content, including new postings and favorite links (Figure 16.53).

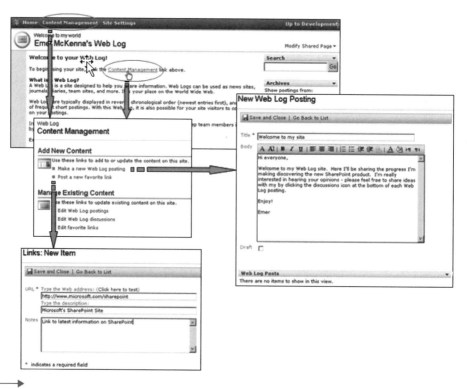

Figure 16.53   *Adding content.*

Figure 16.54   *Web log ready for viewing.*

To create a Web log posting, do the following:

1.   In the navigation bar, click the **Content Management** link.

2.   Click the **Make a New Web Log Posting** link.

3.   Populate the *Title* and *Body* fields with the text of your choice.

4.   Click **Save** and **Close**.

Your posting is now visible in the Web Log Web Part on the Home page (Figure 16.54).

To add links to the Links Web Part, do the following:

1.   In the navigation bar, click the **Content Management** link.

2.   Click **Post a new favorite link**.

3.   Populate the *URL* field with the URL of the Web site of interest.

4.   Populate the *Description* and *Notes* fields with the text of your choice.

5.   Click **Save** and **Close.**

Your new link is now visible in the Links Web Part on the Home page (Figure 16.54), and your Web log site is ready for viewing.

16.9 Ghosting and FrontPage 2003

FrontPage 2003 provides an extremely versatile environment for customizing SharePoint sites; however, this customization comes with a hit on performance. The pages and list schema of a SharePoint site are read from the site definition files and cached at IIS process startup. The pages appear to be physically part of the site; however, when a page is requested, it is not in the actual database but on the file system and is pulled from the cache at run time. This concept is known as ghosting, and Microsoft uses ghosting for both pages and metadata in SharePoint. So, for example, if you examine the CAML code associated with a view definition, you will notice that there is a lot of XML generated to inform SharePoint how to render specific views within a Web Part Page such as `allitems.aspx`. Giving everybody a copy of the same XML would waste resources and affect the scalability of the system; therefore, ghosting tells SharePoint to use the page that's already available in the site definition. So, if you have 10,000 sites, as far as ASP.NET is concerned it is only serving 1 page as opposed to 10,000 pages. ASP.NET dynamically renders different content into that one page depending on the request—but it is still only one page. From a performance perspective ghosting significantly reduces the memory footprint required to serve those pages and the I/O hit on SQL Server to serve these pages.

When you perform customizations through the browser, such as customizing your Contact view, you are actually customizing the CAML associated with the view. However, SharePoint does not copy the complete view XML to the database; instead, it stores a variant of the file containing the differences.

If you examine the content column of the Docs table in the site's SQL database, you can see ghosting in action. For example, if you look at the row assigned to `default.aspx` in a virgin site, you will see that the content column is NULL. This tells SharePoint that the page is still ghosted and to use the page that is already available in the setup area. Even if you customize the `default.aspx` page of the site through the browser by adding and removing Web Parts, the content column remains NULL, meaning that the page is still ghosted. The page remains ghosted because customizations performed through the browser do not actually change the physical file.

Using FrontPage to customize a page in a SharePoint site effectively unghosts the page, resulting in its entire contents being stored in the database. This means that each time the page is requested, instead of retrieving it directly from disk, it is retrieved from the database, which, in turn, reduces the site's overall performance. So it's easy to see that if you have 10,000 sites and each one has been customized using FrontPage 2003, you could run into some performance issues. In addition, any future updates made to the site definition files will not apply to unghosted pages.

16.10 Setting up your site to restrict access through FrontPage

One way to prevent pages in SharePoint sites from being unghosted is to prohibit editing sites through FrontPage. This can be enforced for your entire SharePoint deployment by adding the `wdfopensite` value to the `DisableWebDesignFeatures` attribute of the `Onet.xml` file of each site template.

To prohibit users from opening a SharePoint site in FrontPage 2003, do the following:

1.   On the server running SharePoint, navigate to the XML folder of the site template to which you want to restrict access. If you want to prevent all WSS sites in your deployment from being edited using FrontPage 2003, you would apply the modification to the STS site template. The file location for the XML directory in the STS site template is

     ```
     Drive:\Program Files\Common Files\Microsoft Shared\
     Web Server Extensions\60\Template\localID\STS\XML
     ```

2.   Open the file `Onet.XML`.

3.   Locate the Project Title tag.

4.   Check for the existence of a `DisableWebDesignFeatures` attribute within the Project Title tag. The tag may already include a `DisableWebDesignFeatures` attribute, especially if you are editing an SPS site template as opposed to a WSS site template. If the `DisableWebDesignFeatures` attribute does not exist, simply add it to the tag, as follows:

     ```
     <Project Title="Team Web Site" ListDir="Lists"
     xmlns:ows="Microsoft SharePoint"
     DisableWebDesignFeatures="wdfopensite">
     ```

5.   Using IIS, restart the SPS Application Pool (`MSSharePointPortalAppPool`).

Figure 16.55
SharePoint site editing in FrontPage disabled.

6.   In your browser open a site that uses the site template you just modified.

7.   From the File menu, select **Edit with Microsoft Office FrontPage**. A message box should appear informing you that the editing feature has been disabled for the site (Figure 16.55).

16.11 FrontPage 2003 features disabled when editing an SPS site

If you perform the previous modification on any site template other than the STS site template, you will notice that the `DisableWebDesignFea-tures` attribute of the Project Title tag already exists and has a number of other values defined. Each of these values represents a function, or feature, that is prohibited from use within FrontPage 2003 and is defined mainly to prevent you from making changes that could possibly compromise the functionality of your portal. The following list details the functions that are not available when editing an SPS site through FrontPage.

- **Publishing**: You cannot publish an SPS site from one server to another server. If you wish to move a portal site and its contents to another location, Microsoft recommends that you use the SPS Data Backup and Restore utility (`SPSBackup.exe`) or the SharePoint Migration Tool (`smigrate.exe`) for team sites.

- **Navigation and link bars**: In order to ensure that the navigational structure of the portal remains intact, the link bars' functionality in FrontPage 2003 is disabled when you edit an SPS site.

- **Navigation view**: The Navigation view pane is disabled when you open an SPS site in FrontPage 2003, because SPS uses a different mechanism for maintaining its navigational structure.

- **Themes**: As mentioned earlier in this chapter, you cannot apply a theme to a page in SPS if you use FrontPage 2003. If you want to apply a theme to your portal, you should do so using the Site Settings page in the browser.

- **Creating subsites in an area or subarea**: Although you can create subsites under the root folder of the portal and under other subsites, areas are treated differently. Areas and subareas cannot have nested subsites. When you open an area or a subarea in FrontPage 2003 and right-click on the area or subarea icon, the *Subsite* menu option is not available on the New menu.

- **Web Package import and export:** The importing and exporting of Web Packages is disabled at the portal level. If you open an SPS site in FrontPage 2003, the *Packages* option on the Tools menu is disabled. When editing a WSS site, the same menu is available.

17

Customizing and Extending SharePoint

So far, we have discussed the basics of SharePoint development with respect to building and deploying Web Parts and customizing your site using FrontPage 2003. With this final chapter, we take a look at some of the more advanced methods of customizing and extending your SharePoint implementation. SharePoint development in and of itself is a huge topic, and this book merely skims the surface of the product's extensibility. We highly recommend that you sift through the SharePoint Product and Technologies SDK, in addition to MSDN, for more detailed information and lots of sample code.

17.1 Basic customizations

One of the first requests that a developer or Web designer is likely to encounter when SharePoint is introduced to his or her company is, "Can we apply our company's branding?" The answer to this question is undoubtedly yes; however, there are some caveats with respect to the methods of customizations that are officially supported by Microsoft. The previous version of SPS had many limitations when it came to applying custom color schemes, banners, layouts, and navigational structure. This release of SharePoint has significantly improved the customization capabilities with the introduction of site definitions and custom templates, in addition to tight integration with FrontPage 2003. Site definitions are basically a set of files used in the site-generation process that provide information about the site's lists, views, Web Parts, Web Part Pages, and navigational structure. Custom templates are created through the user interface or by using the SharePoint object model, and instead of residing on the file system, they are stored in the SharePoint database. Many of the customization capabilities of STS have been improved upon and incorporated into both SPS and WSS. For example, STS had the concept of a single site definition, the "team

Figure 17.1
*Default SPS
Home page.*

site," from which sites could be instantiated. SPS and WSS extend the templating architecture to enable the use of multiple site definitions and templates; this means that you can create sites that reflect the needs of the target audience by enabling the appropriate functionality up front through the use of custom lists, Web Parts, and Web Part Pages.

Figures 17.1 and 17.2 show the default layout of the Portal Server Home page and a team site Home page respectively. While the default layout looks very professional and uses a complementary color scheme, chances are it does not meet your company's branding guidelines. At the very least, you will most likely want to replace the Microsoft logo with a logo that represents your site and change the name of the Home page to something more

Figure 17.2
*Default Windows
SharePoint Services
team site.*

relevant. For the remainder of this section, we'll take a brief look at some of the common basic customizations.

17.1.1   Changing the title of the Web Part Page

When you create a site in SharePoint, whether it is a portal site or a team site, the name you provide appears as a caption on each Web Part Page in the site. In addition, each Web Part Page has a title, which you may want to change to reflect the terminology used within your company. The steps to change the Web Part Page title vary, depending on whether you are customizing an SPS or a WSS site.

Changing the Web Part Page title in SPS

The following steps detail how to change the title of a Web Part Page in SPS.

1. Using your browser, navigate to the portal's Web Part Page for which you wish to change the title.

2. From the Actions menu, click **Change Settings**.

3. From the *Title and Description* section in the General property page, change the *Title* field to reflect the new title for your Home page.

4. Click **OK**.

Modifying the Web Part Page in this manner automatically updates the corresponding menu item in the horizontal navigation bar.

Changing the Web Part Page title in WSS

Unfortunately, changing the title for a default Web Part Page in a WSS site is not possible through the user interface out of the box. While it is still a straightforward process, it requires editing the Web Part Page using FrontPage 2003, which in turn unghosts the page, reducing its overall performance.

1. Using your browser, navigate to the WSS Web Part Page for which you wish to change the title.

2. From the browser's File menu, click **Edit with Microsoft Office FrontPage**. Alternatively, you can open the site through FrontPage directly.

3. In design mode, edit the Web Part Page title text directly.

4.   Save your changes.

Modifying the Web Part Page in this manner does not automatically update the corresponding menu item in the horizontal
navigation bar. Additional steps must be taken in order for this to
happen.

5.   While still in design mode, double-click the horizontal navigation
bar. The Link Bar Properties dialog appears.

6.   From the Links list, select the menu item that you wish to change
and click **Modify Link**. The Modify Link dialog appears.

7.   In the *Text to Display* field, change the text to match the title of
the corresponding Web Part Page.

8.   Click **OK** to close the Modify Link dialog.

9.   Click **OK** to close the Link Bar Properties dialog and commit
your changes.

10.   Save your changes.

If you refer to Chapter 14, you will notice that we demonstrated a way
to rename the Web Part Page in a WSS site using the browser user interface.
Unfortunately, this method applies to new Web Part Pages that have been
created through the user interface's Create pages and not to the default
pages generated on site creation. The Web Part Page templates used when
creating a page through the user interface provide the title of the Web Part
Page through a dynamic Web Part. This Web Part is customizable when in
design mode, removing the need to edit the page in FrontPage.

17.1.2   Replacing the logo

The default logos that appear in SharePoint sites are stored in the `\Program
Files\Common Files\Microsoft Shared\web server extensions\
60\TEMPLATE\IMAGES` directory. If you want to replace the default logos
with your own custom logos, you can simply copy your logos to this directory, delete or rename the default images, and rename your logos to the
original SharePoint names. Figure 17.3 shows some of the images you may
wish to replace.

1.   To replace the SPS site logo, there is an alternative method to
replacing the default Microsoft file.

Figure 17.3
Default site logos.

Image	Filename	Description
Microsoft Office SharePoint Portal Server 2003	sitelogo.gif	The logo that appears in the banner on each page in the portal site. (actual image appears without background color)
	spshome.gig	The logo that appears next to the Web Part Page title on the Home page in the portal site.
	spstopic.gif	The logo that appears next to the Web Part Page title on the Topic page in the portal site.
	spsnews.gif	The logo that appears next to the Web Part Page title on the News page in the portal site.
	spssites.gif	The logo that appears next to the Web Part Page title on the Sites page in the portal site.
	spsmysh.gif	The logo that appears next to the Web Part Page title on the My Site page in the portal site.
	home.gif	The logo that appears next to the Web Part Page title on the Home page in a WSS Team site.
Microsoft Windows SharePoint Services	homepage.gif	The logo that appears by default in the Image Web Part that appears on a WSS Team site.
	dwshome.gif	The logo that appears next to the Web Part Page title on the Home page in a WSS Document Workspace site.
	meethome.gif	The logo that appears next to the Web Part Page title on the Home page in a WSS Meeting Workspace site.

Create your custom logo and copy the file to the `\Program Files\ Common Files\Microsoft Shared\web server extensions\60\TEM- PLATE\IMAGES` directory.

2.   Using your browser, navigate to the portal Home page.

3.   From the top-level menu, click **Site Settings**.

4.   Click **Change Portal Site Properties and SharePoint Site Creation Settings**.

5.   From the *Custom Portal Site Logo* section, change the location of the logo file to map to your new custom logo. For example:

```
/_layouts/images/mylogo.gif
```

Note: If you replace any default image files with your own custom image, it is a good practice to keep a copy of your image in a safe place, since future service packs and hotfixes may overwrite these files. In fact, the installation of Service Pack 1 replaces `sitelogo.gif` and `logo.gif` with the default Microsoft images.

17.1.3   Merging the SPS horizontal menu bars

Applying a company banner across the top of each Web Part Page in a SharePoint site is a common customization request. The default installation of SPS already includes a type of banner that hosts the SharePoint logo and additional menu options, such as My Site, Site Settings, and Help. Adding an additional banner above the default SharePoint banner will most likely make the page appear cluttered; therefore, in order to make the most of the real estate on the page, we need to merge the two horizontal navigation bars into one, thus freeing up the space at the top that previously housed the portal site logo and site settings menus.

This can be achieved by making a simple modification to the appropriate Web Part Pages. Simply edit the `default.aspx` of each area in which you wish to merge the menus and replace the code shown in Figure 17.4 with the code shown in Figure 17.5. This code appears toward the beginning of the `.aspx` file.

You can edit the `default.aspx` file using FrontPage 2003, but keep in mind that editing a Web Part Page in this manner unghosts the page. Once a Web Part Page is unghosted, it is no longer directly retrieved from the file system; instead, SharePoint retrieves the customizations from the database, which results in some performance overhead. An alternative to editing through FrontPage is to edit the file directly from the file system; however, editing Web Part Pages in this manner introduces the added risk of any of the modifications you make being overwritten by subsequent product releases or service packs and is therefore not supported by Microsoft. The

```
<tr> <td colspan="3" width="100%">
    <SPSWC:PageHeader id="PageHeaderID" runat="server" PageContext="SitePage" ShowTitle="false" />
    <div class="ms-phnavlwrapper ms-navframe">
        <SPSWC:CategoryNavigationWebPart runat="server" id="HorizontalNavBar" />
    </div>
</td> </tr>
```

Figure 17.4   *Default SPS horizontal navigation bar code.*

```
<tr><td colspan="3" width="100%">
   <table width="100%" border="0" cellpadding="0" cellspacing="0">
      <tr>
         <td>
            <div class="ms-phnav1wrapper ms-navframe">
               <SPSWC:CategoryNavigationWebPart runat="server" id="HorizontalNavBar" />
            </div>
         </td>
         <td>
            <SPSWC:PageHeader id="PageHeaderID" runat="server" PageContext="SitePage" ShowTitle="false" />
         </td>
      </tr>
   </table>
</td></tr>
```

Figure 17.5   *Code to merge SPS horizontal navigation bars.*

.aspx files that require modification are stored in the \Program Files\ Common Files\Microsoft Shared\web server extensions\60\TEM-PLATE\<locid> directory. We'll discuss the location of each of these files in more detail in section 17.4.

Figure 17.6 shows the result of applying this code. If you compare this figure with Figure 17.1, you will see that the SharePoint menus have merged; however, you will also notice that the menus are slightly offset and that the default site logo is still present in the navigation bar. These settings are controlled by the SPS stylesheet. In order to completely remove the logo and adjust the height, width, and color of the menus so that they merge successfully, we must customize the stylesheet.

It should be noted that the .aspx files located in the \Program Files\ Common Files\Microsoft Shared\web server extensions\60\TEM-PLATE\<locid> directory only pertain to the dynamic Web Part Pages

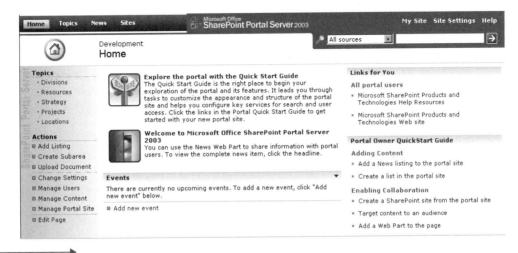

Figure 17.6   *Merged menus.*

within the portal site. If you wish to have a consistent look and feel throughout the portal site, there are many other static Web Part Pages in the portal site that also require the merged-menu modification. These static pages are located in the `\Program Files\Common Files\Microsoft Shared\web server extensions\60\TEMPLATE\LAYOUTS\<locid>` directory; however, modifying the files in this directory is not supported by Microsoft, so proceed with caution. The majority of these files use the `AlternateHeader` attribute; consequently, you can apply the merged-menu technique to these files by simply customizing the `Portal-Header.aspx` file or specifying your own alternate header. For personal sites, the alternate header file is `MySiteHeader.aspx`. Keep in mind that if you edit the `PortalHeader.aspx` and `MySiteHeader.aspx` files directly, you may have to reapply your changes with subsequent service pack and hotfix releases. For more information on the alternate-header technique, please refer to section 17.4.

17.2 Customizing the SharePoint stylesheets

SharePoint uses cascading stylesheets (`.css`) to define the color scheme and layout of both SPS and WSS. Cascading stylesheets allow you to assign several properties at once to all of the elements on an HTML page marked with a particular tag. The term *cascading stylesheets* implies that two or more stylesheets can cascade together to produce the final look of the page. The language used for creating cascading stylesheets is CSS, a simple declarative language that allows you to apply stylistic information, such as the font and color, to documents written in HTML or XML. Elements on the page are associated with properties and values in the stylesheet. For example, Figure 17.7 declares that BODY elements are 10-point blue text.

The main stylesheets that control the color scheme and layout for SPS and WSS are `sps.css` and `ows.css`, respectively. These files can be found in the `\Program Files\Common Files\Microsoft Shared\web server extensions\60\TEMPLATE\LAYOUTS\<localid>\STYLES` directory.

In addition, the `owspers.css` stylesheet controls the color scheme and layout of the My Site team site. Each file contains numerous classes that are

Figure 17.7
Sample CSS code.

```
Body
{
  Font-size: 10pt;
  Color: blue;
}
```

Figure 17.8
Script code to identify CSS classes.

```
<body>
...
<!-- CSS Script Start -->
<script language="jscript">
function ClassInfo()
{
    if (window.event.srcElement.className != null)
    {
        stsclass.innerText = window.event.srcElement.className;
    }
    else
    {
        stsclass.innerText = "";
    }
}

window.document.body.onmouseover = ClassInfo;</script>

<div style="border-style:solid;border-width:1px; width: 281px; height: 34px;
position: absolute; left: 286px; top: 41px; z-index:15; padding-left:4px;
padding-right:4px; padding-top:2px; padding-bottom:2px; background-
color:#EEEEF4">
<p id="stsclasstitle"><font face="Tahoma" id="stsclasstitle">Classname:
</font>
<font face="Tahoma"id="stsclass"> </font>
</p></div>
<!-- CSS Script End -->
...
</body>
```

used to define specific elements on a Web Part Page. For example, both `sps.css` and `ows.css` contain the `ms-bannerframe` class, which controls the background color of the navigation bar that appears at the top of the page. So, how do you know which class controls which element on the page? The SharePoint Products and Technologies SDK provides tables that define each class and, in most cases, display an image to show you the element the class controls.

The SDK also provides sample code that you can add to a Web Part Page, which applies a tool tip to each element, describing the class that controls that element. The code is shown in Figure 17.8.

Insert this code within the BODY element of the Web Part Page for which you wish to determine the class mapping. The code basically adds an area on your page that displays the title of the class applied to the area that your mouse is hovering over (Figure 17.9). Notice that the mouse pointer is hovering over the top right area of the navigation bar. Since we have merged the top SPS menu with the horizontal navigation bar, the `ms-bannerframe` applies only to the right-side merged menu bar. The left side is controlled by the `ms-phnav1wrapper ms-navframe` class.

To demonstrate the type of customizations you can make by creating a custom stylesheet, we'll make the following changes to SPS:

1.   Remove the logo that appears on the menu bar.

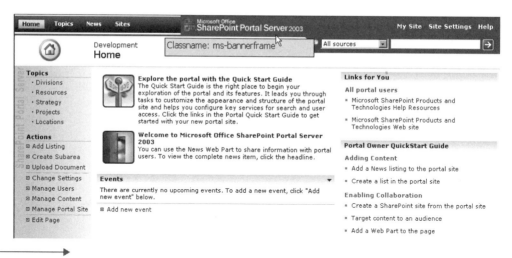

Figure 17.9   *Home page with CSS script code applied.*

2.   Change the background color across the top menu bar, including any merged menus.

3.   Reduce the height of the menu bar to increase the real estate on the page.

4.   Remove the background color associated with the search boxes.

Microsoft recommends that you do not modify the sps.css and ows.css directly; instead, create a custom stylesheet that includes the classes you wish to override and apply the custom stylesheet to your Web Part Pages. SPS provides a user interface mechanism that allows you to apply a custom stylesheet to your Web Part Pages, which allows you to override the default classes. Unfortunately, there is no such user interface for WSS, but you can include a link to your custom stylesheet by editing the appropriate Web Part Pages directly or by applying them through code. The best option would be to create a custom site definition, edit the appropriate .aspx files to include a link to the custom stylesheet, and then create a custom template based on the new site definition from which users can generate their WSS sites.

17.2.1   Creating the custom stylesheet

Since we want to customize the portal look and feel, we need our customizations to override the settings in the sps.css. You can create your custom stylesheet from scratch, or you can make a copy of the sps.css, rename it to your own custom stylesheet, and then edit the classes that you would like to customize. One thing to note is that if your customization requires the removal of an attribute that is set in the default stylesheet, you should keep the attribute in your custom stylesheet and set its value to null or an equivalent value that suits the attribute type. For example, if you want to remove the `background-image` attribute, instead of deleting the attribute definition altogether, you should set the `background-image` to `none`. This ensures that your custom stylesheet will override the attribute setting in `sps.css`. If you find that some of your customizations are not taking effect, check to make sure that all of the attributes defined in the default `sps.css` are also defined in your custom stylesheet.

Custom stylesheets should be placed in the `_layouts` folder of each front-end server. For convenience and consistency, you can place them in the same folder as the default stylesheets; just remember to give them a different name—for example, `customsps.css`. Once you have created your stylesheet, you can instruct SharePoint to add a reference to the new stylesheet.

1. Using your browser, navigate to the Home page of your portal.

2. From the top-level menu, click **Site Settings**.

3. Click **Change Portal Site Properties and SharePoint Site Creation Settings**.

4. From the *Custom Cascading Style Sheet* section, enter the location of the custom stylesheet—for example, `/_layouts/1033/styles/customsps.css`.

Any changes that you apply to the custom stylesheet will affect the portal site. This is very convenient when testing customizations, since a simple browser refresh will show you the updated effect.

17.2.2 Removing the logo that appears on the menu bar

Removing, or giving the appearance of removing, the site logo on an SPS or WSS page is simply a matter of replacing `sitelogo.gif` or `logo.gif`, respectively, with an image representing a pixel of the color you want to apply to the menu bar. The image still appears, except that it blends with the rest of the banner and, given that it is only a pixel, does not significantly reduce the real estate of the page.

→
Table 17.1   `SPS.CSS` *Classes to Change Background Color of Merged Menu*

Class	Sample Code	Description

`.ms-phnav1wrapper`	`{`
	`border-top: #7795cb 1px solid;`
	`background-image: url(/_layouts/`
	`images/hptoolgrad.gif);`
	`width: 100%;`
	`background-repeat: repeat-x;`
	`background-color: #3e6d9c;`
	`}`
		Changes the background color of the left region of the merged menu and makes use of a custom image that matches the new color scheme. On a default installation this class controls the background color for the horizontal navigation bar.

`.ms-bannerframe`	`{`
	`border-top: #7795cb 1px solid;`
	`background-image: url(/_layouts/`
	`images/hptoolgrad.gif);`
	`background-repeat: repeat-x;`
	`background-color: #3e6d9c;`
	`padding-top:2px;`
	`padding-bottom:4px;`
	`}`
		Changes the background color of the right region of the merged menu and makes use of a custom image that matches the new color scheme. Additionally, the padding at the top and the bottom of the region is reduced, and the bottom border is removed.

17.2.3 Changing the background color of the top menu bar

Continuing with our SPS example, since we are customizing the merged menus, we want the two menus to have a consistent look and feel. Table 17.1 details the classes we need to override in order to provide the same background color across the entire navigation bar.

Figure 17.10 shows the results of applying these modifications to override the classes in `sps.css`. As you can see, there are still customizations required to make this menu production ready.

17.2.4 Reducing the height of the menu bar

Figure 17.10 shows that the merged menus still appear offset. Table 17.2 details the classes we need to override in order to provide a consistent navigation bar height.

Figure 17.10   *Merged menu with new color scheme and site logo removed.*

Table 17.2 `SPS.CSS` *Classes to Reduce Height of Merged Menu*

Class	Sample Code	Description

`.ms-phnavtableone`	`{`
	`padding-top: 0px;`
	`padding-right: 0px;`
	`padding-bottom: 0px;`
	`padding-left: 0px;`
	`}`
		Removes all the padding code that appears by default, which significantly reduces the size of the navigation bar

`.ms-phnavmidc1,`
`.ms-phnavmidc0`
	`{`
	`padding-top: 0px;`
	`padding-right: 8px;`
	`padding-bottom:0px;`
	`padding-left: 8px;`
	`}`
		Removes the top and bottom padding from the default settings of the unselected menu options

`.ms-phnavmidc1sel,`
`.ms-phnavmidc0sel`
	`{`
	`padding-top: 1px;`
	`padding-right: 8px;`
	`padding-bottom:1px;`
	`padding-left: 8px;`
	`background-color:#b0d9f5;`
	`background-image: url(/_layouts/`
	`images/navgradp.gif);`
	`background-repeat: repeat-x;`
	`BORDER-top: 0px;`
	`BORDER-left: #3E6D9C 1px solid;`
	`BORDER-bottom: 0px;`
	`BORDER-right: #3E6D9C 1px solid;`
	`}`
		Reduces the top and bottom padding of the default settings for the currently selected menu option and also removes top and bottom borders

`Div.ms-titleareaframe`	`{`
	`border-top: 0px;`
	`background-image: none;`
	`background-repeat: no-repeat;`
	`}`
		Removes the background image and the border

Figure 17.11 shows the results of applying these modifications to override the classes in `sps.css`. The two menus are now successfully merged, their colors consistent, and their heights appropriately aligned. All that remains is to remove the background color for the search area so that the search boxes appear as part of the main page.

Figure 17.11 *Merged menu with height aligned.*

Table 17.3   SPS.CSS *Classes to Remove Search Area Background Color*

Class	Sample Code	Description

.ms-sbtopcorner	`background-color: #FFFFFF;`
	`background-image: none;`
	`background-repeat: no-repeat;`
	`background-position: left top;`
	`border-bottom-width: 0px;`
		Removes the background image from the default setting of the top left corner of the search area

.ms-sblbcorner	`background-color: #FFFFFF;`
	`background-image: none;`
	`background-repeat: no-repeat;`
	`padding-left: 0px;`
	`padding-right: 5px;`
	`padding-bottom: 4px;`
		Removes the background image from the default setting of the bottom left corner of the search area

.ms-sbtable	`background-color: #FFFFFF;`
	`font-family: Verdana;`
	`font-size: .7px;`
	`font-style: normal;`
	`font-weight: normal;`
		Changes the background color of the search area to white

17.2.5   Removing the background color associated with the search boxes

Table 17.3 details the classes we need to override in order to remove the background color associated with the search boxes.

Figure 17.12 shows the final results of applying our modifications to override the classes in sps.css. The two menus are now successfully merged, their colors consistent, their heights appropriately aligned, and the background color for the search area removed so that the search boxes appear as part of the main page.

Figure 17.12   *Search box area with background color removed.*

17.3 Custom themes

In Chapter 16, we saw how to customize a WSS site using FrontPage themes. To recap, themes are professionally designed style packages that define the color, fonts, and graphical page elements of Web pages within a site. For WSS sites, themes can be applied using both FrontPage and the browser.

The following steps show how to apply a theme to a WSS site through the browser.

1. Using your browser, navigate to the Home page of the SharePoint site to which you would like to apply the theme.

2. Click the **Site Settings** link on the horizontal navigation bar at the top of the page.

3. From the *Customization* section of the page, click the **Apply theme to site** link. The Apply Theme to Web Site page appears.

4. Select the theme to apply to the site from the list box on the right of the page. A preview of the theme is shown.

5. Click **OK**.

While the application of themes to an SPS site using FrontPage is not supported, you can apply a theme to the portal using the custom stylesheet settings described in the previous section. Instead of specifying a path to a custom stylesheet, you define the path to the stylesheet (theme.css) for the theme. If you are applying a theme in this manner, you can copy the theme to the _layouts directory for easier access. Figure 17.13 shows the application of the Breeze theme to a default portal site. If the theme does not accommodate all of the SPS styles, you can simply modify the theme stylesheet to suit your needs.

SharePoint comes equipped with 20 themes out of the box; this list is available to you from the Apply Theme to Web Site page in WSS. If these themes do not suit your needs, you can also create a new theme or customize an existing theme for use in your deployment. SharePoint retrieves the list of themes from the theme template definition file (SPTHEMES.XML), which is located in the \Program Files\Common Files\Microsoft Shared\Web Server Extensions\60\TEMPLATE\LAYOUTS\<localid> directory. If you create a new custom theme, you must add a template definition for the new theme in this file for it to appear as a selection in the list. In addition, you should provide thumbnail and preview image files for your theme.

The following steps show how to create a new custom theme and display it as an option in the Apply Theme to Web Site page in WSS.

1. Navigate to the `\Program Files\Common Files\Microsoft Shared\Web Server Extensions\60\TEMPLATE\THEMES` directory.

2. Make a copy of the theme that most closely matches your needs, and rename the folder with a unique name that describes your custom theme, for example, `CustomTheme`.

3. Open the new folder and locate the `.INF` file. Rename this file to match the name of the new folder, for example, `Custom-Theme.INF`.

4. Edit the `.INF` file and assign the same name to the title attribute in the `[info]` section of the file.

5. Customize the styles defined in the cascading stylesheets associated with this theme (`theme.css`, `graph0.css`, and `graph1.css`). Include any SPS and WSS classes that may be missing from the theme.

6. Customize the image files in the new folder as desired.

Figure 17.13
Applying a theme to the portal site.

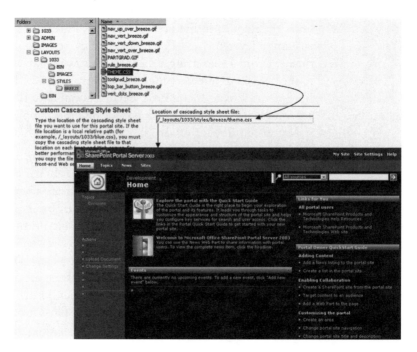

7.   Create a thumbnail and preview image for your theme, and save the files to the \Program Files\Common Files\Microsoft Shared\Web Server Extensions\60\TEMPLATE\IMAGES directory.

8.   Navigate to the \Program Files\Common Files\Microsoft Shared\Web Server Extensions\60\TEMPLATE\LAYOUTS\ <localid> directory, edit the file SPTHEMES.XML, and add a definition for your new theme. The order in which the themes are defined in the XML file is the order they will appear in the list. So, if you want your custom theme to appear at the top of the list, then make it the first definition in the XML file. Figure 17.14 shows the code required for the template definition and the final result of the modification, with the custom template appearing at the top of the theme list in the Apply Theme to Web Site page.

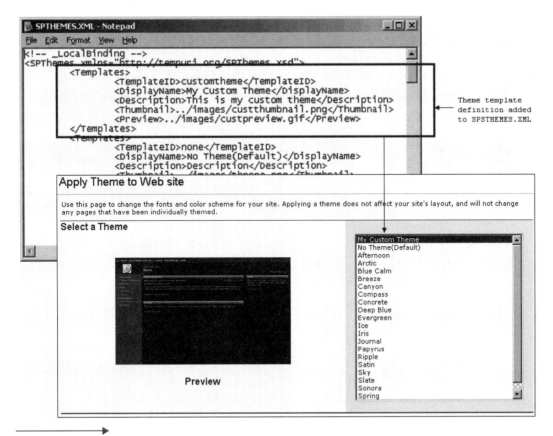

Figure 17.14   *Custom theme template definition.*

17.4 Site definitions

With respect to look and feel, site definitions provide the basic foundation for SharePoint sites. A site definition comprises a set of files that reside in the `\Program Files\Common Files\Microsoft Shared\web server extensions\60\TEMPLATE\<localid>` directory. If you examine this directory, you will notice a set of folders with an SPS prefix, each of which represents a specific site definition (Figure 17.15). For example, the SPS folder contains all the files required to build the SharePoint portal site; this includes the Web Part Pages, such as the default Home page, and the Web Part Zones, Web Parts, and navigational structure that appear on those pages, group listings, site Web Part Gallery, available lists, and libraries. When a team site, portal site, or portal area is instantiated, SharePoint uses files from the appropriate site definition to build the structure and layout of the site. In addition, there are two folders specific to WSS: STS and MPS. The STS folder represents a specific type of site definition that defines the team site, blank site, and document workspace configurations, and the MPS folder represents a specific type of site that defines the basic meeting workspace, blank meeting workspace, decision meeting workspace, social meeting workspace, and multipage meeting workspace configurations.

Table 17.4 lists the site definitions that are available by default with SPS.

SharePoint extracts the site structure and layout information for a site from a set of XML files, the most prominent of which are ONET.XML,

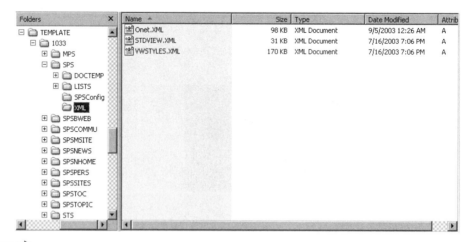

Figure 17.15   *Default site definitions.*

`SCHEMA.XML`, `WEBTEMP.XML`, `DOCICON.XML`, and `FLDTYPES.XML` (listed in Table 17.5).

In the following sections, we review some of the customization capabilities of these files, with particular attention given to `ONET.XML`.

Table 17.4   *SharePoint Site Definitions*

Site Definition Folder	Description
MPS	WSS site definition that defines the configuration of the basic meeting workspace, blank meeting workspace, decision meeting workspace, social meeting workspace, and multipage meeting workspace.
SPS	SPS site definition that defines the configuration of the portal site.
SPSBWEB	SPS site definition that defines the configuration of the SPS bucket web.
SPSCOMMU	SPS site definition that defines the configuration of the SPS community area.
SPSMSITE	SPS site definition that defines the configuration of the SPS My Site Home page. This works in conjunction with the SPSPERS to define the overall My Site effect. SPSMSITE basically maps to the public/private pages in My Site.
SPSNEWS	SPS site definition that defines the configuration of the SPS News area.
SPSNHOME	SPS site definition that defines the configuration of the SPS news area Home page.
SPSPERS	SPS site definition that defines the configuration of the SPS My Site team site. This controls the lists and fields available on the lists in the My Site. Changing the `default.aspx` of this site definition has no effect on the My Site, since it is hidden. If you want to make changes to the `default.aspx` of My Site, edit the `default.aspx` file in the SPSMSITE site definition instead.
SPSTOC	SPS site definition that defines the configuration of the SPS topic area Home page.
SPSTOPIC	SPS site definition that defines the configuration of the SPS topic area.
STS	WSS site definition that defines the configuration of the team site, blank site, and document workspace.

Table 17.5 *SharePoint Schema Files*

XML File	Description
ONET.XML	Each site definition has one ONET.XML file, which defines various components of the site, including the navigation areas of the Home page, list views, the list and document templates available, and the Web Parts that appear on the Home page and in the Web Part Gallery by default.
SCHEMA.XML	Each list definition defined in the ListTemplate area of the ONET.XML includes a folder that contains the files that comprise the list, including a SCHEMA.XML file. SCHEMA.XML is used to create custom views, custom forms, and action areas that appear in the side navigational area of the list views.
WEBTEMP.XML	Each front-end Web Server in a SharePoint deployment has at least one WEBTEMP.XML file. The WEBTEMP.XML file contains the site definitions that are available on the Template Selection page when creating a new site.
DOCICON.XML	Each front-end Web Server in a SharePoint deployment has one DOCICON.XML file. The DOCICON.XML maps ProgIDs and file extensions to file icons and maps a file type to a specific control to be used when opening a file of that type. Changes to the contents of this file are global to a SharePoint deployment and affect all site definitions on the front-end Web Server; therefore, care must be taken when editing this file.
FLDTYPES.XML	Each front-end Web Server in a SharePoint deployment has one FLDTYPES.XML file. The FLDTYPES.XML file determines how the various field types are rendered in the different viewing modes for list data. Once again, changes to the contents of this file are global to a SharePoint deployment and affect all site definitions on the front-end Web Server; therefore, care must be taken when editing this file.

17.4.1   ONET.XML

When creating your own site definitions, you will likely find that most of your customizations take place in the ONET.XML file. If you examine the ONET.XML file, you will see that it comprises a number of significant elements that give a good idea of the types of items controlled by this file. Figure 17.16 shows the top-level elements in the XML file.

To understand the customization potential of this file, we'll examine the main elements in detail.

```
<?xml version="1.0" encoding="utf-8" ?>
<!--  _lcid="1033"  _version="11.0.5704.0"   -->
<!--  _LocalBinding  -->
- <Project Title="Team Web Site" ListDir="Lists" xmlns:ows="Microsoft SharePoint" AlternateHeader="PortalHeader.aspx"
    DisableWebDesignFeatures="wdfbackup; wdfrestore; wdfpackageimport; wdfpackageexport; wdfthemeweb; wdfthemepage;
    wdfnavigationbars; wdfnavigationview; wdfpublishview; wdfpublishselectedfile">
  + <NavBars>
  + <ListTemplates>
  + <DocumentTemplates>
  + <BaseTypes>
  + <Configurations>
  + <Modules>
  + <Components>
  </Project>
```

Figure 17.16   ONET.XML *structure.*

The Project element

The Project element is the top-level element of the ONET.XML file and has a number of associated attributes that can be set to control various aspects of the site. For example, you can set the DisableWebDesignFeatures attribute to prevent certain features from being editable from Microsoft FrontPage. Table 17.6 lists the Project element's attributes.

Table 17.6   Project *Element Attributes*

Attribute	Required	Description
Title	Yes	Defines the default name for the SharePoint site.
ListDir	Yes	Defines the directory in which to create new lists.
AlternateHeader	No	Defines an .aspx page located in the \Program Files\Common Files\Microsoft Shared\web server extensions\60\TEMPLATE\LAYOUTS\ directory that is to be used to create the top of the SharePoint page; for example, Alternate-Header="myPortalHeader.aspx" instructs SharePoint to use the myPortalHeader.aspx file located in the _layouts directory as an alternate header. This only affects SharePoint pages that have code that looks at the AlternateHeader property and processes the header accordingly.
AlternateCSS	No	Defines an alternate .css file located in the \Program Files\Common Files\Microsoft Shared\web server extensions\60\TEMPLATE\LAYOUTS\<localid>\STYLES directory. For example, the SPSMSITE site definition points the AlternateCSS attribute to the owspers.css file, which tells SharePoint to use this stylesheet when instantiating the My Site team site.

Table 17.6   `Project` *Element Attributes (continued)*

Attribute	Required	Description
CustomJSUrl	No	Defines a custom JavaScript file located in the `\Program Files\Common Files\Microsoft Shared\web server extensions\60\TEMPLATE\LAYOUTS\` directory to run within the site created from the site definition.
DisableWebDesignFeatures	No	Defines which FrontPage features are disabled for the site. Possible values include: the following.

		Value	*Description*
		wdfbackup	Disables the ability to back up a site using the *Backup* menu command
		wdfrestore	Disables the ability to restore a site using the *Restore* menu command
		wdfpackageimport	Disables the ability to import a Web Package using the *Import* menu command.
		wdfpackageexport	Disables the ability to export a Web Package using the *Export* menu command
		wdfthemeweb	Disables the ability to apply a theme to a site using the *Apply as Default* command from the Task Pane
		wdfthemepage	Disables the ability to apply a theme to the pages in a site using the *Apply to Selected Pages* command from the Task Pane
		wdfnavigationbars	Disables the ability to insert navigation bars using the *Navigation* menu command
		wdfnavigationview	Disables the ability to view the navigation using the *Navigation* command on the View menu

Table 17.6 `Project` *Element Attributes (continued)*

Attribute	Required	Description	
		Value	*Description*
		`wdfpublishview`	Disables the ability to import a remote Web site using the *From Site* command on the Import dialog, in addition to disabling the ability to view a remote Web site using the *Remote Site* command from the View menu
		`wdfpublishselectedfile`	Disables the ability to publish the selected files using the *Publish Selected Files* command available when you right-click a file in the Folder list
		`wdfopensite`	Disables the ability to open a SharePoint site within FrontPage using either the *Open Site* command on the File menu or the *Edit with Microsoft Office FrontPage* command on the File menu in Internet Explorer.
		`wdfnewsubsite`	Disables the ability to create a new subsite from a site folder in the folder list

The `AlternateHeader` attribute

The `AlternateHeader` attribute is worth special mention, since it controls the banner area at the top of the page for `.aspx` files that leverage this attribute. If you examine the `ONET.XML` files of the various SPS site definitions, you will see that this attribute is set to `PortalHeader.aspx`, with the exception of `SPSPERS`, which is set to `MySiteHeader.aspx`. These `.aspx` files contain the header style and layout; for example, they display the horizontal navigation bar in addition to the SharePoint logo. So, which pages are affected by the `AlternateHeader` attribute? The `.aspx` pages located in the `\Program Files\Common Files\Microsoft Shared\web server extensions\60\TEMPLATE\LAYOUTS\<localid>\` directory provide generic functionality to SharePoint sites. For example, the `spsviewlists.aspx` and `viewlsts.aspx` files display all the libraries, lists,

Figure 17.17
Alternate header code in .aspx *file.*

```
...
<%
string alternateHeader = SPControl.GetContextWeb(Context).AlternateHeader;
if (alternateHeader == null || alternateHeader == "")
{
%>
    ...HTML code to build header
<%
}
else
{
    Server.Execute(alternateHeader);
}
%>
...
```

discussion boards, and surveys in a portal site and WSS site, respectively. Many of the files located in this directory contain code that references the AlternateHeader property for the site (Figure 17.17), and only these files are affected by the AlternateHeader attribute in ONET.XML.

You can apply your own custom header by either modifying the default PortalHeader.aspx and MySiteHeader.aspx files or creating your own file and editing the AlternateHeader attribute in the ONET.XML to reference the new file. If you edit the default .aspx files directly, make sure you keep a copy of your customizations, since future service packs and hot fixes may overwrite your changes.

Upon creation of a site or subarea, SharePoint retrieves the value of the AlternateHeader attribute in the ONET.XML file, if one exists, and applies this value to the AlternateHeader property of the SPWeb object for the site. The SPWeb object is used to programmatically access a SharePoint site. Notice that we say "upon creation"; any changes to the AlternateHeader attribute in the ONET.XML file after site creation will *not* affect existing sites and areas. That said, you do have the ability to change the content of the header files that the AlternateHeader property references, which will affect existing sites that reference that header file. As usual, it is recommended that you modify the contents of custom header files only to prevent your customizations from being overwritten by future service pack and hotfix releases.

Figure 17.18 shows the result of customizing the AlternateHeader and AlternateCSS attributes in the SPSTOPIC site definition.

To see the AlternateHeader attribute in action, perform the following steps on your development server:

1.   Create a custom header file, apply the desired customizations, and save the file to the \Program Files\Common Files\ Microsoft Shared\web server extensions\60\TEMPLATE\

LAYOUTS\<localid>\ directory. You can easily create a custom header file by using the PortalHeader.aspx file as your base. If you want to use a custom stylesheet, leave the code that references the CustomCSSResourceElement control.

2. Edit the ONET.XML file of the SPSTOPIC site definition.

3. Change the AlternateHeader attribute to map to the custom header file you created in step 1—for example, Alternate-Header="myPortalHeader.aspx."

4. If you want to use a custom stylesheet, change the AlternateCSS to map to the custom .css file.

5. Save your changes, and close ONET.XML.

6. Using your browser, navigate to the Topics Home page on your portal site.

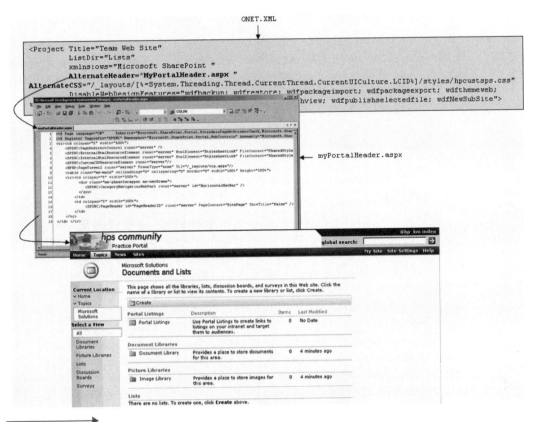

Figure 17.18   *Alternate header applied to the* SPSTOPIC *site definition.*

7.   Ensure that the subareas created under the Topics Home page use the topic area template. You can check these settings by viewing the Page tab of the Change Settings page.

8.   From the Topics Home page, create a subarea.

9.   Navigate to the newly created topic area.

10.   From the vertical navigation bar, click **Manage Content**. This displays the `_layouts/<localid>/spsviewlsts.aspx` file, which should display your custom header and use your custom stylesheet, if specified.

You can, of course, change this property programmatically after site creation. In fact, programmatically changing values such as the `Alternate-Header` is a valid and supported method for customizing your site, whereas customizations to the default Microsoft ONET.XML files run the risk of being overwritten with service pack and hotfix releases. We revisit programmatically changing the `AlternateHeader` attribute later in this chapter.

It is unfortunate that all the pages in a SharePoint site, including the `default.aspx`, do not reference the `AlternateHeader` property; if they had, then applying custom banners to your entire deployment could be easily achieved. Alas, this is not the case, and applying banners to all your pages is a challenge to say the least! As we proceed through this chapter, we will present some of the options you have for addressing other pages in the site, such as the site definition's `default.aspx` page.

The `AlternateCSS` attribute

The `AlternateCSS` attribute is also worth a special mention if you intend to use custom stylesheets as opposed to customizing the default stylesheets. If you examine the ONET.XML files of the SPSPERS site definition, you will see that this attribute is set to `/_layouts/[%=System.Threading.Thread.CurrentThread.CurrentUICulture.LCID%]/styles/owspers.css`, which is the SharePoint stylesheet used for My Site team sites. The `\Program Files\Common Files\Microsoft Shared\web server extensions\60\TEMPLATE\LAYOUTS\<localid>\` directory contains .aspx files that provide generic functionality to these sites. For example, the `viewseclsts.aspx` file displays all of the libraries, lists, discussion boards, and surveys in the My Site team site. Some of the files contain code that references the `AlternateCSS` attribute from the site definition (Figure 17.19). The `CustomCSSResourceElement` control is specific to SPS and, consequently, cannot be used on WSS pages. The `CSSLink` control is specific to WSS; however, since WSS provides the

Figure 17.19
*Code that
references the*
AlternateCSS
attribute.

foundation for SPS, this control can be used on both SPS and WSS pages. Files that use either control are affected by the AlternateCSS attribute in the ONET.XML.

Upon creation of a site or subarea, when SharePoint encounters the CssLink control or the CustomCSSResourceElement control, it retrieves the value of the AlternateCSS attribute in the ONET.XML file, if one exists, inserts a matching link element into the resulting HTML page, and applies the external stylesheet.

As previously mentioned, not all pages in the _layouts directory reference the AlternateCSS attribute; in fact, many of the .aspx files that reference the AlternateHeader attribute make no allowance for the AlternateCSS attribute. However, this is easily rectified by simply including the CustomCSSResourceElement control (Figure 17.20) and CSSLink control (Figure 17.21) in your SPS and WSS header files, respectively.

```
myWSSHeader.aspx  myPortalHeader.aspx
 1  <%@ Page language="C#"      Inherits="Microsoft.SharePoint.Portal.SiteAdminPageNoBrowserCheck,Microsoft.SharePoint.P
 2  <%@ Register Tagprefix="SPSWC" Namespace="Microsoft.SharePoint.Portal.WebControls" Assembly="Microsoft.SharePoint.P
 3  <tr><td colspan="3" width="100%">
 4      <SPSWC:PageRedirectControl runat="server" />
 5      <SPSWC:ExternalHtmlResourceElement runat="server" HtmlElement="StylesheetLink" FileContext="SharedStyle" FileNa
 6      <SPSWC:ExternalHtmlResourceElement runat="server" HtmlElement="StylesheetLink" FileContext="SharedStyle" FileNa
 7      <!-- Apply AlternateCSS setting, if defined -->
 8      <SPSWC:CustomCSSResourceElement runat="server"/>
 9      <!-- Insert HP Top Banner -->
10      <HPVP:PageViewer2 runat="server" FrameType="none" Url="/_layouts/top.aspx"/>
11      <!-- Merge SPS menus -->
12      <table class="ms-main" cellpadding="0" cellspacing="0" border="0" width="100%" height="100%">
13      <tr><td colspan="3" width="100%">
14          <div class="ms-phnav1wrapper ms-navframe">
15              <SPSWC:CategoryNavigationWebPart runat="server" id="HorizontalNavBar" />
16          </div>
17      </td>
18      <td colspan="3" width="100%">
19          <SPSWC:PageHeader id="PageHeaderID" runat="server" PageContext="SitePage" ShowTitle="false" />
20      </td>
21  </tr>
22  </td> </tr>
```

SPS code to insert link to .css file defined in ONET.XML

Figure 17.20   myPortalHeader.aspx *code to reference* AlternateCSS.

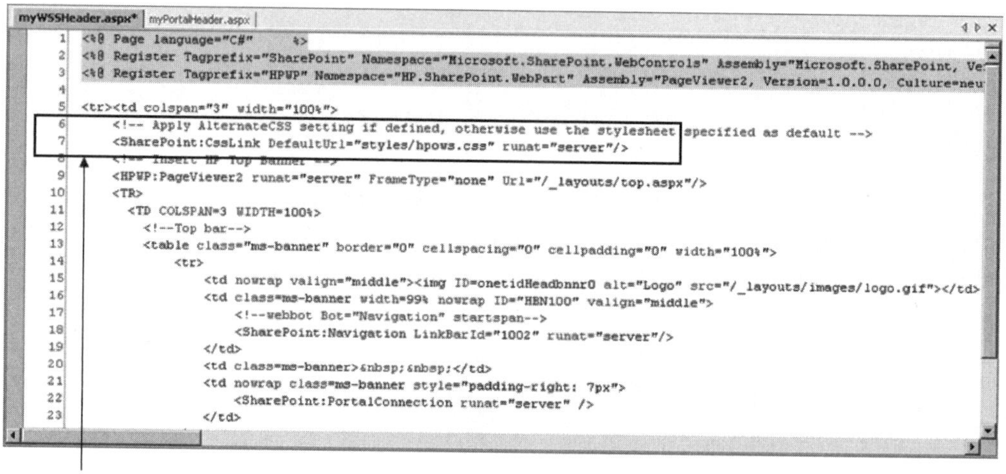

WSS code to insert link to .css file defined in ONET.XML

Figure 17.21   `myWSSHeader.aspx` *code to reference* `AlternateCSS`.

Once again, changes to the `AlternateCSS` attribute in the `ONET.XML` file after site creation will not affect existing sites and areas. However, as with the `AlternateHeader` property, you can insert the `CssLink` and `CustomCSSResourceElement` controls onto a page programmatically postsite creation.

The `NavBars` element

The `NavBars` element, as one would expect, controls the navigation bars that appear on a WSS page and comprises one or more `NavBar` elements. The navigation bar that appears at the top of the page is defined by the first `NavBar` element, which is named the "SharePoint Top Navbar." This `NavBar` may contain `NavBarLink` elements that define hyperlinks to add to the top navigation area. All subsequent `NavBar` elements define the quick launch area of the page, in other words, the vertical navigation area that appears on the left of the default WSS site.

The horizontal and vertical navigational structures that appear on the SPS pages are controlled by specific SPS Web controls, and, as such, customizations to the `NavBar` elements in the `ONET.XML` file do not affect SPS portal sites or portal areas.

Adding an additional menu item to the top menu of a future WSS site created through a site definition is straightforward; simply add a new `NavBarLink` element to the SharePoint Top `Navbar` element in the site definition's `ONET.XML` file. Figure 17.22 shows sample code that adds a **Cus-**

```
<NavBars>
        <NavBar Name="SharePoint Top Navbar" Separator="   "
Body="&lt;a ID='onettopnavbar#LABEL_ID#' href='#URL#' accesskey='J'&gt;#LABEL#&lt;/a&gt;"
ID="1002">
        <NavBarLink Name="Documents and Lists"
Url="_layouts/[%=System.Threading.Thread.CurrentThread.CurrentUICulture.LCID%]/viewlsts.aspx">
        </NavBarLink>
        <NavBarLink Name="Create"
Url="_layouts/[%=System.Threading.Thread.CurrentThread.CurrentUICulture.LCID%]/create.aspx">
        </NavBarLink>
        <NavBarLink Name="Site Settings"
Url="_layouts/[%=System.Threading.Thread.CurrentThread.CurrentUICulture.LCID%]/settings.aspx">
        </NavBarLink>
        <NavBarLink Name="Custom App" Url="_layouts/customapps/customapp.aspx">
        </NavBarLink>
        <NavBarLink Name="Help" Url='javascript:HelpWindowKey("NavBarHelpHome")'>
        </NavBarLink>
    </NavBar>

    ...quick launch nav bars defined here...

</NavBars>
```

Figure 17.22   *Sample code to add Custom App link to top navigation bar.*

tom App link to the title bar of a SharePoint team site, and Figure 17.23 shows a new site created from the customized site definition.

Adding a link to an existing navigation bar on the quick launch area follows the same steps as adding a link to the top navigation bar. For example, to add a new document library link to the Documents navigation bar, simply insert a new NavBarLink element to the Documents NavBar definition in ONET.XML, with the URL referencing the specific document library. Adding a new navigation bar to the quick launch of a future WSS site created through a site definition requires slightly more work. First, you need to add a new NavBar entry. The easiest way to

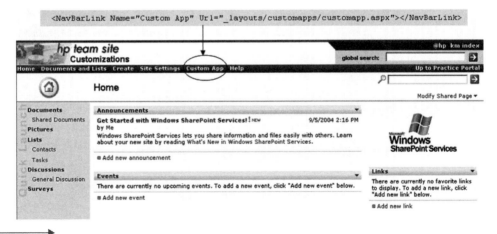

Figure 17.23   *Result of custom navigation bar.*

```
<NavBar Name="Team Sites" Prefix="&lt;table border=0 cellpadding=4 cellspacing=0&gt;"
Body="&lt;tr&gt;&lt;td&gt;&lt;table border=0 cellpadding=0
cellspacing=0&gt;&lt;tr&gt;&lt;td&gt;&lt;img src='/_layouts/images/blank.gif' ID='100'
alt='Icon' border=0&gt; &lt;/td&gt;&lt;td valign=top&gt;&lt;a
ID=onetleftnavbar#LABEL_ID#
href='#URL#'&gt;#LABEL#&lt;/td&gt;&lt;/tr&gt;&lt;/table&gt;&lt;/td&gt;&lt;/tr&gt;"
Suffix="&lt;/table&gt;"
ID="1010">
            <NavBarLink Name="HPS Women Technologists"
                Url="http://myportal.hp.com/sites/HPWTS/default.aspx">
            </NavBarLink>
            <NavBarLink Name="Technical Career Path"
                Url="http://myportal.hp.com/sites/TCP/default.aspx">
            </NavBarLink>
            <NavBarLink Name="HP Technical Conference"
                Url="http://myportal.hp.com/sites/TechCon/default.aspx">
            </NavBarLink>
</NavBar>
```

Figure 17.24   ONET.XML *code to create a new navigation bar.*

achieve this is to make a copy of an existing NavBar entry, rename it, and
provide it with a unique ID. Figure 17.24 shows sample code that creates
a navigation bar named "Team Sites."

Next, we need to modify the navigational structure defined in the
default.aspx associated with the site definition to include the new navigation bar (Figure 17.25). The code is inserted after the Surveys navigation
bar code in the *Navigation* section of default.aspx. Obviously, if you

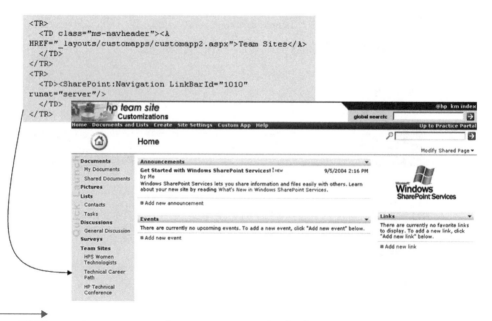

```
<TR>
  <TD class="ms-navheader"><A
HREF="_layouts/customapps/customapp2.aspx">Team Sites</A>
  </TD>
</TR>
<TR>
  <TD><SharePoint:Navigation LinkBarId="1010"
runat="server"/>
  </TD>
</TR>
```

Figure 17.25   Default.aspx *code to create a new navigation bar.*

want the new navigation bar to appear earlier in the quick launch area, you must position your code appropriately.

Note: IIS needs to be reset before modifications to the `NavBars` element in `ONET.XML` take effect.

The `ListTemplates` *element*

The `ListTemplates` element defines the lists included in the site definition. Each list is defined by a separate `ListTemplate` element. The `List-Template` element has a number of associated attributes that define the type of list it is, the folder that contains the list details such as the `SCHEMA.XML`, whether the list can appear in the quick launch area, and whether it should appear as an option on the Create page of the site. Table 17.7 shows the attributes associated with the `ListTemplate` element.

Table 17.7   `ListTemplate` *Element Attributes*

Attribute	Description	
Name	A mandatory text value that maps to the folder name in the site definition that represents the list. *Note:* This field must map exactly to the name of the new list folder.	
DisplayName	A mandatory text value that defines the display name for the list in the site definition.	
BaseType	A mandatory integer value that defines the `BaseType` used to create the list and maps to an existing value defined in the `BaseTypes` element within `ONET.XML`. Possible values include 0 through 4.	
Type	An optional integer value that uniquely identifies the list definition in the SharePoint site. This value should be assigned a unique value within the site definition. According to the CAML documentation, this value should be less than 1,000. For example, `Type=160` is most likely a unique list type within your site. If you create a `ListTemplate`, and it does not appear in your site as expected, check to make sure that the `Type` value is correct. The following lists the values for the default list template types.	
	Unique ID	*Description*
	100	Generic list
	101	Document library
	102	Survey
	103	Links list
	104	Announcements list
	105	Contacts list

Table 17.7   `ListTemplate` *Element Attributes (continued)*

Attribute	Description	
	Unique ID	*Description*
	106	Events list
	107	Tasks list
	108	Discussion board
	109	Picture library
	110	Data sources
	111	Site Template Gallery
	113	Web Part Gallery
	114	List Template Gallery
	115	XML form library
	120	Custom grid for list
	200	Meeting Series list
	201	Meeting Agenda list
	202	Meeting Attendees list
	204	Meeting Decisions list
	207	Meeting Objectives list
	210	Meeting text box
	211	Meeting Things to Bring list
	212	Meeting Workspaces Pages list
	300	Portal Sites list
	1100	Issue tracking
	2002	Personal document library
	2003	Private document library
	The value defined in this attribute maps to a corresponding `Type` attribute of the `List` element in the `SCHEMA.XML` file for the list.	
`OnQuickLaunch`	An optional Boolean value that determines whether the user is presented with the option to add a link to the list in the quick launch area.	
`SecurityBits`	An optional text value that defines the security of the list. This attribute does not apply to document libraries. The first bit in the text defines the read security, and the second bit defines the write security. Each bit has a number of possible values:	
	Read bit: Possible values include 1 or 2, where 1 gives all users read permission to items on the list, and 2 gives users read permission only to items they create.	
	Write bit: Possible values include 1, 2, and 4, where 1 gives all users permission to modify items in the list, 2 gives users permission to modify only items they create, and 4 denies users the ability to modify items in the list. For example, the value 12 allows users permission to read all the items in the list but only to modify the items they create.	

Table 17.7   `ListTemplate` *Element Attributes (continued)*

Attribute	Description
`Description`	Optional text value that describes the list's function.
`Hidden`	Optional Boolean value that determines whether the list template is available as an option on the list Create page. If the value is set to `true`, the list does not appear on the Create page.
`HiddenList`	Optional Boolean value that determines whether a list that is created from the list definition is hidden. If the value is set to `true`, the newly created list is hidden.
`Image`	Optional `URL` value that maps to an icon that represents the list.
`Unique`	An optional Boolean value that determines whether the list definition or list template is only accessible during site creation. If this value is set to `true`, the template cannot be used to create a list through the user interface or via the object model post site creation. A value of `true` hides the list from the Create page and the Documents and Lists page of the site.
`DontSaveInTemplate`	An optional Boolean value that determines whether the contents of the list can be saved in a custom list or custom site template. A value of `true` specifies that the list content cannot be saved to a template.
`Catalog`	An optional Boolean value, which, when set to `true`, indicates that the list definition defines a gallery (site, list, or Web Part).
`Path`	An optional text value that specifies the name of the site definition that contains the list definition, for example, `STS` or `MPS`.
`RootWebOnly`	An optional Boolean value, which, when set to `true`, indicates that a list created from the definition is only available in the root Web site of a site collection.

Creating a List Definition

The following steps show how to create a list definition in your site definition using the `ListTemplates` element. For the purpose of this example, we'll use the Announcements list definition as our foundation and keep the list field structure and layout the same.

1. Using Windows Explorer, navigate to the Lists subfolder of the site definition to which you want to add the new list definition.

2. Make a copy of the Announce folder and rename it to `Mylist`.

3. Edit the `SCHEMA.XML` file in the new folder and change the `<List>` element to match the code shown in Figure 17.26:.

4. Search `SCHEMA.XML` for descriptive text containing the word "Announcement" and replace the text with your own custom

```
<List xmlns:ows="Microsoft SharePoint" Name="MyList" Title="My Custom List"
Direction="0" Url="Lists/My List" BaseType="0" >
```

description. For example, replace the text "Add new announce-ment" with "Add new entry." Take care not to replace any of the stylesheet tags, such as ms-announcementtitle.

5.   Save your changes and exit SCHEMA.XML.

6.   Navigate to the XML folder of the site definition to which you want to add the new list definition.

7.   Edit ONET.XML.

8.   Locate the <ListTemplates> element.

9.   Make a copy of the Announcements list template definition and change the code to match the code shown in Figure 17.27.

10. Save your changes, and exit ONET.XML.

11. Reset IIS.

12. Using your browser, create a new site based on the modified site definition.

13. Navigate to the Create page of the site. The My List template should appear under the *Lists* section of the Create page (Figure 17.28). The security of the new list should be such that users have read permission for all items in the list but may only edit the items they create.

Note: Changes to the ListTemplate element affect both new and existing sites created from the site definition.

```
<ListTemplate Name="mylist"
              DisplayName="My List"
              Type="160"
              BaseType="0"
              OnQuickLaunch="TRUE"
              SecurityBits="12"
              Description="Create this list to test the ListTemplate element!"
              Image="/_layouts/images/itann.gif">
</ListTemplate>
```

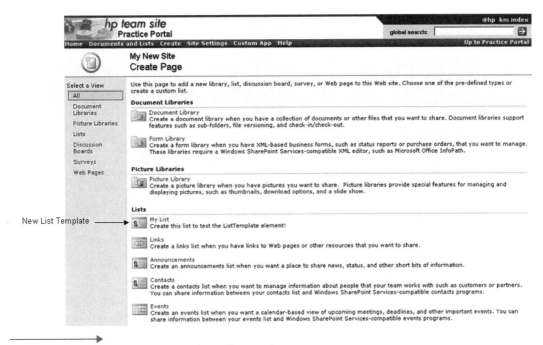

Figure 17.28   *Create page with new list template.*

The `BaseTypes` element

The `BaseTypes` element provides the structure and layout for the default base list types in SharePoint. This section should not be modified; doing so may result in breaking the site definition, which can negatively impact existing sites as well as new sites.

The `Configuration` element

The `Configuration` element in `ONET.XML` determines the lists and modules to be generated when a site is instantiated from a site definition. A site definition may have more than one configuration element defined within a parent `Configurations` element. For example, the `STS` site definition contains three configuration definitions: team site, blank site, and document workspace; the `MPS` site definition contains five configuration definitions: basic meeting workspace, blank meeting workspace, decision meeting workspace, social meeting workspace, and multipage meeting workspace.

A `Configuration` element has a number of associated attributes that describe the configuration (Table 17.8).

Table 17.8 Configuration *Element Attributes*

Attribute	Description
ID	A mandatory integer value that uniquely identifies the configuration within the configuration element. This attribute maps to the ID attribute of the configuration element in WEB-TEMP*.XML.
Name	An optional text value that contains the configuration name.
Type	An optional text value that identifies the configuration with a specific site definition.
Title	An optional text value that defines the title of the configuration that appears on the Template Selection page.
Description	An optional text value that defines the description of the configuration that appears on the Template Selection page.
ImageUrl	An optional URL value that defines the location of a preview image that appears on the Template Selection page.
Hidden	An optional Boolean value that determines whether the configuration appears as an option on the Template Selection page; a value of true determines that the configuration will not appear as an option.

The Configuration element can contain Lists and Modules elements, which identify the lists and modules to be generated upon site creation. The Lists element may contain multiple List elements, which identify the lists to be included in the site. The Type attribute of the List element maps to a specific ListTemplate definition in the ONET.XML. An error will occur upon site creation, stating "Invalid list template," if a list is specified for a

Figure 17.29
Instantiating a list in ONET.XML.

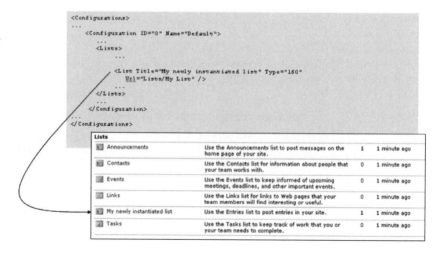

ListTemplate that is not defined. Figure 17.29 shows the instantiation of a list created using our custom list template. Note that the title corresponds to the title of the instantiated list. The list appears on the Documents and Lists page and, if specified, a link will appear on the quick launch area. Table 17.9 shows the attributes associated with the List element.

Table 17.9   List *Element Attributes*

Attribute	Description
Name	A text value that maps to the internal name for the list.
Type	A mandatory integer value that determines the type of list to instantiate. This value must map to a corresponding ListTemplate definition in the ONET.XML file.
Title	A mandatory text value that defines the display name ' r the list.
Url	An optional URL value that defines the path to the folder that contains the list definition.
DisableAttachments	An optional Boolean value that determines whether attachments are allowed in the list.
Default	An optional Boolean value that determines whether the list is created upon site creation. If this value is set to false, the list is not created but is available for later instantiation.
QuickLaunchUrl	An optional text value that specifies the URL of the list's View page to open when the link is clicked in the quick launch area.
OrderedList	An optional Boolean value that allows users to reorder the list from the Edit View page.
PrivateList	An optional Boolean value that, when set to true, specifies that the list is private.
RootOnlyWeb	An optional Boolean value that, when set to true, specifies that the list created from the definition exists only in the root web of the site collection.
EventSinkAssembly	An optional text value that specifies the strong name of an assembly in the GAC that provides an event handler for document library events.
EventSinkClass	An optional text value that specifies the name of the class that implements the event handler for document library events.
EventSinkData	An optional text value that contains a string used by the event handler for document library events.
ThumbnailSize	An optional integer value that determines the width of the thumbnails to display in a picture library.
WebImageHeight	An optional integer value that determines the height in pixels of an image in a picture library.

Table 17.9   List *Element Attributes (continued)*

Attribute	Description
WebImageWidth	An optional integer value that determines the width in pixels of an image in a picture library.
URLEncode	An optional Boolean value that, when set to true, determines that special characters, such as spaces, are converted to UTF-8 format.

In addition to the Lists element, the Configuration element may also contain a Modules element that determines which modules to contain within a configuration. ONET.XML contains two Modules elements, the first of which is a child element of the Configuration element. The individual modules specified in this section of ONET.XML map to the individual

```
1.   ...
2.   <Configurations>
3.   ...
4.       <Configuration>
5.           ...
6.           <Modules>
7.               <Module Name="Default"/>
8.               <Module Name="WebPartPopulation"/>
9.           </Modules>
10.          ...
11.      </Configuration>
12.  ...
13.  </Configurations>
14.  ...
15.  <Modules>
16.  ...
17.      <Module Name="Default" Url="" Path="">
18.          <File Url="default.aspx" NavBarHome="True">
19.              <View List="104" BaseViewID="0" WebPartZoneID="Left"/>
20.              <View List="106" BaseViewID="0" WebPartZoneID="Left" WebPartOrder="2"/>
21.              <View List="160" BaseViewID="0" WebPartZoneID="Right" WebPartOrder="1"/>
22.              <AllUsersWebPart WebPartZoneID="Right" WebPartOrder="2">
23.                  <![CDATA[
24.                  <WebPart xmlns="http://schemas.microsoft.com/WebPart/v2"
xmlns:iwp="http://schemas.microsoft.com/WebPart/v2/Image">
25.                      <Assembly>Microsoft.SharePoint, Version=11.0.0.0,
Culture=neutral, PublicKeyToken=71e9bce111e9429c</Assembly>
26.
<TypeName>Microsoft.SharePoint.WebPartPages.ImageWebPart</TypeName>
27.                      <FrameType>None</FrameType>
28.                      <Title>Site Image</Title>
29.                      <iwp:ImageLink>/_layouts/images/homepage.gif</iwp:ImageLink>
30.                  </WebPart>
31.                  ]]>
32.              </AllUsersWebPart>
33.              <View List="103" BaseViewID="0" WebPartZoneID="Right" WebPartOrder="3"/>
34.              <NavBarPage Name="Home" ID="1002" Position="Start">  </NavBarPage>
35.              <NavBarPage Name="Home" ID="0" Position="Start">  </NavBarPage>
36.          </File>
37.      </Module>
38.  ...
39.  </Modules>
40.  ...
```

Figure 17.30   Modules *element.*

Module elements defined in the second Modules element, which is found toward the bottom of the file. In other words, the list of modules that appears in the Configuration element references the actual module definition defined in the second Modules element.

Figure 17.30 shows the code for the default module for a site definition, and Figure 17.31 shows the outcome of this code. The default module includes a default.aspx file (line 18). The module defines the content for the default.aspx page of the site, including the navigation area and the Web Parts that appear on the page. Lines 19, 20, and 33 use the View element to define the List View Web Parts for the Announcements, Events, and Links lists, respectively. WebPartZoneID and WebPartOrder determine in which zone the Web Part appears on the page and also the order in which the Web Part appears within the zone. Line 21 shows the code required to add a List View Web Part to the default.aspx that represents our newly instantiated list. We want the Web Part to appear as the first Web Part in the right Web Part Zone. You need to make sure that all the Web Parts within a specific zone are ordered correctly; failure to do so may return unpredictable results. For example, if you have two Web Parts with the WebPartOrder set to 1, SharePoint will order them on a first-come, first-served basis.

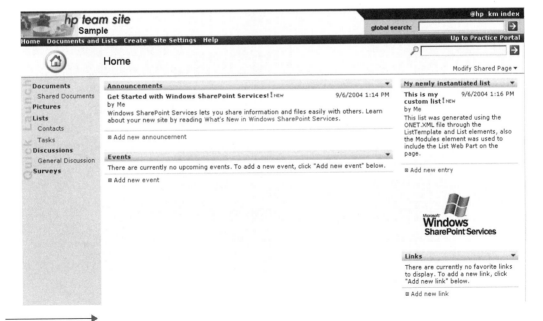

Figure 17.31   *Result of customized* Module *element.*

```
...
<AllUsersWebPart WebPartZoneID="Right" WebPartOrder="1">
  <![CDATA[
    <WebPart xmlns="http://schemas.microsoft.com/WebPart/v2" >
            <Title>Calendar Web Part</Title>
            <FrameType>None</FrameType>
            <Assembly>BookWebParts,
                    Version=1.0.0.1,
                    Culture=Neutral,
                    PubliKeyToken=0b6be9364fd482d7
            </Assembly>
            <TypeName>BookWebParts.TestWP</TypeName>
    </WebPart>
  ]]>
</AllUsersWebPart>
...
```

Figure 17.32   `AllUsersWebPart` *code.*

The `AllUsersWebPart` element is used to implement Web Parts on the page. This is a particularly useful element, since it provides a mechanism for you to activate your own custom Web Parts upon site creation, instead of relying on the users to import the Web Parts postsite creation. This allows you to create truly functional sites from the start. Implementing a Web Part using the `AllUsersWebPart` element is fairly straightforward regardless of whether you are implementing a custom Web Part or a default SharePoint Web Part. Simply include the Web Part definition in a `CDATA` section of the `AllUsersWebPart` element (Figure 17.32). For this example, we have reordered the Web Parts in the previous example so that the custom List View

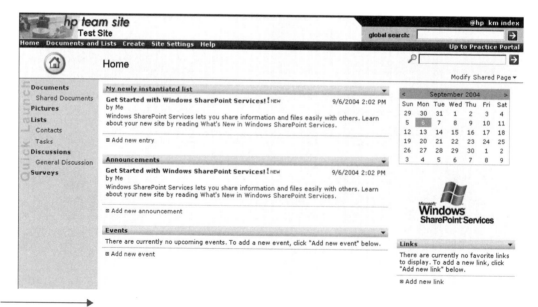

Figure 17.33   *Outcome of* `AllUsersWebPart` *code.*

Web Part appears on the left and our custom calendar Web Part appears in the right Web Part Zone (Figure 17.33).

17.4.2 Site-definition banners and footers

The zone layout for a Web Part Page can be used in conjunction with the `AllUsersWebPart` element to implement a banner and footer for the `default.aspx` page in a site definition. The `default.aspx` page can be edited and code inserted to add new Web Part Zones—for example, My Banner Zone and My Footer Zone. You can then create custom Web Part controls that implement the banner and the footer for your site and insert the Web Part definition for each into a separate `AllUsersWebPart` element in `ONET.XML`, mapping each Web Part to the appropriate zone (Figure 17.34).

The same strategy can be used to implement the banner and footer on the `.aspx` pages associated with the lists in your site definition. The various

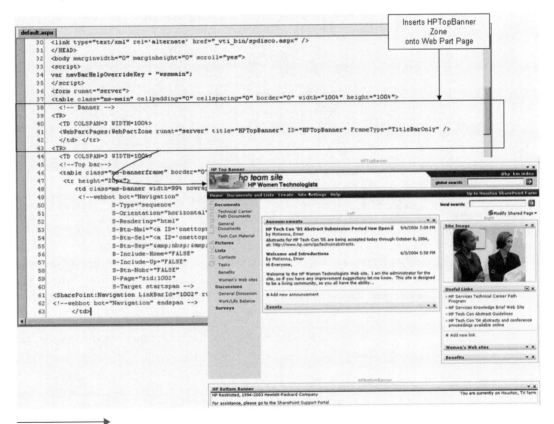

Figure 17.34   *Inserting a Web Part Zone onto a Web Part Page.*

Figure 17.35
SCHEMA.XML
WebPart *element*
code.

```
<List ...
    <MetaData>
        <Fields>
            ...
        </Fields>
        <Views>
            <View BaseView="0" FreeForm="TURE" Type="HTML">
                ...
            <WebParts>
                <View BaseViewID="1" WebPartZoneID="HPTopBanner" WebPartOrder="1">
                <![CDATA[
                    <WebPart xmlns="http://schemas.microsoft.com/WebPart/v2">
                        <Assembly>PageViewer2,
                                  Version=1.0.0.0,
                                  Culture=neutral,
                                  PublicKeyToken=4da912aecbdb8e3e
                        </Assembly>
                        <TypeName>HP.SharePoint.WebPart.PageViewer2</TypeName>
                        <Title>HP Top Banner</Title>
                        <FrameType>None</FrameType>
                        <Description>Custom version of Page Viewer that does not use an
iFrame and executes the request server-side.</Description>
                        <Url xmlns="PageViewer2">../../_layouts/top.aspx</Url>
                    </WebPart>
                ]]>
                </View>
                <View BaseViewID="1" WebPartZoneID="HPBottomBanner" WebPartOrder="1">
                <![CDATA[
                    <WebPart xmlns="http://schemas.microsoft.com/WebPart/v2">
                        <Assembly>PageViewer2,
                                  Version=1.0.0.0,
                                  Culture=neutral,
                                  PublicKeyToken=4da912aecbdb8e3e</Assembly>
                        <TypeName>HP.SharePoint.WebPart.PageViewer2</TypeName>
                        <Title>HP Bottom Banner</Title>
                        <FrameType>None</FrameType>
                        <Description>Custom version of Page Viewer that does not use an
iFrame and executes the request server-side.</Description>
                        <Url xmlns="PageViewer2">../../_layouts/bottom.htm</Url>
                    </WebPart>
                ]]>
                </View>
            </WebParts>
            </View>
            ...
        </Views>
        ...
    </MetaData>
</List>
```

list .aspx pages can be edited and code inserted to add the new Web Part Zones. Then the Web Part definitions for the Banner and Footer controls can each be inserted into a separate View element contained within the WebParts element of each list's SCHEMA.XML file (Figure 17.35).

You can use this method in conjunction with the AlternateHeader and AlternateCSS attributes to apply custom banners to the majority of pages on your site.

17.4.3   WEBTEMP.XML

Each configuration has a corresponding ID that uniquely identifies the configuration within a Configuration element; this identifier maps directly to an entry in the `WEBTEMP*.XML` file. `WEBTEMP*.XML` defines the configurations that appear as site template options when creating a site from a site definition. The default files that come with SharePoint are `WEBTEMP.XML` and `WEBTEMPSPS.XML`. The `WEBTEMP.XML` file represents the `STS` and `MPS` site definitions, and the `WEBTEMPSPS.XML` represents all of the SPS site definitions. `WEBTEMP.XML` is the base file; at run time SharePoint merges the contents of this file with other `WEBTEMP*.XML` files to determine the sites templates available for site creation.

If you wish to customize the settings in this file, you should make a copy of the default `WEBTEMP.XML`; rename it `WEBTEMP*.XML`, where the * represents the name of your site definition, for example, `WEBTEMPMYSTS.XML`; and apply your customizations to the newly created file. The `WEBTEMP*.XML` files are located in the `\Program Files\Common Files\ Microsoft Shared\web server extensions\60\TEMPLATE\1033\XML` directory.

Two main elements compose the structure of this file: the `Template` and `Configuration` elements. The `Template` element maps to a specific site-definition folder. For example, if you examine the `WEBTEMP.XML` file, you will see there are two `Template` elements defined: `STS` and `MPS`. The `Template` element has two basic attributes: `Name` and `ID`. The `Name` attribute corresponds to the name of the folder that contains the site definition, and the `ID` attribute uniquely identifies the site definition. In order to avoid collisions with built-in site definitions, it is recommended that you set `ID` to a value greater than 10,000. A single `Template` element comprises one or more `Configuration` elements.

The `Configuration` elements represent a specific configuration within a template and map to the configurations defined in the `ONET.XML` of the corresponding site definition. The `Hidden` attribute for a given configuration determines whether the configuration appears as an option on the Template Selection page when creating a site. If you are defining a configuration for an SPS area, you should always set this value to `Hidden`; failure to do so results in the area template appearing as a template option during team site creation, and a user who selects this template will receive an error indicating that the action cannot be completed. The `Hidden` attribute does not prevent SPS area templates from being shown as an option for subarea creation.

SharePoint includes the configurations of each site definition that has an SPS prefix in the subarea template list and ignores all other site definitions. This assumes of course that an appropriate entry exists in the `WEBTEMP*.XML` file. The exception to this rule is that the SPS site definition is

```
1.   <?xml version="1.0" encoding="utf-8" ?>
2.   <!-- _lcid="1033" _version="11.0.5510" _dal="1" -->
3.   <!-- _LocalBinding -->
4.   <Templates xmlns:ows="Microsoft SharePoint">
5.     <Template Name="MYSTS" ID="10001">
6.       <Configuration ID="0" Title="HP Team Site" Hidden="FALSE"
7.       ImageUrl="/_layouts/images/stsprev.png" Description="..."></Configuration>
8.       <Configuration ID="1" Title="HP Blank Site" Hidden="FALSE "
9.       ImageUrl="/_layouts/images/stsprev.png" Description="..."></Configuration>
10.      <Configuration ID="2" Title="HP Document Workspace" Hidden="FALSE"
11.      ImageUrl="/_layouts/images/dwsprev.png" Description="..."></Configuration>
12.    </Template>
13.    <Template Name="MYMPS" ID="10002" >
14.      <Configuration ID="0" Title="HP Basic Meeting Workspace" Hidden="FALSE "
15.      ImageUrl="/_layouts/images/mwsprev.png" Description="..."></Configuration>
16.      <Configuration ID="1" Title="HP Blank Meeting Workspace" Hidden="FALSE"
17.      ImageUrl="/_layouts/images/mwsprev.png" Description="..."></Configuration>
18.      <Configuration ID="2" Title="HP Decision Meeting Workspace" Hidden="FALSE"
19.      ImageUrl="/_layouts/images/mwsprev.png" Description="..."></Configuration>
20.      <Configuration ID="3" Title="HP Social Meeting Workspace" Hidden="FALSE "
21.      ImageUrl="/_layouts/images/mwsprev.png" Description="..."></Configuration>
22.      <Configuration ID="4" Title="HP Multipage Meeting Workspace" Hidden="FALSE"
23.      ImageUrl="/_layouts/images/mwsprev.png" Description="..."></Configuration>
24.    </Template>
25.    <Template Name="SPSCUST" ID="10003">
26.      <Configuration ID="0" Title="My New Area Template" Hidden="TRUE"
27.      ImageUrl="../images/spshome.gif" Description=" ..."></Configuration>
28.    </Template>
29.  </Templates>
```

Figure 17.36   WEBTEMPCUST.XML *code.*

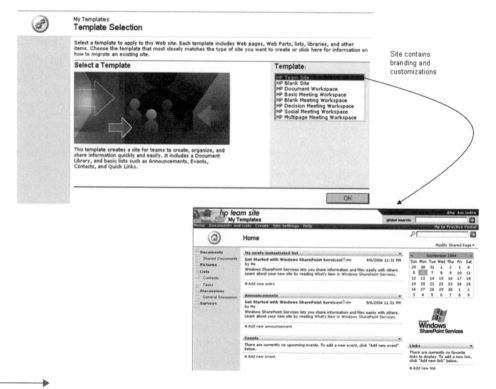

Figure 17.37   *Outcome of customized* WEBTEMP*.XML.

also excluded from this list, which makes sense given the fact that it represents the Home page of the portal site. The subarea template list is accessible from the Page tab on the Change Settings page of the portal.

Figure 17.36 shows the code for the WEBTEMPCUST.XML file. The code defines custom template configurations for the site definitions MYSTS, MYMPS, and SPSCUST. MYSTS and MYMPS are customized versions of the STS and MPS site definitions, and SPSCUST represents a custom SPS area. A general rule of thumb with respect to creating site definitions is, if you want to define a custom area, you should prefix your site definition and WEBTEMP*.XML template entry with SPS; this differentiates an area template from a site template.

If you want only your custom configurations to appear as options on the Template Selection page, edit the WEBTEMP.XML file and set the Hidden value to true for each of the default configurations. Figure 17.37 shows the outcome of the WEBTEMPCUST.XML file combined with the customized WEBTEMP.XML file. Notice that only the custom templates appear as options on the Template Selection page.

17.5 Creating a custom site definition

So far, we have shown many of the customization capabilities available to you using the XML files associated with a site definition, and, on numerous occasions, we have mentioned that modifying the default SharePoint site definitions is not supported by Microsoft. Microsoft recommends that if you want to perform customizations to a site definition, instead of modifying the existing files you should create your own custom definition. Creating a custom site definition is a very simple process; however, there are a few idiosyncrasies that you should keep in mind during the process, such as the naming of the site definition. It is recommended that when naming the site-definition folder, you use all caps; in addition, if you are creating a site definition for SPS, you should prefix your folder with SPS—for example, SPSCUST. The naming of this folder should map to a template entry in the WEBTEMP*.XML file.

The steps to creating a custom site definition are as follows:

1.   Using Windows Explore navigate to the \Program Files\Common Files\Microsoft Shared\web server extensions\ 60\TEMPLATE\<LocalID> directory.

2.   Make a copy of the site-definition folder that resembles the function of your custom site definition. For example, if you are creat-

ing a site definition that represents a subarea within SPS, make a copy of one of the SPS area site definitions, such as SPSTOPIC.

3.   Rename the newly created site definition, for example, SPSMY-CUST if it is an SPS site definition and MYCUST if it is a regular WSS site definition.

4.   Customize the site-definition files as desired. For example, you can add lists, change the navigation, add and remove Web Parts, and apply an alternate header and stylesheet; the possibilities are endless.

5.   Using Windows Explorer navigate to the \Program Files\Common Files\Microsoft Shared\web server extensions\60\TEMPLATE\<LocalID>\XML directory.

6.   Make a copy of the WEBTEMP.XML file and rename it as desired. The name of the file should have the WEBTEMP prefix, for example, WEBTEMPMYCUST.XML.

7.   Edit the new WEBTEMP*.XML file. Add a template entry for your new site definition, including each of the configurations that you want to make available. Remove all other template entries.

8.   Save your changes and close the file.

9.   Reset IIS.

If you want to replace the default WSS templates with your own custom version, the easiest way to achieve this is to create your own custom site definitions of the STS and MPS templates and set the current configurations to Hidden in the WEBTEMP.XML.

17.6 Custom templates

A site is instantiated from a site definition. Any changes made to a site or a list within the site postcreation can be saved and stored in a template known as a custom template. Custom templates consist of the differences between the original site definition and the site or list's current state. Unlike site definitions, custom templates are stored in the database. A custom template can optionally store all the content associated with the site or list; however, there is a maximum 10-MB limit on the content size. Once a custom template is created, it is always tied to the site definition from which it was originally created; if a custom template is applied and the site definition no longer exists, an error will occur.

List templates can be created using the browser user interface, or through code using the `SaveAsTemplate` method of the `SPList` class. When you save an existing list as a template, SharePoint creates a `.stp` file and saves it to the List Template Gallery. The `.stp` file is basically a `.cab` that contains a single `manifest.XML` file in CAML that the server generates. The `manifest.XML` is a subset of the migrate format that is generated with the Microsoft SharePoint Migration Tool (`smigrate.exe`). You can examine the contents of the `.stp` file by extracting the template from the List Template Gallery using the Save As menu command and renaming the file with a `.cab` extension.

The following steps show how to save a list as a template:

1. Using your browser, navigate to the list that you want to save as a template.

2. From the vertical navigation area, click **Modify settings and columns**.

3. From the *General Settings* section, click **Save list as template**. The Save as Template page appears (Figure 17.38).

4. Enter the filename, title, and description of the template. If you want to include the list content, check **Include Content**.

5. Click **OK**. Your list template is now saved in the List Template Gallery.

When a list template is added to the List Template Gallery, the list appears as an option on the Create page, which allows users to create a list based on the template. If you want a list template to be available in another site collection, you can simply download it from the List Template Gallery of the source site and upload it into the List Template Gallery of the target site.

Site templates can also be created using the browser user interface or through code using the `SaveAsTemplate` method of the `SPWeb` class. When you save an existing site as a template, SharePoint creates another `.stp` file but this time saves it to the Site Template Gallery. Once again, if you are interested, you can extract the `.stp` and examine its contents. When you save a site as a template, the template file includes any list templates contained in the List Template Gallery for the site.

The following steps show how to save a site as a template:

1. Using your browser, navigate to the site that you want to save as a template.

Figure 17.38

*Save a list
template.*

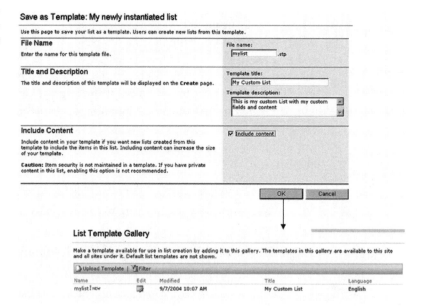

2.   From the horizontal navigation area, click **Site Settings**.

3.   From the *Administration* section, click **Go to Site Administration**. The Top-Level Site Administration page appears.

4.   From the *Management and Statistics* section, click **Save site as Template**. The Save as Template page appears (Figure 17.39).

5.   Enter the filename, title, and description of the template. If you want to include the list content, check **Include content**.

6.   Click **OK**. Your site template is now saved in the Site Template Gallery.

When a site template is added to the Site Template Gallery, the template appears as an option on the Template Selection page when you create a subsite of the site that contains the template. As with the list template, if you want a site template to be available in another site collection, you can simply download it from the Site Template Gallery of the source site and upload it into the Site Template Gallery of the target site. Additionally, if you want a site template to be available to all site collections in your deployment, you can add it to the Central Site Template Gallery using the stsadm.exe tool. Site templates added to the Central Site Template Gallery are available for self-service site creation in addition to all subsites. Figure 17.40 shows the command to add a site template to the Central Site Template Gallery. You must reset IIS after adding a site template to the

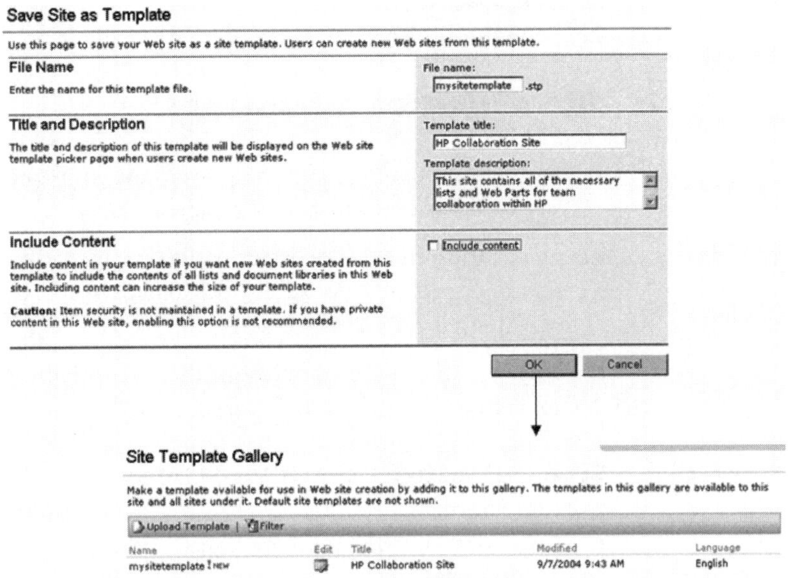

Figure 17.39
Save a site
template.

Central Site Template Gallery in order for it to appear as an option on the Template Selection pages.

You can also add a site template to the Central Site Template Gallery through code using the `AddCustomGlobalTemplate` method of the `SPGlobalAdmin` class.

Note: Site templates are only applicable to WSS sites. The only site template mechanism that is available to SPS is the site definitions, and, unfortunately, there is no user interface mechanism for managing customizations to site definitions. That said, you still have the ability to save lists as templates with SPS.

Custom templates and site definitions provide many options for customizing your site; however, it is difficult to know when to use a custom template and when to use a site definition to perform your customizations. There are a number of differences between the two that may sway your

Figure 17.40
Add site template
to Central Site
Template Gallery.

```
stsadm.exe -o addtemplate -filename "c:\mysitetemplate.stp"
-title "My Site Template" -description "My description"
```

decision towards one specific technique over another, full details of which can be found in the SDK. Here are some of the main points:

17.6.1   Site definition advantages

- Site definitions have a lot of power, and you can typically perform very complex customizations using CAML.
- Site definitions have a performance advantage in that they do not require SharePoint to access the database for the customizations; everything is on the file system.
- There are specific customizations that can only be implemented using site definitions, such as defining new view styles.

17.6.2   Site definition disadvantages

- Customizations take place by directly editing the file; there is no user interface.
- Changes to a site definition are difficult to deploy post site creation.
- You have the potential to break existing sites.
- You cannot apply themes to a site definition.
- You have to have access to the file system on the front-end Web Servers.

17.6.3   Custom template advantages

- A user interface makes creation of custom templates easy. Most customizations that can be achieved through the user interface can be saved in the template.
- Custom templates can be modified without affecting existing sites using the template.
- Custom templates are easy to deploy.

17.6.4   Custom template disadvantages

- Custom templates do not perform as well as site definitions, especially in large-scale environments.
- If the site-definition that the custom template is based on does not exist, the template will not work.

17.7   SharePoint object model overview

So far, we have examined customizations that you can apply to your site through Web Parts, site definitions, templates, and FrontPage 2003. In addition to these types of customizations, both WSS and SPS provide object models that expose various classes, methods, and properties to allow you to perform many tasks programmatically. For example, you can use the object model to create sites and lists, apply custom templates and headers, and even perform administrative tasks such as adding and removing Web Part Packages from the Web Part Gallery; the possibilities are endless. While we can't go into detail about all the classes, methods, and properties exposed by the object model (this information is available in the SDK), we provide you with enough information to get started with your own exploration.

The object models are implemented in C# and can be accessed through ASP.NET or any .NET Framework process. The WSS object model provides an easy mechanism for navigating through the various components that make up your WSS deployment. The `Microsoft.SharePoint` and `Microsoft.SharePoint.Administration` namespaces provide access to the various types, members, and methods for working with and managing SharePoint data such as lists, sites, subsites, and WSS servers. Each namespace contains many classes for working with SharePoint; however, four deserve special attention, since they are the classes that provide the most functionality.

- `SPWeb`: The `SPWeb` class represents the top-level object for an individual Web site and provides access to all its lists, files, folders, Web Parts, and any additional objects.

- `SPSite`: The `SPSite` class represents the top-level object for a SharePoint site and provides access to its collection of subsites and templates.

- `SPVirtualServer`: The `SPVirtualServer` class represents the top-level object for a virtual server and is used to implement serverwide configuration settings. This class can be used to create, delete, and access sites under a specific virtual server.

- `SPGlobalAdmin`: The `SPGlobalAdmin` class represents the top-level object for administering a SharePoint deployment. This class can be used to install and enable a Web Part Package and add it to the Web Part Gallery.

The `SPWeb` object is of paramount importance, since it acts as the entry point for accessing SharePoint objects, such as lists, items, documents,

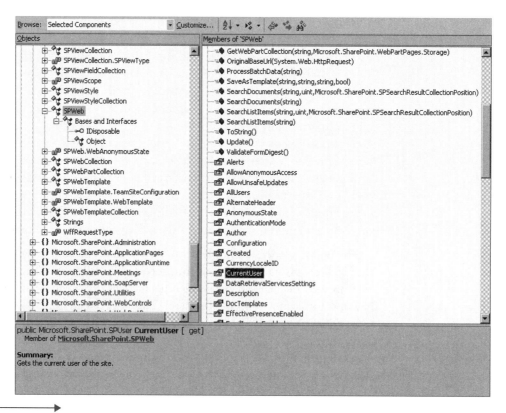

Figure 17.41   SPWeb *class viewed in object browser.*

users, and alerts for your Web site. Figure 17.41 shows the SPWeb class through the Visual Studio .NET object browser. As you can see, the SPWeb object contains numerous properties and methods. For example, the CurrentUser property returns the current user of the site, and the SaveAsTemplate method saves the site as a template.

The SPS 2003 object model builds on top of the WSS object and provides access to portal objects, such as user-profile objects and Single Sign-On objects. Most of the new portal functionality is written in ASP.NET managed code, with the exception of legacy aspects of the portal. The document-management functionality that was available in SPS 2001 and accessible through the Publishing and Knowledge Management Collaboration Data Objects (PKMCDO) object model is still available in SPS 2003 for backward compatibility. Additionally, some of the advanced search features such as protocol handlers and iFilters are all still using essentially the same old COM-based object model used in SPS 2001.

SPS 2003 introduces two new assemblies that you can reference if you want to programmatically reference the portal functionality: `Microsoft.SharePoint.Portal.dll` (`Portal.dll`) and `Microsoft.SharePoint.Portal.SingleSignOn.dll` (`SingleSignOn.dll`). `Portal.dll` hosts the vast majority of the portal functionality, whereas `SingleSignOn.dll` hosts user and password information implemented by the `SingleSignOn` functionality. If you examine each component through the Visual Studio .NET object browser, you will see the namespaces, classes, properties, and methods accessible. The `Portal.dll` component introduces a large number of subnamespaces for each set of objects.

17.7.1   Creating a SharePoint ASP.NET Web application

If you want a custom ASP.NET page to run in the same context as your SharePoint deployment, you need to store the page in the layouts directory of your SharePoint server. This ensures that your application is accessible from all sites in your SharePoint deployment.

The following steps show how to create a custom ASP.NET application in the context of a SharePoint deployment.

1.   Launch Visual Studio .NET.

2.   From the File menu, click **New** and then click **Project**.

3.   From the list of templates, select **ASP.NET Web Application**.

4.   In the *Locations* field, enter the location for your new Web application, for example, `http://spdev01/_layouts/myapps`, where `myapps` is a subfolder of the `_layouts` folder that contains all your custom Web applications.

5.   Click **OK**. A progress dialog should appear informing you that the new Web is being created. If you are creating the application from a remote computer, see the following section.

6.   Add some "Hello World" code to your application.

7.   Save your application.

The new `.aspx` page should be available via the `_layouts` path of any site. For example, if you have a WSS site called "Development," the path to your new `.aspx` page would be `http://spdev01/sites/development/_layouts/myapps/myapp.aspx`.

Figure 17.42
*Register SharePoint
namespaces.*

```
<%@ Register Tagprefix="SharePoint" Namespace="Microsoft.SharePoint.WebControls"
   Assembly="Microsoft.SharePoint, Version=11.0.0.0, Culture=neutral,
PublicKeyToken=71e9bce111e9429c" %>
<%@ Register Tagprefix="Utilities" Namespace="Microsoft.SharePoint.Utilities"
   Assembly="Microsoft.SharePoint, Version=11.0.0.0, Culture=neutral,
PublicKeyToken=71e9bce111e9429c" %>
<%@ Import Namespace="Microsoft.SharePoint" %>
<%@ Register Tagprefix="WebPartPages" Namespace="Microsoft.SharePoint.WebPartPages"
   Assembly="Microsoft.SharePoint, Version=11.0.0.0, Culture=neutral,
PublicKeyToken=71e9bce111e9429c" %>
```

Creating a Web application from a remote computer

If you are creating the Web application from a remote computer and followed the previous steps, you may have received an error when you reached step 5. To overcome this error, perform the following steps:

1. You will be prompted with a Web Access Failed dialog box, informing you that the file path does not match the specified URL. From the *What would you like to do?* section, select the *Retry using a different share path* option.

2. Enter the path to the SharePoint server's layouts directory and append your application directory, for example, `\\SPDEV01\C$\ Program Files\Common Files\Microsoft Shared\Web Server Extensions\60\TEMPLATE\LAYOUTS\myapps`.

3. Click **OK**.

If you want to use the object model with your new Web application, you will need to register the appropriate namespaces in your code. Figure 17.42 shows the registration code for the Microsoft SharePoint, `Microsoft.SharePoint.WebControls`, `Microsoft.SharePoint.Utilities`, and `Microsoft.SharePoint.WebPartPages` namespaces in a typical `.aspx` page.

For code behind files or console applications, use the `using` or `Imports` directives, as shown in Figure 17.43.

To gain the benefit of the Intellisense, you should set a reference to the relevant SharePoint assemblies, for example, `Microsoft.Share-`

Figure 17.43
*Register namespaces
in C# and
VB.NET.*

```
C# Code
using Microsoft.SharePoint;
using Microsoft.SharePoint.WebControls;
using Microsoft.SharePoint.WebPartPages;

VB.NET Code
Imports Microsoft.SharePoint
Imports Microsoft.SharePoint.WebControls
Imports Microsoft.SharePoint.WebPartPages
```

Point.dll. If the assembly does not appear in your list of available .NET references, you can browse to the C:\Program Files\Common Files\ Microsoft Shared\web server extensions\60\ISAPI directory and select the .dll.

Now you are all set to start writing some SharePoint code!

17.7.2   Coding a SharePoint application

Obviously, the complexity of the coding process will vary depending on the type of application you are creating. Let's look at a simple Web Form application that sets the AlternateHeader property for a site. Figure 17.44 shows the purpose of our simple application; the application retrieves the current AlternateHeader value for the current site, then, when the user hits the **Apply** button, the filename he or she entered in the text box becomes the new AlternateHeader for the pages in that site. The application isn't particularly pleasing to the eye, but it should give you a feel for the relative ease with which you can extend the functionality of your Share-Point deployment without jeopardizing your support contract with Microsoft.

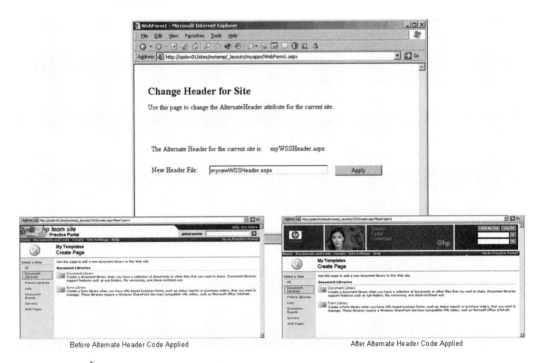

Figure 17.44   *Simple application to change alternate header for a site.*

We'll pick up from the previous section and assume that you have your application open in Visual Studio .NET and have declared the various SharePoint namespaces. Next, add the following HTML elements to the page:

- A <DIV> element that represents the title of the page
- A <DIV> element that represents the description of the page
- A <DIV> element to display the leading text "The Alternate Header for the current site is"
- A <DIV> element to display the value of the AlternateHeader attribute for the site
- A <DIV> element to display the leading text "New Header File:"
- An <INPUT> element of type Text to enter the new header file
- An <INPUT> element of type Button that the user will click to set the AlternateHeader attribute equal to the new header file
- A <DIV> element to display error messages at the bottom of the page

Visual Studio .NET provides an HTML toolbox to make the addition of these elements easier. The following steps show you how to access the toolbox:

1.   View your .aspx page in design mode.

2.   From the View menu click **Toolbox**.

3.   From the Toolbox pane, select the HTML tab.

4.   Simply drag and drop the appropriate tools onto your page. The Label represents a <DIV> element, the Text Field represents an <INPUT> element of type Text, and the Button represents an <INPUT> element of type Button. If you view your page in HTML mode, you will see that the appropriate HTML code has been generated behind the scenes.

You can populate the various elements with the desired text directly in code or using the Properties window of the elements in design mode. Once you have your Web Form configured, you can add the SharePoint-specific code to the class file associated with the .aspx file, for example, myapp.aspx.cs. To access the class file, double-click the button on your Web Form. Figure 17.45 shows the code for this class file.

Visual Studio .NET's code generator creates much of the code for you. In our example, short of adding the appropriate using declarations, the only code that we had to add was to declare our site attribute and then add the content code for the `Page_Load` event and the `Button1_Click` event; the shell for each of these events was automatically created.

The `AlternateHeader` is a property of the `SPWeb` class; consequently, we need to declare our own SPWeb object for use in the events (line 12). Lines 13 through 18 define the `Page_Load` event, which, as its name implies, is invoked when the ASP.NET page loads in the browser. Line 15 establishes the context of our site using the `GetContextWeb` method of the `SPControl` class. This method returns an `SPWeb` or `SPSite` object. Since the `AlternateHeader` property belongs to the `SPWeb` class, our implementation returns an `SPWeb` object. Line 16 clears any previous errors from the display, and line 17 retrieves the current value of the SPWeb's `Alternate-Header` property. Lines 39 through 52 define the `Button1_Click` event; if the text field is not empty, then the code sets the `AlternateHeader` property of the `SPWeb` object to the value the user entered into the text field.

Security validation

Testing the application at this stage results in an error message (Figure 17.46), indicating that the security validation for this page is invalid. To prevent malicious attacks on a SharePoint server, Microsoft does not allow you to make posts from a Web application to update content in the database without first providing the appropriate security validation on the page. Since our application is updating the content of the `AlternateHeader` attribute for the site in the database, we need to include this security validation by adding a `FormDigest` control to our page. The `FormDigest` control is a Web control provided by the `Microsoft.SharePoint.WebControls` class; consequently, you must first ensure you have registered a valid page directive for the `Microsoft.SharePoint.WebControls` namespace (Figure 17.42). To add a `FormDigest` control, insert the following code within the `form` element on the page:

```
<SharePoint:FormDigest runat="server"/>
```

Once you have added this code to your `.aspx` page, then saved and compiled the project, you are now ready to test your application.

Testing the application

To test your application, simply navigate to your Web Form within the context of a SharePoint site. The URL will take the following form:

```
http://myserver/sites/mysite/_layouts/myapps/WebForm1.aspx
```

Change the header to the name of your custom header .aspx file located in the \Program Files\Common Files\Microsoft Shared\web server extensions\60\TEMPLATE\LAYOUTS\<localid>\ directory, such as myCustomHeader.aspx. If your site currently does not have an AlternateHeader property defined, your code will still set the property, and your custom header will override the default Microsoft header on all

```
1.    public class WebForm1 : System.Web.UI.Page
2.    {
3.        protected System.Web.UI.WebControls.Button Button1;
4.        protected System.Web.UI.WebControls.TextBox TextBox1;
5.        protected System.Web.UI.WebControls.Label Label2;
6.        protected System.Web.UI.WebControls.Label Label3;
7.        protected System.Web.UI.WebControls.Label Label4;
8.        protected System.Web.UI.WebControls.Label Label5;
9.        protected System.Web.UI.WebControls.Label Label1;
10.       protected System.Web.UI.WebControls.Label Label6;
11.
12.       private SPWeb cursite;
13.       private void Page_Load(object sender, System.EventArgs e)
14.       {
15.         cursite = SPControl.GetContextWeb(Context);
16.         Label6.Text = "";
17.         Label2.Text = cursite.AlternateHeader.ToString();
18.       }
19.       #region Web Form Designer generated code
20.       override protected void OnInit(EventArgs e)
21.       {
22.         //
23.         // CODEGEN: This call is required by the ASP.NET Web Form Designer.
24.         //
25.         InitializeComponent();
26.         base.OnInit(e);
27.       }
28.
29.       /// <summary>
30.       /// Required method for Designer support - do not modify
31.       /// the contents of this method with the code editor.
32.       /// </summary>
33.       private void InitializeComponent()
34.       {
35.         this.Button1.Click += new System.EventHandler(this.Button1_Click);
36.         this.Load += new System.EventHandler(this.Page_Load);
37.       }
38.       #endregion
39.       private void Button1_Click(object sender, System.EventArgs e)
40.       {
41.         string newHeader = TextBox1.Text;
42.         if (newHeader != String.Empty)
43.         {
44.           cursite.AlternateHeader = TextBox1.Text;
45.           cursite.Update();
46.           Label2.Text = cursite.AlternateHeader.ToString();
47.         }
48.           else
49.         {
50.           Label6.Text = "You must first enter a header file!";
51.         }
52.       }
53.   }
```

Figure 17.45   WebForm1.aspx.cs *class code.*

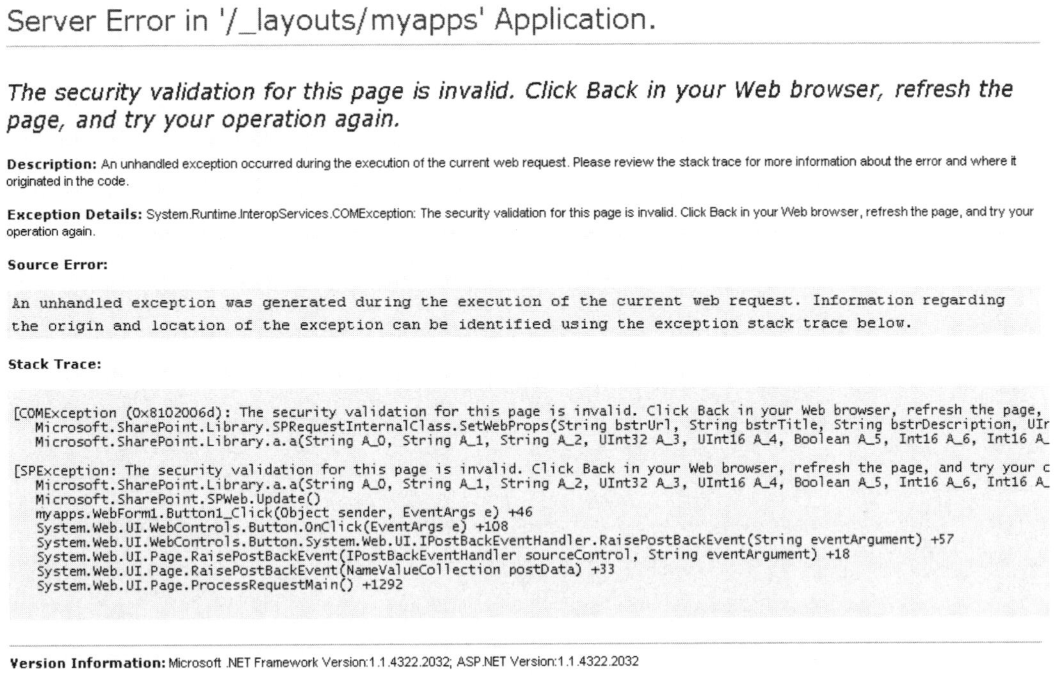

Server Error in '/_layouts/myapps' Application.

The security validation for this page is invalid. Click Back in your Web browser, refresh the page, and try your operation again.

Description: An unhandled exception occurred during the execution of the current web request. Please review the stack trace for more information about the error and where it originated in the code.

Exception Details: System.Runtime.InteropServices.COMException: The security validation for this page is invalid. Click Back in your Web browser, refresh the page, and try your operation again.

Source Error:

```
An unhandled exception was generated during the execution of the current web request. Information regarding
the origin and location of the exception can be identified using the exception stack trace below.
```

Stack Trace:

```
[COMException (0x8102006d): The security validation for this page is invalid. Click Back in your Web browser, refresh the page,
   Microsoft.SharePoint.Library.SPRequestInternalClass.SetWebProps(String bstrUrl, String bstrTitle, String bstrDescription, UIr
   Microsoft.SharePoint.Library.a.a(String A_0, String A_1, String A_2, UInt32 A_3, UInt16 A_4, Boolean A_5, Int16 A_6, Int16 A_

[SPException: The security validation for this page is invalid. Click Back in your Web browser, refresh the page, and try your c
   Microsoft.SharePoint.Library.a.a(String A_0, String A_1, String A_2, UInt32 A_3, UInt16 A_4, Boolean A_5, Int16 A_6, Int16 A_
   Microsoft.SharePoint.SPWeb.Update()
   myapps.WebForm1.Button1_Click(Object sender, EventArgs e) +46
   System.Web.UI.WebControls.Button.OnClick(EventArgs e) +108
   System.Web.UI.WebControls.Button.System.Web.UI.IPostBackEventHandler.RaisePostBackEvent(String eventArgument) +57
   System.Web.UI.Page.RaisePostBackEvent(IPostBackEventHandler sourceControl, String eventArgument) +18
   System.Web.UI.Page.RaisePostBackEvent(NameValueCollection postData) +33
   System.Web.UI.Page.ProcessRequestMain() +1292
```

Version Information: Microsoft .NET Framework Version:1.1.4322.2032; ASP.NET Version:1.1.4322.2032

Figure 17.46   *Security validation error due to missing* FormDigest *control.*

.aspx pages that reference the AlternateHeader property, such as the Create page of a site (http://myserver/sites/mysite/_layouts/ 1033/create.aspx).

17.8   Leveraging the event architecture

You may want to extend the default behavior of SharePoint by providing your own workflow-type process to control the life cycle of a document on your site. Those of you familiar with SPS 2001 may be aware that the product shipped with an event architecture, which made it easy to control the life cycle of a document. SPS 2001 shipped out of the box with approval and routing functionality that could be extended further using the Web Storage System event sinks. While the current version of SharePoint does not offer this routing behavior out of the box, the WSS architecture does offer the developer document library events. As a developer, you can create your own workflow functionality by writing custom event handlers and binding them to the document library. Table 17.10 shows the document library events supplied by WSS.

Table 17.10   *WSS Document Library Events*

Event	Description
Check in	A document is checked in
Check out	A document is checked out
Cancel check out	Changes made to a checked-out document are undone
Insert	A new document is saved to the document library
Delete	A document is deleted from the document library
Copy	A document in the document library is copied
Move or rename	A document in the document library is moved or renamed
Update	A document in the document library is edited, or a value of a custom column in the library is edited

To work with event handlers you need to ensure that events are enabled for your site, which can be achieved from the Virtual Server Settings page of the SharePoint central administration:

1. Using your browser, navigate to the SharePoint Central Administration page.

2. From the *Virtual Server Configuration* section, click **Configure virtual server settings**.

3. From the Virtual Server list, click the virtual server for which you want to enable event handlers. The Virtual Server Settings page appears for the selected virtual server.

4. From the *Virtual Server Management* section, click **Virtual server general settings**. The Virtual Server General Settings page appears.

5. Scroll to the bottom of the page. In the *Event Handlers* section, ensure that Event Handlers are turned on (Figure 17.47).

6. Click **OK**.

From a development perspective, a document library event handler is basically a .NET class that implements the IListEventSink interface. The IListEventSink interface contains one method, the OnEvent method, which is used to respond to changes that occur to a document stored in a document library. The OnEvent method receives the events as they occur as an SPListEvent object. The SPListEvent object is accessible through

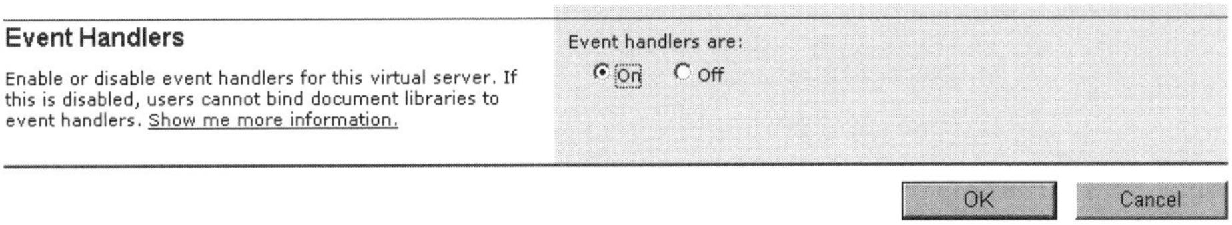

Event Handlers

Enable or disable event handlers for this virtual server. If this is disabled, users cannot bind document libraries to event handlers. Show me more information.

Event handlers are:
○ On   ○ Off

[OK]   [Cancel]

Figure 17.47   *Enabling event handlers on virtual server.*

code, and all you need to do as a developer is insert code into the OnEvent method that listens for the specific events you are interested in and process them accordingly.

Coding the event handler

For our first example, we'll create an event handler that outputs information about the events to a text file as and when they occur. This simple application is quite useful if you want to see which events are actually triggered when items are processed in the document library. For example, when you rename a document in the document library, the process triggers both a Move event and an Update event. Armed with this knowledge, you can ensure that you are capturing all the appropriate events when developing more functional event handlers.

Before we begin, it is important to note that document library event handlers run in the context of the IIS Application Pool Identity Account, which typically does not have access to the WSS object model. In this example, we assume that you are coding on a development machine in which the Application Pool Account has sufficient permission to access the SharePoint Services namespaces required to manage the document life cycle. The following steps show you how to check the account associated with the SharePoint application pool.

1.   Launch IIS Manager.

2.   Navigate to the SharePoint application pool, for example, MSSharePointPortalAppPool.

3.   From the application pool's shortcut menu, click **Properties**.

4.   Select the Identity tab to view the account associated with the application pool.

In a typical production environment, the account under which the application's worker process runs has the least user rights required to run Web applications, thus providing security against malicious attacks. If your development server mimics the security of a production environment, then

```
1.  using System;
2.  using Microsoft.SharePoint;
3.  using System.IO;

4.  namespace DocLibraryEventHandler
5.  {
6.      /// <summary>
7.      /// This is a simple class that traps events and outputs info to a file
8.      /// </summary>
9.      public class OutputEvents : IListEventSink
10.     {

11.         void IListEventSink.OnEvent (Microsoft.SharePoint.SPListEvent listEvent)
12.         {
13.             // TODO: ***** IF REQUIRED INSERT YOUR IMPERSONATE CODE HERE ****
14.
15.             StreamWriter objStreamWriter = new StreamWriter("c:\\eventoutput.txt",true);
16.             objStreamWriter.WriteLine("An event was triggered on: " + DateTime.Now);
17.             objStreamWriter.WriteLine("The event type is: " + listEvent.Type.ToString());
18.             objStreamWriter.WriteLine("-----------------------------------------------");
19.             objStreamWriter.Close();
20.         }
21.     }
22. }
```

Figure 17.48   *Simple document library event handler C# code.*

your code will need to leverage the `LogonUser` API to impersonate a Windows account that has appropriate access to the document library and SharePoint object models. Our second example in this section shows how to use the `LogonUser` API.

First, we need to create a new class project that represents our event handler assembly. Next, we need to add the code shown in Figure 17.48 and rename the namespace, class, and output file as desired.

Lines 1 through 3 provide the directives required by our code. The code requires the `System` directive in order to use the `DateTime` function, the `Microsoft.SharePoint` directive in order to access the `SPListEvent` class, and the `System.IO` directive in order to use the `StreamWriter` class. When creating a document library event handler, the class created must implement the `IListEventSink` (line 9). Lines 11 through 21 define the code to be executed when a document library event occurs in a document library linked to the event handler. We basically use the `StreamWriter` object to write information about a triggered event to a file. The `Type` property of the `SPListEvent` class tells us the type of event triggered, such as an `Update` event.

As with Web Parts, document library event handlers must be strongly named in order to run successfully. Additionally, they must be deployed to the GAC. As a quick refresh, you can use the Strong Name Tool (`sn.exe`) to strongly name your assembly. Make sure that you associate your `Assembly.info` file with the same key file used with the `sn.exe` tool. More information on strongly named assemblies and the GAC is found in Chapters 14 and 15.

All that remains is to compile and deploy your event handler assembly.

Deploying the event handler

Deploying an event handler involves installing the assembly to the GAC, ensuring that event handlers are enabled, and finally associating the document libraries with the event handler. The following steps show how to deploy an event handler:

1. Install your assembly to the GAC. You can use the `gacutil.exe` tool to deploy your assembly to the GAC or simply drag and drop your assembly into the `\windows\assembly` directory on your server.

2. On the Virtual Server General Settings page in SharePoint Central Administration, ensure that the use of event handlers is enabled.

3. Navigate to the document library with which you wish to associate the event handler.

4. Click **Modify Settings and Columns**. The Customization page appears.

5. From the *General Settings* section, click **Change advanced settings**. The Advanced Settings page appears.

6. In the *Event Handler* section, enter the details for the *Assembly Name* and *Class Name* fields. Figure 17.49 shows the settings we used for our example. You can retrieve the value for the `Public-KeyToken` attribute from the properties pane of the assembly deployed in the GAC or by using the `sn.exe` tool with the `-T` parameter. The class name should be set to the fully qualified, case-sensitive name of the class.

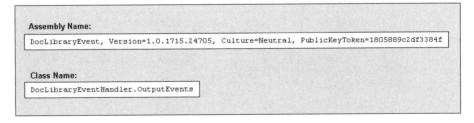

Figure 17.49   *Event handler document library settings.*

Note: If you have set your assembly versioning to automatic, or if you change the version number in subsequent updates of your assembly, you must update the `Version` attribute in the *Assembly* field of this page if you want the document library to attach to the new version.

---

7.   Reset IIS. IIS must be reset with each update of the assembly.

The event handler is now successfully deployed and ready to be launched. To see your event handler in action, simply invoke an event; for example, if you upload the file specified in the code, the output file should contain text notifying you that the `Insert` event fired. Figure 17.50 shows sample output from the file.

Document workflow example

Our next example creates an event handler that performs some workflow on items in the document library. The basic premise of the workflow is that a folder exists in a site that receives submissions from employees. These sub-

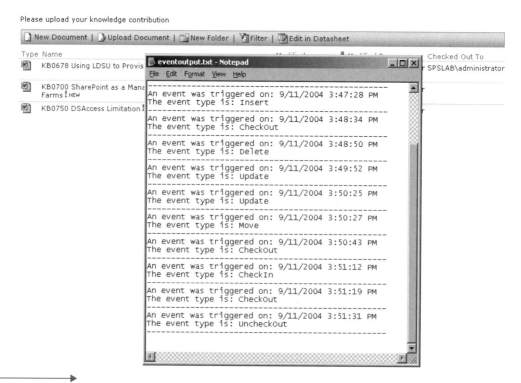

Figure 17.50   *Event handler output file.*

missions are typically in the form of a document containing specific knowledge that the employee would like published to the Published Knowledge Briefs (KBs) document library. This document is known as a KB. The publication process requires that an employee upload his or her contribution to the Knowledge Contributions folder. Once the document is uploaded, a KB reviewer reviews the content and determines whether it is suitable for publication to the site by updating the status to either Approved or Rejected. The employee receives confirmation e-mails after first uploading the contribution and when the reviewer updates the status. If the submission is approved, the document is automatically moved to the Published KBs document library, and an e-mail is sent to the employee notifying him or her of the approval. If the submission is rejected, the document is deleted from the Knowledge Contributions folder, and a message is sent to the employee to inform him or her that more work is required.

The code performs a specific process when the item is in each of the following states:

1.   The item is uploaded to the site.

2.   The status property associated with the item is set to Approved.

3.   The status property associated with the item is set to `false`.

Figure 17.51 provides the class structure; the class contains two methods: `IListEventSink.OnEvent` and `SendEmail`. The `IListEventSink.OnEvent` method listens for `Insert` and `Update` events from the document library and processes the items accordingly. The `SendEmail`

```
using System;
using System.Web.Mail;
using Microsoft.SharePoint;
using System.IO;

namespace DocLibraryEventHandler
{
    /// <summary>
    /// Summary description for Class1.
    /// </summary>
    public class SendConfirmation : IListEventSink
    {
        void IListEventSink.OnEvent (Microsoft.SharePoint.SPListEvent listEvent)
        {
            ///code in here to handle events
        }

        void SendEmail (string to, string subject, string content)
        {
            ///code in here to send email
        }
    }
}
```

Figure 17.51   *Code structure.*

method sends an e-mail to the employee with the current status of his or her submission.

Figure 17.52 shows the code for `IListEventSink.OnEvent`. Lines 3 through 9 set up the various properties and objects that will be used throughout the rest of the method. The `SPListEvent` object represents the event from which we can access other properties and methods, such as the

Figure 17.52

`OnEvent` *code.*

```
1.    void IListEventSink.OnEvent (Microsoft.SharePoint.SPListEvent listEvent)
2.    {
3.        SPWeb site = listEvent.Site.OpenWeb();
4.        SPUser curUser = site.SiteUsers[listEvent.UserID];
5.        SPFile docFile = site.GetFile(listEvent.UrlAfter);
6.        usrEmail = curUser.Email;
7.        string subject;
8.        string publishUrl = "Published KBs/";
9.        string msgContent;
10.       switch (listEvent.Type)
11.       {
12.         case SPListEventType.Insert:
13.             docFile.Item["Status"] = "Pending";
14.             docFile.Item.Update();
15.             // send email to confirm the receipt of submission
16.             subject = "Thank you for your knowledge contribution.";
17.             msgContent = "<html><body>Your document is currently being";
18.             msgContent += " reviewed.<br>";
19.             msgContent += "Thank You!<br>The KM Team</body></html>";
20.             SendEmail(usrEmail, subject, msgContent);
21.             return;
22.         case SPListEventType.Update:
23.             //get email address of document Author
24.             usrEmail = docFile.Author.Email;
25.             //get information about the uploaded item
26.             string docTitle = docFile.Title;
27.             string docFileName = docFile.Name;
28.             string docSubDate = docFile.TimeCreated.ToString();
29.             string docDetails = "File Name: <B>" + docFileName;
30.             docDetails += "</B><br>Document Title: <B>" + docTitle;
31.             docDetails += "</B><br> Submission Date: <B>";
32.             docDetails += docSubDate + "</B><br>";
33.             //check item status and process accordingly
34.             if (docFile.Item["Status"].ToString() == "Approved")
35.             {
36.                 //copy document to Published Document Library
37.                 docFile.MoveTo(publishUrl + docFile.Name,true);
38.                 //Send approval notification email
39.                 subject = "Your Knowledge Contribution has been approved!";
40.                 msgContent = "<html><body>" + docDetails;
41.                 msgContent += " has been approved! <br><br>";
42.                 msgContent += "Thank You!<br>The KM Team</body></html>";
43.                 SendEmail(usrEmail, subject, msgContent);
44.             }
45.             else if (docFile.Item["Status"].ToString() == "Rejected")
46.             {
47.                 //delete the document from the repository
48.                 docFile.Item.ListItems.DeleteItemById(docFile.Item.ID);
49.                 //Send rejection notification email
50.                 subject = "Your Knowledge Contribution requires rework!";
51.                 msgContent = "<html><body>" + docDetails + " has been reviewed and ";
52.                 msgContent += "requires edits before resubmission. <br><br>";
53.                 msgContent += "Thank You!<br>The KM Team</body></html>";
54.                 SendEmail(usrEmail, subject, msgContent);
55.             }
56.             return;
57.        }
58.    }
```

ID of the user who initiated the event and the URL of the document associated with the event. We use the SPWeb object to access the data in the site. Using this object in conjunction with the SPListEvent object, we retrieve the user who initiated the event, the document associated with the event, and the e-mail address of the current user (lines 4, 5, and 6).

A switch statement is used to handle two event types, the Insert event (lines 12 through 21) and the Update event (lines 22 through 56). Lines 13 and 14 access the *Status* field of the item associated with the document being processed and set the value of this field to Pending. The Pending status lets reviewers know that the document requires review. Reviewers can then proceed to use the *Check Out* functionality to provide feedback that they are reviewing the document. After the *Status* field is updated, an e-mail is sent to the user who uploaded the document to inform him or her that it is currently being reviewed.

The Update event handler monitors the *Status* field and, depending on its value, either publishes the document to another document library in the site or deletes it from the site. If the document is approved, the MoveTo method of the SPFile class is used to move the document to the Published KBs document library. It is important to note that the MoveTo and CopyTo methods apply to the context of a single site; you cannot use either of these methods to copy or move content to another site. If the document is rejected, the DeleteItemByID method is used to delete the document from the Knowledge Contributions document library.

Figure 17.53 shows the code used for the SendMail method. The Send-Mail method uses the MailMessage class to construct and submit e-mail messages. The MailMessage class is a member of the System.Web.Mail namespace.

Figure 17.53
SendEmail
C# code.

```
void SendEmail (string to, string subject, string content)
{
    MailMessage myMail = new MailMessage();
    myMail.From = "KBReviewer@hp.com";
    myMail.To = to;
    myMail.Subject = subject;
    myMail.Priority = MailPriority.Normal;
    myMail.BodyFormat = MailFormat.Html;
    myMail.Body = content;
    try
    {
        SmtpMail.Send(myMail);
    }
    catch (Exception e)
    {
        //error code here
    }
}
```

Figure 17.54
*Custom event
handler in action.*

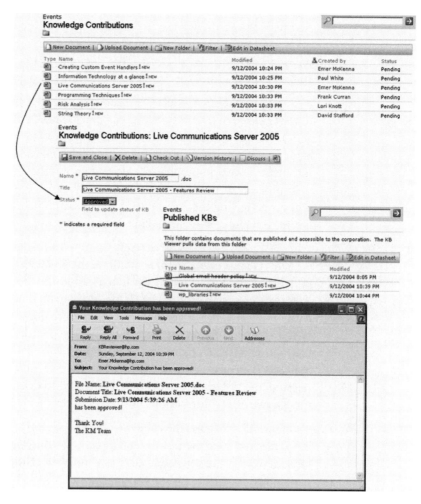

Figure 17.54 shows the results of the approval of a submitted contribution. Notice that the document is eventually moved to the Published KBs document library, and an e-mail is distributed to the contributor.

Creating an impersonation identity

As previously mentioned, the account under which the application's worker process runs does not have access to the SharePoint object model. As a result, any code you develop should leverage the `LogonUser` API to impersonate a user who has the appropriate permissions. Figure 17.55 shows the code for the `CreateIdentity` method that establishes the identity under which the event handler will run. The code is well documented in various resources, including the SDK; it basically calls the Windows API to connect the impersonation user on to the system. The impersonation user is defined by the developer. The `CreateIdentity` method ultimately returns a `WindowsIdentity` object to the main code for further processing, allowing SharePoint to perform various tasks on behalf of the impersonation account. The account defined as the impersonation account must have the appropriate permissions to perform the various tasks.

The code requires the `System.Security.Principal` directive in order to use the `WindowsIdentity` class and the `System.Runtime.InteropServices` directive in order to use the `DLLImportAttribute` class.

Before we depart from this topic, it is important to note that the event model in WSS is asynchronous only, which means that you cannot stop an action from happening; you can only be notified that it has happened. For example, there is no way to prevent an item that you are currently processing through workflow from being deleted; the only way to restore the item is to reinsert it into the library yourself. That said, you are passed the before and after states with your event handler, which allows you to compare the state of a document in the document library before it was modified with the state after it was modified.

Those of you familiar with the event architecture that came with SPS 2001, courtesy of the Web Storage System, may be disappointed by the fact

Figure 17.55
Impersonation C# code.

```
protected static WindowsIdentity CreateIdentity(string usrName,
                string domain, string   password)
{
  const int LOGON32_PROVIDER_DEFAULT = 0;
  const int LOGON32_LOGON_NETWORK= 3;
  //The Windows NT user Token
  IntPtr tokenHandle = new IntPtr(0);
  tokenHandle = IntPtr.Zero;

  //Call LogonUser to logon the user and get a token

  bool returnValue = LogonUser(usrName, domain, password,
      LOGON32_LOGON_NETWORK, LOGON32_PROVIDER_DEFAULT, ref tokenHandle);
  if (false == returnValue)
  {
    //There was an error
    int retError = Marshal.GetLastWin32Error();
    StreamWriter objErrorWriter = new StreamWriter("c:\\errorlog.txt",true);
    objErrorWriter.WriteLine("Logon failed 0: " + DateTime.Now);
    objErrorWriter.WriteLine("Error: " + retError.ToString());
    objErrorWriter.Close();
  }

  //Create a new Windows Identity and pass it back
  WindowsIdentity id = new WindowsIdentity(tokenHandle);
  CloseHandle(tokenHandle);
  return id;
}
[DllImport("advapi32.dll", SetLastError=true)]
private static extern bool LogonUser(string lpszUsername, string lpszDomain,string
    lpszPassword, int dwLogonType, int dwLogonProvider, ref IntPtr phToken);
[DllImport("kernel32.dll", CharSet=CharSet.Auto)]
private static extern bool CloseHandle(IntPtr handle);
}
```

that document library events are asynchronous only. We can only hope that subsequent releases of the product improve in this area.

If you want to play with sample document library event handlers, you should download the Document Library Event Handler Toolkit available on the Microsoft Web site.

17.9 Accessing SharePoint data using Web Services

The object models that we have been working with to date are server-side object models. If you need to access SharePoint objects and items remotely through code, you can leverage the Windows SharePoint Services Web Service provided by the `Microsoft.SharePoint.SoapServer` namespace. The `Microsoft.SharePoint.SoapServer` namespace has numerous methods for accessing SharePoint data. Table 17.11 shows the Web Services offerings.

The Simple Object Access Protocol (SOAP) interfaces leveraged by these services provide developers with an object model that can access WSS data remotely from a client or custom application. In fact, Web Services are built on top of the WSS object model and, as such, provide much of the same basic functionality, such as working with lists, webs, views, and users. In an

Table 17.11 *WSS Web Services*

Service	Description
Administration	Provides methods for managing a WSS deployment. Methods include the ability to create and delete sites, retrieve the languages used in the WSS deployment, and refresh the configuration cache for the virtual server. `http://<your server:PortNumber>/_vti_adm/admin.asmx`
Alerts	Provides methods for retrieving and deleting alerts. `http://<your server>/_vti_bin/Alerts.asmx`
Document workspace	Provides many methods for managing document workspace sites and their associated data. Methods include, but are not limited to, creating a document workspace site, creating subfolders in the document library of a document workspace site, and performing a batch update of items and data for the document workspace site. `http://<your server>/_vti_bin/DWS.asmx`
Forms	Provides methods for returning data for forms that are used in the user interface when working with the contents of a list. For example, the `GetForm` method returns the schema of a form for a specified list based on the name of the list and the URL. `http://<your server>/_vti_bin/Forms.asmx`

Table 17.11   *WSS Web Services (continued)*

Service	Description
Imaging	Provides many methods that enable you to create and manage picture libraries. Methods include, but are not limited to, deleting specific files from a list on the site and downloading files to a list on the site. `http://<your server>/_vti_bin/Imaging.asmx`
List data retrieval	Provides a query method that allows developers to perform queries against lists in WSS. `http://<your server>/_vti_bin/.asmx`
Lists	Provides many methods for working with lists and list data. Methods include, but are not limited to, adding lists, deleting lists, and updating items in a list. `http://<your server>/_vti_bin/Lists.asmx`
Meetings	Provides many methods for creating and managing meeting workspace sites. Methods include, but are not limited to, creating a meeting workspace, deleting a meeting workspace, and associating a meeting with a specific meeting workspace. `http://<your server>/_vti_bin/Meetings.asmx`
Permissions	Provides methods for adding, removing, and retrieving the permissions for a site or list. `http://<your server>/_vti_bin/Permissions.asmx`
Site data	Provides methods that return metadata or list data from WSS sites or lists. `http://<your server>/_vti_bin/SiteData.asmx`
Sites	Provides a method for returning information about the site templates for a site collection. `http://<your server>/_vti_bin/sites.asmx`
Users and groups	Provides many methods for working with users, site groups, and cross-site groups. Methods include, but are not limited to, adding cross-site groups to the current site collection, adding specific cross-site groups to a specific site group, and adding a user to a specific site group. `http://<your server>/_vti_bin/UserGroup.asmx`
Versions	Provides methods for working with file versions, such as the deleting all versions of a file, deleting only a specific file version, restoring a specific file version, and retrieving information about the versions associated with a specific file. `http://<your server>/_vti_bin/versions.asmx`
Views	Provides methods for working with views, such as the ability to add, delete, retrieve, and update views. `http://<your server>/_vti_bin/views.asmx`
Webs	Provides methods for working with sites and subsites. For example, you can use the method to retrieve the titles and URLs of all the sites within the current site collection. `http://<your server>/_vti_bin/webs.asmx`

effort to improve the performance of the provided SOAP interfaces, Microsoft optimized their behavior to reduce the number of roundtrips required to the server. For example, the `GetList` method of the Lists Web Service returns the schema of the specified list and assigns it to an `XmlNode` object; in order to retrieve additional information from the list, the developer simply queries the `XmlNode`.

If you are hesitant about pursuing Web Services as a suitable option when developing SharePoint-aware applications, you should be comforted by the fact that Office 2003 uses Web Services extensively to provide its SharePoint integration.

Viewing available Web Services

Visual Studio can be used to view more information on the Web Services that are provided by WSS.

1.   Open your application in Visual Studio .NET, or, alternatively, create a new application.

2.   From the Project menu, select **Add Web Reference**.

3.   Enter the URL to the Web Service in which you are interested. For example, to see more information on the Lists Web Service enter `http://<yourserver>/sites/<yoursite>/_vti_bin/ Lists.asmx`. The Web Service and its corresponding URL can be found in Table 17.11.

4.   Click the **Go** button.

The dialog displays the various methods exposed by the service (Figure 17.56), and clicking on a specific method displays information about the SOAP request. To be able to work with a particular service, you should add it as a Web reference to your project. To add a Web Service as a reference, resume the previous steps and simply click the **Add Reference** button.

Leveraging the Lists Web Service

To provide a quick review of this Web Service capability, we'll create a simple Windows application that will create a new custom list in a SharePoint site.

1.   Open Visual Studio .NET, and create a new project using the Windows Application template. This example uses C#.

2.   Once the project is open, add a Web reference to the Lists Web Service.

Figure 17.56
*Adding a reference
to the Lists Web
Service.*

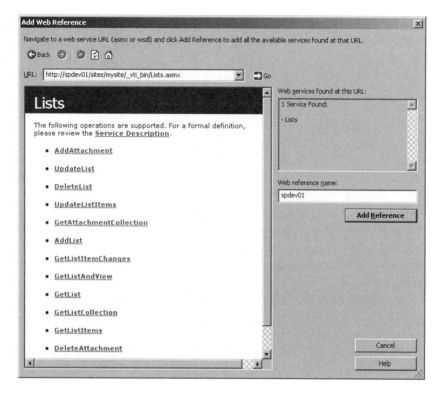

3.   Next, add a Button control and a Text Box control to your form.

4.   The user will enter the name of the new list and click the Button
control to create the list. The Button control will call the
AddList method of the Lists Web Service.

Defining credentials

When leveraging the WSS and SPS Web Services, the first set of coding
tasks that you will most likely perform is to instantiate your Web Service
and then to establish your credentials. Figure 17.57 shows the code required
to create a new list; as you can see, there's not much to it. Line 3 instantiates
the Lists Web Service; spdev01 represents the Visual Studio folder name

Figure 17.57
*Web Services code
to add a list.*

```
1.    private void button1_Click(object sender, System.EventArgs e)
2.    {
3.      spdev01.Lists listSvc = new spdev01.Lists();
4.      listSvc.Credentials = System.Net.CredentialCache.DefaultCredentials;
5.      XmlNode ndLst = listSvc.AddList(textBox1.Text, "Created by Web Service", 100);
6.      MessageBox.Show(ndLst.OuterXml);
7.    }
```

for the reference to the Web Service, and `Lists` represents the Web Service to which we are connecting. Line 4 authenticates the user running the code to the Web Service by passing the user's credentials from the system credential cache. Line 5 creates the new list using the `AddList` method from the Lists Web Service; the text entered by the user in the Text Box control determines the name of the new list. If you enter the code directly to your own application, be sure to add a directive for `System.XML`.

Line 6 is merely to show you the XML that is returned by the service (Figure 17.58). This can be quite useful when you are deciphering the structure of existing lists, since it provides you read access to the associated list schema.

Figure 17.59 shows the outcome of our sample code. Please note that the code shown in the examples throughout this book does not contain adequate exception and error handling; therefore, you are advised to use this code for learning purposes only.

Figure 17.58   *OuterXML display.*

Figure 17.59
Result of Lists Web Service application.

Figure 17.59
Result of Lists Web Service application.

When working with the Lists Web Service, knowing the various attributes and their values is essential. For example, if you want to update items in a list, you need to know the internal name of the list, such as {17991794-81BB-494F-9910-CFBF1093A7CF}. Fortunately, this information is readily available from the XML node returned from the GetList and GetListCollection methods of the Lists Web Service. Our final example demonstrates an application that retrieves the lists associated with a specific site and displays their names in a List Box control representing the available lists. A second list box displays the attributes, along with their cor-

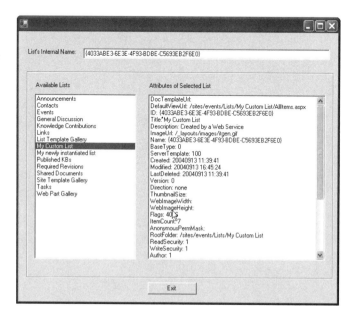

Figure 17.60
Sample list-retrieval application.

responding values, of the currently selected item in the list of available lists.
Figure 17.60 shows the running application. Notice that the internal name
of the list also appears in a text box at the top of the form; as a developer,
you can use this simple application to retrieve the internal name of the various lists with which you want to work by copying the name directly from
the text box.

Figure 17.61
*List-retrieval
application
C# code (1).*

```
1.   using System;
2.   using System.Drawing;
3.   using System.Collections;
4.   using System.ComponentModel;
5.   using System.Windows.Forms;
6.   using System.Data;
7.   using System.Xml;
8.   using System.Text;

9.   namespace WindowsApplication2
10.  {
11.  /// <summary>
12.  /// Sample Application.
13.  /// </summary>
14.    public class Form1 : System.Windows.Forms.Form
15.    {
16.      private System.Windows.Forms.Button button1;
17.      private System.Windows.Forms.Label label1;
18.      private System.Windows.Forms.GroupBox groupBox1;
19.      private System.Windows.Forms.ListBox listBox1;
20.      private System.Windows.Forms.ListBox listBox2;
21.      private System.Windows.Forms.Label label3;
22.      private System.Windows.Forms.Label label4;
23.      private System.Windows.Forms.TextBox textBox1;
24.      //declare custom types
25.      private spdev01.Lists listSvc = new spdev01.Lists();
26.      private XmlNode ndLstCol;
27.      private XmlNode ndLst;

28.      /// <summary>
29.      /// Required designer variable.
30.      /// </summary>
31.      private System.ComponentModel.Container components = null;

32.      public Form1()
33.      {
34.        InitializeComponent();
35.      }

36.      /// <summary>
37.      /// Clean up any resources being used.
38.      /// </summary>
39.      protected override void Dispose( bool disposing )
40.      {
41.        if( disposing )
42.        {
43.          if (components != null)
44.          {
45.            components.Dispose();
46.          }
47.        }
48.        base.Dispose( disposing );
49.      }
50.      //Windows Form Designer generated code
51.      ...
52.      static void Main()
53.      {
54.        Application.Run(new Form1());
55.      }
```

The application code is listed in Figures 17.61 and 17.62. Figure 17.61 contains mostly Windows Form design-generated code; however, lines 25 and 26 contain code specific to the Lists Web Service. Figure 17.62 contains the crux of the application, and there are two main methods that provide the functionality for our application: `Form1_Load` and `listBox1_SelectedChanged`. `Form1_Load` is called when our application initially loads the Windows form; consequently, this method contains the code necessary to populate our list boxes with the appropriate data. Line 74 authenticates the user running the application to the appropriate Web Service. Line 75 calls the `GetListCollection` method of the Lists Web Service to retrieve the collection of lists associated with the referenced site. Lines 77 through 80 traverse the collection and extract the title of each list; each title is subsequently added to `listBox1`. Line 81 extracts the internal name of the first list and populates the text box with this value.

`ListBox1_SelectedIndexChanged` is called when the user selects another item in `listBox1`. Since we have already established our credentials during the form load, we can immediately start working with the List Web Service. This time we leverage the `GetList` method of the Lists Web

Figure 17.62

List-retrieval application C# code (2).

```
56.      private void button1_Click(object sender, System.EventArgs e)
57.      {
58.          Form1.ActiveForm.Dispose();
59.      }

60.      private void listBox1_SelectedIndexChanged(object sender, System.EventArgs e)
61.      {

62.          ndLst = listSvc.GetList(listBox1.Text);
63.          listBox2.Items.Clear();
64.          for (int nNode = 0; nNode <= ndLst.Attributes.Count - 1; nNode++)
65.          {
66.              string lstItem = ndLst.Attributes.Item(nNode).Name.ToString();
67.              lstItem += ": " + ndLst.Attributes.Item(nNode).Value.ToString();
68.              listBox2.Items.Add(lstItem);
69.          }
70.          textBox1.Text = ndLstCol.ChildNodes.Item(listBox1.SelectedIndex).
                 Attributes.GetNamedItem("Name").InnerText;
71.      }

72.      private void Form1_Load(object sender, System.EventArgs e)
73.      {
74.          listSvc.Credentials = System.Net.CredentialCache.DefaultCredentials;
75.          ndLstCol = listSvc.GetListCollection();
76.
77.          for (int nNode = 0; nNode <= ndLstCol.ChildNodes.Count - 1; nNode++)
78.          {
79.          listBox1.Items.Add(ndLstCol.ChildNodes.Item(nNode).
                 Attributes.GetNamedItem("Title").InnerText);
80.          }

81.          textBox1.Text = ndLstCol.ChildNodes.Item(0).
                 Attributes.GetNamedItem("Name").InnerText;
82.      }
83.  }
84.  }
```

Service by passing the name of the currently selected item in `listBox1` (line 62). The `GetList` method returns the schema for the specified list in an XML node. Lines 64 through 69 traverse the schema and extract the name and value of each attribute associated with the list. The name and its corresponding value are then added to the second list box (`listBox2`). Finally, line 70 extracts the internal name of the selected list and populates the text box with this value.

17.10 Conclusion

This book has provided you with the basic knowledge and tools to begin applying the common customizations applicable to many organizations. Obviously, your requirements may be more specialized and require additional knowledge beyond what we were able to provide. Fortunately, there are many more resources at your disposal, such as the SharePoint Products and Technologies SDK, resource kits, newsgroups, and blogs, not to mention the multitude of community sites devoted to the SharePoint technology. Each of these resources provides more information on specific items, such as the object model, Web Services, and the event model.

That said, we hope that you found the content in this book helpful when deploying SharePoint and appreciate the fact that you used us as a resource.

Index

managing, 29–31

opening, 34

LightWeight Directory Access Protocol
(LDAP), 41

Line-of-business (LOB) applications, 107,
109

back-end, 111

integrating via SOAP and OLEDB, 234

Link Bar Properties dialog, 522

Link bars, 522–23

creating, 522

modifying, 523

SPS sites and, 548

List Data Retrieval Web service, 621

List definitions

creating, 583–85

defined, 581

List element, 586–88

attributes, 587–88

multiple, 586

List items

attachments, 22

contacts, adding, 58–60

List-retrieval application, 625, 626–27

Lists, 22–26

actions, 36

approval enabled on, 27

bulleted, 506

content indexing, 142

contents, 25–26

converting, to Data views, 519–20

creating, 23

custom templates, 22–23

Datasheet view, 67–69

default view, 24

defined, 22

exporting, 22, 25

FrontPage 2003 and, 494–98

history, 507

horizontal, 507

importing/saving from Excel to, 66–67

indexing, 149–51

inserting, 497–98

linking, to Outlook, 77–80

manipulating, 25

numbered, 507

in personal sites, 121

saving, as template, 597

as single documents, 149, 151

views, 26–27

working with, 66–70

XML representation, 32

See also Windows SharePoint Services
(WSS)

Lists Web service, 621, 622–28

adding, code, 623

adding references to, 623

application results, 625

leveraging, 622–28

working with, 625

See also Web services

ListTemplates element, 581–85

BaseType attribute, 581

Catalog attribute, 583

code, 584

Description attribute, 583

DisplayName attribute, 581

DontSaveInTemplate attribute, 583

Hidden attribute, 583

HiddenList attribute, 583

Image attribute, 583

list definition creation with, 583–85

Name attribute, 581

OnQuickLaunch attribute, 582

Path attribute, 583

RootWebOnly attribute, 583

SecurityBits attribute, 582

Type attribute, 581–82

Unique attribute, 583

See also ONET.XML

Live Communications Server (LCS), 12, 207

defined, 12, 207